Suspended License

CENSORSHIP

AND THE VISUAL ARTS

Suspended License

CENSORSHIP AND THE VISUAL ARTS

Edited by Elizabeth C. Childs

A Samuel & Althea Stroum Book

UNIVERSITY OF WASHINGTON PRESS

Seattle and London

For my son, William. May his generation fear no art.

This book is published with the assistance of a grant from the Stroum Book Fund, established through the generosity of Samuel and Althea Stroum.

Printed in the United States of America

COMPOSITION: Wilsted & Taylor Publishing Services

Library of Congress Cataloging-in-Publication Data
Suspended license : censorship and the visual arts / edited by Elizabeth C. Childs.
p. cm.
Includes bibliographical references and index.
ISBN 0-295-97627-6 (alk. paper)
1. Art—Censorship. I. Childs, Elizabeth C.
N8740.S87 1998
701′.03—DC21 97-16469
CIP

The paper used in this publication meets the minimum requirements of American National Standard for Information Sciences—Permanence of Paper for Printed Library Materials, ANSI Z39.48–1984.

CONTENTS

ACKNOWLEDGMENTS

THE TASK OF CREATING an anthology belongs to no one person, and each of the contributors here has demonstrated both commitment and patience over the long course of the realization of this book. Without their perseverance and generous cooperation, the book quite obviously could never have been finished. We all owe a debt to Shreve Simpson, assistant director for curatorial affairs at the Walters Art Gallery, and Joseph Ansell, dean of faculty and instructional programs, School of the Museum of Fine Arts, Boston, who first gave our subject a platform at the College Art Association conference in Washington, D.C., in 1991. I am particularly grateful to Naomi Pascal, editor-in-chief at the University of Washington Press, whose unflagging enthusiasm for the anthology was a constant source of encouragement. Julidta Tarver and Leila Charbonneau, also at the University of Washington Press, devoted their expert talents to the production and copyediting of the volume. Christiane Andersson, Jerome Silbergeld, and Gerald Silk contributed valuable counsel, in addition to contributing essays. I owe a personal debt to the faculty at Purchase College, State University of New York, who first encouraged me in this endeavor, and to my current colleagues at Washington University in St. Louis, who have supported me in the final stages. Stephen Poelker of the Arts and Sciences Computing Center at Washington University saved me from a computer crisis that threatened the project at a crucial moment. My husband, John Klein, read drafts of my essays and generously provided both his astute commentary and his steadfast support throughout this long process. A final note of thanks must go to the artist Honoré Daumier, whose inventive and powerful caricature got me thinking about censorship in the first place.

ELIZABETH C. CHILDS
St. Louis, September 1996

Suspended License

CENSORSHIP

AND THE VISUAL ARTS

We painters take the license which poets and madmen take.

Paolo Veronese, 1573,
at his hearing before the Venetian Inquisition

One of the artist's and the humanist's great values to society is the mirror of self-examination which they raise so that society can become aware of its shortcomings as well as its strengths. Moreover, modes of expression are not static but are constantly evolving.

Senate Report on establishment of the NEA and NEH, 1965

Introduction

ELIZABETH C. CHILDS

HISTORIANS OF CULTURE OFTEN ASK how the preoccupations of an era shape creativity. Our best insights are frequently revealed not so much by the clarity of connections, or the union of expression and dominant ideology, as through the chaos and rupture caused by the dissenting voice. It is often when an artist seems most at odds with his or her world, most subject to critical debate, that we glimpse the dominant values of a society, the meaning and function of art, the dynamics of reception and interpretation, and the often painful process of cultural debate and transformation. We owe to the artists of our time not only a sense of our own self-consciousness, but also a possibility of self-criticality.

For the historian, then, much is revealed by the tensions and conflicts surrounding polemical art and controversial artists. If each artist in post-Renaissance Western society has assumed Veronese's "license" to create (as proclaimed in the epigraph to this book), we may well ask what can be learned from the moments when artistic license is suspended by political, religious, or moral authority. What, if anything, do we learn from the history of conflict and failure that is traced by a history of censorship of the arts?

Certainly, not every example unearthed from the historical record is instructive. But it is the position of the contributors to this volume that the present has a great deal to gain by pulling out for reconsideration the record of suspended artistic licenses. As has long been acknowledged in subaltern studies, the traces of the silenced and the powerless can speak volumes about the shape and function of the world of authority, about that of the repressed, and about the constantly changing relations between the two. Records of rupture and discord can be the fault lines that expose the truly heterogeneous terrain of a given historical moment, leading us to a richer model of history that accommodates dissent from regulatory discourse. Fractures of controversy dissolve illusory monolithic contours of the historical record, revealing the particular and material evidence of human desire and expression that is found in art.

An exploration of the history of censorship demands some consideration of the usefulness of the term censorship itself. Some authors concerned with the politics of controversial art have declined altogether to use the word, as its meanings are so varied and mutable.[1] Some authors see its existence in some form as a given in any society; others define it much more stringently.[2] In a historical sense, we may begin by defining censorship narrowly as a "regulative" operation—that is, a process by which works of art that have entered the public sphere are controlled, repressed, or even destroyed by the representatives of political, religious, or moral authority.[3] Traditionally, the agency for such action derives from the powers of church and nondemocratic states such as monarchies, empires, and totalitarian regimes.

In post-Enlightenment society, democracy generally promotes a sense of individual entitlement to a censor-free milieu, in which the term censorship invokes the interruption, manipulation, or eradication of the right of free speech. Although "speech" literally means spoken words, the legal concept has expanded to include most forms of personal expression, including text, images, individual performances, and symbolic conduct. For American citizens, the promise that Congress shall make no law "abridging the freedom of speech, or of the press" is guaranteed by the First Amendment.[4] The initial province of the First Amendment in the Revolutionary era was the expression of individual opinion in the realm of politics and public affairs, but the concept now also applies to opinion in the realms of religion, sexuality, morality, and aesthetics. In our society, the protection of free speech of course has its limits. One function of polemical art has been to test the boundaries of those limits.

The progressive thought of the post-Enlightenment era that dismantled the old authority of state and religious censorship resulted in the creation of open criticism and debate, ostensibly free of censorship, in the arena that Jürgen Habermas has called the modern public sphere.[5] But that sphere may not be as generally free of censorious activity as liberalism presumes. Sue Curry Jansen has argued that the Enlightenment actually gave birth to new forms of censorship, which she describes as constitutive. Following a generally Foucaultian model, she proposes that there is a more covert or insidious form of censorship than the overt actions of regulatory censorship that operates when a work enters (or attempts to enter) the public sphere. Constitutive censorship depends on obtaining and controlling the power of naming—such as naming what is true, beautiful, natural, perverse, sacrilegious, seditious, and so forth. This model of censorship acknowledges that cultural formations permit and encourage the privileged to express the discourses of the dominant ideology, while condemning other viewpoints to derision, to marginal venues, or to silence altogether. Jansen argues that in post-Enlightenment society, civic trust was essentially transferred to private trust, and constituent censorship still occurs in liberal democracy through the manipulation of economic opportunity, a process she terms market censorship.

This distinction begs us to open up the conventional definition of censorship and move beyond the model of regulatory action, which presumes that there is a stable opposition of good and bad, permitted and proscribed, official and unofficial expression. The sociologist Pierre Bourdieu proposes that in addition to "manifest" or regulatory censorship, a structural censorship defines the very field of what is possible to accept or discuss. It is that more subtle delimitation of expression by society that stands behind the promotion of one ideology at the expense of another, and keeps dissenting or minority voices from being heard:

> The manifest censorship imposed by orthodox discourse, the official way of speaking and thinking about the world, conceals another, more radical censorship: the overt opposition between "right" opinion and "left" or "wrong" opinion, which delimits the universe of possible discourse, be it legitimate or illegitimate, euphemistic or blasphemous, masks in its turn the fundamental opposition between the universe of things that can be stated, and hence thought, and the universe of that which is taken for granted.[6]

This structural censorship may coexist with and reinforce overt regulatory policies (as in socialist regimes), or it may operate (like Jansen's constitutive model) in a liberal democracy that is ostensibly free of regulatory censorship. Thus, while we may comfort ourselves that certain actions are not strictly censorious (such as Jesse Helms's assertion, discussed later in this Introduction, that the denial of federal sponsorship to the arts is not the same as censorship), it is crucial to keep a historical and critical eye not only on the regulatory power of censors, but on the ways in which certain kinds of expression are repressed through the exclusionary operations of the dominant ideology within institutions. In the present study, we have cast the term censorship in the broadest possible sense to consider the varied conditions in which the ideological content of artistic proposals or products has somehow been repressed or altered as a result of the political interaction of the art or artist with the public spheres of exhibition, publication, patronage, and criticism. This interaction often occurs through the overt regulation of art in the public sphere; but some of the essays also address the practice of a more structural or constitutive censorship in which the very field of possible opportunities in the public sphere is limited by a kind of self-regulating cultural system that renders the expression of minority or dissenting viewpoints not only impractical but generally inconceivable.

This collection of twelve essays developed from a session I chaired at the annual meeting of the College Art Association in Washington, D.C., in 1991.[7] Each essay addresses a specific cultural moment, ranging from Reformation Germany to contemporary America and China. No attempt has been made to offer a comprehensive analysis of censorship throughout world history; nor has our goal been to explore in depth one genre of censorship, such as the repression of religious or political imagery.[8] Our aim has been to introduce the reader (who may or may not be an art historian) to a wide range of the political, social, and artistic circumstances in which censorship of the visual arts has occurred. We also hope to stimulate consideration of the dynamics of censorship, and to lead the reader to reflect on the presence of censorious policy and action in our own time.

One could conceivably begin this anthology at many chronological points. We have included three essays from the Renaissance period of European history to exemplify the operations of regulatory censorship in the pre-Enlightenment world. These essays offer the contemporary reader useful insights into artistic life in the early modern era, a time when the comprehensive institutional powers of church and state dominated key aspects of artistic patronage, production, and criticism. In the nineteenth century, our case studies demonstrate how visual culture was still largely regulated by monarchical or imperial governments, which promoted an orthodox political vision.[9] The manifestation of oppositional political and aesthetic discourses in both periods is evidence of the determination of artists and the limitations of the forced regulation of creativity.

Our twentieth-century examples are drawn both from American democracy and from fascist and Communist regimes. Four case studies trace the charged interaction of modern American artists with various conservative institutions and critics over the last forty years. Yet these struggles are placed in perspective through comparison with the more severe fate not only of art but of artists themselves in the repressive culture of Nazi Germany, and with the constitutive system of censorship imposed by Communist China.

In these twelve essays, we have examined the careers of acknowledged canonical masters, of lesser-known figures, and of controversial contemporary artists to offer the reader a broad spectrum of the interaction of artists with censorial authority. Taken as a whole, these studies examine several of the most common operations and motivations of censorship, as well as a wide range of artistic response in the face of repressive action. The authors demonstrate how particular objects become the material focus of ideological disputes that are only superficially reducible to a single artistic act or a single critical response. These operations are mostly examples of the practice of regulatory censorship, exercised in the public sphere by established political and social institutions. Several examples of structural censorship may also be identified, some of which reinforce regulatory action. Following a discussion of the practice of censorship as framed by these essays, I will address the question of the appropriateness of censorship in today's society, and what relevance the problem of censorship has for the understanding of our current cultural wars in America.

ARTISTS ON TRIAL

The essays in this book document the wide range of restrictions and punishments imposed on artists whose work has entered the public sphere and been censored. Some artists have merely been questioned; others have been tried and, if found guilty, either fined, imprisoned, or publicly censured. In my essay, we see that Daumier was not only prosecuted and fined by the government, but was actually imprisoned in 1832 for his caricature. Such extreme measures were used occasionally during the July Monarchy and the Second Empire in France to set an example for those who would produce politically sensitive imagery. Yet such sentences often worked to the benefit of the opposition, by transforming a troublemaker into a martyr.

As Jerome Silbergeld points out, however, few of the punishments levied in the West rival the serious consequences suffered by artists in China who produce work found "dissident" in the view of the ruling Communist Party. In 1966 , the artist Li Huasheng's use of traditional Chinese painting styles led to his being labeled a "contradiction among the people" and to a sentence of hard labor. Later, in 1983, the government and Party journals charged him with counterrevolutionary behavior, using an illicit love affair to unfairly accuse the artist with rape and submit him to public disgrace. Only through extraordinary political canniness was he able to restore his reputation and avoid further repressive action.

Of course, not all artists charged with infractions receive such severe treatment. One who is well established may be insulated from such prosecution. Janis Tomlinson relates how Francisco Goya was called before the Spanish Inquisition in 1815 once it was discovered that he had painted the *Naked Maja* and the *Clothed Maja*, works denounced to the Inquisition after the end of the Napoleonic Wars in 1814. Yet, as Tomlinson speculates, the lack of any record of his testimony or any punishment suggests that Goya, salaried as court painter at that time by the newly restored King Fernando VII, probably avoided the embarrassment of appearing in person before the tribunal. Particularly in autocratic regimes, censorship often proves an inconsistent practice that bends to the political will of the enforcer and to the political savvy of the artist and the artist's protectors.

OBJECTS UNDER SIEGE

Even if the artist is not punished, the offending work may become the target of "corrective" action, such as physical alteration, or exclusion or removal from public exhibition; in extreme cases, it may be confiscated and destroyed. Such precautions may even take place before the work enters the public domain.

Throughout much of the nineteenth century in France, prior censorship of images was the principle of the elaborate press laws controlling publication of political caricature in illustrated journals. Such censorship policies are usually ideological and not aesthetic in nature (although it is not always possible to separate the two). In his essay on Manet, John House distinguishes between the normal process of rejection from the Paris Salon, in the nineteenth century, and the few explicit examples of political censorship by the Salon jury. Notably, Manet was informed prior to the submission of his canvas *The Execution of the Emperor Maximilian* (see p. 186) to the Salon of 1869 that it would be rejected; moreover, he was denied permission to publish a related lithograph. As House shows, it was not Manet's subject that was problematic, since other artists had successfully exhibited canvases in 1868 relating to the execution. The jury objected to Manet's failure to celebrate Maximilian as an innocent and pious martyr, or to promote the heroism of French troops in the Mexican campaign. Moreover, Manet's style, which rejected the traditional dramatic rhetoric of gesture and narrative in grand history painting, was incomprehensible to the Salon authorities. They feared that in the puzzling inexpressiveness of the figures and the generalized setting of the drama lay an implicit message of political critique. In the painting's illegibility, or its refusal to present a clear moral that could easily be read by the public, the jury found a failure to conform to either artistic or political convention. For this double betrayal, they judged the image too seditious to exhibit.

When an offending work is permanently installed in a public or ceremonial space, some alteration or modification, often without the artist's participation or consent, is sometimes the most expedient "solution" for church or state. Michelangelo's monumental *Last Judgment* (p. 60), discussed in the essay by Bernadine Barnes, was repainted on several occasions after the artist's death. These changes, made in the name of decorum and piety, ranged from the addition of loincloths to the replacement of nudity with full dress and the substitution of one pose for another. Had the image been a smaller, portable oil painted on canvas, or had the artist been less famous and the commission less celebrated, church officials might have simply carried the objectionable work out of the Sistine Chapel, or replaced it with another fresco.

The simplest form of repression is probably just to sweep the object away from the public eye. This is a solution often favored today, when the artist may be considered untouchable but public space is still regulated by curatorial or even legal authority. As Gerald Silk recounts in his essay, Edward Kienholz was never arrested because of his controversial works of art, but the forces of public opinion joined to forcibly remove some of his work from exhibition.

Censorship may include not only removal of an offensive work from the public sphere but its complete (or attempted) destruction. Given the severity of Daumier's sentence for his caricature of King Louis Philippe as Gargantua (p. 152), it is not surprising that the lithographic stone itself was seized and destroyed, as were all impressions of the print that could be located. Treasured Renaissance masterpieces have also been the object of such destructive desires. Tomlinson recalls that twice in the second half of the eighteenth century, Spanish Kings Carlos III in 1762 and Carlos IV in 1792 threatened to excoriate sacrilegious nudity by burning offending paintings in their royal collections. If not for the timely intervention of such fast-thinking connoisseurs as Anton Mengs, who moved these canvases from the palace to his studio, we would no longer have such masterpieces as Titian's *Venus and Adonis* and *Venus and Cupid with an Organist* (now safely harbored in the Prado). As Joseph Kosuth documented in his compelling installation at the Brooklyn

Museum in 1990, the urge to destroy the offensive object is a materialist passion that has erupted repeatedly throughout human history.[10] David Freedberg has observed in his study of iconoclasm that "people who assail images do so in order to make clear that they are not afraid of them, and thereby prove their fear. It is not simply fear of what is represented: it is fear of the object itself."[11] And this violence, acted out on either creator or object, serves to reassure nervous authorities that the power of art may be contained and regulated by the exercise of power. Yet eliminating objects does not stop art; cultural memory and new acts of creation often render futile such attempts at repression of counterideology.

THE POLITICS OF EXHIBITION AND PUBLICITY

We also need to consider that while censorship usually targets polemical works of art, the suppression of those works can be achieved not only through their *exclusion* from public presentation, but also by their *inclusion* in exhibitions and propaganda intended to discredit proscribed art and artists. Christoph Zuschlag demonstrates how the Nazis used art to link modernism with the alleged degeneration of German culture under the government of the Weimar Republic, which had ensured freedom of expression in its Constitution until it was repealed in 1933. Expressionist and abstract art was now labeled "rubbish," and "the monstrous offspring of insanity, impudence, ineptitude, and sheer degeneracy."[12] Nazi officials employed various strategies to ridicule the art, and by extension the allegedly degenerate and subversive culture that had created it. Their tactics ranged from the simple to the elaborate. For example, a single Chagall painting of a Jewish scene was paraded through the streets of Mannheim in 1933 in a pull cart, like a prisoner turned out for public ridicule.

But one of the Nazis' most highly refined tools of propaganda was the art exhibition. The series of shows that culminated in the famous "Entartete Kunst" ("Degenerate Art") show (p. 222) in Munich in 1937 featured modernist pictures removed from their frames and hung in chaotic fashion in darkened rooms, an installation style intended to discredit the artistic merit of the work. The viewer was informed that his tax dollars had been "wasted" to buy these works for public museums. This appeal to "common man" values has been used by fascists and democracies alike in antimodernist discourse. The taxpayers' "unfair" subvention of a threatening minority (so-called Communist, Elite, Homosexual, etc.) has been central to conservatives' objections to local and federal funding of controversial contemporary art in America.[13]

The defamation of controversial art need not depend on public spaces such as exhibition or trial. In our age of desktop publishing and mass mailing (let alone the Internet), there are relatively simple means for special interest groups to target an artist's work and circulate unflattering press to a sympathetic readership. The art of the late David Wojnarowicz fell victim to calculated selection and misrepresentation in a number of brochures circulated by Donald Wildmon's American Family Association (AFA) in a mailing campaign against the National Endowment for the Arts (NEA). As Peter Spooner summarizes in his essay, Wildmon excerpted details from Wojnarowicz's work and printed the images out of context to support his assertions about Wojnarowicz's creation of federally supported pornography.

The media can of course shape public opinion about art and generate controversy where little or none had existed. In the case of the obscenity scandal surrounding Edward Kienholz's retrospective at the Los Angeles County Museum of Art in 1966, adverse publicity in the local papers so prepared viewers to be offended that several naive visitors mistook paintings of nudes in the European Baroque galleries to be the highly publicized "obscene" work of Kienholz. The discourse of obscenity was appropriated by an opportunistic politician, Warren Dorn, who was then running for governor of California. Dorn exploited the occasion to promote himself as a grand protector of public morality, and he continued his public diatribes against Kienholz and the museum for his own political gain long after other public officials had ceased to press their objections. As Silk astutely points out, the extent of the scandal surrounding Kienholz's works had as much to do with the politics of the museum and the coincidence of the timing of a national Supreme Court hearing on pornography as it had to do with the actual works by Kienholz, many of which had been exhibited in previous years without stirring controversy.

DAMAGE CONTROL AND THE QUESTION OF AUDIENCE

Regulation may also be achieved by controlling access. Limit the audience, and one restricts the power of the unruly object. Such was the idea behind the decision by Spain's King Carlos IV to move paintings of female nudes in his royal collection to the Royal Academy, where admission could be limited to those persons deemed sophisticated enough to appreciate the paintings. An alternative to audience regulation is the control of viewing conditions. Silk cites a modern example in the career of Kienholz, whose works have occasionally been manipulated to be made "acceptable" for public viewing. A museum stepped in as moral guardian when Kienholz included his *Back Seat*

Dodge '38 (p. 261) in his retrospective at LACMA in 1966. The sculpture, which depicted a couple engaged in sex in the back seat of a car, was not removed from the exhibition; authorities simply closed the car door, thereby hiding the lovers. Yet the constant demands by viewers for the guards to open the door suggests that the public's curiosity and voyeurism flourished in the wake of the ambivalent moralizing gesture of the institution.

The exhibition also restricted the viewing of controversial art to an audience of a particular age (in this case, eighteen and older). As Silk observes, the advocacy of age restrictions goes back to Aristotle's *Politics*. Admission restrictions in the "Degenerate Art" exhibitions in Germany enhanced the titillating appeal of a high art peep-show flaunting modernism's corruption and decadence—a spectacle allegedly suitable for viewing only by mature adults.[14] As Steven Dubin points out in the case of the exhibition of Mapplethorpe's photographs, different institutions imposed varying conditions of access: some museums adopted disclaimers to advise potential viewers about the highly charged subject matter of the *X* portfolio, and other venues (such as Cincinnati) admitted no minors at all.

Audience response is often key in the formulation of censorship policies. In the case of Michelangelo's *Last Judgment*, Barnes claims that Aretino first argued for some censorship of the masterpiece in the 1540s, precisely when the image was first disseminated through engravings to a popular audience beyond the literati and church officials in the Vatican. Thus it was an awareness of a changing and expanding popular audience, she contends, that led the famous critic to revoke his initial support of Michelangelo, and to raise the charges of impiety and indecorousness against the artist. Interestingly enough, she charts how the engraving of the *uncensored* version of the fresco enjoyed a wide audience well into the seventeenth century: as with many examples of polemical work in our own time, the publicity surrounding a controversial work fans the fires of notoriety rather than extinguishing them. For example, the opening at the Mapplethorpe exhibition in Cincinnati was overrun by visitors seeking a glimpse of the contentious photographs.

Another strategy of suppression, one we might describe as the tactic of antithetic viewing, is not to cancel the public exhibition of controversial art but instead add a companion exhibition to show work that is ostensibly better, more beautiful, morally superior, more skillful, or more patriotic. Clearly not an overt or manifest example of suppression, such action is nonetheless aimed at framing the art objects within an ideology of preferable alternatives, a method that appears to leave judgment up to the viewer while limiting the field of options to a clear opposition, and leading to preestablished conclusions.

In his essay, Zuschlag explores the ideological underpinnings of such a principle. The Nazis developed antithetic exhibition techniques with their "Great German Art Exhibition" which was presented simultaneously in Munich with the "Degenerate Art" exhibition of 1937. Such a double-barreled program reinforced predetermined, pro-Nazi conclusions about the inferior quality and integrity of modern art (yet interestingly enough, the nationalistic Great German Art show in the vast new House of German Art pulled in only one-fourth the crowd of the more sensational and less familiar "Degenerate Art" exhibition housed nearby).

ASSAULTS ON INSTITUTIONS

The American protection of freedom of speech can of course cut both ways: all viewers have a right to express themselves. Those critical voices can sometimes rally powerful support by sensationalizing their mission, and by serving up a few isolated scapegoats for self-righteous public scrutiny. As we learn from Francine Carraro's essay, a coalition of local arts groups joined together to form the Dallas County Patriotic Council in 1955. What started as a ladies lunch club's complaint that the Dallas Museum of Fine Arts was exhibiting the art of "known Communists" exploded into a full-fledged battle over whether the city should cancel all contributions to the museum's operating budget because of the museum board's unshakable commitment to opening a traveling exhibition entitled "Sport in Art."

Forty years later, it is astonishing to realize that at the center of this storm were four works of art by such acknowledged modernists as Shahn, Kuniyoshi, Zorach, and Kroll (pp. 246–52). Their "un-American" art represented such typically American sports activities as fishing, skating, and baseball. Yet the patriots of Dallas were reinforced in their fear of modernism by antimodernist discourse that found its national voice in Congress in the inflammatory speeches of Senator George Dondero. The mere listing of these artists' names in the infamous files of the House Un-American Activities Committee was enough to brand them as dangerous Communist sympathizers, whose modernist styles were intended to corrupt American morality. (One is reminded here of Helms's rhetoric of fear and intolerance evident in his plea to "put an end to the use of federal funds to support outrageous 'art' that is clearly designed to poison our culture."[15]) While this denunciation failed to achieve the closing of the show, the public pressure did apparently force our government's hand, and led to a decision to cancel the Australian venue of the exhibition at the 1956 Olympics. And the episode may have had further ramifications: for several years the United States failed to send contemporary American art abroad, apparently in the belief that only American works painted before the Russian Revolution of 1917 were unquestionably free of any taint of pro-Communist sympathy. We may do well to recall today the power of effective lobbyists in the shaping of national art policies.

RESPONSIBILITY AND THE FIRING LINE

Creators are not the only targets for censorious action; the individuals responsible for bringing controversial art to the public arena often pay a steep personal price. In the case of public exhibitions, the museum director often takes the heat. As Carraro points out, Jerry Bywaters, director of the Dallas Museum of Fine Arts, received considerable hate mail that labeled him a Communist or a fool. An arts administrator also faced the threat of jail in 1990 when Director Dennis Barrie was tried for obscenity charges after the Cincinnati Contemporary Arts Center opened the Mapplethorpe exhibition. Both Barrie and his institution were acquitted, but he had clearly risked personal liberty in deciding to exhibit art photography subsequently branded by local officials as elitist pornography. In the more desperate circumstances of authoritarian regimes, individuals have occasionally given their lives to protect controversial works of art that authorities sought to confiscate or destroy.[16] The artist is certainly not the only individual whose freedom may be at stake in a censorship battle.

STACKING THE DECK: THE POLITICS OF SCANDAL

Political or religious authorities often appropriate the arts, or even use the public spectacle of the censorship process itself, in ideological campaigns that promote the censors' own interests. Governments, for example, have often attempted to appease religious authorities by putting censorship laws "on the books," even though officials were inconsistent or even lax about enforcing those laws. In Reformation Germany, the official punishment for printing, buying, selling, and owning libelous or sacrilegious texts and images was officially quite harsh, but the sentences handed down were often mild; as Christiane Andersson points out, such policies probably existed to dispel imperial suspicions of the loyalty of local authorities. This is particularly clear in her discussion of the case of Nuremberg. In 1521, in response to the Edict of Worms, the Nuremberg town council prohibited the sale of all portraits of Martin Luther that included the Holy Spirit; by 1524, Nuremberg had banished images of Luther altogether. This may seem curious when we realize that Nuremberg was officially a *Protestant* city, but as Andersson proposes, the town council appears to have been most concerned about mending relations with the Catholic Holy Roman Emperor. Such censorship laws were therefore a public testimony to the city's political allegiance, and served more the interests of diplomatic relations than the ideological concerns of religious dogma.

Similarly, in the case of Paolo Veronese's interrogation by the Inquisition, Paul Kaplan argues that the hearing was not really called to evaluate the theological decorum of the painting, as the Church claimed, but was rather a political ploy by the Venetian-dominated Inquisition panel to curry favor with the pope. At the time the unfortunate Veronese finished his painting of *The Last Supper* (p. 86), Venice happened to be embroiled in a controversy with Rome over the adoption of a papal bull that would prohibit Venice from renewing its vital trade links with the nearby Ottoman Empire. Veronese's uncanonical inclusion of both Protestant and Muslim observers in his sacred scene gave the Venetian Republic a timely opportunity to demonstrate to Rome that in spite of Venice's secular trade interests, its adherence to Counter Reformation ideology was pure. That Veronese was never punished for not changing the actual imagery of the painting; that the brief hearing itself was held in private and was reported only to papal authorities and not to the Venetian public sympathetic to the successful painter; and that Venice temporarily avoided any great break with Rome in that year over the Republic's choice not to adopt all provisions of the papal bull—all reinforce Kaplan's compelling interpretation of the geopolitical motivation of this hearing.

ARTISTIC RESPONSE TO CENSORSHIP

Thus far we have considered how these essays explore the operations of censorship and the results of repressive action in specific instances. Yet the history of censorship is not just a matter of institutional "solutions" to embarrassing or threatening art; it is also a history of individual artistic decisions made in the face of such policies. Repressive political climates have inspired artists to make censorship the very subject of their work, or to work around it in a covert manner, as demonstrated by Daumier's satirical maneuvers to represent taboo images of government leaders.

One obvious response to censorship, even among the most forceful personalities of the modernist avant-garde, has been to accept the realities of contemporary political life and keep the polemical object under wraps. Manet, it will be recalled, never challenged the Salon by submitting his *Maximilian* once he had been warned off; he even declined to show it in a studio exhibition several years later. For many artists, the reasonable reaction to censorship is to move on to the next project, the next image, the next issue.

Yet what about the artists who cannot passively accept the censor's verdict or tolerate the system? For some, the answer is to break the rules and pay the price, whether it be a fine, imprisonment, or public censure. But this is certainly not the only option, particularly if an artist is willing to experiment or make modest political compromises. As these essays suggest, there are many possible artistic strategies for working inside or around a censorious art system while exercising one's artistic license. These tactics include changing the venue for the exhibition of the work; changing the image itself; changing the context for viewing the work; appearing to follow the rules while encoding prohibited sentiment in art; or perhaps the most effective ploy, turning the tables and attacking the censoring institution through art itself.

Exile and relocation provide an obvious alternative to suffering from strict censorship, if one is willing to take the show on the road. As Andersson demonstrates, the bans on antipapal literature in Nuremberg did little to stem the sale of small, cheap illustrated pamphlets at fairs outside the jurisdiction of the town council's bans. The Reformation's widespread censorship campaigns only became necessary due to the flourishing production of texts made possible by the invention of the printing press. The press was also the object of the strictest censorship codes in Second Empire France. Yet while anti-Napoleonic imagery was proscribed within the French borders, an active industry in oppositional caricature flourished in Belgium and England, and many of these images were covertly smuggled back into France by Republican sympathizers. The threat of jail sentences for possession of such contraband seems to have had only limited effect on the commerce in such material. A more extreme option for the persecuted artist is emigration. Following the targeting of modern artists by the Nazi government, most fled to England or the United States in search of a home where freedom of expression was guaranteed. When the going gets tough, some of the tough just move the studio.

For those willing to make changes in controversial art, there is often the reasonable hope that the censor will be placated. For those unwilling to make physical charges, a shift in the title of the offensive work was sometimes a sufficient modification. As Kaplan explains, the upshot of Versonese's hearing in 1573 was a sentence that he "correct and amend" his painting in three months at his own expense in order to alleviate the Inquisition's fear that his

Last Supper was not only indecorous but perhaps even crypto-Protestant. Yet Veronese's response was not to alter the painting itself, but simply to rename it *Feast in the House of Levi* (p. 86). Kaplan argues that the new title carries a clever rebuke to the Inquisitors themselves, reminding them that in spite of their objections to the many noncanonical figures in his sacred feasting scene, it is precisely those "heretics and infidels" appearing in his picture who should be the objects of Christ's mission and His Church. Thus even in carrying out the Inquisition's sentence, Veronese asserted his own critical perspective.

For some artists, rules are chains; for others, they are a challenge. In the world of political caricature in nineteenth-century France, censorship laws often laid down a gauntlet before inventive and resilient artists, such as the satirists working for the moderate Republican journal *Le Charivari*. As I propose in my discussion of the caricatures of the Haitian Emperor Soulouque in the 1850s, Daumier staged a spirited oppositional critique of the empire of Napoleon III, in spite of the rigorous censorship policies of the regime. By appropriating an exotic personage for his caricature, he managed to slip these images past the literal eyes and minds of the police censors who could not always decode the symbols of oppositional discourse.

For an artist who wishes neither to roll over in the face of censorious attacks nor to engage in clever strategies of accommodation, there is (at least in most Western liberal democracies) the possibility of legal recourse and appeal. A notable case is the decision made by Wojnarowicz in 1990 to sue his would-be censor, Wildmon and AFA, for copyright infringement and defamation of character. The artist won an injunction demanding that the AFA send out a correction to their inflammatory brochure, explaining that their reproductions of the artist's work had been taken out of context. While Veronese hardly had the option of suing the pope, or Daumier of suing his king, there are at least in modern democracy the options of public discourse and legal challenge.

THE DYNAMICS OF CENSORSHIP

We may have a tendency to view censorship as a stable and unchanging force in society, as laws purport to establish authority, consensus, and consistency. But laws and regulations often fall out of touch with the will of a society, or at least with the will of a ruling elite that has not updated the rules. Highly polemical art at times finds unexpected allies. Such, we learn from Tomlinson, was true of Manuel Godoy, prime minister in the Spanish court in the 1790s. Some in the Bourbon court, including Godoy, saw the Catholic Inquisition as old-fashioned and as a hindrance to Spain's entrance into the modern world. His decision to form a collection of paintings of female nudes for his own private delectation might be better understood as one manifestation of an enlightened challenge to censorship at the turn of the eighteenth century; he probably even commissioned Goya's *Naked Maja* (p. 128) for that collection.

Moreover, censorship is not always a self-evident system of regulations that artists may learn, dodge, or confront. Silbergeld's essay suggests that modern China combines subtle constitutive censorship with regulatory practices. The Chinese government relies on a system of education and expectation to create an atmosphere of necessary compliance with political mandates. Seldom are individual works censored, because the art system itself promotes complete adherence to Communist Party policy. In such a world, the same state agency plays the role of both patron and censor, and the artist learns to regulate individual will in order to survive in the system.

WHERE CAN WE DRAW THE LINE?

The range of examples leaves us with a wide array of valuable works of art that have been destroyed or censored in the past. When we look at the fate of controversial art by such artists as Cranach, Michelangelo, Manet, and Goya, we might well ask if censorship can ever be desirable, since history reminds us that great art has often been decried in its own time. How many more significant contributions to the artistic record will we never know, either because the work vanished under repression or because of the historical practice of privileging the "successful" and celebrated works of an era? We might well ask: If censorship is permitted in any form today, what cultural era will be permanently effaced? What regrettable lacunae will we write into our own history?

It is easy for an advocate of democratic civil liberties to point a finger at other societies, and to denounce the inequities of religious and state-authorized censorship of the arts, such as the *fatwa* declared against writer Salman Rushdie. It is harder to look at the culture wars in our own society and judge where the limits of artistic freedom can and should be drawn. Much of what has given dynamism to art in the modern era can be described, as Kirk Varnedoe has put it, as a "fine disregard" for the conventional rules of art making.[17] Sometimes breaking the rules opens the doors to new perspectives, new expression, new forms to fit new times. But how can we draw a reasonable line between encouraging or simply permitting ground-breaking creativity and condoning unlawful or dangerous expression couched in artistic terms?

American jurisprudence draws many clear-cut boundaries. One of the most abiding principles of our law is the protection of private property. Thus creative expression in the form of graffiti scrawled across another's property or bashing a sculpture in a museum is prohibited. The same laws, however, have traditionally permitted destruction of property, including art, at whim by its owner.[18] In the United States we have adopted only limited aspects of a principle the French describe as the *droit moral* of the artist—the artist's right to demand respect for the physical and aesthetic integrity of the created object once it has been sold. In the United States, clashes over the treatment of an artwork may seem to the artist to constitute censorship, whereas the owner may claim to be exercising property rights or executing some action in the name of a larger public good.

A famous recent conflict in this domain was the controversy surrounding the dismantling and removal of the sculpture *Tilted Arc* by Richard Serra in 1989. The General Services Administration commissioned the piece as a site-specific sculpture for the public plaza in front of the federal building in downtown Manhattan; in 1981, Serra completed the 120 foot long, 12 foot high arc of rusted steel and installed it on a diagonal across the plaza. The GSA eventually held hearings to consider charges that not only was the work displeasing aesthetically but it attracted graffiti and litter, and posed a public safety threat. These complaints masked the major reason for the objections: an aesthetic conservatism of a minority of the sculpture's audience. When the GSA decided to remove the sculpture, Serra claimed an abridgment of his freedom of expression, arguing that dismantling his site-specific piece was tantamount to its destruction. The court dismissed his case in 1987, arguing that Serra had "sold his free speech to the government." In other words, he abandoned his right to free speech in this matter when he was paid in 1981 for the work by the government, which became its owner.

In the wake of this conflict, Serra and many artists lobbied for moral rights legislation that would acknowledge the connection between an artist and his or her work after it has been sold. In 1986, Senator Edward Kennedy introduced the Visual Artists Rights Act to prohibit distortion, mutilation, and destruction of an artwork after it has been sold. The bill, which finally passed in 1990, guarantees some (but not unconditional) federal protection to works of art during an artist's lifetime.[19]

Other significant limitations to artistic prerogatives protected under the

First Amendment are recognized by our legal system. These include some instances of libel and slander, threats, extortion, perjury, and fraud.[20] Free speech is also limited by the determination of when "speech" constitutes a clear and present danger, or threatens to incite imminent violence—a condition easy to envision but hard to prove. Modern law requires artists to respect the physical safety of the viewer in a public space. As Silk recounts, Kienholz's installation *Still Live* (p. 263) in 1974 pushed German authorities to enforce a firearms law. Kienholz invited the viewer to sign a release form and then to sit in an armchair in the direct path of a rifle set to fire at one random moment in the next hundred years. The artist's interest in invoking the viewer's sensations of curiosity, fear, vulnerability, and anxiety was clearly superseded by the inherent risk of physical injury to the viewer/participant if the firearm discharged. The sculpture was removed from exhibition and returned to the artist.

One kind of speech declared by American courts to be outside the range of First Amendment protection is obscenity. There were no specific laws against obscenity in the United States until the nineteenth century, when movements such as that sponsored by Anthony Comstock attempted to regulate art and literature in the name of morality. Since the Comstock Law of 1873 set the tone for limiting the distribution of materials deemed obscene, lewd, and lascivious, American courts have struggled to define obscenity. The difficulty of this task was highlighted by the obscenity debate of the 1950s—a debate Silk relates to the controversy over Kienholz's art. In 1957, the Supreme Court declared that obscenity is speech about sex with no redeeming social importance. But Justice William Brennan pointed out that some art and literature about sex deserves constitutional protection, as it explores "a great and mysterious motive force in human life."[21]

For some critics, the very existence of obscenity laws is tantamount to censorship and the violation of civil liberties.[22] For others, the laws are not strict enough, as they still permit some pornography (defined simply as images or texts designed to arouse sexual desire). Since the 1973 case of *Miller v. California*, the courts have respected a three-part obscenity test, weighing whether the "average person, applying contemporary community standards would find that the work, taken as a whole, appeals to the prurient interest; whether the work depicts or describes in a patently offensive way, sexual conduct specifically defined by the applicable state law; and whether the work, taken as a whole, lacks serious literary, artistic, political or scientific value."[23] This law permits the definition of obscenity to change with locale, depending on community mores. The varied receptions given the Mapplethorpe exhibit, as characterized by Dubin, demonstrate the contentious range of response one artist can generate in different venues.

To battle the obscenity charges in Cincinnati, the defense in the Mapplethorpe case focused on the third principle of the *Miller* test. Convinced by expert witnesses that the photographs had redeeming artistic merit, the jury acquitted Barrie. Of course, what is prurient, what is patently offensive, and what is serious artistic value is determined on a case-by-case basis, and censorship of "obscene" material is legal whenever there is local consensus on these matters. What these principles of "community consensus" do not protect are the interests of individuals whose tastes may be legal in another community but subject to censorship in their own.

Efforts to regulate free speech can of course arise from all directions in a free society; conservatives have no monopoly on proposing limitations. Some universities propose to banish "hate speech" from the campus, even though such speech may be protected by the First Amendment. And some feminists have recently found themselves curiously allied with conservatives in a battle to make pornography illegal. Catharine MacKinnon and Andrea Dworkin, among others, argue that pornography is not merely degrading to women, but that it is both a metaphor for and an actual means of subordinating women.[24] MacKinnon argues that the First Amendment was written by men to protect a freedom they already had; but if the access to means of speech is precluded for some due to race, class, or gender, then freedom from government restriction still doesn't guarantee universal freedom of speech. In this view, "censoring" pornography is not a violation of men's free speech; it would simply be an act of affirming the civil rights of women, recognizing that pornography is a form of sex discrimination. MacKinnon and Dworkin drafted an antipornography ordinance that banned the production, sale, distribution, or exhibition of any work considered pornographic according to a complex set of criteria that could be judged only from subjective viewpoints. This law, adopted by Indianapolis in 1984, was found by the Supreme Court to violate the First Amendment.[25] As Marjorie Heins has pointed out, the law would have made illegal images ranging from a demonstration of the use of a speculum in a medical journal (in that it shows the penetration of the female body) to Judy Chicago's *Dinner Party*, which celebrates female sexual organs.[26] In a free society that does not discriminate against viewpoints or mandate any one religion, there is no clear justification for giving legal privilege to a feminist or fundamentalist Christian definition of pornography over a more libertarian definition of eroticism, however distasteful this form of protected speech may be to some audiences.

WAGING THE CULTURE WARS

Since 1989, Americans have been locked in debate over whether or not federal sponsorship of the arts is tantamount to censorship.[27] In other words, is the availability of government funding to an individual or an arts institution to be considered simply a patronage question, or is it a form of market control, or even market censorship? If we think of censorship in the simple regulatory sense—as action taken against works that have already entered the public sphere—then obviously the funding of art and exhibitions is not strictly a form of censorship. But if we endorse a broader definition of censorship that acknowledges (as in Bourdieu's model) the structural limit set by the field of opportunities, and if we consider the significant generative impact of federal funding on the vitality of the arts in America, the question is more complex. The key element becomes access to opportunity and support for artists during critical creative years—an access that is determined by criteria other than the marketability of the artistic product in the private sphere. The measure of the value of an artist should not be reduced to predicting whether he or she will attract a large audience or sell well, any more than federal grants to writers should be given out, as Newt Gingrich has suggested, as speculative seed-money for lucrative best-sellers that can pay royalties back to the government.[28] Not all important art sells well, particularly in its own time.

This is no simple issue, particularly since the terms of the debate over the culture wars have shifted since we first started work on this anthology in 1991. In the immediate wake of controversies over the art of Mapplethorpe, Wojnarowicz, and Andres Serrano, the debate focused on what genre of art the government should be funding, and how the government could limit or set restrictions on art funded by federal appropriation. Hence the proposal by Senator Helms of an amendment in 1989 that prohibited the NEA from supporting any art the agency might deem obscene, including "depictions of sadomasochism, homoeroticism, the sexual exploitation of children, or individuals engaged in sex acts and which, taken as a whole, do not have serious literary, artistic, political or scientific value."[29] The terminology here clearly invoked that of the obscenity test drafted in the Supreme Court case *Miller v. California*. Although this language was not as restrictive as Helms had originally proposed, his bill nonetheless placed the first content-specific restriction on the NEA since the Endowment's inception in 1965. A second restriction was soon forthcoming, charging the NEA to ensure that all grants respected "general standards of decency and respect for the diverse beliefs and values of the American people." Artists Karen Finley, Holly Hughes, Tim

Miller, and John Fleck (the so-called NEA Four) sued the NEA over this restriction, and in June 1992 a federal court ruled that the "decency requirement" was vague and hindered free speech.[30] As Judge Tashima ruled, "The right of artists to challenge conventional wisdom and values is a cornerstone of artistic and academic freedom."[31]

Since the Helms amendment was struck down in 1992, there have been further initiatives to delimit the content of federally supported art or exhibitions.[32] It is surely no coincidence that the art that has sparked the most congressional and popular controversy—Mapplethorpe, Serrano, Wojnarowicz—is often photographic or cinematic. There remains some of the conventional mistrust that photography, while a good tool for documentation, can never be a medium of fine art. Moreover, the medium insists on the facticity of its subjects; for some viewers, Mapplethorpe's photographs representing lifestyles of some homosexuals, for example, are offensive precisely because the viewer confronts the actuality of the models in an uncompromising way.

In particular, conservatives appear threatened by art that explores the sexual, political, and religious views of minorities, and spokespersons ranging from former National Endowment for the Humanities (NEH) Chairwoman Lynne V. Cheney to Speaker of the House Newt Gingrich seem baffled and offended that so much contemporary art, including some of that funded by the National Endowments, is politicized. The former bemoans that many artists "now see their purpose not as revealing truth or beauty, but as achieving social and political transformation."[33] The latter, for example, condemns the NEA and NEH for funding "skillfully presented political statements masquerading as art," as if the realms of art and politics could be so neatly separated. Indeed, the mere exhibition of modern political art has been a lightning rod for recent conservative complaint and for public controversy, even when no federal or state funding is involved.[34] In the post-Enlightenment world that produced the art of Jacques-Louis David, Trumbull, Goya, Daumier, and Picasso, political passion has often fueled artistic vision, and it is naive to imagine that artists can, as Gingrich wishes, "celebrate legitimate cultural issues" without often moving into the political sphere.[35] The Endowments' detractors assert that government should avoid artists with any "agenda," and fund only those artistic visions that support some fictive consensual viewpoint of what modern American civilization is or should be. But the Endowments were founded with an awareness that the critical capacity of art is healthy, and even essential to our culture, and that dissenting views contribute to debate and self-awareness. As the Senate Report on the establishment of the Endowments in 1965 observed, "One of the artist's and the humanist's great values to society is the mirror of self-examination which they raise so that society can become aware of its shortcomings as well as its strengths. Moreover, modes of expression are not static but are constantly evolving."

So the question facing Congress of what kind of art should be funded remains unresolved, largely because the content of artistic expression has proved to be hard to define and nearly impossible to regulate. The Endowments' critics have therefore driven the debate onto more general grounds by asking whether there should be government sponsorship of the arts at all. Advocates of ending federal arts funding point out that fine art flourished in America before the founding of the Endowments in 1965. But they overlook the impressive record of government sponsorship and support of the fine arts throughout American history.[36] Although critics such as Hilton Kramer charge that federal funding produces only a utilitarian art compromised by its political and social agenda, there is ample visual proof—from the historical murals executed by John Trumbull in the early 1800s to the powerful photographs by Walker Evans and Dorothea Lange funded by the Farm Securities Administration in the Depression—that government involvement has fostered and advanced American artistic culture.

As this book goes to press, the future of the NEA and NEH is uncertain, and the debate continues. Funding for the NEA has steadily decreased since 1992, when appropriations reached an all-time high of $175.9 million. In 1996 both Endowments saw eviscerating cutbacks from the previous fiscal year, as the NEA budget fell from $162.4 million to $99.5 million, and NEH's dropped from $172 million to $110.5 million. Recommendations were passed in 1996 by the House Committee on Economic and Educational Opportunity to dismantle, or "zero-out," the NEA in 1998, and the NEH in 1999. The Senate, however, supported continued reauthorization, and President Clinton has attempted to restore the Endowments' budgets to recent levels. Every year, a new recipient of an Endowment grant is made a scapegoat by those who claim that the Endowments "waste" federal support. Mapplethorpe and Serrano have been replaced by performance artist Ron Athey, photographer Joel Peter-Witkin and filmmaker Cheryl Dunye in the discourse of congressional debate; names of other controversial artists will undoubtedly be brought forward until the larger question of government support of the arts—especially contemporary art—is resolved.[37]

Those in favor of dissolving the Endowments claim that privatization of the arts will result in ample prosperity for the arts and the disempowerment of an academic, elitist culture out of touch with mainstream America. But isn't it elitism to argue that we should let the private sector become the economic arbiters of taste in all public venues? It is true that aristocratic French patrons of the Old Regime sponsored some great art; it is also true that it took a revolution to make that same art accessible to the people by turning the Louvre palace into a public museum. There seems little hope that our private sector today will step forward to cover all of the public work currently done by the National Endowments. The Rockefeller Foundation's 1996 survey of private foundations reported that arts and culture are *at the very bottom* of the list of American funding priorities.[38] To leave the arts to the mercy of private funding is to put art back in the power of market censorship, and to abdicate the responsibility of government as a public trust.

Those who would end government support of the fine arts argue that as long as there are private competitors who can provide some arts subsidy, the government is not repressing free speech by failing to sponsor art.[39] But to argue that federal funding is simply replaceable by private sponsorship is to ignore the particular power the government has in the marketplace of ideas and artistic goods: the government's name is good for the business of art. Federal grants draw many times their own value in matching funds.[40] Those like Helms who advocate content restrictions on cultural funding argue that government should be able to use allocative discretion like any sponsor, freely choosing what kind of art it wishes to sponsor. But the government is never just another sponsor, just another NYNEX or Mobil Oil underwriting the show. Government participates in and shapes culture, even as it regulates it. Gingrich has complained that the NEA's contribution to the funding of an exhibition of Andres Serrano's work put the government imprimatur on mockery and blasphemy.[41] He misses the point here; the message the government sends is not about approval of what some deem to be sacrilege. Federal support of controversial art proclaims that the United States does not discriminate against viewpoints, and can openly sponsor the public exhibition of diverse individual response to religious heritage. The message would not be the same if Philip Morris were the sole sponsor of such a show. Federal support of such an exhibition advocates tolerance and open-mindedness, and serves to remind us that what is labeled sacrilege or blasphemy by one viewer may be understood by another as the earnest artistic exploration of the intersection of the realms of the divine and the human.[42]

In our society, there should be significant government support for the arts. To shut down cultural funding is to effectively censor diverse viewpoints by restricting access to support, exhibition, publication, and criticism of creative work. As feminists have long recognized, opportunity, encouragement, and validation in the public sphere are necessary for the successful nurturing of any talent. As a sponsor of culture, our government can affirm that art teaches the essential values of tolerance and curiosity by challenging us to examine perspectives we might otherwise miss.

In a liberal democracy, where regulatory censorship is largely prohibited by First Amendment protections, we still need to be vigilant in recognizing the less obvious structural mechanisms that limit the expression of diverse values. Mere adherence to our laws will not protect the pluralism that defines and invigorates our culture; we must actively create opportunities to ensure the development and display of creativity. In totalitarian societies, structural and regulatory censorship achieve the same result, as both are fully representative of a dominant ideological position. In our democratic society, where the Constitution prevents ideology and regulation from being coincident (in that viewpoints may not usually be restricted), we should be aware that their very separation challenges us to recognize how a dominant culture restricts without regulating. What we must protect is not just artistic expression, but our very access to the multiplicity of viewpoints—to that profoundly important "mirror of self-examination"—our artists can offer.

NOTES

1. Steven C. Dubin, *Arresting Images: Impolitic Art and Uncivil Actions* (New York and London: Routledge, 1992), 8–9.

2. For a brief summary of recent efforts to define censorship, see Richard Burt, ed., *The Administration of Aesthetics: Censorship, Political Criticism, and the Public Sphere*, Cultural Politics, vol. 7 (Minneapolis: University of Minnesota Press, 1994), xxvi–xxvii, note 6.

3. I have adapted the term "regulative censorship" from Sue Curry Jansen's *Censorship: The Knot that Binds Power and Knowledge* (New York: Oxford University Press, 1991), 7–8.

4. In this essay, America and American will designate the United States and its citizens, and not North America(n) more generally.

5. Jürgen Habermas, *The Structural Transformation of the Public Sphere: An Inquiry into a Category of Bourgeois Society*, trans. Thomas Burger (Cambridge, Mass.: MIT Press, 1989). The standard view is that the Enlightenment paved the road for the revolutionary thought that ended state censorship, yet recent work asserts that the

idea of the public sphere is a pre-Enlightenment formulation. See Burt, *The Administration of Aesthetics*, chapters 1 and 2.

6. Pierre Bourdieu, *Outline of a Theory of Practice*, trans. Richard Nice (New York: Cambridge University Press, 1977), 169–70. My attention was drawn to Bourdieu's analysis of censorship by Burt, *The Administration of Aesthetics*, xvi–xviii. Burt's ambitious project is to explore the meaning of the "new" censorship of the last decade, not in terms of legitimating progressive politics per se, but by reconsidering the forms of institutional power that are evidenced by the controversies.

7. The session was entitled "Censorship and the Visual Arts: A Historical Perspective." The essays in this volume that are based on talks presented in that College Art Association session are by Christiane Andersson, Francine Carraro, Jerome Silbergeld, Peter Spooner, Janis Tomlinson, and Christoph Zuschlag.

8. Several compendia of instances of censorship have been published. See for example Jane Clapp, *Art Censorship: A Chronology of Proscribed and Prescribed Art* (Metuchen, N.J.: Scarecrow Press, 1972). On contemporary America, see People for the American Way, *Artistic Freedom under Attack*, vols. 1–4 (Washington, D.C.: P.F.A.W., 1992–96).

9. In spite of the relative absence of regulatory censorship in political and religious matters in nineteenth-century America, structural censorship certainly existed. Access to professional opportunities was clearly limited according to race, class, and gender in nineteenth-century America, even though freedom of the press and freedom of speech were constitutionally protected rights. Recent scholarship addresses an instructive case in Boston, where a talented young woman sculptor won a blind competition but was denied the commission once her gender was revealed. See Eleanor Tufts, "An American Victorian Dilemma, 1875: Should a Woman Be Allowed to Sculpt a Man," *Art Journal* 51, no. 1 (Spring 1992): 51–56.

10. *The Play of the Unmentionable: An Installation by Joseph Kosuth at the Brooklyn Museum*, essay by David Freedberg (New York: The New Press, 1992), 129–31.

11. David Freedberg, *The Power of Images: Studies in the History and Theory of Response* (Chicago: University of Chicago Press, 1989), quoted in Kosuth, *The Play of the Unmentionable*, 129.

12. Quoted in Zuschlag essay, at note 18, from Peter-Klaus Schuster, ed., *Die "Kunststadt" München 1937, Nationalsozialismus und "Entartete Kunst,"* exh. cat. (Munich: Prestel, 1987), 217.

13. In the Dallas Museum controversy discussed by Francine Carraro, newspaper editorials debated the question "Shall art by Reds be exhibited at taxpayers' expense in our museum?" The American Family Association used a similar tactic in their anti-NEA campaign, asking readers "Is this how you want your tax dollars spent?" (Peter Spooner's article).

14. One is reminded here of the strategies used by the conservatives in Congress. When Jesse Helms argued in 1989 to reduce the NEA's appropriation, he announced

that all women ("the ladies") and pages should leave the floor of the Senate before he could unveil the allegedly obscene photographs of Robert Mapplethorpe for viewing. Dubin, *Arresting Images*, 180.

15. Helms, "It's the Job of Congress to Define What's Art," as quoted in Richard Bolton, ed., *Culture Wars: Documents from the Recent Controversies in the Arts* (New York: The New Press, 1992), 101.

16. See Danuta Batorska, "The Political Censorship of Jan Matejko," *Art Journal* 51, no. 1 (Spring 1992): 57–63.

17. Kirk Varnedoe, *A Fine Disregard: What Makes Modern Art Modern* (New York: Abrams, 1990).

18. The classic case here is *Crimi v. Rutgers Presbyterian Church*, 89 N.Y.S. 2d 813 (Sup. Ct. 1949), in which the court upheld a church's right to destroy a fresco it had commissioned. See John Henry Merryman and Albert E. Elsen, *Law, Ethics and the Visual Arts* (New York: Matthew Bender, 1979), vol. 1, 4-12 to 4-16.

19. See Richard Serra, *The Destruction of Tilted Arc: Documents* (Cambridge, Mass.: MIT Press, 1991). On the Visual Artists Rights Act of 1990, see Martha Buskirk, "Moral Rights: First Step or False Start," *Art in America* 79, no. 7 (July 1991): 37, 39, 41, 43, 45.

20. Marjorie Heins, *Sex, Sin, and Blasphemy: A Guide to America's Censorship Wars* (New York: The New Press, 1993), 2–3.

21. Ibid., 20.

22. Donna Demac, *Liberty Denied: The Current Rise of Censorship in America* (New York: PEN American Center, 1988), 48. For example, see the American Civil Liberties Union's position on the Meese commission in 1985.

23. *Miller v. California*, 413 U.S. 15 (1973).

24. Catharine A. MacKinnon, *Feminism Unmodified: Discourses on Life and Law* (Cambridge, Mass.: Harvard University Press, 1987) and Andrea Dworkin, *Pornography: Men Possessing Women* (New York: G. P. Putnam's Sons, 1981).

25. MacKinnon, *Feminism Unmodified*, 210.

26. Heins, *Sex, Sin, and Blasphemy*, 159.

27. An anthology of essays by artists, administrators, and arts advocates directly involved in these controversies is by Jennifer Peter and Louis Crosier, eds., *The Cultural Battlefield: Art Censorship and Public Funding* (Gilsum, N.H.: Avocus Publishing, 1995). Short accounts of recent efforts to censor the fine and popular arts in America are published periodically by "artsave," a project sponsored by People for the American Way. See *Artistic Freedom under Attack*, vols. 1–4.

28. See Newt Gingrich, "Cutting Cultural Funding: A Reply," *Time*, August 21, 1995, 71.

29. Quoted in Heins, *Sex, Sin, and Blasphemy*, 131. Also see Dubin, *Arresting Images*, 180.

30. On Finley, see Dubin, *Arresting Images*, 149–58, and Heins, *Sex, Sin, and Blasphemy*, 133–34.

31. Quoted in Heins, *Sex, Sin, and Blasphemy*, 134.

32. When Congress passed the NEA appropriations for fiscal year 1996, the bill included new content restrictions. Section 331 (b) of the Conference Report on H.R. 3019 (the omnibus appropriations spending bill) reads: ". . . No funds . . . made available under this Act to the National Endowment for the Arts may be used to promote, disseminate, sponsor, or produce any material or performances that (1) denigrates the religious objects or religious beliefs of the adherents of a particular religion, or (2) depicts or describes, in a patently offensive way, sexual or excretory activities or organs, and this prohibition shall be strictly applied without regard to the content or viewpoint of the material or performance." That the language here restricts freedom of speech is admitted by the following section, that states nothing in the provision "shall be construed to affect in any way the freedom of any artist or performer to create any material or performance using funds which have not been made available [by the NEA]." See *The Congressional Record—House*, 104th Cong., vol. 142, no. 55 (April 25, 1996): H3898. These provisions obviously open up questions of First Amendment protection, and as of September 1996, the restrictive language is under review by the Justice Department.

33. Quoted in Stephen Burd, "Cultural Crossfire," *Chronicle of Higher Education*, February 3, 1995, A22.

34. The Gingrich quotation on political art is from his "Cutting Cultural Funding: A Reply," 70. In April 1996, both Gingrich and Senator Robert Dole called for the removal of Kate Milliett's *The American Dream Goes to Pot* from the exhibition "Old Glory: The American Flag in Contemporary Art" at the Phoenix Art Museum. The sculpture, made in the early 1970s in protest of the Vietnam War, included an American flag stuffed partly into a toilet. The Phoenix Art Museum did not cancel or alter the exhibit.

35. Gingrich, "Cutting Cultural Funding: A Reply," 70–71. Gingrich here defends a great tradition in American culture, which he identifies with the work of Twain, O'Neill, Gershwin, and Ellington. But he ignores how federal funds have supported development of our knowledge of these canonical artists. Between 1980 and 1995, seventy-nine grants were awarded by the NEH to individuals and organizations to sponsor research on these four Americans. The funds have resulted in books, film, radio productions, TV dramas, and exhibitions available to the widest possible audience. The NEH has also helped with unglamorous but essential work that no corporate entity has rushed to sponsor, such as installation of climate control systems for a museum of Mark Twain artifacts in Hartford, Connecticut. Moreover, the recent exhibition of Whistler (another member of Gingrich's pantheon of American greats) at the National Gallery of Art was made possible by an indemnity provided by the Federal Council on the Arts and the Humanities. The indemnity program, started in 1975 and administered by the NEA, makes major international loan shows possible by underwriting prohibitively expensive insurance costs. By 1996, the Federal Council had approved indemnity coverage for 501 exhibitions, saving the orga-

nizers more than $90 million in insurance costs. The government's costs, in contrast, have been minimal—only two claims have been paid in twenty years. This is an outstanding example of how a modest federal subsidy can enhance our cultural life immeasurably.

36. See Lillian B. Miller, *Patrons and Patriotism: The Encouragement of the Fine Arts in the United States, 1790–1860* (Chicago: University of Chicago Press, 1966), and Vivien Green Fryd, *Art and Empire: The Politics of Ethnicity in the U.S. Capitol, 1815–1860* (New Haven: Yale University Press, 1992). My thanks to Angela Miller for these references.

37. For example, in June 1996, Congressman Peter Hoekstra (Republican, Michigan) unsuccessfully attempted to reduce the NEA's proposed 1997 budget of $99.5 million by $31,500, the specific amount of a Media Arts grant made in 1995 to Women Make Films, Inc., New York, in support of Cheryl Dunye's feature film *The Watermelon Woman*. The internationally acclaimed film is a fictional account of a black lesbian filmmaker who explores her identity as an African American woman through her fascination with the "Watermelon Woman," a particular "mammy" character she sees in a movie from the 1920s. For a revealing exchange between Congressman Hoekstra, who attacked the film and the NEA simultaneously, and Congresswoman Sheila Jackson-Lee (Democrat, Texas), who defended the film on the grounds of First Amendment protection for artists, see *The Congressional Record—House*, 104th Cong., vol. 142, no. 92 (June 20, 1996), H6636–38. More generally on the debate over NEA and NEH funding, see also ibid., H6641–46. Among the valuable NEH-sponsored projects derided by some members of the House as evidence of "a Federal feel-good agenda" were a 1994 national summer institute for college professors on the construction of sex and gender in the High Middle Ages, sponsored by the University of Notre Dame; and a research conference on the study of gender in the history of opera, sponsored by the SUNY Research Foundation/Stony Brook. (Debate in the House attacking federally funded gender studies seems particularly dismissive, as typified by the comment of one congressman who glibly reduced the opera project to a one-sentence "free lesson," sniping that sopranos are usually women and men are usually basses.) In arguing for arts funding reductions, such detractors often emphasize the size of the U.S. national debt. Yet the economic stakes are relatively small: 1996 appropriations for the NEA were only 0.02 percent of the annual federal budget. The NEA cost each American only 38 cents in 1996, small change indeed compared to the public expenditure on the arts made by European nations (for statistics from other countries, see Robert Hughes, "Pulling the Fuse on Culture," *Time*, August 7, 1995, 64).

38. See Nina Kressner Cobb, *Looking Ahead: Private Sector Giving to the Arts and Humanities* (Washington, D.C.: President's Committee on the Arts and the Humanities, 1996).

39. My discussion of the rhetoric of sponsorship/censorship is indebted to a lecture given at Princeton University in 1993 by Kathleen M. Sullivan, professor of law at

Stanford University, entitled "Art and Government: Lessons from the NEA Wars." Also see her essays, "The First Amendment Wars," *New Republic* 207, no. 14 (September 28, 1992): 35–36, 38–40; and "Artistic Freedom, Public Funding and the Constitution," in Stephen Benedict, ed., *Public Money and the Muse: Essays on Government Funding for the Arts* (New York: Norton, 1991), 80 ff.

40. According to the NEA, one Endowment dollar currently attracts twelve dollars for the arts from state, regional, and local arts agencies, foundations, businesses, and individuals. The Challenge Grant program has generated more than $1.05 billion in additional funds since 1965. An additional $307 million has been raised through the NEH "matching grants." Data from "Point of View," *Chronicle of Higher Education*, February 3, 1995, A56. Regrettably, the NEA's Challenge Grant program is scheduled to end in 1996 due to budget cuts. The NEH also has a very successful Challenge Grant program which stimulated three and one half dollars for each federal dollar in 1996. Since that program began in 1977, $330 million of federal money has brought in over $1.1 billion from state and private sources.

41. Gingrich, "Cutting Cultural Funding: A Reply," 70.

42. That we do not live in a theocratic state that restricts viewpoints was confirmed by the Supreme Court's refusal to support New York State's ban on Roberto Rossellini's allegedly sacrilegious film *The Miracle* in 1952.

The Censorship of Images in Reformation Germany, 1520–1560

CHRISTIANE ANDERSSON

IN WESTERN SOCIETY, some form of censorship by the state or religious authorities has always existed. Indeed, before the Enlightenment in the eighteenth century, censorship was a standard procedure, a right customarily accorded to those in power. Especially religious heresy and criticism of political authority were considered intolerable, certainly in print. Regarding religious orthodoxy, even the early apologists for free speech in the sixteenth century had second thoughts. For instance, in his *Utopia* of 1516, Sir Thomas More demanded freedom of thought, but within certain limits. He did not tolerate a diversity of opinion about divine providence or the immortality of the soul.[1] Even John Milton, whose *Areopagitica* propounds freedom of the press, did not grant this right to the papacy or to Catholic dogma generally.[2]

Up until the eighteenth century, freedom of thought was subordinated to so-called higher values, such as religious orthodoxy and preservation of the political status quo. Freedom of thought and freedom of the press were rooted in the ideas of the Enlightenment. In America in 1776, the Declaration of Rights of the Virginia Constitution recognized those rights as "one of the great bulwarks of liberty." In France in 1789, the *Declaration of Rights of Man and of Citizens* (*Déclaration des droits de l'homme et du citoyen*) named freedom of expression "un des droits les plus précieux de l'homme." In Germany the Reformation has often been credited with establishing the right to freedom of conscience. The liberation from a rigid Catholic dogma initiated by Erasmus and other humanists and the dissemination of new social ideas first espoused by the radical Reformers, such as Thomas Müntzer (1489?–1525), certainly were significant steps in that direction. But the Protestant reformers were far from granting freedom of thought in questions of belief. Martin

Luther (1483–1546) used censorship against his former allies in 1525, and Huldrych Zwingli (1484–1531) instituted censorship in 1523 in Reformed Zurich.[3]

Before the modern era, Germany functioned as a unified nation only in limited ways, being an agglomeration of small states and free imperial cities, each of which established its own policies and regulations. In the eighteenth century when the Americans and the French were proclaiming that the rights of man included freedom of thought, this concept was still in its infancy in Germany. One of its most influential proponents was Immanuel Kant. Freedom of the press was established around 1815 only in a few German states, and even there with some limitations. The more liberal policies were usually not of long duration. The Nazi regime in the 1930s again halted what progress had been made. In Germany, freedom of expression in the modern democratic sense is a post–World War II phenomenon. In view of these widespread repressive tendencies, it is well to remember that unlimited freedom of expression does not exist, even today. And we have seen how easily even a relative degree of such freedom can be called into question in the controversy over Robert Mapplethorpe's photographs beginning in 1990,[4] and in the strict censorship of news coverage of the Gulf War against Iraq early in 1991.

Censorship became a major political factor in Germany only at the onset of the Reformation. In 1517, Martin Luther, an Augustinian monk and later professor of theology at Wittenberg University in Saxony, initiated the Protestant Reformation, and his intense study of the Bible led to a new understanding of how mankind could achieve salvation through faith alone, thus rejecting the traditional Catholic dogma of salvation through good works. Luther's objection to the sale of indulgences, understood as a means of buying one's way out of purgatory and into heaven, provoked an uproar in 1517 and led within four years to his open defiance of the pope. Excommunication by the Church and the ban of the Empire soon followed. Luther initially considered his activities directed at reforms within the Church, but the basis of compromise was lacking on both sides. The dramatic and widespread denunciation of papal authority by Luther and his followers had far-reaching consequences also in the political and social realms in Germany.

Although it had existed earlier in pursuit of individual heretical texts, censorship was not implemented with any incisiveness by the Catholic Church until the invention of printing using movable type in about 1454 brought with it the danger of a rapid spread of heresy via the printed word. Various papal bulls demanded preventive censorship, requiring manuscripts to be submitted to the Church authorities prior to publication; but such measures remained fairly ineffective, since at that time the Church had no means of local enforcement.[5]

The situation changed radically, however, in reaction to the new Lutheran theology. The crucial document was the Edict of Worms of 1521,[6] in which the Catholic emperor of the Holy Roman Empire of the German Nation, Charles V (1500–1558), adapted a papal censorship bull of 1515 to the new circumstances.[7] He joined forces with the pope, and that seemed to now make the regulations enforceable. Their political alliance resulted from common interest: both realized how gravely their power was endangered by the new faith, which in spiritual and secular terms called into question the basic tenets of the medieval view of the world. Luther was by no means alone in questioning the authority of the Church hierarchy, and many were willing to begin questioning secular authority as well, resulting in such actions as the Peasants' War of 1525.

The Edict of Worms, promulgated after Luther's refusal to disavow his heretical beliefs at the Diet of Worms in the presence of the emperor and the German princes, condemned Luther and his adherents and decreed the censorship of all of Luther's writings and of all printed material deemed contrary to Catholic belief or directed against the pope, the prelates of the Church, princes, or university theological faculties. Nothing injurious to these parties was to be printed, bought, sold, or even owned, openly or secretly; and any libelous material already in circulation was to be confiscated and publicly burned. The edict's jurisdiction was the Holy Roman Empire, which at that time included Germany, the Netherlands, Burgundy, Naples, and Sicily.

The edict expressly stated that texts and images were equally subject to censorship, and included the artist along with the author and printer among those who would be punished for violating the edict's regulations. The Nuremberg town council, for example, when banning offensive tracts, was especially mindful to confiscate the woodblocks from which the woodcut illustrations had been printed. Censoring images as well as texts was entirely plausible, considering the low rate of literacy in Germany at the beginning of the sixteenth century.[8] Luther himself recognized the potential persuasiveness of printed images, as is evident in the care he devoted to the woodcut illustrations in his tracts published in Wittenberg, designed in the workshop of his friend, Lucas Cranach the Elder. Among numerous polemical works on which Luther and the Cranach workshop collaborated, the *Passional Christi et Anti-Christi* (1521) is probably the best known.[9]

Censorship of printed pictures was handled no differently from that of texts partly because in Reformation propaganda they were often inseparable. Text and image were printed together in a variety of combinations. The cheapest and most popular form united the polemical text with one or more woodcut illustrations on a single sheet of paper as a broadsheet. An example published in Wittenberg is the *Satire on the Papal Coat of Arms* (fig. 1).[10] The woodcut has been attributed to the Monogrammist BP, an artist of the Cranach school, and can be dated 1538, as it is described on February 17 of that year in a diary entry by Anton Lauterbach (1502–69). The text, signed at bottom right, is considered to be by Martin Luther himself. This broadsheet was censored by the authorities in Nuremberg as we know from an undated letter written by Veit Dietrich (1506–49) to Hieronymus Baumgartner (1498–1565), in which Dietrich expresses his opposition to such censorship. The popularity of the broadsheet is demonstrated by its reprinting in Latin the following year with sixty distichs of additional text (fig. 2).[11] This second edition no longer divulges the name of the author, Martin Luther.

The heraldic image, normally showing the bearer's honors and insignia of office, has been subverted in the woodcut into an accusatory litany on the pope's misuse of office. The papal shield, surmounted by the tiara, is supported by the shafts of Saint Peter's two crossed keys, the shattered parts of which lie scattered as signs of the pope's power destroyed. The keys serve as the gallows from which two victims dangle: the pope and Judas. As Robert W. Scribner has shown,[12] the satirical hanging is based in part on late medieval letters of reprimand (*Scheltbriefe*), which often portrayed death by hanging of those they attacked. The depiction of hanging was to become a common form of Reformation satire. The antipapal satire here also derives from traditional images of shame (*Schandbilder*). Such publicly displayed small posters offered an outlet for outrage and feelings of injustice in an era when legal redress of grievances was often difficult to obtain. They named the crime and the offender, depicting him through his coat of arms.

In the later Middle Ages, heraldic devices had a totemlike significance and were often used to substitute for the person they signified. Four money bags in the central shield refer to Judas's betrayal of Christ for thirty pieces of silver and to the pope's avarice. The implication of the image and text is that the pope is not—as he claims—the heir of Saint Peter, but rather of Judas. The verses in dialogue form surrounding the woodcut accuse the pope of abusing the power of the keys to fill his purse through annates and palliums. The pope's methods of exercising his greed are suggested by the bishops' miters, royal crowns, and the cardinal's hat protruding from the money bags

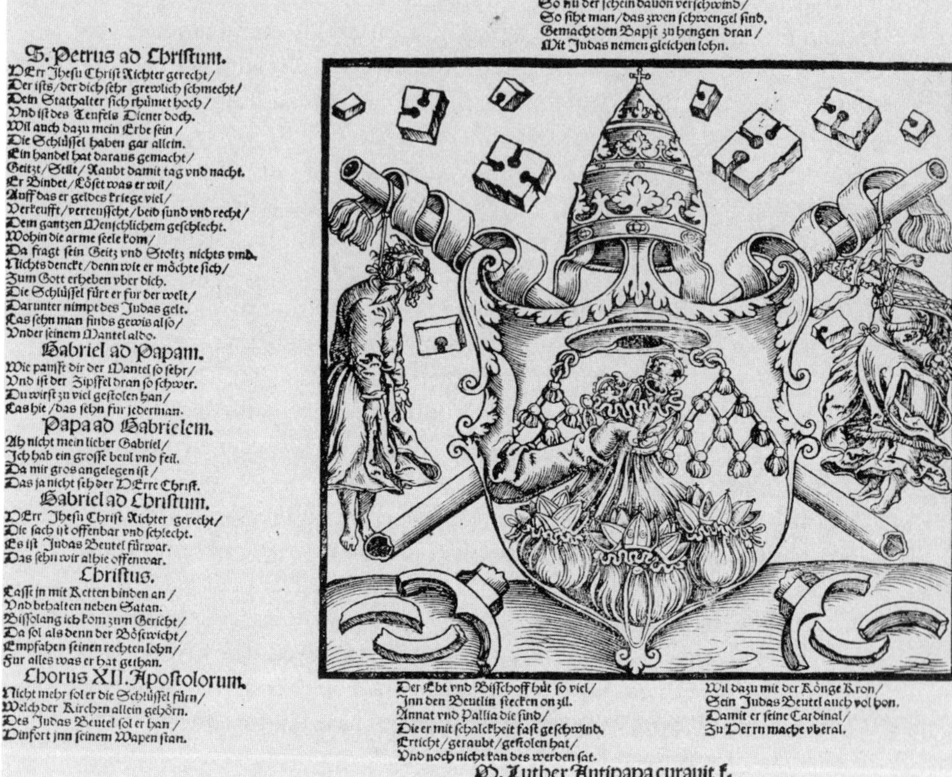

FIG. 1. Monogrammist BP, *Satire on the Papal Coat of Arms*, with German text by Martin Luther, 1538.
Woodcut, 27.7×32.3 cm (11×12¾ in.). Kunstsammlungen der Veste Coburg, Coburg.

—headdresses alluding to the henchmen who assist in fleecing the pope's flock.

The Edict of Worms delegated the responsibility of enforcing its censorship regulations to professors of theology for specifically theological materials and to local city councils for all other printed matter, such as the multitude of satires of the type just described (fig. 1). The councils in turn issued local censorship ordinances, which tended to follow closely the wording of the Edict of Worms, and as stipulated in the edict, usually appointed themselves as the censoring body. The ordinances were publicized by being

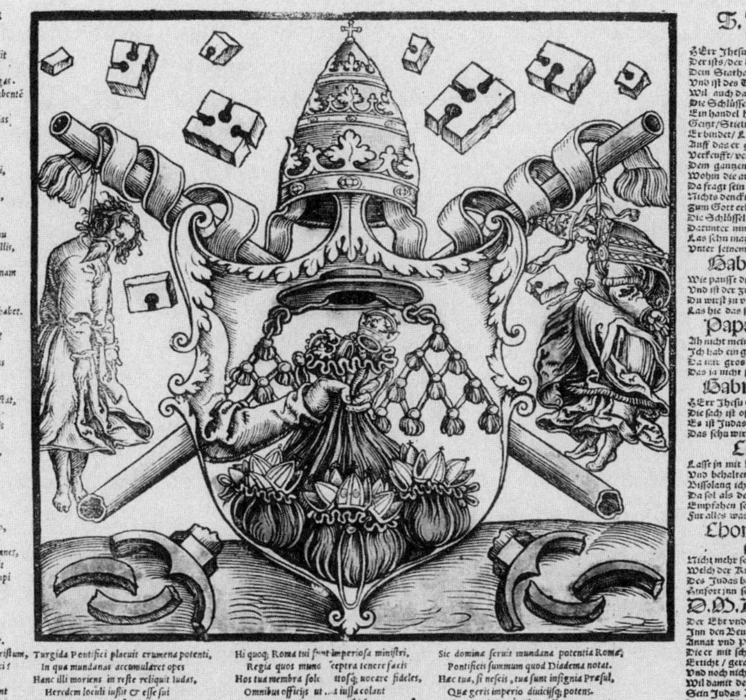

FIG. 2. Monogrammist BP, *Satire on the Papal Coat of Arms*, with Latin text by Martin Luther, 1539.
Woodcut, 28.6×34.3 cm (11¼×13½ in.). Herzog August Bibliothek, Wolfenbüttel.

read aloud from the pulpits and by posting in public places. They required printers to swear an oath of compliance with the rules and to offer for advance inspection copies of everything intended for publication, so that permission to print could be granted or denied.

The responsibility to carry out the imperial edict forced city councils in many German towns with a substantial Protestant population to walk a fine line between the emperor's demands for strict censorship and their own citizens' passionately held evangelical beliefs.[13] Especially the Protestant-leaning free imperial cities, such as Nuremberg, Augsburg, and Strassburg, were obliged to appease the Catholic emperor, since they stood directly under his jurisdiction, deriving their political power and free status originally from him alone. The punishments locally set forth for contravening the regulations, including, for example, heavy fines or exclusion from the printing profession, may seem unduly harsh, but in the case of magistrates with Lutheran sympathies, one suspects that to some extent these official guidelines were intended to dispel imperial suspicions about the willingness of councils to prosecute offenders. By contrast, the punishments actually meted out in individual cases often showed great leniency. The degree to which local authorities enforced censorship regulations was always determined by the political circumstances of the moment. The examples of censorship cited here have been chosen primarily from the free imperial cities Nuremberg, Augsburg, and Strassburg, because their archives are preserved nearly intact and thus offer the most complete documentation.[14]

Central to Reformation imagery were the portraits of Martin Luther himself. As the initiator of the new faith, even his likeness had a polemical character and was thus subject to censorship after the Edict of Worms was proclaimed in 1521. In Nuremberg particular images of Luther were not tolerated after the edict; several years later, all images of him were censored, corresponding to the changing political climate. Prior to the edict, in 1520 the Nuremberg artist Hans Sebald Beham created a small woodcut portrait of Luther in profile, shown in his doctor's cap and gown writing at his desk, with the dove of the Holy Spirit hovering above (fig. 3). Surrounded by the rays of a halo, Luther is cast in the guise of a saint or an evangelist. Beham's woodcut, based on traditional medieval author portraits of the evangelists writing the Gospels, gives Luther all the trappings of a divinely inspired man of God,[15] and thereby characterizes Luther's writings as divine revelation. On March 3, 1521, responding to the newly issued Edict of Worms, the Nuremberg town council forbade the sale of all portraits of "Luther with the Holy Spirit."[16] The ban must have been directed against Beham's small woodcut and against Hans Baldung Grien's woodcut portrait of Luther, dated 1521 (fig. 4), which also shows Luther as a saint with halo and dove.

Baldung created his woodcut in Strassburg but the demand for Luther's portrait was so great among his followers throughout Germany that impressions were surely circulated to Nuremberg and other cities. The portrait appeared as a single-sheet woodcut and was also used to illustrate tracts by Luther published in 1521, thus becoming precisely the type of author portrait

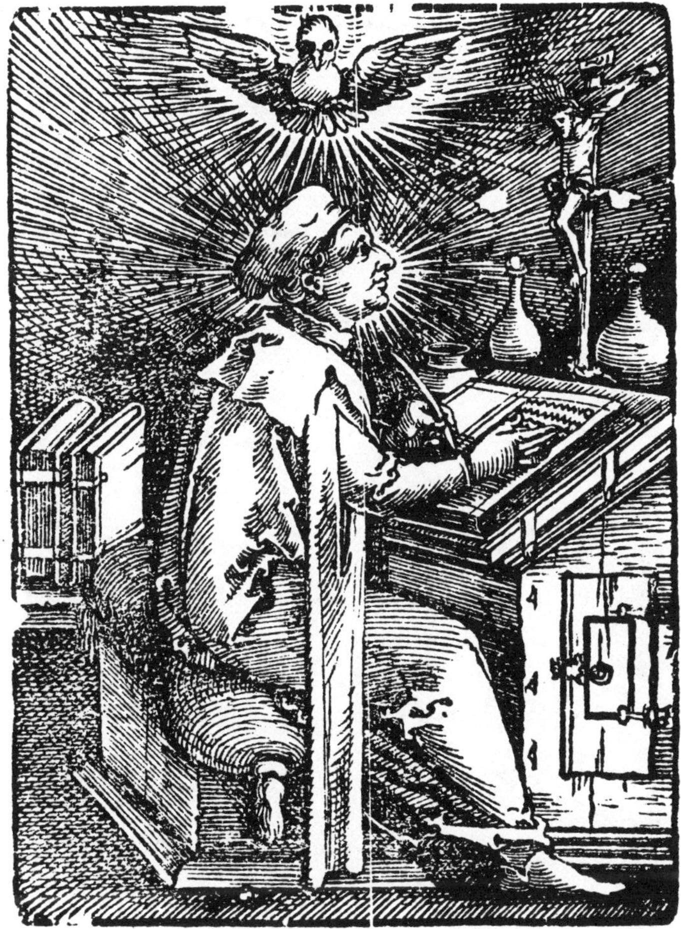

FIG. 3. Hans Sebald Beham, *Luther as an Evangelist*, 1520.
Woodcut, 10.8×7.6 cm (4¼× 3 in.).
Staatliche Museen Preussischer Kulturbesitz,
Kupferstichkabinett, Berlin.

upon whose medieval precedents the image was based. Baldung's woodcut was also used to illustrate various reports about Luther's appearance before the Diet of Worms in 1521.[17] The papal nuncio Aleander attending the Diet complained about Baldung's woodcut of Luther, which he observed simple people carrying about and kissing, a practice previously reserved for images of the saints. Baldung's woodcut must also have elicited intense emotions in

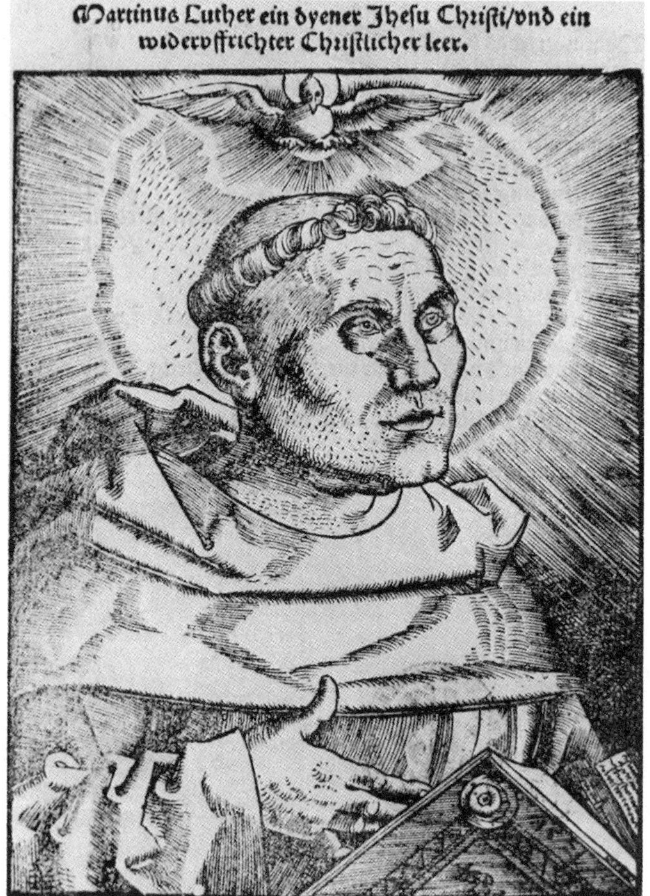

FIG. 4. Hans Baldung Grien, *Luther with the Bible, Halo and Dove*, 1521.
Woodcut, 15.6×11.5 cm ($6\frac{1}{8}\times4\frac{1}{2}$ in.).
Kunsthalle, Hamburg. Andersson photo.

the Catholic camp, as mutilated impressions of the portrait demonstrate (fig. 5). Baldung had copied his likeness of Luther from an engraved portrait of 1520 by Cranach the Elder (fig. 6). Cranach's engraving was also copied by other artists, such as Hieronymus Hopfer, who realized that there was money to be made with Luther's image. Hopfer's etching (fig. 7) shows Cranach's prototype in reverse, like Baldung's woodcut—a result of the printing process. But Hopfer extends the figure below the waist, including Luther's left hand holding the Bible, and copies Baldung's nimbus of radiant light and the

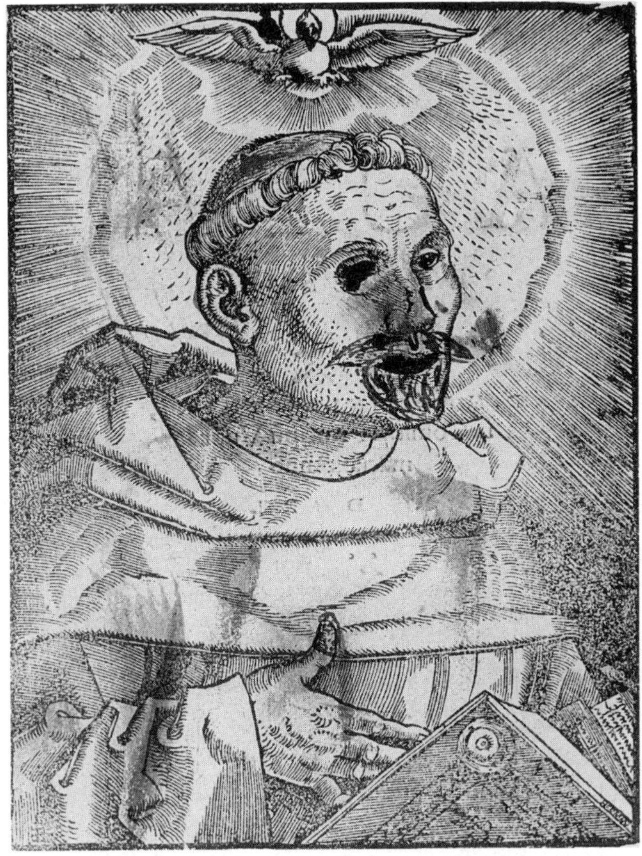

FIG. 5. Hans Baldung Grien, *Luther with the Bible, Halo and Dove*, mutilated impression of the previous image, 1521.
Woodcut, 15.6×11.5 cm (6⅛× 4½ in.).
Universitätsbibliothek, Marburg an der Lahn.

dove. Working in Augsburg, Hopfer was not subject to Nuremberg's mandate to censor Luther's image with the dove.

Three years after the Nuremberg council banned images of Luther with the dove, all portraits of Luther were censored.[18] By 1525, Nuremberg had officially become a Protestant city. What may appear illogical in so strongly Lutheran an environment was in fact an urgent attempt to mend diplomatic relations with the outraged Catholic emperor. Again it is uncertain whether the ban was consistently carried out, since Hans Sebald Beham's woodcut

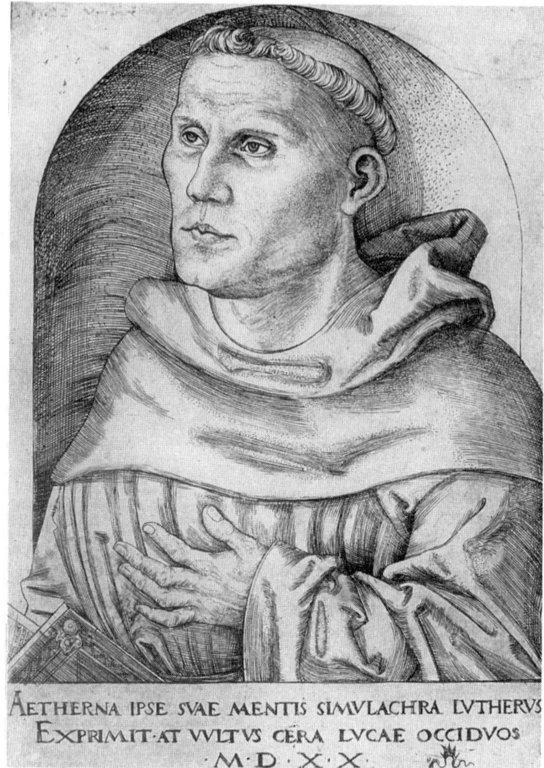

FIG. 6. Lucas Cranach the Elder, *Luther as an Augustinian Monk Preaching before a Niche*, 1520. Engraving, 16.5×11.8 cm (6½×4½ in.). Staatliche Graphische Sammlung, Munich.

portrait (fig. 3) was reused in 1524 in Nuremberg by the Protestant publisher Hans Herrgott as the title-page illustration in a vernacular edition of the New Testament (*Das new Testament Deütsch*). The Nuremberg archives offer no evidence that this edition was interfered with by the censors.

The woodcut portraits of Luther by Beham and Baldung were printed and sold as single sheets or incorporated as illustrations in books. Most polemical images, however, appeared in so-called pamphlets, a flimsier type of book with usually only a paper binding. The cheap and lightweight binding kept costs low and facilitated transport. This was essential because pamphlets were sold at fairs in distant towns and it allowed offending material to evade

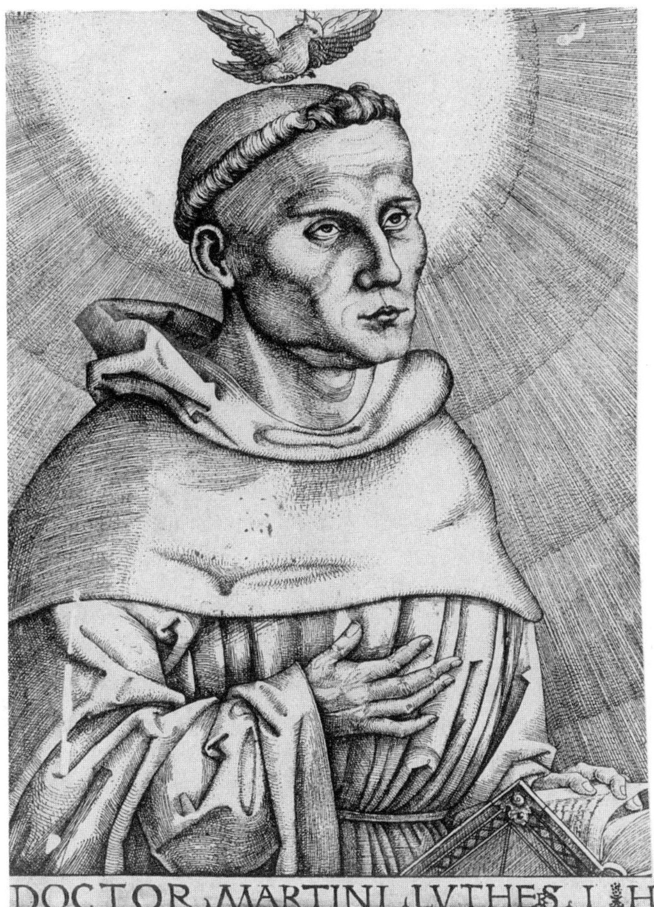

FIG. 7. Hieronymus Hopfer, *Luther with the Bible, Halo and Dove*, after 1520.
Etching, 21.1×15.3 cm (8⅓×6 in.).
Staatliche Graphische Sammlung, Munich.

local censors by moving it rapidly beyond their jurisdiction. One of the best documented examples of the censorship of an antipapal pamphlet occurred in Nuremberg in 1527 upon publication of *A Wondrous Prophecy of the Papacy* (*Eyn wunderliche Weyssagung von dem Babstum*, fig. 8).[19] The pamphlet is illustrated with thirty allegorical woodcuts by Erhard Schön depicting the history and ultimate defeat of the papacy, with brief explanations of the im-

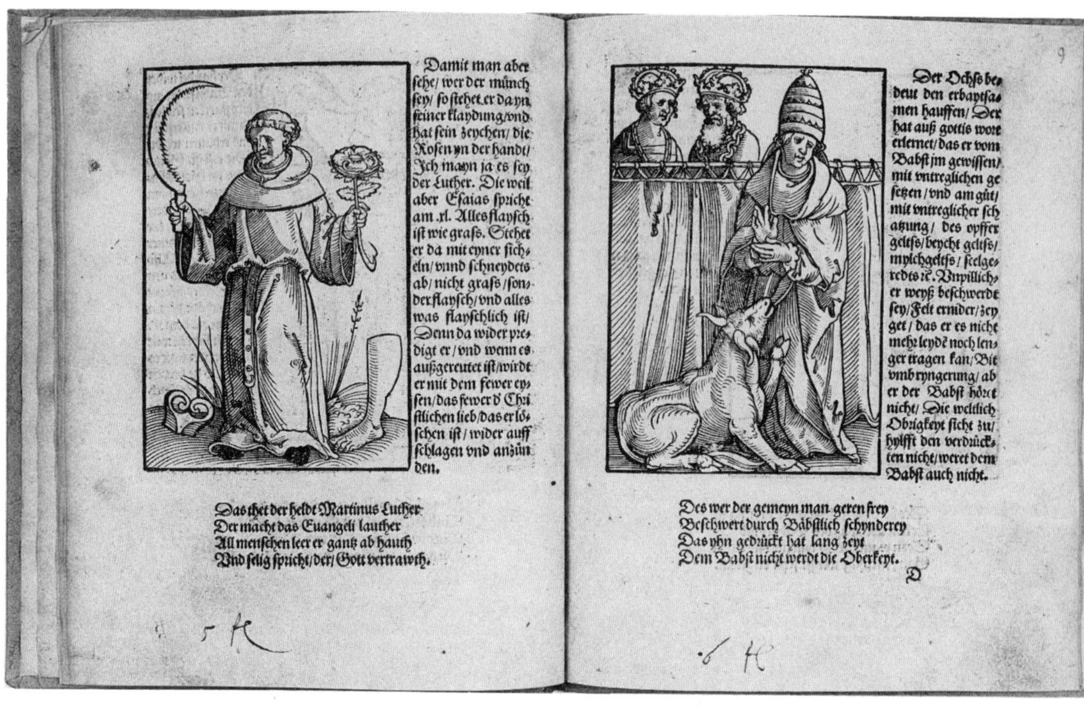

Damit man aber sehe/ wer der münch sey/ so stehet er da yn seiner klaydung/vnd hat sein zeychen/ die Rosen yn der handt/ Jch mayn ja es sey der Luther. Die weil aber Esaias spricht am .xl. Alles flaysch ist wie grafs. Stehet er da mit eyner sicheln/ vnnd schneydets ab/ nicht grafs/sonder flaysch/ vnd alles was flayschlich ist/ Denn da wider predigt er/ vnd wenn es außgereutet ist/wirdt er mit dem fewer eysen/das fewer d' Christlichen lieb/das erlöschen ist/ wider auff schlagen vnd anzünden.

Das thet der heldt Martinus Luther
Der macht das Euangeli lauther
All menschen leer er gantz ab hauth
Vnd selig spricht/der/Gott vertrawth.

Der Ochfs bedeut den erbaytsamen hauffen/ Der hat auß gottis wort erlernet/ das er vom Babst jm gewissen/ mit vntreglichen gesetzen/vnd am gůt/ mit vntreglicher schatzung/ des opffer geltfs/beycht geltfs/ mylchgeltfs/ seelgeredts rc. Vnpillicher weyß beschwerdt sey/Felt ernider/ zeyget/ das er es nicht mehr leydē noch lenger tragen kan/ Bit vmb ryngerung/ aber der Babst hört nicht/ Die weltlich Obrigkeyt sicht zu/ hylfft den verdrückten nicht/ weret dem Babst auch nicht.

Des wer der gemeyn man geren frey
Beschwert durch Bäbstlich schynderey
Das yhn gedrückt hat lang zeyt
Dem Babst nicht werdt die Oberkeyt.

D

FIG. 8. Erhard Schön, two illustrations from *A Wondrous Prophecy of the Papacy* (*Eyn Wunderliche Weyssagung von dem Babstum*), 1527.
Woodcuts, 11×7.5 cm (4⅓× 3 in.). Harry Ransom Humanities Research Center, University of Texas at Austin.

ages written by Nuremberg's Lutheran preacher, Andreas Osiander, accompanied by two rhyming couplets per image, composed by the poet Hans Sachs. The *Wondrous Prophecy* is based on a much older prophetic source, the *Vaticinia de summis pontificibus*, attributed to the medieval sectarian Joachim of Fiore (1145?–1202?) and to a certain bishop Anselmus. Osiander had discovered the text in a Bolognese edition of 1515 in the library of the Carthusian monastery in Nuremberg. Suspecting that the Bolognese edition obscured the full extent of criticism of the medieval Church, Osiander composed his own text to elucidate the images. The woodcuts were copied from the Bolognese ones with minimal changes by Schön.[20]

The medieval prophecy served Osiander's polemical purposes as evidence of the increasing sinfulness of the papacy that dated from an era well before Luther. Following a strategy of Reformation polemics that by 1527 was well established, Osiander equates the pope with the Antichrist, dwells at length on his worldly habits and misuse of authority as a temporal lord and war-monger, and then tries to show that all these ills prophesied in the twelfth-century text were fulfilled in later centuries. Finally, the last five images with their texts foretell the pope's eventual unmasking and deposing. To achieve the desired topical relevance, Osiander and Schön took a few liberties with their prototype. For instance, Luther himself appears among the opposition to the pope. The Wittenberg Reformer is shown as an Augustinian monk, holding his heraldic emblem, the rose, and the sickle with which he will mow down the flesh, symbolized by the severed foot, a reference to Isaiah 40:6 (fig. 8). The flint at the lower left Luther will use to rekindle the fire of Christian love, which Osiander suggests the pope has allowed to extinguish. The pamphlet speedily found its way to Wittenberg, as we know from a letter Luther wrote to Wenzeslaus Link on May 19, 1527, in which he expressed approval of his identification with the reaper monk.[21] The adjacent allegorical woodcut shows the pope standing next to an ox, symbol of patient, hardworking Christians, who have long submitted to the pope's financial demands. Now having learned from God's Word that these payments are unjust, they refuse to pay any longer.

Osiander's pseudorehabilitation of a medieval prognostic to give prophetic legitimacy to his personal beliefs was a common tactic during the Reformation. Nuremberg's town councilors, however, felt Osiander's pictorial prophecy was far too inflammatory so soon after the city had officially espoused the Lutheran faith, when every effort was being made to steady the city's precarious relations with the Catholic emperor. The tract, they explained, would only offend and embitter simple folk and had no redeeming qualities. After reprimanding the participants in the project for not having cleared it with the censors in advance, as required by law, the councilors censored the *Wondrous Prophecy*, confiscated the six hundred copies remaining at Hans Guldenmund's printing shop, and even wrote to the town council in Frankfurt, requesting their colleagues there to look out for any copies of the offending tract at the fairs and instructing that they be bought up and sent to the Nuremberg council at the latter's expense.

The care taken to apprehend all copies of the *Wondrous Prophecy* indicates how damaging the councilors feared it would be in the eyes of the emperor. They forbade Osiander to publish anything without their prior consent and advised Hans Sachs to cultivate his shoemaker's trade instead of composing provocative verses. Erhard Schön, the artist involved in the project, is not expressly mentioned in the censorship proceedings, presumably because his woodcuts were merely copied from those in the Bolognese prototype with certain changes, but they were not in themselves offensive. In this instance, the explanatory texts by Osiander and Sachs were what the councilors considered dangerous, not the images. They generously compensated the printer, Guldenmund, for his loss in sales with twelve florins, due to alleged financial hardship. They also returned the confiscated woodblocks to him and suggested he publish the text of the original Bolognese edition using these woodblocks, if he so desired.[22] Such a book, however, would not have found a market in Reform-minded Nuremberg. Both the expression of one's Lutheran beliefs and the profit to be made on such a publishing venture were critical factors in any decision to print a work and try to circumvent the censors. Antipapal polemics were far more popular during these years than most other titles.

The financial motive was cited outright as the deciding factor by David de Negker when he published *The Heinous Destruction and Defeat of the Papists* (*Von der Erschrocklichen Zurstörung und Niderlag des gantzen Bapstums*), a satirical antipapal comedy written by the Anabaptist Martin Schrot, which appeared in an edition of one thousand copies in Augsburg in 1558. As soon as the publication came to the attention of the imperial court, the councilors in Augsburg were instructed to apprehend and punish the publisher and to destroy all remaining copies. The well-documented proceedings against de Negker, son of the famous Augsburg woodcutter Jost de Negker,[23] who executed many of the woodcuts for Emperor Maximilian I's graphics projects such as the *Weisskunig* and cut chiaroscuro woodcuts for Hans Burgkmair,[24] record that the reason for assuming the book would sell especially well lay in its entertaining and comic content (*ein schwänkig lächerig ding*).[25]

During lengthy interrogations, whose results were reported to the emperor, David de Negker justified publishing an obviously polemical book illegally by admitting that he had hoped to use the anticipated income to pay his considerable debts. A factor in the comedy's favor was certainly the popularity it had attained when performed publicly in Augsburg in more liberal times, in 1546. Following the emperor's victory over the Protestant princes in the Schmalkaldic Wars and the publication of the Interim in May 1548, however, a more repressive period had begun. The councilors imprisoned de Negker for four months and when they let him free, forbade him to practice his trade. Only after seven and a half months and several pleas for leniency did the emperor relent. In this case, de Negker was the designer and cutter of the woodcut illustrations (fig. 9) as well as the printer. His collaboration with the Anabaptist author Schrot was based on friendship and common reli-

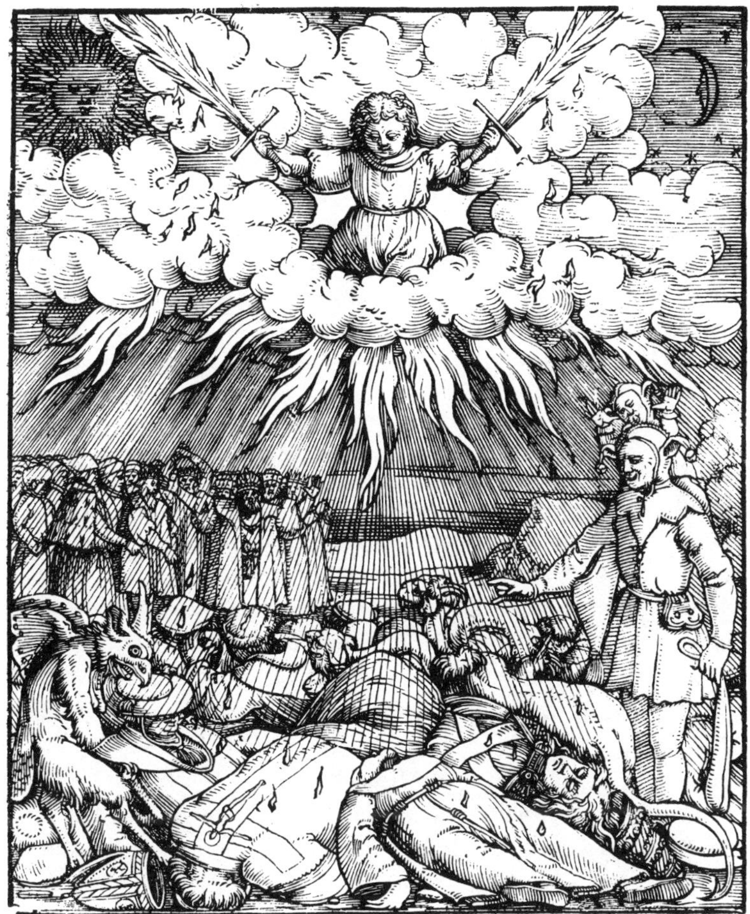

FIG. 9. David de Negker, *The Avenging Angel over the Defeated Papists*, from Martin Schrot, *The Heinous Destruction and Defeat of the Papists* (*Von der Erschrocklichen Zurstörung*), 1558.
Woodcut, 19.6×15.8 cm (7¾×6¼ in.). Chapin Library, Williams College, Williamstown, Massachusetts.

gious convictions. In danger of being apprehended for another censored text, Schrot had entrusted his manuscript of the comedy to de Negker before he fled Augsburg to join the Moravian Brethren. Once de Negker realized that the text required additional work, Schrot secretly returned to Augsburg to make corrections and additions while hiding from the authorities for over a month during the summer of 1557. He risked imprisonment in order to ensure that his antipapal comedy could be properly published.

The text of his comedy combines the standard polemic attacks against the venality of the papacy with stories from the prophets and the Apocalypse, interspersed with Bible quotations. The polemical drama was intended to reveal the Catholic Church as a creation of the devil and to demonstrate a deserved divine retribution. The third full-page illustration (fig. 9), for instance, shows God's avenging angel holding two flaming swords of retribution while hovering over the defeated heap of the papists. In the left foreground Satan attempts to help a cardinal rise to his feet, while at the right a fool uses the "fig" gesture to make fun of the defeated. In the background the pope's henchmen, who had recently sworn loyalty to him, do not offer assistance. The book's last full-page illustration (fig. 10) shows an allegory of the new Protestant faith. The resurrected Christ stands atop a rocky peak to which twelve steps lead, signifying the twelve articles of faith. Christ has defeated Satan, who tumbles in midair at the left, pursued by avenging angels. Above God the Father is seated on his throne. At the right, cherubs adore the lamb of God. In the center a believer ascends the staircase welcomed by an angel and the dove of the Holy Spirit. To the right of the stairs, angels armed with swords prevent the unworthy from attempting to enter the kingdom of God—for instance, by climbing a ladder. In the foreground, believers are ministered to by Saint John the Baptist and the prophets. The multitude at the right are the nonbelievers, shown behind Moses holding the tablets of the law.

The archival documents of de Negker's interrogation also reveal how and where the books were sold. He gave the first copy as a gift to the well-known bibliophile Elector Ottheinrich, the second to Margrave Karl of Baden, and then sold a large number to a local itinerant bookseller, who in turn sent them to an agent in Leipzig. De Negker sold some copies in Augsburg to local book collectors and gave a few to Schrot's wife. The majority, however, he took to sell at the fair in Frankfurt. Generally fairs and church festivals where throngs gathered were the best markets. Itinerant peddlers (*Buchführer*) offered their wares in the market squares and even under the main portal of the Church of Our Lady in Nuremberg, a practice prohibited in

Ich Glaub ein Heilige Christliche Kirchen.

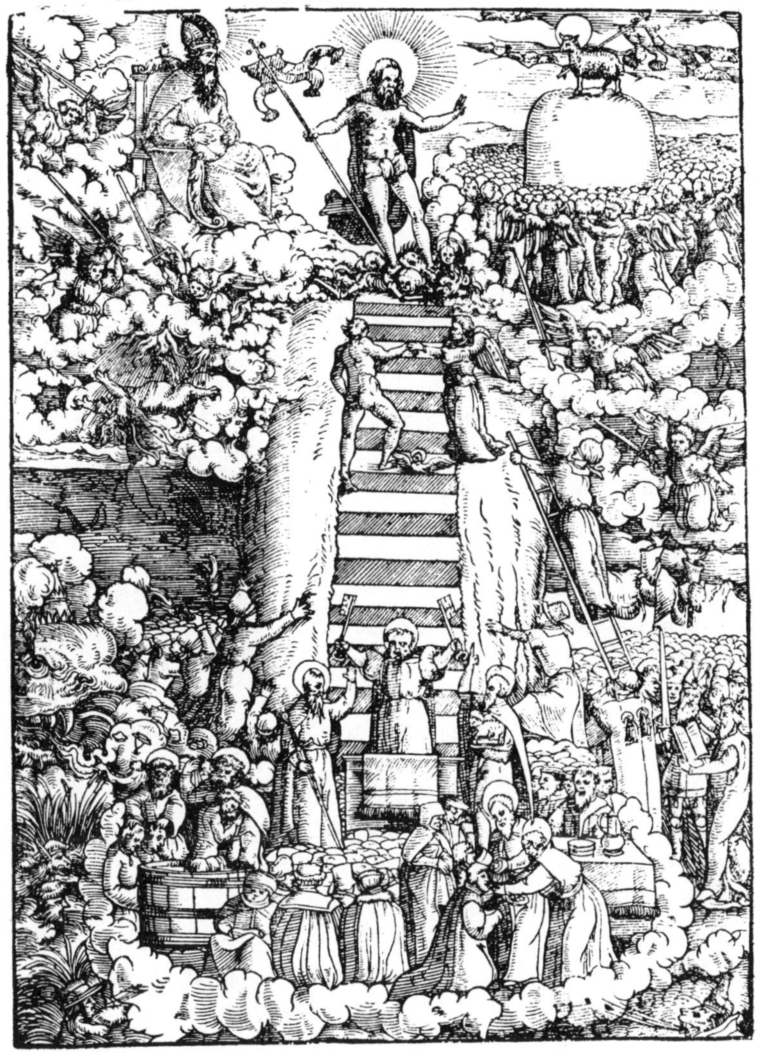

All Hällisch pforten werden sy nit vbersigen/Mathei 16.

FIG. 10. David de Negker, *Allegory of Faith*, from Martin Schrot, *The Heinous Destruction and Defeat of the Papists* (*Von der Erschrocklichen Zurstörung*), 1558. Woodcut, 19.6×15.8 cm (7¾×6¼ in.). Chapin Library, Williams College, Williamstown, Massachusetts.

1547.[26] In 1560 in Augsburg itinerant booksellers complained of unfair competition to the city council about a book vendor who had opened a shop rather than working the streets and fairs.[27] During this period it was customary for itinerant vendors to offer paperbound pamphlets, not larger books, displayed on small, portable tables along with single-sheet prints and broadsheets held together by a string, so that each sheet could be torn off when sold.[28]

The political situation in the Alsatian capital, Strassburg, was quite different from conditions in Nuremberg or Augsburg. Strassburg was known for a high degree of religious tolerance and thus became a haven for religious mavericks, though their activities and publications were closely monitored. Early on, the population of Strassburg was almost entirely Lutheran. The town council, responsible for maintaining the peace, exercised censorship primarily by suppressing Catholic tracts, in particular those by the virulently polemical Franciscan, Thomas Murner (1475–1537).[29] His pamphlet *The Great Lutheran Fool* (*Von dem grossen Lutherischen Narren wie in doctor Murner beschworen hat*) of 1522 was seized by the censors.[30] The title-page woodcut (fig. 11) depicts a scene of satirical exorcism. The author, shown in his Franciscan habit and with a cat's head (an onomatopoetic pun on the name Murner and theriomorphic form in which Murner was customarily portrayed in evangelical propaganda[31]), frees the "great fool," signifying the folly of Lutheran belief: not demons but rather many smaller fools issue from the great fool's mouth in the process of exorcism. Murner was known as a best-selling author of fools literature such as his *Narrenbeschwörung*, in the tradition of Sebastian Brant's *Ship of Fools* (*Narrenschiff*, 1494), before becoming one of the most eloquent and satirical defenders of the Catholic faith. In this anti-Lutheran tract he employed for polemical purposes the tradition of fools literature, with its imagery drawn from popular culture. On March 21, 1521, Murner had requested permission to reply in print to recent Lutheran attacks against him. The councilors allowed him only to post his rebuttal at twelve public spots in Strassburg. Instead on December 19, 1522, Murner published his tract on the "Great Fool" without prior permission, and the council immediately confiscated and burned almost the entire edition, except for a few copies that must have escaped the censor's grasp. The printer, Johann Grüninger, tried to claim compensation for his financial loss but received only a severe reprimand. Grüninger, known for his Catholic sympathies, had consistently printed Murner's diatribes but due to effective censorship in Strassburg, soon could no longer afford to do

Von dem grossen Lutherischen Narren wie in docto: Murner beschworen hat. ꝛc.

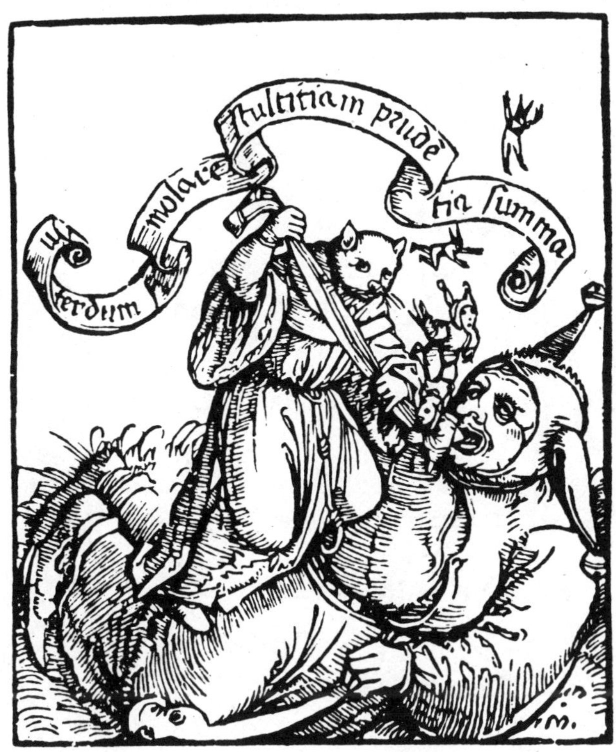

FIG. 11. Anonymous Strassburg artist, Title-page illustration from Thomas Murner, *The Great Lutheran Fool* (*Von dem grossen Lutherischen Narren*), 1522. Woodcut, 11.7×9.4 cm (4½× 3¾ in.). Bayerische Staatsbibliothek, Munich.

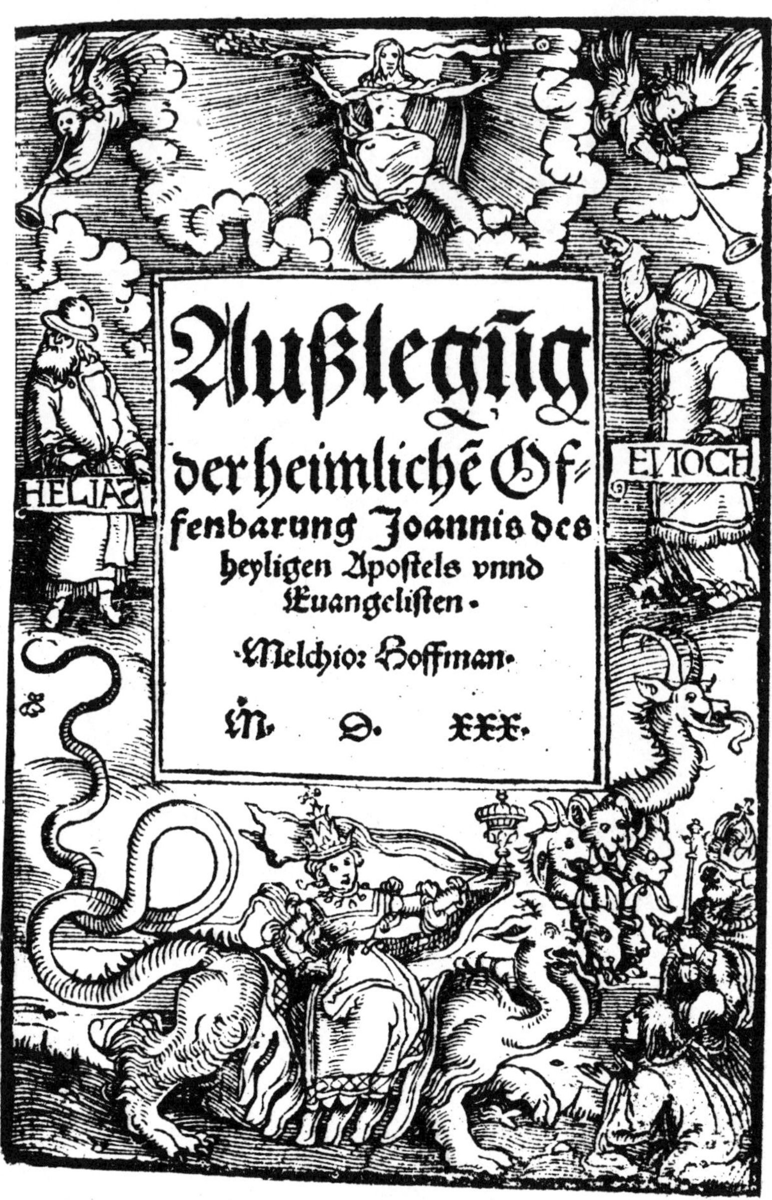

FIG. 12. Anonymous Strassburg artist, *The Whore of Babylon Riding the Seven-Headed Beast of the Apocalypse*, title-page illustration from Melchior Hoffman, *Interpretation of the Mysterious Revelations of Saint John* (*Ausslegung der heimlichen Offenbarung Joannis*), 1530.
Woodcut, 12.6×8.1 cm (5×3¼ in.). Bayerische Staatsbibliothek, Munich.

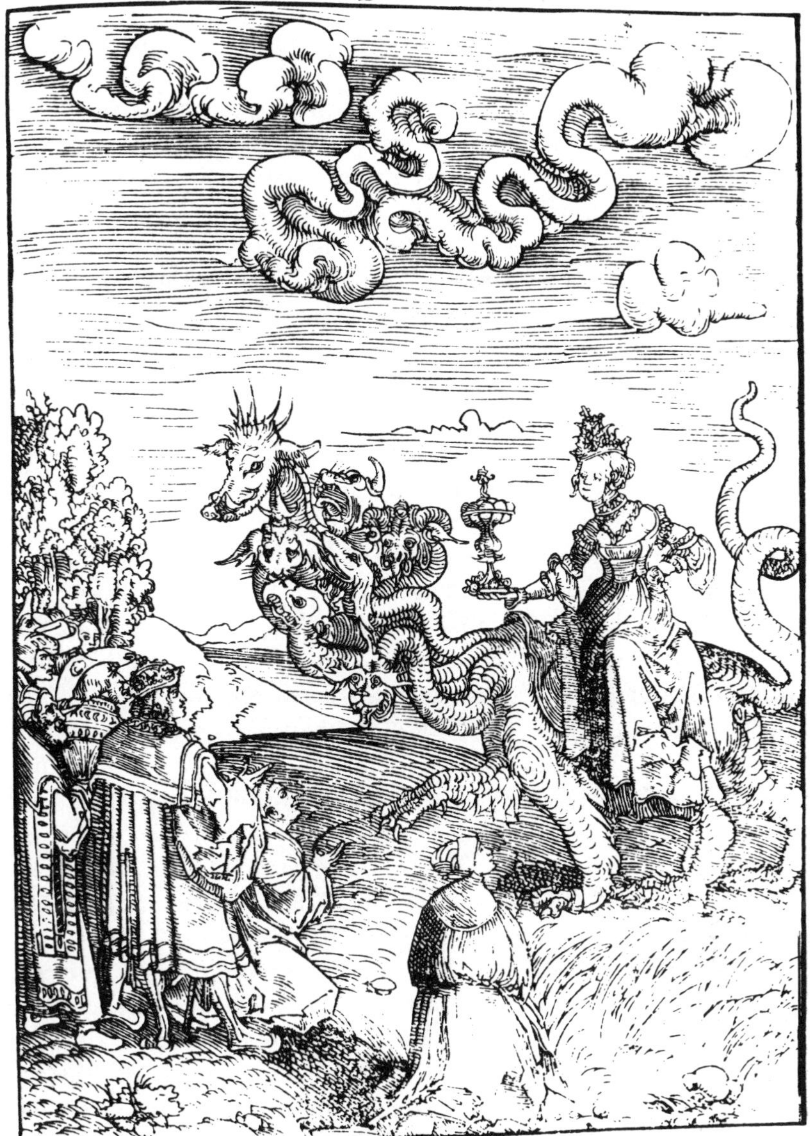

FIG. 13. Lucas Cranach the Elder and workshop, *The Whore of Babylon Riding the Seven-Headed Beast of the Apocalypse*, illustration from Martin Luther's translation of the *New Testament*, 1st edition, 1522. Woodcut, 23.5×16.0 cm (9¼×6⅓ in.). Kunstbibliothek mit Museum für Architektur, Staatliche Museen Preussischer Kulturbesitz, Berlin.

so. Murner was silenced primarily because he could find no printer willing to publish his texts.

Strassburg's city council, committed to orthodox evangelical belief, was careful to prevent the circulation of heretical tracts by Anabaptists or religious fanatics. In 1530 the councilors censored the self-styled "revelations" of the Anabaptist Melchior Hoffman,[32] which he published in his *Interpretation of the Mysterious Revelations of Saint John* (*Ausslegung der heimlichen Offenbarung Joannis*). His new interpretation of the Book of Revelations focused on his personal vision of the Last Judgment. The pamphlet's title-page illustration (fig. 12) shows Christ the Judge flanked by two angels announcing Judgment Day with their trumpets, the prophets Elias and Enoch, who foretold the end of the world and exposed the Antichrist's identity, and below, the apocalyptic woman seated on the seven-headed beast of the Apocalypse, adored by three figures. The lower scene with the apocalyptic woman shown as the Whore of Babylon wearing the papal tiara is a reversed copy after Lucas Cranach's illustration for Luther's Bible of 1522 (fig. 13), which in turn is based loosely on one of Albrecht Dürer's *Apocalypse* woodcuts of 1498. The identification of the papacy with the Whore of Babylon was already considered highly provocative in Cranach's woodcut, so much so that in the next Wittenberg edition in December 1522, the triple tiara was cut out of the woodblock, leaving only a simple crown. But the papal tiara was not what the Strassburg councilors objected to. As in Nuremberg, they were concerned to avoid any personal attacks against the emperor, and they considered the standing figure at the right edge of the title-page illustration an obvious portrait of Charles V. The council confiscated all remaining copies of the pamphlet plus the woodblock, held a hearing with the parties involved, and imprisoned both the author and the printer, Balthasar Beck.

Ultimately the imperial court was unable to enforce the anti-Lutheran censorship decrees of Charles V.[33] This is evident from the frequent and ever more emphatic reissuing of regulations, sometimes with identical texts. In an edict of 1524, Charles stated his intention of reinforcing what he had proclaimed in the Edict of Worms only three years earlier, and in 1548 he complained outright that previous decrees had been ineffective. In the Edict of Speyer of 1570, he outlawed the operation of printing presses located in out-of-the-way places, which were difficult for the authorities to control; and he allowed presses to operate only in free imperial cities or in towns in which a princely court or a university was located, the implication being that he could rely only on representatives of these institutions. Despite official disapproval, the censors were often lenient, as we have seen, and German pamphleteers flourished on the whole. They benefited from cheap paper, good trade routes, and the ease with which forbidden broadsheets and pamphlets could be smuggled. The authorities by contrast had to contend with all the impediments to effective censorship: a multitude of political jurisdictions; overburdened, easily bribed, or outright sympathetic censors; conflicts between lay and ecclesiastical authorities; lax magistrates and popular pressure; and consistent mutual aid among Protestant publishers. They in fact exercised their own form of "reverse" censorship in many parts of Germany by refusing to print any pro-Catholic material. The official policies were ineffective also because often those charged with enforcing them were sympathetic to Luther.

An assessment of the censorship of images in Germany during the Reformation era must take account of the political circumstances in each case. As we have seen, these changed radically over the period considered here, sometimes in only a few weeks, and varied from place to place. The limits of tolerance continued to be tested by fervent believers on both sides of the religious conflict. Predictably, however, the "underdog" Protestants were vastly more inventive and productive in their polemical output. The printer was usually considered by the censors to be the "guiltiest" participant and was more likely to be punished than the author or artist. When the woodcutter David de Negker masterminded such a project, he acted essentially as a printer. The question of relative guilt and retribution will be included in a more comprehensive future study.

NOTES

For their generous support of this research project, I would like to thank the Institut für Europaische Geschichte of the University of Mainz, where I was a Senior Fellow in 1993–94.

1. Edward Surtz and Jack H. Hexter, eds., *Thomas More, Complete Works* (New Haven: Yale University Press, 1965), 4:10–20.

2. Frank Allen Patterson, ed., *The Works of John Milton* (New York: Columbia University Press, 1931), 4:301.

3. Adalbert Erler and Ekkehard Kaufmann, eds., *Handwörterbuch zur deutschen Rechtsgeschichte* (Berlin: E. Schmidt, 1984), 3: col. 1910.

4. See Steven S. Dubin's essay in this volume and his recent book, *Arresting Images: Impolitic Art and Uncivil Actions* (New York and London: Routledge, 1992).

5. Arndt Müller, "Zensurpolitik der Reichsstadt Nürnberg: Von der Einführung

der Buchdruckkunst bis zum Ende der Reichsstadtzeit," *Mitteilungen des Vereins für die Geschichte der Stadt Nürnberg* 49 (1957): 70.

6. Paul Kalkoff, *Die Entstehung des Wormser Ediktes* (Leipzig: Heinsius, 1913), and *Das Wormser Edikt und die Erlasse des Reichsregiments und einzelner Reichsfürsten*, Historische Bibliothek, 37 (Munich and Berlin: Oldenbourg, 1917).

7. Müller, "Zensurpolitik," 74.

8. Rolf Engelsing, *Analphabetentum und Lektüre, Zur Sozialgeschichte des Lesens in Deutschland zwischen feudaler und industrieller Gesellschaft* (Stuttgart: Metzler, 1973), 32 ff.

9. Dieter Koepplin and Tilman Falk, *Lukas Cranach: Gemälde, Zeichnungen, Druckgraphik*, exh. cat., Kunstmuseum Basel (Basel: Birkhäuser, 1974 and 76), 1:330, cat nos. 218–20, figs. 178–79 and 2:586, fig. 302.

10. Hermann Meuche and Ingeborg Neumeister, eds., *Flugblätter der Reformation und des Bauernkrieges*, vol. 1 (Leipzig: Insel-Verlag, 1975), 41 and 119–20, with pl. TA18. See also Wolfgang Harms and Beate Rattay, eds., *Illustrierte Flugblätter aus den Jahrhunderten der Reformation und der Glaubenskämpfe* (Coburg: Kunstsammlungen der Veste Coburg, 1983), 40–41, cat. no. 20.

11. See Michael Schilling's commentary on the 1539 edition in Wolfgang Harms, *Deutsche illustrierte Flugblätter des 16. und 17. Jahrhunderts, vol. 2 Die Sammlung der Herzog August Bibliothek in Wolfenbüttel, 2: Historica* (Munich: Kraus, 1980). Luther's authorship is confirmed in Anton Lauterbach's letter, cited in *D. Martin Luthers Werke, Kritische Gesamtausgabe* (Weimar: Hermann Böhlaus Nachfolger, 1933), *Tischreden III*, no. 3749, and in *Briefe VIII*, 200, 23 and 206, 3–5. Veit Dietrich's letter is cited in D. Albrecht and P. Flemming, "Das sogenannte Manuscriptum Thomasianum, III," *Archiv für Reformationsgeschichte* 13 (1916): 29–30.

12. Robert W. Scribner, *For the Sake of Simple Folk: Popular Propaganda for the German Reformation* (Cambridge: Cambridge University Press, 1981), 78–81.

13. Müller, "Zensurpolitik," 74.

14. The archives consulted are the *Stadtarchiv* in Nüremberg, the *Stadtarchiv* in Augsburg, and the *Archives Municipales* in Strassburg.

15. Cf. Beham's woodcut of Saint Paul with the Sword, dated 1530 in F. W. H. Hollstein, *German Engravings, Etchings and Woodcuts, 1400–1700* (Amsterdam: Menno Hertzberger, n.d.), 3:191–92 with illustration.

16. Theodor Hampe, *Nürnberger Ratsverlässe über Kunst und Künstler im Zeitalter der Spätgotik und Renaissance* (Vienna: Gräser; Leipzig: Teubner, 1904), 205, no. 1339.

17. Maria Consuelo Oldenbourg, *Die Buchholzschnitte des Hans Baldung Grien, ein bibliographisches Verzeichnis ihrer Verwendungen* (Baden-Baden: Heitz, 1962), p. 125, no. 358, and fig. 188.

18. Hampe, *Ratsverlässe*, 221, no. 1455.

19. Müller, "Zensurpolitik," 82–84, Scribner, *Popular Propaganda*, 142 ff, Jeffrey Chipps Smith, *Nuremberg, a Renaissance City, 1500–1618*, exh. cat. (Austin, Texas: Archer M. Huntington Art Gallery, University of Texas, 1983), 167, cat. no. 65, and David

Landau and Peter Pershall, *The Renaissance Print, 1470–1550* (New Haven and London: Yale University Press, 1994), 224.

20. Jeffrey Chipps Smith (1983) illustrates only one page opening. The majority of the woodcut illustrations are unpublished.

21. Luther's letter written from Wittenberg to Wenzeslaus Link in Nuremberg states: *Nihil novi apud nos nisi libellus vester imaginarius de Papatu, in quo imaginem meam cum falce valde probo, ut qui mordax et acerbus tot annis ante praedictus sum futurus, sed rosam pro meo signo interpretari dubito, magis ad officium etiam pertinere putarim. Caetera nunc placent, si vera sunt, quae vulgastis* (There is nothing new with us except your illustrated pamphlet about the Papacy, in which I thoroughly approve of my image with a sickle, as one of whom it was predicted so many years ago that I was destined to be biting and sharp, but I am dubious about interpreting the rose as a symbol for me, I would have thought it also referred rather to my office. With the other things you reported, I am satisfied, if they are true). Martin Luther, *D. Martin Luthers Werke: Kritische Gesamtausgabe, Briefwechsel* (Weimar: Hermann Böhlaus Nachfolger, 1933), 4:203.

22. Hampe, *Ratsverlässe*, 238, no. 1580, and 274, no. 1921.

23. Hildegard Zimmermann in Ulrich Thieme and Felix Becker, *Allgemeines Lexikon der bildenden Künstler von der Antike bis zur Gegenwart* (Leipzig: Seemann, 1931), 25:377–78, and Jane Turner, ed., *The Dictionary of Art* (London: Macmillan, 1996) 8: 723.

24. Tilman Falk, Rolf Biedermann, et al., *Hans Burgkmair: Das graphische Werk*, exh. cat. (Stuttgart: Staatsgalerie, 1973), cat. nos. 21–22, and for the *Weisskunig* illustrations, cat. nos. 178–203.

25. Friedrich Roth, "Zur Lebensgeschichte des Augsburger Formschneiders David Denecker und seines Freundes, des Dichters Martin Schrot; ihr anonym herausgegebenes 'Schmachbuch' Von der Erschrocklichen Zurstörung vnnd Niderlag deß gantzen Bapstumbs," *Archiv für Reformationsgeschichte* 9 (1912): 199–200.

26. Hampe, *Ratsverlässe*, no. 3010.

27. G. Costa, "Die Rechtseinrichtung der Zensur in der Reichsstadt Augsburg," *Zeitschrift des historischen Vereins für Schwaben und Neuburg* 42 (1916): 14–15.

28. Vendors offered their wares in 1560 *auf den Schragen und an den Stricken*, according to Costa, "Rechtseinrichtung," 14. The *Schragen* was the customary means of table display used by many different kinds of merchants in public places. Jacob and Wilhelm Grimm, *Deutsches Wörterbuch* (Leipzig: S. Hirzel, 1899), 15: cols. 1621–22.

29. *Allgemeine Deutsche Biographie*, 23:67–76.

30. Paul Merker, ed., *Thomas Murner, Von dem grossen Lutherischen Narren*, in *Thomas Murners Deutsche Schriften, Kritische Gesamtausgabe der elsässischen Schriftsteller des Mittelalters und der Reformationszeit* (Strassburg: Trübner, 1918).

31. Compare the illustration of the cat-headed portrait of Murner in an anonymous illustrated broadsheet with text of about 1521 in the Germanisches Nationalmuseum, Nuremberg, illustrated in Christiane Andersson, "Polemical Prints in Ref-

ormation Nuremberg," in Jeffrey Chipps Smith, ed., *New Perspectives on the Art of Renaissance Nuremberg: Five Essays* (Austin: Archer M. Huntington Art Gallery, University of Texas, 1985), 47, fig. 10.

32. On Melchior Hoffman, see Peter Kawerau, *Melchior Hoffman als religiöser Denker* (Haarlem, Netherlands, 1954); Hans Hillerbrand, ed., *The Oxford Encyclopedia of the Reformation* (New York: Oxford University Press, 1996), 2: 240–43; and Klaus Deppermann, *Melchior Hoffman: Social Unrest and Apocalyptic Visions in the Age of the Reformation* (Edinburgh, 1987), esp. 192–93 and no. 11 in his list of Hoffman's publications. The censorship of his *Ausslegung der heimlichen Offenbarung* is briefly discussed by Karl Schottenloher in "Beschlagnahmte Druckschriften aus der Frühzeit der Reformation," *Zeitschrift für Bücherfreunde* n.s. 8 (1917): 317.

33. Maurice Gravier, *Luther et l'opinion publique* (Paris, 1942), 60, and Elizabeth L. Eisenstein, *The Printing Press as an Agent of Change: Communications and Cultural Transformations in Early Modern Europe*, 2d ed. (Cambridge and London: Cambridge University Press, 1980), 405, and cf. Christiane Andersson, "Polemical Prints during the Reformation," in New York Public Library, *Censorship: 500 Years of Conflict*, exh. cat. (New York: Oxford University Press, 1984), 50–51.

Aretino, the Public, and the Censorship of Michelangelo's *Last Judgment*

BERNADINE BARNES

MICHELANGELO'S *LAST JUDGMENT* (fig. 1) was the focus of a vehement public debate. Painted on the wall above the altar in the Sistine Chapel, the image of the Last Day seems to be a mass of contorted nudes. Even to those who sympathize with the Renaissance love of the nude, some of the figures are puzzling and seem intentionally offensive. Included among these are a man being pulled to hell by his testicles (fig. 6); the prominent figure of Minos, whose penis is being bitten by a snake; and Saint Blaise, who in the original version hovered over a naked Saint Catherine with his currycombs raised, suggesting some kind of sadistic activity, or even sodomy. These images were all "censored" in a series of repainting campaigns that began in 1564.[1] Most often this involved the rather perfunctory addition of loincloths (compare figs. 6 and 7, a print preserving the original appearance of the fresco), but in the case of Saints Blaise and Catherine more drastic measures were taken. Catherine was given full dress, while the plaster on which Blaise's head was painted was chipped out and an entirely new head, now looking at Christ, was substituted (compare figs. 4 and 5).

Why was this painting subjected to such treatment? It was not the first work that used nudity in a religious setting—Michelangelo's own frescoes on the ceiling of the same chapel are full of nudes that were not painted over. The Sistine Ceiling, painted between 1508 and 1512, simply did not generate the same kind of debate that confronted the *Last Judgment* after its unveiling in 1541.[2] The criticisms of the ceiling remained isolated remarks; the debate over the *Last Judgment* continued throughout the century, with opinions ranging from the highest praise to biting satire. Comments appeared in pasquinate, in sermons, in poetry, and in extensive theoretical discussions.

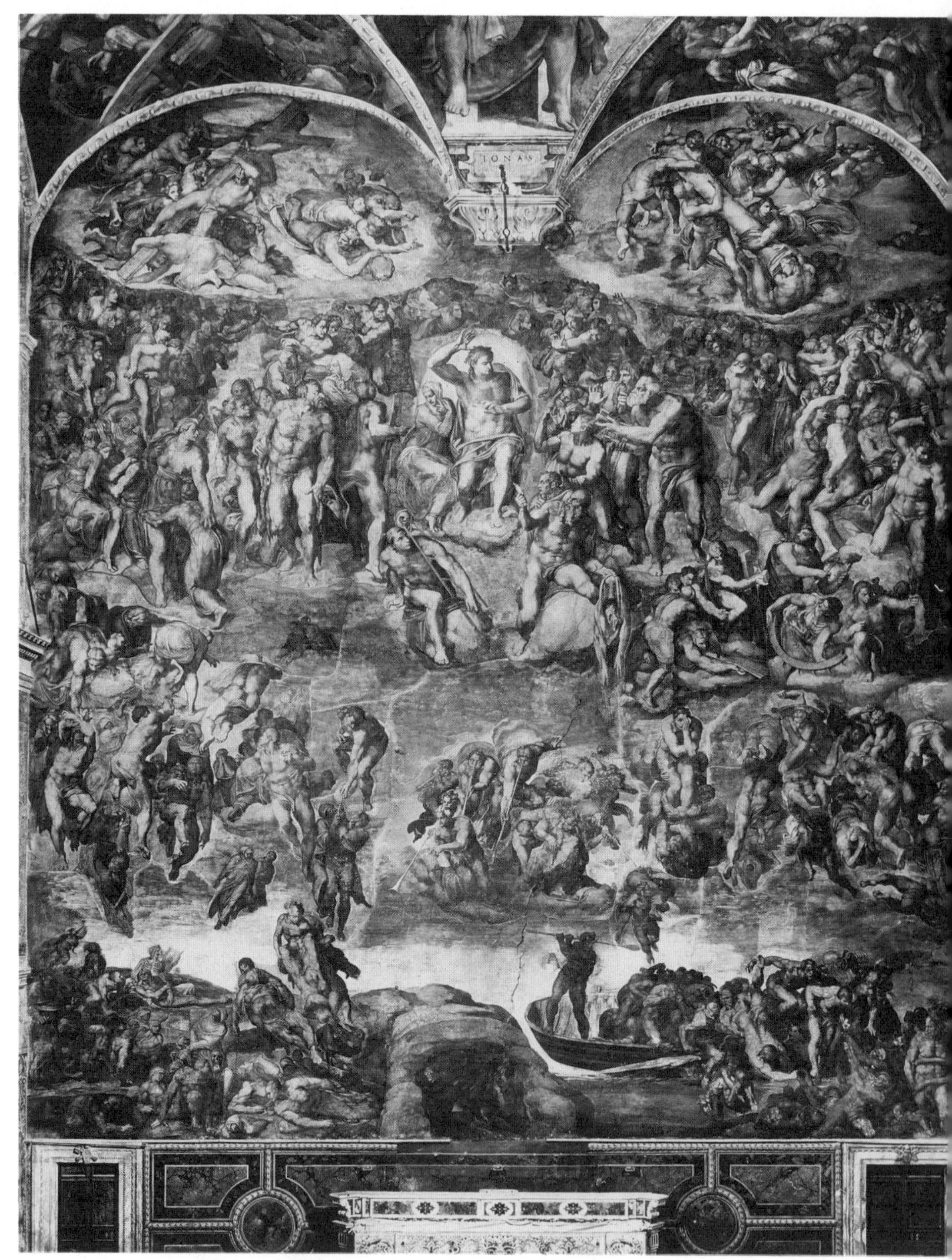

FIG. 1. Michelangelo, *Last Judgment*, completed 1541.
Fresco, 1,464×1,342 cm (576×528 in.). Vatican, Sistine Chapel.

These last especially include responses to earlier criticisms, creating a true dialogue.

The answer to why this painting drew so much attention, and why it was finally subjected to repainting, is publicity. And the person behind that publicity, at least at the beginning, was Pietro Aretino. His remarks on the *Last Judgment* are found in a series of letters written between 1537 and 1550, some addressed to Michelangelo himself, others to friends who might be interested in the work. These letters have been discussed before, usually to gain insight into the personalities of the two men or to discern Aretino's theory of art.[3] I believe they reveal much more about Aretino's perception of his own audience, and about his changing ideas regarding who the audience might be for the *Last Judgment*. What makes Aretino's comments so interesting is that they show him learning the potential of the press, discovering both his audience and how to appeal to them. They also show him discovering that a new audience for art was developing through widespread distribution of reproduced prints. Neither printmaking nor the book publishing industry originated in the 1530s, but both were becoming more profitable businesses and were attracting wider audiences.[4] Aretino's letters show his awareness of these new audiences, and in directing his own work toward them he fueled the fires that eventually led to the censorship of the *Last Judgment*.

The infamous Aretino (1492–1556) was raised in modest circumstances in Arezzo (his name refers to his city of birth). He discovered his talent for writing as a young man, and moved to Rome to seek a position in the papal court.[5] In 1527 he settled in Venice, where he became the center of a circle of artists and writers, a group that included the painter Titian and the architect Jacopo Sansovino. He was a prolific writer, and became most famous for his letters commenting on the people and events of his times. Often addressed to high-ranking government and religious officials, these letters frequently contained scathing criticism and received equally strong responses. As a result, he acquired the epithet the Scourge of Princes, and took on the motto "Veritas odium parit" (Truth begets hatred).[6] Both are displayed with his portrait in figure 2. Despite his purported honesty, Aretino's own literary production—indeed his own personality—is so multifaceted that it is almost impossible to discern a "real" Aretino. In addition to his letters, he wrote extremely explicit pornography as well as popular religious books; and there is every reason to believe that his religious works were taken quite seriously in the sixteenth century.[7] Aretino himself proudly pointed out the variety in his writings in a passage from the pornographic *Dialogo quale la Nanna insegna la Pippa* (1536): "Over there are my *Psalms*, further along is

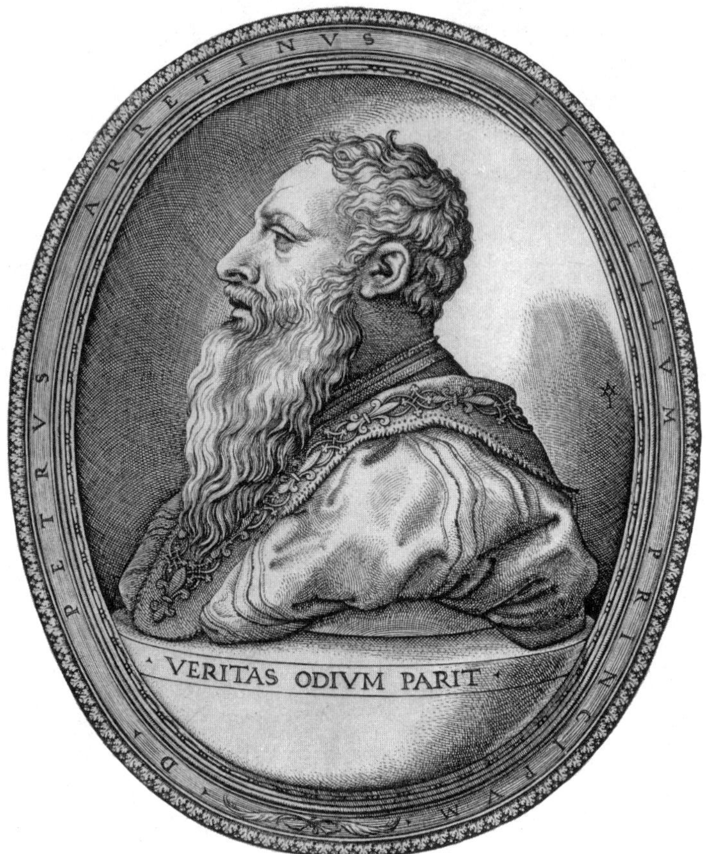

FIG. 2. Giovanni Jacopo Caraglio, *Pietro Aretino* (after Titian?), ca. 1534. Engraving, 19.3×15.3 cm (7⅝×6 in.). Metropolitan Museum of Art, New York, Harris Brisbane Dick Fund, 1927. (27.78.2 leaf 53).

my *History of Christ*, beyond that are my plays and here are my *Dialogues*: devout or entertaining works, according to the subject."[8]

In the past, this diversity was scorned as the mark of a hypocrite, although recently Aretino scholars have become interested in examining his varying "personae"—the authorial fictions that he takes on to fit his particular purposes. Those purposes are often connected to his perceived audience. For example, he may adopt the guise of scholar or courtier to gain entrance into the powerful circle of patricians in Venice. He may take on the role of satirist in order to describe the perversity of human behavior while distancing himself from it. He may act as a connoisseur in order to promote the careers of his friends, or he may act as the man without much learning to appeal to a wider, unschooled audience.[9]

A similar kind of diversity is seen in Aretino's letters on the *Last Judgment*. All scholars notice the striking change that takes place between the beginning of the correspondence in 1537 and his final reference to the *Last Judgment* some thirteen years later. Aretino's interest changes from an evident desire to collaborate on the fresco by supplying a literary "invention" for it, to lavish praise of the finished result (in spite of Michelangelo's rejection of his offer of service), and finally to sharp criticism of the fresco. Several reasons have been suggested for this change. Aretino's increasing frustration at Michelangelo's refusal to send him drawings is most frequently proposed, and surely it was an important factor. It may also be that the puritanical stance evident in the last letters has something to do with a rumor that Aretino might be made cardinal.[10] However, Aretino had religious ambitions even in the early 1530s, so in itself this could not account for his abrupt change of tone. Nevertheless, by 1550 Counter Reformation forces were gaining strength in Venice, and Aretino may have felt some pressure to modify his licentious reputation. Even this remains conjectural, since Aretino's own works were not censored until 1559, three years after his death.[11]

My purpose is not to refute these explanations for Aretino's vicissitudes, since any or all of them could have been at work. Rather, I would like to suggest that here too Aretino is keying his writing to particular audiences. He was aware from the beginning that his letters would be read not only by the addressee but also by those who purchased his book of letters. By 1537 his plan to publish such a collection was firmly in mind. This would be the first collection in Italian of letters gathered by the author himself and modeled after the highly crafted Latin letters of Renaissance humanists.[12] It would seem that from 1537 on Aretino thought of his letters as public letters, but that the public toward which he directed them changed over time. The letters reveal that Aretino was aware of that change, and that he was also aware of the wide audience that the *Last Judgment* had by midcentury. In response to these changed conditions, Aretino constructed his persona, revealing his motivations and expectations. In the process we learn, above all, the conditions that were necessary to make this painting the object of censorship.

The first letter by Aretino dealing with the *Last Judgment* is dated September 15, 1537.[13] Michelangelo had already begun painting by then, but his work progressed in secrecy. Still, news of the commission had spread rapidly throughout Italy. Aretino, writing from Venice, responded to the anticipatory excitement with his own long description of what the Last Judgment might be like. In the opening paragraphs he establishes his persona: he presents himself as a courtier, a humble servant to a great man. He tells Michelangelo that he would not even have dared to address him, "had not my name, accepted by the ears of every prince in Europe, lost much of its former indignity." This reference to his epithet, the Scourge of Princes, seems to be less a threat than an apology, suggesting that he is no longer as mean spirited as he once was. His tone is obsequious and flattering, although he makes it clear that he knows a great deal about art. To demonstrate that knowledge he expounds on drawing, talking like an insider to the artist famous for *disegno*:

> For in your hands there lives hidden the idea of a new nature, so that the difficulty of outlines—the highest science in the subtlety of painting—is so easy for you that you bind within the outlines of the bodies the end of art, a thing which art itself confesses to be impossible to bring to perfection, because the outline (as you know) should surround itself in such a way that, in showing what it does not show, it can suggest the things that the figures of the Sistine Chapel suggest to those who know how to judge them rather than merely gape at them.

Indeed he shows his awareness of current discussions of Michelangelo's art, bringing up not only *disegno* but also *difficultà*, and, in the following lines, the fact that Michelangelo excelled in painting, sculpture, and architecture.[14] But even more important, he presents himself as a member of an elite group—a man of judgment—who not only understands the subtleties of such ideas but truly appreciates Michelangelo's art, as opposed to those who "merely gape" at it.

Aretino *did* have close ties to the world of art, so not all of this is empty boasting, but he did not usually treat artists to this much adulation. With established artists he took a familiar tone; with lesser artists he was more critical. Usually it was the artist who wrote to Aretino with an air of respect, and (one suspects) with the hope of getting some publicity from him.[15] But here the tables are turned. Michelangelo was now, at the age of sixty-two, a mature artist and the acknowledged master of painting in Italy. This letter shows Aretino offering his services to a man he clearly ranks above himself, and, as the closing line of the letter makes clear, the service he offers is that of a publicist, someone who will "proclaim his powers."

The body of the letter, in which the Last Judgment is described, is in fact a display of Aretino's talents as a writer. It is often said to be a proposal for the painting, as if Aretino intended Michelangelo to use it as the basis for his design, but the style of the description makes it seem rather to be an *ekphrasis*—that is, a vivid description of a painting (in this case an imagined painting) that makes it seem as though it is a real event or object.[16] It is Aretino's style of writing that I think is important here, not whatever use Michelangelo might have made of the description.

Aretino presents the description as if it were a vision, beginning nearly every phrase with *Veggo*—"I see." Given the context, the reader might easily associate this with the divinely inspired vision of Saint John on Patmos, or with the vision of Dante. Indeed, echoes of this description are found in even more elaborate form in one of Aretino's religious works, *Il Genesi*, published in 1538, and there the description is included as part of the vision of Noah, again divinely inspired.[17] In keeping with such a grand conceit, Aretino strives for dramatic effect. Emotions are exaggerated, sound effects are added, actions are powerful and often violent. We hear the crashing of the arrows, see the world disintegrate, watch Fame being thrown down and crushed. Repetition is used to increase the force of the description, series of nouns are used instead of simple labels, and words that suggest terrible noise and brilliant light abound.

Aretino's description is not based on the visual tradition of the Last Judgment, nor is it derived from the literary works most often pointed to as sources for that tradition. There is little that derives from a biblical source, even less that might refer to the popular poems and plays written about the end of the world. The main characters are neither saints nor devils, nor are they the resurrected dead who so often figure in the popular tradition. Rather, they are personifications: Life and Death, Hope and Despair, Time seated on a throne, Fame crushed below the wheels of a chariot. These last two figures suggest a possible source in Petrarch's *Triumphs*, particularly the Triumph of Time, although the similarities are not precise. Nevertheless, this arrangement of paired personifications is more closely related to sophisticated literary works, counterposing figures of speech rather than relying on the characters and narratives commonly heard in sermons or plays.

The elaborate description of the Last Judgment stands out in Aretino's letters. Descriptive *ekphrases* in general are scarce in Aretino's work—there are only about a dozen among more than three thousand letters—and even rarer are dramatic descriptions based on works or events not really seen by him.[18] However, there is a significant cluster of *ekphrases* dated around 1537.[19] This was a time when Aretino was preparing to publish his first book of letters. He actively collected examples of his writing that he thought were his best works, and he wrote many new letters expressly for publication.[20] The description of the Last Judgment was surely one of these. It fits into a section of the first book of letters in which Aretino is most concerned with poetics, and its style suggests a conscious attempt to write in the grand manner.[21] The fact that Aretino was so concerned with style, and with creating a suitably grand image that would parallel a subject as glorious and terrifying as the Last Judgment, shows that he was writing not only to Michelangelo but also to a literary audience. He seems to have thought that the function of description, and of the work of art, was to delight the highly trained connoisseur. The audience as he perceived it was sophisticated, literate, and skilled in the perception of style.

Aretino had more than one purpose in writing the letter on the Last Judgment. He wanted to serve Michelangelo as his publicist, but he also wanted to demonstrate to people of good taste that he could create a literary description appropriate for such grand subject matter. Connected to this latter purpose is the notion that a person as great as Michelangelo deserved a higher style of address. He confirms this in his next letter to Michelangelo, dated January 20, 1538: "Certainly you are a divine person, and anyone who writes about you must use more than human language, unless he wants either to prove that he is ignorant, or to tell lies by talking in an everyday manner."[22]

There was yet another reason for writing to Michelangelo in this way. By being addressed to a great artist at work on what many thought would be the high point of his career, Aretino's letter would have attracted the reader's attention.[23] He very likely was hoping to attach himself to Michelangelo's fame, and in giving an "advance review" of what was expected to be the artist's greatest work it is also likely that Aretino was hoping to sell more copies of his *Lettere*. Aretino was himself a famous man by now, but his fame rested mostly on his scandalous writings. In the book of letters he was creating a new, more intellectual image for himself, and it was not at all clear how well it would sell.[24]

The book of letters containing the description turned out to be extremely popular. It was reprinted at least seven times in just over a year of its publication, with a second edition appearing in 1542.[25] A friend wrote to tell Aretino about the crowds at the bookshops to buy his book: "In opening the door of the Rota in Rome I have never seen such a rush of litigants to be first in line at the entrance, as I saw in the buying of your work when they read on a sheet of paper: Letters of the Divine Pietro Aretino."[26]

The letter on the Last Judgment also seems to have attracted the attention that Aretino sought. At least two of Aretino's admirers wrote high-sounding letters praising the *Last Judgment*, and since neither had seen the fresco they were most likely inspired by Aretino's letter.[27] Later another friend, Anton Francesco Doni, wrote to Aretino saying that Michelangelo's response to the letter was "some of the best praise that you have ever had."[28]

As for Michelangelo himself, Aretino had sent him a copy of the letter before it was published, and Michelangelo replied in turn.[29] Aretino later wrote that he would have included the artist's reply in the *First Book of Letters* but was prevented from doing so ("because the envious omitted it" he complained, but more likely because of an editorial decision not to publish letters other than Aretino's in the book).[30] In his response Michelangelo was noncommittal about using any of Aretino's ideas, but the artist recognized the offer that had been made, saying, "Now as to your writing about me, I not only say in reply that I should welcome it, but I entreat you to do so. . . ." He also generously offered to send Aretino something by his own hand. Aretino never forgot this offer, and his letters for the next six years contain repeated requests for drawings, which he never received. In spite of that affront, his flattery continued unabated. Throughout this period he maintained the persona of one who appreciated Michelangelo in a way that the common people could not, and as one who had the ability to write about Michelangelo's works in the style they deserved.[31]

The first published hint of Aretino's changed opinion of Michelangelo's fresco is found in the *Third Book of Letters*, in a letter dated January 1546 addressed to the printmaker Enea Vico. In it Aretino refers to an engraved copy of the *Last Judgment* by another artist, whom he calls Bazzacco.[32] Aretino praises Bazzacco's skill, but because he has copied the fresco without alterations, the engraving lacks the decorum that a religious work should have. He asks Vico to create an amended version of the print because he is afraid that the nudity will cause a scandal among the Lutherans. Such an enterprise, he assures Vico, will not only bring blessings from God but rewards from the duke of Florence. Aretino also implies that Vico would find the sale of these prints rewarding, and he suggests that a much wider public would be interested in the print. He points out that the whole world will participate in the Last Judgment, and so it is only right that Vico should be credited with everyone's enjoyment of an image of the Last Day. It is not coincidental that this new interest in everyone's enjoyment of the fresco, as well as concern over the scandal it may cause, is brought up in connection with engraved copies.

These same concerns are voiced in a far more famous letter, the invective against the *Last Judgment*. The handwritten version of this letter is not securely dated. It bears the date MDLXV (1565), which is surely incorrect since Aretino died in 1556. Most scholars believe that the L and the X have been inverted, and thus the correct date is 1545; a revised version of the letter bears the date July 1546.[33] I believe that the letter is closely related to the one addressed to Enea Vico; whether it precedes or follows may never be resolved. This letter ends with a postscript telling Michelangelo that the author was only letting off steam and that the letter should be torn up, but quite clearly it was not. Aretino himself must have kept a copy and thought it good enough to publish, for it appears in revised form readdressed to Alessandro Corvino in the *Fourth Book of Letters*, which came out in 1550. In keeping with Aretino's approach to letter writing in general, it is probable that he intended to publish this letter from the beginning.[34]

After a brief word of praise in which he compares Michelangelo's invention to the designs of Raphael, Aretino launches into his tirade. His criticism relies on the Renaissance concept of decorum, and in that regard is comparable to the earlier letters to Michelangelo. Before, he had made a point of using a more elaborate style in deference to both the artist and the subject of the painting. Now he is concerned that the painting fit the place and the audience who might see it. However, the audience is no longer composed of connoisseurs and literati, but rather of more common viewers. The following is taken from the body of the letter:

> However, as a baptized man, I am ashamed of the license, so unallowable to the spirit, that you have taken in expressing the ideas . . . of our absolutely true faith. For how can that Michelangelo of such stupendous fame, that Michelangelo of outstanding prudence, that Michelangelo of admirable habits, have wanted to show to the people no less religious impiety than artistic perfection? Is it possible for you, who through being divine do not condescend to the company of men, to have made this in the foremost temple of God? . . . You, in a subject of such a high history, show the saints and angels, the former without any of the decency proper to this world, and the latter deprived of celestial ornament. Here even the pagans in their sculpture—I'm not speaking of the clothed Diana, but the nude Venus—make her cover with her hand those parts that may not be revealed. And yet he who is a Christian, by valuing art more than faith, makes such a genuine spectacle out of both the lack of decorum in the martyrs and virgins, and the gesture of the man grabbed by his genitals, that even in a brothel the eyes would shut so as not to see it. . . . It would be less of a sin for you not to believe than by believing in this manner to weaken the faith of others.

Thus as a result of seeing Michelangelo's work, the people will have their faith shaken, they will be hindered in doing good, they will lose their love of devotion. To go along with this, Aretino makes it clear that Michelangelo considers himself above them—for example, he says that Michelangelo does not condescend to associate with mere mortals—and toward the end of the letter there are numerous scornful references to Michelangelo's pride, his intellect, and his learning. His tomb of Julius II (a work that caused Michelangelo much agony) is called a "haughty machine" (*altiera machina*), and the reason it has not been finished is that God wants Julius's remains to lie in a simpler tomb. This cutting remark goes along with all Aretino has said about the *Last Judgment.* By devoting himself to making the greatest work of art he could make, Michelangelo is working against the will of God. Art and religion are set against each other, as though they are mutually exclusive. By valuing art so highly, Michelangelo has shown himself to be without religion. Finally Aretino calls for censorship—either by the artist himself, who should cover the "shameful" parts with flames (for the damned) or rays of the sun (for the blessed), or by the pope, following the example of Gregory the Great, who "devoted himself to removing from Rome all the prideful statues of idols, rather than hinder the good in their devotion to the humble images of the saints."

Aretino has now become a representative of the simple folk who don't really care very much about art. This is in striking contrast to the persona of the first letter, where he touted himself as one with a particularly subtle understanding of Michelangelo's work. Aretino has not, of course, lost any of his sophistication. He now sees the audience for the *Last Judgment* to be wider than he had anticipated. It should be noted that Aretino had not gone to Rome to see the fresco itself; at the beginning of his letter he says that he has in hand a *schizzo* of the whole fresco—literally a sketch, but most likely a print, very probably the print mentioned in the letter to Enea Vico.[35]

The *Last Judgment* had by this time been made into prints by several artists. Niccolò della Casa's engraving of 1543 reproduced here (fig. 3) is one of the earliest; it proved so popular that it was reissued in 1548.[36] Another popular engraved version by Giulio Bonasone came out in 1546, around the time this letter was written. This is certainly the way that most people would have known the fresco. The Sistine Chapel was not a place to which the public was regularly invited; even though half of the chapel was nominally open to the laity, evidence from the diaries of the masters-of-ceremonies indicates that one had to be an invited guest of the papal court to gain entrance to the chapel. These diaries also indicate a genuine annoyance on those rare occasions when the public was allowed into the chapel.[37] Aretino, however, was probably not concerned about those who could see the fresco in person. Ludovico Dolce, who borrowed many of his ideas from Aretino, claimed that "infants, mothers and girls" would be scandalized by the *Last Judgment*—all people who would rarely (or never, in the case of infants) have had access to the chapel.[38] Aretino's criticisms make sense only if an untutored public could easily see Michelangelo's *Last Judgment.* By 1546 this was increasingly possible because of the availability of copies.

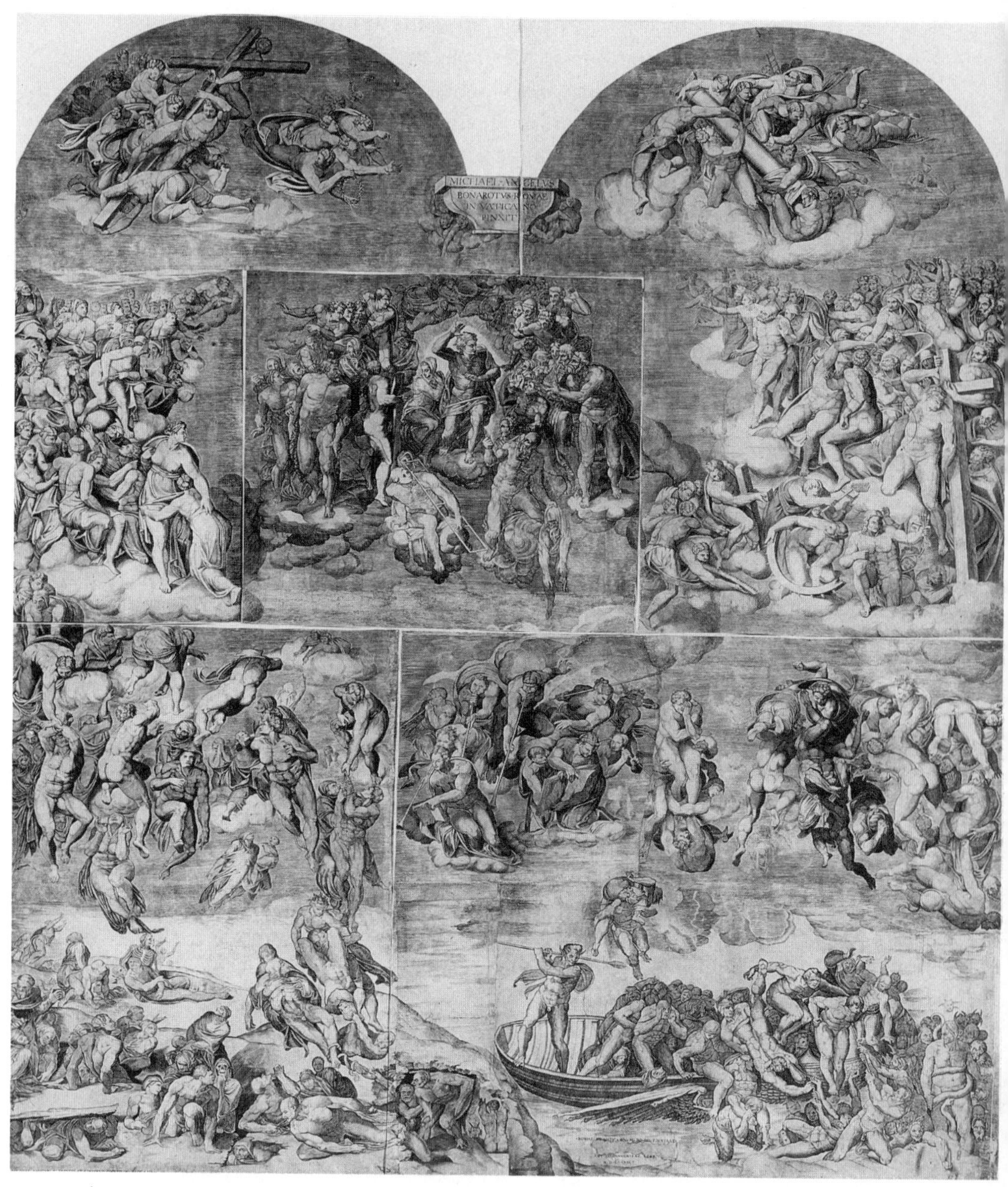

FIG. 3. Niccolò della Casa, copy of Michelangelo's *Last Judgment*, 1543.
Engraving, 154.5×130 cm (60¾×51¼ in.). Metropolitan Museum, New York, Rogers Fund, 1962;
Elisha Whittelsey Collection, The Elisha Whittelsey Fund, 1959.

If Aretino's knowledge of the fresco came through a popularized route, it is likely that his criticism did as well. His complaints are not specific: the angels have no "celestial ornament," there are too many nudes, and the martyrs and virgins behave in an indecorous manner (perhaps a reference to the infamous grouping of Saints Blaise and Catherine). The only clearly described figure is one of the damned who is pulled to hell by his genitals. It is likely that such criticism was circulated widely by persons with little knowledge of the fresco. In a letter written from Rome shortly after the unveiling of the fresco, Nino Sernini says that "there is no end to the talk" about the nudes and the lack of majesty in some of the figures. He attributes these remarks to conservative Theatine cardinals, and they surely would have voiced their complaints to others.[39] Sernini's letter, unlike Aretino's, was not written for publication, so it is not a direct source for Aretino's comments. Still, it is a good indication of the kind of gossip that surrounded the work and that surely spread beyond the walls of the Vatican. The generality of Aretino's remarks suggests that he was just quoting what "they" say. There is, in fact, evidence that these are not Aretino's sincere feelings. Another letter written the year before says that after seeing prints of the fresco he is "moved to tears," and in one written to his friend Titian, who was then visiting Rome for the first time (this letter is dated only one month before the invective), he warns Titian not to lose himself in wonder before the *Last Judgment*.[40]

Perhaps inadvertently, many of the venomous remarks in the manuscript version of the letter reveal Aretino's personal motivations for writing it. He complains that Michelangelo only gives drawings to his "Gherardos" and "Tommasos," references to two young men with whom Michelangelo was close, and probably also a reference to rumors about Michelangelo's homosexuality. He also says that his own invention—that is, his description of the Last Judgment in the 1537 letter—was done "with honor, glory and fear," and if Michelangelo had used it he would not have been subjected to such criticism.

In the version of the letter published in 1550, all of these insults are omitted. The criticism themselves remain essentially unchanged, but Aretino takes on yet another role. Now he is the detached observer: in one passage he wonders how Michelangelo "could have allowed envy" the chance to say all the things that he in fact said in the earlier version, and he changes another line to read, "Someone, I don't know who, said that it would be better not to believe than, by believing in this manner, to diminish the belief of others." He eliminates all references to his personal motivations for criticizing the fresco, so that his remarks seem objective and based solely on the merits or

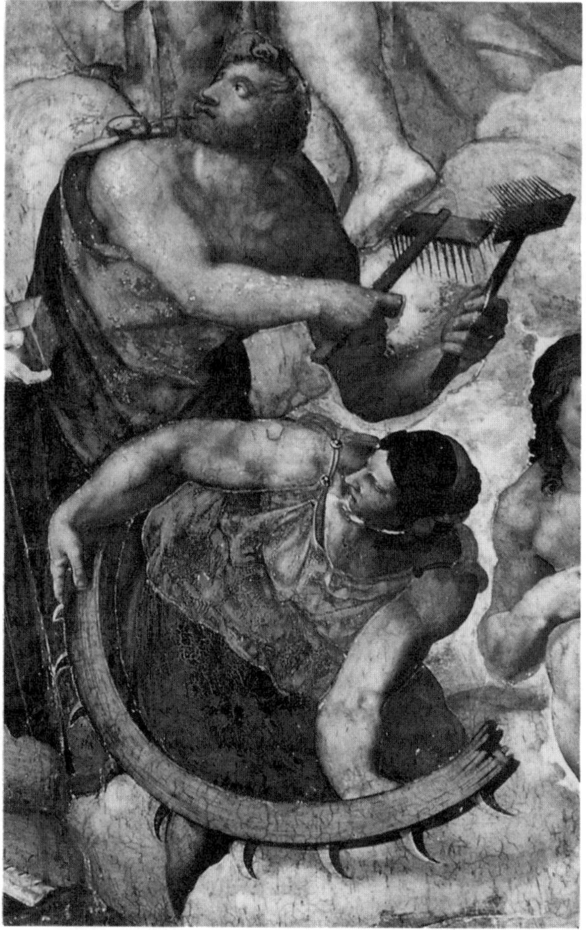

FIG. 4. Michelangelo, *Last Judgment*, detail showing Saint Blaise and Saint Catherine. Detail of fig. 1.

faults of the fresco. In one sentence he reveals that he is depending on his readers' lack of precise knowledge of the fresco: he changes the wording of the description of the man "dragged away by his genitals" to the plural so that it seems as though many figures are being grabbed by the genitals. And yet he again sets himself up as a connoisseur who is above getting upset about such things: "but as regards its being Christian, I can only shrug my shoulders amiably at the licentiousness of his brush . . ."

The changes made in the published version of this letter show how much

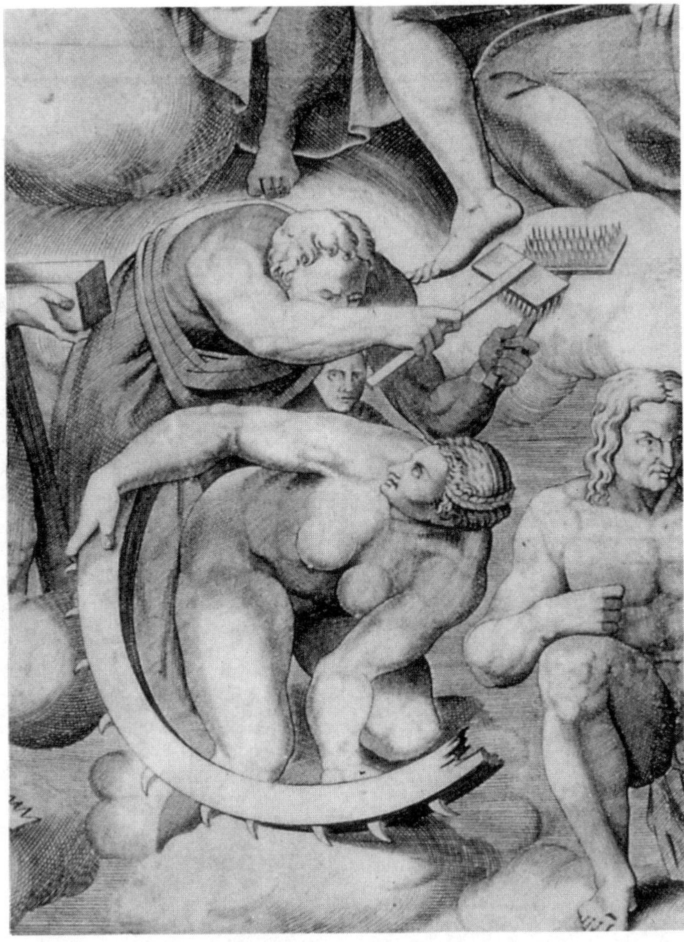

FIG. 5. Niccolò della Casa, copy of Michelangelo's *Last Judgment.* Detail of fig. 3.

Aretino adjusted his ideas to suit his audience. While the first version may have drawn on popular criticism in order to provoke a more violent public reaction, in publishing his invective he shows greater awareness of his actual readers. I believe that Aretino still desires to address his published work to the upper classes, the collectors and connoisseurs who appreciate the arts. In his earlier letters he had done this by appealing to their appreciation of literary style; now he takes on a more "knowing" attitude toward art. He surely realized by now that the appeal of his books of letters was not due to his great

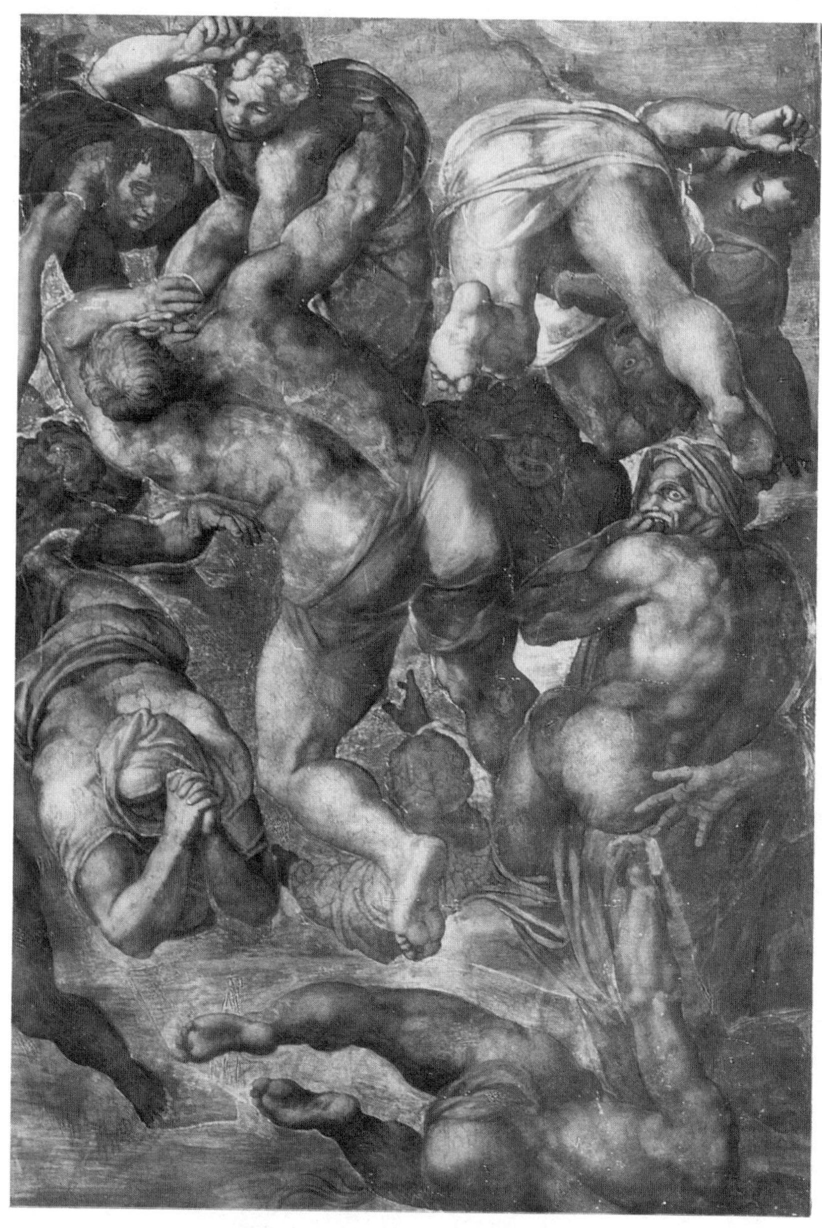

FIG. 6. Michelangelo, *Last Judgment*, detail at right showing sinner dragged to hell. Detail of fig. 1.

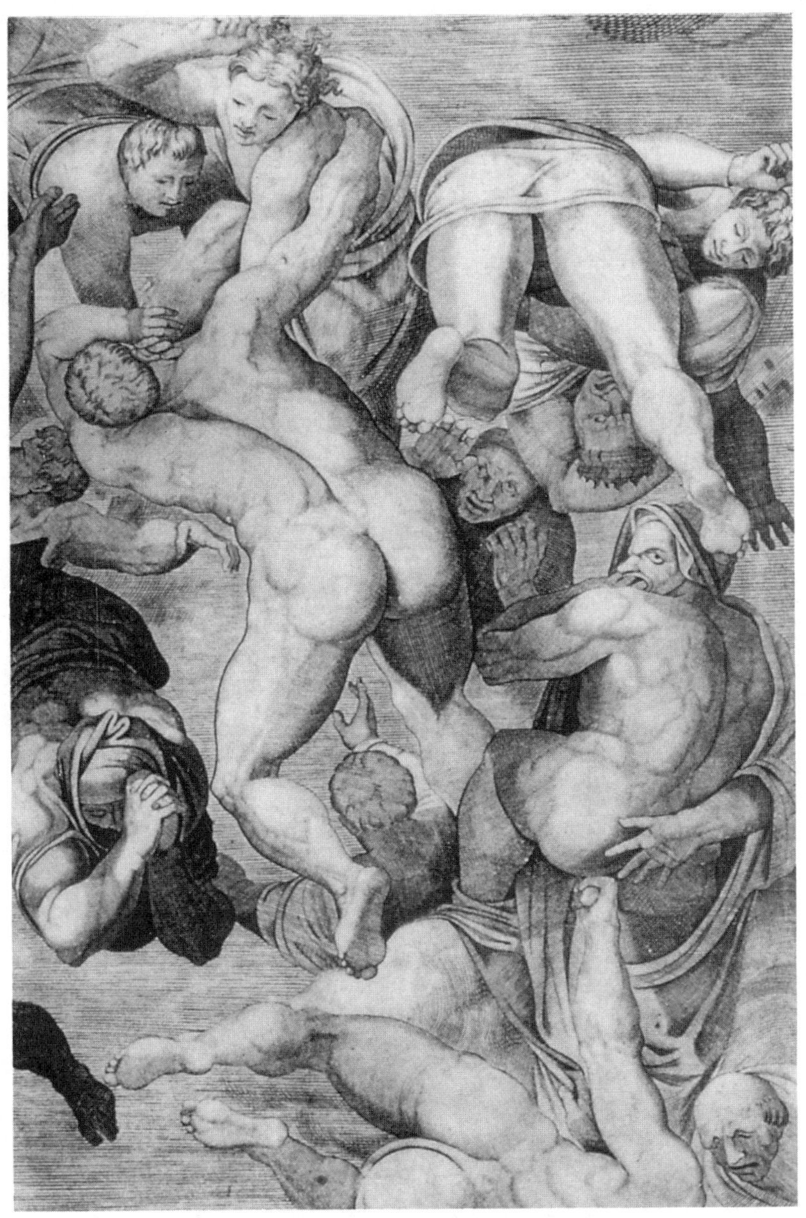

FIG. 7. Niccolò della Casa, copy of Michelangelo's *Last Judgment*. Detail of fig. 3.

literary skills, but to his reporting on the rich and famous. After the first two books, the collections are more loosely structured, with very few literary exercises.[41]

The readers of his letters are not necessarily literati, but they are literate, and so he uses more subtlety to express the anti-intellectualism so evident in the first version of the letter: "But if the immortal intellect resents hearing what I write, I accept that since it is better to displease [Michelangelo] by talking about these things, than to hurt Christ by keeping silent." Yet he still wants to include the criticisms of the fresco that were most often associated with the clergy and, through them, the lower classes. To do this he takes on the role of guardian or protector. He himself is not personally upset about the fresco, but he can see how such a work might be misunderstood by others, and especially by innocent minds. This position allows him to continue to call for the censorship of the fresco: he still hopes that the pope (now Julius III) will follow the example of Gregory the Great and have such a work destroyed rather than weaken the faith of the common people.

Aretino wanted to call attention to the fresco to tarnish Michelangelo's reputation and perhaps even to have the work destroyed, but he achieved neither of these goals in his own lifetime. The effect of his words began to be felt strongly in 1557, the year after he died, when Ludovico Dolce wrote and published *L'Aretino*, a dialogue in which a fictionalized Aretino converses with a Florentine about art. At the heart of the dialogue is a discussion of the *Last Judgment* based on Aretino's published criticism of the fresco.[42] Dolce was himself a member of Aretino's circle in Venice and one of the literati; his attempt to create a theory of painting similar to literary theory suggests that he expected his dialogue to be read by people like himself. However, when he begins to speak about the *Last Judgment*, he adopts a more populist attitude: "If Michelangelo does not want anyone to understand his inventions, apart from a small number of intellectuals, then I, who am not one of the intellectual few in question, leave thinking about them to him."[43] Through Dolce, Aretino's ideas became part of the discourse on art in the late sixteenth century, as calls for ease, grace, and sensual beauty began to replace the emphasis on difficulty in painting.

Echoes of Aretino's words are also heard in Giovanni Andrea Gilio's *Degli errori de' pittori*, published in 1564.[44] As in Dolce's dialogue, the discussion of the *Last Judgment* is set within a larger framework in which Gilio tries to establish rules for secular and religious paintings. He emphasizes subject matter, which in the case of religious painting should be straightforward and help the viewer to understand orthodox beliefs. He also brings up formal elements like foreshortening, which he says should be done so that a proper attitude of respect is created in the minds of the "ignorant" who may not understand the artistic value of such tricks. The specific and very detailed criticism of the *Last Judgment* begins, not surprisingly, when one of the interlocutors brings out a print of the fresco.[45] It is also at this point that references to Aretino's letters, as well as Dolce's dialogue, enter the conversation. Probably the greatest reliance on Aretino's criticism is found in the idea that Michelangelo values art more than religion, or as one of Gilio's interlocutors says: "Not everyone wants to learn to paint, but everyone should learn to be a good Christian."[46] Although in this dialogue too there are literary pretensions, Gilio's concern with the unlearned seems less contrived than in Aretino's or Dolce's writings.[47] Here most of the negative criticism of the fresco is voiced by a theologian, and because these ideas are set in a religious context there is a less ambiguous interest in the unsophisticated viewer. Gilio recognizes that painting has a direct and powerful effect on the unlearned, although it may not be the effect the artist intended. He describes vividly how untrained viewers are startled by foreshortening, amused by complex movements, and aroused by nudity.

Published works like these generated defenses, which in turn stimulated even more interest in the *Last Judgment*. In 1563, more than twenty years after the fresco's completion, the problem of the *Last Judgment* was brought up at the last session of the Council of Trent, where it was resolved that the objectionable areas should be painted over. At that point Daniele da Volterra, Michelangelo's friend and disciple, was commissioned to begin the repainting. The fact that an artist was chosen who would treat Michelangelo's work with respect, and the effect of the repainting would be minimal, testifies that many within the Vatican continued to value the work highly. As Aretino had guessed, the audience for the *Last Judgment* was still composed of connoisseurs as well as those who saw art as something that could be misinterpreted by the common people.

In one regard, Aretino seems to have been completely out of touch with what the public wanted. In his letter to Enea Vico of 1546, he implied that much profit would come from creating a censored engraving of the *Last Judgment*. In fact, many printmakers profited from making copies of the fresco in its *uncensored* state. At least seventeen printmakers made copies of the fresco in the sixteenth and early seventeenth centuries, all showing the nudes without loincloths, and Saint Catherine and Saint Blaise in their original "indecorous" postures. Of these at least twelve were made after the fresco was overpainted.[48] Of course, part of the explanation for this is that the engravers relied on earlier copies rather than using the fresco itself for their model. But it seems that there was really very little demand for censored versions, while uncensored copies continued to be made and reissued well into the seventeenth century. If the sheer number of copies was not testimony enough, Vasari in his 1568 edition of the *Lives* comments that many copies were quite poor, having been pulled "more for profit than honor."[49] It would be impossible to say exactly how much of this sustained interest in copies of the fresco was due to Aretino's publicity, but similar effects have been seen in our own time when labels warning of pornographic content boost music or book sales tenfold.

Aretino's letters give powerful testimony to the ways that the audience for art was changing in the sixteenth century. His attempt to accommodate both the connoisseur and the unsophisticated viewer is symptomatic of problems with religious art in general. Largely through the example of Michelangelo, artists had begun to use increasingly more complex devices in their works, aiming, no doubt, to gain the approval of an audience skilled in the appreciation of these techniques. Since patrons of important religious works were usually of this same class of connoisseurs, artists were given the freedom to use striking artistic inventions in religious works. This scenario is especially true of the *Last Judgment*, commissioned for a restricted setting by highly sophisticated popes who allowed Michelangelo complete artistic freedom.

With the greater availability of prints and published discussions of works of art, other voices began to be heard. Aretino, and later Dolce and Gilio, became the unlikely representatives of the lower class—a class unskilled in the appreciation of artistic style.[50] This was a public accustomed to responding to works directly, relying on their efficacy—the power to stimulate a strong emotional response—to strengthen religious beliefs.[51] This group now let it be known that highly valued artistic achievements, like the ability to paint the nude in complex poses, did not inspire piety, but rather laughter and lust. Aretino may not have personally shared these sentiments, but it was politically useful for him to give voice to them. His writings circulated these opinions widely, encouraging more response and more criticism. The *Last Judgment*, because of its widespread distribution in prints and in the printed word, became an obvious example to use in these discussions, a symbol of "degenerate" art. Its censorship was, in turn, a symbolic response to the demands of a new audience.[52]

NOTES

1. As part of the restoration of the *Last Judgment*, completed in 1994, the repainting has been carefully studied recently. The repainted areas are even more obtrusive than before the cleaning, since they were painted to match the fresco when it had already accumulated dirt for over thirty years. For a report on the restoration, see Fabrizio Mancinelli, G. Colalucci, and N. Gabrielli, "The *Last Judgment*: Notes on Its Conservation History, Technique, and Restoration," in P. de Vecchi, ed., *The Sistine Chapel: A Glorious Restoration* (New York: Abrams, 1994), 236–55.

2. For criticism of the Sistine Ceiling, see Giorgio Vasari, *La vita di Michelangelo nelle redazioni del 1550 e del 1568*, ed. Paola Barocchi (Milan: R. Ricciardi, 1962), 1:234–35 and 3:761, and Eugenio Battisti, "La critica a Michelangelo prima del Vasari," *Rinascimento* 1 (1954): 117–23. Many of the criticisms of the *Last Judgment* are collected in André Chastel, *A Chronicle of Italian Renaissance Painting*, trans. Linda and Peter Murray (Ithaca: Cornell University Press, 1984), 188–207.

3. See, for example, Sergio Ortolani in "Pietro Aretino e Michelangelo," *L'Arte* 25 (1922): 15–26, and Lionello Puppi, "Michelangelo und Aretino," in *Michelangelo Heute: Materialien der Michelangelo-Konferenz* (Berlin, 1964), 123–31. For Aretino's "theory," see Mario Pozzi, "Note sulla cultura artistica e sulla poetica di Pietro Aretino," *Giornale storico della letteratura italiana* 145 (1968): 293–322, and Lora Anne Palladino, "Pietro Aretino: Orator and Art Theorist," Ph.D. dissertation, Yale University, 1981, 390–94.

4. On printmaking see Paolo Bellini, "Printmakers and Dealers in Italy during [the] 16th and 17th Centuries," *Print Collector* 13 (1975): 17–45. The output of Aretino's own publisher is discussed in Amedeo Quondam, "Nel Giardino del Marcolini," *Giornale storico della letteratura italiana* 157 (1980): 75–116.

5. A concise summary of his career can be found in Giuliano Innamorati's entry in the *Dizionario Biografico degli Italiani* (Rome: Instituto della enciclopedia italiana, 1962), 4:89–105. Since the text of this essay was completed, two works in English have been published that offer insights into specific aspects of Aretino's career, as well as supplying general biographical information: Joanna Woods-Marsden, "Toward a History of Art Patronage in the Renaissance: The Case of Pietro Aretino," *Journal of Medieval and Renaissance Studies* 24 (1994): 275–99; and Luba Freedman, *Titian's Portraits through Aretino's Lens* (University Park: Pennsylvania State University Press, 1995).

6. Raymond B. Waddington, "A Satirist's *Impresa*: The Medals of Pietro Aretino," *Renaissance Quarterly* 42 (1989): 655–81.

7. Both the pornography and the religious works have only recently been given scholarly attention. On the former, see David O. Frantz, *Festum Voluptatis: A Study of Renaissance Erotica* (Columbus: Ohio State University Press, 1989), 43–901. There is also an essay by Paula Findlen on censorship and pornography in the Renaissance (see note 52 below), which includes a discussion of Aretino's writings, in Lynn Hunt,

ed., *The Invention of Pornography: Obscenity and the Origins of Modernity, 1500–1800* (New York: Zone Books; distrib. by MIT Press, 1993). On the religious writings, see Christopher Cairns, *Pietro Aretino and the Republic of Venice: Researches on Aretino and His Circle in Venice, 1527–1556* (Florence: L. S. Olschki, 1985), 69–73, and Jaynie Anderson, "Pietro Aretino and Sacred Imagery," in David Rosand, ed., *Interpretazioni Veneziane: Studi di storia dell'arte in onore di Michelangelo Muraro* (Venice: Arsenale Editrice, 1984), 275–90, both with further references. One of Aretino's religious works, *I Quattro libri de l'Humanita di Cristo*, went into eight editions between 1535 and 1551.

8. Aretino, *Sei Giornate*, ed. Giovanni Aquilecchia (Bari: Laterza, 1969), 162–63. Quoted and translated in Frantz, *Festum*, 84.

9. For studies of these personae, see Cairns, *Pietro Aretino*, 24 and passim; Waddington, "Satirist's *Impresa*," 655–81; and Patricia H. Labalme, "Personality and Politics in Venice: Pietro Aretino," in David Rosand, ed., *Titian: His World and His Legacy* (New York: Columbia University Press, 1982), 119–32.

10. Romeo De Maio, *Michelangelo e la Controriforma* (Rome and Bari: Laterza, 1981), 22 and 28–29; Ortolani, "Aretino e Michelangelo," 25; LaBalme, "Personality and Politics," 128; and Cairns, *Pietro Aretino*, 97 ff.

11. Paul F. Grendler, *The Roman Inquisition and the Venetian Press, 1540–1605* (Princeton: Princeton University Press, 1977), 116. Grendler's chapter "The Growth of Censorship" gives a good account of the sporadic enforcement of the Inquisition in Venice until the 1560s.

12. Giuliano Innamorati, *Tradizione e invenzione in Pietro Aretino* (Messina and Florence: G. d'Anna, 1957), 230–36. Some letters of Saint Catherine and of Francesco Filelfo had been published in Italian in the earlier part of the sixteenth century, but in neither case were the letters written with publication in mind, nor were they selected or arranged by the author. Erasmus's letters have been proposed as the direct inspiration for Aretino's enterprise.

13. The Italian text is transcribed in Pietro Aretino, *Tutte le opere, I: Lettere, il primo e il secondo libro*, ed. Francesco Flora (Milan: A. Mondadori, 1960), no. 191. An English translation of the entire letter is in Robert Klein and Henri Zerner, *Italian Art, 1500–1600: Sources and Documents* (Englewood Cliffs: Prentice-Hall, 1966), 56–58. My translation is adapted from this.

14. See David Summers, *Michelangelo and the Language of Art* (Princeton: Princeton University Press, 1983), 177–85 and 259–61.

15. Paul Larivaille, *Pietro Aretino fra Rinascimento e Manierismo* (Rome, 1980), 324–25. See, for example, *Lettere*, ed. Flora, nos. 134 and 148.

16. Palladino, "Pietro Aretino," 392–93, has also pointed out the ekphrastic nature of the letter. On this subject in Renaissance writings about art, see Svetlana Alpers, "*Ekphrasis* and Aesthetic Attitudes in Vasari's *Lives*," *Journal of the Warburg and Courtauld Institutes* 23 (1960): 190–215; Norman E. Land, "*Ekphrasis* and Imagination: Some Observations on Pietro Aretino's Art Criticism," *Art Bulletin* 68 (1986):

207–17; Norman E. Land, *The Viewer as Poet: The Renaissance Response to Art* (University Park: Pennsylvania State University Press, 1994); and Amy Golahny, ed., *The Eye of the Poet* (Lewisburg: Bucknell University Press, 1996).

17. Pietro Aretino, *Scritti Scelti*, ed. G.G. Ferrero, 2d ed. (Turin: Unione tipografico-editrice torinese, 1970), 973–75.

18. There is one other comparable example, a letter to Giorgio Vasari, which Aretino based on a description that Vasari had sent him. In this case Aretino's reworking of the description is clearly meant to be a writing lesson to Vasari. Karl Frey, *Der literarische Nachlass Giorgio Vasaris* (Munich: Georg Müller, 1923), 1:xviii, xxi, xxii, and xxiii.

19. Most of the examples discussed in Land's article date to 1537.

20. Larivaille, *Pietro Aretino*, 298–99, has noted that two-thirds of the letters in the first book, including the letter to Michelangelo, were written between June and December of 1537—that is, after the decision to publish the work was made and the first group sent off to the publisher.

21. Innamorati, *Tradizione e invenzione*, 242–45, notes that the letters dated from 1535 to 1537 are most often literary works, written on topics that have little personal relevance; Aretino is most concerned with explaining his "poetic" in letters from the summer of 1537. The characteristics of a high literary style were probably suggested to him by Bernardino Daniello, who sent Aretino a copy of his *Della Poetica* soon after it was published in 1536. In a letter dated December 22, 1536, Aretino praises the book, and compares the author's judgment to Michelangelo's; *Lettere sull'arte di Pietro Aretino*, ed. Ettore Camesasca (Milan: Edizioni del Milione, 1957), 1:35–36, no. XVII. Daniello's high style is reserved for grave and sublime subjects. It is characterized by "ornate composition made up of grave, high, magnificent and sonorous words" which can have either a simple or metaphorical meaning. Amplification and "all the ornaments" should be used to give the sentences the same gravity as the words. See Bernard Weinberg, ed., *Trattati di poetica e retorica del cinquecento* (Bari: Laterza, 1970), 1:276, 280.

22. *Lettere*, ed. Flora, no. 9. This letter was published in his second book of letters.

23. Aretino himself gives evidence of this expectation in a letter to Leone Leoni, dated July 15, 1539; *Lettere sull'arte*, 1:130–31, no. LXXXIII. In addition, Pope Clement VII, who commissioned the fresco in 1533, expected an extraordinary work, as is seen in Sebastiano del Piombo's words to Michelangelo regarding the commission: the pope had in mind "things you never would have imagined"; quoted in Vasari, *Vita di Michelangelo*, 1156.

24. See Cairns, *Pietro Aretino*, 160–61, and Innamorati, *Tradizione e invenzione*, 223–32. Aretino's first book of letters was published by Marcolini, who was also the publisher of his religious and pornographic works. Since at that time Aretino was Marcolini's main author, there would surely have been pressure on him to make this a strong seller. See Quondam, "Giardino del Marcolini," 89–99 and 113.

25. See the publication history given in *Lettere*, ed. Flora, 975–79.

26. Quoted in Innamorati, *Tradizione e invenzione*, 232.

27. Examples written by Francesco Maria Molza and Niccolò Martelli, both correspondents of Aretino, were probably written before either had seen the fresco. Both are quoted in Vasari, *Vita di Michelangelo*, 1254–55 and 1258. Martelli's letter is dated December 4, 1541, and was published in 1546. Molza's poem was first published in 1565.

28. A. F. Doni, *Disegno*, 1549, f. 60 v.; cited in Vasari, *Vita di Michelangelo*, 1257, note 563.

29. E. H. Ramsden, ed. and trans., *The Letters of Michelangelo* (Stanford: Stanford University Press, 1963), 2: no. 199.

30. See Ortolani, "Aretino e Michelangelo," 21.

31. Other examples are dated April 1544 and April 1545; *Lettere sull'arte*, nos. CLXXVIII and CCXXI. Both were published in the *Third Book of Letters* in 1546.

32. The Italian text and a translation can be found in Chastel, *Chronicle*, 200 and 280. Bazzacco, also called Zabacco, is Ponchino di Castelfranco; see De Maio, *Michelangelo e la Controriforma*, 71; *Lettere sull'arte*, 3, pt. 2, 416–17. De Maio refers to a drawing Bazzacco made, although the letter to Vico clearly refers to a print. Neither print nor drawing survives. Vico's print, if indeed it was made, also does not survive.

33. The manuscript version is transcribed in Chastel, *Chronicle*, 278–79, with a translation on pages 191–95. On the dating, see Erica Tietze-Conrat, "Neglected Contemporary Sources Relating to Michelangelo and Titian," *Art Bulletin* 25 (1943): 154–56; and Mark W. Roskill, *Dolce's "Aretino" and Venetian Art Theory of the Cinquecento* (New York: New York University Press, 1968), 27–28. The published version is transcribed in *Lettere sull'arte*, 2:175–77, no. CCCLXIV. Adding to the confusion of dates, the letter is inserted in *Fourth Book of Letters* amid the 1547 letters (no. 183). However, the added reference to Pope Paul III's death, which occurred in 1549, implies that it was revised in 1549–50, just prior to publication.

34. On the issue of whether or not the manuscript letter was sent, see Tietze-Conrat, "Neglected Sources," 154–56, and Chastel, *Chronicle*, 196. I was able to examine the letter at the Archivio di Stato (Strozziana filza 133). The body of the letter is a fair copy in another hand, which would be expected since Aretino regularly used scribes because of his crippled right hand. The postscript is more hastily written, possibly by Aretino himself. There is also an "envelope" with Michelangelo's name on it (unfortunately, postmarks did not exist then). The addition of the postscript raises several questions: if Michelangelo received the letter, why did he not rip it up? Did he send it to someone else, and, if so, to what purpose? Is it possible that Aretino wrote the letter only for publication, never intending to send it to Michelangelo, and added the postscript as an explanation of why he kept it so that it could appear in print later? (This is a suggestion made by Elizabeth Childs.) If this was the case, did he send it to someone in Florence (where it is to this day) who may have suggested some toning down, as in fact it was in its published version?

Corvino was a Roman collector of antiquities and the secretary of Ottavio Farnese. He was introduced to Aretino and his circle in 1545. See Giorgio Padoan, "A casa di Tiziano, una sera d'Agosto," in *Tiziano e Venezia* (Vicenza: N. Pozza, 1980), 366. Tietze-Conrat, "Neglected Sources" (155), notes that he served as a go-between for Aretino and the papal court, and says that Aretino probably addressed the letter to him with the assumption that he would circulate it in Rome. Since this was a published text, however, I think it hardly matters if Corvino circulated the letter, and the choice of addressee may have been arbitrary.

35. Tietze-Conrat, "Neglected Sources" (154), discusses other copies Aretino might have seen.

36. On the copies of the *Last Judgment*, see Mario Rotili, ed., *Fortuna di Michelangelo nell'incisione* (Benevento: Azienda Beneventana Tipografia Editoriale, 1964); also Alida Moltedo, ed., *La Sistina riprodotta: gli affreschi di Michelangelo dalle stampe dal cinquecento alle campagne fotografiche Anderson* (Rome: Fratelli Palombi, 1991) and *Michelangelo e la Sistina*, 245–57.

37. One example comes from the diaries of Paris de Grassis, who was papal master-of-ceremonies from 1504 to 1521. For the feast of the Purification, when candles were distributed to the public from the Loggia, guards were posted at the doors of the Sistine Chapel with wooden sticks, so that no one except the "necessary and usual" people could enter (BAV, Vat. lat. 5634, f. 192v).

38. Roskill, *Dolce's "Aretino,"* 167. When the masters-of-ceremonies mention women in the Sistine Chapel, they are generally noblewomen; it seems, in any case, that they were made to sit in a room next to the chapel, which had a window through which they could view the ceremonies. See the entry of May 28, 1531 (BAV, Vat. lat. 12276); the entry of November 18, 1520, in the same manuscript, mentions that the pope gave a special dispensation so that another duchess could be seated in the chapel itself.

39. Nino Sernini's letter is dated November 19, 1541; transcribed in Chastel, *Chronicle*, 278, with English translation on 188–89. For others, see De Maio, *Michelangelo e la Controriforma*, 17–21. A similar point has been made by Leo Steinberg, *Michelangelo's Last Paintings* (London: Phaidon, 1975), 42–43, and Palladino, "Pietro Aretino," 394.

40. *Lettere sull'arte*, no. CCLXIV, dated October 1545. For other letters praising Michelangelo's painting, see *Lettere*, ed. Flora, nos. 156, 247, 323 (from the first book of letters), and nos. 384 and 391 (from the second book). There is only one letter that is critical of Michelangelo's art before 1545. It is dated December 17, 1537, and in it Aretino complains that in the *Pietà* Michelangelo has made the Virgin too young and that in the Sistine Ceiling he has made the figures *in aria* (that is, weightless and incongruous with the architectural setting). This passage was omitted from the second edition of the first book of letters (transcribed in *Lettere*, ed. Flora, no. 298 and pp. 1083–84, note 2).

41. See Cairns, *Pietro Aretino*, 160–61.

42. Roskill, *Dolce's "Aretino,"* 27–29, 163, and passim; Pozzi, "Cultura artistica," 298.

43. Roskill, *Dolce's "Aretino,"* 167.

44. Gilio's treatise has been edited by Paola Barocchi, in *Trattati d'arte del cinquecento* (Bari: Laterza, 1961), 2:5–115.

45. Ibid., 53.

46. Ibid., 86; similarly on 55. Another reference to one of Aretino's letters is in the description of the Last Day (59), drawn from the 1537 letter.

47. The beginning of the dialogue is very poetic in tone, and throughout there are detailed discussions of literary and theological matters. At one point he even asserts that painters would make fewer mistakes if they were literati.

48. The following lists most of the copies of the *Last Judgment* which I have seen or to which I have found references; I make no claims about its completeness. Niccolò della Casa, 1543 (2d ed., 1548); Bazzacco, ca. 1546 (not extant); Giulio Bonasone, 1546; Giorgio Ghisi, ca. 1556 (reprinted by Dei Rossi publishers in mid-seventeenth century); Domenico del Barbiere, n.d., probably after Ghisi; Nicolas Beatrizet, after Ghisi, 1562 (possibly an earlier version ca. 1542 or 1543 as well); Giambattista de' Cavaliere, 1567 (with biblical passages, gives Christ a beard, retains nudity); Martino Rota, 1569; Jan Wierix after Rota, after 1569; Leonard Gualtier, after Rota, last quarter of sixteenth century; Anonymous, after Rota, 1576, published in Venice by Nicolò Nelli; Etienne Duperac, after Rota (two versions; he was also the publisher of Beatrizet's prints); Ambrogio Brambilla, with text by Jacopo Vivo, 1588; Michele Grechi, late sixteenth century; Cherubino Alberti, 1591 (five figures); Francesco Villamena, 1594 and 1603; Phillippe Thomassin, 1606–20.

49. G. Vasari, *Le vite de' più eccelenti pittori scultori ed architettori nelle redazioni del 1550 e 1568*, ed. Paola Barocchi and Rosanna Bettarini (Florence: Sansoni, 1966–87), 5 (Testo): 19. This comment comes immediately before he discusses copies of the *Last Judgment*. In general Vasari praises reproductive printmaking, since it makes known the works of great masters to those who cannot go to see the originals.

50. Pozzi, "Cultura artistica," 311.

51. Carlo Ginzburg, "Titian, Ovid, and Sixteenth-Century Codes for Erotic Illustration," in his *Clues, Myths, and the Historical Method*, trans. John and Anne C. Tedeschi (Baltimore and London: Johns Hopkins University Press, 1989), 79–80. For the late sixteenth-century application of this idea, see David Freedberg, "Johannes Molanus on Provocative Painting," *Journal of the Warburg and Courtauld Institutes* 34 (1971): 229–45.

52. Since this article was first written, an article by Paula Findlen has appeared that is quite similar in approach to mine, but it is focused on Aretino's pornographic writings: "Humanism, Politics and Pornography in Renaissance Italy," in Lynn Hunt, ed., *The Invention of Pornography: Obscenity and the Origins of Modernity, 1500–1800* (New York: Zone Books, 1993), 49–108. She gives similar attention to print culture and the growing market for reproductions. She also notes Aretino's ambiguous relationship to the intellectuals of his time. His pornographic works are at once the product of humanist culture and the means by which the values of the humanists are revealed as false and pretentious.

Veronese and the Inquisition: The Geopolitical Context

PAUL H. D. KAPLAN

ONE OF THE MOST NOTORIOUS confrontations between an artist and the authorities of church and state took place in Venice on July 18, 1573. On that day Paolo Veronese was questioned by the Venetian branch of the Catholic Church's Holy Office, otherwise known as the Inquisition, about a picture of the Last Supper (fig. 1) he had finished three months earlier for the refectory of the Dominican monastery of SS. Giovanni e Paolo.[1] The interrogation probably lasted only twenty minutes, but in the past century it has become an emblem of those conflicts that pit the right of creative artists to determine their own imagery against the perennial tendency of powerful institutions to interfere in such matters.[2]

The painting that provoked this conflict, today in the Accademia in Venice, is a vast canvas of extraordinary elegance. Beneath a nobly ornamented Renaissance loggia, seated at a long and lavishly equipped table set off against the background's stylish edifices and cool evening sky, Christ and his apostles are served an ample supper by a teeming crowd of servants; there are well over twice as many waiters and attendants as there are banqueters. These retainers are a cosmopolitan group: among them are seven liveried black pages, five turbaned Moslems (fig. 2), a dwarf holding a parrot, a prominent dark-skinned man (in the right foreground), and two soldiers in German dress (fig. 3).

The tribunal that summoned Veronese to defend, among other things, his inclusion of a mass of varied servants never mentioned in the Gospels or later sacred legend had little experience in questioning an artist about his art. Writers were often targets of the Inquisition's pursuit of heresy and sacrilege, but painters were not: the surviving records of the Holy Office in Venice re-

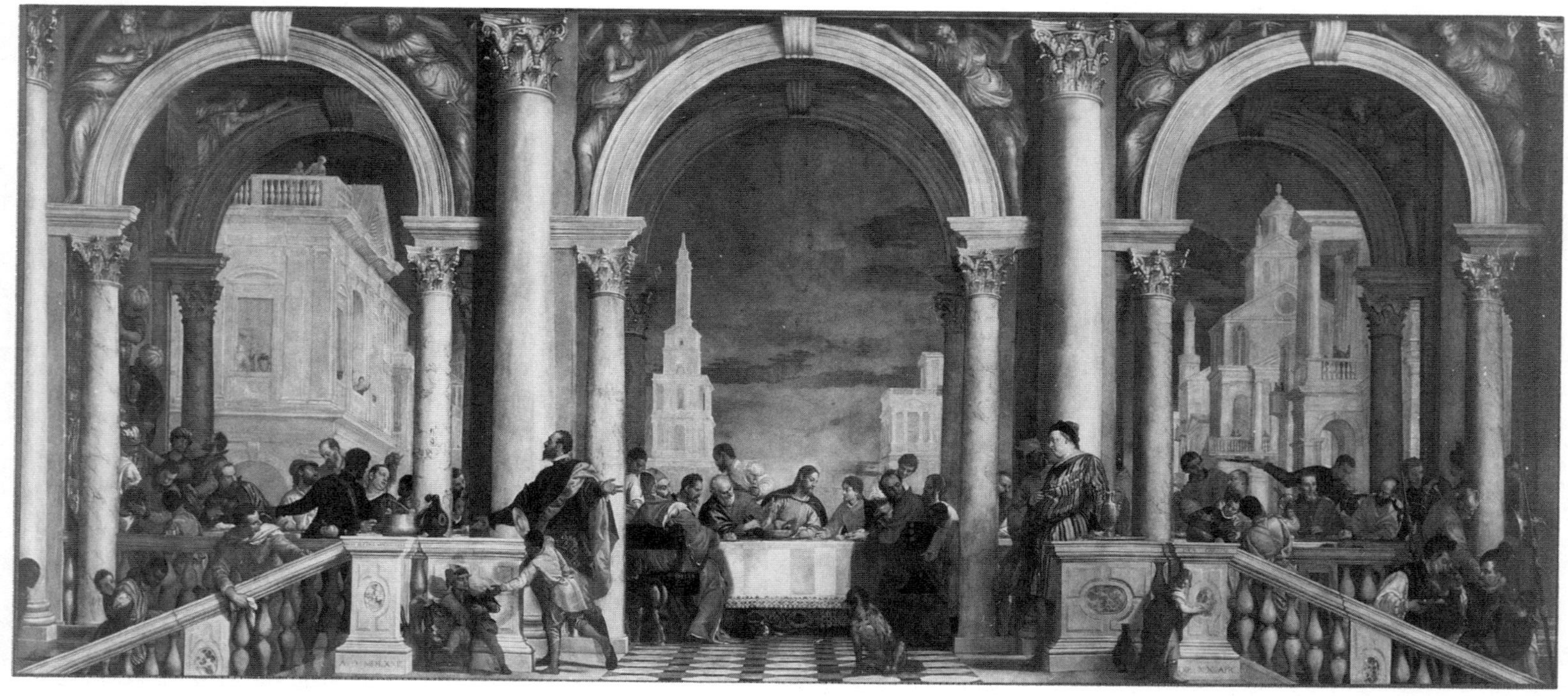

FIG. 1. Paolo Veronese, *Last Supper/Feast in the House of Levi*, 1573.
Oil on canvas, 555×1,310 cm (218×516 in.). Accademia, Venice. Photo: O. Boehm, Venice.

veal nothing remotely similar to the Veronese episode,[3] and indeed no other example of a judicial interrogation of a Renaissance artist about his imagery has come to light. Thus the transcript of Veronese's hearing (see the appendix below) is a unique document, and perhaps—though we can never be sure—it records a unique event for its time.

Though it is easy to romanticize this encounter between a painter and the authorities, at bottom the modern view that it represents a significant departure from earlier norms of artistic behavior is justified. In defending his work against the Inquisition's hostile questions about the presence of so many extraneous and uncanonical persons at the sacred supper, Veronese asserted, "We painters take the license, which poets and madmen take," that is, the license of creative imagination. At another point he said: "But the commission was to embellish the picture as I thought fit, which picture is large and capable of holding many figures, as it seemed to me."[4] But let us be clear: for centuries Italian painters had indeed been expected to fill up sacred pictures with appropriate detail, much of it drawn from the texture of contemporary life. Patrons, theorists like Alberti, and standard workshop practices demanded it. The novelty in Veronese's statements lies in the context: he was responding to a group of officials at a formal hearing.

Renaissance artists were, of course, sometimes criticized for their imagery in print or in public forums. Art critics like Vasari, for instance, objected to the obscurity or eccentricity of the subject of particular paintings, and with the onset of the ideological struggles of the Reformation period, sacred art in particular became a battleground. Representatives of various Protestant and Catholic positions attacked certain types of subjects and approaches as well as individual works. There were also attempts to suppress pornographic images and to punish those who had produced and distributed them. A considerable scandal erupted over the nudity of Michelangelo's figures in his Sistine Chapel *Last Judgment*.[5] So well known was this case that Veronese cited it during his hearing, implying that it was far more grave a breach of decorum than anything in his own work. But Michelangelo was never summoned to a formal interrogation; his fresco was altered by the addition of clothing, but only after the master's death.

One might expect Michelangelo to have run into problems of this sort, given his frequently personalized sacred images and his affiliation with a controversial segment of the Counter Reformation. Veronese, on the other hand, had a very different artistic personality. There is no record of any serious disputes with his patrons, and no evidence of his intentionally assuming any independent or unorthodox ideological position with regard to religious theory or practice.[6] Biographers from Borghini (1584) to Ridolfi (1648) and

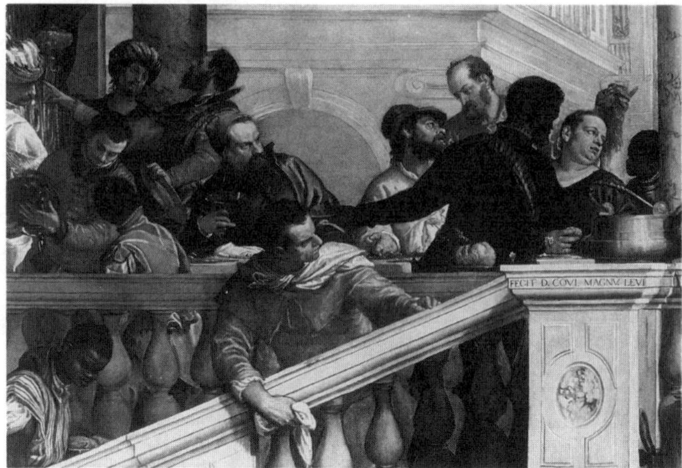

FIG. 2. Paolo Veronese, *Last Supper/Feast in the House of Levi*, detail of left side. Photo: O. Boehm, Venice.

Zanetti (1771) characterized Paolo's career as a smooth progression from success to success, with nary a hint of any crisis threatening his growing reputation and prosperity.[7] No whisper of the Inquisition's hostile attention appeared in print for nearly three hundred years. Veronese's images of sacred feasts—he executed at least five vast canvases with this general theme in the fifteen years prior to 1573—were especially praised by critics, and one of these epic paintings was resold to the Spinola of Genoa in 1646 for the fabulous sum of 8,000 ducats; another (fig. 5) was eagerly sought and acquired by Louis XIV.[8] When the French historian and archival researcher Armand Baschet in 1867 accidentally rediscovered the transcript of Veronese's interrogation, he was surprised not so much that such an event had occurred as that it had occurred to the mild and agreeable Paolo Veronese.[9] And finally, since Baschet's discovery, even with the knowledge of Veronese's contretemps, no scholar has been able to turn up another breath of this (or any other) scandal in unpublished documents.

To summarize: Veronese's interrogation was in many respects unprecedented, and it cannot be explained by something deliberately provocative in the artist's personality or body of work as a whole. Yet the *Last Supper* for SS. Giovanni e Paolo clearly *was* provocative to at least a few influential contemporary viewers, in a way that Veronese's earlier and similar feast paintings for nearby monastic refectories were not. In order to understand what brought about this unusual episode, we shall need to look briefly at Vero-

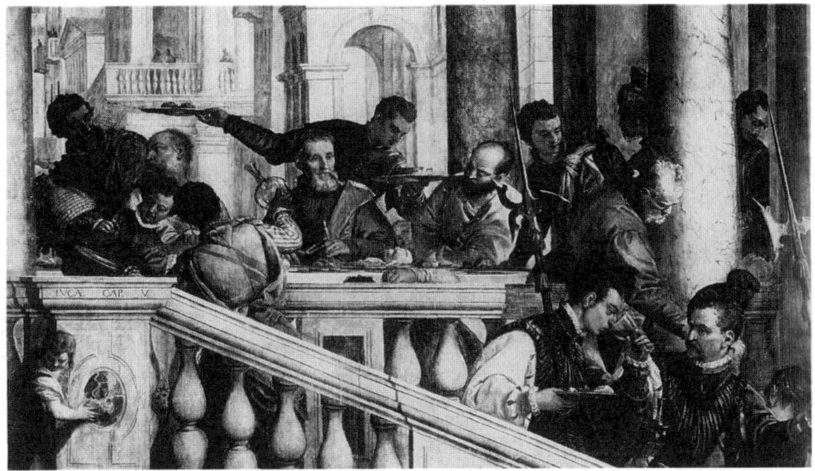

FIG. 3. Paolo Veronese, *Last Supper/Feast in the House of Levi*, detail of right side. Photo: O. Boehm, Venice.

nese's career, somewhat more carefully at his earlier feast paintings and their sources, and then intensively at the makeup of the Venetian Inquisition and the discourse of the hearing itself. Once these matters are clarified, we shall turn to an analysis of the challenges then being faced by the monastery of SS. Giovanni e Paolo, the sensitivity of the Last Supper as a subject, and the complex political relations between Venice, the papacy, and the Ottoman Empire which shaped the most dramatic events of 1573. Ultimately, as I hope to demonstrate, Veronese's hearing resulted from a Venetian need to placate the pope, not so much for purely theological reasons as for immediately political ones.

Paolo Spezapreda, later called both Paolo Caliari and Paolo Veronese, was born in 1528 in Verona. As a young artist he quickly outstripped his rather mediocre teachers; by the early 1550s he was beginning to work not only for patrons in Verona but also for distinguished Venetians. His early subjects included portraits, altarpieces, political allegories for the Ducal Palace in Venice, and fresco cycles for patrician villas. By 1560 he had taken up permanent residence in Venice, and enjoyed the favor of several of the most powerful and culturally engaged noblemen of the city; he was also the chosen artist of the Girolamite monastic church of S. Sebastiano, whose inner surfaces he eventually blanketed with his compositions.[10]

Between 1556 and 1560, Veronese carried out his first commission for a picture to decorate a monastic dining hall: *Supper in the House of Simon*. This

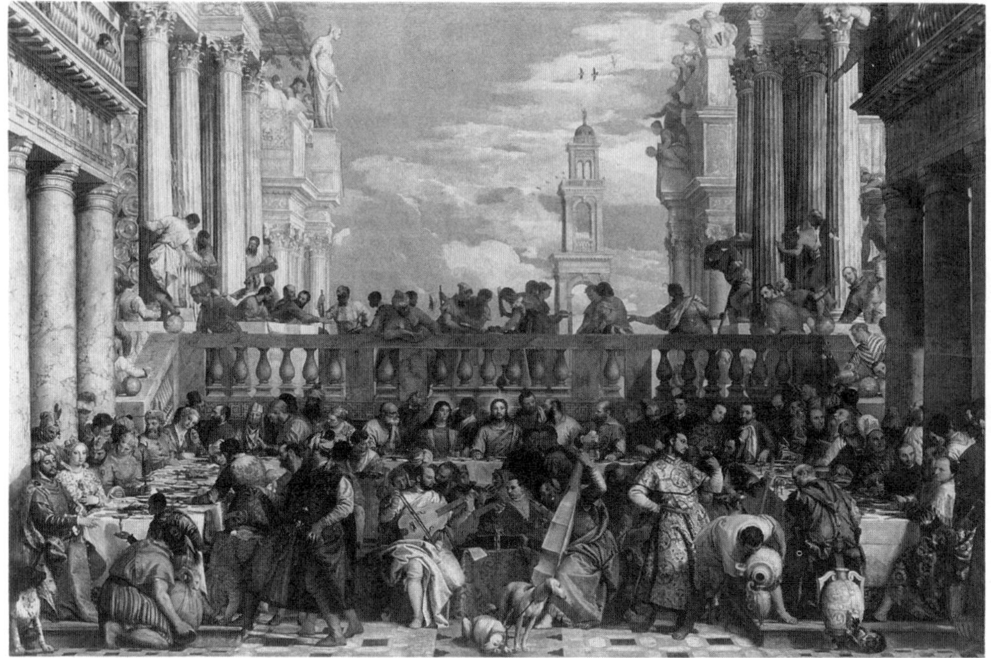

FIG. 4. Paolo Veronese, *Marriage Feast at Cana*, 1562–63.
Oil on canvas, 669×990 cm (263×390 in.). Musée du Louvre, Paris.
Photo: Cliché des Musées Nationaux, Paris.

painting, which focuses on Mary Magdalene anointing Christ's feet, was made for the Benedictine monastery of SS. Nazzaro e Celso in Verona.[11] At three by four and a half meters (almost ten by fifteen feet), it was larger than anything Veronese had undertaken on this kind of support, except for a few works of roughly similar scale being made for S. Sebastiano in these years. However, in 1562–63 he painted a *Marriage Feast at Cana* (for the Benedictines of S. Giorgio Maggiore in Venice, and now in the Louvre) (fig. 4) that was five times larger (677 by 994 cm).[12] There is nothing summary or imprecise about either of these works; they are enormous oil paintings with the fine handling typical of much smaller compositions.

From 1567 to 1570, Veronese produced another *Supper in the House of Simon*, this time for the refectory of his beloved S. Sebastiano.[13] He seems to have painted still another version (now lost) for the dining hall of the Fathers of the Maddalena in Padua, who belonged to the same Girolamite order as the monks at S. Sebastiano.[14] By 1572 Veronese had completed two further

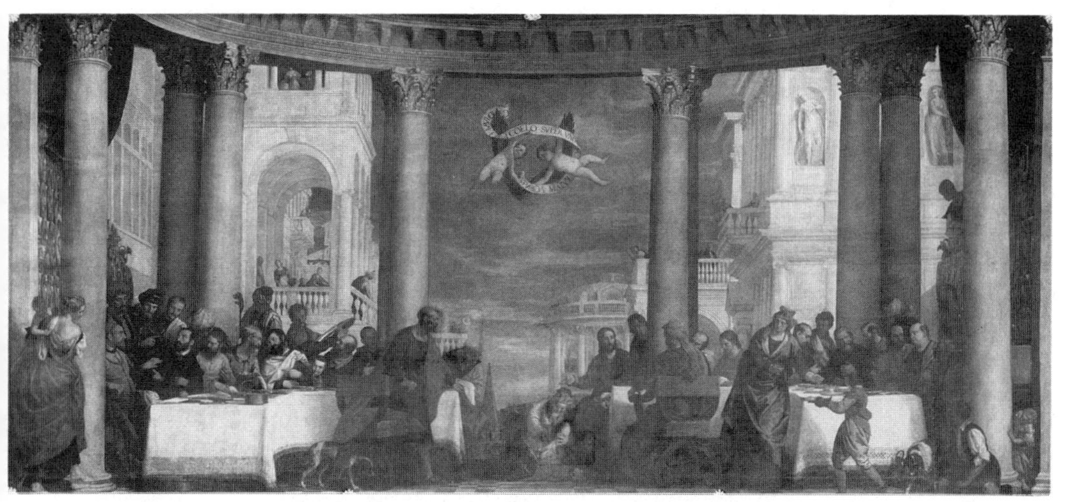

FIG. 5. Paolo Veronese, *Supper in the House of Simon*, ca. 1570–72.
Oil on canvas, 454×874 cm (178×344 in.). Musée National, Versailles.
Photo: Cliché des Musées Nationaux, Paris.

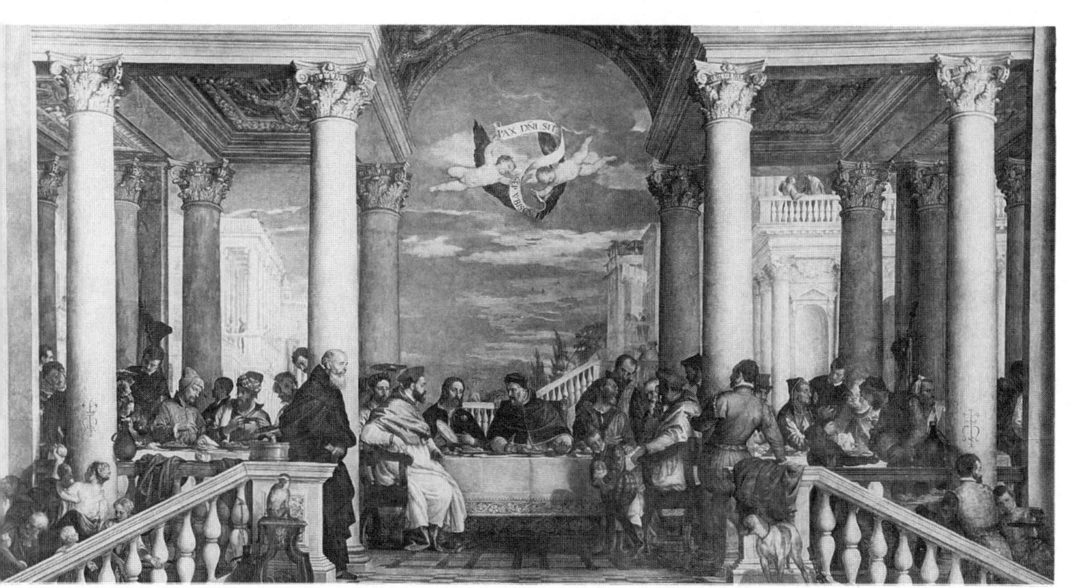

FIG. 6. Paolo Veronese, *Feast of Saint Gregory*, 1572.
Oil on canvas, 477×862 cm (188×339 in.). Sanctuary of Monte Berico, Vicenza.
Photo: Alinari/Art Resource, New York.

huge refectory canvases for Servite monks: a *Supper in the House of Simon* for S. Maria dei Servi in Venice (fig. 5),[15] and a *Feast of Saint Gregory the Great* at the Sanctuary of Monte Berico in the suburbs of Vicenza (fig. 6).[16] This sort of commission had become one of the artist's great specialties.[17]

Veronese's 1573 *Last Supper* was thus no radical departure, but another variation on a theme that had brought the artist success and fame for more than a decade. Moreover, the notion of a lavish and elegant refectory feast painting was hardly his invention; several works by major Central Italian painters predate Veronese's efforts, and other Venetian masters also helped to shape his ideas. The genre was first developed in Tuscany, especially in Florence, and it was from that tradition that Leonardo's immensely influential Milan *Last Supper* of the 1490s was derived.[18] Produced for the Dominican monastery of S. Maria delle Grazie, Leonardo's dramatic image was probably in the minds of the leaders of the Venetian Dominican monastery of SS. Giovanni e Paolo when, around 1550, they asked Titian to produce a very large canvas of the *Last Supper* for their refectory.[19] Titian's painting, completed by 1557, was one of the first—and by far the largest—sacred feast images for a Venetian monastic dining hall. But during the night of February 13–14, 1571, it was destroyed in a fire that swept through the refectory and the rooms beneath it. Fortunately, closely related compositions survive[20] (fig. 7), and thus we know that the lost work was a vast but sober reevocation of Leonardo's masterpiece; the only notable additions were a monumental arched loggia, and two attendants at the margins. Although Titian's composition was essentially conservative, it did give the refectory feast painting an instant importance in Venetian art.[21]

Veronese, however, probably knew depictions of sacred feasts far more lavish than Titian's. Between 1525 and 1550, North and Central Italian painters began to produce images of biblical feasts in which genre details from contemporary refections were increasingly emphasized. In the works of Bonifazio de' Pitati (Venice), Garofalo (Ferrara), Francesco Salviati (Rome), and Giorgio Vasari (Bologna and Arezzo), the luxury of Italian aristocratic banquets is repeatedly reflected,[22] and fortunately for us Vasari the art critic was eager to explain what Vasari the painter had in mind. Writing of his *Marriage Feast of Esther and Ahasuerus* (1548–49) for the refectory of the Benedictine Badia of Arezzo (fig. 8), Vasari affirmed that he was seeking greatness and majesty through the depiction of

> all kinds of servants, pages, ensigns, soldiers of the guard, vessels with wine, credenzas, musicians, and a dwarf, and every other thing which is required at a royal and magnificent banquet. There one sees among others the steward

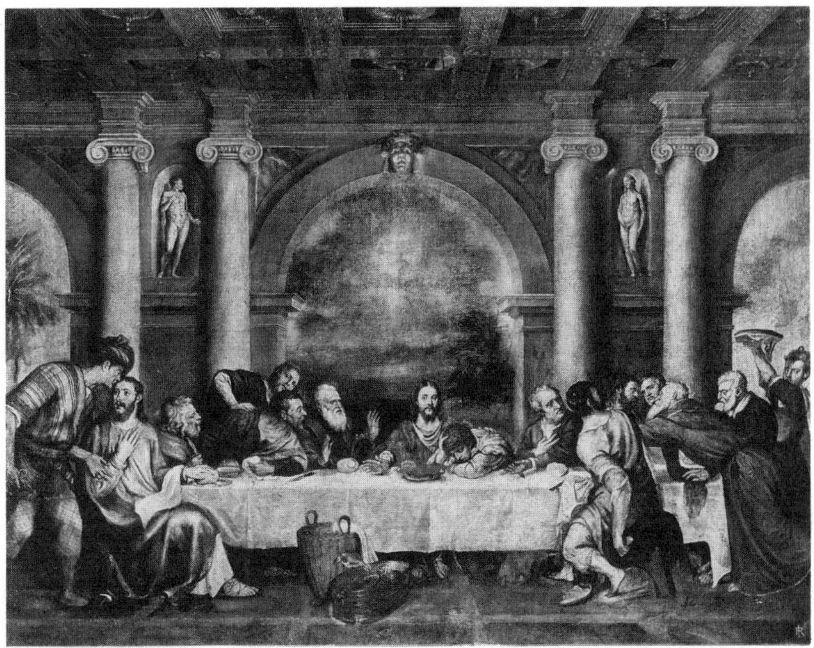

FIG. 7. Titian (?) or copy after Titian, *Last Supper*, ca. 1550 or later. Oil on canvas, 170×216 cm (67×85 in.). Brera, Milan. Photo: Alinari/Art Resource, New York.

> bringing the dishes to the table accompanied by a good number of pages dressed in livery, and other ensigns and servants. At the heads of the table, which is oval, are lords and other great personages and courtiers, who are standing up, as one typically sees at a banquet.[23]

This passage, first published in the 1568 edition of Vasari's *Lives*, evokes both Veronese's own feast pictures and, even more dramatically, parts of his self-defense before the Inquisition. Paolo, for example, justified his inclusion of two German soldiers (and implicitly all other attendants): "They are placed there, that they may do some service, it seeming to me fitting that the owner of the House, who was great and rich according to what I have heard, should have such servants."

Many of these earlier efforts may have been known to Veronese, but his ideas about sacred feast paintings must have been colored even more strongly by the works of his great Venetian rival Jacopo Tintoretto. Tintoretto's teeming *Marriage Feast at Cana* of 1561 for the refectory of the Crociferi

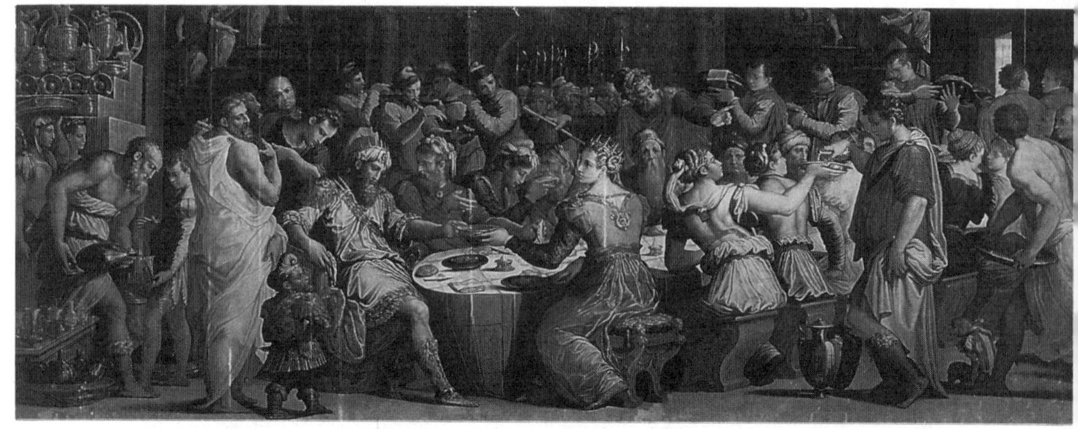

FIG. 8. Giorgio Vasari, *Marriage Feast of Esther and Ahaseurus*, 1548–49.
Oil on canvas(?). Museo, Arezzo. Photo: Alinari/Art Resource, New York.

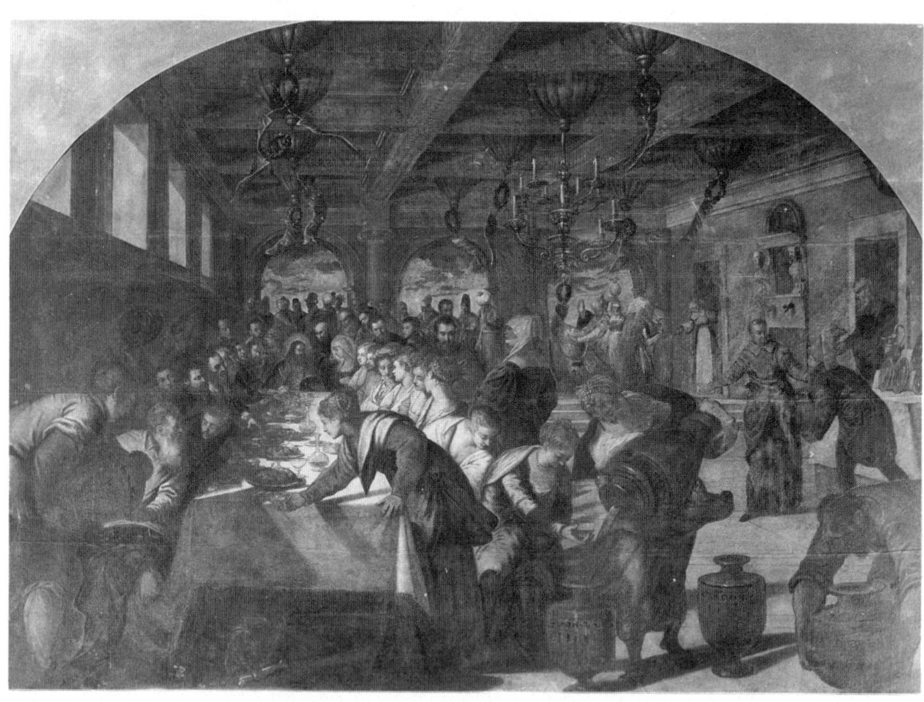

FIG. 9. Jacopo Tintoretto, *Marriage Feast at Cana*, 1561.
Oil on canvas, 435×545 cm (171×214 in.). S. Maria della Salute, Venice.
Photo: O. Boehm, Venice.

(fig. 9)[24] was undoubtedly the main prototype for Veronese's *Cana* of 1562–63 for S. Giorgio Maggiore. Yet the two pictures belong to different orders of magnitude: Veronese's is three times larger and has nearly three times as many figures.

Among this group of luxurious feasts painted after 1525, the subject of the Last Supper itself is conspicuously absent. Tintoretto, beginning in 1547, had painted a series of dramatic and ingenious *Last Supper*s, but all of them were intimate in feeling, and none of them, remarkably, were for refectories.[25] From 1557 to 1571 the only major Venetian refectory with a *Last Supper* was that at SS. Giovanni e Paolo.

The destruction of Titian's *Last Supper* and the refectory that contained it in February 1571 prompted the immediate resolve to replace them. We know that the state contributed money to the architectural project, but no contractual documents survive pertaining to Veronese's commission.[26] It is easy to imagine what happened. Titian was perhaps approached, but begged off on the grounds of his age—he was at least in his eighties, conceivably over ninety. Veronese was one of the two major active painters in the city (with Tintoretto), and he was by this time more renowned than his rival for feast paintings in refectories. Though he had had no previous dealings with the Dominicans of SS. Giovanni e Paolo, he was chosen.[27] According to an apparently trustworthy seventeenth-century tradition, an otherwise obscure monk named Andrea de' Buoni volunteered to pay for the picture; we do not know what he was charged.[28] Naturally, the subject of the new work would remain the same, though as the room itself was to be enlarged, the new canvas would also be enlarged to fill one of its shorter sides.

Veronese did not sign the canvas, but he did inscribe on it the date of its completion: A.D. MDLXXIII DIE. XX APR. (This is the only such inscription giving date as well as year in Veronese's oeuvre. It is presumably a proud expression of accomplishment—and relief—in having brought the vast project to completion.) From this date we may infer that work was begun sometime in 1572. Its current dimensions are 555 cm high by 1,310 cm wide, having lost a small strip at the top.[29] In addition to the thirteen canonical sacred figures, there are sixty-one other participants or observers, plus two birds, two dogs, and a cat. The subject, as originally intended, is without question the Last Supper.[30] Christ, his apostles, a monk (the donor de' Buoni?), and an elegant man, whom Veronese describes as the owner of the inn where the supper takes place, are gathered at a long thin table parallel to the picture plane. The table stands within a monumental loggia, behind which a vista of classicizing buildings extends into the distance. The structural similarities with Veronese's earlier feasts are pronounced. The closest link is undoubtedly with the Monte Berico *Feast of Saint Gregory* of 1572 (fig. 6), and sensibly so, since the event celebrated in that image was Pope Gregory's imitation of the Last Supper itself.[31]

We do not really know how Veronese's *Last Supper* came to the attention of the Inquisition. There is a gap of three months between the completion date (April 20)—which may or may not be the date the work was fully installed at SS. Giovanni e Paolo—and the hearing (July 18). The monks no doubt saw the picture, but whether any lay persons were invited to view it is unclear. At any rate, from Veronese's comments at the hearing, we know that the prior of the monastery was summoned to speak with the Inquisitors—perhaps more informally, since no transcript of this discussion survives—and he was to convey to Veronese instructions about changing the picture. The painter said he had been asked to insert a figure of Mary Magdalene in place of a dog, which would have meant changing the subject to a *Supper in the House of Simon*.[32] Veronese then indicated that he was not inclined to accept the advice, and this, he imagined, was what had earned him an invitation to appear before the Inquisitors. His interrogators did not dispute this account of what had prompted the hearing.

What, then, was the nature of the official body before which Veronese appeared? The Venetian incarnation of the Holy Office, as the Inquisition was usually known, was very different from its harsher and papally controlled Roman counterpart. It had been founded in 1547. In Veronese's day, four of its six members were Venetian functionaries, and of these four only one was a churchman.[33] A fifth participant, at the time of Veronese's hearing, was a native of Venice's territories on the mainland. Let us look at all of these men and their allegiances more closely.

The chief and perhaps only active interrogator was a Dominican monk named Aurelio Schellini, who was not so much the chair of the committee as its counsel. Nominated by Rome, the person who held this post was by statute subject to confirmation by the Venetian state. Schellini was from Brescia, a provincial city of the Venetian empire, and not much else is known about him.[34] The fact that he was a Dominican, like the monks at SS. Giovanni e Paolo, may be significant. The other clergymen were a papal legate (envoy) to Venice, Giovanni Battista Dei, archbishop of Rossano in Southern Italy, and Giovanni Trevisan, patriarch (effectively archbishop) of Venice.[35] Trevisan, like virtually all Venetian patriarchs, belonged to an aristocratic family from Venice itself, and had been nominated by the Venetian government and merely confirmed by the pope.

The three laymen were also Venetian patricians. They had been elected by their peers in the Collegio—a select legislative body—to serve a two-year term as the Tre Savi sopra Eresia ("three overseers on heresy") and their principal function was to participate in the proceedings of the Holy Office. Two of these men, Nicolò Venier and Alvise Zorzi, were distinguished though unremarkable,[36] but the third man, the senior member, was a powerful politician. Giacomo di Michele Foscarini was a learned patrician with a history of involvement in politics and pious works.[37] In 1557 he had been one of the founders of the Venetian institution of the Catecumeni, a home and school for those Jews and Moslems who could be induced to convert to Christianity.[38] Foscarini was among the forty-one nobles chosen to elect the doge of Venice in 1559, 1567, and 1570, and held many major elective offices. (In the ducal election of 1578, Foscarini may himself have been the recipient of a number of votes.) In 1572–73 he was a member of the Council of Ten, the much feared state security committee which was the strongest executive body of the Venetian government, and he served at least two month-long terms as one of its three chairs, in July and September.[39] Foscarini's stature, however, was not unusual for the Savi sopra Eresia; the state wanted sophisticated and high-level representation on this sensitive body.

While the charge of the Venetian Holy Office was to search out and suppress heresy, its investigations frequently had political ramifications. On the one hand, the presence of so many lay officials emphasized that the physical powers of the state stood ready to enforce the Inquisition's dictates. Indeed, since the Venetian state prized the scrupulous observance of orthodox religious practices by its subjects as a hallmark of social order, the government was often eager to support the rulings of the Holy Office. On the other hand, the Venetian government had long been suspicious of the Roman Church's tendency to assert the primacy of ecclesiastical law and practice over local secular legal systems. The presence of at least four powerful Venetian subjects—three of them laymen—at the deliberations of the Holy Office was therefore calculated to prevent those excesses of pious zeal which might compromise Venetian secular authority, both in principle and in practice. The result was an overall mildness in the pronouncements of the Inquisition in Venice compared with its Roman counterpart.[40]

The transcript of Veronese's hearing presents several technical problems. As the most thorough editor of the text, Philipp Fehl, has pointed out, "it does not represent a verbatim account of all that was said [at the hearing]. The scribe appears to have concentrated on the essential elements of the transaction and to have edited what he heard."[41] Fehl also carefully noted a number of crossed-out words and phrases. A translation of the transcript is provided here in the appendix, but a summary of the main points raised might be helpful.

After identifying himself and indicating why he thought he had been summoned, Veronese proceeded to respond to questions about the subject, location, and dimensions of his picture. The subject, he said, was the "last Supper, that Jesus Christ took with his apostles." The painter was then requested to describe the more important noncanonical figures in the work, whom he identified as the owner of the inn and his chief steward in charge of the meal. Veronese was then asked about the "Suppers of the Lord" he had previously painted, and he listed them; the Inquisitor disqualified the *Marriage at Cana* for S. Giorgio Maggiore from this list, but accepted the several versions of the Supper in the House of Simon. Veronese did not mention the Vicenza *Feast of Saint Gregory.*

Schellini next asked about an attendant with a bloody nose, and about the two soldiers outfitted in the German style at the right (fig. 3). Sensing that his interrogator was fishing for sacrilegious implications, Veronese in reply made a more general defense of the innocence of his imagery:

> We painters take the license, which poets and madmen take, and I made these two Halberdiers, one who drinks and the other who eats, near a blind staircase. They are placed there, that they may do some service, it seeming to me fitting that the owner of the House, who was great and rich according to what I have heard, should have such servants.

Veronese was then asked about the dwarf with the parrot in the foreground, and about the actions of several apostles, especially Peter, who is cutting up a roast lamb.

The questions then become more tendentious. Veronese denied that anyone had asked him specifically to include "Germans and buffoons and similar things," but this only earned him a scolding about inventing things "without any discretion and judgment." "Did it seem to you fitting," asked Schellini, "that at the last supper of the lord it was fitting to paint buffoons, drunkards, Germans, dwarfs and similar scurrilities?" "Do you not know," continued the Inquisitor, "that in Germany and other places infected with heresy they are accustomed, with various paintings full of scurrilities and similar inventions, to spread [lies?], vituperate and pour scorn on the things of the Holy Catholic Church, in order to teach bad doctrine to idiotic and ignorant people?"[42]

Here Veronese introduced the idea that his own iconographic idiosyncrasies were nothing next to Michelangelo's in the Sistine *Last Judgment*, but this earned another rebuke.[43] The painter concluded his testimony by saying he did not want to defend his picture, "but I thought I was doing right." The scribe then gives—now in Latin rather than Italian—a kind of sentence: Veronese is "held and obliged to correct and amend the painting" within three months at his own expense, or face other unspecified penalties. Significantly, the phrase "that it would be fitting as a last supper of the Lord" is crossed out.

Several conclusions can be drawn from Schellini's questions and statements. The Inquisitor's principal concern about the picture was that its profane elements made the painting sacrilegious. The eating and drinking Germans, and the man with the bloody nose, were evidently taken as parodies of the eucharistic meaning of the event. (We shall return to this point in more detail shortly.) Schellini feared that the image was crypto-Protestant, and tried to find out if some suspect individual had influenced Veronese in this direction.[44] (The Dominican did not suggest that Veronese himself was tainted by Lutheranism.) The Inquisitor evidently was persuaded by Veronese's replies that he had no subversive intent in composing the picture, and therefore concluded by scolding him for not having anticipated that many of the profane details ("scurrilities") might be seen as attacks on the doctrines and authority of the Catholic Church. This sort of concern, of course, corresponds to the tenor of Catholic religious discourse in the 1560s. In the decrees of the final phase of the Council of Trent in 1563, and in the book of the Flemish censor Johannes Molanus in 1570, artists and especially ecclesiastical patrons were instructed to exclude fantastic and potentially sensual elements from religious images.[45] But, it must be emphasized, these statements had no apparent impact on the acceptability of Veronese's feast paintings executed in the 1560s and in 1570–72. To put it another way, we are still left with the problem of understanding why the 1573 canvas, so similar to its predecessors in many ways, was the one to create scandal. Only three major features really set this work apart from the others: (1) it was made for the Dominican monastery of SS. Giovanni e Paolo; (2) it was Veronese's first depiction of the Last Supper; (3) it was completed in the spring of 1573.

The vast Gothic church of SS. Giovanni e Paolo (S. Zanipolo in Venetian dialect) was one of the principal centers of Venetian ecclesiastical life, and, one might say, political afterlife. As the greatest church of the influential Dominican order of preaching monks in the city, it attracted the attention of the powerful as well as the poor, and from the fourteenth century it gradually became the favored site for the lavish tombs of Venetian doges and military leaders.

During the period around 1573, the monastery of SS. Giovanni e Paolo was a troubled institution; unfortunately a full understanding of its problems still eludes us. Here is what we do know. The monastery was on the defensive, struggling as best it could with efforts at reform and attempts by Rome to control its fate. The Venetian Senate wrote to the Venetian ambassador in Rome on August 6, 1569, telling him to thank the general (chief administrator) of the Dominican order for his cooperation in the new reform of the monastery.[46] On December 23, 1570, the papal nuncio in Venice was urged in a letter from his Roman superiors to press harder for reform at SS. Giovanni e Paolo, and on January 13 of the following year Facchinetti, the nuncio, reported on his slow progress in this matter.[47]

Meanwhile—and we do not know if it was the cause or result of this crisis—an extraordinarily large number of monks at the monastery seem to have left its walls and died after abandoning the Catholic faith. An internal monastic chronicle lists two such deaths in 1568, four in 1571, six in 1572, two in 1573, three in 1574, three in 1575, and seven in 1576, and these apostates represent more than 75 percent of the deaths of monks recorded for those years.[48] This is an astonishing result, and many details are unclear. The chronicle does not indicate when the monks left SS. Giovanni e Paolo; from the dates of death, one would presume that the exodus took place well before 1568, but this cannot be proven.[49] Most of the monks evidently turned to Protestant sects, but one, the chronicle indicates, became a Moslem. If the chronicler's data are correct, SS. Giovanni e Paolo was in turmoil nearly to the point of disintegration. Veronese's inclusion of Germans (fig. 3) and turbaned Moslems (fig. 2) in his refectory picture may have produced a bitter reaction among those concerned about the monastery's difficulties with apostasy.

Another document from the Venetian archives is even more suggestive of a connection between Veronese's troubles and the monastery's precarious state. On May 3, 1573, the two Venetian ambassadors to the pope sent a dispatch to the chairs of the Council of Ten.[50] (Veronese's *Last Supper* had been completed on April 20.) The dispatch, with some obliqueness, indicated that one of the Venetian envoys had spoken with the general of the Dominicans of Brescia to obtain the absolution—by the father Inquisitor of Venice (Schellini)—and reinstatement of the vicar of the monks of SS. Giovanni e Paolo. The general had finally conceded to these requests. The Venetian state had thus successfully intervened with the Dominican order and the Dominican Inquisitor in an attempt to protect, at least to some degree, the Venetian monastery. But we remain ignorant of why the vicar (perhaps another word for the prior or head of the monastery, or perhaps his principal subordinate) had been suspended and why he required absolution.[51] Even if it had nothing to do with Veronese's painting, the precarious position of the monastery in the eyes of the authorities is obvious.

In this difficult situation, the Last Supper was bound to be a sensitive subject for a painting. Though it might have been wiser for the Dominican patrons to have commissioned some less theologically central feast, the urge to replace Titian's incinerated *Last Supper* was too strong. Veronese had not painted this subject before, and as a layman was possibly unaware of how loaded the event had become in the preceding half-century.

Since early Christian times, of course, the Gospel account of Christ's final meal with the apostles had been understood as a critical event in his life. His statement that in offering bread and wine to his apostles he was offering them his sacrificial flesh and blood[52] provided the basis for the recurring eucharistic miracle of the mass, where the priest reenacted the transformation for the Christian faithful. The Lutheran challenge to certain doctrinal aspects of the mass immediately began to make its biblical prototype a delicate subject. In 1523, Dürer produced an austere woodcut of the scene with reformist overtones.[53] Luther himself wrote in 1530:

> Whoever is inclined to put pictures on the altar ought to have the Lord's Supper of Christ painted, and with these two verses written around it in gold letters: "The gracious and merciful Lord has instituted a remembrance of His wonderful works." Then they would stand before our eyes for our heart to contemplate them, and even our eyes, in reading, would have to thank and praise God. Since the altar is designated for the administration of the Sacrament, one could not find a better painting for it. Other pictures of God or Christ can be painted somewhere else.[54]

This recommendation was evidently not followed, perhaps because Luther did not give further guidance on what should be shown in such an image.

Indeed, the many controversies surrounding Holy Communion in this period tended to scare artists off the Last Supper as a subject altogether, especially in Northern Europe. And depictions of sacred feasts in general began to come in for pointed criticism by the 1530s. The Catholic reformer Erasmus wrote:

> Some artists, when they paint something from the Evangelists add impious absurdities to it. For example, when they depict our Lord received to supper at the house of Martha and Mary, they show the young John secretly chatting in a corner with Martha, and Peter downing a tankard, while He is speaking to Mary.

> And again, at the supper, they show Martha sitting behind John with one hand thrown on his shoulder and the other as if making fun of Christ, who is unaware of it all. Also there is Peter already flushed with wine still putting a tankard to his lips. And although these things are blasphemous and impious, they still pass for humour. In sacred matters it is proper that the same standards apply to painting as to speech.[55]

As with Saint Bernard's famously lyrical castigation of the impious fantasies of Romanesque sculpture, one senses a certain rhetorical pleasure in Erasmus's description of these lapses in painterly decorum; this, along with the absence of a named work of art as its object, separates Erasmus's critique from that of the inquisitor Schellini. But the Counter Reformation notion that profanities must be banished from sacred narrative painting is shared by the urbane humanist and the Dominican interrogator.[56] Still, one has to ask again why the Inquisition did not confront Veronese about one of his several earlier *Suppers in the House of Simon*, especially since this is the very feast which concerns Erasmus in the passage above. And one of the answers must be that although the Inquisition was willing to list the Simon feasts as "suppers of the Lord," the Last Supper remained in a class by itself. Only at this final meal was the Eucharist instituted, and thus only here could the gluttonous Germans and the servant with the bleeding nose really be seen as a potential attack on vital dogma. Schellini's idea that these might have been deliberately parodic elements must be understood in light of Catholic attitudes toward Protestant celebrations of "Holy Suppers," like the one publically mounted in Lyon in 1562; an unsympathetic observer called this chaotic and crowded affair "diabolical" and likened it to a bacchanal.[57] And Protestants attacked Catholics in similar terms: a trenchant and mocking Calvinist treatise of 1560, *Satyres chrestiennes de la cuisine Papale*, compared Catholicism in general and the mass in particular to a disordered and gluttonous banquet.[58]

But there is more. In Veronese's case, the charged nature of the Last Supper as a subject was further exacerbated, in the eyes of papal and Venetian officials, by the fact that one of the two most serious contemporary conflicts between Venice and the pope centered on a papal bull entitled "In Coena Domini" (At the Lord's Table). Traditionally issued each year on Maundy Thursday, the anniversary of the Last Supper, this formal and public papal document essentially declared which sins were so grievous that their absolution was reserved to the pope rather than to any priest. The practice went back to at least the 1300s, but became more structured and standardized from 1511.[59] No great controversy was attached to this bull until the election of the militantly zealous Dominican Pope Pius V in 1566. Pius quickly transformed the "In Coena Domini" into a threat to excommunicate the leaders of other Christian states if they resisted Pius's substantial limitations on their temporal powers.

The first series of disputes broke out in 1568, with Spain and its Italian dependencies (Milan and Naples) leading the attack on papal "usurpation" of the right to prosecute, tax, and otherwise control the clergy in their dominions.[60] Perhaps emboldened by Spanish resistance, in 1569 the Venetian Senate resolved to ban the new version of "In Coena Domini" which had been issued on April 1 of that year.[61] This precipitated a substantial crisis in relations with the papacy, but despite much maneuvering Venice remained firm in refusing to publish or post the bull anywhere in its dominions, all the while protesting its loyalty to the Roman Church.[62]

In addition to the clauses related to control over the clergy, Venice also had reason to be concerned about the severe strictures Pius had added to the bull concerning heretics, Jews, and Muslims. Venetian trade with Lutheran Germany and the Ottoman Empire was considerable and vital. Yet the new "In Coena Domini," narrowly interpreted, forbade allowing Lutherans or Muslims to enter the Venetian republic, and it placed many kinds of commerce off limits as giving aid to the enemies of the Roman Church.[63] Between 1569 and early 1573, however, Venice could not have been too preoccupied with this aspect of the bull, since it was continuously at war with the Turks. This conflict also explains the pope's failure to actually excommunicate the Venetians; they were fighting the crusade-like war Pius had always wanted, and in fact in 1571 Spain and the papacy joined Venice in the so-called Holy League. (In February 1570, Rome had offered help against the Ottomans as a reward for accepting the banned bull, but the Venetians did not agree to this, knowing that the pope would support them militarily anyway.[64]) In March 1570, Venice moved to detain Turks and Eastern Jews in the city,[65] and in the aftermath of the Holy League's great naval victory at Lepanto in October 1571, the Venetian ruling classes became even more strongly xenophobic. On December 18 the Senate ordered the expulsion of the entire Venetian Jewish community, which in the preceding half-century had become an important factor in Venice's economic vitality.[66] Venice was falling in with several parts of Pius's program for a Church Militant.

The victory at Lepanto was, however, an end rather than a beginning, and the Holy League soon began to come apart. Venice's prosperity—indeed, even the survival of the republic—depended on its key role as a fulcrum of international commerce between Northern Europe, the Christian nations of the Mediterranean basin, and the Ottoman Empire. Venice simply could not afford to be at war with one of its principal trading partners indefinitely, and early in 1573 it negotiated with the Turks for a separate peace.[67] The papal nuncio in Venice expressed a fear that such a peace might be made on February 21.[68] Maundy Thursday fell on March 19, and the new "In Coena Domini" issued by the recently elected Pope Gregory XIII contained a special clause directed as a warning to Venice: any state that abandoned the Holy League would be excommunicated.[69] But a Venetian treaty with the Ottomans had been secretly drawn up in Istanbul on March 7.[70] Two weeks after the issuance of the bull, on April 6, Venetian envoys—with elaborate instructions as to how to couch an apology from the Senate—revealed the treaty to a disgusted pope.[71] On April 16 the Venetian ambassador Paolo Tiepolo, still trying to placate the pontiff, wrote the Senate that Gregory feared that Venice's betrayal would lead Spain to abandon the war, and that then the Turks would "form an alliance with the Protestants, and turn the world upside down."[72] Four days later the unlucky Veronese completed his painting.

Venetian apologies and excuses continued to be made to the pope on into May, and they achieved their aim: Gregory, who lacked Pius's obsessive intensity, did not enforce the sections of his "In Coena Domini" that prohibited defection from the League, commerce with the Turks, and the admission of heretics and infidels into Venetian territory.[73] Venice was thus not placed under an interdict despite its refusal either to abide by certain clauses or to publish any section of the bull. Indeed, the Senate dared to go further: on July 7 the Senate revoked the official expulsion of the Jews —which, incidentally, had never been carried out—and on the 11th the Jewish community received a new charter.[74] (This may have been a reward for Jewish help in making peace with the Ottomans.[75]) But despite these economically pragmatic actions, Venice could scarcely afford to give the impression—least of all to Rome—that it was relaxing its guard against enemies of the Catholic Church.[76]

In this sense, Veronese's hearing on July 18 was a kind of smokescreen. The artist's picture had appeared at the wrong place (in a troubled monastery whose monks were suspected of heresy), at the wrong time (just as Venice desperately needed to assure the papacy that despite its political actions the republic's Counter Reformation heart was pure), and with the wrong subject (one that was doctrinally most sensitive, and could only remind both Venice and the pope of their dispute about the "In Coena Domini" bull). One of

Schellini's questions, it should be noted, focused on the depiction of Peter cutting up the lamb. The Inquisitor no doubt feared this was a veiled criticism of papal greed, an issue that was a staple of Protestant attacks and also a feature of Catholic complaints about the "In Coena Domini" bull's usurpation of the tax-levying rights of secular states.[77]

But although the Venetian state permitted and participated in Veronese's interrogation, its leaders were not really interested in punishing or making a public example of him. The hearing was secret, and no word of it was leaked. The papal court was of course informed, since one of those present at the hearing was the papal legate himself, and this was really the most important audience. At no cost to itself, the republic could act to assure the pope that it would clamp down on even the suspicion of heresy and sacrilege.[78] There was, however, no point in really damaging or destroying an artist highly valued by the Venetian ruling class. So the Inquisition's sentence imposed no penalty but a vague instruction that the painting be corrected. By crossing out the phrase "that it would be fitting as a last supper of the Lord" the Inquisition was probably hoping that Veronese would accept the suggestion that had first been made to him—to add Mary Magdalene and thus convert the composition into a Supper in the House of Simon.[79]

Instead, and with the connivance of some learned person of more emphatic antipapal tendencies, Veronese's "correction" answered the Inquisition and militant Counter Reformation ideology with a daring and witty theological repartee. Since the rebuff would have been fully intelligible only to those few who knew of the charges against the painter, contemporary discussion of the painting does not refer to it, but it is odd that modern critics have never noted it. This is probably because these critics have emphasized Veronese's apolitical and nonideological stance at his hearing,[80] but the rebuff suggests that, as with so many artists in our own day, Veronese's reluctance to accept the authorities' ideological interference with his imagery did not mean he was unwilling to make a political comment of his own.

Thanks to the recent cleaning and conservation of the SS. Giovanni e Paolo canvas, we now know for certain that Veronese made *no* changes in his picture after April 20, except the one which has long been evident: he added the inscriptions "FECIT D.COVI.MAGNU.LEVI" and "LUCAE CAP. V."[81] He thus retitled the work as the *Feast in the House of Levi*, by which name it has been known since 1573. This feast, described in the Gospels of Matthew and Mark as well as Luke, is a celebration of the apostle Matthew's calling by Christ:

> After this he [Christ] went out, and saw a tax collector, named Levi [Matthew], sitting at the tax office; and he said to him, "Follow me." And he left everything and rose and followed him. And Levi made him a great feast in his house; and there was a large company of tax collectors and others sitting at table with them. And the Pharisees and their scribes murmured against his disciples, saying, "Why do you eat and drink with tax collectors and sinners?" And Jesus answered them, "Those who are well have no need of a physician, but those who are sick; I have not come to call the righteous, but sinners to repentance."[82]

As a subject for artists, Matthew's calling is well known, but there is no tradition of representing the ensuing feast except in medieval manuscripts.[83] As far as we know, Veronese's painting was the first large-scale work to be so entitled, and the choice of this scene therefore must have been both deliberate and meaningful. Veronese's painting does not really fit this subject—where are the conversing apostles and Pharisees?—but the subject was suited to the rebuke Veronese wished to make. If the Inquisitors had castigated Veronese for inserting Germans, a dwarf, buffoons (black and turbaned white characters as well as the dwarf are evidently meant by this term[84]), his reply to them would be in Christ's words: "I have not come to call the righteous, but sinners to repentance." The Lord's mission is to preach to, not expel or excommunicate, the heretic, the infidel, the tax collector; and the exclusionary Pharisees are stand-ins for the pope and the Inquisition.[85]

That Veronese got away with his "correction" is perhaps not so remarkable in the light of political shifts toward the end of 1573. The "In Coena Domini" crisis was moving toward a solution, and the pope had come to terms with Venice's peace treaty and the end of the League.[86] Veronese's value as a state artist soared even higher after the Ducal Palace fires of 1574 and 1577, since so many new triumphal images of the republic were now required. Paolo continued to work on major sacred commissions, but he was no fool: he never resumed his specialty in vast sacred feasts. A request for a huge *Marriage at Cana* for the refectory of Benedictine nuns in Treviso was turned over to Veronese's brother Benedetto.[87] Paolo did paint another *Last Supper*, but this much smaller and soberer canvas, made for a confraternity of the Most Holy Sacrament in the small Venetian parish church of S. Sofia, has an ingenious Counter Reformation iconography that the Inquisition would have found beyond reproach.[88]

After Paolo's death in 1588 his refectory feast paintings (including the one for SS. Giovanni e Paolo) were taken by his critics and biographers as among his greatest creations, and their sumptuousness and elaboration were con-

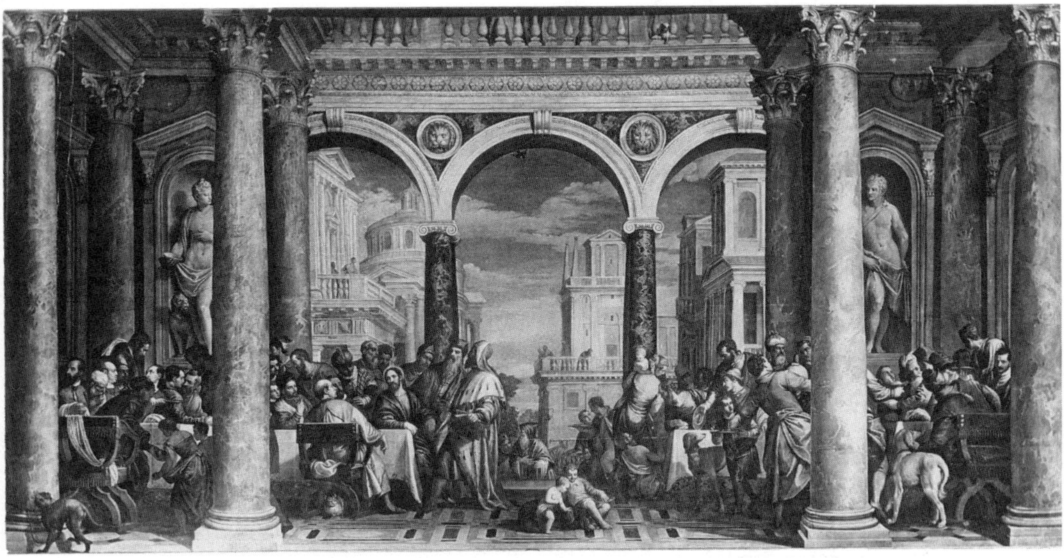

FIG. 10. "Heirs" of Veronese, *Feast in the House of Levi*, ca. 1588–1610. Oil on canvas, 550×1,010 cm (216×397 in.). Accademia, Venice, on deposit at Municipio, Verona. Photo: O. Boehm, Venice.

sidered central to his achievement as an artist. The *Feast in the House of Levi* was simply held to be one of a distinguished group of compositions; these writers give not the slightest hint that the picture had been retitled, or that it had ever been the subject of controversy. But there is a peculiar epilogue to that controversy, albeit a possibly fortuitous one. Paolo's heirs—his brother, two sons, and a nephew—either did not know of his brush with the Holy Office, or if they did it meant little to them two decades later. For at some point after 1588, perhaps even after 1600, they accepted a commission from the Servite monks at S. Giacomo on the Giudecca for a refectory painting (fig. 10) with the subject of the *Feast in the House of Levi*![89]

This vast work survives, and it is apparently the only example in postmedieval Christian art of a real illustration of the biblical event. The composition is a pastiche of Paolo's earlier feasts, but in the center several Pharisees—one holding the text of the Law—argue with Christ and his apostles. It may only be coincidence that the intellectual leader of Venice's next and stronger challenge to the papacy, Fra Paolo Sarpi, was also one of the leaders of the Servite order in the city.[90] This new conflict, again inflamed by a Venetian refusal to publish the "In Coena Domini" bull, culminated in the interdict placed upon Venice by the pope in 1606–7.[91] A destructive breach of this kind was, perhaps, what Veronese's hearing paradoxically had helped to avoid in 1573.

APPENDIX

The transcript of Veronese's hearing before the Inquisition is found in the Archivio di Stato of Venice, Sant'Ufficio, Processi, 6, busta n. 33, 1572–1573. The best published version of the original Italian/Latin text is in Philipp Fehl, "Veronese and the Inquisition: A Study of the Subject Matter of the So-called 'Feast in the House of Levi,'" *Gazette des Beaux-Arts*, 6th ser., 58 (1961): 325–54 (reprinted in his *Decorum and Wit: The Poetry of Venetian Painting*, Vienna, 1992, 223–43); text also reprinted in Terisio Pignatti, *Paolo Veronese: Convito in casa di Levi*, Hermia, 10 (Venice, 1986), 9–13. What follows is a very literal translation of this text into English, using the previously standard English version (in Elizabeth G. Holt, ed., *A Documentary History of Art*, vol. 2, Garden City, 1958, 65–70) as a point of departure; many of my adjustments and changes—though they often make for inelegant prose—clarify the nuances of the statements recorded; others simply reflect Fehl's more accurate transcription, which Holt did not have access to. Two other recent and somewhat freer English translations should be noted: by Peter and Linda Murray, from Fehl, in André Chastel, *A Chronicle of Italian Renaissance Painting* (Ithaca, 1984), 214–20; by Brian Pullan in David Chambers and Brian Pullan with Jennifer Fletcher, eds., *Venice, a Documentary History, 1450–1630* (Oxford, 1992), 232–36, from Fogolari. Minor crossed-out words are not included.

SATURDAY 18TH DAY OF THE MONTH OF JULY 1573

Paolo Caliari of Verona painter resident in the parish of S. Samuele, summoned to the holy office in the presence of the holy Tribunal, and questioned as to his name and surname. Answered as above. Questioned as to his profession. Answered: I paint and make figures. Said to him: Do you know the reason why you were summoned? Answered: No, sir. Said to him: Can you imagine it? Answered: I can well imagine. Said to him: Say what you imagine it is. Answered: From that which was said to me by the Holy Fathers, that is, the Prior of SS. Giovanni e Paolo, whose name I don't know, who told me that he had been here, and that Your Illustrious Lordships had given instructions that he should have had made the Magdalene in the place of a dog, and I responded that, I would have freely done that and other things for my honor and that of the painting; But that I did not feel that such a figure of the Magdalene could appear as if it were right, for many reasons, which I will give at any time, if I am given a chance to say them. Said to him: What picture is this of which you have spoken? Answered: This is a picture of the last Supper, that Jesus Christ took with his apostles. [Crossed out: Said to him.] In the house of Simon. Said to him: Where is this picture? Answered: In the refectory of the monks of SS. Giovanni e Paolo. Said to him: Is it on the wall, on panel or on canvas? Answered: On canvas. Said to him: How many feet high is it? Answered: It would be seventeen feet. Said to him: How wide is it? Answered: About thirty-nine feet. Said to him: At this Supper of the Lord have you painted Ministers [representatives, i.e., figures besides Christ and the Apostles]? Answered: Milord, yes. Said to him: Say how many Ministers, and the effect made by each. Answered: There is the owner of the inn, Simon, beyond this I have made below this figure a steward, whom I pretended had come for his own pleasure to see how things were going at the table. Then he added: that there are many figures, and because there are many, and because I finished the painting some time ago, I cannot recall them. Said to him: Have you painted other suppers than this? Answered: Yes, sir. Said to him: How many have you painted and in what place? Answered: I made one in Verona for the Reverend Monks of S. Lazar [scribe's error for S. Nazzaro]; which is in their refectory. Said: I made one in the refectory of the Reverend Fathers of S. Giorgio here in Venice. It was said to him: This is not a supper, one is asking of the Supper of the Lord. Answered: I made one in the refectory of the Servi of Venice, and one in the refectory of S. Sebastiano here in Venice. And I made one in Padua at the Fathers of the Maddalena, And I do not recall having made any others. Said to him: In this Supper, which you made at SS. Giovanni e Paolo, what is the meaning of the depiction of he who has blood coming out of his nose? Answered: I made him for a servant, who due to some accident had a bloody nose. Said to him: What is the meaning of those armed men dressed as Germans each with a halberd in hand? Answered: It is necessary that I say twenty words. Said to him: Say them. Answered: We painters [crossed out: have the] take the license, which poets and madmen take, and I made those two Halberdiers, one who drinks and the other who eats, near a blind staircase. They are placed there, that they may do some service, it seeming to me fitting that the owner of the House, who was great and rich according to what I have heard, should have such servants. Said to him: That man dressed as a Buffoon with the parrot in his fist, for what purpose did you paint this in that Canvas? Answered: For ornament, as is customary. Said to him: At the table of the lord, here there are? Answered: The Twelve apostles.

[Crossed out: Said to him: You know Saint Peter who is the first to cut up the lamb.] Said to him: What is the effect of Saint Peter, who is the first? Answered: He divided the lamb to give it to the other End of the Table. Said to him: What is the effect of the other one who is near him? Answered: He has a plate to receive that which Saint Peter will give him. Said to him: Say what is the effect of the other one who is near him. Answered: He is one, who has a fork, who picks his teeth. Said to him: Who do you believe was really to be found at that Supper? Answered: I believe that Christ with his apostles were to be found; but if in a picture space is provided I adorn it with figures [crossed out: as I am instructed] according to the stories. Said to him: Were you instructed by any person that you should paint in that picture Germans and buffoons and similar things? Answered: No, sir: But the commission was to embellish the picture as I saw fit, which picture is large and capable of holding many figures, as it seemed to me. Said to him: Are not the ornaments which you the painter are accustomed to place around paintings and pictures supposed to be fitting and proper to the subject and principal figures or are they to be truly [crossed out: by chance] at your pleasure according to what comes to your imagination without any discretion or judgment? Answered: I make paintings with that consideration of what is fitting, that my intellect can grasp. Asked if it seemed to him fitting that at the last supper of the lord it was fitting to paint buffoons, drunkards, Germans, dwarfs and similar scurrilities. Answered: No, sir. Asked: Why then have you painted this, [Answered:] I did it because I supposed these people were outside the place where the supper was to be held. Asked: Do you not know that in Germany and other places infected by heresy they are accustomed, with various paintings full of scurrilities and similar inventions, to spread [lies?], vituperate and pour scorn on the things of the Holy Catholic Church, in order to teach bad doctrine to idiotic and ignorant people? Answered: Sir, yes, this is bad: but I return again to what I have said, that I am obliged to follow what those greater than me have done. Said to him: What have those greater than you done, have they perhaps done something similar? Answered: Michelangelo in Rome [crossed out: in the clothes] in the Pontifical Chapel painted our Lord Jesus Christ, his mother and Saint John, Saint Peter and the Celestial Court, all made nude from the Virgin Mary on down in different poses with little reverence. Said to him: Do you not know that in painting the last judgment, in which no clothing or similar things are presumed, it was not necessary to paint clothing, and in those figures there is nothing which is not spiritual, nor are there buffoons, nor dogs, nor weapons, nor similar buffooneries? And does it seem to you because of this or any other example that you did right in having painted this picture in that way which it is, and do you want to argue that the picture is right and decent? Answered: Illustrious Lord[s?] no, I do not want to defend it; but I thought I was doing right. And I did not consider so many things, Thinking even so much not to make disorder, that those figures of buffoons are outside the place where Our Lord is. [Now entirely in Latin.] Of which it is held [i.e., ruled]. The Lords decreed that the said Paolo would be held and obliged to correct and amend the painting here considered [crossed out: so that it would be fitting as a last supper of the Lord] at the judgment of the Holy Tribunal within the limit of three months numbered from the day of this correction, making it according to the aforesaid judgment of the Holy Tribunal at his [i.e., Veronese's] expense, with the threat of penalties to be imposed by the Holy Tribunal. And thus they decreed in the best of all manners.

NOTES

I would like to thank the staff of the Archivio di Stato in Venice for their assistance. Some of the research on this project was carried out while I held a National Endowment for the Humanities Summer Stipend in 1987, and I am grateful to the Endowment for its support.

1. The most important treatments of this work are: Terisio Pignatti, *Veronese*, 2 vols. (Milan, 1976), 1:136, no. 177, 2: fig. 455 (catalogue entry in the standard monograph); idem, *Paolo Veronese: Convito in casa di Levi*, Hermia, 10 (Venice, 1986), a useful pamphlet with the text of the artist's interrogation; Giovanna Nepi Scirè, ed., *Il restauro del 'Convito in Casa di Levi' di Paolo Veronese*, Quaderni della Soprintendenza ai Beni Artistici e Storici, 11 (Venice, 1984); Gino Fogolari, "Il processo dall'Inquisizione a Paolo Veronese," *Archivio Veneto* 17 (1935): 352–86, the first detailed examination of the problem; G. Delogu, *Paolo Veronese: la Cena in casa di Levi* (Milan, 1952), with a facsimile of the transcript of the interrogation; Emerich Schaffran, "Der Inquisitionsprozess gegen Paolo Veronese," *Archiv für Kulturgeschichte* 41, no. 2 (1960): 178–93; Philipp Fehl, "Veronese and the Inquisition: A Study of the Subject Matter of the So-called 'Feast in the House of Levi,'" *Gazette des Beaux-Arts*, 6th ser., 58 (1961): 325–54, reprinted in Fehl's *Decorum and Wit: The Poetry of Venetian Painting* (Vienna, 1992), 223–43, the most thoughtful treatment and best text of the transcript (not translated); Michelangelo Muraro, "La Cena di Paolo Veronese: nuove interpretazioni" (typescript; Padua, 1980–81), in the Biblioteca Marciana, Venice; André Chastel, *A Chronicle of Italian Renaissance Painting* (Ithaca, 1984), 208–27, 284–89; Massimo Gemin, "Riflessioni iconografiche sulla cena in casa di Levi," in Massimo Gemin, ed., *Nuovi Studi su Paolo Veronese* (Venice, 1990), 367–70.

2. See, for example, Sandra Moschini Marconi, *Gallerie dell'Accademia di Venezia: Opere d'arte del secolo XVI* (Rome, 1962), 83–85.

3. See the thorough study of the Venetian Inquisition's files in Philipp Fehl and Marilyn Perry, "Painting and the Inquisition at Venice: Three Forgotten Files," in David Rosand, ed., *Interpretazioni Veneziane: Studi di storia dell'arte in onore di Michelangelo Muraro* (Venice, 1984), 371–83, reprinted in Fehl, *Decorum and Wit*, 243–60. For a case from the 1600s of artists questioned about illicit changes in a portrait tending to sanctify a living sitter, see Anne Jacobson Schutte, "'Questo non è il ritratto che ho fatto io': Painters, the Inquisition and the Shape of Sanctity in Seventeenth-Century Venice," in Peter Denley and Caroline Elam, eds., *Florence and Italy: Renaissance Studies in Honour of Nicolai Rubinstein* (London, 1988), 419–31. For two painters from Verona prosecuted by that city's Inquisition in 1559 and 1584 for offenses unrelated to their art, see Giulio Sancassani, "Il pittore Girolamo Vaienti da Vicenza in carcere a Verona per eresia nel 1559," *Atti e memorie dell'Accademia di agricoltura, scienze e lettere di Verona* 151 (1976): 191–98.

4. For this and all other quotations from the transcript of the hearing, see the appendix.

5. See Pierluigi De Vecchi, "Michelangelo's Last Judgment," in C. Pietrangeli et al., eds., *The Sistine Chapel: The Art, the History, and the Restoration* (New York, 1986), 190–97; and the essay in the present volume by Bernadine Barnes.

6. As is true of most artists in this era, no records survive (apart from the transcript of the hearing) which shed light on his personal religious beliefs or practices, but one would assume that he was a conventional Catholic. At the hearing, Veronese made every effort to disassociate himself from heretical beliefs.

7. R. Borghini, *Il Riposo* (Florence, 1584), 561–63; Carlo Ridolfi, *Le Maraviglie dell'Arte*, 2 vols. (Venice, 1648), 1:283–338; Antonio Maria Zanetti, *Della pittura veneziana e delle opere pubbliche dei veneziani maestri* (Venice, 1771), 172–90.

8. The work bought by the Spinola was the *Supper in the House of Simon* from the monastery of SS. Nazzaro e Celso in Verona, now in the Galleria Sabauda in Turin; Pignatti, *Veronese* (1976), 1:117, no. 93, 2: fig. 188; the picture that the Venetian state purchased and sent to Louis XIV was also a *Supper in the House of Simon*, from the monastery of S. Maria dei Servi in Venice, and now at Versailles; Pignatti, 1:135–36, no. 176.

9. "Paul Véronèse appelé au tribunal du Saint Office à Venise (1573)," *Gazette des Beaux-Arts*, 1st ser., 23 (1867): 378–82, including the first published version of the transcript. Baschet had long been familiar with the Venetian archives, but he was so astonished by the Veronese hearing transcript that he claimed its discovery in a dated inscription (May 2, 1867) he added to the document's folder. The date of discovery is interesting in two respects: (1) the discovery was probably made possible by Venice's incorporation in the kingdom of Italy one year earlier in 1866—the antipapal Italian state would have had few objections to the study of secret Inquisitional documents; (2) Baschet's publication of this document in a major French periodical in 1867 may reflect a more general climate of interest in policies of censorship in late Second Empire France; see the essay by John House in this volume.

10. For a detailed account of the artist and his career, in addition to Pignatti, *Veronese*, see: Remigio Marini, *L'opera completa del Veronese*, Classici dell'Arte, 20 (Milan, 1968); Terisio Pignatti and Filippo Pedrocco, *Veronese: Catalogo completo dei dipinti* (Florence, 1991); Rodolfo Pallucchini, *Veronese* (Milan, 1984); W. R. Rearick with Terisio Pignatti, *The Art of Paolo Veronese, 1528–1588*, exh. cat. (Cambridge, 1988).

11. Now Turin, Galleria Sabauda; 315 by 451 cm; see above, note 8.

12. Pignatti, *Veronese*, 1:126, no. 131, 2: fig. 375. See also *Les Noces de Cana de Véronèse: Une oeuvre et sa restauration* (Paris, 1992); David Rosand, "Theatre and Structure in the Art of Paolo Veronese," *Art Bulletin* 55 (1973): 217–39, revised and reprinted in his *Painting in Cinquecento Venice: Titian, Veronese, Tintoretto* (New Haven and London, 1982); and Philipp Fehl, "Veronese's Decorum: Notes on the *Marriage at Cana*," in Moshe Barasch, Lucy Freeman Sandler, and Patricia Egan, eds., *Art, the Ape of Nature: Studies in Honor of H. W. Janson* (Englewood Cliffs, 1981), 341–65, reprinted in Fehl, *Decorum and Wit*, 261–81.

13. Now at Milan, Brera; 275 by 710 cm; Pignatti, *Veronese*, 1:132–33, no. 164, 2: fig. 431.

14. Veronese referred to this work at his Inquisitional hearing (see appendix) but did not specify its subject, except that it was a "cena." However, since this monastery was a Girolamite house like S. Sebastiano, and since it was dedicated to the Magdalene (who plays a crucial role in the Supper in the House of Simon story, anointing Christ), the presumption must be that the Paduan picture was similar in title and composition to the work at S. Sebastiano. It was probably executed around 1570. See Fogolari, "Il processo," 370.

15. Now at Paris, Louvre, on deposit at Versailles; ca. 1570–72, 454 by 874 cm; Pignatti, *Veronese*, 1:135–36, no. 176, 2: fig. 454.

16. Still in situ; completed 1572, 477 by 862 cm; Pignatti, *Veronese*, 1:135, no. 175, 2: fig. 453.

17. The present essay is part of a larger project examining all of the feast paintings of Veronese and his Venetian contemporaries; for a section already published, see my article listed in note 88 below. Irina Smirnova's brief "Le cene veronesiane: Problemi iconografici," in Gemin, ed., *Nuovi Studi*, 359–64, takes a step in this direction. Veronese did make feast paintings for sites other than refectories: a medium-sized (207 by 457 cm) *Marriage at Cana* painted ca. 1571 for the Palazzo Cuccina in Venice, now in Dresden; Pignatti, *Veronese*, 1:134, no. 170, 2: fig. 445; two images of the Supper at Emmaus for domestic display, one rather large (in the Louvre, ca. 1560, Pignatti, no. 91) and one small (Rotterdam, ca. 1574, Pignatti, no. 171), and a late *Last Supper* for the parish church of S. Sofia to which are related several works by Paolo's shop; on this final group, see below, p. 106. See also Luisa Vertova, "I chiaroscuri di casa Muselli," in Gemin, ed., *Nuovi Studi*, 172–82, fig. 137, for an unusual drawing of a sacred meal.

18. On the Tuscan tradition see Luisa Vertova, *I Cenacoli Fiorentini* (Turin, 1965);

also Creighton Gilbert, "Last Suppers and Their Refectories, " in Charles Trinkaus with Heiko A. Oberman, eds., *The Pursuit of Holiness in Late Medieval and Renaissance Religion* (Leiden, 1974), 371–407.

19. See Brian T. D'Argaville, "Titian's 'Cenacolo' for the Refectory of SS. Giovanni e Paolo Reconsidered," in *Tiziano e Venezia*, Convegno Internazionale di Studi, Venice, 1976 (Vicenza, 1980), 161–67. Until 1582, SS. Giovanni e Paolo was administratively subordinate to S. Maria delle Grazie.

20. A large but cut-down work (Escorial) and a small intact work (Brera) (D'Argaville, figs. 52–53)—this last (fig. 7) a late copy, or even a modello by Titian himself; see entry by Carlo Bertelli, in Rodolfo Pallucchini et al., *Da Tiziano a El Greco: Per la storia del Manierismo a Venezia, 1540–1590* (Milan, 1981), 115, no. 22.

21. Possibly predating but more likely postdating Titian's painting is a modest *Last Supper* by Giuseppe Salviati made for the refectory of the monastery of S. Spirito in Isola and now in the sacristy of S. Maria della Salute. See Rodolfo Pallucchini, "Per gli inizi veneziani di Giuseppe Porta," *Arte Veneta* 29 (1975): 159–65, at p. 164.

22. Bonifazio: Simonetta Simonetti, "Profilo di Bonifacio de' Pitati," *Saggi e Memorie di Storia dell'Arte* 15 (1986): 83–134, 235–77, nos. 27, 28, 35, 37, 38, 58, and by shop nos. A54, A61, A82, A162, A167, A168, A240, A241. Garofalo: *Marriage Feast at Cana*, 1531, now St. Petersburg, Hermitage. Salviati: *Marriage Feast at Cana*, early 1550s, fresco, refectory of S. Salvatore in Lauro, Rome (discussed in conjunction with Veronese by Fehl, "Veronese's Decorum"; Tracy Cooper, "Un modo per 'la riforma cattolica'? La scelta di Paolo Veronese per il refettorio di San Giorgio Maggiore," in Vittore Branca and Carlo Ossola, eds., *Crisi e rinnovamenti nell'autunno del rinascimento a Venezia* (Florence, 1991), 271–92, at p. 276; Christian Lenz in *Les Noces de Cana*, 228–29, fig. 76. Vasari: *Christ in the House of Martha* and *The Feast of Saint Gregory*, 1539–40, for S. Michele in Bosco, Bologna, and *The Marriage Feast of Esther and Ahasuerus*, 1548–49, now Arezzo, Museum; Paola Barocchi, *Vasari Pittore* (Milan, 1964), 92, 102–3, pls. IV, V, XVII. Salviati and Vasari both worked in Venice for a time, and Vasari produced an actual (as opposed to painted) feast for a fashionable Venetian club; *Le vite de' più eccelenti pittori scultori ed architettori*, vol. 7, ed. G. Milanesi (Florence, 1906), 664–66.

23. Quoted in Barocchi, *Vasari Pittore*, 102–3; Vasari-Milanesi, *Le vite*, 7:687–88.

24. Now in the sacristy of S. Maria della Salute; 435 by 545 cm; Rodolfo Pallucchini and Paola Rossi, *Tintoretto: Le opere sacre e profane*, 2 vols. (Milan, 1982), 1:180–81, cat. no. 230, 2: pl. 300.

25. The 1547 work was for S. Marcuola; ibid., 1:155–56, cat. no. 127, 2: pls. 162–66; for some smaller and perhaps earlier feasts, see cat. nos. 42, 46, 49, 99, and 113. The major works which follow the S. Marcuola picture were made for the churches of S. Simeon Grande (1562–63), S. Trovaso (1566), S. Polo (ca. 1570), S. Rocco (1579–81), S. Margherita (1580), and S. Giorgio Maggiore (1592–94); Pallucchini and Rossi, *Tintoretto*, cat. nos. 232, 259, 305, 351, 410, 467. The biggest canvas was the one for San Rocco, 538 by 487 cm; the others were about 2 to 3.5 by 5 meters. Discussions of Tintoretto's im-

pact on the conception of Veronese's feasts can be found in Pignatti, *Paolo Veronese* (1986), 26; and Smirnova, "Le cene veronesiane," 359.

26. On the 400 ducat contribution to the reconstruction, see Pignatti, *Paolo Veronese*, 6 (from Archivio di Stato di Venezia, hereafter ASV, Senato Terra, reg. 49, carta 152).

27. Veronese, as far as we know, had not yet worked directly for the Dominicans. He did carry out his *Allegory of the Battle of Lepanto* for a lay donor who placed it in the Dominican church of S. Pietro Martire in Murano; this work was executed after October 1571, but not necessarily before the spring of 1573; see Pignatti, *Veronese* (1976), 1:133. After 1573, Veronese did paint two works for Dominican churches: an *Adoration of the Magi* for S. Corona in Vicenza (lay donor); ibid., 1:144–45, no. 231, 2: pls. 545–46; a *Dead Christ with Mary and Angel* for SS. Giovanni e Paolo, early 1580s, now in the Hermitage; ibid., 1:167.

28. The mysterious Fra Andrea appears in the 1648 Ridolfi account (314): "Fra Andrea de' Buoni, wishing to see Painting renewed [or, the painting replaced], offered to Paolo for this purpose a certain sum of money, which he had put aside from charity and confessions, which price one would not risk asking a gentleman to accept these days for such a big canvas. But since the poor monk could not spend more, Paolo, obliged by his prayers, finally wished to satisfy him, taking on such a big job, urged on more by his [i.e., Paolo's] desire for glory than by business sense." Ridolfi also indicated that the elderly man seated at the table—one of the fifteen seated figures, with Christ, the twelve apostles, and the host—was a portrait of Fra Andrea. This may well be so, though it is puzzling that this character is dressed in brown rather than the black and white of the Dominican habit. His age would correspond to that of Fra Andrea, who is also mentioned in the "Emortuale fratrum SS. Jo e Pauli ab anno 1500 usque 1739" compiled by Urbano Urbani (Venice, Museo Correr, cod. Cicogna 822, first section, p. 45, last section f. 11r): this document also says that de' Buoni paid for the work, and says that he died in 1588 at the age of ninety-two, which would have made him seventy-seven in 1573. The "Emortuale" further indicates that Fra Andrea had commissioned a monstrance for use on Holy Thursday which was used at SS. Giovanni e Paolo. See Fogolari, "Il processo," 356–57, 363. Andrea de' Buoni's name cannot be found in other documents of the period, and his last name is an unfamiliar one in Venice, unless it is a version of Bon, a common nonpatrician surname; Pignatti, *Paolo Veronese* (1986), 6.

29. On the work's physical history and conservation, see Nepi Scirè, *Il restauro*.

30. Despite much obvious evidence to the contrary, several modern scholars have claimed that the SS. Giovanni e Paolo picture was not commissioned as a Last Supper. Anthony Blunt (*Artistic Theory in Italy, 1450–1600*, Oxford, 1940, 116) asserted it had always been a *Feast in the House of Levi*, but it does not come close to illustrating this rarely depicted story; see below. Elizabeth G. Holt (*A Documentary History of Art*, Garden City, 1958, 2:66) suggests the commissioned subject was the Supper in the House of Simon, and Richard Cocke argues vigorously in defense of this idea; see

both his *Veronese's Drawings* (Ithaca, 1984), 166, and his "Venice, Decorum and Veronese," in Gemin, ed., *Nuovi Studi*, 241–55, at p. 251. For more on this matter, see Fehl, "Veronese and the Inquisition," 342, note 16. There are two sources for the confusion about Veronese's initial subject for this canvas. First, all later critics (until 1867) knew the work as the *Feast in the House of Levi*—the result of Veronese's retitling later in 1573 (see below). Second, even when the transcript of the Inquisition's hearing was discovered, there was Paolo's evidently confused statement: he indicated that his subject was the Last Supper which Christ took with his apostles, in the house of Simon. Cecil Gould, in "Veronese's Greatest Feast: The Inter-Action of Iconographic and Aesthetic Factors," *Arte Veneta* 43 (1989–90): 85–88, speculates that Veronese, having been warned of the Inquisition's interest before his hearing, changed his *Last Supper* to *Supper in the House of Simon*, and finally after the hearing to *Feast in the House of Levi*; but the evidence for this complicated trajectory is slight and unpersuasive. As Fehl suggested, Veronese probably believed that the Last Supper did take place in Simon's house, but this did not mean that he could not distinguish the Last Supper from the Supper in the House of Simon at which the Magdalene appeared. In fact, the Bible does not indicate who owned the house in whose upper room the Last Supper was held (see Mark 14:12–16), and Christian writers have guessed that it might have been the dwelling of John the Evangelist, Joseph of Arimathea, or Simon (see Fehl, "Veronese and the Inquisition," 352, note 4, and 354, note 41). At the beginning of his interrogation Veronese acknowledged that the prior of SS. Giovanni e Paolo had recently told him that the Inquisition had advised him to add a figure of the Magdalene—which would have gone some way toward making the picture a Supper in the House of Simon—but that he had refused. It is in fact very hard to see how Veronese could easily have added a Magdalene anointing Christ, since Jesus is placed behind the table in an inaccessible spot with most of his body obstructed. A major repainting of this section of the canvas would have been necessary, and this may be why Veronese refused to take the Inquisition's first hint. For another detailed affirmation of why Veronese's intended subject was the Last Supper, see Gilbert, "Last Suppers," 397–99.

31. According to legend, Pope Gregory the Great had reenacted the Last Supper as a banquet for twelve of the poor, at which a thirteenth guest—Christ—mysteriously appeared; see Fehl, "Veronese and the Inquisition," 327.

32. See above, note 30.

33. Apart from Veronese himself, the names of those present at the artist's hearing are not listed in the transcript and must be inferred from other documents from the same file; see Fogolari, "Il processo," 365–66. My data about the Venetian Inquisition is drawn from Paul Grendler, "The *Tre Savi sopra Eresia* 1547–1605: A Prosopographical Study," *Studi Veneziani*, n.s., 3 (1979): 283–340, and also Fehl and Perry, "Painting and the Inquisition at Venice."

34. Schellini served as Inquisitor from July 1569 until November 1574; Fogolari, "Il processo," 365–66. Gemin, "Riflessioni iconografiche," 368–69, speculates about

Schellini's theological orientation, but presents no new hard information about the man.

35. Dei was evidently a Florentine, from his surname. Trevisan participated in the Council of Trent; Fehl, "Veronese and the Inquisition," 353, note 29.

36. Venier received votes in the ducal elections of 1578 and 1585; Zorzi was known to be well disposed toward ecclesiastical powers; Grendler, "The *Tre Savi sopra Eresia*," 294, 319, 321–22, note 56.

37. Foscarini, 1507–83; for a detailed vita see ibid., 296, 318–19, note 52.

38. *Capitoli, ed ordini per il buon governo delle pie case de' Catecumeni di Venezia* (Venice, 1802), 5.

39. Foscarini is named as a *capo* (chief) of the Council of Ten on July 4 and September 26; ASV, Capi Cons. X Parti Secrete Rome, filza 1, 1573–1582. Thus he was probably serving in this capacity when Veronese appeared before him on July 18. Grendler indicates that Foscarini served two further terms as a Savio sopra Eresia (1576–78, and 1580–81), other terms on the Council of Ten (one in 1569), and as a ducal counselor, another important post.

40. See Fehl and Perry, "Painting and the Inquisition at Venice"; but see Fehl, "Veronese and the Inquisition," 341, note 3, who points out that it was nevertheless a serious matter to be interviewed by the Venetian Inquisition, which often imposed prison terms and exile.

41. Fehl, "Veronese and the Inquisition," 349.

42. Veronese might have been tempted to suggest that his German soldiers were echoes of the drunken German soldiers billeted at SS. Giovanni e Paolo in 1571 who were said to have caused the fire that destroyed the refectory and Titian's painting (see above), but he made no such comment. See Muraro, "La Cena di Paolo Veronese," 17; also Nepi Scirè, "Il restauro," 13, note 3. Nepi Scirè notes that the document cited by Fogolari ("Il processo," 356) asserting that these soldiers were German and in Venice because of Venice's war with the Turks can no longer be found in the ASV, but D'Argaville, "Titian's 'Cenacolo,'" 164, note 8, refers to a microfilm copy at the Cini Foundation.

43. See above (note 5); and see also the interesting observations in Fehl, "Veronese and the Inquisition," 354, note 37, and in Gemin, "Riflessioni iconografiche," 369, who points out that Schellini—in contrast to the Church's standard position in these years—actually defends Michelangelo.

44. On Veronese and at least one Protestant patron, see Michelangelo Muraro, "Un celebre ritratto: Sir Philip Sidney a Venezia nel 1574 sceglie Veronese per farsi ritrarre," in Gemin, ed., *Nuovi Studi*, 391–96.

45. For the decrees of the Council of Trent, see Holt, *Documentary History of Art*, 62–65. On Molanus see David Freedberg, "Johannes Molanus on Provocative Paintings," *Journal of the Warburg and Courtauld Institutes* 34 (1971): 229–45. Both the Council and Molanus were particularly preoccupied with lasciviousness in images, but the sensuousness of a lavish banquet could be seen in similar terms in this period.

In 1608, Saint Francis de Sales wrote: "There is some resemblance between shameful voluptuousness and that of eating, because both are concerned with the flesh, such that the former, because of its brutal vehemence, is simply called carnal. I will thus explain that which I cannot say of the one sort by what I can say of the other." *Introduction à la vie dévote*, in *Oeuvres*, ed. A. Ravier (Paris, 1969), pt. 2, chap. 39, "De l'honnêteté du lit nuptial," 240.

46. ASV, Senato Decreti Roma Ordinaria, r. 2, 1566–1570, f. 87r.

47. Aldo Stella, ed., *Nunziature di Venezia*, 9 (Rome, 1972), 413, no. 301, and 426–28, no. 309; see also xiii. Complaints about unspecified misbehaving mendicant monks were made on August 4 and September 9, 1571; Aldo Stella, ed., *Nunziature di Venezia*, 10 (Rome, 1977), 68, 95, nos. 32, 52. See also the brief reference to the process of reform in the nuncio's letter of February 14, 1571, quoted in D'Argaville, "Titian's 'Cenacolo,'" 164.

48. The chronicle is the "Emortuale" cited above, note 28. This material was first brought forward by Fogolari, "Il processo," 377–78, note 1; Gemin, "Riflessioni iconografiche," 369, gives it greater importance. Neither author alludes to the Rome-Venice correspondence about the monastery just discussed.

49. Perhaps the "deaths" recorded here are really departures from the faith rather than physical demise.

50. ASV, Capi Cons. dei X, Dispacci degli Ambasciatori, Roma, busta 25, 1566–1573, f. 205 (from Nicolo da Ponte and Paolo Tiepolo): "Il General delli padri di S:Domenico Bressano, et molto servitor di quel ser.mo Dominio, al quale io Paulo parlai per l'asolutione del padre Inquisitor di Venetia, et per la restitutione del Vicario delli padri di S. Giovanne Paulo superando tutte le difficoltà, ch'egli havea finalmente hà concessa l'una et l'altra cosa molto favorabilmente mandandi per questo corriero, l'una, et l'altra spedittione gu." Unfortunately, I have not been able to find further documents that might clarify the suggestive but murky implications of this letter. It should be noted that Giacomo Foscarini (the Savio sopra Eresia) was on the Council of Ten at this point.

51. I have not been able to identify the leading administrators of SS. Giovanni e Paolo during these years; Brian Pullan has identified the prior as Adriano Alviani, but does not indicate his source; David Chambers and Brian Pullan with Jennifer Fletcher, eds., *Venice, a Documentary History, 1450–1630* (Oxford, 1992), 233, note 29.

52. Mark 14:17–25.

53. See Erwin Panofsky, *Albrecht Dürer*, 2 vols. (Princeton, 1948), 1:222–23, 2: figs. 277–78.

54. In his *Commentary on Psalm CXI*, cited in James Snyder, *Northern Renaissance Art* (Englewood Cliffs, 1985), 346.

55. From his *Christiani Matrimonii Institutio*, in *Opera*, vol. 5, ed. Jean Leclerc (Leiden, 1703–6), cols. 696F–697A. This passage is discussed by Erwin Panofsky, "Erasmus and the Visual Arts," *Journal of the Warburg and Courtauld Institutes* 32 (1969): 200–227, at 211–12, notes 30, 31; and by Keith Moxey, "Erasmus and the Ico-

nography of Pieter Aertsen's *Christ in the House of Mary and Martha* in the Boymans–Van Beuningen Museum," *Journal of the Warburg and Courtauld Institutes* 34 (1971): 335–36. Erasmus did, however, recommend that an ideal secular dining room be decorated with images of the Last Supper as well as other sacred and mythological feasts; *The Colloquies of Erasmus*, trans. Craig R. Thompson (Chicago, 1965), 76–77, "The Godly Feast" (1522).

56. In fact, the Counter Reformation writer on art Johannes Molanus approvingly quoted Erasmus's very words in chapter 42 of his 1570 treatise *De Picturis et Imaginibus Sacris*; Freedberg, "Johannes Molanus," 242–43. In the same breath Molanus also quoted another passage from Erasmus (*De Amabili Ecclesiae Concordia*, in *Opera*, vol. 5 [Antwerp?, 1733], col. 501D): "To twist sacred literature into unsuitable and profane jokes is a kind of blasphemy; for the same reason those who on their own initiative add details which are ridiculous and unworthy of the saints when they paint subjects from the scriptural canon deserve punishment." This should be understood as the basis of Inquisitor Schellini's attitude toward Veronese; and the appropriation of Erasmus's statement by Molanus demonstrates that in this matter two otherwise very different approaches to Catholic reform were in full agreement. This is a point not grasped by Gemin, "Riflessioni iconografiche," 368–69.

57. Six to seven hundred armed men attended the event, which lasted from January 11 to 13; note that the Venetian Inquisitors objected to the *armed* Germans in Veronese's picture. See Jean Guéraud, *La chronique lyonnaise de Jean Guéraud, 1536–1562*, ed. Jean Tricou (Lyon, 1929), 147, no. 284. See also Natalie Zemon Davis, "The Rites of Violence: Religious Riot in Sixteenth-Century France," *Past and Present* 59 (1973): 51–91.

58. Geneva, 1560 (republished in Geneva in 1857), esp. satire 5 (pp. 56–77). The tract was written by learned Protestant apologists, probably including Theodore de Beze; Y. Giraud, "Le Comique engagé des *Satyres chrestiennes de la cuisine papale*," *Studi di letteratura francese* 177 (1983): 52–72; Michel Jeanneret, *A Feast of Words: Banquets and Table Talk in the Renaissance* (Chicago, 1991), 206. This text has not previously been related to Veronese's interrogation.

59. Since Maundy Thursday was the day of the first communion, its anniversary became the most popular day for popes to excommunicate. It is clear that portions of the bull existed in 1363 (perhaps earlier), but the first full text is from 1511, during the reign of the aggressive Pope Julius II. See the entries on "Bulla in Coena Domini" in *New Catholic Encyclopedia* and *Dictionnaire de Droit Canonique* (1937).

60. Mario Bendiscioli, "La Bolla 'In Coena Domini' e la sua pubblicazione a Milano nel 1568," *Archivio Storico Lombardo* 54 (1927): 381–99; Ludwig Pastor, *The History of the Popes*, 18, ed. Ralph F. Kerr (London, 1952), 35–60; Stella, *Nunziature*, 9:xii–xiii.

61. For the text of the 1569 bull, see F. Gaude, ed., *Bullarium Diplomatum et Privilegiorum Sanctorum Pontificum*, 7 (Naples, 1882), 744–46, no. CXXVII, called "Si de protengendis caeteris." The bull was drafted six days before Holy Thursday, which fell

on April 7 that year. On April 6 the papal nuncio to Venice, Facchinetti, first mentioned the new bull (Stella, *Nunziature*, 9:39–40, no. 4), and on April 16 Rome ordered Venice to publish it (ASV, Senato Secreta Deliberazioni Roma, filza 3, 1567–1569). On April 22 the Venetian Senate decided, however, to ban it by a vote of 163 to 4, and notified their Roman ambassador (ASV, Senato Secreta Deliberazioni Roma, filza 3, 1567–1569, and Senato Decreti Roma Ordinaria, r. 2, 1566–1570, fs. 78r–79r).

62. April 23: Nuncio points out that the patriarch of Venice had published the 1568 version of the bull (Stella, *Nunziature*, 9:49, no. 11). April 30: Patriarch writes to Rome of ban (Stella, 9:54, no. 16). May 4: Nuncio asserts that cause of ban is the Venetian fear of losing tax revenues (Stella, 9:55–56, no. 18). May 5: Venice defends the ban as a defense of its liberty, and believes the pope is trying to get around the ban (ASV, Senato Secreta Deliberazioni Roma, filza 3, 1567–1569, and Senato Decreti Roma Ordinaria, r. 2, 1566–1570, fs. 80r–80v). May 14: Senate writes to monasteries to enforce ban (Bartolomeo Cecchetti, *La repubblica di Venezia e la corte di Roma nei rapporti della religione*, 2 vols., Venice, 1874, 1:448, and 445–51 on the controversy as a whole). May 26–28: The Senate writes to the nuncio, agreeing to carry out all "spiritual" portions of the bull, affirming its loyalty to the pope, but defending its right to refuse limits on its temporal power; the nuncio informs Rome that he believes the Venetians are conspiring with the Spanish in this matter (ASV, Senato Secreta Deliberazioni Roma, filza 3, 1567–1569, and Senato Decreti Roma Ordinaria, r. 2, 1566–1570, fs. 82v–83v; Stella, 9:72–73, no. 31). For further communications on June 17, July 1, September 19, November 26, and December 10, see Stella, 9:169, no. 108, and ASV, Senato Secreta Deliberazioni Roma, filza 3, 1567–1569, Senato Decreti Roma Ordinaria, r. 2, 1566–1570, fs. 85r, 87r, 87v, 89r, and Senato Dispacci Ambasciatori 1569, filza 4, nos. 38–39. See also Christopher Cairns, *Domenico Bollani, Bishop of Brescia: Devotion to Church and State in the Republic of Venice in the Sixteenth Century*, Bibliotheca Humanistica & Reformatorica, 15 (Nieuwkoop, 1976), 209–13, who notes that this conflict also involved the Venetian Inquisition.

63. See article 7 in Gaude, *Bullarium*, 744–46; and also the analysis in Pastor, *History of the Popes* (appendices 2–3), 463–66, esp. 464–65.

64. Stella, *Nunziature*, 9:200–201, no. 131, February 4. On April 18, 1571, the nuncio was instructed to allow the absolution of some Venetians who had failed to observe the bull; Stella, 9:487, no. 351.

65. Ibid., 9:226, no. 156, March 5.

66. Benjamin Ravid, "The Socioeconomic Background of the Expulsion and Readmission of the Venetian Jews, 1571–1573," in F. Malino and P. Cohen Albert, eds., *Essays in Modern Jewish History: A Tribute to Ben Halpern* (Rutherford, N.J., 1982), 27–55, at 41–43.

67. Mario Brunetti, "La crisi finale della Sacra Lega (1573)," in *Miscellanea in onore di Roberto Cessi*, 2 vols. (Rome, 1958), 2:145–55.

68. Stella, *Nunziature*, 10:405–10, no. 229.

69. This version of the bull is not published in the usual compilations, but the section on the League is alluded to by Paolo Tiepolo, the Venetian ambassador to Rome, in a letter to the Senate of March 23: "Giovedi fo' segondo l'ordinario publicata la bolla in cena Domini, con molte aggiunte, a' far buona parte delle quali vien detto, che ha' dato occasione il Cardinal Granvella co'l severo modo da lui tenuto nelle attioni sue, ma anco alcune toccano la lega, si come mi è stato referito, perciòche io stando alquanto lontano non la ho' udita, se potrò questa sera haverla stampata la mandarò, se non, questa futura settimana al tutto si manderà." ASV, Senato Dispacci Ambasciatori Roma, filza 9, f. 37r. I have never been able to find a copy of any of the controversial "In Coena Domini" bulls in the Venetian archives; it is as if every copy was so threatening that it could not be allowed to survive. The League-related contents of the 1573 bull are discussed in William J. Bouwsma, *Venice and the Defense of Republican Liberty* (Berkeley and Los Angeles, 1968), 329; Ludwig Pastor, *Storia dei Papi*, 9 (Rome, 1925), 238; Luciano Serrano, *La liga de Lepanto entre España, Venecia y la Santa Sede (1570–1573)*, 2 vols. (Madrid, 1918–20), 2:249; also Cairns, *Domenico Bollani*, 213.

70. Pastor, *Storia dei Papi*, 239.

71. ASV, Senato Decreti Roma Ordinaria, reg. 4, 1573–1580, fs. 7v–9v, also f. 12r; ASV, Senato Deliberazioni Secreta Roma, filza 6, 1573; Pastor, *Storia dei Papi*, 239.

72. ASV, Senato Dispacci Ambasciatori Roma, filza 9, f. 124r.

73. For Venetian apologies, see ASV, Senato Deliberazioni Secreta Roma, filza 6, 1573, documents dated April 23 and May 15, Senato Decreti Roma Ordinaria, reg. 4, 1573–1580, fs. 13v–17r. For papal grumbling, see Serrano, *La liga de Lepanto*, 2:413–26, documents, XXIV–XXX. For evidence that all commercial enterprises with the Ottomans were in theory banned by the bull, see Stella, *Nunziature*, 10:409, no. 229 (February 2, 1573).

74. The first crack in the expulsion order appeared on June 29. See Ravid, "Venetian Jews," 47.

75. Ibid., 49–50.

76. It was a commonplace that Venice's political and economic interests required a delicate balance in its relations with the papacy and the Ottomans. One might simply describe Veronese's problem with the Inquisition as a breach of decorum potentially jeopardizing that balance. Gilio, the Counter Reformation critic of the arts, exemplifies the concept of decorum by saying "it would not be right to dress the pope in Turkish garments, nor to dress the Turk in the pope's robes"; Giovanni Andrea Gilio, *Due dialogi* (Camerino, 1564), reprinted in Paola Barocchi, ed., *Scritti d'arte del cinquecento*, 2 vols. (Milan and Naples, 1971), 1:303–25, at 308.

77. On visual images of papal greed characterized as gluttony, see the *Lazarus and Dives* woodcut of 1556 by Hans Lautensack discussed in Fehl, "Veronese and the Inquisition," 353–54, note 35, fig. 20. See also *Satyres chrestiennes*, above (note 58).

78. For a similar phenomenon, see Cairns, *Domenico Bollani*, 202–4: in 1565 the

powerful and humorless ecclesiastic Saint Charles Borromeo was upset by unorthodox religious views expressed by the mayor of Brescia, a Venetian appointee. The dispute quickly became politicized. The Venetians settled it by apologizing to Borromeo, protecting the mayor from arrest or prosecution, and telling him firmly to shut up. Schellini, a Brescian, probably witnessed this dispute.

79. Fehl, "Veronese and the Inquisition," 354, note 41.

80. Pignatti (*Paolo Veronese* [1986], 15), for example, says that "the pure painter had defeated censorship."

81. Before the 1980–83 cleaning, some writers had claimed to be able to see clear marks of figurative changes (Schaffran, "Der Inquisitionsprozess," 190—a painted-out Magdalene—and Brian D'Argaville, in a talk at the College Art Association annual meeting in 1976). The cleaning revealed no figurative changes had been made after completion, but did reveal one interesting pentimento which must have been made in the middle of the work's initial execution: a page, serving the seated owner of the house, was eliminated; Nepi Sciré, *Il restauro*, 16; Pignatti, *Paolo Veronese* (1986), fig. 7. In 1771 Zanetti (*Della pittura veneziana*, 174) had in fact mentioned this pentimento, indicating that it had been made for purely aesthetic reasons. As the page's removal gives a clearer view of the controversial motif of Peter's plate with the lamb, the figure must have been erased before the hearing. For another view, see Gould, "Veronese's Greatest Feast."

82. Luke 5:29–32; cf. Matthew 9:10–13; Mark 2:15–17.

83. Fehl, "Veronese and the Inquisition," 342, note 13. The story appears in medieval manuscripts that provide a small illumination for virtually every event in the New Testament, and these miniatures are never elaborate; see for example Bibliothèque Nationale, Paris, ms. gr. 74, fs. 17r, 67v, 116v. A fresco in the church of Spas-Mirojski in Pskov, Russia, of 1156, and a catacomb fresco in the Hypogeum of the Aurelii, Rome, ca. 200—neither one unquestionably of this subject—are the only large-scale images known.

84. Both Veronese and Schellini use this abusive term in the plural, which means it must apply to more than the dwarf with the parrot. In the sixteenth century, Italians referred to black pages and other "exotic" non-European peoples in this way.

85. Veronese's retitling has sometimes been described as a slap in the face of the Inquisition, but only because by doing so he seemed to evade the instruction to correct the picture; Pignatti, *Paolo Veronese* (1986), 15. Marion Leathers Kuntz, in her talk "The Inquisitor as *Medicus*: Religion and Politics in Renaissance Venice," at the Renaissance Society of America 1995 annual meeting, revealed that a Venetian Inquisitor of the early 1560s actually referred to Luke chapter 5 as a model for the duties of an Inquisitor, who must heal the sick and not the healthy. In this light, Veronese's use of Luke chapter 5 seems an even more pointed reproach to the particular Inquisitor who interrogated him.

86. The dispute about the bull was fully settled only in 1575, but it drops out of the

diplomatic correspondence by the end of 1573. See Cairns, *Domenico Bollani*, 213. Prosecutions by the Venetian Inquisition, which had shot up from about 30 a year to about 50 a year in 1572 and 1573, dropped off to 35 in 1574 and 24 in 1575; ASV, Sant'Ufficio, Savi all'Eresia, index 303.

87. For S. Teonisto, Treviso; now Rome, Palazzo di Montecitorio; 379 by 970 cm, 1580; Pignatti, *Veronese*, 1:205, no. A276, 2: pl. 952.

88. 230 by 523 cm, ca. 1585, now Milan, Brera. See Paul Kaplan, "Veronese's Last *Last Supper*," *Arte Veneta* 41 (1987): 51–62.

89. Venice, Accademia (since 1910 on deposit in the Municipio of Verona). Little attention has been paid to this work in the last few centuries, and consequently many errors have crept into the very brief published accounts of it. Pignatti (*Veronese*, 1:218, no. A365) gives what appear to be correct dimensions—550 by 1010 cm—but mistakenly calls it a *Supper in the House of Simon*. (There is no Magdalene.) He attributed it to Veronese's brother Benedetto. Moschini Marconi (98–99, no. 159, inv. no. 339, cat. no. 1017) gets the title right but the dimensions wrong (she gives 550 by 1,280, the dimensions of the SS. Giovanni e Paolo picture before its recent repair); she also cites Ruskin's proposal to take it off the wall and burn it. Bernard Berenson (*Italian Pictures of the Renaissance: Venetian School*, 2 vols. [London, 1957], 1:138) titled it *Christ in the House of the Pharisee*. It has been said that Veronese did not care about which subject he was painting, but in reality it is sometimes the art historians who seem not to care about this. G. Martinioni (*Venetia città nobilissima et singolare*, Venice, 1663, 252) clearly describes it: "These fathers [at S. Giacomo] have in their refectory the story told by the evangelist Saint Luke in chapter five, where is depicted the Savior at the table with Levi the banker, and many scribes, and Pharisees, of whom it appears, that some are scandalized, and ask the disciples: why does their master eat with sinners and publicans?" Some of the details which caused problems for Veronese in 1573 (bloody nose, Germans, dwarf, fork, apostles preoccupied with food) are notably absent in this work. Giovanna Nepi Scirè ("Paolo Veronese: Restauri recenti alle Gallerie dell'Accademia," in Gemin, ed., *Nuovi Studi*, 399) gets the title right and names Benedetto as the painter. On small copies of the SS. Giovanni e Paolo canvas, see Nepi Scirè, "Paolo Veronese" (398) and *Il restauro* (22, fig. 8).

90. Sarpi was born in 1552, and entered the Servite order in 1566. He became regent at S. Maria dei Servi (the major monastery of the order in Venice, to which S. Giacomo was attached) in 1578, and prior of the entire Venetian province of the order in 1579. In 1585 he became second in command of the entire order in Rome. In 1594 he was accused of unorthodox theological opinions and of holding theological conversations with Venetian Jews, but he was finally absolved by the Venetian Inquisition. See David Wooton, *Paolo Sarpi between Renaissance and Enlightenment* (Cambridge, 1983), 8–10, and Paolo Sarpi, *Opere*, ed. G. and L. Cozzi (Milan and Naples, 1969), 3–25. In Sarpi's own monastery of S. Maria dei Servi there was, of course, a great *Supper in the House of Simon* by Veronese (fig. 5), installed in the early 1570s when Sarpi was

already in residence there. Sarpi was also in a position to know something of the acts of the Venetian Inquisition, having written a history of it (*Discorso della origine, forma, leggi, ed uso dell'uffizio della inquisizione nella città, e dominio di Venezia*, 1613, in Sarpi's *Scritti giurisdizionalistici*, ed. G. Gambarin, Bari, 1958, 119–212), and he may have been one of the few in Venice who were aware of Veronese's brush with that institution.

91. Bouwsma, *Venice and the Defense of Republican Liberty*, 350.

Goya and the Censors

JANIS A. TOMLINSON

THE TITLE OF THIS ESSAY may lead some to expect a discussion of Francisco Goya's best known work, *Los Caprichos*, a series of eighty aquatint etchings. Advertised for sale in 1799, these prints satirize contemporary social customs and also explore a fantasy world of witches, goblins, and other imaginary creatures (fig. 1). Although *Los Caprichos* is usually cited as an example of Goya's daring under a repressive regime, the issue of censorship appears to have been overstated, for the evidence is fairly tenuous. Goya's decision to offer the prints for sale in a perfume shop—rather than through a bookshop or print dealer—has been interpreted as a mode of subterfuge. Further testimony of Goya's strategy of evasion is seen in the seemingly erratic ordering of the prints in the series (though that might be expected, given the tradition of "caprice" in art) as caution led him to interrupt his sequence of thoughts and themes.[1]

It has been argued that the "publication of a set of prints that attacked the vices of the clergy and the highest nobility constituted a risk for Goya, one that could be justified only if the cultivated, enlightened audience for whom the prints were intended were able to understand what he said covertly in them."[2] But one might ask whether Goya's anticipation of an "enlightened" audience would in fact have offset such a risk. It is also unlikely that the artist would have advertised his prints in the *Diario de Madrid* if he had been afraid of censure by the Holy Office. Finally, if Goya's decision to give the etched plates for the series to the Royal Calcography in 1803 was motivated by Inquisitional pressure, it is curious that the artist received in exchange a pension for his son, Francisco Xavier.

The shortcomings of such explanations become apparent when they are

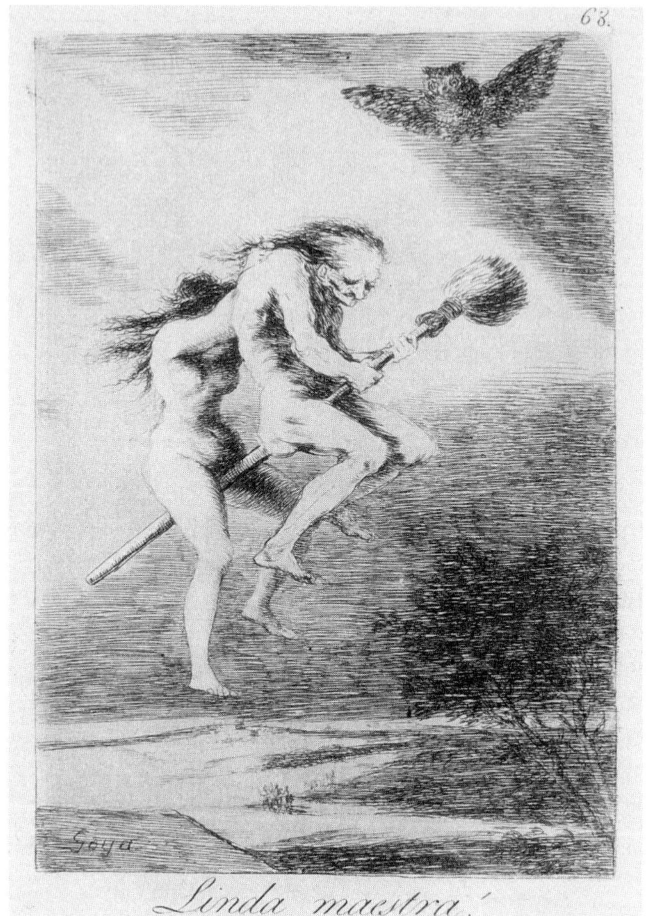

FIG. 1. Francisco Goya, *Linda Maestra* from *Los Caprichos*, plate 68, 1797.
Aquatint etching, 21.3×15 cm ($8\frac{3}{8} \times 5\frac{7}{8}$ in.).
Arthur Ross Foundation, New York. Photo: Pollitzer, Strong and Mayer.

examined in light of approaches literary historians have tended to use in considering the role of censorship. As Hans Gumbrecht has pointed out, these might be formulated as a series of rules. One of them is: "Whenever *variants* are stated among the different versions of one identical 'work' one is bound to see them as 'objectivations' of the author's effort to anticipate interventions of censorship."[3] Thus changes made by Goya from preliminary drawings to the final etchings lend themselves as evidence of efforts to tone down meaning.[4] Another pertinent literary rule suggests: "Whenever you *simply don't understand what a text means*, you can claim that censorship forced the author to remain unclear—and you then are free to present the meaning you personally wish to impute to a text as the now-possible concretization of what the author really wanted to say." And in order to explain Goya's continued success as court painter until his death in 1828, we might call up another of these rules: "Whenever you are finally confronted with the *problem that an author was never repressed*—or with the problem that the author was successful despite the undeniable existence of censorship, you may attribute such a case to the stupidity of the censors or to the author's highly intelligent textual strategies."[5]

One immediately thinks of how easy it has been to accept the stupidity of Goya's would-be oppressors: we need only recall the unflattering comments made about the members of royalty pictured in *The Family of Carlos IV*. Fred Licht, for example, sees the portrait as a "drastic description of human bankruptcy" and asks how such "fiercely intransigent realism was acceptable to its sitters."[6] That interpretations of Goya's *Los Caprichos* fit so neatly into this system of rules, or assumptions, does not of itself prove these readings to be invalid. Yet such correspondences might give us pause before accepting them at face value, and lead us to reconsider the documentary evidence.

In doing so, we discover that there is no documentary support for the assumption that Goya was persecuted by the Inquisition at the time of *Los Caprichos*' publication. The artist was comfortably situated at court, having attained the position of painter to the king in 1786, court painter in 1789, and first court painter in 1799 (about eight months *after* publishing the etchings). He donated the copper plates for *Los Caprichos* to the Royal Calcography in 1803 under no apparent pressure, but rather in exchange for a pension for his son. The plates were not destroyed—as they probably would have been if deemed subversive—and are today exhibited in the same establishment.

Admittedly, Goya was later challenged by the Inquisition in 1815 for having painted the *Naked Maja* (*Maja desnuda*) and the *Clothed Maja* (*Maja vestida*). But even here, theories of an Inquisitional vendetta against the artist must be rejected. As we shall see, the Inquisitional investigation has focused on the painting of the *Naked Maja*, discovered at the close of the Napoleonic Wars, and only in the course of the inquiry was it revealed that its artist was the court painter, Francisco Goya. The absence of any testimony by the artist in the documents pertaining to this case suggests that he was able to avoid an appearance before the tribunal.

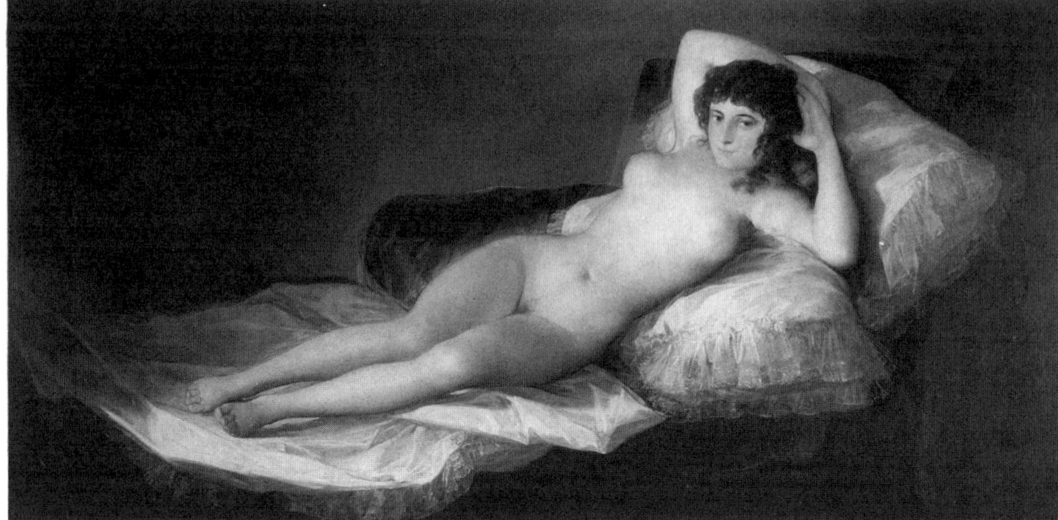

FIG. 2. Francisco Goya, *Naked Maja*, 1795–97(?).
Oil on canvas, 97×190 cm (38⅖×74⅘ in.). Museo del Prado, Madrid. Photo: Museum.

The sole document that can be cited in support of Goya's run-in with the Inquisition over *Los Caprichos* is his own letter of December 20, 1825, written in Bordeaux, to the Paris-based publisher Joaquin Ferrer.[7] We surmise from this letter that Ferrer was reluctant to publish a lithograph of a bullfight subject that Goya had sent him, and had inquired about the possibility of republishing *Los Caprichos*, the work for which Goya was best known in Paris. Goya responded:

> Lo que me dice Usted de los caprichos no puede ser, por que las láminas las cedi al Rey más ha de 20 años como las demás cosas que he grabado que están en la calcografia de Su Magestad, y con todo eso me acusaron a la Santa ni yo las copiaría por que tengo mejores occurrencias en el día. . . .
>
> (That which you say of *Los Caprichos* cannot be done, because I gave the plates to the King more than twenty years ago, as I did with the other things I engraved that are in the Calcography of His Majesty, and they nevertheless accused me before the Inquisition, nor would I copy them because I have better projects now in mind. . . .)

Goya's own words show that his confrontation with the Inquisition postdated his donation of the plates for *Los Caprichos* to the Calcography. The In-

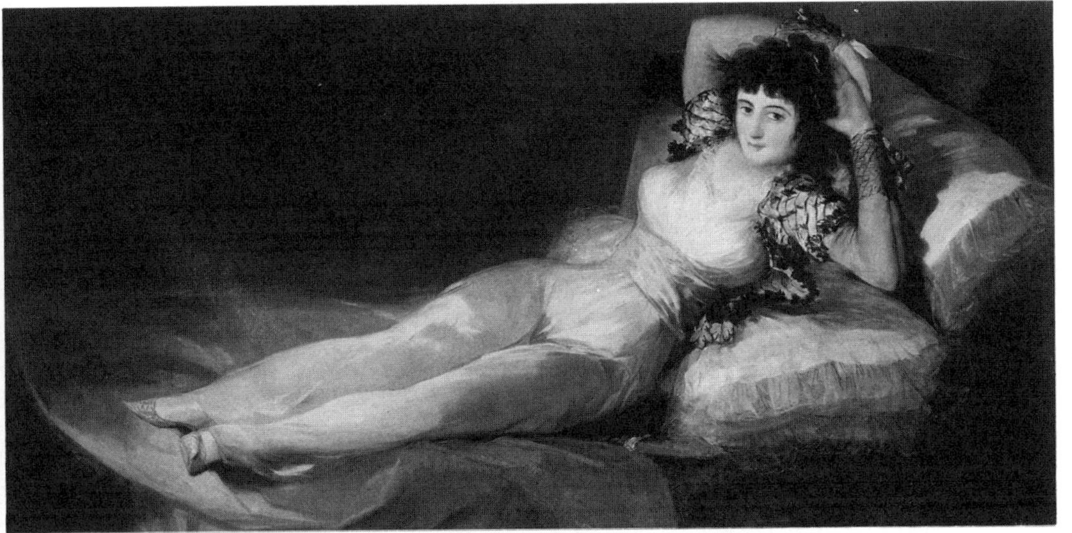

FIG. 3. Francisco Goya, *Clothed Maja*, 1803–5 (?).
Oil on canvas, 95×180 cm (37⅖×74⅞ in.). Museo del Prado, Madrid. Photo: Museum.

quisition did not target Goya; he was denounced by an anonymous "they," who may have used his engravings—as prosecutors might today—as part of a case being built against him.

When, then, did Goya appear before the Inquisition? The absence of any documented confrontation involving *Los Caprichos* suggests that it was not until 1815, after Goya had been identified as the painter of the *Naked Maja* and the *Clothed Maja* (figs. 2, 3), that he was asked to appear before the Holy Inquisition (or, in brief, the Santa). It is this confrontation that I would like to consider here. But before turning to that case, a brief discussion of Inquisitorial censorship of images in late eighteenth- and early nineteenth-century Spain is in order.

By attributing to the Inquisition such a major role in determining the course of Goya's career, we are also adhering to a romanticized notion of Spain as a land of intolerance and oppression. In fact, the history of the Inquisition is not so monolithic. In Spain, its authority was delegated to regional councils, and the degree and nature of its intervention varied widely. In censoring books a general list would probably be drawn up and followed, although special licenses to read censored works could be obtained by the learned or the powerful. The censorship of images was far more haphazard.

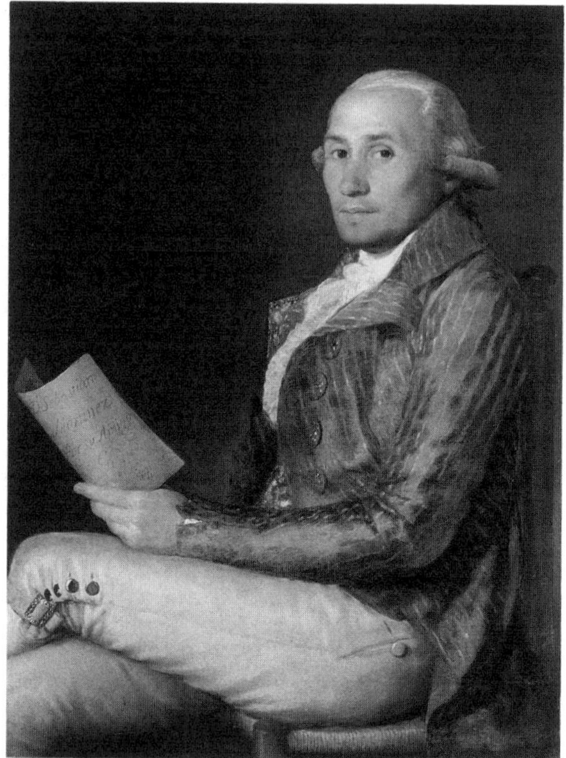

FIG. 4. Francisco Goya, *Sebastián Martínez*, 1792.
Oil on canvas, 96.9×67.6 cm (38⅛×26⅝ in.).
Metropolitan Museum of Art, New York,
Rogers Fund, 1906. (06.289). Photo: Museum.

A case to be discussed below involving Goya's patron, Sebastián Martínez (fig. 4), shows that images confiscated in the provincial town of Cádiz might go unnoticed in Madrid. Documents pertaining to Inquisitional censorship of the visual arts at the end of the eighteenth century in Madrid usually dealt with anonymous works publicly exhibited—for example, the statue of a nude Venus for sale in a Madrid shop, or fans being sold in the Puerta del Sol that when held up to the light showed a man and woman in various indecent postures.[8]

There is no historical evidence that Inquisitional wrath was aimed at any individual artist: the sole purpose in dealing with images seems to have been to safeguard public morality. Works in private collections of powerful individuals at court were never subjected to inquiry. Thus Manuel Godoy was able to create a cabinet of paintings dedicated to the female nude (including Goya's *Naked Maja*) that came under Inquisitional surveillance only after his fall from power.

Most discussions of Inquisitorial censorship have focused on the written word, and it is to such discussions that we turn for our framework. As Stephen Haliczer has pointed out, the censorial role played by the Inquisition became, during the eighteenth century, a contested issue.[9] To summarize his argument: Inquisitorial censorship came into direct conflict with the need to assimilate foreign ideas, recognized by a progressive elite active at the Bourbon court. Many perceived the Inquisition as a deterrent to the program of modernization, championed by members of an increasingly liberal government. Carlos III curtailed certain powers of the Inquisition, decreeing in 1762 that it could no longer prohibit books without royal permission; eight years later a royal edict largely confined the Inquisition's jurisdiction to works dealing with theology and morals. Although these actions are often seen as evidence of Carlos's enlightenment, they were also part of an ongoing power struggle between the church and the Bourbon monarchy. Carlos III was no friend of the papacy that had sided with the Austrians in their attempt to take over his former kingdom of Naples.

Conflicts arose between zealous Inquisitors and the central government, as conservatives became increasingly alarmed by the licenses given to read formerly prohibited material. By 1812, when the very existence of the Inquisition was being debated by the Cortes (or parliament) at Cádiz, liberals such as Antonio Puigblanch vehemently condemned Inquisitorial censorship for having "obstructed the progress of science, by persecuting, either through ignorance or malignancy, its professors, as well as by suspending and proscribing their works."[10] With the restoration of Fernando VII in 1814, the Inquisition was reinstated, though without its former autonomy. It now served as a kind of security police for the restored monarchy that sought the moral regeneration of Spain.

The division of civil and religious authority advocated by progressives had first been jeopardized after 1789, when the Inquisition was enlisted by the government to help stem the flow of information entering Spain from revolutionary France. The once progressive minister of state, the count of Floridablanca, now ordered that the Inquisition collect any writings, whether published or in manuscript, that were "directly or indirectly opposed to the subordination, vassalage, obedience, and reverence owed to our venerated monarch and to the vicar of Jesus Christ because such ideas are anti-evangelical and expressly opposed to the doctrines of the holy apostles Peter and Paul."[11] During this period, Inquisitorial censorship effectively shifted from protecting a cosmological order of good versus evil to protecting a political status quo that guaranteed the alliance of throne and altar.[12] Although the stringent, reactionary censorship of the early 1790s would be relaxed during the course of that decade, the godless French Revolution had affirmed the conservative opinion that the Inquisition was essential in safeguarding Spanish tradition. On the other hand, those of a more liberal persuasion, including Godoy, the royal favorite and minister of state (from 1792 to 1798), continued to view the Inquisition as a nemesis dogging Spain's progress in the modern world. Although there is no indication that Godoy was in any way an intellectual, he was, as minister and subsequently as personal friend and counselor of Carlos IV and María Luisa, a powerful advocate of enlightened ideas in Spain from 1792 to 1808.[13]

It was in Godoy's collection that Goya's *Naked Maja* was first documented in November 1800. The style suggests that Goya had painted the work during the late 1790s. The earliest identification of its subject as a *maja*, or young woman from the popular classes of Madrid, occurs in the Inquisitional records of 1815. Since a *maja* had a reputation for her streetwise, brazen manner, and for her overt sexuality, the identification seems appropriate to Goya's nude, who so boldly confronts the viewer.[14] The *Naked Maja* will be considered here in the context of the progressive defiance of censorship that took place in late eighteenth-century Spain. Although ideological debate is most often discussed by historians, another manifestation of defiance was the growing interest in things sexual. These trends blossomed in opposition to attempts made by both the monarchy and the church to repress certain themes—efforts that not surprisingly had the opposite effect of making them more appealing.[15] The structure of my argument has been anticipated by Richard Terdiman's *Discourse/Counter Discourse*, which examines works of nineteenth-century French literature and art created to attack the hegemonic discourse of an increasingly bourgeois society, showing the extent to which such "counter discourses" in fact participate in the dominant discourse.[16] Goya's *Naked Maja* and her clothed counterpart, the *Clothed Maja*, can be seen on one level as an attempt to defy the traditional association of the female nude with evil—an association perpetuated by the censorship of the nude. But as Goya responds to this traditional discourse, his imagery intimates his own ambivalence before his subject as well as his susceptibility to the censorial attitudes involving the female nude.

Social, literary, and visual manifestations in late eighteenth-century

Spain of a will to challenge traditional sexual taboos offer a context for the *Naked Maja*. The most frequently mentioned indication of these is the rise and dissemination among the upper classes of the custom of the *cortejo*, a single man who served as escort to a married woman.[17] Contemporary opinion seems to have been divided between those who regarded the relationship as an innocent diversion and those who branded it outright adultery. The *cortejo* nevertheless became a stock character in the one-act comic interludes known as *sainetes*, and also inspired a wave of satiric literature. The liberal acquiescence in this custom is voiced by the enlightened husband in a satirical theatrical interlude (described in its title as a *saynete crítico*), *The Good Temper of a Husband, and Enlightenment of These Times*:

> Don Pedro [i.e., the *cortejo*] enters:
> They do whatever they please,
> but what does it matter to me?
> Isn't it all the rage to live like this?
> Well, I swear by fashion,
> for if I didn't
> I wouldn't be an *ilustrado* of the times.[18]

Clearly, the author of this anonymous play is mocking not only the custom of the *cortejo* but also the political correctness of the (apparently) betrayed husband. Like many texts concerning the *cortejo* and his lady, this one is circumspect about the nature of the relationship. We learn only that "they do whatever they please," a statement that offers an implicit appeal to read between the lines of these very general descriptions. This intentional ambiguity is hardly surprising, since the *cortejo* was an accessory of the upper classes, whose sexual activities were rarely acknowledged or discussed.

More graphic description of sexual activity would lead us away from the polite classes to the marginal society that inspired Moratín the Elder's *Art of Whoring* (*Arte de las Putas*), perhaps the best known of several erotic verses penned—and circulated in manuscript—in Spain in the late eighteenth century. The earliest notice we have of this work is its Inquisitional censure of 1777, in which it is "prohibited entirely, even for those who have the license to read prohibited books, because it is full of false and scandalous propositions, provocations to falsehoods injurious to all states of Christianity."[19] Moratín details procedures ranging from bargaining for better prices to protecting against venereal disease, in a work that pays tribute to Ovid's *Art of Love* as well as to the original ancient Greek definition of pornography as writing about prostitutes.[20]

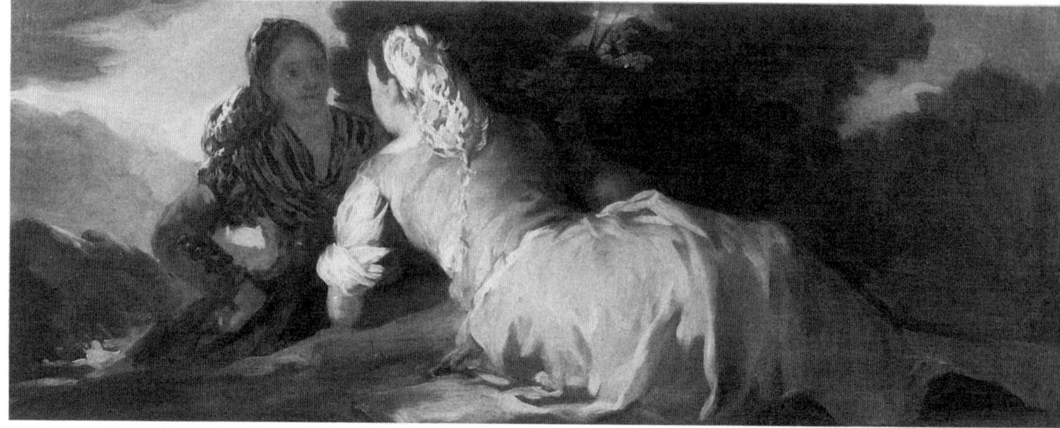

FIG. 5. Francisco Goya, *Gossiping Women*, ca. 1785.
Oil on canvas, 59×146 cm (23¼× 57½ in.). Wadsworth Athenaeum, Hartford, Connecticut, Ella Gallup Sumner and Mary Catlin Sumner Collection. Photo: Museum.

By 1770, around the time that Moratín wrote the *Art of Whoring*, the poet was well established at the Madrid court, his circle of readers undoubtedly from the upper and more educated classes. One might suggest that it was for a similar audience that Goya painted canvases that show women lounging, chatting, or sleeping, such as *Gossiping Women* (fig. 5) and *Sleeping Woman* (fig. 6), from about 1791. These or similar paintings may have belonged to a group of three overdoors documented in the collection of the Cádiz merchant Sebastián Martínez (fig. 4). Such a provenance would suggest the willingness of at least one of Goya's bourgeois patrons to challenge Inquisitorial censorship.[21]

This attitude is documented by Martínez's confrontation with the Inquisition of Cádiz from 1783 onward.[22] In that year, he intervened on behalf of an art dealer, from whom four "indecent" paintings with nudes had been confiscated. Martínez promised to "correct" the paintings, and was given three months to do so. By 1785, it was clear that he had no intention of altering the paintings; what is more, by that date he had been denounced for having in his collection "two paintings of a nude man and woman in the act of fornication," as well as paintings of nudes and prohibited books. The suspicions of the Inquisition had been aroused, and in August 1788, Pedro Sánchez Manuel Bernal, commissioner of the Inquisition in Cádiz, singled out from Martínez's collection some paintings of nudes, which in fact remained in Martínez's hands, with the stipulation that they not be shown to anyone. Bernal also took the key to the cabinet where Martínez kept his books and prints. Drawings after the paintings, included with Martínez's subsequent appeal to Madrid, allow us to identify a fragment of a painting by Giulio Romano, *Cleopatra and Lucretia* by Andrea Vaccaro, *Acis and Galatea* by Luca Giordano, *Samson and Delilah* by Alonso Cano, and three anonymous works (*Allegories of Justice and Peace*, a painting of a reclining nude seen from the back, and an academic drawing of a female nude, also seen from the back). On September 25, 1788, Bernal again visited Martínez, seizing the ten volumes of Montfaucon's engravings of Greek and Roman antiquities and a painting on copper of the Three Graces. Martínez complained to friends in Madrid, and ultimately to Floridablanca, who prior to the outbreak of the French Revolution was one of the more powerful progressive members of the court. Floridablanca responded that the Cádiz commissioner was out of line, for the issues concerning these paintings had nothing to do with religion, and his behavior served only to discredit the Inquisition. Surviving records show that by April 1789 the case remained unresolved; we might surmise that with the fall of the Bastille the Inquisition turned its attention to other matters, as did Floridablanca. His stance regarding the division between civil and religious censorship changed markedly after 1789, when he recruited the Inquisition to assist in his campaign against revolutionary propaganda.

How does this "censorial mentality" inform Goya's *Naked Maja* and *Clothed Maja*? It had long been apparent that lascivious women—particu-

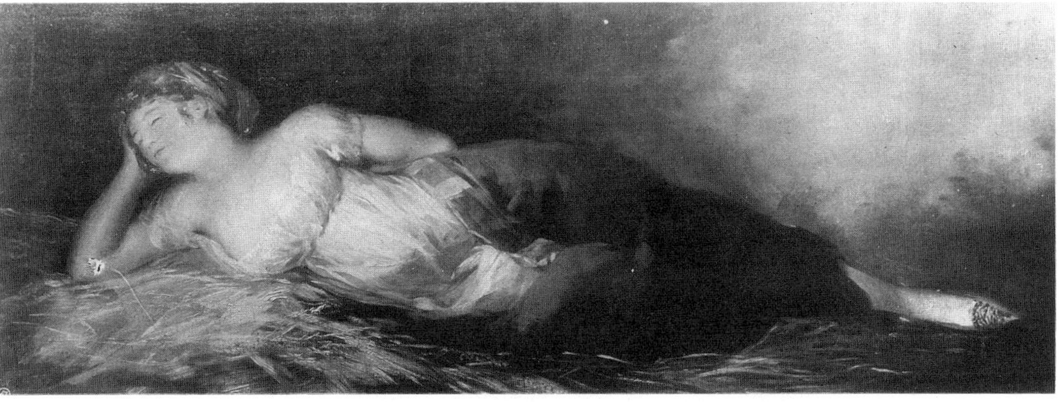

FIG. 6. Francisco Goya, *Sleeping Woman*, ca. 1790.
Oil on canvas, 59×146 cm (23¼× 57½ in.). MacCrohan Collection, Madrid. Photo: Mas.

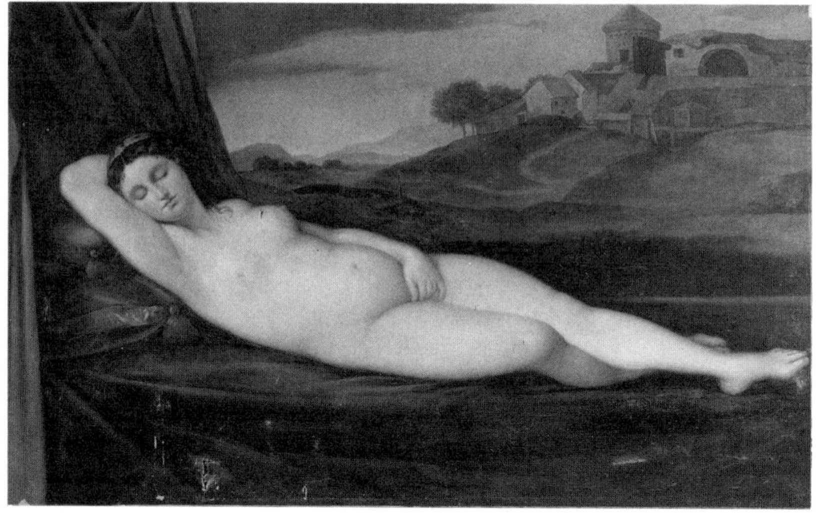

FIG. 7. After Titian, *Sleeping Venus*, ca. 1800.
Oil on canvas. Museo de la Real Academia de Bellas Artes, Madrid. Photo: Museum.

larly those without clothes—were not a subject universally favored by Goya's patrons. In 1762, King Carlos III ordered Anton Rafael Mengs, first court painter, to assemble all the paintings in the royal collection that showed "too much nudity" so that they might be burned.[23] Since these included five paintings by Titian—a *Sleeping Venus* (now lost, but known through a late eighteenth-century copy, fig. 7), two versions of *Venus and Cupid with an Organist* (1545–48), *Venus and a Dog with an Organist* (ca. 1550), *Venus and Adonis* (1553–54), and *Danae* (1553–54; all today in the Prado, Madrid)—as well as works by Veronese, Annibale Carracci, Guido Reni, and Rubens, we may be thankful that Mengs suggested the alternative solution of moving the paintings to his studio in the Casa del Reveque, where they were seen by Antonio Ponz in 1776.[24] The incendiary passion seems to have been hereditary, for in 1792 Carlos IV sought once again to burn this group of paintings. The reason for this reiteration of his father's threat has never been clarified, but given its suddenness and the date of 1792, one may wonder if Carlos IV intended these unholy pictures as an ex-voto, offered in response to the worsening situation of his Bourbon cousin, Louis XVI. This time it was the Marqués de Santa Cruz who intervened, suggesting that the works be moved to the Royal Academy, where they could be seen only by those with sufficient knowledge to appreciate their artistic merits.[25] During the reign of the intruder king Joseph Bonaparte (who suppressed the Inquisition on December 4, 1808), they were displayed in the Academy; but upon the restoration of the Spanish king, Fernando VII, in 1814 they were again sequestered. In 1827 they were transferred to what later became the Prado Museum.[26]

This censorship by Carlos III and Carlos IV was not motivated by a concern for the public good, since these paintings of nudes could easily be hidden from public view (a solution Carlos III had adopted as king of Naples when confronted with a Roman statuette, of a satyr fornicating with a goat, that had been entrusted to the royal sculptor).[27] The censorship of both Spanish kings was apparently motivated by a view of the world that confused image and reality, and in this coincided with the censorial rationale of the Inquisition.[28] To this way of thinking, naked women, whether painted or real, who displayed themselves to male eyes offended a divinely ordained cosmology. What saved the paintings was a rationalization of this view: in anticipation of nineteenth-century arguments against censorship, Mengs (and, we may suppose, the Marqués de Santa Cruz) asserted that between a real naked woman and a painting of one there *was* a difference, grounded in the painting's aesthetic qualities.[29] Thus, if the paintings were placed under the care of the first court painter (or, subsequently, in the Royal Academy), to be seen only by those able to appreciate their higher qualities, their subject matter would become secondary and the threat they posed would be mitigated. Apparently the need for censorship was determined by the prospective audience; and perhaps it is not coincidental that the Spanish kings became concerned with the issue as the royal collections were opened to visiting dignitaries to Madrid and others with an introduction to the court.[30]

It does not seem coincidental that, as paintings of female nudes were being escorted to the Royal Academy in the mid-1790s, Godoy was busy assembling his own collection. Given his role as first minister and consequently as protector of the Royal Academy, he was clearly aware of the controversy surrounding the nudes in the royal collection. The formation of his own cabinet can only be seen as a premeditated challenge to such controls. Whether his motive was to show his liberal stripes or to test his power against that of the censors remains a matter of speculation.

The earliest known reference to Goya's *Naked Maja* was made November 12, 1800, by academician Pedro González de Sepúlveda, who described in Godoy's palace a "room or cabinet in which hung various paintings of Venus."[31] Among other paintings mentioned were Velázquez's *Venus* (fig. 8, today known as the *Rokeby Venus*), its pendant (then attributed to Luca Giordano and recently identified with a painting, now lost, of the Venetian school),[32]

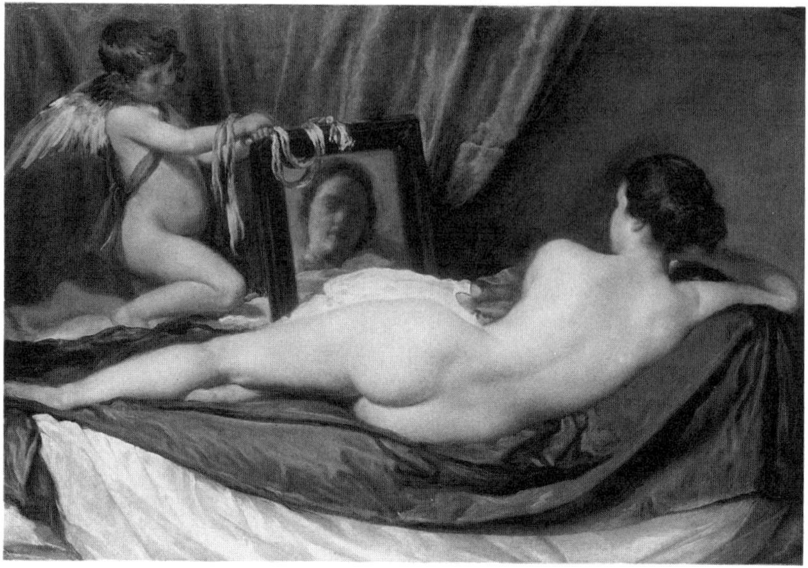

FIG. 8. Diego Velázquez, *Reclining Venus*, ca. 1650.
Oi! on canvas, 122.5×177 cm (48¼× 69½ in.). National Gallery, London. Photo: Museum.

and a copy of a *Sleeping Venus* by Titian, the original of which had been moved to the Royal Academy but is now lost. That no reference is made to the *Clothed Maja* suggests that she had not yet been painted.

Godoy's cabinet reflects a preoccupation with those themes that were the targets of Inquisitional censorship. The use of a private cabinet to exhibit paintings with nude figures was in itself not new: the duke of Alba had such a *gabinete reservada*, and Wilhelm Humboldt remarks in his Spanish diary that fine paintings by Rubens and Guido Reni were often relegated to darkened rooms.[33] But Godoy went further. The newly appointed grandee and promulgator of enlightened reforms flaunted his defiance of censorial attitudes by forming a gallery that isolated and objectified the female nude, scrutinizing her representation through the centuries. To complete the tradition, he apparently commissioned copies of well-known works, enlisting the services of Madrid's foremost painter, Goya. What is more, the paintings in this room were not simply paintings with nudes; they were works that removed the nude from any narrative context. The nude was transformed into icon, enshrined and sequestered for private adoration in an obsessive manner that implicitly acknowledged the prohibitions that Godoy, on one level at least, so brazenly challenged. If the discourse of sexuality was in fact defined in the West by the tradition of religious confession, as Michel Foucault has argued, Godoy's cabinet might be seen as an enlightened alternative to the confessional, where the male viewer obsesses about female sexuality behind closed doors, albeit without the benefit of priestly absolution.[34]

Given the highly controversial nature of its subject, it is likely that Godoy commissioned the *Naked Maja*, thereby calling on Goya not only to respond to tradition but to pander to Godoy's compulsive scrutiny of the female nude. Isolated from narrative, the *Maja* is also removed from nature: the painting is not a response to external reality, but to the tradition of representing the unclothed female. For Goya, tradition and commission were equally loaded: for if one who contemplates such images risks damnation, what of one who paints such pictures? Scholars of seventeenth-century Spanish painting have long been aware of the controversial status of the nude in the aftermath of the Council of Trent. Velázquez's father-in-law, the theorist Francisco Pacheco, so abhorred the nude that he recommended that even the Christ child appear dressed.[35] These prohibitive attitudes did not vanish with the (admittedly tempered) advent of the Enlightenment in Spain. During the annual awards ceremony of the Royal Academy in 1790, Joseph Manuel Quintana delivered a poem condemning the painter Lucidio, who had strayed from his call to commemorate great events and abandoned his sublime talent in order to paint effeminate works such as "Julia uncovering her breast, and Cupid sleeping in her arms."[36] Although Quintana formulates this as a criticism of effeminate tastes (implicitly contrasted with the commendable virility of historical subjects), it betrays a moralistic attitude toward the nude similar to that voiced by seventeenth-century writers.

Can we be certain that Goya and his patron cast off the mentality that equated a painting of a nude with an evil reality? To answer this question with a definite "yes" would be to deny the religious tradition that was their heritage. And the *Maja* hardly suggests that Goya was at ease with his subject. This stilted representation of the attributes of female sexuality imposed on a rococo doll intimates an inability to transcend the dogmatic relationship of sin and female flesh. In defense of this hypothesis of Goya's discomfort with his subject, it might be noted that it was never repeated: all his other representations of nudes are small-scale, private works—drawings, miniatures, or preliminary oil sketches.[37] That Goya did not hesitate to paint equally seductive women clothed (as in the overdoors mentioned above) suggests his adherence to the prevailing proscription not of lascivious females, but of nudes: even Carlos III had in his bedchamber a painting by Titian showing a clothed Venus looking at herself in a mirror supported by a single cupid (today lost).[38]

It is now generally accepted that the *Clothed Maja* was painted several years—perhaps as much as a decade—after the *Naked Maja*.[39] We recall that no mention of the *Clothed Maja* is made in Sepúlveda's 1800 account of Godoy's collection; it is first recorded, with its pendant, in an 1808 inventory by Frédéric Quilliet as *Goya: Gitana nue/Gitana habillée/tous deux couchées* (Goya: Nude gypsy/Clothed gypsy/both lying down). The manner in which the paintings were related within the chamber remains a matter of speculation. According to Charles Yriarte, who credits his information to *quelques vieillards*, the *Naked Maja* once hung on the verso of the *Clothed Maja*, and the paintings were exhibited back to back, in the middle of the room. In 1914, Pedro Beroquí related the tradition that by means of a mechanism the *Clothed Maja* could be lifted to reveal the *Naked Maja*.[40]

Differences in the two paintings support the hypothesis that these works were not intended to be seen side by side, but in succession. Although the poses are similar, the *Clothed Maja* is brought forward to dominate the pictorial surface. Her multiple charms receive new emphasis: golden brocade slippers set off her delicate feet, a dark shadow calls attention to her pubis, her waist curves deeply inward to enhance the protrusion of her breast, her formerly blasé expression becomes more immediately intelligible as a slyly provocative smirk, set off against her raised elbow, now defined not as flesh but as the intersection of two curves, in seeming anticipation of Picasso's *Demoiselles d'Avignon*.

The palette chosen for the *Clothed Maja* corroborates her forthright character. Examining the canvas, one detects a mustard-tone underpainting (in contrast to the sepia tone used for the *Naked Maja*), suggesting that Goya's intent was from the outset to key up the tonality of the entire work. While in the *Naked Maja* the highlights are light gray, those of the *Clothed Maja* are a far more strident yellow. In her costume, the warm tones of her mustard-colored jacket and rose sash dominate; even the green of the couch is now liberally tinged with yellow. These colors reinforce the presence of the figure against the pictorial surface, in contrast to the recessive and, comparatively speaking, timid presence of her nude counterpart.

The *Clothed Maja* flaunts her sexuality, which becomes a masklike shell that perhaps originally opened to reveal the *Naked Maja*—who would have been seen as innocent by comparison. In other words, by identifying female sexuality with gaudy artifice, the *Clothed Maja* leaves the nude comparatively bereft of sexual power. In the context of such hyperbole, the nude is no longer threatening: her sexuality, which had seemed so blatant compared to that of the *Rokeby Venus*, has now been travestied by her flamboyant, costumed counterpart. What is more, by creating a clothed figure far more seductive than her nude counterpart, Goya makes a mockery of the Inquisitional solution—as exemplified by the case of Sebastián Martínez—of "correcting" nude figures by painting over them.

Paired with the *Clothed Maja*, Goya's nude is removed from the traditions of Titian and Velázquez that engendered her; and her significance is altered as she becomes inseparable from her clothed pendant. When seen together with the *Clothed Maja*, the nude, who had formerly seemed so flat, is perceived as set back into space, with the result that her timidity is emphasized and the staged space essential to voyeurism is reinstated. In short, when juxtaposed with the confrontational *Clothed Maja*, the *Naked Maja* is put back in her place.

What, then, might we say about the *Clothed Maja*? Doesn't she now become a threatening force, by assuming the role once assigned the *Naked Maja*? I would argue not. The *Clothed Maja* doesn't seem to be a real person: if the nude is taken as a standard, the clothed version is larger than life and the palette used suggests an artificiality that may well have been identified with masquerade. As mask, she invites dis-covering—an invitation that her owner might take up if he could unveil her at the pull of a rope. The second factor undermining her power is the identity that Goya gives her by dressing her. We recall that in 1808 she was inventoried as a gypsy, a member of a powerless and marginalized class. Here Goya returns to a ploy that he had used frequently in his tapestry cartoons, identifying female sexuality with a stereotypical character of the lower classes.[41] The implication is clear: sexuality is no longer a threat but a potential commodity.

What induced Goya to take the nude through the permutations here witnessed? I would suggest that the artist participated to some degree in the view of the world that underlay the censorial attitudes of late eighteenth-century Spain. Accordingly, image and reality became confused, making it impossible for Goya to treat the female nude on a purely aesthetic level. This very contemporary nude, who so boldly addresses the viewer, becomes an embodiment of perversion somehow to be contained. As we have seen, Goya's solution is to dress her in a manner that identifies her sexuality with commodity and masquerade, thus divorcing it from the female form, which in turn is emptied of the sexual.

The subsequent history of the *Majas* attests to the transformation in the nature of censorship. On March 19, 1808, Godoy was overthrown in a mob uprising at Aranjuez. The paintings in his Madrid palace were seized; several—including the *Rokeby Venus*—were taken from Spain during the course of the Napoleonic war; those that remained were found in storage in 1814 with other confiscated goods. Among them were Goya's *Clothed Maja* and *Naked Maja*. Although it was not then known who had painted them, they were denounced to the Inquisition on November 18, 1814, and delivered to its officials ten days later. On January 7, 1815, it was reported that the painting of a "nude woman on a bed" was by Goya, as was "the woman dressed as a *maja* on a bed." (As mentioned earlier, this is the first identification of the subject as a *maja*, implying the figure's lowly social class, forthright character, and contemporaneity.) On March 16, 1815, Goya was ordered to appear before the tribunal to explain his motivation in painting these works; his testimony does not survive, and it is possible that the painter, still salaried at court, was able to circumvent an appearance.[42]

The Inquisitional intervention of 1814 illustrates a new type of censorship, now placed in the service of the state. The censor's main target was no longer the subversive or unorthodox imagery of the work, but rather the intentions of its creator. This interest in the artist's intent was also political, since in Restoration Spain moral subversion was identified with treason, with the French, and with the fallen Godoy (who became, in effect, the scapegoat of the old order). The initial denunciation of Goya's *Majas* on November 18, 1814, illustrates the identification. Its author opens by condemning the general collapse of morals under the government of the "intruder king," Joseph Bonaparte:

> These modern Attilas, not content with infusing the religious Spanish people with the venom of heresy that they held in their hearts, and that had produced as many ills as disgrace in the kingdom, to carry forth their execrable mission, tried to corrupt our customs with dishonest books, prints, and the most provocative and obscene paintings. . . .[43]

In all likelihood, the author of this statement had little idea that his investigation of "provocative and obscene paintings" would lead him to Spain's most senior court painter. That in itself might have made a more objective observer reconsider the ostensible correlation between sexual imagery and subversive politics; but such a thought was not to be entertained by the Inquisition in 1815.

Another artist brought before the Inquisition during these years was the

Parisian trained academic painter José Aparacio, summoned to explain his role in producing a deck of cards (referred to as *cartitas de amor*, or erotic little cards) with "thirty entertaining questions and answers," advertised for sale in the *Diario de Madrid* on December 2, 1814. The record of Aparicio's appearance before the Inquisition on January 17, 1815, does survive. He admitted to engraving the vignettes for the cards, but said that the questions and answers were the work of Josef Asensio, whose whereabouts were not known. He pointed out that the cards were sold only in two bookstores, and he agreed to surrender those that he had at home. He explained that he undertook the project without malice, and without intending to offend morality, since such cards were sold before the invasion of the French, and never confiscated.[44] It would seem that Aparicio did not sense the new conservatism to which the confiscation of these cards itself attests. One of the illustrated cards (of which no photograph could be obtained) is included in the file pertaining to Aparicio's case. It is an innocuous roundel, about one and a half inches in diameter, showing a neoclassical engraving of a Cupid about to kiss Venus, who is shown half-length and dressed in a tunic that falls to reveal one breast. The file does not contain any document referring to the Inquisition's ruling, but given Aparicio's appointment as court painter to Fernando VII on August 23, 1815, we might surmise that the painter was let off with a reprimand.[45]

Like Aparicio's cards, Goya's *Majas* had by 1815 acquired a significance far different from what might have been attributed to them under Spain's old regime. Formerly titillating additions to a gentleman's private cabinet, they now became emblematic of the moral decline that had led to the downfall of Carlos IV and María Luisa—by this time, living in exile in Rome. Yet these monarchs were, in effect, above reproach, since it was their son who now ruled Spain. Thus Godoy served as a perfect scapegoat, embodying the absolute evil, the flabby sensuality, and the political liberalness that the conservatives—now restored to power—saw as the cause of Spain's near ruination.[46] He too was now living in exile, following his king and queen as an ever faithful servant. So in Madrid, the restored government could take revenge on him only in effigy: bringing the *Majas* to trial offered an opportunity to do so.

The inquiry into the *Majas* should not be interpreted as typical of Inquisitional censorship. The case of Sebastián Martínez suggests that earlier attempts to censor images of the nude in private collections were exceptional in late eighteenth-century Spain. The case of the *Majas* represents a final, perhaps somewhat desperate attempt to assert Inquisitional power, made possible by the reactionary climate that surrounded the restoration of Fernando VII. As mentioned, the Inquisition had been abolished by Joseph Bonaparte in 1808, and by the Cortes of the Spanish government in exile at Cádiz on February 22, 1813. Eager to identify himself with Spanish tradition, Fernando VII restored the Inquisition on July 21, 1814, and conservatives rallied to its cause. Yet it soon became clear that the Inquisition's time was past: it was again abolished with the *pronunciamento* of Colonel Riego in 1820, as for a three-year period the Constitution of Cádiz was restored. In 1823, with the aid of the Holy Alliance, Fernando was reinstated. Wiser now, he resisted the demands of ultraconservatives to restore the Inquisition to its former powers. It was finally abolished by his widow, María Cristina, on July 15, 1834.

NOTES

1. Edith Helman, *Trasmundo de Goya* (Madrid: Alianza, 1983), 54.

2. Alfonso Pérez Sánchez and Eleanor Sayre, *Goya and the Spirit of Enlightenment* (Boston: Museum of Fine Arts, 1989), page 20.

3. Hans Ulrich Gumbrecht, "Censorship and the Creation of Heroes in the Discourse of Literary History," in Wlad Godzich and Nicholas Spadaccini, eds., *The Institutionalization of Literature in Spain*, Hispanic Issues no. 1 (Minneapolis: Prisma Institute, 1987), 233.

4. An example of this is the interpretation of the changes in the preliminary drawings for *Capricho* 70, discussed in Pérez Sánchez and Sayre, *Spirit of Enlightenment*, 132.

5. Gumbrecht, "Censorship and the Creation of Heroes," 233–34.

6. Fred Licht, *Goya: The Origins of the Modern Temper in Art* (New York: Universe Books, 1979), p. 68.

7. Francisco de Goya, *Diplomatario*, ed. Angel Canellas López (Saragossa: Librería General, 1981), 389.

8. Antonio Paz y Melia, *Catálogo abreviado de papeles de Inquisición* (Madrid: Revista de Archivos, Bibliotecas y Museos, 1914), 81–87.

9. Stephen Haliczer, "Inquisitional Myth and Inquisition History: The Abolition of the Holy Office and the Development of Spanish Political Ideology," in Angel Alcalá, ed., *The Spanish Inquisition and the Inquisitorial Mind* (Boulder, Colo.: Atlantic Research and Publications, 1987), 539–41.

10. Antonio Puigblanch, *The Inquisition Unmasked*, trans. William Walton (London, 1816), 2:80. In addition to being translated into English, Puigblanch's book, first published in Cádiz in 1811, was reprinted in Lima (1813) and in Mexico (1824).

11. Reference made in Inquisición de Toledo to Consejo de la Inquisición, October 3, 1789, A.H.N. Inq., leg. 4430, no. 1, cited by Richard Herr, *The Eighteenth-Century Revolution in Spain* (Princeton: Princeton University Press, 1958), 243.

12. Ibid., 243–68.

13. For further discussion of Godoy as an advocate of the Enlightenment, see Janis Tomlinson, *Goya in the Twilight of Enlightenment* (New Haven: Yale University Press, 1992), chapter 4.

14. For further discussion of the *maja*, and her appearance in Goya's earlier tapestry cartoons, see Janis Tomlinson, *The Tapestry Cartoons and Early Career at the Court of Madrid* (New York: Cambridge University Press, 1989), 33–35, 80–85.

15. Scott Kendrick, *The Secret Museum: Pornography in Modern Culture* (New York: Viking, 1987), 29.

16. Richard Terdiman, *Discourse/Counter Discourse: The Theory and Practice of Symbolic Resistance in Nineteenth Century France* (Ithaca: Cornell University Press, 1985).

17. On the custom of the *cortejo*, see Carmen Martín Gaite, *Usos amorosos del dieciocho en España* (Madrid: Siglo Veintiuno Editores, 1972), chapter 1. On the appearance of the *cortejo* in Goya's tapestry cartoons, see Tomlinson, *The Tapestry Cartoons*, pp. 82–84. The custom is also satirized in a working proof, undoubtedly prepared for *Los Caprichos* but never published; see Tomas Harris, *Goya: Engravings and Lithographs* (San Francisco: Alan Wofsy Fine Arts, 1983), vol. 2, cat. 118.

18. Anonymous, *El Buen genio de un Marido, e Ilustración de estos tiempos / Saynete Crítico*, Ms. 14496, no. 39, Biblioteca Nacional, Madrid.

19. Nicolás Fernández de Moratín, *Arte de las Putas*, ed. Manuel Fernández Nieto (Madrid: Ediciones Siroe, 1977), 13–14.

20. Kendrick, *Secret Museum*, 1.

21. Pierre Gassier and Julie Wilson, *The Life and Work of Francisco Goya* (New York: William Morrow, 1971), cat. nos. 307, 308; Sarah Symmons, *Goya in Pursuit of Patronage* (London: Gordon Fraser, 1988), 142.

22. The following information on Martínez and the Inquisition is based on José Manuel Cruz Valdovinos, "Inquisidores e ilustrados: las pinturas y estampas 'indecentes' de Sebastián Martínez," in *El Arte en Tiempo de Carlos III: IV Jornadas de Arte* (Madrid: Editorial Alpuerto, 1989), 311–19.

23. Narciso Sentenach, "Cuadros selectos condenados al fuego," *Boletín de la Real Academia de San Fernando*, 2d ser., 4, no. 57 (1921): 50.

24. Antonio Ponz, *Viaje de España* (Madrid: Aguilar, 1947), 6:533. Other works included were: Veronese's *Venus, Adonis and Cupid*; Carracci's larger version of the same subject; *Hippomenes and Atalanta* by Guido Reni; *The Rape of the Sabines*, *Diana at Her Bath*, and *Bacchanal* by Rubens; and *Perseus and Andromeda*, *Juno, Palas and Venus*, and the *Judgment of Paris*, said by Ponz to be after designs by Rubens.

25. Sentenach, "Cuadros selectos," 46–48.

26. Pedro Beroquí, *Tiziano en el Museo del Prado* (Madrid, 1946), 153.

27. Kendrick, *Secret Museum*, 6.

28. Gumbrecht, "Censorship and the Creation of Heroes," 239–40.

29. Sentenach, "Cuadros selectos," 46–50.

30. One result of the opening up of the royal collections was the publication of guides such as Richard Cumberland's *An accurate and descriptive catalogue of the several paintings in the King of Spain's palace at Madrid* (London: Dilly, 1787).

31. E. Pardo Canalis, "Una Visita a la galería del Principe de la Paz," *Goya*, 148–50 (1979): 308.

32. Duncan Bull and Enriqueta Harris, "The Companion of Velázquez's *Rokeby Venus* and a Source for Goya's *Naked Maja*," *Burlington Magazine* 128 (September 1986): 648.

33. Isadora Joan Rose Wagner, *Manuel Godoy: Patrón de las artes y coleccionista* (Madrid: Universidad Complutense, 1983), 317–18.

34. As Foucault writes: "On the face of it at least, our civilization possesses no *ars erotica*. In return, it is undoubtedly the only civilization to practice a *scientia sexualis*; or rather, the only civilization to have developed over the centuries procedures for telling the truth of sex which are geared to a form of knowledge-power strictly opposed to the art of initiations and the masterful secret: I have in mind the confession." Michel Foucault, *The History of Sexuality*, vol. 1, *An Introduction*, trans. Robert Hurley (New York: Vintage, 1980), 58.

35. Julián Gallego, *Visión y símbolos en la pintura española del siglo de oro* (Madrid: Cátedra, 1987), 68–70.

36. "Lucidio, aquel Pintor cuyo gran Genio / Frutos tan excelentes prometia, / Y que á inmortalizar los hechos grandes / Solo parece que nacido habia / De algunos Sibaritas corrompidos / Por adular el gusto afeminado, / Su talento sublime ha abandonado, / Su robusto pincel y sus ideas. / Y en vez de dedicarse a las acciones / De los antiguos ínclitos Varones,/Se encuentra enteramente embebecido, / Pintando á Julia descubierto el seno, / Y al Amor en sus brazos adormido. . . ." Joseph Manuel Quintana, "Epistola," in *Distribución de los Premios* (Madrid: Real Academia de Bellas Artes de San Fernando, 1790), 87.

37. Cf. Gassier and Wilson, *Life and Work of Francisco Goya*, cat. nos. 366, 375, 696, 1682, 1688.

38. Harold Wethey, *The Paintings of Titian* (London: Phaidon, 1975), cat. no. L-27.

39. Relevant scholarship is summarized by Wagner, *Manuel Godoy*, vol. 2, cat. nos. 246, 247. She proposes a date for the *Maja desnuda* of 1792–95 and for the *Maja vestida* of 1803–6. I am indebted to her research for the factual information on the paintings cited in this paragraph.

40. Charles Yriarte, *Goya* (Paris: Henri Plon, 1867), 89; Pedro Beroquí, "Adiciones y correcciones al catálogo del Museo del Prado," *Boletín de la Sociedad Castellana de Excursiones* 6 (1913–14), 502.

41. Tomlinson, *Tapestry Cartoons*, 102–3.

42. Archivo Histórico Nacional, Madrid, *Inquisición*, legajo 4499, no. 3. The case is summarized by A. Paz y Melia, *Catálogo abreviado de la Inquisición* (Madrid: Archivo Histórico Nacional, 1947), 85.

43. Letter signed *Doctor Don Valentin Zorrilla de Velasco y Ollauri*, dated November 18, 1814, in AHN, Madrid, *Inquisición*, legajo 4499, no. 3.

44. AHN, Madrid, *Papeles de Inquisición*, legajo 4493, no. 23.

45. On Aparicio, see Musée Goya, Castres, *Les élèves espagnols de David* (Saint Sebastian: Editions ACL Crocus, 1989), 23–38.

46. Richard Herr, "Good, Evil and Spain's Rising Against Napoleon," in Harold Parker, ed., *Ideas in History* (Durham: Duke University Press, 1965).

The Body Impolitic: Censorship and the Caricature of Honoré Daumier

ELIZABETH C. CHILDS

In the face of censorship, the only thing one can possibly do is to keep working.
—*Salman Rushdie*

POLITICAL CARICATURE OFTEN THRIVES at the margins of repressive government.[1] Throughout much of the nineteenth century in France, censorship laws attempted to define strict parameters within which social and political caricature could be published and circulated. Yet the various proscriptions, while largely effective, never completely eradicated political critique in satirical journals. In some instances, the laws, the seizures, the prosecutions, and the rhetoric of restriction served only to provoke a more creative response to taboo themes. Some of the most charged political satire of the modern era emerged from the caricaturists who created their art in the face of severe political and economic repression.

In the early years of the July Monarchy, satirists worked in a volatile environment ruled by a government that promised freedom of expression but then increasingly became repressive and interventionist. Beginning in 1830, caricature developed a momentum of open nose-thumbing and risk-taking that escalated dramatically until 1835, when strict regulations were imposed and the rigid curtain of the September press laws seemed to fall on the stage of satiric political critique. The defiant heroics of 1830–35 are characteristic of artists working in embattled periods of revolution when ideological opposition is most evident and lines of conflict are clearly drawn. Less obvious, but perhaps more revealing about the dynamics of creativity, are cases of subtle political expression during periods of rigorous surveillance of the arts and the press by political agencies. These are times when the rules and their enforcers appear to reign with uncontested authority; two such periods were the July Monarchy between 1835 and 1848 (when the September Laws regulating political caricature were in effect) and the early years of the Second Empire.

By focusing on periods when law and regulation appear to be most fully in force, and comparing them with periods of greater artistic freedom, we may examine the dynamic relationship between the practice of censorship and artistic response. In the case of nineteenth-century French political caricature, the historical record suggests that government could not, despite official policy and extensive bureaucratic effort, ever fully silence oppositional voices in political caricature. While appearing to comply with laws that forbade political critique, satirists and their publishers could, on occasion, cast their political expression in a coded *argot* that slipped through the official nets of censorship. The very concept of freedom of the press, a key legacy of the age of revolution, was thus perpetuated not only by political theorizing, where one might expect to find it, but through public artistic practice, where by official decree it was supposed to be absent. The integrity of such work, at once defying the laws governing its production while appearing to follow the rules, is not compromised. On the contrary, it draws its significance not only from the deeply felt political belief of the artists, but also from the implicit and self-conscious critique of the political mechanisms that attempt regulation.

French caricaturists found their most powerful weapon of political resistance in the humor of the body politic. This essay examines the development of Honoré Daumier's use of a particular form of physiognomic satire in caricature produced between 1831 and 1872. By turning the image of the head of the French state into a subject for laughter, Daumier and his fellow caricaturists created an unofficial but persuasive political art. I will argue that the very mutability of the image of the leader's body—its distortions, exaggerations, and exotic and literary reincarnations—in the hands of the satirists became a visual repudiation of the political authority that attempted to regulate representation. The subject of the leader's body was a loaded one. The image of the king (and, by extension, the image of his self-appointed successor, the emperor) was well protected not only by established codes of aristocratic French art but also by the mythology of absolute monarchy, which held that the king had in fact two bodies—the mere flesh and bones common to all men, and the body politic consisting of his policy and government.[2] Prerevolutionary tradition held that while the king's physical body was vulnerable, the God-given powers of his body politic were inviolable. Revolutionary acts of decapitation, regicide, the dissolution of monarchy, and the establishment of a republic had violently dismantled the old system of political symbols. By the end of the Bourbon Restoration in 1830, it was abundantly clear to Monarchists and Republicans alike how vulnerable and replaceable the French head of state was. What followed in the July Monarchy was the birth of a hybrid figure, the Citizen King, at once divine and bourgeois. At this time, the image of the absolute leader became a focus for a compensatory assertion of the old royal authority and power; but it was also a contested focus for Republican opposition to any monarch, even a compromised one. Caricaturists asserted new liberties of the crayon that were at one stroke both political and artistic. These freedoms came, of course, at the expense of the decorum and idealized perfection of the royal (and later, the imperial) body politic.

The metaphoric power of the leader's body is made explicit in a caricature by Charles-Joseph Traviès, in which a crowd gathers in front of the lithograph shop of Aubert to view a display of caricatures of King Louis Philippe (fig. 1). The caption "Got to Admit that the Government Has a Very Funny Head" makes it clear that the target of the people's laughter is as much the body politic as the body of the king. By claiming the body as sign of political authority through the discourse of satirical humor, caricaturists affirmed that visualized political expression is not some stable commodity that may be harnessed and controlled, but an adaptive, dynamic process, beyond prediction and often beyond entrapment. There is also a compelling suggestion in the history of caricature that when the dominant ideology seeks to repress its opposition, the less powerful may forge solidarity and identity through humor and satire.[3] To turn the opposition into a good joke in the public forum of the press is to regain the upper hand symbolically. As a consensus-building strategy, laughter is one of the most powerful tools of propaganda, precisely because it may seem so innocuous, spontaneous, and natural (and therefore truthful). Funny as these political caricatures were (and often still are), they were no mere laughing matter in nineteenth-century France.

The most significant political caricaturist to work throughout both the July Monarchy and Second Empire was Honoré Daumier (1808–79). He published his first political caricature in 1830 at the age of-twenty-two, and as an older man his crayon attested to the ravages of Paris in the Franco-Prussian War and in the Commune. His commitment to Republican politics informed his graphic work for more than four decades, and over a third of his lithographic oeuvre of some four thousand prints concerns the political life

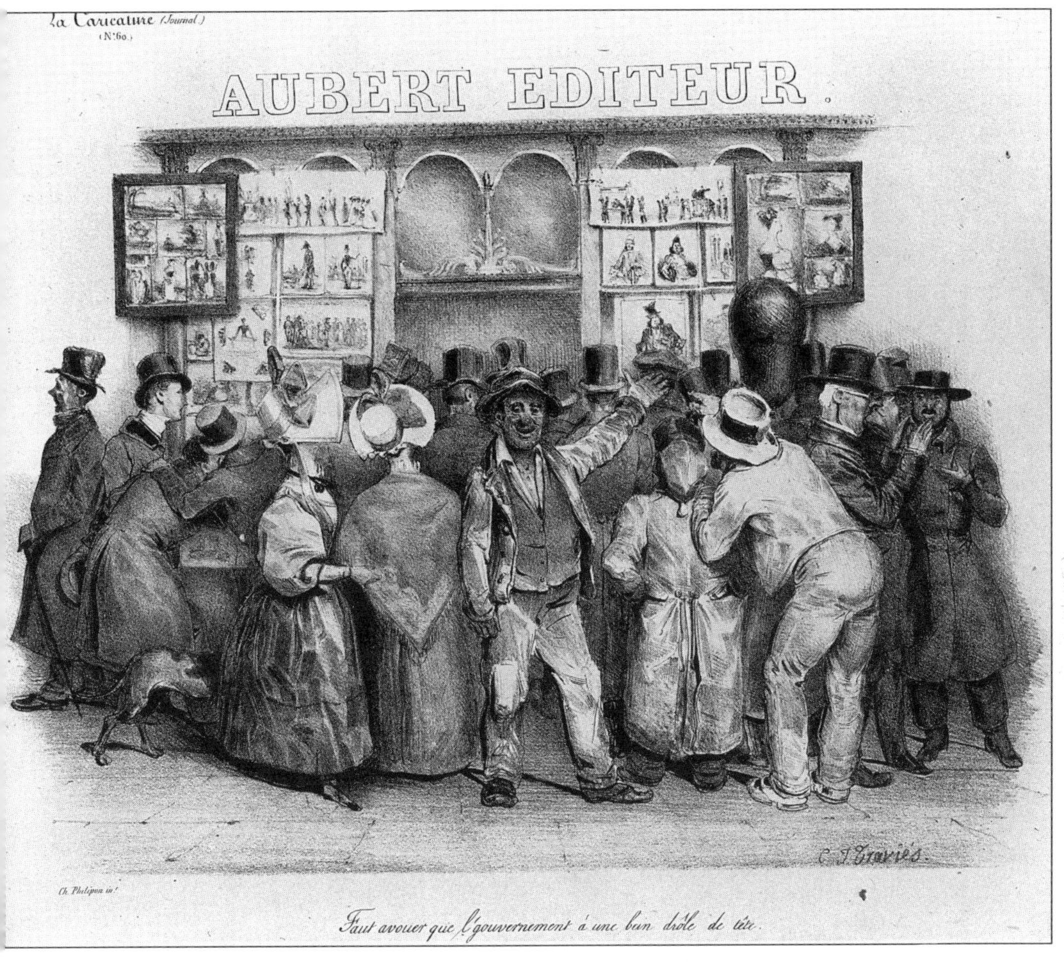

FIG. 1. Charles-Joseph Traviès de Villars,
Got to Admit that the Government Has a Very Funny Head, 1831.
Lithograph, 24.5×28 cm (9⅝×11 in.). Courtesy of the Fogg Art Museum,
Harvard University Art Museums, Cambridge, Gift of Philip Hofer.

of Paris. His dramatic career lent itself to legend-making. After his death, Daumier was claimed as both artistic genius and political martyr by Republicans of the Third Republic.[4] Many of these accounts characterize him as a martyr-hero—praising him for suffering public scandal and personal hardship while displaying moral courage in his early, dramatic encounter with censorship in the July Monarchy.

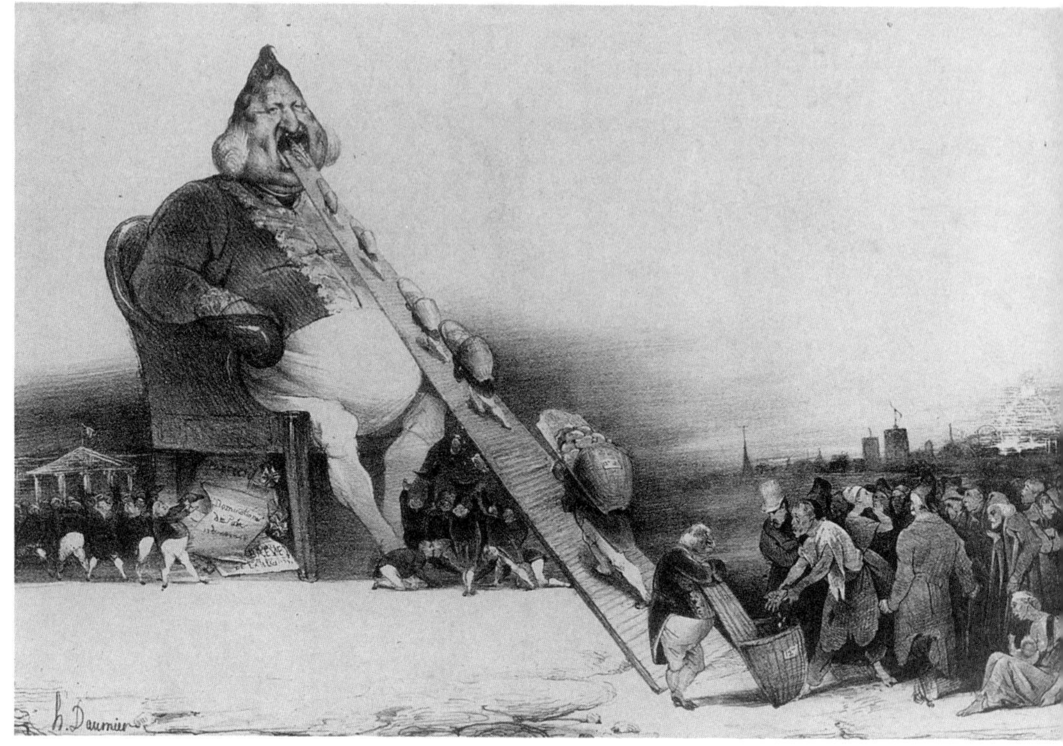

FIG. 2. Honoré Daumier, *Gargantua*, deposited December 16, 1831. Lithograph (2d state), Delteil 34, 24×30.5 cm (9½× 12 in.). Rose Art Museum, Brandeis University, Waltham, Massachusetts. The Benjamin A. and Julia M. Trustman Collection, Brandeis University Libraries, Waltham.

Almost every biography of the artist mentions that in 1832, at the age of twenty-four, he went to jail because of his art. He served six months in Ste. Pélagie prison for drawing a satirical lithograph of King Louis Philippe as the Rabelaisian character Gargantua (fig. 2). This episode was the most celebrated of the artist's many encounters with censorship over his long career. In the eyes of fellow caricaturist Étienne Carjat, Daumier was the consummate Republican artist who could inspire subsequent generations to be "toujours fidèles à l'art, à la fraternité et à la République."[5] After his death in 1879, obituaries trotted out the familiar tale of Daumier's trial and imprisonment, mourning the artist with melodramatic recollections of how his arrest in 1832 was allegedly witnessed by his impoverished, grief-stricken parents.[6] Police archives, which reveal how nervously the Third Republic kept an eye on the remnants of the old left guard, testify that at the 1880 ceremonies at Daumier's reburial in Père-Lachaise cemetery in Paris, Carjat praised Daumier for suffering imprisonment in 1851 at the hands of Louis Napoleon.[7] In fact, no such second imprisonment occurred. On the contrary, by this time, Daumier had learned how to negotiate the delicate boundary between the permitted and the proscribed in caricature. Carjat's error draws our attention to the political implications of artistic reputation in the modern era. The Gargantua episode solidified Daumier's association with Republican entrepreneurs who were cultivating a middle-class market for political satire. It was the start of a business relationship that lasted thirty years. While we may acknowledge Daumier's political integrity in defending artistic liberty, we should also note that there was some self-interest in courting notoriety in the name of Art and Freedom. The scandal that surrounded Daumier's *Gargantua* was not completely uninvited by the idealistic and ambitious artist; a certain amount of grand-standing must be acknowledged. In 1832, artistic freedom was a charged topic in France—the cult of individualism fostered romantic ideals about Truth linked to independent expression. It was also not a bad career move for a struggling young caricaturist to get involved in the politics of censorship.

Daumier's early career would surely not have been so eventful had he not, at age twenty-two, joined the stable of artists employed by artist and entrepreneur Charles Philipon, the "Duc de Lithographie, Marquis de dessin, comte de Bois gravé, Baron de Charge et chevalier des caricatures," as he was affectionately addressed by Balzac.[8] As Daumier later recalled, "If Philipon had not been behind me to prod me unceasingly like one does to an ox with a plow, I would never have done anything."[9] Philipon's establishment, La Maison Aubert, dominated the growing caricature business in Paris in the first decade of the July Monarchy.[10] The Revolution of 1830 had made a recently politicized middle class conscious of its new role in government, and a large audience emerged with a certain self-interest in political satire. Just as this self-interested class now desired a greater role in government and business, they also desired images of themselves and their leaders. For this generation of consumer-connoisseurs, possession and viewing were complementary activities. Caricature, a quintessential urban art form, offered a new social space where a world of rapidly shifting identities of class and power could be frozen in the comforting, summarizing lines of various urban types.[11]

The new caricature industry also opened a new political space where images of dissent and criticism could be circulated, their seditious content mediated by the screen of laughter. For mere funny papers, caricatures were starting to do serious political work. After the Revolution of 1830, an explosion of political caricature sympathetic to Republican philosophy occurred in a climate of disillusionment and broken promises. Louis Philippe had promised to protect the freedom of the press, a freedom that had been brutally curtailed by his predecessor, Charles X. In the Constitutional Charter of 1830, he had promised that censorship would never be reestablished. But even by the end of 1830, new press laws began to introduce new restrictions. The offenses now punishable under French law fell into three areas: attacks against the person of the king; debate over succession to the throne; and questioning the legitimate domain of the legislature.[12] The government was, it became clear, nervous not only about demonstrations and strikes, but also about the press's ability to incite unrest. Soon, as had been the case before 1830, papers were required to pay security deposits, a forced prepayment of the government fines they would owe if found guilty of infractions. The press, in short, was now repressed.

In this increasingly embattled atmosphere, Philipon led the satirical charge against Louis Philippe. First in the weekly journal *La Caricature* (founded in 1830) and then later in the daily illustrated *Le Charivari* (founded in 1832), he published ardently Republican fare. Between November 1831 and May 1833, Philipon was arrested three times for press offenses, sentenced to a total of thirteen months in prison, and was fined 4,600 francs. His employees and cohorts at La Maison Aubert were often engaged in similar volleys with authority—by July 1832, Philipon boasted that he and his publications had endured twenty seizures by Louis Philippe's press censors, six arrests, and three prison sentences and fines.[13] Philipon even bragged, with the pride of a bustling entrepreneur, that he had gained subscribers from members of the juries that had heard his cases. He knew that bad press could mean good business.

At stake in the trials was not just Philipon's freedom to do business but the very question of artistic freedom in the political arena—freedom to choose a subject, freedom to render it as one pleased, freedom to put the work on public view in a shop window or in the pages of a journal. Significantly, the satire that first brought the editor-artist to trial was a satiric depiction of the head of state. The specific charge was injury to the person of the king, the form of treason known as *lèse majesté*, made illegal by the press law of November 1830. Philipon's first trial was in 1831 over the caricature *Soap Bubbles*, in which he depicted Louis Philippe nonchalantly blowing soap bubbles in a Chardinesque parody.[14] Each bubble represents a promise made

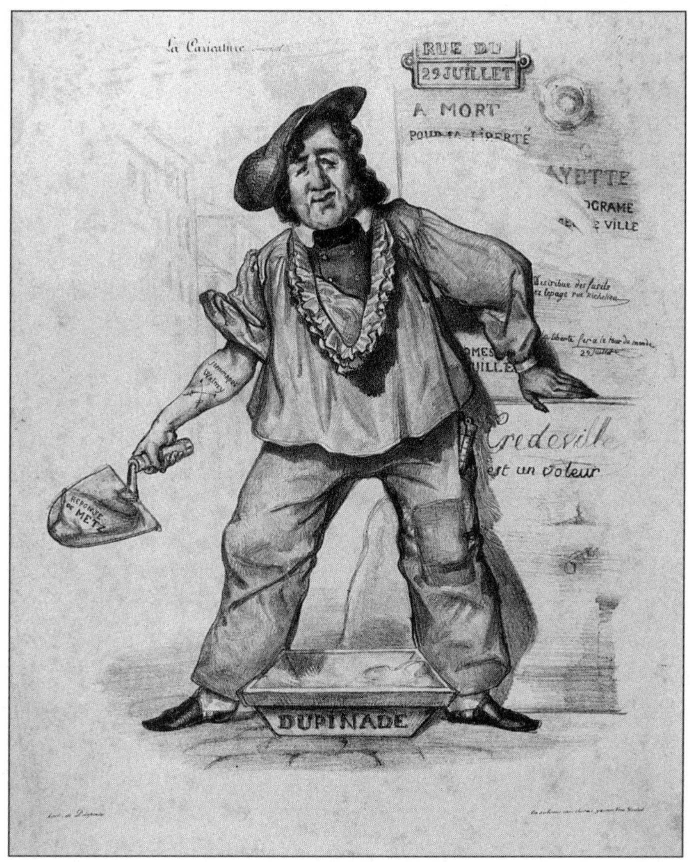

FIG. 3. Charles Philipon, *The Replastering* in *La Caricature*, June 30, 1831. Lithograph, 36.8×27.6 cm ($14\frac{1}{2}\times10\frac{7}{8}$ in.). Mount Holyoke College Art Museum, South Hadley, Massachusetts. Gift of Mr. and Mrs. Howard P. Vincent (Mary Wilson Smith, Class of 1926), 1991.

during the Revolution of 1830 (the "mousse de juillet"). Prominent among these fragile pledges is liberty of the press ("liberté de la presse")—demoted from a serious moral right to an ephemeral child's toy of the whimsical monarch.

Although acquitted for *Soap Bubbles*, Philipon was not as fortunate at his trial on November 14, 1831, for a print entitled *The Replastering* (fig. 3) in which the king, dressed as a common mason, whitewashes the past by plastering over his forgotten promises of 1830.[15] Philipon was convicted for publishing this print and received a prison sentence of six months and a heavy fine. He had argued unsuccessfully that the caricature only represented the government through the symbolic resemblance of the king, but was not intended as a specific attack on the king's person—a strained defense necessitated by the concept of *lèse majesté*.

While Philipon may have lost the battle at this trial, he nonetheless managed to set out the terms on which he and other caricaturists would ultimately win the war. In his defense he had pointed out the absurdity of creating any precedent that would require every satire to be tried on the issue of resemblance, whether it suggested the physionomy of the king. In a grand gesture that combined wit, skill, and a flair for visual drama, Philipon drew the famous four-part sketch for the court in which the bulbous face of Louis Philippe mutates into a common pear (fig. 4). The metonymic substitution was not only canny but insulting, as *poire* in French slang had the derogatory connotation of fathead or simpleton. Using the sketch, he argued that law cannot regulate the realm of resemblance, or soon artists would be thrown in jail for merely drawing fruit. He also predicted that the more the courts attempted to impose such restrictions, the more caricaturists would take malicious pleasure in testing their skills and the sacred liberty of the crayon. The gauntlet was down. Ten days after Philipon's conviction, *La Caricature* reproduced his courtroom sketch of the king as pear, and La Maison Aubert began to sell a separate poster of the motif. Authorities stepped in, predictably, and seized the lithograph, but not before the image had made its mark.

Almost immediately, artists adapted the new visual code. As Philipon had predicted, the image was beyond the control of the law. If the king's body was off limits to satirists, the fruit was not, even when used metonymically. "Poire-o-mania" exploded among Philipon's satirists.[16] Between the moment of its invention in the courtroom in 1831 and its demise at the hands of the repressive September laws of 1835, La Poire's currency was high. As a sign of opposition to the Orléanist regime, it appeared in caricature journals, in print shop windows, in the homes of some bourgeois Republicans, and even on the prison walls of caricaturists jailed for censorship infractions. Years later in 1850, Flaubert noted that the pear had also toured Egypt, where he found the image among the French graffiti on the great pyramid at Giza. The defiant pear thrived as a symbol of resistance in the margins of the law, and in the margins of official culture.

In the early July Monarchy, even the outline of the pear carried a political message. Accounts in *Le Charivari* of the censorious actions of the police were printed in pear-shaped articles.[17] The pear literally gave form to opposi-

LES POIRES,

Faites à la cour d'assises de Paris par le directeur de la CARICATURE.

Vendues pour payer les 6,000 fr. d'amende du journal le *Charivari*.

Sur la demande d'un grand nombre d'abonnés des départemens, nous donnons aujourd'hui dans le *Charivari* les poires qui servirent à notre défense, dans l'affaire où la *Caricature* fut condamnée à six mois de prison et 2,000 fr. d'amende.

Si, pour reconnaître le monarque dans une caricature, vous n'attendez pas qu'il soit désigné autrement que par la ressemblance, vous tomberez dans l'absurde. Voyez ces croquis informes, auxquels j'aurais peut-être dû borner ma défense :

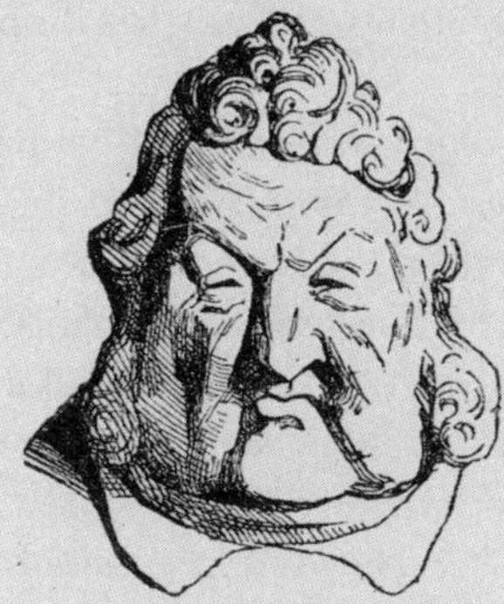

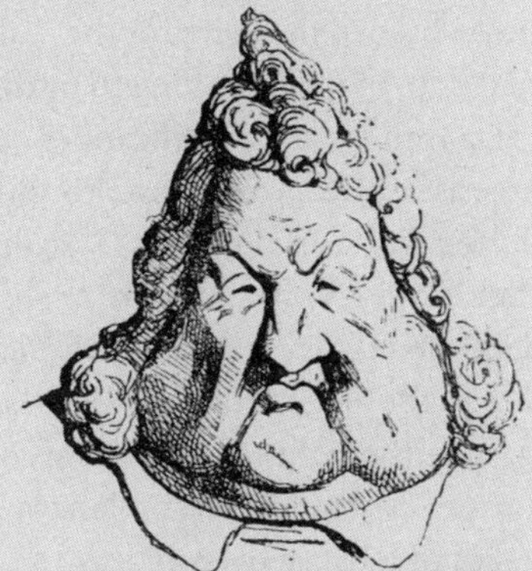

Ce croquis ressemble à Louis-Philippe, vous condamnerez donc ?

Alors il faudra condamner celui-ci, qui ressemble au premier.

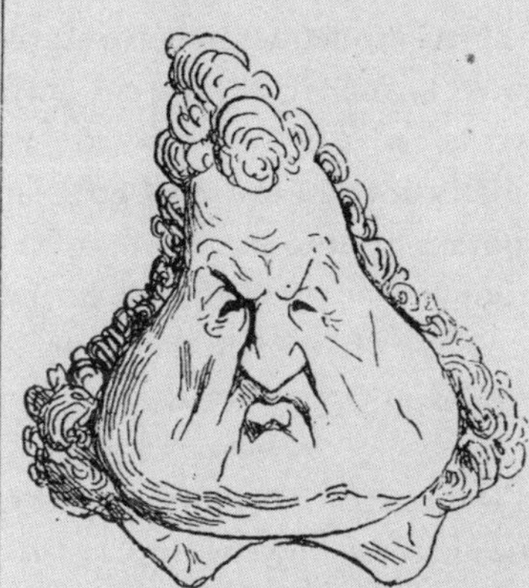

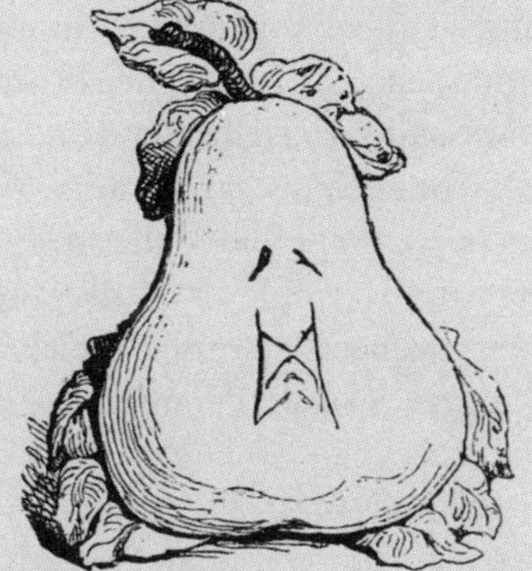

Puis condamner cet autre, qui ressemble au second.

Et enfin, si vous êtes conséquens, vous ne sauriez absoudre cette poire, qui ressemble aux croquis précédens.

Ainsi, pour une poire, pour une brioche, et pour toutes les têtes grotesques dans lesquelles le hasard ou la malice aura placé cette triste ressemblance, vous pourrez infliger à l'auteur cinq ans de prison et cinq mille francs d'amende !!

Avouez, Messieurs, que c'est là une singulière liberté de la presse !!

FIG. 4. Charles Philipon, *The Pears* in *Le Charivari*, January 17, 1832. Lithograph, Print Collection, Miriam and Ira D. Wallach Division of Art, Prints, and Photographs, New York Public Library, Astor, Lenox, and Tilden Foundations, New York.

tion discourse, and flaunted its power to defy regulation. Caricaturists exploited its formal potential for obscene and scatological humor. For example, the ponderous jowls of the pear-king invited comparison with his other cheeks, those of his buttocks, in a comic inversion of top and bottom, front-side and back-side that was a stock joke of earlier political satire. As fruit, the pear also bore the constant potential of rot and decay, as well as the bi-spherical shape of a fat human ass, the source of excremental filth. As in the caricature of 1832 by Traviès, *Le Juste Milieu se crotte*, stagnation, decay, and waste are all posited as the realm of *la poire*.[18] In other words, it is the natural state of the pear-king to be dirty and foul.

Daumier's first significant encounter with censorship coincides with the genesis of this provocative, inventive, and insulting imagery of *la poire*. He started work on the print *Gargantua* in November and December 1831, just after Philipon's invention of *la poire* at his trial for *The Replastering*. Philipon published both his drawing of *The Pears* (*Les poires*) (fig. 4) and his exhortation to the artists of his time: "Yes, we have the right to personify power. Yes, we have the right to take for this personification whatever resemblance suits our needs! Yes, all resemblances belong to us!"[19] Thus Philipon raised the stakes of a battle over images to a veritable crusade for the artistic freedom of the satirist. With *Gargantua*, Daumier consciously and somewhat rashly entered the censorship fray. Although he had recently left several provocative prints deliberately unsigned in order to protect himself from prosecution, he now boldly signed his last name at the lower left edge of *Gargantua* so there could be no doubt as to its authorship. He might not have chosen to go to jail, but he was not blind to the advantages of notoriety, or to the benefits of siding with his employer on the issue of freedom of the press. Indeed, he may even have been aware of the celebrated martyrdom of such Republican artists as Pierre Jean de Béranger, the famed author of oppositional songs and poems.[20]

The links between Philipon's *poire* and Daumier's *Gargantua* are incontestable. The pyramidal shape of Gargantua's head, defined by ample whiskers and pointed coiffure, emphatically re-figures *la poire*. Even Gargantua's pointed cowlick mirrors the stem of Philipon's pear. The rounded shape of the king's entire body, jammed into its chair, echoes the contours of the ripe fruit. From fat head to fat belly, Daumier's royal figure recalls the newly crowned surrogate, the pear-king.

In *Gargantua*, Louis Philippe sits on a large *chaise percée*, or toilet, and defecates rewards to the tiny ministers of his government gathered beneath the chair. Other ministers collect tribute from the destitute and crippled populace of Paris, and then march up a gangplank to feed the baskets of wealth to the ravenous king. The king's body—obese, passive, and immobilized by gluttony—is the agent of his own physical corruption. And it is here that Daumier transgressed the law of 1830 with its proscription of attacking the royal person of the monarch. Daumier's *Gargantua* is the vehicle for insulting both the royal body and the body politic.

Had the image been a mere retelling of the *poire* joke, however, Daumier would probably not have been the target of such rigorous censorship. After all, Philipon was not tried again for creating or printing the pear. But, as I have argued elsewhere, the *Gargantua* image was laden with reference to libelous scatological traditions and to controversial recent events.[21] Its implications clearly made the relatively new and somewhat unstable monarchy nervous. Within days of its appearance in the windows of Aubert's shop, the police confiscated it, and ordered Aubert to destroy the original lithographic stone and all remaining proofs; the extreme rarity of impressions of *Gargantua* today suggests they were largely successful.[22]

In February 1832, Daumier was tried for *Gargantua*, along with two of his collaborators: Gabriel Aubert (Philipon's brother-in-law and owner of the publishing house, and therefore responsible for selling the print to the public) and Hypolite Delaporte (the printer of the lithograph). All were found guilty of arousing hatred and contempt of the king's government, and of offending the king's person (the crime of *lèse majesté*). Although all received a sentence of six months in prison and a heavy fine, in the end only Daumier had to serve. *He* was held responsible, as it was his "seditious crayon that had traced the guilty image." The court determined that his goal had been to "figure with exaggerated and monstrous features the person of the king, represented devouring under the eyes of his starving people a feast in the style of Rabelais." What was at stake in this judgment was clearly fear: the government feared, and punished, the artist more than his business collaborators. Moreover, pictures were, from the government's point of view, more dangerous than words. This was not only because of widespread illiteracy but also because images were relatively easy to disseminate among various classes and regions. There was also a threat in the rapidity with which images conveyed messages and could incite group action. An open fear of caricature surfaced time and again in the debates over censorship in the July Monarchy and later in the Second Empire. One articulation of the threat appeared in a memo from the minister of police in 1852: "Among the means employed to shake and destroy the sentiment of reserve and morality so essential to a well-ordered society, drawings are one of the most dangerous. Drawing offers a sort of personification of thought, it puts it in relief, it communicates it with movement and life, so as to thus present spontaneously, in a translation everyone can understand, the most dangerous of all seductions."[23]

Daumier's conviction did little to alter his commitment to political caricature. In the six months between his trial in February 1832 and his imprisonment later that year, he produced six more satires that were seized by the government (Delteil 35–39). He seems to have teased the government with ever more brazen caricatures to see if they would actually enforce the sentence of his conviction. By the end of summer 1832 he was in Ste. Pélagie prison, which appears in several of his later caricatures as a metaphor for the pervasive climate of Orléanist political repression and control.[24] He amused himself in jail by drawing variations of Gargantua on the wall, and later in Dr. Pinel's Maison de Santé, where he finished serving his sentence, he joined Philipon in drawing new caricatures to be published by La Maison Aubert. Making caricature was clearly one of the few meaningful acts of political resistance possible while sitting in jail.

After his release in 1833, and for the next two years, Daumier participated fully in Philipon's business of political caricature. One of his key targets continued to be the king. From 1832 until the September laws of 1835 forbade further political caricature, Daumier produced more than two hundred lithographs. Over a third of these depict either Louis Philippe or his surrogate form, *la poire*.[25] Daumier toys with the issue of resemblance, often coyly covering or turning the king's head away from the viewer to avoid dealing directly with royal facial features. Rather, Louis Philippe is often identifiable through his typical attributes: his umbrella and top hat (signs of the so-called Citizen King), his corpulent profile, his muttonchop sideburns, and his pointy coiffure. Daumier casts the king in a variety of demeaning roles, figuring him as beggar (Delteil 108), as bloodletting doctor (Delteil 73), as pickpocket (Delteil 95), as villainous butcher (Delteil 97), and as clown (Delteil 86).

In spite of his conviction for *Gargantua*, Daumier did not abandon the general theme of the monarch's despotic greed that fueled the Rabelaisian image. He did, however, generally avoid mocking the king with overtly scatological humor, as this particular form of degrading the royal body seems to have been a deciding factor in the government's decision to press charges for *Gargantua*.[26] In 1834, Daumier satirized Louis Philippe's avarice by simultaneously exoticizing and trivializing the king in *The Magot of China* (*Magot de la Chine*) (fig. 5). Here the king appears as a grimacing Chinese porcelain bibelot, his legs crossed, his eyes slanted, and his earlobes extended in a vul-

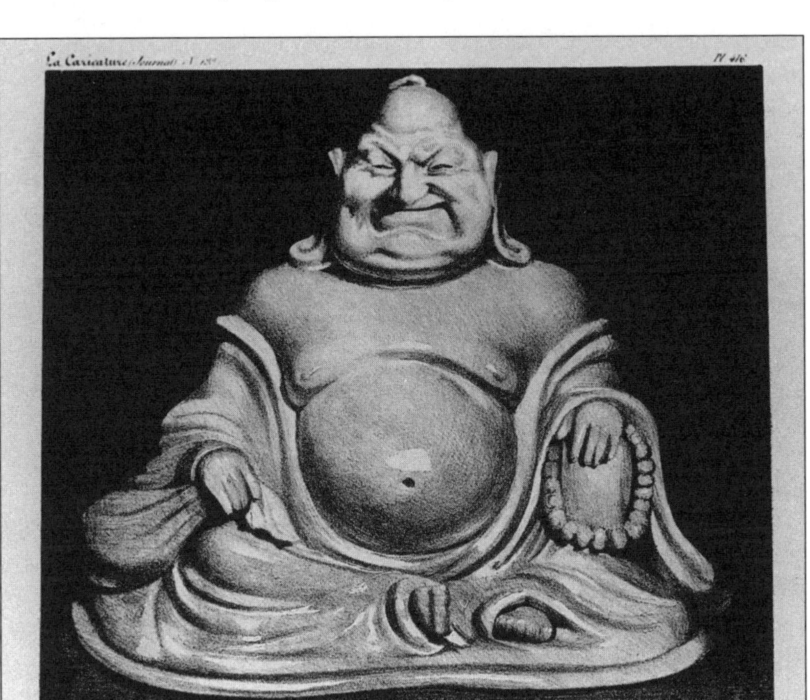

FIG. 5. Honoré Daumier, *The Magot of China*, in *La Caricature*, August 28, 1834. Lithograph, Delteil 83, 25.5×34.8 cm (10×13¾ in.). Armand Hammer Daumier and Contemporaries Collection, UCLA at the Armand Hammer Museum of Art and Cultural Center, Los Angeles.

gar parody of imported Buddha figurines. This little statue reflects the middle-class taste for such *chinoiserie* in the July Monarchy, when the antique *magots* and *potiches* so popular in prerevolutionary France were once again in fashion.[27] Daumier's satire invokes both senses of the word *magot*, which can mean either a grotesque figurine or a hidden treasure or cache of money. Louis Philippe clutches a money bag, a sign of greed that resonates with other signs of excess—the swollen belly of the Magot or the memory of the gluttonous belly of Gargantua. Yet another strain in this heterogeneous satiric discourse is that of the *poire*: from the polished head of the *magot* sprouts the distinct stem of a pear. Moreover, the rounded pyramidal shape of the figure also echoes the bulbous contours of the infamous fruit. References to greed, stupidity, and excess thus unite in this exoticized body of the ruler. In figuring his monarch as a greedy oriental, Daumier cracks the same joke as George Cruikshank, who two decades earlier had satirized King George IV as a rotund Chinese emperor, enthroned in his new "Chinese Palace" at Brighton.[28] Cruikshank's caricatures of the English king as oriental despot reflected widespread public criticism of the extravagance of the royal pavilion. Daumier successfully adopts a similar trope of orientalism to re-embody the French monarch, distancing his subject (and thereby the direct threat of the image) through the strategy of exoticism.

In other satires of Louis Philippe, Daumier's humor of the body depends not only on the physical dislocation of exoticism, but also on the pointed violation of regal decorum. In *Honest compensation . . .* (*Recompense honnête . . .*) (fig. 6) he unveils Louis Philippe in bed with two aboriginal women, "savages of North America." The ménage à trois reclines beneath a hanging quiver of arrows, an exotic parody of the amorous symbol of Cupid. The print illustrates a fictional anecdote, recounted in *La Caricature* about Louis Philippe's youthful adventures in North America, where during his exile of 1796–99 he supposedly saved the life of an ailing Cherokee chief and was given the reward of spending the night with the two eldest noblewomen of the tribe. The satire not only destabilizes the king's authority by removing him physically from Paris and the throne room, placing him *face-à-face* with a cultural "other," but also demeans his power sexually by placing him at the mercy of two partners who are older, aggressive, and conventionally unattractive—typically unsuited to be consorts of a French king. Daumier does not cross over the line of vulgarity here into pornography; he clearly circumvents the risks of a charge of *lèse majesté*. But the bawdy circumstances nonetheless humorously compromise the king's royal decorum, as we voyeuristically enter a most private space, that of the king's bed. Had Daumier attempted a similar joke with less exotic partners, the satire would probably not have been tolerated.

Until the September Laws forbade political caricature in 1835, Daumier remained a public defender of freedom of the press. A diminutive figure of Louis Philippe rants and raves in the margins of *Don't mess with it!!* (*Ne vous y frottez pas*) of 1834 (fig. 7), in which a young and defiant lithographic printer stands down all interference with freedom of the press. Through his heroic scale and defiant posture, Daumier's worker claims his victory over the impotent efforts of government. But in this final year before the official suppression of political caricature, the government was growing less and less tolerant of oppositional voices. Daumier's sober and poignant *Rue Trans-*

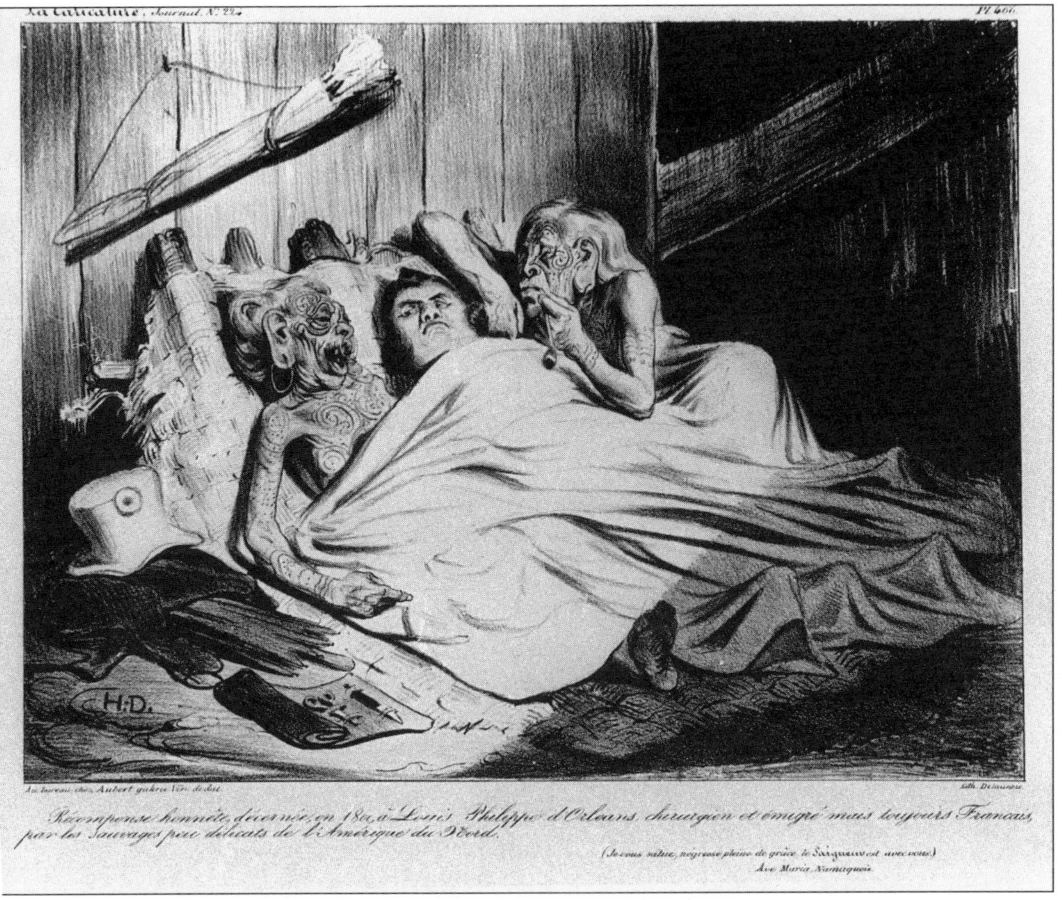

FIG. 6. Honoré Daumier, *Honest compensation bestowed in 1800 on Louis Philippe d'Orléans, surgeon and immigrant, but forever French, by the crude North American savages (I hail thee, Negress full of grace, the Savior [and the Surgeon] is with you. Ave Maria, Namaquois)* in *La Caricature*, no. 224, February 19, 1835. Lithograph, Delteil 109, 26.5×34.7 cm (10½×13⅝ in.). Armand Hammer Daumier and Contemporaries Collection, UCLA at the Armand Hammer Museum of Art and Cultural Center, Los Angeles.

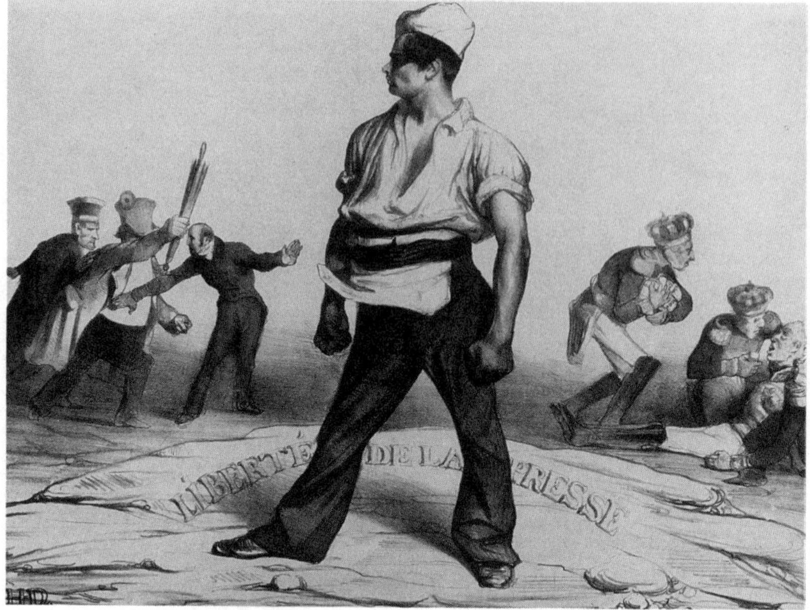

FIG. 7. Honoré Daumier, *Don't mess with it!!* in *L'Association menseulle*, plate 20, March 1834. Lithograph, Delteil 133, 36×54.6 cm (14¼×21½ in.). Armand Hammer Daumier and Contemporaries Collection, UCLA at the Armand Hammer Museum of Art and Cultural Center, Los Angeles.

nonain (Delteil 135), an indictment of military repression, was seized as soon as it appeared on public display, and the police destroyed all available prints, as they had in the case of *Gargantua*. Freedom of the press was not as unassailable as Daumier's heroic caricature had asserted.

After the demise of *La Caricature* at the hands of the September Laws of 1835, Philipon's major publication was the sister journal *Le Charivari*. (Philipon and Daumier both figure at the center of its masthead, beating the noisy instruments characteristic of the festive rituals of folk charivari. The title of the journal is apt to its mission of social and political critique. As historian Charles Tilly has demonstrated, the "charivari" was a form of popular action, transferred from country to city, that laid the groundwork for political demonstration and revolution in the modern era in France.[29]) *Le Charivari* developed as a less politically aggressive journal than *La Caricature*: its articles and images were largely devoted to the lampooning of bourgeois society. But it was not without its occasional political edge; Philipon used it as a mouthpiece of resistance whenever he thought he could get away with it. After 1835, prior police approval was necessary for the caricatures printed in all illustrated journals. Since text was considered much less a threat than imagery, it was not reviewed by censors *before* publication. Therefore, the journal often resorted to publishing textual descriptions of prints that had been rejected.[30]

In truth, the task of a censor was difficult. In the year 1840 alone, the office of censorship at the Ministry of the Interior had to judge the political content of almost eight thousand images.[31] Archival records suggest that the types of lithographs most frequently censored in the July Monarchy included depictions of the King's Guard in undignified actions; views of extreme carnage or crime; particular scenes in the history of the French Revolution; sexually explicit scenes (often located in bathhouses); and political critique of Louis Philippe's person and government.[32] Censors had only one shot at these images: once an image had passed, it could not be recalled for second judgment if it was subsequently deemed to be offensive or unacceptable.

Knowing these rules, the editors of *Le Charivari* often played a clever game of cat and mouse. One example is the front page of an issue of *Le Charivari* in July 1841 (fig. 8). On the date of the anniversary of the July Revolution of 1830, *Le Charivari* published this memorial issue, featuring commemorative songs of the Revolution and small vignettes by Daumier depicting the ministers of the July Monarchy. These caricatures are recycled images, taken from *en-tête* headings printed in the journal in 1833.[33] The heads of the politicians are arranged like fairy lights (*lampions*) hung on a large light-stand shaped like a pine tree (*l'if monstre*) of the government. The journal envisions the delight with which the French people would attend the light show if these *lampions* were to be lit by two thousand municipal guards.

The insult intended to the ministers was clear—it was literally incendiary—but the individual drawings had been submitted one by one, and not in this particular "ensemble" to the censor. Correspondence between the minister of justice and the minister of the interior about this image reveals their deep frustration in trying to monitor the journal. Even the most vigilant surveillance of individual images as required by the September laws could not prevent editors from giving certain drawings "un caractère répréhensible" by adding oppositional commentary or creating a certain effect by a suggestive arrangement of the drawings.[34] Not every manipulation of the relationship between images, or between images and text, could be foreseen and regulated.

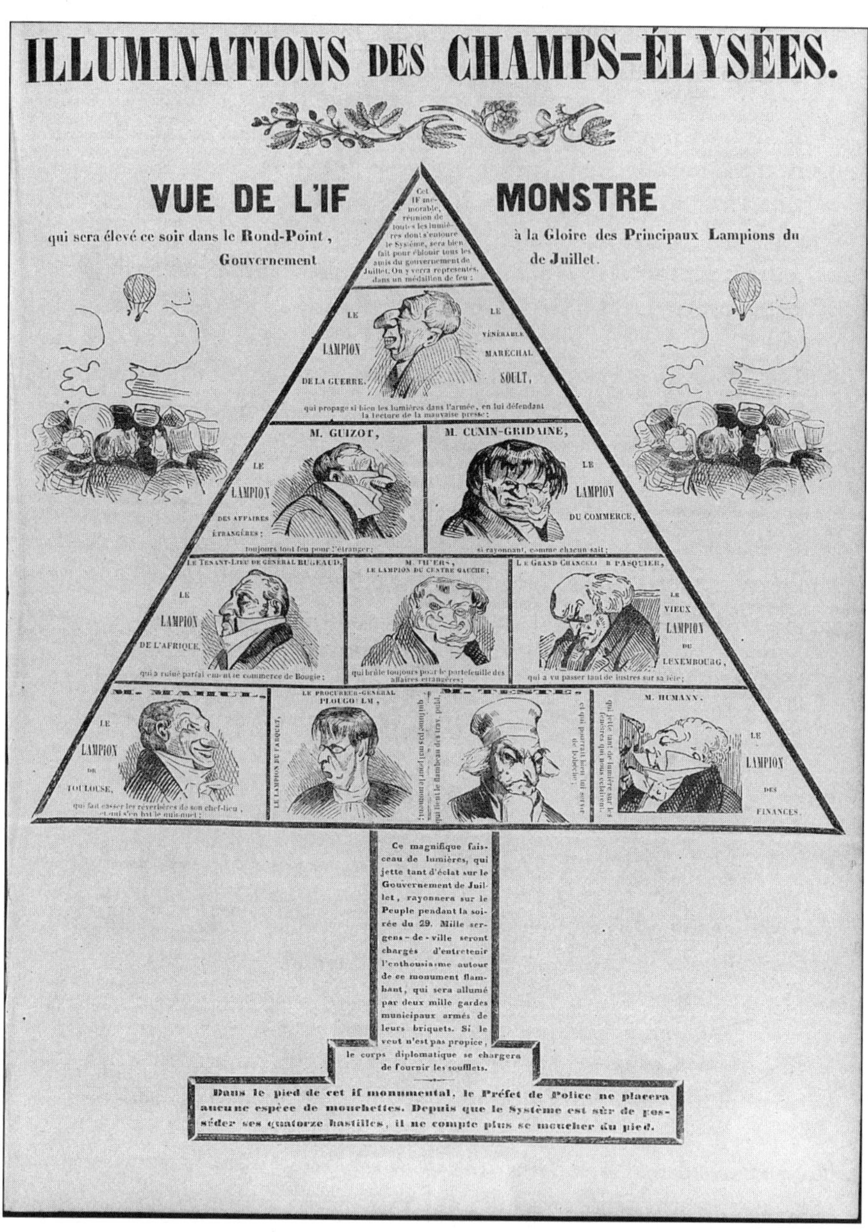

FIG. 8. Honoré Daumier, *Illuminations of the Champs-Élysées, View of the monstrous light-stand* in *Le Charivari*, July 29, 1841. Woodcut, 36.3×25.1 cm (14⅓×9⅞ in.). The Beinecke Rare Book and Manuscript Library, Yale University Library, New Haven.

A review of the censorship records of *Le Charivari* between 1835 and 1848 reveals that the number of issues signaled as potentially offensive was far greater than the number that was suppressed; furthermore, the high number of acquittals of press infractions suggests that *Le Charivari* had learned how to negotiate the delicate boundary between the permissible and the proscribed in political satire.[35] The artists, undoubtedly keenly aware of Daumier's history, avoided making that same costly error of *lèse majesté* in caricature. Between 1835 and 1848, the only infraction committed by *Le Charivari* that drew a conviction with a prison sentence resulted from an essay, not an image. In 1839 the journal's manager Beauger was convicted of publishing an article "offensive to the person of the King."[36] The article, which plays on a fictional confusion between the king and a common umbrella thief, had represented Louis Philippe as extremely fat. In 1838, censors were still striving to repress the satirical discourse of royal obesity linked with corruption, as established several years earlier by the *Gargantua* and pear caricatures. Archival records clearly demonstrate that during the July Monarchy the artists at *Le Charivari* did not avoid political subjects. At least fifty prints submitted by La Maison Aubert to the censor between 1835 and 1848 were rejected; and at least nine of these were by Daumier.[37] As Michael Driskel has demonstrated, Nicolas Charlet published many prints that contained subtle Republican protests in the July Monarchy, in spite of the considerable number of his prints that were censored.[38] Further study of the Republican caricature journals of the period will undoubtedly continue to reveal the pervasiveness of oppositional political discourse, even in this period of surveillance and attempted regulation.

With the Revolution of 1848 and the establishment of the Second Republic, press censorship was once again abolished. Daumier and fellow Republicans could once again openly express political sentiment in caricature as well as in more high-minded forms such as in the official competition for the painted representation of *The Republic*.[39] But in the volatile days at the end of the Second Republic, President Louis Napoleon began to reinstate censorship. Some of Daumier's more brazen colleagues, such as the younger artist Charles Vernier and the journal's *gérant responsable* Léopold Panier, were imprisoned in 1851 for publishing in *Le Charivari* a satire of Louis Napoleon's acts of favoritism.[40] It is interesting to note here that unlike the earlier case of Daumier, who received a heavier sentence than his business collaborators at the time of his conviction for *Gargantua*, the court under Louis Napoleon now gave a much heavier sentence to the journal's manager than to the artist Vernier.[41] Significantly, the artist was no longer the scapegoat for the business enterprise. In 1832, caricature was still a very new business, and the published image was deemed to be primarily the product of individual artistic intent, or as the court documents regarding *Gargantua* claimed, of the artist whose "seditious crayon had traced the guilty image."[42] By the Second Republic, Louis Napoleon clearly recognized the power of satirical journals as collaborative business enterprises, and held the businessman who managed the day-to-day production as the most guilty party.

Rather than quieting the oppositional spirit of *Le Charivari*, Vernier's conviction seemed to heighten the fervor of the journal's attack on Bonapartism. He was little chastised by the prison sentence; one of his caricatures later in 1851 mocks the frequency with which journalists were being sent to prison.[43] Daumier, however, worked more cautiously. In 1850 he lifted a satirical figure from the humorous texts of *Le Charivari* to portray Louis Napoleon's government—the scurrilous Ratapoil, a fictional, villainous agent of the president's brutal secret police, the "Ten December Society." Ratapoil became a symbol of all that was corrupt and counterfeit about the Bonapartist Second Republic.[44] In a print of 1851 (fig. 9), the sleazy and untrustworthy Ratapoil—whose mustache, beard, and long roman nose echo the familiar visage of Louis Napoleon—extends his arm to a noble and virtuous figure of the Republic. Daumier does not always refer to the Second Republic government through the guise of Ratapoil; occasionally President Louis Napoleon appears as himself, in the company of other identifiable personages of his regime (fig. 10). It is the fictional Ratapoil, however, who dominates Daumier's political caricatures in the closing days of the Second Republic; conversely, the more literal-minded Vernier generally represented Louis Napoleon in direct form.[45] Both satiric personages predictably vanished from the pages of *Le Charivari* with Louis Napoleon's coup d'état of December 2, 1851. At that volatile moment, the journal suspended publication for a week, and then reappeared featuring a "safe" nonpolitical satire of lawyers by Daumier. Caricature's days of openly anti-Bonapartist opposition were, for the moment, over.

Once Louis Napoleon seized political control in 1851, and subsequently declared himself emperor of France in 1852, rigorous press censorship laws were once again reestablished. As in the later July Monarchy, the person of the ruler was off limits to caricaturists. The emperor assembled a massive bureau of censors to police the images of his new regime, and Daumier and colleagues were once again officially ordered to suspend political critique.

The oppositional leadership of *Le Charivari* sought ways to circumvent the new authoritarian restrictions; an obvious ploy was simply to work in ex-

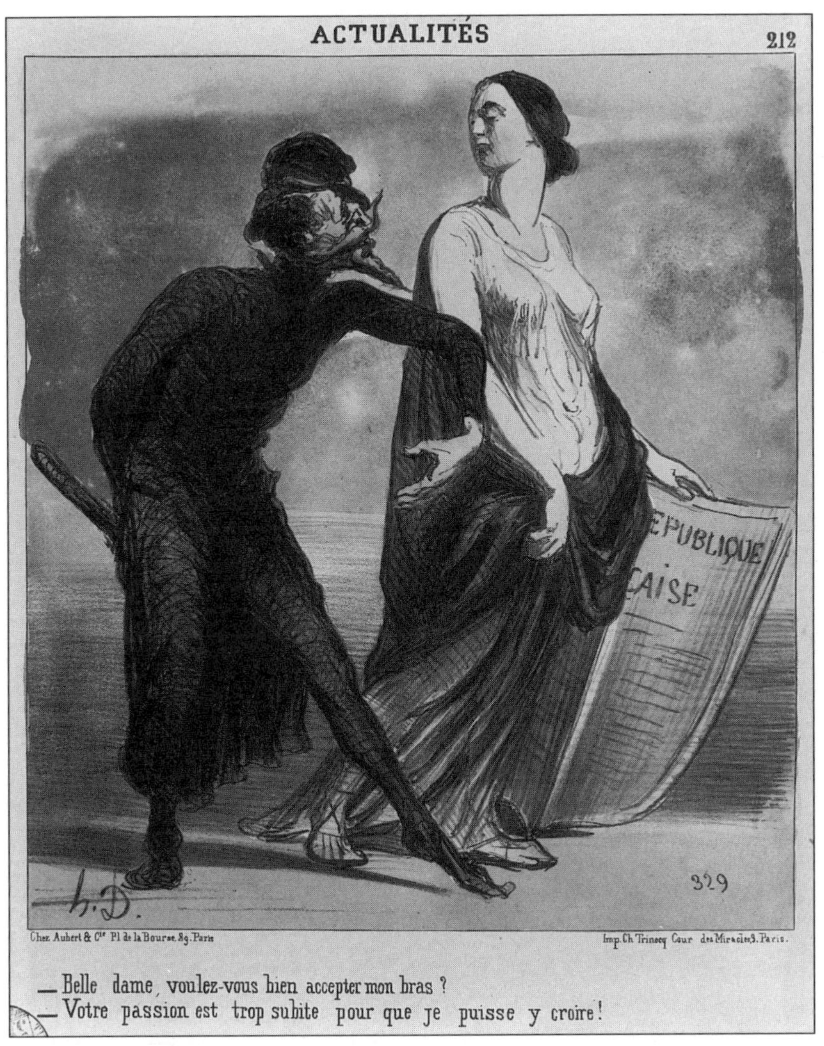

FIG. 9. Honoré Daumier, *—Beautiful lady, would you take my arm? —Your passion is too sudden to be believed!* in *Le Charivari*, September 25, 1851. Lithograph, Delteil 2153, 35.9×28.6 cm (14⅛×11¼ in.). Print Collection, Miriam and Ira D. Wallach Division of Art, Prints and Photographs, The New York Public Library, Astor, Lenox and Tilden Foundations, New York.

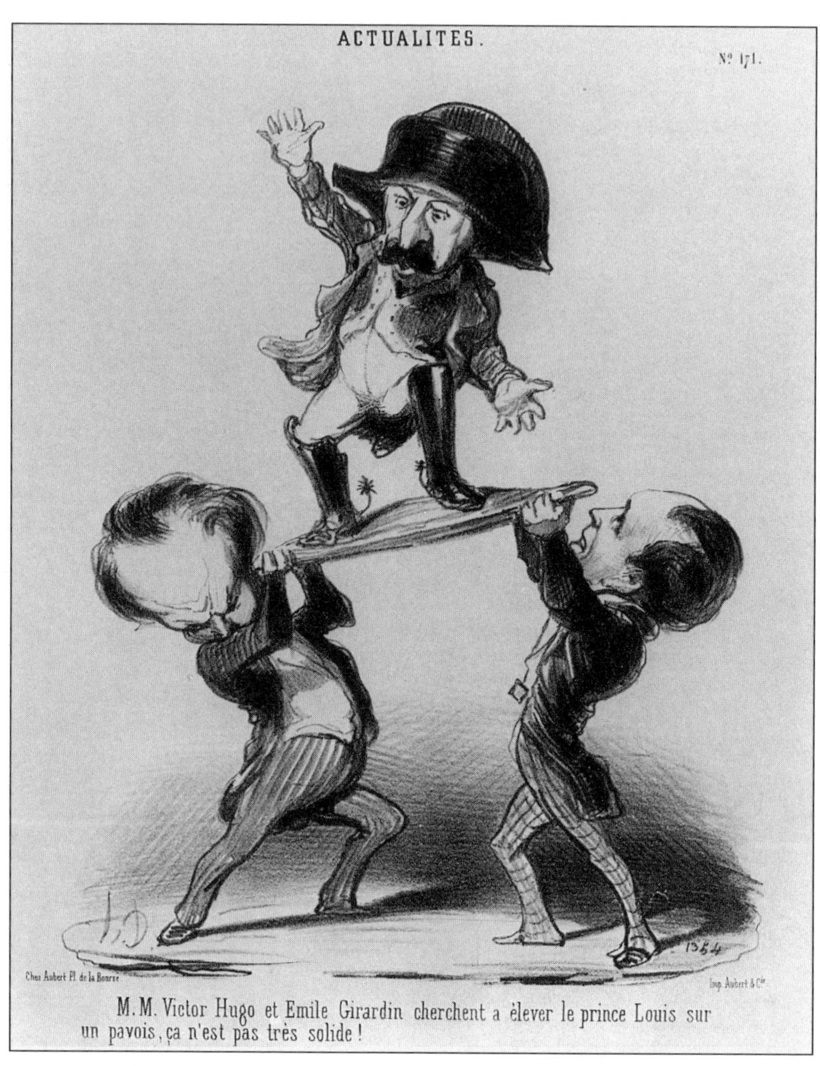

FIG. 10. Honoré Daumier, *Victor Hugo and Emile Girardin trying to lift Prince Louis on the King's shield; it's not very solid!* in *Le Charivari*, December 11, 1848. Lithograph, Delteil 1756, 35.1×26.8 cm (13⅞×10½ in.). Armand Hammer Daumier and Contemporaries Collection, UCLA at the Armand Hammer Museum of Art and Cultural Center, Los Angeles.

ile. A sister journal, *Le Charivari belge*, was published in Brussels during most of the Second Empire.[46] Its articles and images were much the same as those found in the pages of its Parisian version, with one crucial difference: In Brussels, outside the reach of the police censors, oppositional satire could flourish. Anti-Bonapartist caricatures testify to the fires of resistance blazing beneath the surface of the muffled French *Le Charivari*. These images, many by anonymous hands, are keys to the secret agenda of the repressed French journal—marginalized voices that spoke ideas unutterable at the political center. While Daumier did not contribute any political prints to this paper, some of his colleagues, such as the prolific Cham, created political caricatures expressly for the Belgian edition. Daumier and others working for *Le Charivari* in Paris were undoubtedly aware of the agenda of this sister publication, in which the anti-Bonapartist satires are direct and unforgiving. In one example, Louis Napoleon is charged with the murder of Liberty as she lies dead in a coffin marked "Born 1848; died 1851" (fig. 11).[47] In this battle of bodies for the soul of France, the emperor stands as victor and executioner. In the background on a pennant hangs the image of Daumier's Ratapoil—the symbol of repression which had just been forced out of the pages of the Parisian journal by the new censorship laws.

In Brussels, a scatological discourse of opposition could flourish. A print of 1854 shows Louis Napoleon crawling out of the Paris sewers, filthy with the muck of his journey, and admitting (like Louis Philippe earlier, in the pages of *La Caricature*) that he has dirtied himself considerably to arrive at the palace of power (fig. 12). In Belgian exile, the very subject of censorship and representation could be freely addressed. In a variation of the biblical theme of temptation a kneeling figure of the Parisian *Charivari* struggles to resist the lure of taboo political subjects (fig. 13). A complex game of looking is at work here. The magic lantern of political topics presented to *Charivari* frames the political field of events open to the satirical crayon; *Charivari*'s vision in turn is subject to surveillance by the watchful Louis Napoleon in the background. By implication it is the Belgian journal, in the hands of an actual reader, that now keeps Louis Napoleon under the managing surveillance of caricature, and the symbolic empowerment of laughter and disrespect.

The Second Empire viewed the Belgian journal as a threat; even into the 1860s, the mere possession of an issue of *Le Charivari belge* within French borders could result in imprisonment.[48] As of 1852, all political satire of the new emperor, Napoleon III, was illegal. He is generally considered to have been thoroughly successful in censoring the opposition press, particularly during the early years of the Second Empire.[49] Napoleon III constructed a

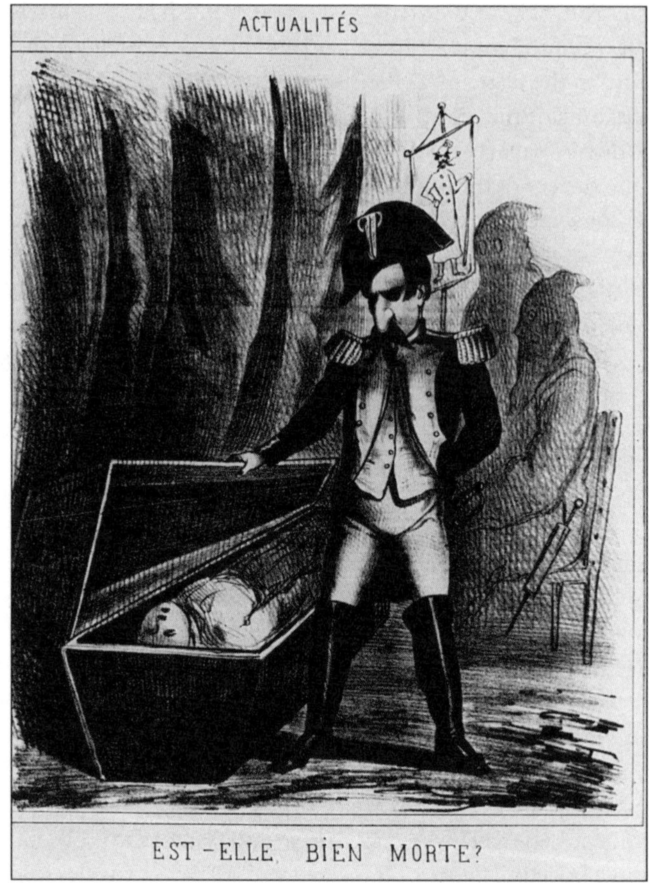

FIG. 11. Anon., *Is she truly dead?* in *Le Charivari* (Brussels), April 18, 1852. Lithograph, 28.3×21.9 cm (11⅛×8⅝ in.). Bibliothèque Royale, Brussels.

public image of himself that drew on the myths of glory associated with his illustrious uncle, Napoleon I. But it is here, with the very image of the ruler, that Daumier took inventive and subtle liberties in order to continue the anti-Bonapartist critique he had begun during the less censorious days of the Second Republic.

This critique begins with the widely understood relationship between Napoleon I and Napoleon III: the latter imitated the former for his own political advancement. During the closing days of the Second Republic, Republicans turned this relationship to their own ends by comparing Louis

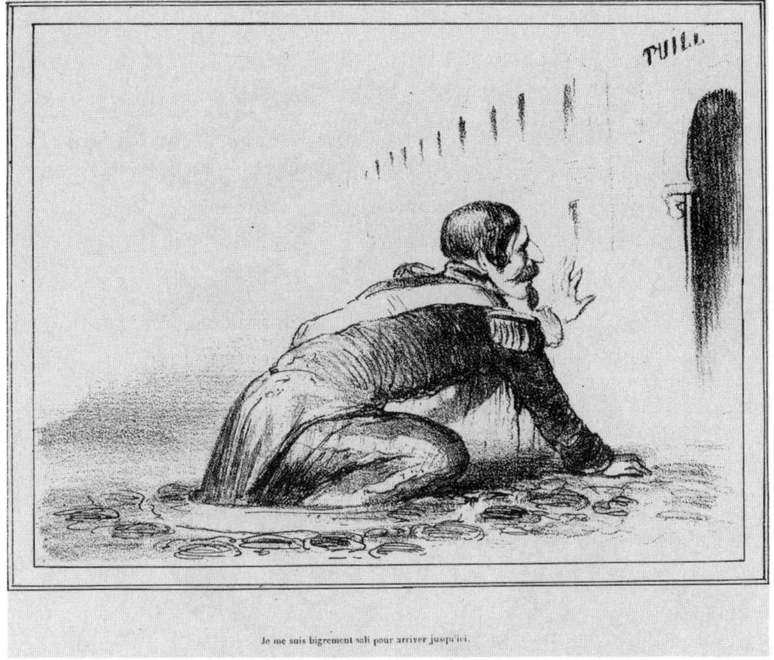

FIG. 12. Anon., *I have dirtied the crap out of myself in order to get this far!* in *Le Charivari belge*, September 14, 1854.
Lithograph, 21.9×28.3 cm ($8\frac{5}{8}\times 11\frac{1}{8}$ in.).
Bibliothèque Royale, Brussels.

Napoleon to another imitator of Napoleon I. Soulouque was the black general who became president of Haiti in 1848, and then proclaimed himself emperor in 1849. A self-declared imitator of Napoleon, he modeled his military and court rituals after the grandeur of the First Empire in France. He was described at length in the French press as an extravagant and authoritarian despot who routinely used violence and intimidation to retain control.

Soulouque emerged in satirical journals of the Second Republic (which did not labor under censorship) as an exotic parallel to President Louis Napoleon. The caricaturist Cham initiated the satire of Soulouque, making more than sixty caricatures of the black emperor between October 1848 and March 1850. Cham's images emphasize Soulouque's barbaric and despotic behavior. Another caricaturist, known as Nadar, turned to the Soulouque topos in 1850, the year the Haitian leader proclaimed himself emperor. In 1850 in *Le Journal pour rire*, Nadar directly asserts the parallel between Sou-

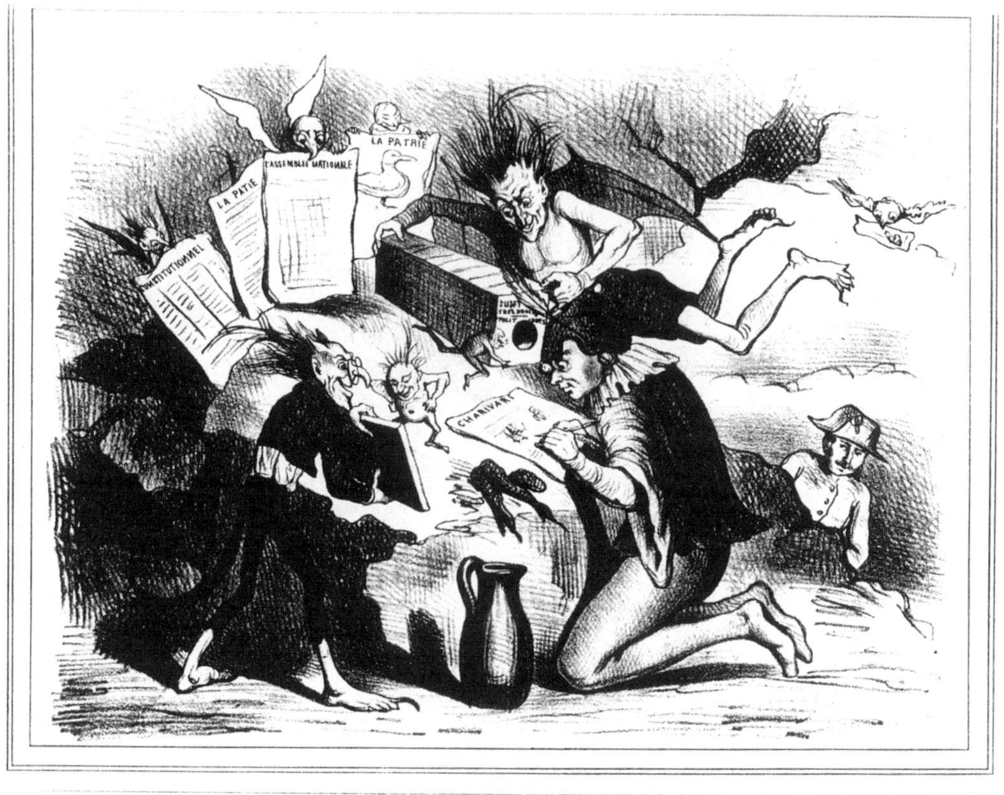

VADE RETRO, SATANAS!
PRIERE du CHARIVARI....... Et ne nos inducas in tentationem, sed libera nos a malo

FIG. 13. Anon., *Get thee behind me, Satan! The prayer of Charivari . . . And lead us not into temptation, but deliver us from evil* in *Le Charivari* (Brussels), May 5, 1852. Lithograph, 21.9×28.3 cm (8⅝×11⅛ in.). Bibliothèque Royale, Brussels.

louque and Napoleon by substituting Soulouque for the statue of Napoleon by Émile Seurre that stood atop the Vendôme column in Paris (fig. 14). Later in the same journal, Nadar clearly linked Soulouque's napoleonic make-over to the political ambitions of President Louis Napoleon.[50] This exotic epithet coined by the caricaturists of the left caught on: at the time of Louis Napoleon's coup d'état in 1851, Republicans ran through the streets denouncing the French president as "Soulouque the Traitor." The international press

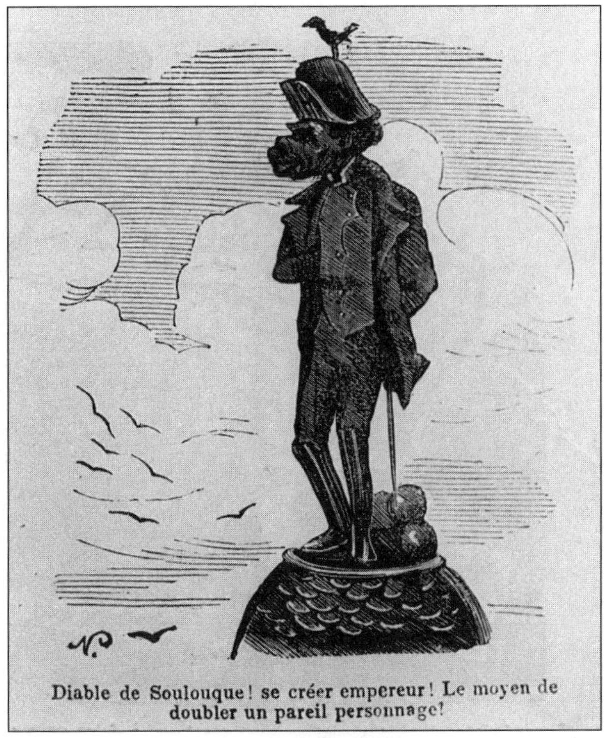

FIG. 14. Nardar [Félix Tournachon]. *That devil Soulouque! Making himself Emperor! What a way to double the same personage!* in *Le Journal pour rire*, March 30, 1850.
Woodcut, private collection.

came to refer to Louis Napoleon as "The French Soulouque—the Grand Imitator."[51]

Daumier first deployed Soulouque in the censor-free period of July 1850 as a barbaric despot who angrily plunges a terrified journalist into a boiling caldron (fig. 15). Soulouque punishes the European for his articles that criticize the black emperor's regime. The satire does not, as we might expect, concern any current event in Haiti, but speaks in the code of established Republican discourse about the repressive action of Louis Napoleon, whose government had just seized an issue of the Republican newspaper *Le Siècle* in Paris. The joke here is undeniably racist: long-standing clichés of barbaric behavior among blacks are invoked to underline the despotic nature of the president.

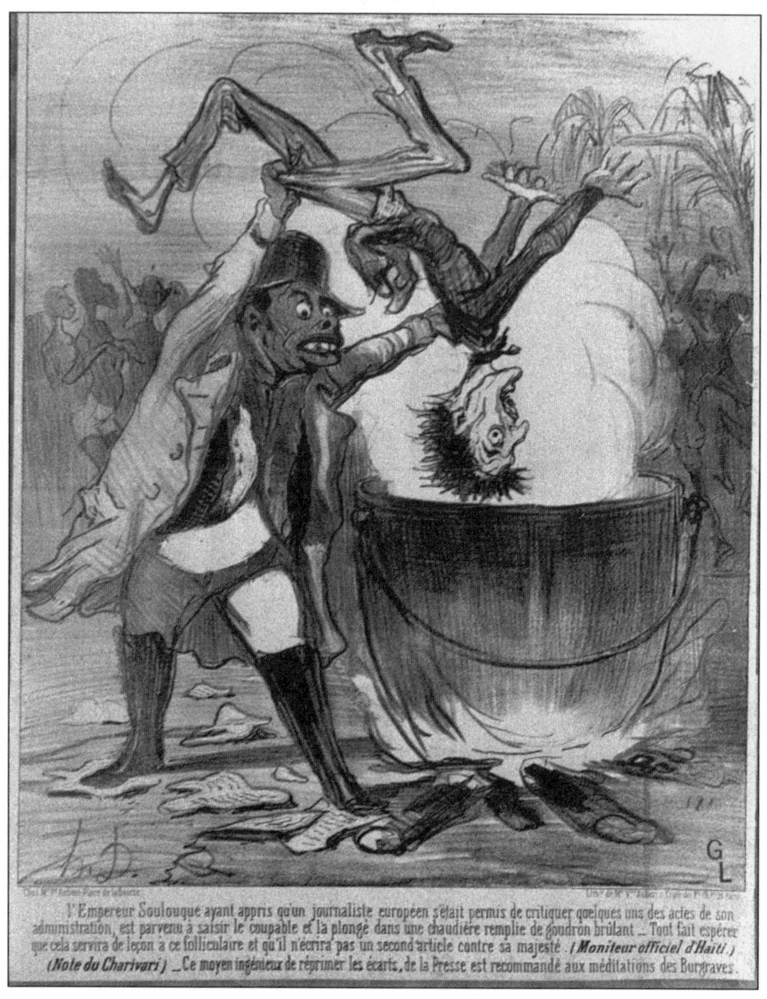

FIG. 15. Honoré Daumier, *The Emperor Soulouque, having learned that a European journalist dared to criticize some of the acts of his administration, has succeeded in seizing the guilty one and plunging him into a cauldron full of boiling tar—in the hopes that this will serve as a lesson to this hack writer and that he will not write a second article against His Majesty (from the newspaper 'Moniteur officiel d'Haiti')* . . . , in *Le Charivari*, June 15, 1850. Lithograph, Delteil 2015, 36.8×24.3 cm (14½×9½ in.). Armand Hammer Daumier and Contemporaries Collection, UCLA at the Armand Hammer Museum of Art and Cultural Center, Los Angeles.

The era's Republican ideals of social equality extended only to white males, and their political idealism did not stop caricaturists from exploiting racist stereotypes in their satiric maneuvers. Once strict censorship laws were in effect again in the Second Empire, the use of Soulouque as an exotic surrogate became part of *Le Charivari*'s strategy for continuing political critique in the face of regulation. The choice of a black surrogate also coincided with the oppositional discourse of scatology we have seen at work in caricature of the July Monarchy: casting Louis Napoleon in blackface may also be seen as a variation of the ruler "dirtying" or blackening himself, another form of self-degradation in the argot of the period.

In defiance of the Second Empire's censorship policy, Daumier and some of his contemporaries at *Le Charivari* continued in the 1850s to parody the regime of Napoleon III through the exotic personage of Soulouque. Daumier used an exaggeratedly simian black body to mock the French emperor as "uncivilized" and "animalistic"—as a coward who hides in the trees while his troops are massacred (a coded reference in 1856 to Louis Napoleon's absence from the bloody and disease-ridden battlefields of the Crimean War); or as a general lazily sleeping in the jungle, a realm of languor that is suggested as his natural habitat by his physiognomic resemblance to his monkey companions (fig. 16). His appearance elsewhere as a brutal despot in a Polichinelle style puppet show (Delteil 2637) clearly invokes Décembriste violence through the baton, a symbol widely associated through Ratapoil with the repressive acts of President Louis Napoleon.

In retrospect, it is perhaps hard to imagine how the censors could let such images pass. Yet it was a brilliant ploy for the caricaturists to ground their Bonaparte surrogate in a contemporary context of foreign politics. The multiplicity of meanings of the Soulouque prints—their connections with a diverse field of cultural referents, as had been the case with *La Poire*—made it impossible for censors to discern a single, stable meaning for any image. (One could imagine Philipon arguing that if you arrest one artist for a Soulouque image, you have to arrest any artist who decides to make an image of any emperor.) The actual practice of censorship was a fast-paced business; one-time judgments of images were meted quickly by censors with little knowledge or understanding of the opposition's culture of argot. These official judges were ill-equipped to follow the transformations of meaning in a humor generated by a competing ideology. It was hard if not impossible to pin down the subtle sentiments of resistance that survived in a network of coded displacement and surrogacy. The strategy of exoticism in political caricature was successful: there is surprisingly no evidence of any Soulouque

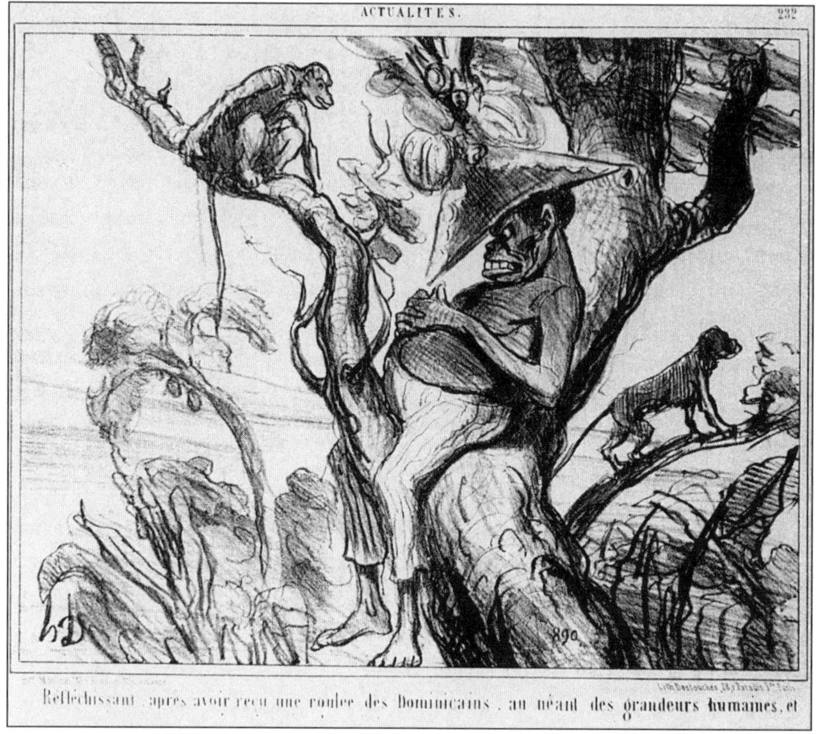

FIG. 16. Honoré Daumier, *After having received a thrashing from the Dominicans, reflecting on the emptiness of human grandeur, and beginning to envy the lot of the simplest monkeys* in *Le Charivari*, March 5, 1856. Lithograph, Delteil 3145, 25.6×37.5 cm (10 1/16×14 3/4 in.). Armand Hammer Daumier and Contemporaries Collection, UCLA at the Armand Hammer Museum of Art and Cultural Center, Los Angeles.

prints ever being censored.[52] In fact, the artists at *Le Charivari* during the Second Empire seem to have been generally more adept in escaping censorship than the team working for the journal during the July Monarchy. This is surely due both to the lessons learned from experience and to savvy strategizing: As Félix Ribeyre observed in 1862, "*Le Charivari* sait se tenir à l'écart du scandale"—they know how to swerve to avoid scandal.[53]

And the caricaturists were not alone in devising artistic strategies to stage political critique in the public arena of the Second Empire. A convincing study of Courbet's *The Artist's Studio*, shown in the Universal Exhibition of

1855, identifies the prominent figure of the *braconnier*, or poacher, in the left section of the painting as a coded portrait of Louis Napoleon, ridiculing him as a common thief who has poached the riches of the Republic of France.[54] Indeed, Linda Nochlin suggests that Courbet intended his massive realist manifesto as "a political cartoon writ large: an allegory of the venality, or at least the futility of present political conduct and hope for a more positive political future."[55] That the ambitious painters of realism shared some of the strategies of the cartoonists for evading the repressive political atmosphere of their time reveals the permeability and cross-fertilization of the so-called spheres of high and low art in this early period of modernism. In spite of Napoleon III's best efforts in the early Second Empire, oppositional political art had its venues and its audiences.

With the liberalization of Napoleon III's government in the 1860s, the reins of press censorship loosened considerably in the late Second Empire. Nonetheless, the Ministry of the Interior continued to watch *Le Charivari*, categorized as a paper of liberal opposition and needing surveillance "as much for its deviations of the pen as for its bad spirit."[53] With the establishment of the Third Republic, fewer press regulations were enforced, and by 1881 the French government gave up altogether attempting to regulate political caricature.[54] Daumier's final productive period as a caricaturist coincided with the censor-free period of the Commune and the early days of the Third Republic. The persistence of his Republican sentiments emerges forcefully in these latter days. In one of Daumier's last caricatures, the infamous personages from his earlier career—Ratapoil and *la Poire* (inscribed on the sleeve of the baton-carrying Ratapoil at left) return in *This chest belongs to no one* (fig. 17), as incarnations of the repressive and exploitative past who have returned to urge the new monarchist Republic to loot the abandoned riches of France.

The great power in the humor of satire is to suggest a potentially different world order. During various trials for press offenses, Philipon's defenders often tried to convince the government that these prints need not be taken too seriously, as they were mere safety valves for the release of political tension. Philipon's lawyer appealed to the jury: "Better these sketches than periodic upheavals."[58] But both caricaturists and government alike knew that political caricature was at some level no laughing matter: its humor and energy nourished the spirit of resistance, critique, and even revolution. Philipon boasted in *La Caricature* of April 28, 1831, that caricature had already become a power, a weapon to strike "the enemies of our liberties." The government of both the July Monarchy and the Second Empire feared the image

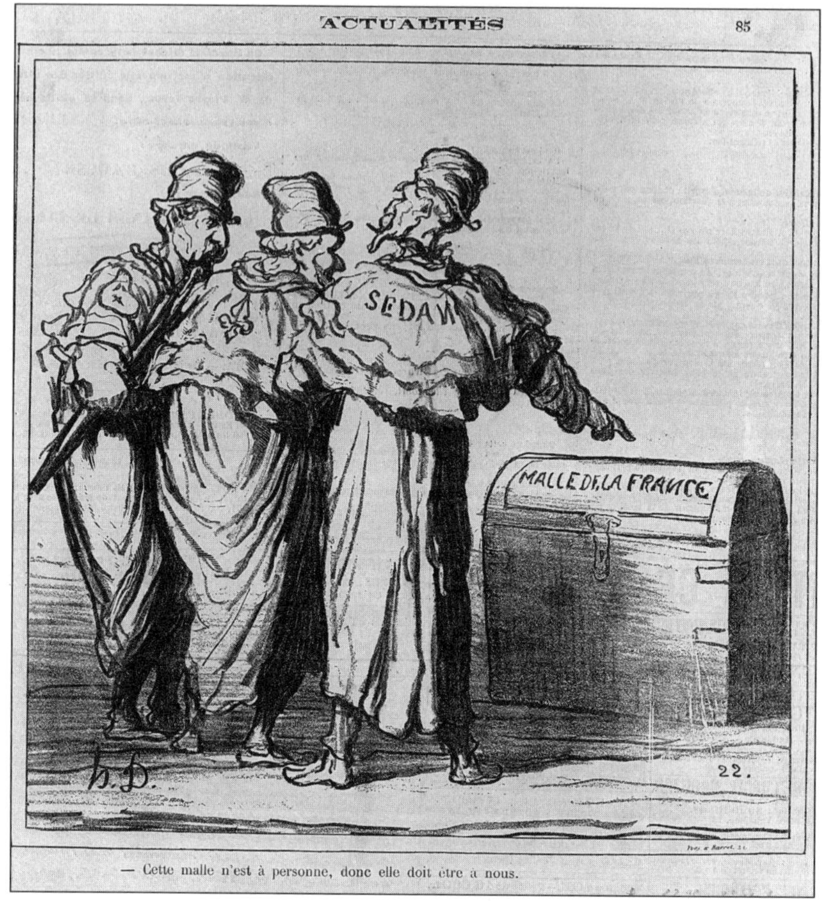

FIG. 17. Honoré Daumier, *This chest belongs to no one; therefore it ought to be ours!* in *Le Charivari*, May 6, 1872.
Lithograph, Delteil 3921, 24.6×23.4 cm (9$\frac{2}{3}$×9$\frac{1}{4}$ in.). All rights reserved, The Department of Drawings and Prints, The Metropolitan Museum of Art, New York.

more than the text, as it conveyed instantaneously an alternative, a different political and social space where radical dislocations of the status quo existed in the suspended moment of the laugh. Its power was openly acknowledged in 1835: as *Le National* observed, "[the government] made these laws in part to escape from Philipon [and his artists]. . . . They suppressed *La Caricature* because they could not fight with it."[59] These caricatures by Daumier and his contemporaries testify that the censorship laws, however ambitious, could not, in the end, eliminate or effectively police the power of the laugh or the liberty of the crayon.

Proving to be a stimulus, a creative irritant in its nettlesome requirements and monolithic restrictions, censorship has at times contributed to the dynamism of modern artistic life. Attempts to stabilize and regulate artistic expression have often had a reverse effect, encouraging some artists to cultivate alternative forms or venues, and to symbolically resist the authority of institutions. This position of opposition characterized much of early avant-garde artistic production. And it is at that juncture, in the reexamination of the province of political art *outside* of the realm of official visual culture, that caricature flourished, and offered visions of a provocative reordering of the modern world.

NOTES

1. I have presented several earlier versions of this essay in lectures, most recently in the Frank B. Davis Memorial Lectures on art and censorship at the Courtauld Institute of Art, London, in November 1993. Much of the research for this study derives from work supported in 1991 by an ACLS Fellowship for Recent Recipients of the Ph.D. All Delteil numbers in the text are from Loys Delteil, *Le Peintre-Graveur Illustré: Honoré Daumier*, 11 vols. (Paris: Chez L'Auteur, 1925–30).

2. See Ernst Kantorowicz, *The King's Two Bodies* (Princeton: Princeton University Press, 1953), p. 7; see also Nicholas Mirzoeff, *Bodyscape: Art, Modernity and the Ideal Figure* (New York: Routledge, 1995), chapter 2.

3. The early history of French caricature supports this idea, as Louis Philippe's government did not in its own turn use satire to demean those factions it wished to repress. Similarly, the government journals of the Second Empire do not contain satirical derision of competing political ideologies. To grant such attention to the opposition might have seemed unnecessary, or perhaps might have been seen as an admission not only of the presence but of the power of the opposition.

4. Michel Melot, "Daumier and Art History: Aesthetic Judgement/Political Judgement," *Oxford Art Journal* 11, no. 1 (1988): 3–24.

5. Étienne Carjat quoted in Edmond Bazire, "Les Obsèques de Daumier," *Le Rappel*, February 19, 1879.

6. Anon., "Échos de Partout," *La Révolution française*, February 13, 1879.

7. See clippings on the dedication of Daumier's grave, April 15, 1880, Archives de la Préfecture de la Police, Paris, file E A/42 2 (document 14, page 3).

8. James Cuno, "Charles Philipon, La Maison Aubert, and the Business of Caricature in Paris, 1829–41," *Art Journal* 43, no. 4 (Winter 1983): 347–54.

9. Quoted in Robert Justin Goldstein, *Censorship of Political Caricature in Nineteenth-Century France* (Kent, Ohio: Kent State University Press, 1989), 125.

10. See Cuno, "Charles Philipon" (1983), 347–54, and his "Charles Philipon and La Maison Aubert: The Business, Politics and Public of Caricature in Paris, 1820–1840," Ph.D. dissertation, Harvard University, 1985.

11. See James Cuno, "Violence, Satire and Social Types in the Graphic Art of the July Monarchy," in Petra Ten-Doesschate Chu and Gabriel P. Weisberg, eds., *The Popularization of Images: Visual Culture under the July Monarchy* (Princeton: Princeton University Press, 1994), 10–36.

12. Goldstein, *Censorship*, 122.

13. Cuno, "Charles Philipon" (1983), 351.

14. The caricature, published in February 1831 by Aubert, is reproduced in Goldstein, *Censorship*, 135.

15. The print was published in *La Caricature* on June 30, 1831.

16. See Elise K. Kenney and John M. Merriman, *The Pear: French Graphic Arts in the Golden Age of Caricature* (South Hadley: Mount Holyoke College Art Museum, 1991).

17. See *La Charivari*, February 27, 1834, and May 1, 1835; also *La Caricature*, August 17, 1835.

18. See Gabriel Weisberg, "In Deep Shit: The Coded Images of Traviès in the July Monarchy," *Art Journal* 52, no. 3 (Fall 1993): 36–40.

19. *La Caricature*, November 24, 1832.

20. I am grateful to Robert Herbert for this suggestion.

21. See Elizabeth C. Childs, "Big Trouble: Daumier, *Gargantua*, and the Censorship of Political Caricature," *Art Journal* 51, no. 1 (Spring 1992): 26–37.

22. The only impressions known to me are at the Rose Art Museum at Brandeis University, the Armand Hammer Museum of Art and Cultural Center in Los Angeles, and at the Bibliothèque Nationale in Paris.

23. Quoted in Goldstein, *Censorship*, 4.

24. See Delteil nos. 197 and 209.

25. For a complete list of the Delteil numbers of these prints, see Louis Provost, *Honoré Daumier: A Thematic Guide to the Oeuvre*, ed. Elizabeth C. Childs (London and New York: Garland, 1989), 26.

26. Childs, "Big Trouble," 31–33.

27. Hugh Honour, *Chinoiserie: The Vision of Cathay* (New York: Dutton, 1961), 204.

28. See M. Dorothy George, ed., *Catalogue of Political and Personal Satire Preserved in the Department of Prints and Drawings in the British Museum*, microfilm, vol. 9, no. 12749; vol. 10, nos. 13889 and 14400.

29. See Charles Tilly, *The Contentious French: Four Centuries of Popular Struggle* (Cambridge: Harvard University Press, 1986), 33. I am grateful to Wayne TeBrake for this reference.

30. Soon after the September Laws went into effect, the journal suffered serious

financial setbacks and lower subscription rates, and Philipon sold *Le Charivari*. For a brief history of the administration of the journal, see Elizabeth Childs, "Honoré Daumier and the Exotic Vision: Studies in French Culture and Caricature, 1830–1870," Ph.D. dissertation, Columbia University, 1989, 76–84.

31. Michael Paul Driskel, "Singing 'The Marseillaise' in 1840: The Case of Charlet's Censored Prints," *Art Bulletin* 69, no. 4 (December 1987): 621.

32. This summary is based on entries in the ledger at the Archives Nationales, Paris, F 18* VI 48.

33. For the woodcut *en-tête* designs, see Eugène Bouvy, *Daumier: l'oeuvre gravé du maître* (Paris: Maurice Le Garrec, 1933), nos. 1 and 7.

34. Letter from Minister of Interior to Minister of Justice, August 6, 1841. Archives Nationales, BB 18 1396 (2289).

35. Archival records of *Le Charivari* for this period include Archives Nationales, BB 17 A 95 (no. 9); BB 18 1242 (no. 4257); BB 18 1233 (no. 2474); and BB 21 412 (S.9 6465).

36. The article was published in *Le Charivari* on December 1, 1838. Beauger served eight months in prison and paid a very heavy fine of 6,000 francs. On his unsuccessful appeal, see Archives Nationales, BB 24 170-186 (S.2884).

37. For a more detailed history of Daumier's censored prints, and the general history of *Le Charivari* and censorship, see Childs, "Daumier and the Exotic Vision," chapter 1 and appendices II and III.

38. Driskel, "Singing 'The Marseillaise.' "

39. See Marie-Claude Chaudonneret, *La Figure de la République: Le concours de 1848*, Notes et documents des musées de France (*Paris: Reúnion des musées nationaux*, 1987).

40. See *Le Charivari*, May 28, 29, and 30, 1851, for reports of the trial. The censored caricature by Vernier is reproduced in Goldstein, *Censorship*, 177.

41. Léopold Panier, the journal's *gérant responsable*, was given a six-month sentence and a 2,000 franc fine; Vernier was given a lighter sentence of two months in prison and a fine of 100 francs. Results of the trial were reported in *Le Charivari* on May 28, 1851, and responses to the verdict appeared on May 29 and 30.

42. Archives Nationales, BB 21 373 (no. 4172-S8).

43. *Le Charivari*, October 10, 1851.

44. For an excellent discussion of the origin of Daumier's Ratapoil figure, see Suzanne Glover Lindsay's entry for the bronze cast of *Ratapoil* in her *French Sculpture of the Nineteenth Century in the Collections of the National Gallery of Art Systematic Catalogue* (New York: Oxford University Press, 1997). My thanks to Suzanne Lindsay for sharing her research with me while it was still in press. See also T. J. Clark, *The Absolute Bourgeois: Artists and Politics in France, 1848–1851* (Greenwich: New York Graphic Society, 1973), 105.

45. Between July 1 and December 2, 1851, seventeen (perhaps eighteen) caricatures

by Daumier and one by Vernier in *Le Charivari* featured Ratapoil. During the same period, two caricatures by Daumier and eight by Vernier depicted Louis Napoleon directly.

46. A Belgian edition of the French *Le Charivari* appeared in February 1852. This paper reproduced most of the articles and caricatures in the French edition, but promoted itself as offering readers two uncensored lithographs per week. In 1852 a purely Belgian edition of the paper appeared.

47. The satire is a chilling parody of a well-known history painting, *Cromwell Examining Charles I's Body*, 1831, by Paul Delaroche (Musée des Beaux-Arts, Nîmes).

48. Archives Nationales, BB 24 687-709 (Registre 5.63, no. 3863).

49. See Natalie Isser, *The Second Empire and the Press: A Study of Government-Inspired Brochures in French Foreign Policy in Their Propaganda Milieu* (The Hague: Nijhoff, 1974).

50. See Nadar, "Odyssée du Prince-Président Soulouque accompagné du E. F. Ragotin et Montalenvers," *Le Journal pour rire*, September 27, 1850.

51. For a more complete discussion of the Soulouque series, see Elizabeth Childs, "The Secret Agents of Satire: Daumier, Censorship, and the Image of the Exotic in Political Caricature, 1850–1860," in *Proceedings of the Annual Meeting of the Western Society for French History* 17 (1990): 334–45.

52. We should note that the censorship records for the Second Empire are incomplete. See Childs, "Daumier and the Exotic Vision," 87. Given the longevity of the Soulouque personage in *Le Charivari*, however, it seems reasonable to surmise that the figure was not condemned by censors.

53. Jules Brazen and Félix Ribeyre, *Grands journaux de France* (Paris: Jouast Père, 1862), 411–12.

54. Hélène Toussaint, "The Dossier on 'The Studio' by Courbet," in *Courbet*, exh. cat., Arts Council of Great Britain, 1978, 265–66.

55. Linda Nochlin, "Ending with the Ending: The Politics of Place, the Place of Hope," in Sarah Faunce and Linda Nochlin, *Courbet Reconsidered*, exh. cat., The Brooklyn Museum, 1988, 38–39.

56. Archives Nationales, report by A. Langlé, October 22, 1866, AN series F 18 294 (193).

57. For a complete history of the breakdown of censorship, see Goldstein, *Censorship*.

58. Ibid., 136.

59. *Le National* as quoted in *Le Charivari*, September 9, 1835.

Manet's *Maximilian*: Censorship and the Salon

JOHN HOUSE

ONE OF THE PERSISTENT THEMES in the histories of modern art has been the rejection of innovative, controversial works of art by exhibition selection committees or other authorities. The activities of the juries at the Paris Salon throughout the nineteenth century have been central to these histories. At first sight the Salon jury would seem to have filled a role comparable to that of formal censors who vetted every published image and stage presentation during most of the century, yet it would be simplistic and misleading to equate Salon rejection with censorship. This essay seeks to explore the distinctions between the two modes of suppression, and the different functions and interests they served. The career of Édouard Manet provides a central focus.

On one occasion Manet was the victim of direct political censorship. He was informed that if he submitted his canvas *The Execution of the Emperor Maximilian* (fig. 1) to the Salon of 1869, it would be rejected; any decision by the jury was thus preempted. By contrast, the most famous instance of his rejection by the jury, his three Salon submissions of 1863, including *Le Bain* (*Le Déjeuner sur l'herbe*), was not in a direct sense a form of censorship, since the pictures were exhibited, with many other works rejected by the jury, in the Salon des Refusés, set up by official decree alongside the Salon itself. By appearing in the Refusés, these works did have the stigma of official disapproval attached to them, and in this sense the exhibition could be seen as a germ of the strategy of the "Entartete Kunst" exhibition in Munich in 1937 (see the essay by Christoph Zuschlag in the present volume). However, viewed from another perspective, the fact that the government allowed them

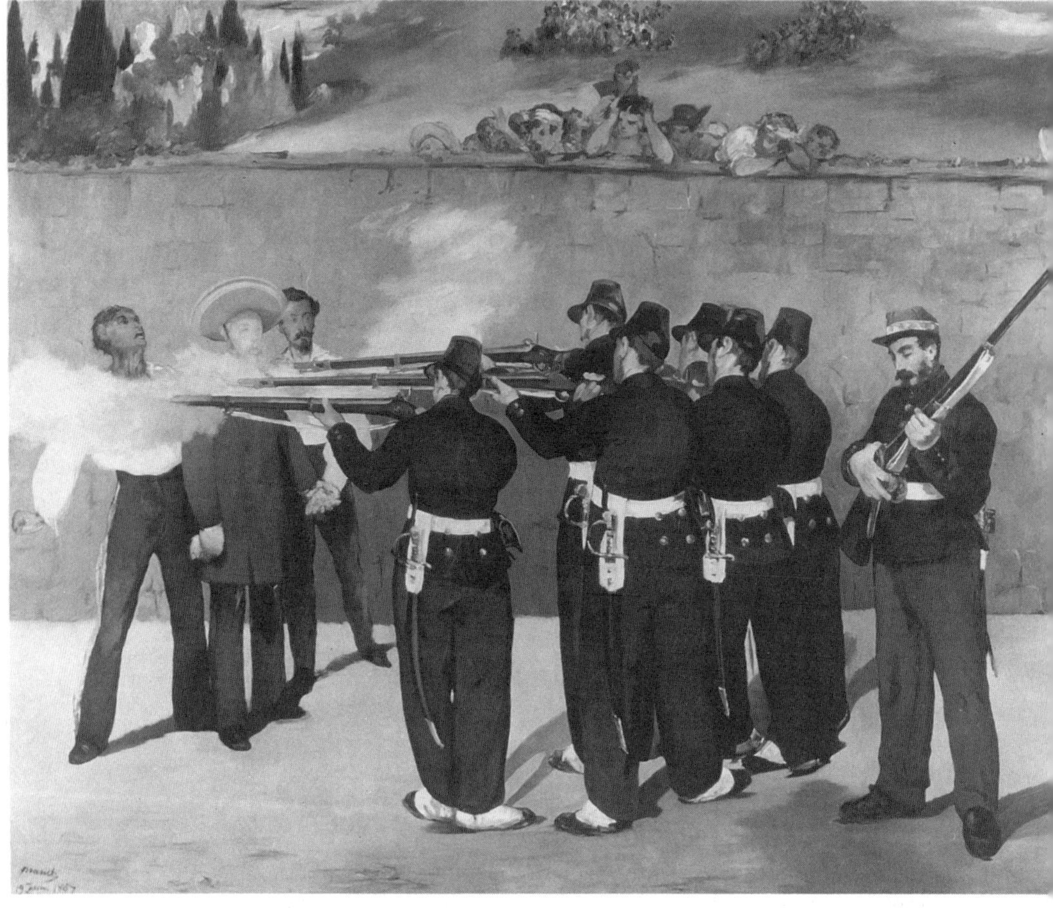

FIG. 1. Édouard Manet, *The Execution of the Emperor Maximilian*, 1868–69. Oil on canvas, 252×302 cm (99×119 in.). Städtische Kunsthalle, Mannheim.

to be displayed at all, in a period of strict censorship, shows that they were not regarded as threatening through their mere appearance. The situation was quite different with *The Execution of the Emperor Maximilian*.

Any discussion of censorship in nineteenth-century France must emphasize the degrees of control applied to different forms of expression, as well as the different structures of surveillance to which they were subject. Only theatrical performances and printed images required prior authorization. The written word in newspapers could be suppressed after publication, and might make the newspaper liable to suspension or closure, and its directors liable to imprisonment and fines.[1]

Two separate issues were at stake in Second Empire censorship—the effect of visual images and the question of social class. The authorities were particularly wary of the potency of visual experience, in the form of a print or a stage representation or a performance of a popular café-concert song;[2] but the question of class—of determining what types of material should be permitted for which social groups—seems to have been the most fundamental concern. A circular from the minister of police at the time of the press laws of 1852 explained the particular reasons for concern about visual images:

> Among the means used to disrupt and destroy the feelings of reserve and morality that it is so essential to maintain at the heart of a well-ordered society, prints [*la gravure*] are one of the most dangerous. The worst page of a bad book needs time to be read and a certain amount of intelligence to be understood, while prints offer a sort of personification of the thought; they throw it into relief and in some sense give it movement and life. . . .[3]

The reasons for theater censorship, as against the considerable latitude offered to printed books, were spelled out by a supporter of censorship in 1862: while books operated on individuals in private and silently, theatrical performances had an immediate impact on whole groups of people, and specifically on the "masses," on "popular imaginations."[4]

The question of class is central in both of these accounts. Books were seen as the province of the bourgeoisie; the theater and prints in newspapers and magazines were accessible even to the illiterate. Yet what was at issue was not simply the question of literacy, as emerges from the long campaign to control the material sold by *colporteurs*, itinerant salesmen in the countryside. *Colportage* presented a dual problem, both because it distributed material to the lowest classes and because the material that *colporteurs* sold was produced by small unregulated printing presses all over the country. The 1849 regulations, in force throughout the Second Empire and supervised by the *colportage* commission set up in 1852, demanded that every copy of every item sold by *colporteurs*, whether verbal or visual, should be individually stamped before sale. The importance of these controls was spelled out in an 1853 report:

> This commission is responsible for directing the lower class press, far more important than the press which is intended to influence the upper classes. *Colportage* is the means by which one can corrupt or moralize the popular classes, and the role of these masses is important for governments. The only stable and truly

> conservative governments are those that understand the necessity of concern for the lower classes and know how to revive their feelings, instincts, beliefs and enthusiasms.[5]

When applied strictly, the censorship regulations during the Second Empire revealed an official sensitivity that verged on paranoia, but there was vigorous debate within government circles as to whether the interests of the regime were best served by strict repression or a measured permissiveness combined with positive propaganda.[6] A report by the government theater censors in 1862 shows how broad their terms of reference were. Four distinct types of material were banned, those that threatened "the interests of public morality, the interests of social order and the politics of the government, the interests of religion, and propriety and taste in references to individuals or things."[7]

A few examples will show the types of imagery that were found threatening or problematic in the theater. Questions of sexual morality were the most frequent, but a wide range of subjects might raise anxieties that were broadly political. Government functionaries, priests, or the military could not be criticized or ridiculed.[8] Contemporary political themes were virtually impossible, and criticism of Napoleon I was particularly excluded, but even themes from past regimes to which the Second Empire was unsympathetic were closely controlled, in case they aroused active political responses.[9] In one case, a chorus in an opera which projected a "sentiment of revolt" was suppressed, not because of the performance itself, "in an outstanding theater and in front of an elite public," but through fears that the slogan *Aux armes* might be repeated in other theaters and cafés-concerts, and in the public street.[10] Again, the question of the class of audiences was crucial.

One example was directly related to events in Mexico. In August 1864, shortly after the Emperor Maximilian's arrival there, the play *The Freebooters of Sonora* by Amédée Rolland and Gustave Aymard was presented to the censors for approval. A melodrama recounting the expedition of a French adventurer in Mexico, it was recognized to be based on the exploits of comte de Raousset-Boulbon, who had been executed in Mexico in 1854 after a bizarre sequence of military ventures. The authorities, fearing that parallels would be drawn with current events, insisted that references to France should be omitted and that the final scene of the count's execution should be toned down. The theme of Raousset-Boulbon's adventures may have been all the more sensitive because there were suspicions that he, like Maximilian, had been supported by the French government.[11] Immediately after Maximilian's execution in June 1867, a commentator in *Le Figaro* compared his fate with that of Raousset-Boulbon.[12]

In the context of Maximilian's execution, the special potency of the visual image emerged most immediately in the suppression of photographs of the firing squad and of Maximilian's coat with bullet holes in July 1867, when verbal descriptions were already being widely printed. Manet, too, recognized the power attributed to images when he noted that his *Maximilian* lithograph had been suppressed even before he had added a title to it: "that speaks well for the work," he wrote to Zola in January 1869.[13]

In this context, the position of the exhibition painting was ambiguous. As a visual image, its effects might be construed as dangerous; yet the Salon public, overwhelmingly bourgeois in its makeup, was clearly regarded as less impressionable—or less dangerous—than the more socially mixed theater audience. In the 1860s there were no regular formalized governmental controls on what was shown at the Salon.

When a state-appointed jury for the Salon was instituted in 1800 under the First Empire, it had as one of its explicit functions to exclude "works whose composition would harm morality by expressing or overtly seeking to recall memories or excite passions contrary to the principles of the government and public calm."[14] It was presumably by criteria such as these that Horace Vernet's paintings dealing with the Napoleonic Wars were excluded from the 1822 Salon.[15] The defeat of the Napoleonic forces at the gates of Paris itself by the allied invaders in March 1814 and the plight of Napoleon's soldiery were presumably unacceptable images under the Restoration because they offered vivid reminders of recent instabilities.

When the jury was placed under the control of the Académie des Beaux-Arts in 1830, there seem to have been no explicit provisions for direct political censorship. Presumably it was felt that the Salon jury would in normal circumstances exercise a regulatory role, though the authorities might step in over the heads of the jury. A number of possible examples of this have been recorded from the July Monarchy, all of them subjects related to the history of the 1790s, and clear evidence of the complexities of Louis Philippe's relationship to the imagery of the French Revolution.[16]

Only one case has been traced where there is a clear indication of orders from the king himself leading to a rejection: Chenavard's 1835 picture of the Convention after voting for the execution of Louis XVI, a subject made the more problematic by the inclusion of Louis Philippe's father prominently among the members of the Convention. But significantly the picture was immediately exhibited elsewhere in Paris; there seems to have been no mechanism for preventing the display of paintings at unofficial exhibitions, though there must have been some general controls dealing with incitement to immorality or unrest. The crucial point in this case was that the work should not be exhibited in a forum that implied that its imagery was officially sanctioned.

Several other pictures were rejected for reasons which may well have been political. In 1831, when Louis's rule was still ostensibly committed to free speech, the jury rejected Louis Boulanger's *Execution of Bailly*, an image of the execution of the ex-mayor of Paris by the sans-culottes. In 1839, Auguste Debay's *An Episode of 1793 at Nantes* (fig. 2) was excluded, despite its evidently sympathetic vision of the victims singing canticles as they await their fate at the hands of the Convention's executioners. Apparently the overliteral rendering of the guillotine was the reason for its exclusion (this was later removed). Lastly in 1841 Émile Verdier's *Mlle de Sombreuil Saves Her Father by Drinking a Glass of Blood* was excluded.

Among the many possible reasons for these rejections, one was concern over the political message displayed, as with the Chenavard. But the exclusion of Debay's *Episode of 1793* may have been as much a question of artistic propriety, if the overemphatic guillotine was really the problem; and Michael Marrinan has argued that a major difficulty raised by Verdier's *Mlle de Sombreuil* may have been its failure to present a clear moral narrative, focusing as it did more on melodrama, in the manner of *genre historique*, than on exemplary values.[17]

In discussing the July Monarchy, we must distinguish these cases from the widespread controversy caused by the Salon jury's rejections. Arguably the jury, when controlled by the Academy, did exercise some form of aesthetic censorship, but this was quite distinct in kind and in purpose from the workings of the formal censors. The rejected pictures, most notably the works of *le grand refusé* Théodore Rousseau, who was excluded from 1836 on, evidently involved none of the factors that concerned the formal censors (*La Descente des vaches dans le Jura*, Mesdag Museum, The Hague, refused in 1836, is perhaps the most celebrated example). In the late 1830s and 1840s, continuous warfare developed between the Academy and the wider artistic community, with the rejections of artists such as Delacroix and Corot and with a succession of concerted protests against the jury's workings;[18] but this, too, would have been of no interest to the censor.

The subsequent history of Debay's *An Episode of 1793 at Nantes* was politi-

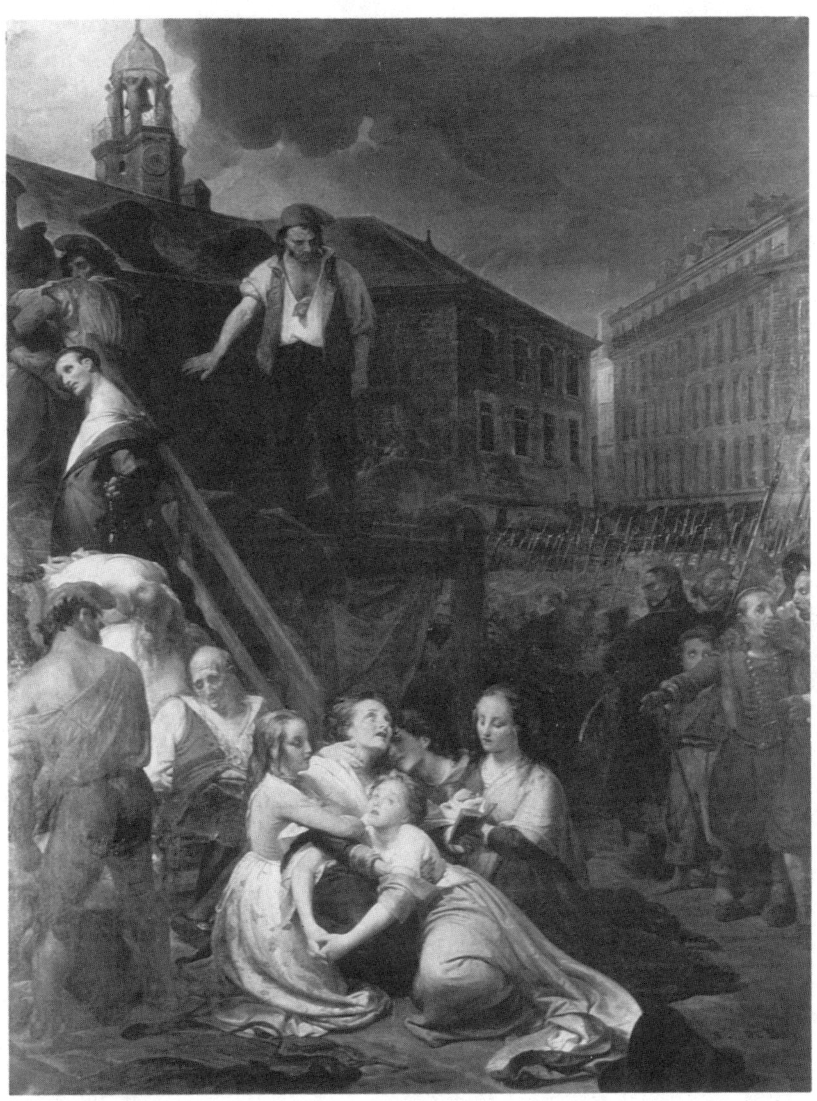

FIG. 2. Auguste Debay, *An Episode of 1793, at Nantes*, 1838, rejected at the Salon in 1839, exhibited at the Salon of 1850–51. Oil on canvas, 227.5×174 cm (89½×68½ in.). Musée départemental Dobrée. Place Jean V, Nantes (Cliché P. J. Ville de Nantes—Musée des Beaux-Arts).

cally complex.[19] The artist submitted the picture to the Salon jury again in 1848, but again it did not appear in the exhibition, though for reasons different from those of nine years earlier. Paintings for the 1848 Salon were submitted before the February revolution, and presumably Debay felt that the tone of the picture would be more acceptable than it had been in 1839; maybe the offending guillotine had also been removed by then. But after the February revolution, the Salon jury was suppressed and all the pictures that had been submitted were in principle granted free access to the Salon. But a number of works did not appear, many of them evidently for political reasons—notably portraits of leading Orléanists, and also Debay's picture, whose counterrevolutionary message was so obviously inappropriate to the post-February situation. In 1850, however, its day finally arrived, in the conservative last phase of the Second Republic under the presidency of Louis Napoleon; it was shown at the 1850–51 Salon, purchased by the state, and sent to the museum at Nantes.

Within the normal workings of the Salon and its jury, there was one area in which some form of censorship might be exercised: in the picture titles published in the Salon *livret* (catalogue). In 1850–51, Courbet suffered this fate. His pictures were not subject to jury scrutiny that year, since he had won a medal at the previous Salon, but his titles were abbreviated and simplified. In one instance, the reason for this must have been political. Courbet submitted his portrait of the itinerant Fourierist philosopher Jean Journet with the title *The Apostle Jean Journet* and an accompanying quotation from Journet: "Departing for the Conquest of Universal Harmony." In the *livret* it appeared as *Portrait of M. Jean Journet*.[20]

After Louis Napoleon's coup d'état of December 1851, the stringent 1852 press laws, with their special concern over visual images, were not accompanied by any explicit controls on the Salon. Yet official intervention might prevent a painting being exhibited at the Salon during the Second Empire, even when, unlike Manet's *Maximilian*, it had not been previously submitted to the censors in print form, just as works of literature, though far less tightly controlled than the theater, might in exceptional circumstances be banned.[21]

There were two clear examples of censorship of exhibition paintings in the early 1860s which go beyond the unofficial policing by the Salon jury: Courbet's *The Return from the Meeting* (fig. 3) was excluded from both the Salon and the Salon des Refusés in 1863, though Courbet was not subject to jury scrutiny, as a past winner of a second class medal; likewise his 1864 submission, *Venus Pursuing Psyche in Her Jealousy*, was excluded. Courbet himself

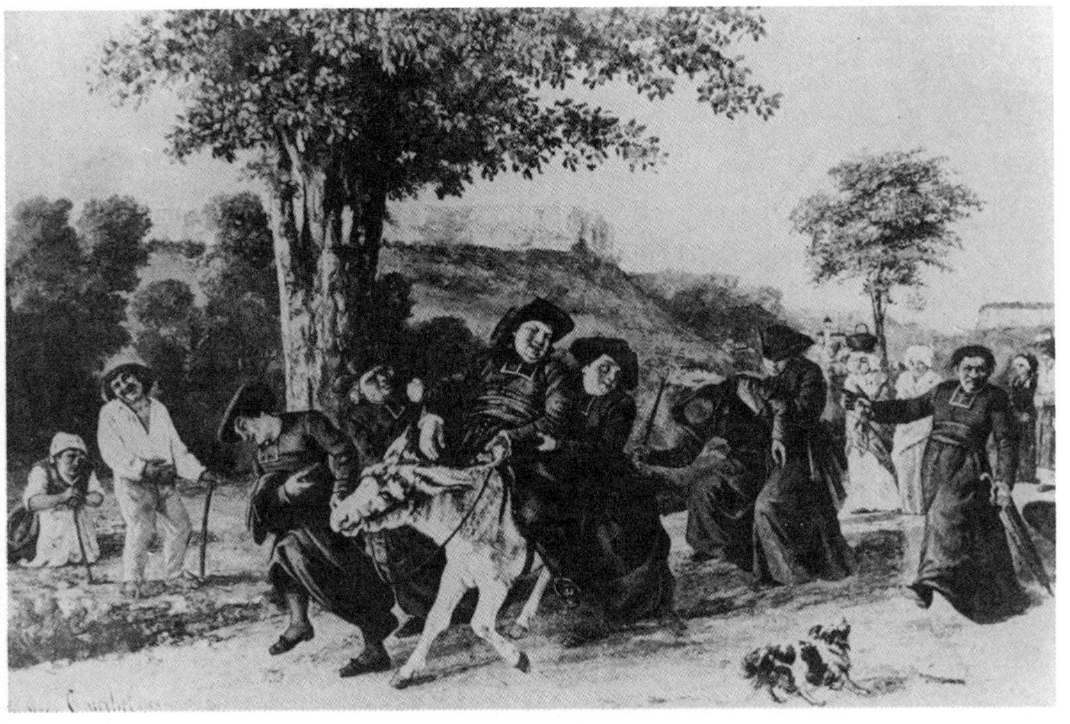

FIG. 3. Gustave Courbet, *The Return from the Meeting*, excluded from the Salon of 1863.
Oil on canvas, 228.5×330 cm (90×130 in.). Destroyed.

said that he had painted his huge canvas of drunken curés lurching down a country road in order to get it rejected, because of the slight he felt he had received in 1861, by not being awarded a first class medal;[22] clearly its suppression came under the "interests of religion" category. In 1868, photographs of the picture were censored, although the verbal descriptions that accompanied them were not—another instance of the power attributed to the visual image, if it appeared in a form that allowed it to circulate to the illiterate and the impressionable—to the "dangerous classes."[23] But, as far as I can see, the authorities could not have stopped Courbet showing the picture itself in Paris, though there is no evidence that he ever succeeded in doing so. A staunch Catholic purchased the original picture around 1900, in order to destroy it—an unusual type of censorship. The 1864 *Venus* may also have been intended to provoke, or else the authorities were extrasensitive to Courbet after *The Return from the Meeting*.[24] It was seemingly a lesbian scene to which a mythological title had been added, and it presumably threatened the "interests of public morality"; but one should emphasize that the next year the jury accepted Manet's *Olympia*, which was more overtly concerned with prostitution, though without overt lesbian overtones. A further incident in Courbet's career suggests that the borderlines between sexual and political concerns were not clear-cut. In 1872, after he had been condemned for his alleged responsibility for the demolition of the Vendôme column during the Paris Commune of 1871, the police kept a watchful eye when his overtly lesbian composition, *Sleeping Women* of 1866 (Musée du Petit Palais, Paris), was put on display in a dealer's window.[25]

We must again emphasize the distinction between censorship and rejection by the Salon jury. The Salon des Refusés of 1863, as an exhibition under imperial patronage showing the paintings rejected by the Académie-controlled jury, is a key point here. The Refusés show demands to be read in several ways. It could be seen as a liberal gesture and a response to the protests of excluded artists; it was also evidently part of the government's warfare against the Académie des Beaux-Arts, which culminated in the reforms of December 1863 (these reforms, too, can be read in contrasting ways, either as a blow for individuality and freedom, or as an extension of state control over the recalcitrant and semiautonomous Académie; after 1863, too, there were government representatives on the Salon jury). However, the Refusés could also be seen largely to vindicate the workings of the jury, since many critics considered that the pictures on view there were evidently inferior to those accepted by the jury. And finally the works included in it were branded with the stigma of jury rejection—indeed many artists withdrew their rejected pictures before the opening of the Refusés so as not to advertise that they had been rejected. But, however it is viewed, the Refusés showed that the government saw no reason to suppress the mass of artworks the jury rejected; such works simply did not come within the censor's sphere of concern.

Looking at Manet's fate at the hands of Salon juries, there was no consistency about which of his paintings were accepted and which rejected at the Salon. *Olympia* was accepted in 1865, and the moral issues raised by *Le Bain* (*Le Déjeuner sur l'herbe*), with its clothed men and naked woman, did not preclude its appearance among the Refusés. But in other years, large canvases with wholly unproblematic subjects were rejected, among them *The Fifer* in 1866 and *The Artist* in 1876. In the main, the rejections seem to have been the result of the aesthetic or personal prejudices of a particular year's jury, though on occasion a jury might react to the severity, or the leniency, of the previous year's jury. Questions of sexuality were presumably a factor in the rejection of Manet's overt image of prostitution, *Nana*, in 1877; and the following year another such image, Henri Gervex's *Rolla*, was excluded, even though Gervex was not liable to jury scrutiny—apparently on the insistence of a government representative.[26] But both *Nana* and *Rolla* were exhibited elsewhere immediately after their exclusion from the Salon. In general, Manet's work did not come within the censors' sphere of interest, both because his primary medium was the fine art exhibition painting, and because his imagery, for all its complexities, was rarely engaged directly with the most problematic political issues. With *The Execution of the Emperor Maximilian* the position was quite different.

The history of Manet's *Maximilian* project is inseparable from the two key threads in the history of the last years of the Second Empire—the ill-fated venture in Mexico, and the gradual moves toward a "liberal Empire."

Maximilian's execution in 1867 was the culmination of France's six-year involvement in the politics of Mexico. Napoleon III dreamed of creating a European, Catholic empire in central America, primarily as a bulwark against the expansionism of the United States. In 1860, the Catholic Miramón was replaced as president of Mexico by the Republican Juárez, who in 1861 refused to honor the huge debts to Europe incurred by his predecessor. The immediate aim of European military intervention was to reclaim the money owed; a combined French, Spanish, and British force reached Mexico in December 1861. But the Spanish and British quickly withdrew when it became clear that French ambitions went far beyond debt reclamation. After a heavy defeat at Puebla in May 1862, the French finally entered Mexico City in June 1863. Meanwhile Napoleon was seeking a prospective European emperor for Mexico, and in early 1864 Archduke Maximilian of Austria, younger brother of the Habsburg emperor, finally agreed to become emperor of Mexico. He reached Mexico during the summer of 1864, and the occupying forces sought to present him as the Mexicans' own choice as ruler.

Things soon began to go wrong for Maximilian and his fledgling empire. Republican supporters of Juárez continued to threaten him militarily, despite an edict of October 3, 1865, which made all military opponents liable to immediate execution; moreover the Mexican Republicans had increased support from the United States after the end of the American Civil War. And French support, on which Maximilian's regime depended, was quickly withdrawn, partly as the result of pressure from the United States, and partly because of a drastic shift in power in Europe: after the defeat of Austria by Bismarck's Prussian forces at Sadowa in July 1866, France's troops were needed at home to confront the growing Prussian threat. The last French forces left Mexico City in February 1867, but Maximilian refused to abdicate; he was soon forced to leave the capital for the better-fortified city of Querétaro, which fell to Juárez's forces in May 16; on June 19, Maximilian was executed by a firing squad with his two leading generals, Miramón and Mejía.[27]

News of Maximilian's death reached Paris on July 1, just before the prize-giving ceremony at that year's Exposition Universelle; ironically, one of the leitmotivs of the Exposition was France as a colonial power.[28] After the immediate shock and indignation, questions were soon asked about responsibility for his fate. Only in papers published outside French censorship could blame immediately be laid at Napoleon III's door. *L'Indépendance belge*, published in Brussels but with many French contributors, led the condemnation.[29] In France itself, direct criticism was confined to two key speeches delivered in the Corps Législatif by Adolphe Thiers and Jules Favre, and to authorized press comment on these speeches. Both speeches made it clear that they considered the ultimate responsibility to lie with France, and implicitly with the emperor himself and his form of personal government.[30] In the months that followed, this attribution of blame became ever more overt, even in France.[31] At the same time, beyond the sympathy for Maximilian's fate, it was argued by Napoleon's opponents that Juárez was doing no more, in ordering his execution, than condemning Maximilian to the fate that he himself had imposed on the Juárists by his savage decree of October 3, 1865.[32]

This severe blow to Napoleon III's national and international prestige took place in a strange period of limbo in French politics. Throughout the 1860s, tentative steps had been taken to liberalize the regime and to relax some of the social and political controls imposed by Napoleon after his coup d'état in December 1851. On January 19, 1867, opening the new parliamentary session, the emperor had promised major reforms of the laws concerning the press and public meetings; but the legislative bodies were unable to agree on details, and the reforms were finally implemented only in the summer of 1868: the new press law was accepted by the Senate on May 11 and became law July 10. Although this law removed some restrictions imposed by Napoleon's press laws of 1852, in practice it did not lead to a wholesale liberalization, and many of the newly launched radical journals were rapidly suppressed.[33] There was no change in censorship laws in the two key areas where they operated, theater presentations and published prints, though there were hopes that the laws would be enforced more permissively.[34]

Manet seems to have begun work on a major painting of the execution quite soon after the event. However, his first attempt (Museum of Fine Arts, Boston) was soon abandoned, without the relationships between the groups being satisfactorily resolved. A second large canvas was started (National Gallery, London), and this was very probably the version of the subject that, according to a report in *L'Artiste*, he planned to submit to the 1868 Salon.[35] But in the end he submitted two other pictures in 1868, and the next we hear of the project is in January 1869, when he sought authorization to publish a lithograph of the execution. Permission was denied, and it was at this time that he was told that his painted version of this subject would be rejected if it was submitted to the 1869 Salon.[36] He did not in the end submit it. This was a third large version of the subject (fig. 1), clearly datable after the lithograph, and thus presumably a different canvas from the one he nearly submitted in 1868.

We do not know why Manet did not submit *The Execution of the Emperor Maximilian* to the jury in 1868, as he initially planned. Perhaps he was dissatisfied with it at this stage; but he would have had good reasons for wanting to show it then, when memories of the episode were still fresh. It is possible that he withheld it in 1868 in the hope that the long promised new and more liberal press laws, finally ratified shortly after that year's Salon opened, would herald a more general liberalization in the display of politically sensitive imagery. The suppression of both print and painting in 1869 proved any such hopes ill-founded.

The authorities could not, it seems, have prevented him displaying the picture in his own studio; as we have seen, Chenavard was able to exhibit his rejected picture elsewhere in 1835. But Manet did not pursue this option, perhaps feeling that it would make its point only in the vast public forum of the Salon. When in 1876 he did open his studio to display the pictures rejected by the jury that year, his *Maximilian* canvas was visible—face to the wall. Though he told a journalist what it was, the image itself remained hidden, its invisible presence a ghostly reminder of the still-potent force of the censor in the mid-1870s, in the aftermath of the Franco-Prussian War and the Paris Commune. Its only appearance in Manet's lifetime was in the United States, in New York and Boston in 1879–80.[37]

To set a context for the suppression of *The Execution of the Emperor Maximilian* we must examine other instances where the difficulties caused by works of art were political. Manet's work is the only instance so far traced of a painting excluded from the Salon during the Second Empire for explicitly politi-

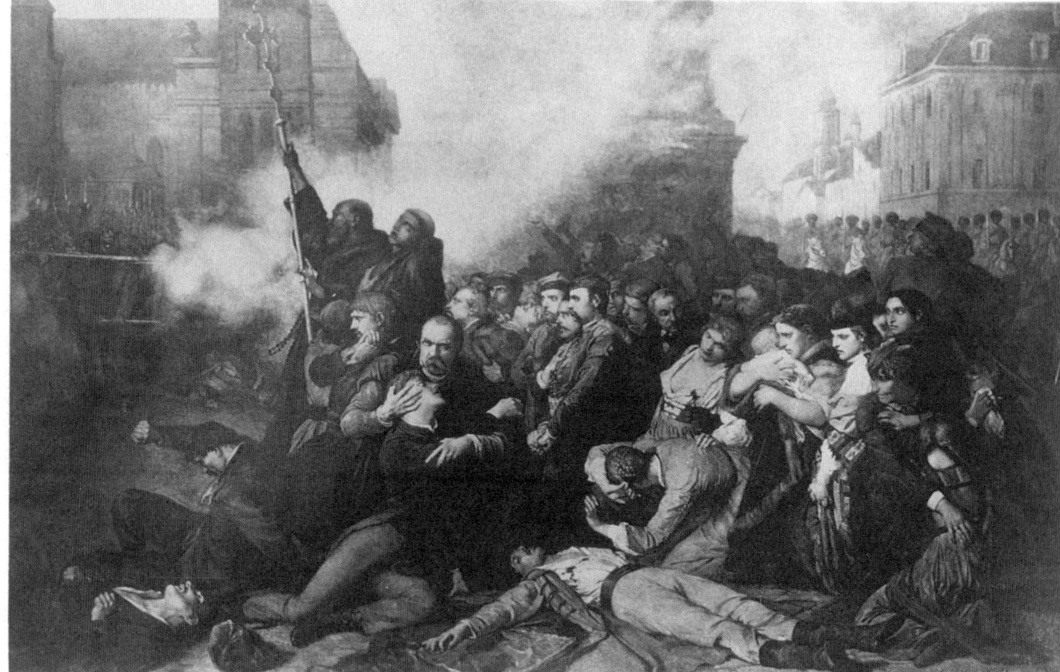

FIG. 4. Tony Robert-Fleury, *Warsaw, 8 April 1861*, Salon of 1866.
Oil on canvas, dimensions and present whereabouts unknown.

cal reasons. However, certain paintings from the period reveal both which types of political engagement were acceptable and which were considered problematic.[38]

First, an example that seemingly raised no problems: Tony Robert-Fleury's *Warsaw, 8 April 1861* (fig. 4) represented Russian troops massacring Polish nationalist protestors.[39] The acceptability of Robert-Fleury's picture and the outspoken responses to it show how readily a painting could tackle an active and polemical political issue, provided two conditions were met: first, its message should be clearly legible; second, its position should be in line with government policy. Anti-Russian sentiment could readily be expressed after Russia's defeat by the Anglo-French alliance in the Crimean War, and subsequent loss of power as an international political force in Europe. In his review of the picture, Charles Clément commented: "I have heard it said that a Russian couldn't safely cross the central hall of the Sa-

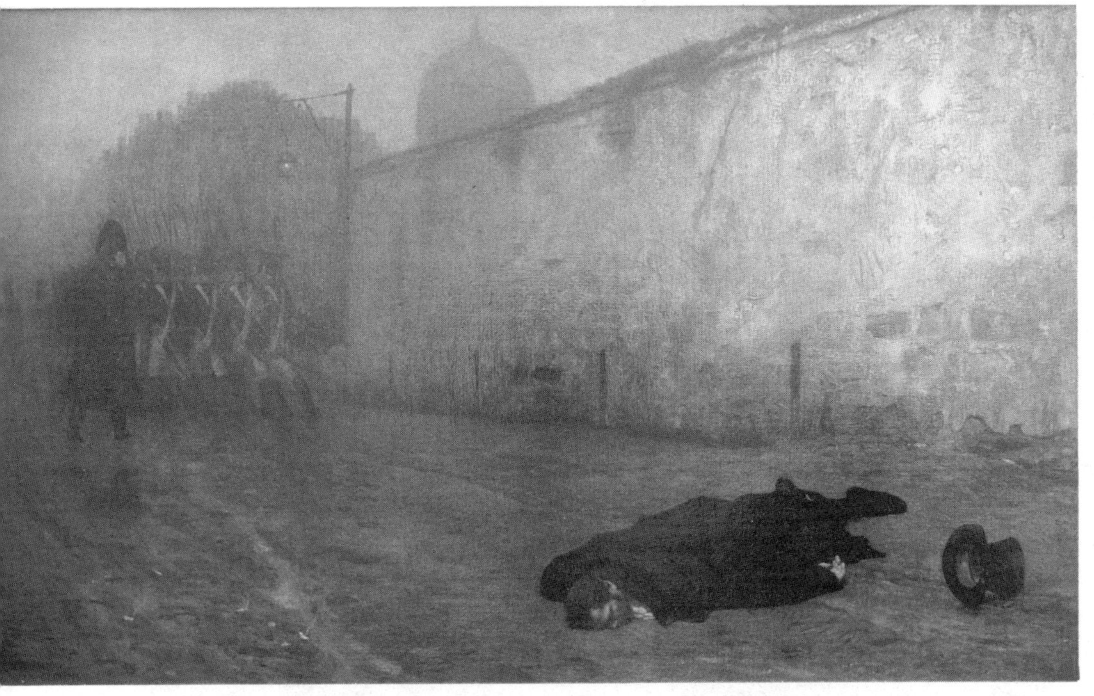

FIG. 5. Jean-Léon Gérôme, *7 December 1815; Nine O'Clock in the Morning*, Salon of 1868. Oil on canvas, 64×103.5 cm (25¼×40¾ in.). City Art Galleries, Sheffield.

lon."[40] We do not know what the tsar thought of the canvas on his state visit to the Exposition Universelle in 1867, where it was again exhibited.

Associations with Maximilian very probably lay behind the controversy that arose around a painting exhibited at the 1868 Salon: Gérôme's *7 December 1815, Nine O'Clock in the Morning* (fig. 5). This shows the immediate aftermath of the execution of Napoleon I's leading associate Marshal Ney, in the "white terror" that followed the restoration of the Bourbon monarchy. Gérôme himself later blamed the affair on Ney's son, who had wanted the painting to be excluded from the Salon.[41] But Edmond About gave a different account of why Gérôme's picture was threatened with rejection: "The administration thought that such a memory should not be evoked, and politely pointed out to the artists that the highest level of propriety dictated that this juridical assassination should not be put on display."[42] Gérôme was presumably able to resist the power of the authorities and insist that his work

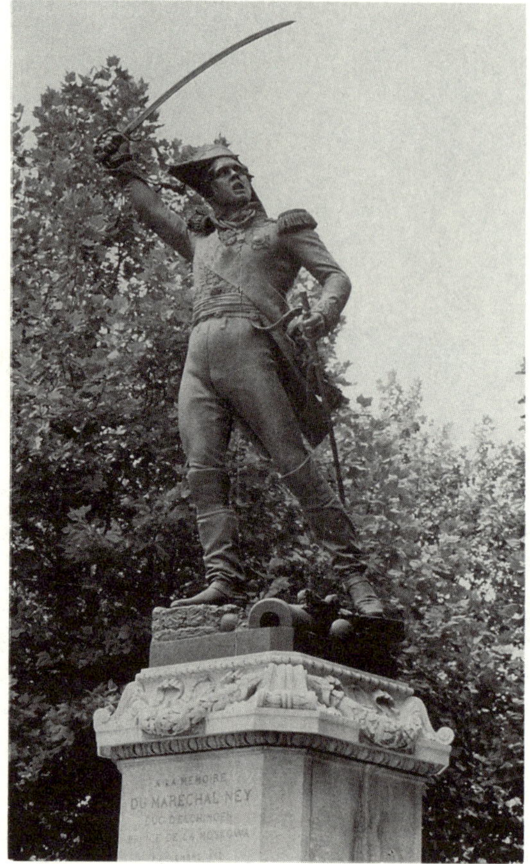

FIG. 6. François Rude, *Marshal Ney*, 1852–53.
Bronze, 267 cm (105 in.) high. Place de l'Observatoire, Paris.
Photo: Conway Library,
Courtauld Institute of Art, London.

was shown because of his close connections with the government, as the government-appointed professor of painting at the École des Beaux-Arts.

The image of Ney had already played an important part in Napoleon III's imperial propaganda, as seen in Rude's monument to Ney (fig. 6), a triumphant image of Ney as the great soldier. Inaugurated with great pomp and amid high security in 1853, this vividly testified to Napoleon III's wish to co-opt for his own regime the imagery of Napoleon I's military might.[43]

About's description of Ney's execution as a juridical assassination evokes comparison with Maximilian's fate at the hands of Juárez; and immediately after Maximilian's death, political commentators drew parallels between the two men's fate.[44] Whether or not Gérôme was responding to this association, the anxiety that his canvas caused shows how sensitive the administration was to historical imagery that was open to interpretation in anti-Bonapartist ways. It seems implausible that Gérôme's choice of subject was coincidental.[45]

Gérôme's treatment of the subject was also controversial. Many critics attacked it for its illegibility and for degrading the image of the heroic Ney. In *The Execution of the Emperor Maximilian*, Manet, like Gérôme, systematically avoided the rhetoric of heroic death; but Gérôme, unlike Manet, deployed anecdotal details—the graffiti, the fallen hat—to heighten the legibility and the piquancy of the scene.

A further episode in 1868 revealed the imperial regime's sensitivity to historical imagery—this time to memories of its own history. After the publication in 1868 of Ténot's narrative of Louis Napoleon's seizure of power, memories were revived of an episode of the coup d'état, the death of Alphonse Baudin, "representative of the people," on December 3, 1851. A demonstration around Baudin's simple grave in the Montmartre cemetery led three Republican journals to launch a subscription for an appropriate monument to this Republican hero. The authorities prosecuted both those who had spoken at the demonstration and the editors of the papers that had launched the subscription, despite its seeming legality. Although the defendants were convicted, the trial provided the forum for a series of savage attacks against the imperial regime, which marked a crucial stage in extending the scope and power of political opposition.[46]

But in 1870, when the gradual process of reform had led, with the so-called liberal empire, to a marked increase in freedom of expression, these issues could be confronted directly in visual terms. In the 1870 Salon, Ernest-Louis Pichio exhibited *The Death of Alphonse Baudin* (fig. 7); Baudin stands on the barricade, a moment before the bullets will strike, holding a copy of the 1789 Declaration of the Rights of Man, while in the shadows on the wall at the right hangs the coup d'état proclamation of December 2, 1851. Yet as far as we know, there was no attempt to suppress the picture. A monument to Baudin was erected by public subscription in the first years of the Third Republic (fig. 8); the bronze by Aimé Millet shows Baudin's corpse, bullet hole in its forehead, clutching a stone tablet inscribed "La Loi."[47]

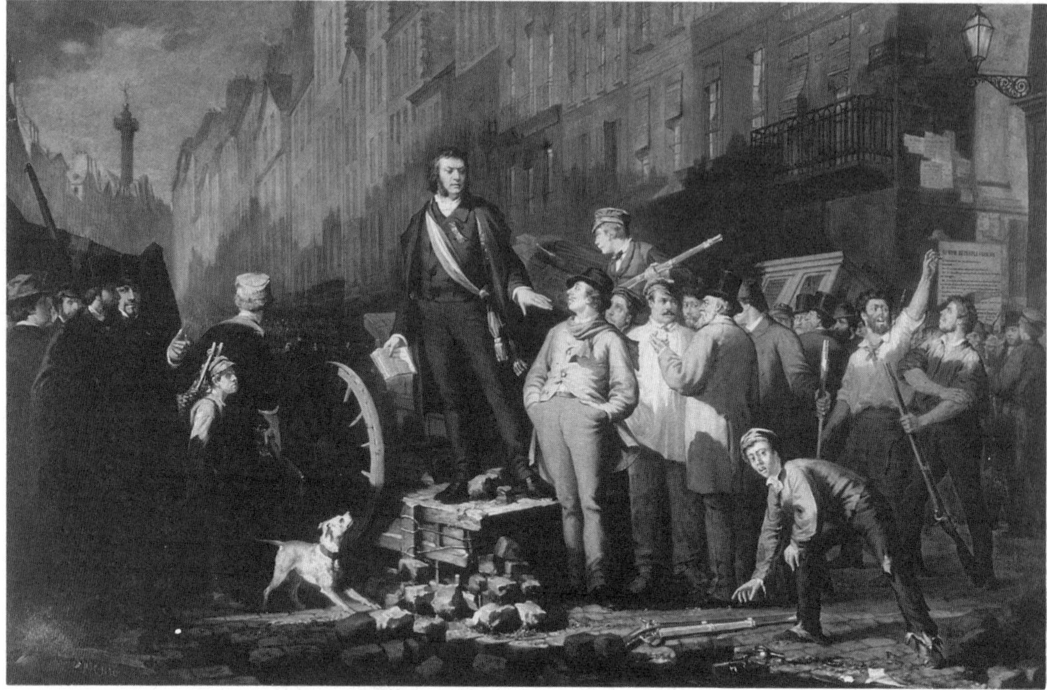

FIG. 7. Ernest-Louis Pichio, *The Death of Alphonse Baudin*, Salon of 1870. Oil on canvas, 128×197 cm (50½×77½ in.). Musée Carnavalet, Paris. Photo: © Photothèque des Musées de la Ville de Paris.

It was not simply the subject that led to Manet's *Maximilian* being suppressed in 1869. Although few images of the execution were published in France, a small number of popular prints were permitted, and at the 1868 Salon, Jules-Marc Chamerlat was able to exhibit two scenes relating to the execution: *The Emperor Maximilian at the Convent of the Capucins* and *The Evening of the Execution of the Emperor Maximilian (Querétaro, 19 June 1867)*. Since these paintings are untraced and no press comment on them has been found, we can only surmise what made them acceptable; but it seems likely, from the titles, that they mainly focused on Maximilian's innocence and piety and the pathos of his fate, as in Jean-Paul Laurens's celebrated canvas of fifteen years later, *The Last Moments of Maximilian*, shown at the 1882 Salon. Also welcomed at the Salons of 1868 and 1869, after the disastrous end of the Mexican enterprise, were scenes of French heroism during the campaign,

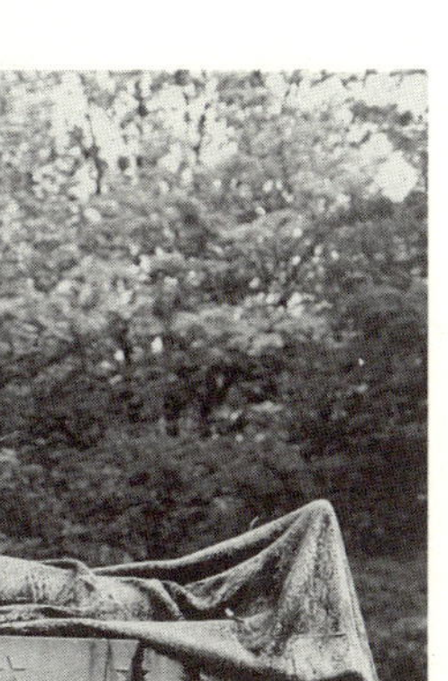

FIG. 8. Aimé Millet, *Monument to Alphonse Baudin*, 1872.
Bronze on stone base designed by Léon Dupré, 163×210×70 cm (64×82¾×27½ in.).
Cimetière de Montmartre, Paris. Photo: Conway Library, Courtauld Institute of Art, London.

notably in canvases commissioned from Jean-Adolphe Beaucé by the government—even one showing the legendary defeat of the French Foreign Legion against impossible odds at Camarone.[48]

In this context, we can suggest why the authorities decided to forestall Manet's *Maximilian* even before he submitted it to the Salon jury. Most obviously, it represented an episode that reflected badly on Napoleon III's foreign policy. But this is not an adequate reason in itself, since other images associated with the Mexican campaign and Maximilian's death could be exhibited in 1868 and 1869, provided they depicted the French in heroic light and showed Maximilian as hero or martyr.

In *The Execution of the Emperor Maximilian*, Manet avoided most of the traditional means of evoking meaning and morality—through gesture, expression, and so on. The picture cannot be read either as an iconic image of tragedy or betrayal, in the terms of Davidian history painting, or as a poignant narrative, in the terms of historical genre. By contemporary standards the treatment of the subject was very problematic, in its seeming detachment from the drama and its refusal to present a clear moral; this was accentuated by the way it was painted—by its summary brushwork and seeming lack of finish. This treatment belonged to a particular sector of the Parisian opposition to Napoleon III's empire, by cultivating a studied aloofness and by repudiating the stock modes of legibility by which late Second Empire society sought to legitimize its authority. This legibility was not simply a matter of social classification but also, and centrally in relation to the *Maximilian*, a question of emotional and moral signposting.[49]

A final comparison will illustrate this, and will emphasize how far, and in what ways, Manet's image refused to function in conventional terms—with Jules David's lithograph of the execution of Monsignor Darboy, the archbishop of Paris, by the Communards on May 24, 1871 (fig. 9). Here, there is a clear contrast between the martyrs, with their eyes on the Beyond, and the mean materialism and callousness of their executioners, and the contrast is stressed by the stock gestural and physiognomical typecasting that Manet's *Maximilian* so overtly rejects. David's print is especially relevant to the image that Manet derived from his *Maximilian*, the *Barricade* lithograph (not published until 1884, after Manet's death). Here, the roles are reversed—Communards are being executed by Versailles government troops in the *semaine sanglante* of May 21–28, 1871; and, as in the *Maximilian*, the conventional rhetorical devices are minimized.

It was the disconcerting combination of ambiguous signs with lack of expressive rhetoric that made Manet's image particularly problematic. Its uncertainties were inseparable from the historical situation itself; Maximilian was universally seen as a victim, but to a considerable degree he was the victim of his own decisions. The soldiers who executed him were only obeying orders, just as any well-trained French soldier would; and even Juárez, by condemning him to death, was doing no more than Maximilian had with his savage decree of October 3, 1865, against his opponents. The only clear blame lay back in Paris, where Manet meant the image to be seen—with Napoleon III, whose ambitions precipitated the whole episode, and whose censors suppressed Manet's image.

It was by its ambivalence, by the studied lack of dramatic rhetoric or moral signposting, that Manet's *Maximilian* could function politically, and it was

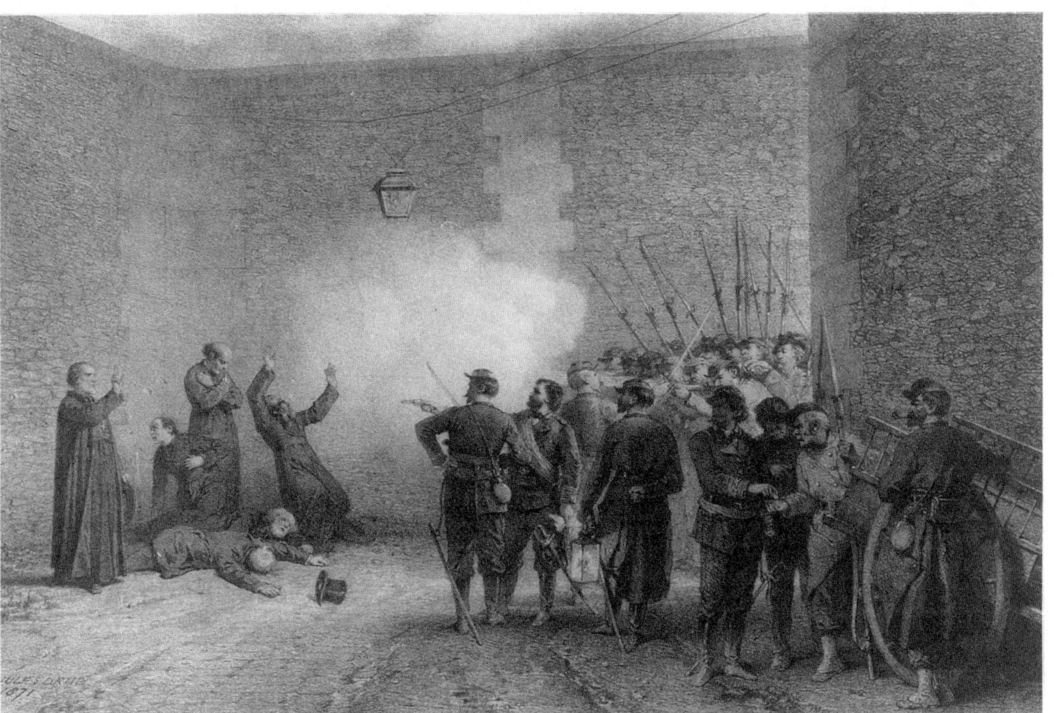

FIG. 9. Jules David, *Massacre of the Hostages*, 1871.
Lithograph from series *Paris et ses ruines*, 24.7×37 cm ($9\frac{3}{4}$×$14\frac{1}{2}$ in.).
Private collection, London.

this that led to its suppression. Its detachment and its open-endedness, a distinctively Parisian language of opposition to Napoleon's empire, set up this image of Maximilian's fate, by a rough wall at Querétaro, as an icon of the perils of imperial and dynastic ambitions.

The dual structures of Salon exclusion highlight the ambivalent position of the Salon itself, suspended between "art" and "politics." In the main, it could be seen as a semiautonomous space, above the daily round of political controls, and the policing of its boundaries could safely be left in the hands of the "artistic" judges. But there was always the possibility that an image might cross these boundaries, and might force itself into the wider political arena. Gérôme's painting of the death of Ney (fig. 5) had trespassed on this borderline in 1868, and the authorities had no doubts that Manet's *Maximilian* crossed it in 1869. As with the refrain in the opera, there was always the danger that the "sentiment of revolt" might spill out from the elite spaces of the Salon onto the streets.

NOTES

A related essay, focusing on Manet's *The Execution of the Emperor Maximilian* in relation to contemporary history painting, was published as "Manet's Maximilian: History Painting, Censorship and Ambiguity," in *Manet and the Execution of Maximilian: Painting, Politics and Censorship*, exh. cat. (London: National Gallery, 1992), hereafter abbreviated as *Manet*, London (1992). I am indebted to Juliet Wilson-Bareau, principal author of that publication, and to Elizabeth C. Childs and Suzanne Glover Lindsay for their searching comments on these essays.

1. In my discussion of censorship I am indebted to Elizabeth C. Childs, who generously allowed me to read her dissertation, "Honoré Daumier and the Exotic Vision: Studies in French Culture and Caricature," Columbia University, 1989, which contains an important section on "Sense and Censorship in the Publication of Caricature" (65 ff), and to Adrian Rifkin, "Cultural Movement and the Paris Commune," *Art History* 2, no. 2 (June 1979): 201 ff.

2. On censorship and the café-concert, see, most recently, Concetta Condemi, *Les Cafés-concerts: Histoire d'un divertissement* (Paris: Quai Voltaire, 1992). On the censorship of popular songs, see also Robert L. Herbert, "Courbet's 'Mère Grégoire' and Béranger," in Klaus Gallwitz and Klaus Herding, eds., *Malerei und Theorie: Das Courbet-Colloquium 1979* (Frankfurt am Main: Städtische Galerie im Städelschen Kunstinstitut, 1980).

3. Quoted in Pierre Casselle, "Le régime législatif," in Roger Chartier and Henri-Jean Martin, eds., *Histoire de l'édition française*, vol. 3, *Le temps des éditeurs* (Paris: Promodis, 1990), 46.

4. Victor Hallays-Dabot, *Histoire de la censure théâtrale en France* (Paris, 1862), viii.

5. Quoted in Jean-Jacques Darmon, *Le Colportage de librairie en France sous le Second Empire* (Paris, 1972), 108–9.

6. For a justification of the most repressive surveillance, see "Rapport à l'Empereur sur le régime de la presse," 1856, in *Documents pour servir à l'histoire du Second Empire: Circulaires, rapports, notes et instructions confidentielles, 1851–1870* (Paris, 1872), 187–93; for an attack on this repression and arguments that the government should concentrate on positive propaganda, see "La Presse et les écrivains sous l'empire: Note remise au Ministre de l'Intérieur par la Direction de la Presse," 1867, ibid., 197–221.

7. Anon., *La Censure sous Napoléon III: Rapports inédits et in extenso (1852 à 1866)* (Paris, 1892), 185.

8. For example, ibid., 41–43, 56–57, 60–65, 66–68, 76–77.

9. For example, ibid., 23, 52–53, 115, 134 ff, 153, 169–71, 177 ff, 260–68.

10. Ibid., 35–36.

11. Ibid., 249–50. For an account of Raousset-Boulbon's remarkable career, with suspicions of French government involvement in his Mexican exploits, see Pierre Larousse, *Grand dictionnaire universel du XIXe siècle*, 13 (Paris, 1875), 689–90.

12. "Mexique: le dernier jour d'un condamné," *Le Figaro*, July 9, 1867, 2.

13. Manet to Zola, January 1869, in *Manet*, exh. cat. (New York: Metropolitan Museum of Art, 1983), 531; on the power of the image without any text, see also Stephen Bann, "The Odd Man Out: Historical Narrative and the Cinematic Image," *History and Theory* 26 (1987): 53 (I am grateful to Stephen Bann for bringing his discussion of Manet's picture to my attention). On the suppression of the photographs, see *Manet*, London (1992), 52–54.

14. Quoted in Christiane Aulanier, *Histoire du palais et du musée du Louvre*, vol. 2, *Le Salon carré* (Paris, 1950), 44; this *jury de censure* continued the functions of the jury set up by the Académie Royale in 1746, whose function was "to exclude works whose exhibition might cause a political or religious scandal"; see Paul Dupré and Gustave Ollendorf, *Traité de l'administration des Beaux-Arts* (Paris, 1885), 2:143. On Salon juries, see Larousse, *Dictionnaire*, 14 (Paris, 1875), 137–38; Jacques Lethève, *Daily Life of French Artists* (London: George Allen and Unwin, 1972), 108–12; William Hauptmann, "Juries, Protests and Counter-Exhibitions Before 1850," *Art Bulletin* 67, no. 1 (March 1985): 95 ff.

15. See Jouy and Jay, *Salon d'Horace Vernet: Analyse historique et pittoresque des quarante-cinq tableaux exposés chez lui en 1822* (Paris, 1822), esp. 4–7, 10–11, 29–32, 94–100, and Charles Blanc, "Horace Vernet," in *Histoire des peintres: École française*, 3 (Paris, 1863), 8–11.

16. My account here is largely derived from Michael Marrinan, *Painting Politics for Louis Philippe* (New Haven and London: Yale University Press, 1988), 125–35.

17. Ibid., 130–31.

18. See Hauptmann, "Juries, Protests and Counter-Exhibitions," 99–107.

19. This account of Debay's picture and the Salons of the Second Republic is derived from the archival research of Valerie Neale ("The Second Republic: Painting and Politics," unfinished Ph.D. thesis, University College London, ca. 1980).

20. The titles as submitted are recorded in the receipts for the paintings in the Archives du Louvre; see John House, "Courbet and Salon Politics," *Art in America*, May 1989, 165.

21. For a listing of suppressed printed books, see Fernand Drujon, *Catalogue des ouvrages, écrits et dessins de toute nature poursuivis, supprimés ou condamnés depuis le 21 octobre 1814 jusqu'au 31 juillet 1877* (Paris, 1879); though most of the repressed material was sexual, wide-ranging political concerns were evident, as with the theater.

22. Letter to Albert de la Fizelière, April 23, 1863, in Petra ten-Doesschate Chu, ed., *Letters of Gustave Courbet* (Chicago and London: University of Chicago Press, 1992),

220–21; cf. also ibid., 216–28, and Georges Riat, *Gustave Courbet, peintre* (Paris, 1906), 201–7, 215.

23. Drujon, *Catalogue*, 114.

24. See Jack Lindsay, *Gustave Courbet, His Life and Art* (London, 1973), 190.

25. *Courbet Reconsidered*, exh. cat. (Brooklyn, New York: Brooklyn Museum, 1992), 176.

26. See Hollis Clayson, *Painted Love: Prostitution in French Art of the Impressionist Era* (New Haven and London: Yale University Press, 1991), 67–93.

27. For further discussion of the historical events, see Douglas Johnson, "The French Intervention in Mexico," in *Manet*, London (1992), and Meredith J. Strang, "Napoleon III: The Fatal Foreign Policy," in *Edouard Manet and the Execution of Maximilian*, exh. cat. (Providence: Brown University, Department of Art, 1981); this publication contains several valuable contributions to the study of Manet's picture.

28. See Paul Greenhalgh, *Ephemeral Vistas: A History of the Expositions universelles, Great Exhibitions and World's Fairs, 1851–1939* (Manchester: Manchester University Press, 1988), 65.

29. "Nouvelles de France," *L'Indépendance belge*, July 4, 1867, 2; "Nouvelles de France," *L'Indépendance belge*, July 6, 1867, 2; the paper had many French subscribers and was circulated in Paris unless a particular issue was banned, as several containing early reports of Maximilian's execution were.

30. *Discours parlementaires de M. Thiers* (Paris, 1881), 11:164–248 (on responsibility, see esp. 219, 222); Jules Favre, *Discours parlementaires* (Paris, 1881), 3:230–48 (on responsibility, see esp. 248). Both speeches were immediately published in *Le Moniteur universel*, July 10, 1867, 910–13.

31. The first detailed history of the expedition to appear in France was Comte Emile de Kératry, *L'Empereur Maximilien et sa chute*. Published initially as articles in the *Revue contemporaine* between July 15 and October 15, 1867, it first appeared in book form outside of France; the first French edition was published late in 1867, with a new preface by Prévost-Paradol, dated November 1867, in which ultimate blame was clearly attributed to the emperor's "personal government."

32. This argument was first used in *L'Indépendance belge* on July 4, 1867, and reiterated several times in the following days.

33. On the press, see especially Roger Bellet, *Presse et journalisme sous le Second Empire* (Paris, 1967).

34. The case of Daumier's lithographs shows how unclear the position was. After a long period when he was forced to avoid political themes, he began, early in 1866, to tackle current international issues, often presented in semiallegorical fashion, and without overt criticism of French foreign policy; he never tackled a Mexican theme. It was only early in 1869 that he began again to treat issues from politics at home in a satirical-critical mode. See Loys Delteil, *Le Peintre-graveur illustré*, vols. 28 and 29 (Paris, 1926, 1926 [1929]).

35. Marc de Montifaud, "Salon de 1868, II," *L'Artiste*, May 1868, 253, announced

that Manet was planning to exhibit *The Death of Maximilian* (cited by Eric Darragon, *Manet* [Paris: Fayard, 1989], 150). For detailed discussion of the chronology of Manet's project, see Juliet Wilson-Bareau in *Manet*, London (1992).

36. All the known documents about the suppression of the print are published in *Manet*, exh. cat. (New York: Metropolitan Museum of Art, 1983–84), 531–34.

37. See *Manet*, London (1992), 69–70.

38. For fuller discussion, see House in *Manet*, London (1992), 95–97, 100–105.

39. The events in Poland were extensively discussed by Charles de Mazade in a series of articles in the *Revue des deux mondes*, republished with a new "Avant-propos" as *La Pologne contemporaine: Récits et portraits de la révolution poloniase* (Paris, 1863); for a vivid description of the massacre of April 8, 1861, see 112–15.

40. Charles Clément, "Exposition de 1866, V," *Journal des débats*, May 28, 1866.

41. Gérôme, quoted in Charles Moreau-Vauthier, *Gérôme* (Paris, 1906), 254. Gérôme also claimed that the picture had been criticized by Bonapartists and Legitimists alike, each side seeing it as supporting the other; clearly it was widely viewed in terms of contemporary politics.

42. Edmond About, "Le Salon de 1868," *Revue des deux mondes*, June 1, 1868, 729.

43. For a richly documented account of the Ney monument, see Louis de Fourcaud, *François Rude, sculpteur: ses oeuvres et son temps* (Paris, 1904), 368–89.

44. For example, *L'Indépendance belge*, July 6, 1867, 2; July 8, 1867, 1; Albert Boime, "New Light on Manet's *Execution of Maximilian*," *Art Quarterly*, Autumn 1973, 189, notes another such reference.

45. Whether or not Gérôme intended such a reference, it is implausible that his picture—an overt updating of his *Death of Caesar* (second version, exhibited at the 1867 Exposition Universelle; Walters Art Gallery, Baltimore)—was somehow a response to Manet's *Maximilian* project, as suggested by Gerald M. Ackerman, "Gérôme and Manet," *Gazette des Beaux-Arts*, September 1967, 169–70.

46. For accounts of the Baudin affair, see Taxile Delord, *Histoire du Second Empire*, 5 (Paris 1874), 345–74; Emile Ollivier, *L'Empire libéral*, 11 (Paris, 1907), 78–104; for contemporary comment, see Charles de Mazade, "Chronique de la quinzaine," *Revue des deux mondes*, November 15, 1868, 491–94 and December 1, 1868, 751–53.

47. On the Baudin monument, see *La Sculpture française au XIXe siècle* (Paris: Grand Palais, 1986), 238–39; on the whole episode, see Rifkin, "Cultural Movement," 206–7.

48. Beaucé's canvases are reproduced in *Manet*, London (1992), 23–24, 102.

49. For further discussion, see House in *Manet*, London (1992), especially 106–8.

"Chambers of Horrors of Art" and "Degenerate Art": On Censorship in the Visual Arts in Nazi Germany

CHRISTOPH ZUSCHLAG

For Stephanie Barron

ON FEBRUARY 24, 1920, ADOLF HITLER announced the program of the National Socialist German Labor Party (NSDAP). There we read: "We demand the legal fight against a tendency in art and literature which exerts a subversive influence on the life of our people."[1] Thus, thirteen years before the fascists came to power, they programmatically planned the systematic and institutionalized fight against "subversive" art and its representatives, an attack which began with ferocity in 1933 and lasted through the fall of the Third Reich.

The Verordnung des Reichspräsidenten zum Schutz von Volk und Staat (Order of the Reichspräsident for the Protection of the People and the State) dates February 28, 1933, repealed all the basic political rights granted in the constitution of the Weimar Republic, including the freedom of the arts. The Gesetz zur Wiederherstellung des Berufsbeamtentums (Professional Civil Service Restoration Act), dated April 7, 1933, was the legal basis for the summary dismissal of unwanted university and academy professors and museum consultants for political or racial reasons. About thirty museum directors were removed from office, among them Ernst Gosebruch (Essen), Gustav Friedrich Hartlaub (Mannheim), Carl Georg Heise (Lübeck), Ludwig Justi (Berlin), and Max Sauerlandt (Hamburg). Others lost their chairs at academies of art, including Willi Baumeister and Max Beckmann (both Frankfurt/Main), Otto Dix (Dresden), Karl Hofer and Käthe Kollwitz (both Berlin), Paul Klee (Düsseldorf), and Gerhard Marcks (Halle/Saale). These massive attacks came as no surprise. They were the culmination of an ideological battle waged by nationalistic groups and conventional artists against both avant-garde artists and those museum directors who had adopted progressive acquisitions policies.

How strongly antimodernist tendencies, which had developed parallel to modern art since the end of the nineteenth century, were interspersed right from the beginning with a conservative and nationalistic ideology is shown by the disputes about French impressionism around the turn of the century. In this context, the director of the Berliner Nationalgalerie from 1896 to 1909, Hugo von Tschudi, should be mentioned. His commitment to French art led to open quarrels with Kaiser Wilhelm II, and finally to Tschudi's dismissal.[2] Other important examples include two publications of 1911 that received great attention. In the massive book *Die Herabwertung deutscher Kunst durch die Parteigänger des Impressionismus* (The Disparagement of German Art by the Party Followers of Impressionism), the Mannheim lawyer Theodor Alt called impressionism a "perverted style of art" and Vincent van Gogh a "mentally ill dilettante." He compared Franz von Defregger to Édouard Manet, Hans Makart to Hans von Marées, and Adolf Hildebrand to Auguste Rodin, and came to the conclusion that nineteenth-century art was classical art, whereas modern art (impressionism, in particular) was nothing but a formalist-subjective and temporary trend. When in the same year (1911) Gustav Pauli bought a painting by van Gogh, *Mohnfeld* (Poppy Field), for the Bremer Kunsthalle, a wave of indignation arose. Carl Vinnen, an unknown landscape painter from Cuxhaven, who was close to the artists' colony of Worpswede, put together a publication entitled *Protest deutscher Künstler* (Protest of German Artists), in which 134 artists participated. In the introduction Vinnen says:

> Given the tremendous invasion of French art . . . it seems to me that the dictates of necessity require that German artists raise their warning voice. . . . Why is the introduction of foreign art so dangerous . . .? Well, in particular, because it overestimates the foreign nature, not adequate to our own, original disposition. . . . And wherever foreign influences . . . want to reorganize fundamental structures here, our cultural traditions are in danger. . . . If one now considers the fact that prices have risen tremendously, it becomes clear that every year millions get lost which could be spent on national art.[3]

The controversy about impressionism was both the beginning and the climax of the dispute over modern art in Germany. During the Kaiserreich and the Weimar Republic, numerous "art scandals" arose concerning the work and public presentation of certain artists. Purchases were prevented, exhibitions censored or closed (such as the Munch exhibition of 1892 in Berlin), and artists had to answer to the courts. Quite often the attacks were sparked by works of art and artists who were later discriminated against in the National Socialist campaign "Entartete Kunst" (Degenerate Art). This was the case with Otto Dix, George Grosz, Ludwig Gies, and Wilhelm Lehmbruck.[4] In the course of these quarrels, the stereotypes and vocabulary for disparaging modern art—as obscene, violating religious feelings, appealing to class struggle, encouraging military sabotage, resembling the artistic efforts of mentally ill persons—were created. In this context special attention must be paid to the role of the *Kampfbund für deutsche Kultur* (Combat League for German Culture). Founded in 1927–29 by Alfred Rosenberg, it was the reservoir of racist and national-conservative associations. The local and openly aggressive agitation pursued by this Combat League, which was organized throughout the country in local groups, against modern art and its defenders led in 1930 to the dismissal of the Zwickau museum director, Hildebrand Gurlitt.[5]

Returning to the events of 1933: the dismissed civil servants in museums and universities were replaced by functionaries and supporters of the NSDAP, who in most cases were closely connected with the Combat League. In many towns, the new directors—some of them artists themselves—began their activities by arranging exhibitions, which in the National Socialist press were frequently and popularly described as "Schreckenskammern der Kunst" (Chambers of Horrors of Art). These were special shows where the respective inventory of modern art, regardless of its style, was presented in order to defame it. In their political function, ideological thrust, and propagandist staging these exhibitions anticipated the 1937 "Entartete Kunst" show in Munich.[6] They were held in Mannheim, with the title "Kulturbolschewistische Bilder" (Images of Cultural Bolshevism); Karlsruhe, "Regierungskunst, 1918–1933" (Government Art, 1918–1933); Nuremberg, "Schreckenskammer" (Chamber of Horrors); Chemnitz, "Kunst, die nicht aus unserer Seele kam" (Art That Did Not Issue from Our Soul); Stuttgart, "Novembergeist—Kunst im Dienste der Zersetzung" (November Spirit—Art in the Service of Subversion); Dessau(?), Ulm, "Zehn Jahre Ulmer Kunstpolitik" (Ten Years of Arts Policy in Ulm); Dresden, "Entartete Kunst" (Degenerate Art); Breslau, "Kunst der Geistesrichtung, 1918–1933" (Intellectual Art, 1918–1933); and Halle/S., "Schreckenskammer" (Chamber of Horrors). The titles of these Schreckenskammern reveal their function as primarily political: the works of art were presented to the public, not for their own sake, but as symptoms of the degeneration of Weimar democracy, to discredit the latter and cele-

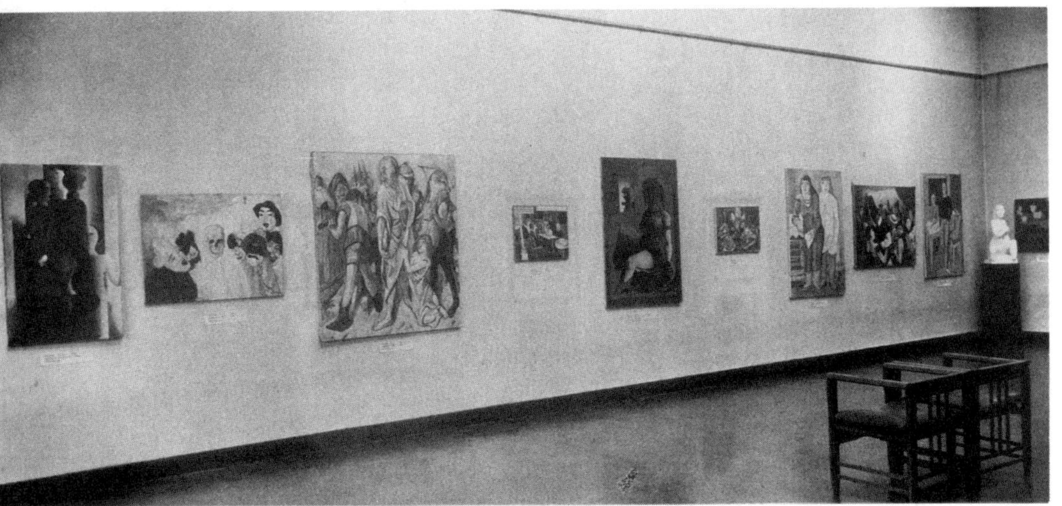

FIG. 1. Gallery in the exhibition "Kulturbolschewistische Bilder" (Images of Cultural Bolshevism), Städtische Kunsthalle, Mannheim, 1933; works by Oskar Schlemmer, James Ensor, Max Beckmann, Jankel Adler, Karl Hofer, Willi Baumeister, and others.
Archiv der Städtischen Kunsthalle, Mannheim.

brate Hitler's victory as a revolutionary new beginning. However, this was an illusion which was to blind the public to the actual continuity of social and economic conditions under Hitler. Provoking the indignation of the public about modern art was not the aim but merely one means of obtaining wide support for the new state and thus contributing to its political stabilization.

Despite the common ideological basis, the forerunner exhibitions came into being independently of each other, as individual local activities. In this lies a significant difference from the show of 1937, which was officially ordered and centrally prepared by the National Socialist government. The content of the Schreckenskammern varied from location to location, depending on the strengths of the local collections; thus in Karlsruhe the main emphasis was on German impressionism, in Chemnitz on expressionism, and in Stuttgart on the sociocritical realism of the 1920s. As examples, two of the forerunner exhibitions, the ones in Mannheim and Dresden, will be described in more detail.

The Mannheim exhibition, presented under the rabble-rousing name "Kulturbolschewistische Bilder" (Images of Cultural Bolshevism) in the Kunsthalle from April 4 to June 5, 1933, was the first of its kind (fig. 1).[7] Otto

Gebele von Waldstein, one of the leading NSDAP functionaries in Mannheim and since April 3 the municipal assistant consultant for the Nationaltheater and the Kunsthalle, arranged it on the instructions of the town leaders only a few days after Gustav Friedrich Hartlaub had been given "time off." The exhibition's 64 paintings, 2 sculptures, and 20 graphics by 55 different artists (Jankel Adler, Willi Baumeister, Max Beckmann, Marc Chagall, Robert Delaunay, André Derain, Otto Dix, Franz Marc, Edvard Munch, Emil Nolde, and others) were depicted as "sorry efforts of cultural Bolshevism" and deserving of public ridicule. The exhibition planners took advantage of all available means of stage management. The paintings were taken out of their frames to emphasize their unworthiness and were hung close together without discernible logic. Works were also exhibited that had never been intended for display in the Kunsthalle. They were, in fact, recent purchases made with a special fund meant for the support of impoverished Mannheim artists. The "images of cultural Bolshevism" were crudely contrasted with an ideal "model cabinet" consisting of framed paintings by conventional Mannheim artists. The National Socialist propaganda exhibitions soon developed such an antithetic principle of display, in which the works of conventional, approved artists would be exhibited next to those of modernists, to the advantage of the former and the defamation of the latter. The purchase price—very high partly as a result of the inflation and deliberately not converted into reichsmarks (the currency introduced in 1924)—was stated on each label in order to evoke the indignation of the "national comrades" about the alleged waste of their tax money. The fact that this show was "for adults only" created an aura of illicitness. The propagandist press blamed the supposedly "fraudulent activities of the Jewish art dealers" for these allegedly inflated, unreasonable prices and equated them with the "penetration by Marxism" in order to stir up anti-Semitic and anti-Communist resentment.

A key work of the Mannheim show was a painting, now in Basle, entitled *Die Prise (Rabbiner)* (A Pinch of Snuff [Rabbi]), by Marc Chagall—the depiction of a "Jewish" theme by a "Jewish" artist born in "Bolshevist" Russia (fig. 2). A spectacle was set up but exactly what happened is not clear. Hartlaub remembered that the painting, "which he himself had purchased, was put on a cart, which was pulled through the city, and then it was so to speak pilloried in a shop window."[8] According to another report, it was a cigar shop where this painting, labeled "Taxpayer, you shall know where your money has gone," was exhibited.[9] The results of this special Mannheim exhibition—with 20,141 visitors it was one of the greatest attractions of the Kunsthalle—

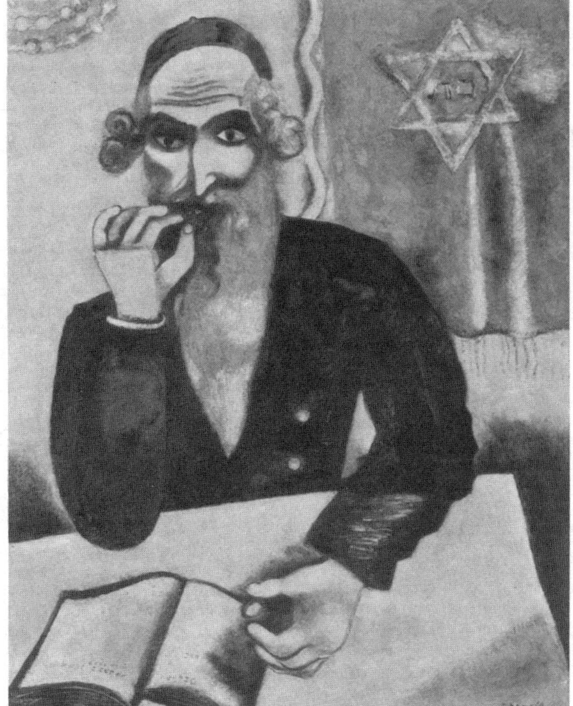

FIG. 2. Marc Chagall, *Die Prise (Rabbiner) (A Pinch of Snuff [Rabbi])*, 1923–26.
Oil on canvas, 117×89.5 cm (46×35 in.).
Öffentliche Kunstsammlung/Kunstmuseum, Basle.
© VG Bild-Kunst, Bonn 1996.

must have greatly satisfied von Waldstein and his associates, because an abridged version was lent to Munich and Erlangen.

Another precursor exhibition deserves special attention, not least as a forerunner of the title given to the major 1937 show. This was "Entartete Kunst," held in the inner courtyard of the Neues Rathaus in Dresden from September 23 to October 18, 1933 (fig. 3). Like other Schreckenskammern it owed its existence to the zeal of a conventional artist, the Nazi and academy director Richard Müller. He now saw his chance to take revenge on his progressive colleagues, such as Otto Dix, who had been expelled from the Dresden academy. The center of the exposition was formed by sociocritical works of the Dresden Secession Group 1919 and the Association of Revolutionary

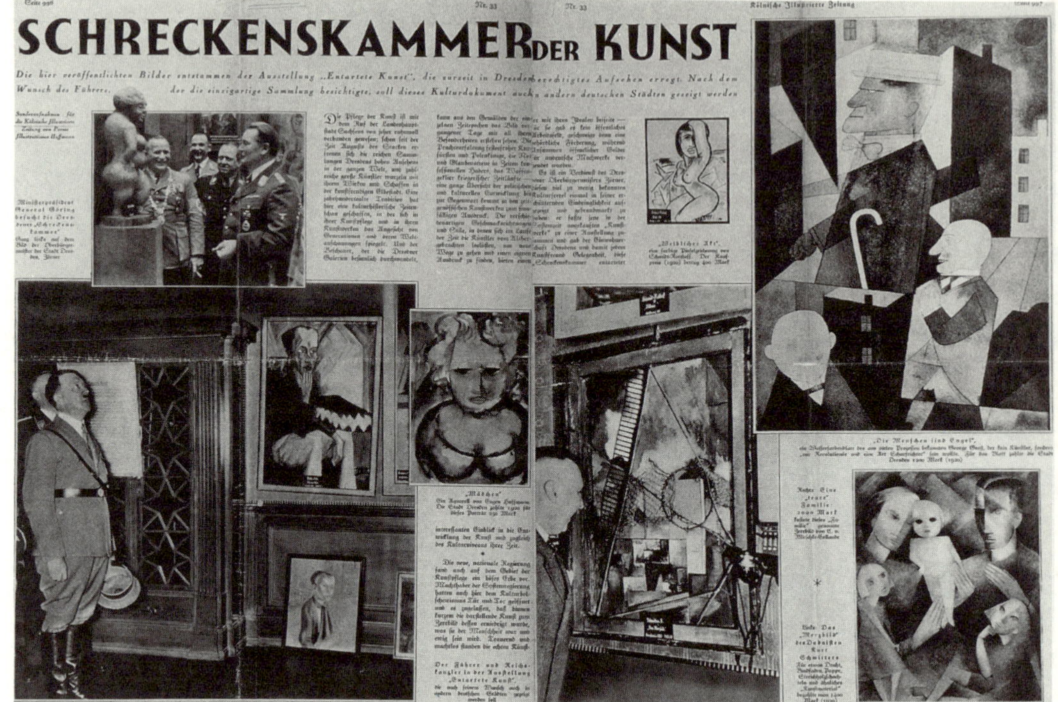

SCHRECKENSKAMMER DER KUNST

Die hier veröffentlichten Bilder entstammen der Ausstellung „Entartete Kunst", die zurzeit in Dresden berechtigtes Aufsehen erregt. Nach dem Wunsch des Führers, der die einzigartige Sammlung besichtigte, soll dieses Kulturdokument auch in andern deutschen Städten gezeigt werden

FIG. 3. Exhibition "Entartete Kunst" (Degenerate Art), Dresden, 1933–35; pages from a review in the *Kölnische Illustrierte Zeitung*, August 17, 1935; *left page, top*: Dresden mayor Ernst Zörner (left) and Hermann Göring (right) examine Christoph Voll's sculpture *Schwangere Frau* (Pregnant Woman); *below*: Adolf Hitler visits the exhibition; displayed are works by Hans Grundig, Erich Heckel, Eugen Hoffmann, Kurt Schwitters, Karl Schmidt-Rottluff, Georg Grosz, and Constantin von Mitschke-Collande.
Private collection, Stuttgart.

German Artists (ASSO) and taken from the inventory of the Dresdner Stadtmuseum. Between 1933 and 1937 it was shown in thirteen cities, the inventory being supplemented by local works in each case. By touring the country during four years, the Dresden show exceeded the otherwise customary local impact of the Schreckenskammern. Individual venues were Hagen/Westfalen, Nuremberg, Dortmund, Regensburg, Munich, Ingolstadt, Darmstadt, Frankfurt, Mainz, Koblenz, Worms, and finally Wiesbaden—before the exhibition was integrated en bloc into the Munich exhibition of the same name in July 1937.

In Frankfurt the exhibition was presented in the so-called Volksbildungsheim (National Education Home) from September 1 to 30, 1936. It was promoted by the National Socialist group Kraft durch Freude (Strength by Pleasure) and the Hans-Thoma-Gesellschaft (Hans-Thoma-Society). From the published reviews it is clear that the Frankfurt show was also based on the antithetic exhibition principle: "But then there is also a small exhibition presenting the justification of the national socialist fight in a sanctuary of real, lasting German art."[10] This "model cabinet" contained paintings and graphics of unknown provenance by Fritz Boehle, Hans Adolf Bühler, Georg Poppe, Otto Scholderer, Hans Thoma, and others. Several sources show that this defamatory show in Frankfurt encountered resistance from some of the viewers. *The Frankfurter Volksblatt* carried a detailed report of the criticism expressed by a group of visitors, who, in the article, were defamed as being "Jewish or of Jewish origin."[11] According to various files of the Stadtarchiv as well as an account by an eyewitness, there was even a stir created in connection with the visit of a high school class, which was dealt with by various authorities over a period of more than two and a half months. A teacher from a public school had made some positive remarks to his class of seniors about the works exhibited, with the result that he got involved in an argument with a Nazi informer, who denounced him to the regional director of the Reichskammer der bildenden Künste (Reich Chamber of Visual Arts) in Hessen-Nassau.[12] Certainly, these controversies, some of which were held in public, reinforced the sensational character of the exhibition.

The total state control of the arts was formed on a legal and organizational-institutional basis. It was part of a process of streamlining, comprising all fields of society, politics, economy, and culture, in the course of which the party and the state were united. Besides the Professional Civil Service Restoration Act, important changes in the cultural sector were the setting up of the Ministry of National Enlightenment and Propaganda under Goebbels (March 11, 1933) and the Reich Chamber of Culture subordinate to this ministry (November 15, 1933).[13] The latter consisted of seven special chambers for the fields of literature, press, broadcasting, theater, music, film, and the visual arts. It was instrumental in controlling all persons working in the cultural field and their products. Only those who were members of a chamber were permitted to practice their profession. A test of the political reliability and racial ancestry of applicants made it possible to exclude unwanted artists and thus impose a professional ban on them. In view of this complete elimination of the autonomy of art, it sounds like pure cynicism when Goebbels promised on the occasion of the inauguration of the Chamber of Culture: "We do not want to restrict the artistic-cultural development but to promote it."[14] The formal streamlining of art was completed by Goebbels's prohibition of art criticism in November 1936.

In spite of these measures, the development of National Socialist art policy up to 1937 did not follow a straight course nor was it free of contradiction. Besides individual protests against both the Schreckenskammern and the widespread condemnation of the avant-garde, an oppositional group arose and began to fight in public for the recognition of expressionism as "German" and "Nordic" art. Unlike most of the museum departments of modern art, which had been closed in 1933 and their collections ordered into storage, the Berliner Kronprinzenpalais remained open until the "year of the Olympics" (1936). The artists ostracized in the precursor shows were able to exhibit in private galleries and art societies and even obtained state commissions. This paradoxical situation was possible because of the power struggle raging among the top leaders of the Nazi party with regard to responsibilities and the future course of cultural policy—particularly involved were the rivals Goebbels, founder of the Combat League Rosenberg, and Minister of Education Bernhard Rust. Last but not least, it was the function of the 1937 exhibitions "Entartete Kunst" and "Große Deutsche Kunstausstellung" (Great German Art) to finally establish definite guidelines for the National Socialist cultural policy.

In order to understand why the show "Entartete Kunst" took place when it did, another important factor has to be taken into account. In 1937, the phase of consolidation in the field of domestic affairs had largely been completed. Hitler's policy vis-à-vis his allies had strengthened Germany's position abroad, and at the same time the economy was beginning to flourish. The time had come for the rulers to account for the first four years of their government and to make sure that the population would consent with enthusiasm to their further activities. As one important instrument of their propagandistic self-portrayal they chose the tool of exhibition. Under the title "Gebt mir vier Jahre Zeit" (Give Me Four Years' Time) a gigantic show promoting economic and military performance was held in Berlin from April 30 to June 20, 1937 (fig. 4). One of the 1.35 million visitors was the French ambassador André François-Poncet, who made the following note in his diary: "One can see only fighter planes, U-boats, and tanks. These are not

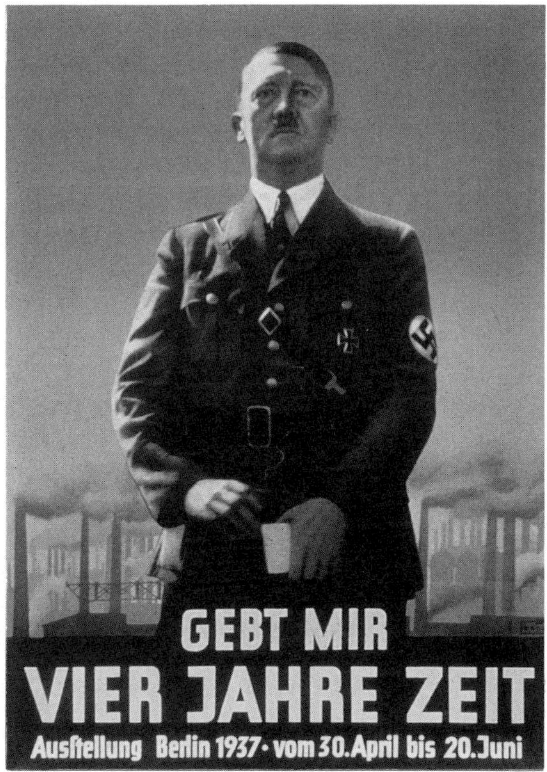

FIG. 4. Exhibition "Gebt mir vier Jahre Zeit" (Give Me Four Years' Time), Berlin, 1937; poster. Bayerisches Hauptstaatsarchiv, Munich.

the only indications of Hitler's thoughts and plans. The tone of his speeches becomes sharper and sharper, especially when he is talking about Soviet Russia."[15]

The "creation of new German art" was another achievement to be celebrated within the framework of a representative show in Munich, the "Hauptstadt der Bewegung" (Capital of Movement). On July 18, 1937, the "Große Deutsche Kunstausstellung" (fig. 5) was solemnly inaugurated in the newly built House of German Art, the building replacing the glass palace that burned down in 1931 was soon popularly called Palazzo Kitschi because of its monstrous size.[16] In forty roomy, brightly lit halls of the temple of art, the visitor was shown about 1,200 sculptures, paintings, and graphics by 557

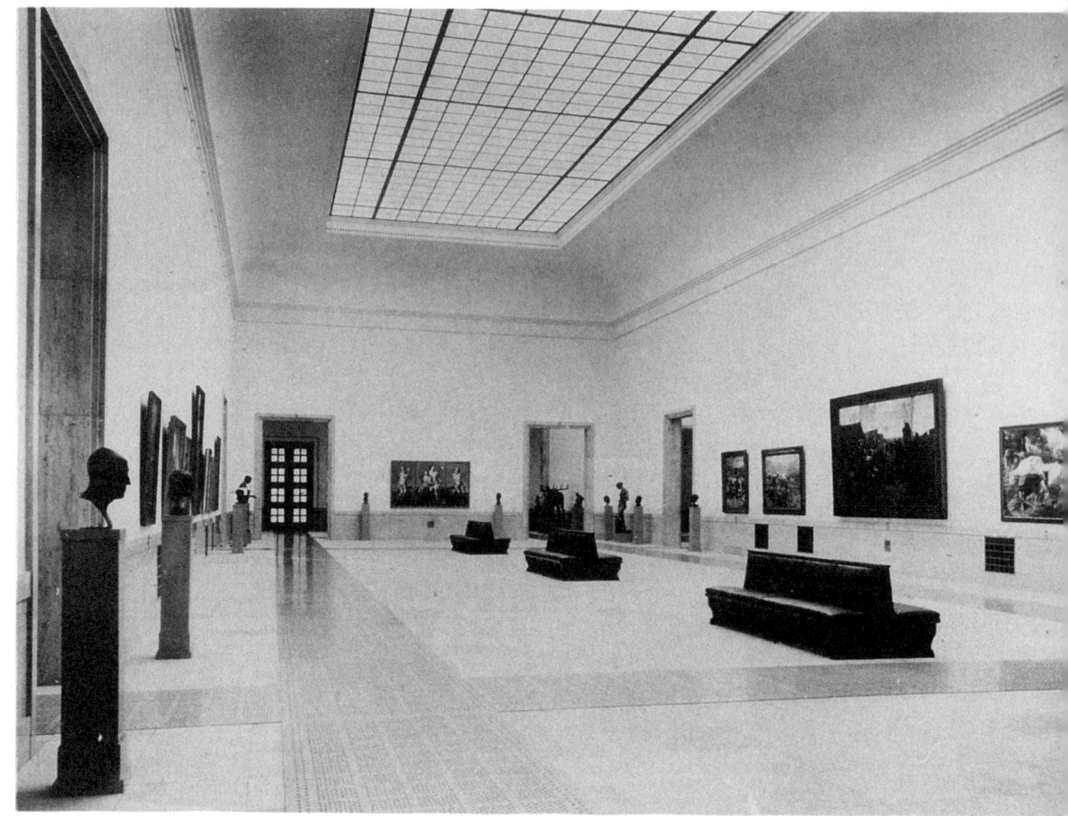

FIG. 5. Gallery in the exhibition "Große Deutsche Kunstausstellung" (Great German Art Exhibition), Munich, 1937; Adolf Ziegler's triptych *Die vier Elemente* (The Four Elements) is on the far wall.
Bildarchiv Staatliche Museen zu Berlin—Preußischer Kulturbesitz.

artists arranged in a deliberately spacious and clear manner. But what was presented as a supposedly new and revolutionary style of art, as the "expression of a new era," was mainly a second- or third-rate rehash of conventional historical scenes, landscapes, and nude paintings. Even filmmaker Leni Riefenstahl admits to having suffered when visiting the show: "How embarrassing Adolf Ziegler's four naked bodies were as 'The Four Elements' . . . or Hitler as a 'knight' on a white nag and another dozen of heroic and allegoric portraits of the Führer."[17] In propagandistic terms as well, the success of the exhibition was mediocre: it is true that according to press reports it attained the considerable number of 420,000 visitors in the three and a half months it was open ("Entartete Kunst," however, recorded approximately two million). The interest in buying "great German art" was also very limited.

While Hitler in his inaugural address in front of the House of German Art announced, snorting with rage, a "relentless purging war" against "decadence in art," feverish work was done in the arcades of the nearby Hofgarten. The rooms usually presenting the collection of plaster casts of the University Institute for Archaeology had been emptied and the defamatory show "Entartete Kunst" hastily set up. As a contrast to the "German" art, it was to be inaugurated the following day with a speech by Adolf Ziegler, president of the Reich Chamber of Visual Arts. Ziegler—furnished with a decree from Propaganda Minister Goebbels and accompanied by a commission—had in a lightning operation from July 4 to 10 descended on the most important collections of modern art in Germany, confiscating hundreds of works of art and shipping them to Munich. In his address broadcast by all German radio stations, Ziegler said: "All around us you see the monstrous offspring of insanity, impudence, ineptitude, and sheer degeneracy. Train wagons would not have been sufficient to remove all this rubbish from the German museums. But this will be done, and it will be done very soon."[18] Only a few weeks later this threat came true: in a second, much more extensive operation throughout the country, several committees appointed by Ziegler confiscated thousands of works of art in more than a hundred museums. The first operation had been a superficial inspection carried out under pressure in order to requisition exhibits for the Munich show. The second operation represented a systematic liquidation of modern art in the whole of Germany. Extremely affected were the major art museums of Essen, Hamburg, Berlin, Mannheim, and Frankfurt. The Gesetz über Einziehung von Erzeugnissen entarteter Kunst (Law on the Confiscation of Products of Degenerate Art) was passed on May 31, 1938, in order to legalize the expropriation of artworks and to establish a legal basis for their sale.

How did the defamatory show manifest itself to the more than two million visitors from both Germany and abroad?[19] Crowded together in nine narrow rooms (figs. 6 and 7), two on the ground floor and seven on the first floor, were about 600 paintings, sculptures, graphics, photographs, and books, by 120 artists. The spectrum of the artistic styles ranged from German impressionism (Corinth) and expressionism (Barlach, Lehmbruck, Heckel, Kirchner, Marc, Mueller, Nolde, Schmidt-Rottluff) to Dadaism (Schwitters)

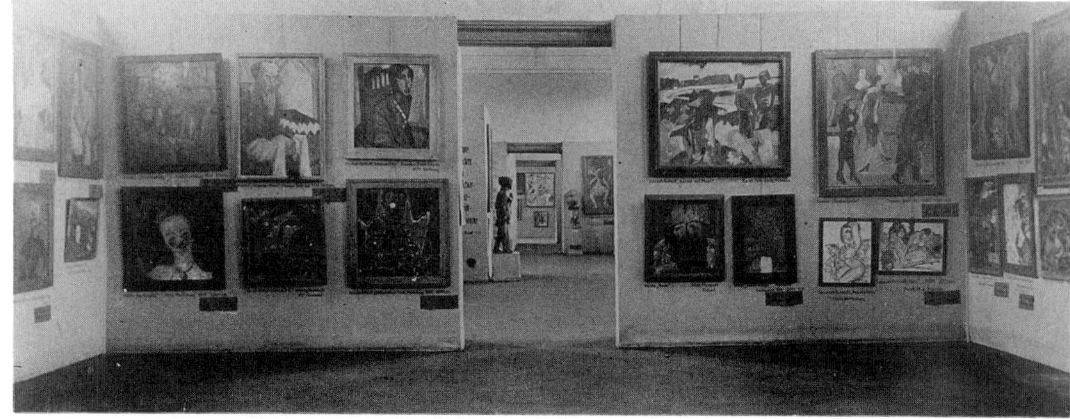

FIG. 6. Galleries in the exhibition "Entartete Kunst" (Degenerate Art), Munich, 1937; works by various expressionist artists.
Archiv der Alten Nationalgalerie, Berlin.

and constructivism (Mondrian, Lissitzky, Dexel), and from artists from the Bauhaus and all forms of abstract art (Feininger, Kandinsky, Klee, Schlemmer) to the New Objectivity (Dix, Schlichter, Scholz). Adler, Beckmann, Chagall, Grosz, Hofer, and Kokoschka were represented as well. It was the expressionists, in particular the artists of Die Brücke (The Bridge), who were subject to extremely violent attacks. An attempt had been made to structure the exhibition according to theme—such as religious subjects, representations of women, scenes from rural life, landscapes—but the plan was not consistently carried out.

The exhibition was characterized by a distinctive form of presentation. Hung close together in narrow and half-dark rooms, the pictures conveyed an impression of chaos and oppressive narrowness. The high purchase prices—partly due to the inflation—were posted in order to provoke indignation about the alleged waste of tax money. The fact that minors were forbidden entry contributed to the exhibition's aura of sensationalism. The crowd of viewers—an average of more than 23,000 persons a day for two and a half months—were confronted with polemically aggressive captions on the walls encouraging resentment toward modern art and raising anti-Semitic and anti-Communist apprehensions. Thus emotions were heightened and hatred was fostered against artists and critics, dealers and museum directors. This created an associative framework with the powerful agenda of reducing all the artworks to the same level, to prevent any single one from

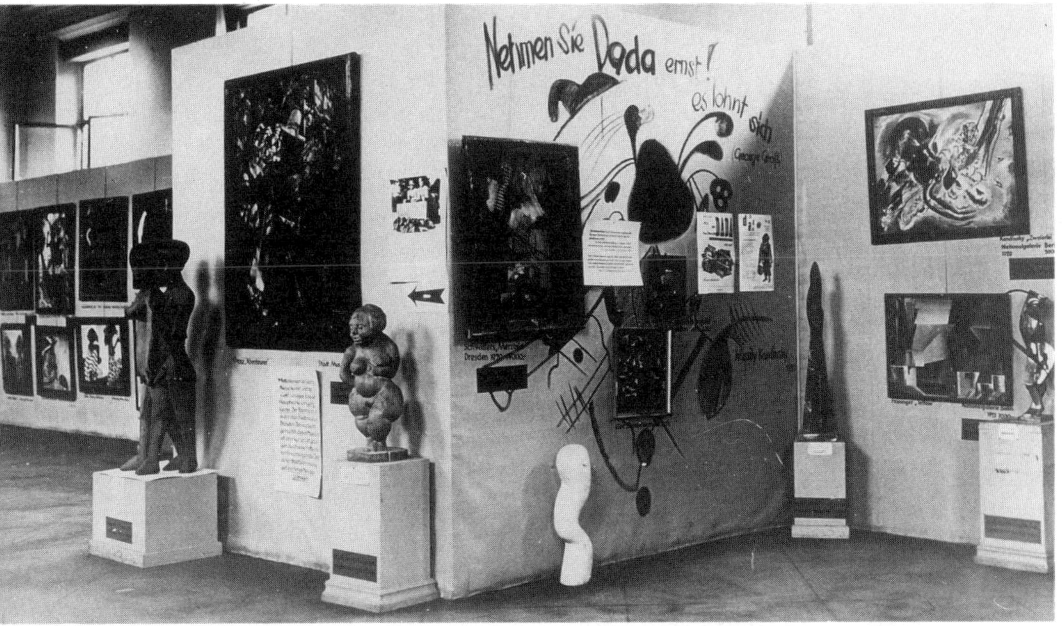

FIG. 7. Gallery in the exhibition "Entartete Kunst" (Degenerate Art), Munich, 1937; Room 3 with the Dada wall; works by George Grosz, Christoph Voll, Kurt Schwitters, Richard Haizmann, Paul Klee, Oswald Herzog, Wassily Kandinsky, Lyonel Feininger, Margarethe Moll, and others; postcard.
George Grosz-Archiv, Stiftung Archiv der Akademie der Künste, Berlin.

having an individual presence, or from being perceived in isolation. The psychological effects thus achieved were given a political function. The art historian Georg Bussmann is worth quoting here:

> Captions and pictures, juxtaposed or arranged in orderless confusion, are intended to stir the viewer's emotions, triggering feelings of repulsion and indignation; these feelings in turn, like the opinions expressed in the captions, are intended to encourage a sense of satisfaction at the demise of this type of art and ultimately to inspire agreement with the "revolutionary" new beginning and political succession.[20]

Even though one can speak of how viewers were conditioned by propagandistic methods, it is necessary to consider the visitors' predisposition. What level of knowledge and expectations did they have? Most of the public were probably extremely suceptible to this rabble-rousing propaganda because few people were familiar with modern art, which had not yet received widespread acceptance in the 1930s. For many visitors such exhibitions were their first encounter with avant-garde art. As far as their expectations were concerned, the sensationalism promoted by the press had played an important role. Carl Linfert wrote in the *Frankfurter Zeitung:* "For a very great number of those present, it is certainly the first time in their life that they are visiting an exhibition. Most of them had come with the will and the awareness that they would be outraged."[21]

It is worth dwelling for a moment on the vocabulary employed by the exhibitions and the publications accompanying them.[22] The concept of "degeneration" had been transferred from the field of psychiatry to the visual arts by Max Nordau, who published his book *Entartung* (Degeneration) in 1892–93. Debates about art policy soon adopted it. A polemic against the Munich Secession written by Martin Feddersen in 1894 was headed "Die Entartung der Münchener Kunst" (The Degeneration of Munich Art). "Jewish-Bolshevist Art," a slogan that was almost synonymous with "degenerate art," was, however, a purely National Socialist construct. It was on this irrational level, and not by seemingly formal distinctions or aesthetic criteria, that modern art could best be appropriated for fascist purposes. The other reproaches (obscenity, violation of religious feelings, appeal to class struggle, military sabotage, relationship to the artistic activities of mentally ill persons) may easily be subsumed under this one concept and applied to very different styles.

After its spectacular start in Munich, the defamatory show was sent on tour by the Propaganda Ministry. In spring 1938 it could be seen in the Berlin House of Art (fig. 8). For this second venue, the works had been reorganized, leading to a fundamental change in the show's appearance: whereas it had been the expressionists who bore the brunt of the attack in Munich, it was the sociocritical, politically committed art of the 1920s that was preponderant in Berlin, such as works by Otto Dix and George Grosz. This tendency also determined the choice of works reproduced in the notorious exhibition guide (fig. 9), a quarter of which clearly demonstrated social criticism. The guide had not been available before the Berlin venue. The 32-page rabble-rousing pamphlet had a clever structure: in a pseudo-scientific manner it divided the "host of manifestations of degeneration" into nine sections, such as "disregard for the basics of technique," "violation of religious feelings," "appeal to class struggle and anarchy," "incitement of military sabotage, ridiculing of the German front soldier," and "representation of moral decline, idealization of the prostitute." It was interspersed with quotations from Hit-

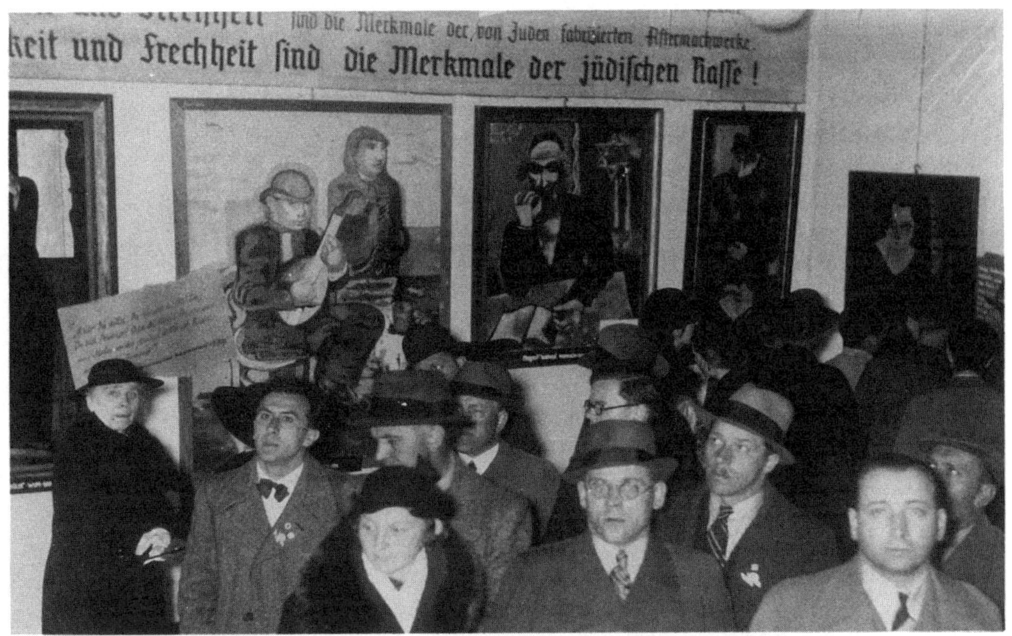

FIG. 8. Gallery in the exhibition "Entartete Kunst" (Degenerate Art), Berlin, 1938; works by Jankel Adler and Marc Chagall.
Bilderdienst Süddeutscher Verlag, Munich.

ler's speeches given at party rallies in 1933 and 1935 as well as on the occasion of the inauguration of the House of German Art. Opposite the text pages were reproductions of individual works, reduced to the size of a stamp and corresponding only in part to the actual objects on display. The pictures were arranged in complete disorder and were explained by cynical comments. The most infamous technique of discrimination is undoubtedly the unscrupulous use of "insane art." On four out of sixteen illustrated pages, works of modern art (such as a self-portrait by Kokoschka done in 1923) are contrasted with works from the famous Prinzhorn Collection of the Psychiatric Clinic of the University of Heidelberg (fig. 10). Depending on the text accompanying the illustrations, the strategy of defamation was applied at different levels: either the visitor was to regard the artists' creations and those of the mentally ill as "similar" and thus be led to the false conclusion that the artists were also "ill" (and in National Socialist terms this meant "racially inferior," and thus ultimately "unworthy of life"); or the "comparison" was to prove that "incurably insane nonartists" still created "better" works (i.e.,

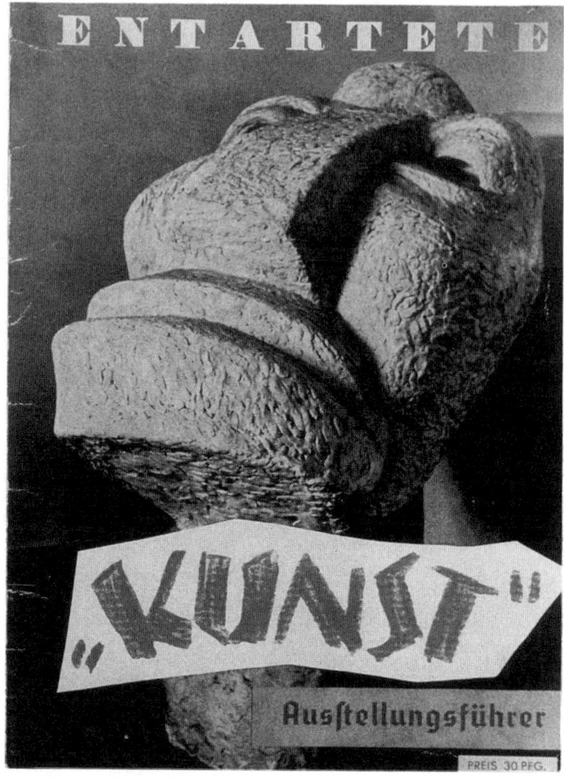

FIG. 9. Cover of the exhibition guide for "Entartete Kunst" (Degenerate Art), 1937–38; image: Otto Freundlich, *Der neue Mensch* (The New Man), 1912. Plaster cast, height 139 cm (54¾ in.); location unknown. Archive of the author.

more similar to the natural model) than modern artists did, thus proving the artist's lack of ability. A third variant was expressed in Hitler's characterization: "deliberate madness."

At this point it becomes clear that the artists of the European avant-garde had in many respects provided antimodernist propagandists with an easy target. In seeking sources of inspiration and new possibilities of expression, and rejecting the more traditional models favored by their predecessors, they had turned to the creations of children, the mentally ill, and so-called primitive tribes. Fascism mercilessly avenged this seeking! Of course, the warning expressed by Doctor Hans Prinzhorn in 1922 in his groundbreaking book der Mitwelt mit Gewalt als Wirklichkeiten aufzuschwätzen versuchen, oder ihr gar als „Kunst" vorsetzen wollen.

Nein, hier gibt es nur zwei Möglichkeiten: Entweder diese sogenannten „Künstler" sehen die Dinge wirklich so und glauben daher an das, was sie darstellen, dann wäre nur zu untersuchen, ob ihre Augenfehler entweder auf mechanische Weise oder durch Vererbung zustande gekommen sind. Im einen Fall tief bedauerlich für diese Unglücklichen, im zweiten wichtig für das Reichsinnenministerium, das sich dann mit der Frage zu beschäftigen hätte, wenigstens eine weitere Vererbung derartiger grauenhafter Sehstörungen zu unterbinden. Oder aber sie glauben selbst nicht an die Wirklichkeit solcher Eindrücke, sondern sie bemühen sich aus anderen Gründen, die Nation mit diesem Humbug zu belästigen, dann fällt so ein Vergehen in das Gebiet der Strafrechtspflege.... Es interessiert mich dabei auch nicht im geringsten, ob sich diese Auch-Künstler die von ihnen gelegten Eier dann gegenseitig begackern und damit begutachten oder nicht! Denn der Künstler schafft nicht für den Künstler, sondern er schafft genau so wie alle Anderen für das Volk! Und wir werden dafür Sorge tragen, daß gerade das Volk von jetzt ab wieder zum Richter über seine Kunst aufgerufen wird.

Durch bewußte Verrücktheiten sich auszuzeichnen, um damit die Aufmerksamkeit zu erringen, das zeugt nicht nur von einem künstlerischen Versagen, sondern auch von einem moralischen Defekt.

Der Führer
Reichsparteitag 1933.

30

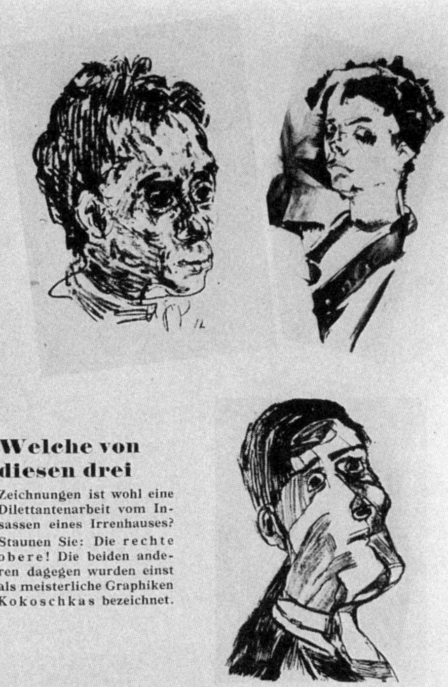

Welche von diesen drei

Zeichnungen ist wohl eine Dilettantenarbeit vom Insassen eines Irrenhauses? Staunen Sie: Die rechte obere! Die beiden anderen dagegen wurden einst als meisterliche Graphiken Kokoschkas bezeichnet.

FIG. 10. Exhibition guide "Entartete Kunst" (Degenerate Art), Berlin, 1937–38; pages 30–31, with works by Oskar Kokoschka and Georg Birnbacher (mentally ill patient of the Psychiatric Clinic of the University of Heidelberg).
Archive of the author.

Bildnerei der Geisteskranken (Image Making by the Mentally Ill), was preached to deaf ears: "It is superficial and wrong to construct out of similarity of outward appearance equality of underlying mental conditions."[23] And as far as sociocritical and left-wing art was concerned, the Nazi reproaches might perfectly mirror the artists' intentions. To accuse Dix of "military sabotage" hits the nail on the head, for what did that combatant intend by his apocalyptic paintings if not to fight against war and militarism?

The propaganda strategists were convinced of the success of their defamatory show. Between 1938 and 1941, a reduced version of the exhibition traveled with changing contents to twelve towns of the Reich: Berlin, Leipzig,

Düsseldorf, Salzburg, Hamburg, Stettin, Weimar, Vienna, Frankfurt, Chemnitz, Waldenburg/Silesia, and Halle. According to press reports, it was visited by more than 3.2 million persons in all. On November 12, 1941, the exhibition "Entartete Kunst" was given back to the Propaganda Ministry. The list stored in the Bundesarchiv Potsdam mentions 7 sculptures, about 50 paintings, and approximately 180 graphics.[24] A comparison with the checklist of objects shown in Munich in the summer of 1937 demonstrates that of the works returned in 1941, only 8 paintings, a sculpture, and 32 graphics belonged to the initial show. These are presumably the only works that were exhibited at all thirteen venues.

In order to adequately estimate the significance of the defamatory art exhibitions as an instrument of National Socialist propaganda, one has to broaden one's horizons and take into account other exhibition projects. The National Socialists had recognized the propagandistic possibilities of such exhibitions staged as *Gemeinschaftsrituale*[25] (community rituals) and made use of them for their own purposes. One of the most effective instruments of mass propaganda used to censor the arts and popularize fascist ideology was undoubtedly the exhibition as such, particularly the traveling show aimed at a large public. The Schreckenskammern, especially the Dresden show "Entartete Kunst" of 1933, marked the beginning of this practice. The strategy was based on the antithetic principle, and the names of the positive, often thematic exhibitions sounded like the topics of a party propaganda catalogue: "The Elite," "Heroic Art," "The Streets of Adolf Hitler in Art," "The German Forest," "The Beauty of Labor," "The Greatness of Germany." From 1939 on, there was a rapid increase in shows glorifying the war and condemning the enemy: "Scenes and Portraits from the Poland Campaign," "Front Art," "The Pirate State of England," "The Soviet Paradise." In contrast, exhibitions dealing with conceptions of the enemy took a negative stance. The precursor exhibitions, which were primarily aimed at the Weimar Republic with its parliamentary system, and the show "Entartete Kunst" of 1937, which was used to generate popular support for the planned war in the East as well as the mass murder of the Jewish people, belonged to this group. Furthermore, from 1936 on the so-called anti-Bolshevist exhibitions, and from 1937 on the show "The Wandering Jew," served to further ideological preparation for war and mass murder.

In our context, it is of interest that in these latter touring exhibitions as well, works of modern art were shown with the intention of ostracizing them. A photograph from the "Anti-Bolshevist Exhibition" in Munich in 1936 (fig. 11) shows several works of art, such as paintings by Beckmann

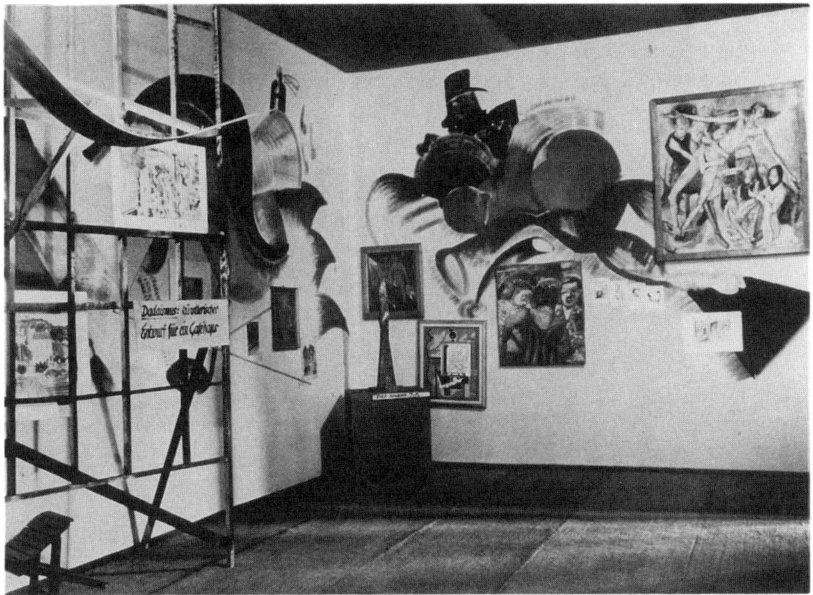

FIG. 11. Gallery in the exhibition "Antibolschewistische Ausstellung" (Anti-Bolshevist Exhibition), Munich, 1936; identifiable works by Ernst Ludwig Kirchner, Willi Baumeister, Paul Kleinschmidt, and Max Beckmann. Bundesarchiv, Koblenz.

(*Kreuzabnahme*, Descent from the Cross; today in the Museum of Modern Art, New York), Paul Kleinschmidt, Baumeister, and Ernst Ludwig Kirchner (*Selbstportrait als Soldat*, Self-portrait as Soldier; now at Allan Memorial Art Museum, Oberlin, Ohio), which had all been confiscated from the Frankfurt Städel Museum, as well as the sculpture *Das Ich* (The Ego) by Oswald Herzog, which had been removed from the Berliner Nationalgalerie. It is quite evident that the exhibition design employed here in 1936 is already that typical of the Munich 1937 show "Entartete Kunst" (figs. 6 and 7)—namely an optically dynamic, spacious mode of presentation combining picture and script, constituting the principles of collage. The installation view (fig. 11) shows the obvious influence of modern exhibition architecture as developed in the late 1920s by El Lissitzky and the members of the Bauhaus, many of whom were denounced by the exhibitions.

The censorship of the visual arts in Nazi Germany ranged from the dismissals of museum staffs and artists via the Schreckenskammern to the closing down of exhibitions and the confiscation of publications; from the elimination of the avant-garde in the museums to the extensive confiscation, sale, and finally methodical destruction of thousands of works of art; from bans on exhibitions, sale, and professional activities, and other reprisals against unwanted artists, to their psychical and physical annihilation. It led to the persecution and flight of numerous intellectuals and artists into exile or inner emigration. The other side of fascist censorship concerned the officially promoted art production. The state cultivated an art that sought only to further a racist human image and the ideological preparation for war, holocaust, and so-called euthanasia: be it with a falsely populistic illustration of the "blood and soil" myth, sloshy landscape idylls, glorification of military virtues, or an idealizing presentation of the "Aryan" family. Art thus served as decoration and at the same time as a stabilizing element for a system that despised human values. Submissive artists worked as collaborators.

The total liquidation of the autonomy of art, replaced by central control of the entire cultural life in the Third Reich, corresponded to the state's claim to total power and authority. With pressure and terror, it confiscated the freedom of the arts warranted and protected in the constitution of the Weimar Republic. This was, by the way, in response to censorship in the Kaiserreich, and was taken up again in 1949 in the constitutional law of the Federal Republic of Germany.[26]

What was the difference between art policy in the Third Reich and censorship of the traditional kind, or the religiously motivated iconoclastic events of the Middle Ages? It was not only that man and work were systematically annihilated without consequence, but that art and art policy were abused for political purposes and the totalitarian rulers turned art policy into a tool with which to lead and dominate the people. And this instrument also served to eliminate a form of art whose effects were feared because it represented individuality, diversity, and intellectual independence in a (partly intentionally) provocative manner—an independence that contained a critical potential as a form of intellectual strength, which those in power might well consider a threat, at least subjectively. As far as the practice and method of National Socialist censorship is concerned, it is remarkable that the objects that were censored were not withheld from the public but were rather systematically exposed.[27]

Until the 1980s the campaign and exhibition "Entartete Kunst" were generally considered as isolated evidence of Nazi cultural barbarism. But more recent research has placed less emphasis on "poor taste" and more on the historical roots of these ideas and the ideology behind the art policies, as well as on the social and political context of the Third Reich. From this approach, it becomes clear that the regime did not consider avant-garde art as one of its main opponents but rather used it as a "spektakuläres Paradefeld ihrer Propaganda"[28] (spectacular and perfect vehicle for propaganda). In the context of the general persecution, the fight against modern art proved to be a "means to further objectives not longer concerned with cultural policy: the campaign thereafter contributed to the construction of racist and anti-Communist concepts of the enemy, which the National Socialist regime needed to persecute minorities, to support its interference in Spain and to prepare its Eastern campaign."[29] The avant-garde was thus *verwertet* (made use of).

Certainly these functions and appearances of censorship are phenomena of a fascist dictatorship and are conceivable only within the framework of a totalitarian state in this particular manner. But when we discuss today the topical question of the dialectics of culture and administration,[30] of public promotion and state censorship in art, it seems to me that we should reflect carefully on this subject. For it clarfies for us the potential dangers and mechanisms of an ideological monopoly and misuse of art for the purpose of materializing overriding interests. The controversy in connection with the National Endowment for the Arts shows not least that the autonomy of art, conceived as a field for experimentation and scope for individual action, is a value for which, even in our democracies, we should never cease to strive.

Translation by Katrin Gatzke

NOTES

1. Program of the NSDAP, § 23 c, section 3; quoted in Werner Maser, *Der Sturm auf die Republik: Frühgeschichte der* NSDAP (Stuttgart: Deutsche Verlags-Anstalt, 1973), 471. The party, founded in January 1919 under the name Deutsche Arbeiter-Partei, was renamed in 1920.

2. Concerning the "affair Tschudi," see Nicolaas Teeuwisse, *Vom Salon zur Secession: Berliner Kunstleben zwischen Tradition und Aufbruch zur Moderne, 1871–1900* (Berlin: Deutscher Verlag für Kunstwissenschaft, 1986), 197–220, and Barbara Paul, *Hugo von Tschudi und die moderne französische Kunst im Deutschen Kaiserreich* (Mainz: Philipp von Zabern, 1993).

3. *Ein Protest deutscher Künstler, Mit Einleitung von Carl Vinnen* (Jena: Eugen Diederichs, 1911), 2–16. See also Ron Manheim, *"Im Kampf um die Kunst": Die Diskussion von 1911 über zeitgenössische Kunst in Deutschland* (Hamburg: Sautter and Lackmann, 1987).

4. As one example, I would like to mention the wooden sculpture *Kruzifixus* (The Crucified Christ; probably destroyed) by Ludwig Gies, the public presentation of

which led to a scandal in 1921–22 culminating in an attack on the work. See Jenns Eric Howoldt, "Der Kruzifixus von Ludwig Gies: Ein Beispiel 'entarteter Kunst' in Lübeck," *Der Wagen* (1988): 164–74; Bernd Ernsting, "Scandalum Crucis: Der Lübecker Kruzifixus und sein Schicksal," in *Ludwig Gies, 1887–1966*, exh. cat. (Leverkusen: Städtisches Museum, Schloß Morsbroich, 1990), 57–71.

5. Concerning the past history of the National Socialist cultural policy and the activities of the Kampfbund für deutsche Kultur, see Stephanie Barron, "1937—Modern Art and Politics in Prewar Germany," in Stephanie Barron, ed., *"Degenerate Art": The Fate of the Avant-Garde in Nazi Germany*, exh. cat. (Los Angeles: Los Angeles County Museum of Art, 1991), 9–23 (with further bibliographical references). Pages 405–11 of that catalogue give a detailed bibliography on the subject.

6. Concerning the National Socialist propaganda exhibitions described in this essay, in particular the precursors and the venues of the show "Entartete Kunst," see Christoph Zuschlag, *"Entartete Kunst": Ausstellungsstrategien im Nazi-Deutschland* (Worms: Wernersche Verlagsgesellschaft, 1995); idem, "An 'Educational Exhibition': The Precursors of 'Entartete Kunst' and Its Individual Venues," in Barron, *"Degenerate Art"*, 83–103; idem, *"Der Kunstverein und die 'Neue Zeit': Der Badische Kunstverein zwischen 1933 und 1945,* in Jutta Dresch and Wilfried Rößling, eds., *Bilder im Zirkel, 175 Jahre Badischer Kunstverein Karlsruhe*, exh. cat. (Karlsruhe: Badischer Kunstverein, 1993), 191–207; idem, "Die verfemte Moderne: Die Ausstellung 'Entartete Kunst'—München 1937," *Kunstpresse*, April 1992, 28–32.

7. See Hans-Jürgen Buderer, *"Entartete Kunst": Beschlagnahmeaktionen in der Städtischen Kunsthalle Mannheim 1937*, Kunst and Dokumentation, 10, exh. cat. (Mannheim: Städtische Kunsthalle Mannheim, 1987; 2d ed., 1990); Karoline Hille, *Spuren der Moderne: Die Mannheimer Kunsthalle von 1918 bis 1933* (Berlin: Akademie Verlag, 1994), 274–309; Christoph Zuschlag, "Das Schicksal von Chagalls 'Rabbiner': Zur Geschichte der Kunsthalle Mannheim im Nationalsozialismus," in Jörg Schadt, ed., *Mannheim unter dem Nationalsozialismus* (Mannheim: Edition Quadrat, 1997).

8. *Mannheimer Morgen*, March 13, 1959; quoted in Buderer, *Beschlagnahmeaktionen*, 37, note 5.

9. According to an account given by Walter Passarge, who, however, did not come to Mannheim until 1936, when he succeeded Hartlaub; quoted in Buderer, *Beschlagnahmeaktionen*, 19.

10. *Nationalblatt*, August 30, 1936; see also the reports in the *Frankfurter Zeitung*, August 30 and September 9, 1936.

11. Hans Pott, "Alljuda contra Nationalsozialismus, Herr Professor Beck und eine Handvoll Judenstämmlinge kritisieren die Frankfurter Ausstellung 'Entartete Kunst,'" *Frankfurter Volksblatt*, September 9, 1936.

12. Stadtarchiv Frankfurt/M., Magistratsakten Az. 6022, Bd. 1, Bl. 258–65 c. Hermann Krämer, "Schubert, die Frankfurter Ausstellung 'Entartete Kunst' und was Kokoschka dazu sagte," in *Jahrbuch der Wöhlerschule* (1986): 51–52.

13. Robert Brady, "The National Chamber of Culture ('Reichskulturkammer')," in

Brandon Taylor and Wilfried van der Will, eds., *The Nazification of Art: Art, Design, Music, Architecture and Film in the Third Reich* (Winchester: Winchester Press, 1990), 80–88; Volker Dahm, "Anfänge und Ideologie der Reichskulturkammer: Die 'Berufsgemeinschaft' als Instrument kulturpolitischer Steuerung und sozialer Reglementierung," *Vierteljahreshefte für Zeitgeschichte* 34 (1986): 53–84.

14. *Völkischer Beobachter*, Berlin edition, November 15, 1933; quoted in Heinrich Dilly, *Deutsche Kunsthistoriker, 1933–1945* (Munich and Berlin: Deutscher Kunstverlag, 1988), 24.

15. André François-Poncet, *Als Botschafter in Berlin, 1931–1938* (Mainz: Florian Kupferberg Verlag, 1947), 285.

16. Today the building is called House of Art. It houses the Staatsgalerie moderner Kunst. However, there is controversy over whether the building should be pulled down or not. See Hans-Joachim Müller, "Die Entsorgung des Kunsttempels," *Die Zeit*, January 26, 1990.

17. Leni Riefenstahl, *Memoiren* (Munich and Hamburg: Knaus, 1987), 293.

18. Quotation from the complete printed version of Ziegler's speech in Peter-Klaus Schuster, ed., *Die "Kunststadt" München 1937, Nationalsozialismus und "Entartete Kunst,"* exh. cat. (Munich: Prestel, 1987), 217.

19. See Mario-Andreas von Lüttichau, "'Entartete Kunst,' Munich 1937: A Reconstruction," in Barron, *"Degenerate Art,"* 45–81.

20. Georg Bussmann, "'Entartete Kunst': Blick auf einen nützlichen Mythos," in *Deutsche Kunst im 20. Jahrhundert: Malerei und Plastik, 1905–1985*, exh. cat. (Stuttgart: Staatsgalerie, 1986), 109.

21. Carl Linfert, "Rückblick auf 'Entartete Kunst,'" *Frankfurter Zeitung*, November 14, 1937.

22. In this context the most important book is Wolfgang Willrich's *Säuberung des Kunsttempels: Eine kunstpolitische Kampfschrift zur Gesundung deutscher Kunst im Geiste nordischer Art* (Munich and Berlin: J. F. Lehmanns, 1937). The painter Willrich (1897–1948) played a decisive role in the organization of the Munich exhibition "Entartete Kunst," with his book providing guidelines.

23. Hans Prinzhorn, *Bildnerei der Geisteskranken: Ein Beitrag zur Psychologie und Psychopathologie der Gestaltung* (Berlin: Springer, 1922; quotation from the 4th ed. 1994), 346.

24. Zentrales Staatsarchiv Potsdam (Abteilungen des Bundesarchivs Koblenz), Best. 50.01–1018, Bl. 29–36.

25. Walter Grasskamp, *Museumsgründer und Museumsstürmer: Zur Sozialgeschichte des Kunstmuseums* (Munich: Beck, 1981), 45.

26. Weimarer Reichsverfassung (constitution of the Weimar Republic), art. 142: "Die Kunst, die Wissenschaft une ihre Lehre sind frei. Der Staat gewährt ihnen Schutz und nimmt an ihrer Pflege teil" (The arts, the sciences, and their teaching are free. The state protects them and participates in their cultivation). Grundgesetz der Bundesrepublik Deutschland (constitutional law of the FRG), art. 5, paragraph 3:

"Kunst und Wissenschaft, Forschung und Lehre sind frei" (The arts and the sciences, research and teaching are free); quotations from Sieghart Ott, *Kunst und Staat: Der Künstler zwischen Freiheit und Zensur* (Munich: Deutscher Taschenbuch Verlag, 1968), 102, 104.

27. This was, of course, a safe choice given that the audience was not already familiar with the work; yet it argues, oddly, for the power of art, since the policy implicitly acknowledges the power of the individual, unique work of art over its reproductions. The question whether an exhibition of reproductions would have been as successful is to be considered.

28. Walter Grasskamp, "Die unbewältigte Moderne: Entartete Kunst und documenta I, Verfemung und Entschärfung," in *Museum der Gegenwart: Kunst in öffentlichen Sammlungen bis 1937*, exh. cat. (Düsseldorf: Kunstsammlung Nordrhein-Westfalen, 1987–88), 15.

29. Hans-Ernst Mittig, "'Entartete Kunst': Künstlerische Rückblicke," *Kritische Berichte*, no. 4, 1990, 34.

30. Theodor W. Adorno, "Kultur und Verwaltung," *Merkur*, no. 2, 1960, 101–21; Hilmar Hoffmann, "Staatliche Lenkung der Kunst?" in Ruprecht-Karls-Universität Heidelberg, ed., *Kunst heute und ihr Publikum: Vorträge im Wintersemester, 1988/89* (Heidelberg: Heidelberger Verlagsanstalt, 1990), 9–18.

Seeing Red:
The Dallas Museum in the McCarthy Era

FRANCINE CARRARO

ON MARCH 15, 1955, THE PUBLIC AFFAIRS LUNCHEON CLUB, a polite and political group of affluent Dallas ladies wearing white gloves and pert hats, issued a statement to the press declaring that the Dallas Museum of Fine Arts (fig. 1) was "over-emphasizing all phases of futuristic, modernistic, and non-objective painting and statuary." They leveled another more serious charge at the art museum for allegedly "promoting the work of artists who have known Communist affiliations to the neglect of . . . many orthodox artists, some of them Texans, whose patriotism . . . has never been questioned." Their public resolution demanded that the museum "correct their policy of sponsoring the work of Communists."[1]

Glancing back today at this curious incident, it would be easy to write it off as merely a comical episode. But at the time, Jerry Bywaters, director of the Dallas Museum of Fine Arts (fig. 2), viewed the accusations seriously. The anti-Communist alarm that the members of the luncheon club sounded was ringing across America. Amid a climate of reaction and intolerance, any criticism or deviation from the "American way" might be viewed as subversive, and motivated either directly or remotely by the Soviets. The use of congressional investigatory committees in the cause of anti-Communism was pioneered by a Texas congressman, Martin Dies, the first chairman of the House Un-American Activities Committee in 1938–44, and later duplicated in the Senate by Joseph R. McCarthy. Across the nation an atmosphere of suspicion was officially fostered. The image of the Soviet threat was forged by the U.S. government and the news media. A *Dallas Morning News* editorial characterized the uneasy peace of the Cold War: "Now is the time for America to be on guard. Now is the hour when all the warnings of recent years against the

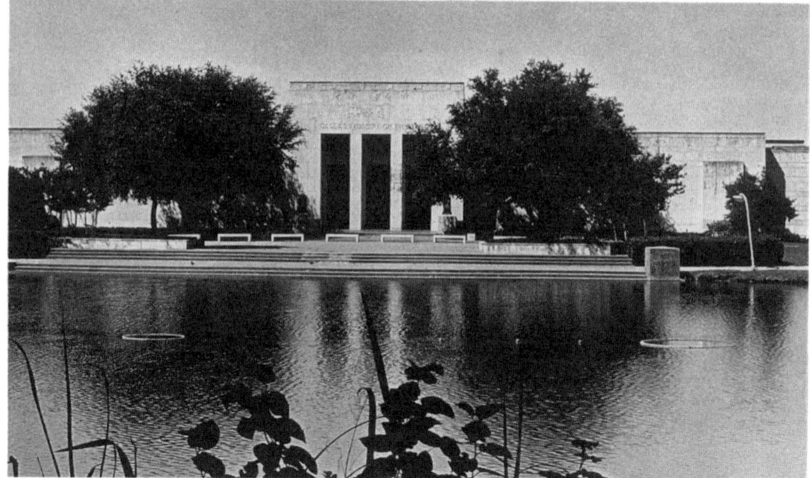

FIG. 1. Dallas Museum of Fine Arts, Fair Park, Dallas. (The building closed in 1984.) Courtesy of Dallas Museum of Art Photography Archives.

world-wide Communist conspiracy take on a newer and deeper meaning."[2] Historian Don Carleton argues in *Red Scare!* that conservative Texans of this period were especially disturbed about the political and economic drift of postwar America. He found: "Instead of contending with a multitude of domestic and international postwar developments as individual and separate issues and events, many Texans and Americans accepted a simple explanation to deal with everything."[3] For the Public Affairs Luncheon Club of Dallas, the Communist threat presented a convenient justification for denouncing all modernist art that they found inscrutable, and therefore subversive.

Beginning in 1955 and ending about four years later, the Dallas Museum of Fine Arts faced a puzzling sequence of politically motivated events and accusations. Symptomatic of the McCarthy era, vigilant superpatriots suspected that abstract art was subversive and they accused the museum of exhibiting artworks by "reds" or "pinko" artists. The right-wing ladies club was joined by a discordant chorus of American Legionnaires and avocational painters who were displeased with the progressive tenor of the museum's exhibitions. Their protests threatened the museum's public funding and they launched a sustained assault of criticism and harassment at an exhibition entitled "Sport in Art," which was organized and toured nationally by the American Federation of Arts. The problems at the museum not only illustrate how

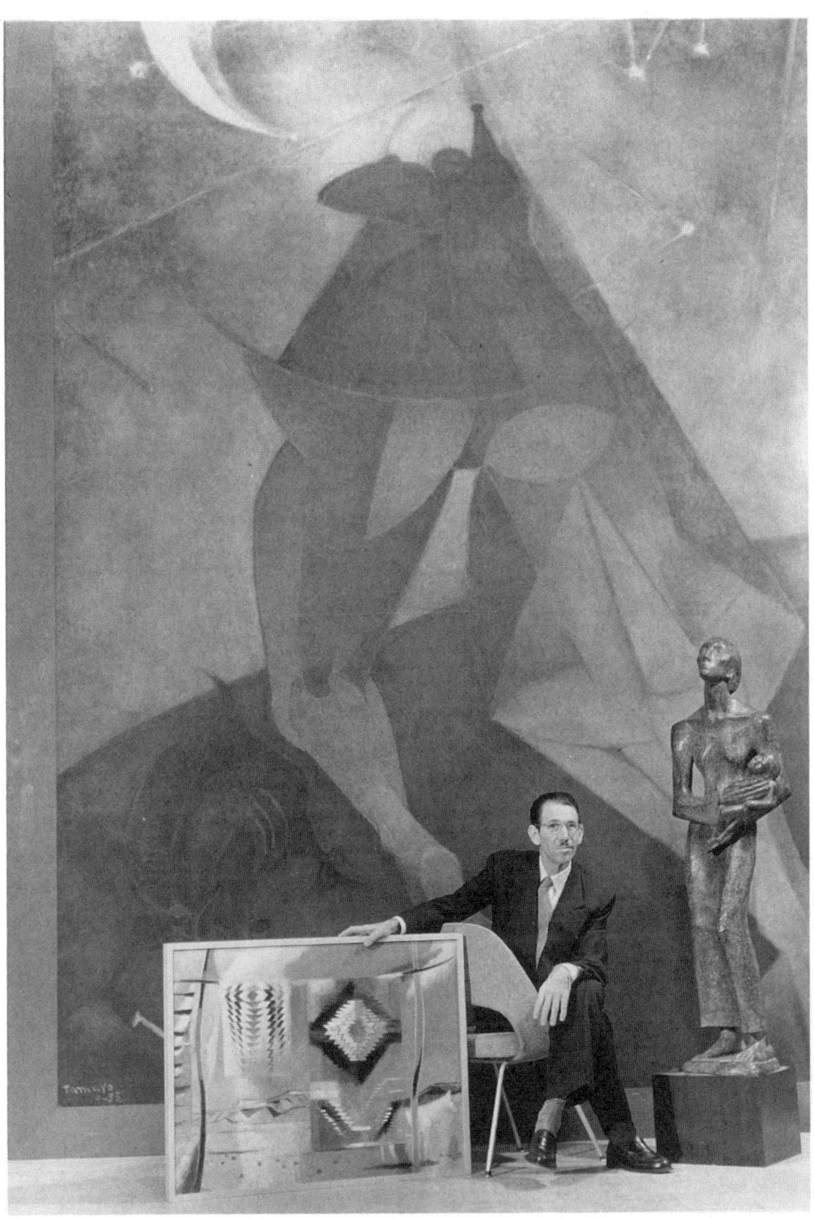

FIG. 2. Jerry Bywaters with mural *El Hombre* by Rufino Tamayo, sculpture *Mother and Child* by Carl Umlauf, and painting *Navajo Blanket* by Otis Dozier. Dallas Museum of Fine Arts, 1953.
Courtesy of The Jerry Bywaters Collection on Art of the Southwest, The Jake and Nancy Hamon Arts Library, Southern Methodist University, Dallas, Texas.

deeply the art world had become embroiled in Cold War politics, but they also demonstrate the symptoms of the Red Scare in the visual arts. The Communist controversy at the Dallas Museum of Fine Arts and the cancellation of the international tour of the "Sport in Art" exhibition provide a case study of the complex and difficult dialogue between postwar politics and the evolution of modern art in America.

The politicization of aesthetics was propelled by the pendulum swing of stylistic change. As the capital of the avant-garde shifted from Paris to New York after World War II, American art moved stylistically from realism to abstraction. And as American culture went through a period of postwar reconstruction buttressed by changes in the world economy, both the art market and the art product were transformed. During the postwar era, the stylistic evolution of art from regionalism and realism to internationalism and abstraction became a political and economic issue. The aesthetic clash between the old guard and the avant-garde turned into a political and economic battle. "Red baiting" discredited artists and damaged careers, and blacklisting was a way of canceling commissions and threatening public funds for museums. In the suffocating atmosphere of McCarthyism, aesthetic issues were sublimated by political concerns. What happened to the Dallas museum illustrates the ramifications of a modernist-traditionalist controversy in American art, and demonstrates how the Cold War brought that aesthetic debate to the surface.

The issues were so complicated that thirty years later Jerry Bywaters struggled to describe the nature of the attacks on the museum. "It's like trying to make a piece of sculpture out of smoke," he explained as he gestured. "It isn't there, it isn't there, you can't pin it down."[4] This discussion intends to pin it down, to describe the chronology of events and the personalities surrounding the controversy, and to analyze the nature of the Communist scare at the Dallas Museum of Fine Arts in the mid-1950s. The controversy did not center on any single event or crisis, but was fueled by chronic harassment, innuendo, unsubstantiated accusations, fear, and intolerance.

In March 1955, when the controversy began, the galleries of the Dallas museum were filled with sculptured jewelry by Salvador Dalí and early American folk art. Attendance at the museum was up and Bywaters anticipated a busy spring planning new exhibitions. Neither he nor the museum board could have anticipated the intensity and duration of criticism the museum would face. As the controversy unfolded, the local press thrived on the scandal and the national press debated the issues. Ultimately, the specific events in Dallas had national and international ramifications.

Certainly no one predicted that the ladies in the Publc Affairs Luncheon Club would cast the first stone. Many were members of the museum and their children attended art classes at the Museum School. The club met once a week and existed "to encourage women to take a thoughtful, informed, and active interest in the affairs and functions of government."[5] Their public accusation that the Dallas museum was exhibiting works by Communists was their first assault in a clumsy tactical battle against an uncertain enemy.

The luncheon club was sponsored by wealthy Dallas oilman Harold Lafayette Hunt, and Mrs. Hunt served on the club's board of directors. H. L. Hunt was a key figure in the museum controversy, not so much as an active participant but as a backer of various organizations and publications that attacked the Dallas Museum of Fine Arts. A substantial supporter of Joseph McCarthy, Hunt founded in 1951 and headed a tax-exempt organization, ostensibly nonpartisan and nonpolitical, called Facts Forum, which produced nationally syndicated radio and television programs and a magazine called *Facts Forum News*. Hunt hired former FBI agent Dan Smoot as commentator of a superpatriotic radio show called *Life Line*. Smoot later founded his own conservative newsletter which became the voice of Dallas's extremist fringe to the rest of the nation. As the controversy unfolded, Hunt's propaganda organs trumpeted alarm.

Women of the luncheon club based their charges against the museum on the information disseminated by *Facts Forum News*, and the ideas of Congressman George A. Dondero, a Michigan Republican who found in modern art a rich source for hidden conspiracies: "Communist art, aided and abetted by misguided Americans, is stabbing our glorious American art in the back with murderous intent." The congressman demanded a full-scale investigation by the House Un-American Activities Committee on the subject of Communist domination of art in the United States.[6]

Dondero's March 17, 1952, speech in the House of Representatives, "Communist Conspiracy in Art Threatens American Museums," was printed in the *Congressional Record*. His purpose was "to expose Red infiltration and control in certain artists' organizations," and he vowed to "show that many great museums are being used by these organizations, and that the critical appraisal of art by some papers and magazines often aids this Marxist cultural conspiracy." A New York arts group, Artists Equity, was a principal target, and by implication any artist who had ever been a member was under suspicion. Central to Dondero's argument was his mission to "expose" abstraction in modern art as dangerous and to show that museums coast to coast were used as agents for communist aggression. Dondero's theory was that abstraction was a vehicle of Communism and therefore museums that exhibited abstract art were Communist front organizations. Members of the luncheon club took Dondero's admonition to heart when he urged, "No immunity should be granted to the red art termites. The loyal American artists . . . are determined to protect our cultural birthright from this horde of art saboteurs who would first destroy in order to control."[7]

Based on Dondero's recommendations and lists of suspect artists, the excited club members checked the museum's catalogues and listed the "most objectionable" artists, including "Joseph Hirsch, Chaim Gross, George Grosz, Jo Davidson, Picasso, Rivera, and Max Webber [*sic*]."[8] The club then published an information bulletin entitled "Is There a Communist Conspiracy in the World of Art?" and distributed it to club members and to the members of the museum board. The publication answered the rhetorical question with a resounding affirmation. Quoting liberally from two Dondero speeches, the pamphlet announced that abstraction was a means of subversion. Using an often quoted phrase of Dondero's analysis of stylistic trends in art, the pamphlet concluded, "These isms can be tagged specifically . . . as instruments of destruction: Cubism aims to destroy by designed disorder; Futurism by the machine myth; Dadism [*sic*] by ridicule; Expressionism by aping the primitive and the insane; Abstractionism by the creation of brainstorms; Surrealism by the denial of reason."[9]

The day after the luncheon club's charges and demands were leveled at the museum, Stanley Marcus, director of Neiman-Marcus and president of the Dallas Art Association which governed the museum, consulted with Bywaters to marshal a response. Before Marcus left for a fashion buying expedition in Europe, he appointed a committee of trustees to study the charges. The committee found no basis for complaints. They decided that the issue was purely "a matter of taste, and neither communism or patriotism is involved." The investigation committee issued a prompt public response denying charges that the museum was "being used for the presentation of the art and concepts of Communists," and they reported that "no tax or City funds have ever been used to acquire any of the Museum's works of art. The collections have been accumulated by the Dallas Art Association with privately donated funds or through gifts. . . . The collection belongs to the City of Dallas under the agreement by which the City provides and maintains the Museum plant."[10]

"That was on a Friday afternoon," Marcus wrote in his autobiography. "On Saturday I paid calls on the publishers of the two daily papers at their homes and asked if they believed in the principle of the freedom of the press.

Naturally they replied affirmatively. I followed up by saying, 'If you believe in freedom of the press, then you must certainly accord similar rights of freedom of expression to writers, actors, and artists.' When they agreed to that proposition, I told them of the efforts being made by a group of super patriots to impinge on freedom of expression at the museum, and enlisted their editorial support."[11] According to Marcus the editors promised to back the museum on both the editorial and news pages. Marcus recalls, "the Dallas papers did stand by the museum's right of free expression for the duration of the problem. Their news stories, of course, reflected the attacks from the opposition, but at no time did the papers pull out their editorial support."[12]

In an effort to defuse any controversy, the museum announced to the press: "We believe the people of Dallas are intelligent enough to decide this matter for themselves."[13] Bywaters hung three paintings near the museum entrance for easy viewing. A bust portrait of a man by Diego Rivera, a scene of workmen washing up by Joseph Hirsch, and a painting of a nude arranging her hair by George Grosz were hung along with a sign, "These paintings are by artists listed by the Public Affairs Luncheon Club resolution as presenting concepts of communism." Also displayed were a few abstract paintings with a sign reading "Abstract art is not communist art."[14] Attendance at the museum that Saturday was larger than usual, and Bywaters reported that the museum added "some 20–25 new members."[15]

Newspapers across Texas covered the controversy. An article in the *Texas Observer* for March 21, 1955, reported that Bywaters said that the club members "are attacking one thing they dislike—contemporary art—and linking with it another thing they dislike—communism."[16] He believed that if the real nature and sources of abstraction in art were understood, the controversy would soon dissipate. Despite his numerous arguments that abstraction was an anathema to Soviet Russia, the museum's critics were not convinced.

It was clear, however, from a March 21 letter from Colonel John W. Mayo, commander of the Dallas Metropolitan Post 581 of the American Legion, that the controversial issue was not based solely on aesthetics. The war veteran's letter to the museum asked urgently if "Communist party membership or Communist-front affiliation . . . have no bearing upon decisions to purchase, accept, or exhibit an artist's work?"[17] Mayo demanded that the investigating committee of the museum board "study the documentation available on those affiliations and then state whether or not the museum will continue to sponsor . . . these artists." He pleaded that "consideration be given to the affiliation of these artists with an international conspiracy that already has enslaved half the world." Mayo obtained newspaper space to make public his position.

J. T. Suggs was uneasy as chairman of the museum board's committee to investigate the accusations that the museum exhibited works by Communists. A staunch conservative, Suggs was vice-president of the Texas & Pacific Railway and had served as legal council and museum trustee since 1947. Under his guidance the museum board responded to Mayo's letter by affirming their Americanism and vowing not to exhibit the works of known Communists. The board issued a public statement affirming that "it is not our policy knowingly to acquire or exhibit work of a person known by us now to be a Communist or of Communist front affiliation."[18] The aesthetic issue of realism versus abstraction was not addressed in the museum's statement.

The museum board's statement was intended to be conciliatory, to prove their patriotism, and to avoid confrontation. But their indecisiveness left them vulnerable. The enraged patriots reasoned that if the board's members did not know their artists were "commies" then it would be necessary to prove it to them. Instead of reassuring the museum's accusers, the statement prompted immediate reaction. A new resolution of the Public Affairs Luncheon Club urged the museum to "consider seriously the documentary evidence that artists with Communist affiliations have been honored in the exhibitions of the museum of Fine Arts."[19] The sources of their documentary evidence were various reports of the House Un-American Activities Committee. The strongest reaction was registered by H. L. Hunt's conservative newsletter, the *American National Research Record*. The publication characterized the museum's position this way: "the Board rejected documented proof of extensive Communist front records compiled from various Congressional reports and hearings. . . . What the Dallas Art Museum board or committee has done is to insist that they will not be moved except by official documentation. . . . This leaves . . . no choice but to force the issue and give the Dallas Art Museum board just what it wants—an official investigation into the whole controversy."[20] Like Dondero, the editorial also called for "a full scale Congressional investigation into the whole question of Communist infiltration in the arts."

Throughout that spring, Bywaters fielded the accusations of suspicious club women, irate legionnaires, and enraged semiprofessional and amateur painters that the museum was regularly exhibiting works by known Communist artists. At a time in Texas when the New Deal was equated with Communism, Bywaters suffered for his close association with the Federal Art Projects of the 1930s. And the fact that he had written an article about Diego

Rivera in 1928 and met the professed Communist in Mexico City in 1951 were not marks in his favor. The museum board decided that it would be unwise to make Bywaters a spokesman because it was too easy to target a single individual. The gesture did not, however, stop the personal attacks on Bywaters. He received unsigned and undated hate mail. One letter clipped to a copy of one of Dondero's speeches admonished, "Inform yourself Mr. Bywaters and do not allow yourself to be a dupe for communist subversion by not knowing the truth." Another letter, addressed "Dear Comrade," urged Bywaters to go to Russia where "there is a real need for your type."[21]

Both the *Dallas Times Herald* and *Dallas Morning News* reported at length the trustees' statement of policy that they denied any knowledge of exhibiting works by Communist artists.[22] The Dallas newspapers were filled with letters to the editor warning people to be alert to Communist infiltration, voicing patriotism, and denouncing modernism, while others pleaded for freedom of expression and an end to paranoia. For many the issue was censorship versus freedom of speech, but many inflamed patriots wanted Communists out of their city museum even if that meant censorship. As one letter to the editor said, "I happen to love America far more than I love art."[23]

The museum board's statement was viewed by many as timid and placative. The controversy received national attention when the May 2, 1955, issue of *Time* magazine quipped, "the Public Affairs Luncheon Club racked up a thumping victory in their campaign to censor the Dallas Museum of Fine Arts." The art world was shocked by the museum board's action. An *Art News* editorial, "Shame in Dallas," in the Summer 1955 issue condemned the action of the trustees. On July 1, Marcus attended the first board meeting after his return from Italy and the last in his elected term as president. He read aloud the *Art News* editorial and informed trustees that he vehemently disagreed with their action. At the next meeting J. T. Suggs was elected president and he recited an acceptance speech that evoked an era of noncontroversy for the museum.

Despite Suggs's optimism, a new firestorm of controversy erupted in the fall of 1955 with a thoroughly inaccurate article in the *American Legion Magazine* entitled "Art for Whose Sake?" and subtitled "Some Modernists Are Peddling More than Pictures." The article, purporting to be an exposé of modern art, was by Esther Julia Pels, the wife of Karl Boarslay, editor of the *American National Research Report.* Without benefit of any art education, she compared the emergence of modern art to the Hans Christian Andersen story about the emperor's new clothes. She wrote: "So called 'modern art' had its origin in socially sick and decadent European art circles before the

First World War. From them sprung Cubism, Dadism [*sic*], Futurism, Symbolism, Expressionism, etc. In the social ferment that was to produce communism, fascism, and nazism, there arose artists who plotted to use art as a means of power over the masses."[24] Pels continued her own version of art history: "Since its inception, 'modern art' has been revolutionary, in the deliberate turning of the human mind from what is true, good, and beautiful to the contemplation and worship of ugliness, disordered visions of madness, 'social protest,' and the use of esoteric and occult symbols for reality." She equated abstraction with perversion and subversion.

Pels tried another line of attack, emphasizing that modern art was not an "American" art. With overtones of anti-Semitism and racism, she pointed to the number of leading modern artists with "foreign names." The crux of Pels's argument remained that modern art is ugly and distorted, and therefore degenerate and meaningless. She believed that modern art, like Communism, strove to break down human dignity and religious reverence, and she maintained that modern artists were predominantly Communists and Communist sympathizers. Pels specifically cited the Dallas Museum of Fine Arts as a leading proponent of Communist-inspired art. And she suggested that the museum ignored the protests of citizens who objected to the exhibition of Communist art in a public institution. The article was later reprinted verbatim in *Facts Forum News*.[25]

The ladies of the Public Affairs Luncheon Club took Pels's article as gospel. Throughout the fall and winter of 1955, the museum's problems were kept alive in club meetings, speeches, and letters to newspapers. Members were urged to cancel their museum memberships and not to send their children to art classes at the museum school. The skirmishes continued when "Sculpture in Silver" opened at the museum on December 11, 1955. The ladies demanded that a work by William Zorach be removed, but the museum stood firm. When the museum opened another touring American Federation of Art exhibition of works by deceased modernists called "In Memoriam," the vigilantes publicly charged that six of the twelve artists represented in the exhibition had Communist-front records.[26]

At the museum board meeting of December 7, 1955, members discussed the current problems and the future of the museum. They were tired of constant harassment. Led by Gerald Mann, a new board member and former attorney general of Texas, they approved a new policy statement to "exhibit and acquire works of art only on the basis of their merit as works of art."[27] The museum announced publicly that they would not ban any pictures from an upcoming "Sport in Art" show and that henceforth decisions would be made solely on artistic grounds.

Immediately after that announcement the museum trustees received a letter from Mayo in the name of a newly formed group called the Dallas County Patriotic Council.[28] The Council comprised several women's clubs, including the Public Affairs Luncheon Club, Pro-America, Daughters of the American Revolution, Daughters of 1812, and the Woman's Chamber of Commerce; also included were chapters of the Dallas Veterans of Foreign Wars, the American Legion, the Inwood Lions, the Matheon Club, and the Southern Memorial Association. A majority of the members of the new Council were artists from local art clubs, including the Frank Reaugh Club, Klepper Club, Federation of Dallas Artists, Bassett Club, and the Oak Cliff Fine Arts Society. Bywaters was the first to recognize that the leaders of the Dallas County Patriotic Council were disgruntled artists—a loose affiliation of Sunday painters, dilettantes, dabblers, and semiprofessionals. The Dallas County Patriotic Council demanded that the museum restate their original policy not to buy or show works by known Communists. The Council also requested deletion of works from the upcoming "Sport in Art" exhibition by four artists: Ben Shahn, Yasuo Kuniyoshi, William Zorach, and Leon Kroll.

"Sport in Art," a touring show organized by a pillar of conservative art, the American Federations of Arts, was scheduled for exhibition in Dallas from March 25 through April 20, 1956. After opening at the Museum of Fine Arts in Boston and traveling to the Corcoran Gallery of Art in Washington, D.C., and the Speed Art Museum in Louisville without incident, the "Sport in Art" exhibition was scheduled to go on tour to art museums in Dallas, Denver, Los Angeles, and San Francisco, and end its tour in Australia as a crowning element of the 1956 Olympic Games. More than one hundred handsome works of art in a variety of styles dealing with the subject of sport were drawn from numerous public and private collections. The exhibition was composed of works by eighty-five artists including such European masters as Daumier and Goya, and such American greats as Winslow Homer, Thomas Eakins, and Arthur Tait. Modern artists included Paul Cadmus, Elaine De Kooning, Peter Hurd, and Fletcher Martin.

Works in the "Sport in Art" exhibition to which the Dallas County Patriotic Council most objected included *National Pastime*, a drawing by Shahn (fig. 3); *Skaters*, a drawing by Kuniyoshi (fig. 4); *Fisherman*, a watercolor by Zorach (fig. 5); and *The Park, Winter*, an oil by Kroll (fig. 6). These four works treat the innocuous subject of sport in a realistic style mediated by ab-

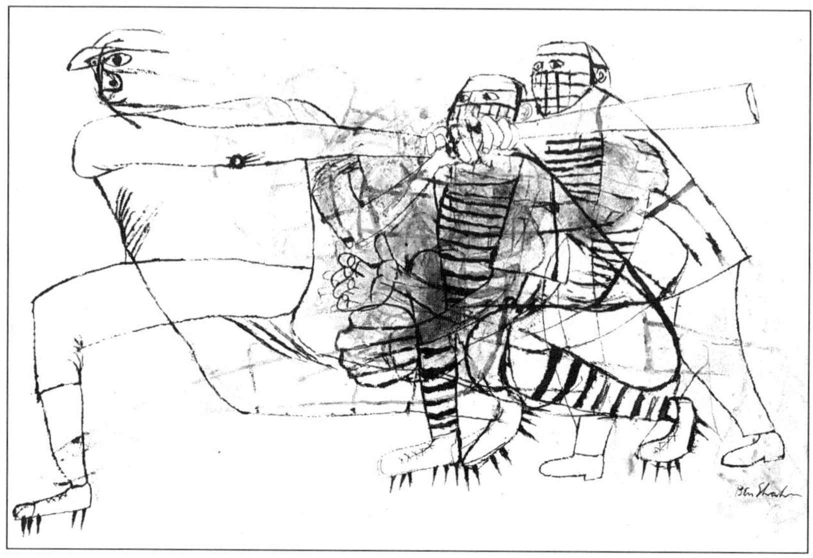

FIG. 3. Ben Shahn, *National Pastime*, 1955.
Ink and wash on paper mounted on board, 68×102.2 cm (26¾×40¼ in.).
The Des Moines Art Center, Des Moines, Iowa.
Purchased with funds from Rose F. Rosenfield, 1958.23.

straction. In actuality, neither the subject nor the style of the artworks was at issue. Despite the critics' complaints about the subversive qualities of abstract art, these four works are not examples of nonobjective abstraction. The Council judged the art not on an aesthetic or stylistic basis, but on a political one.

The fact that the four artists were highly regarded in the art world did not impress the Council. The museum board broadcast information about the artists in an effort to educate the public and turn public opinion. But the museum's efforts to counter the charges that the artists were Communists left little impression; the fact that the artists were merely mentioned in the file of the House Un-American Activities Committee was enough to convince members of the Council that they were indeed Communists and therefore dangerous.

In answer to the Council's demands, the museum board sent a special delivery letter on January 27, 1956, to Colonel Mayo, stating, "The fundamental issue at stake is that of freedom and liberty—not just for the Dallas Museum of Fine Arts, but eventually for our school system, our free press, our library, our orchestra, and the many other institutions of our society. We believe that democracy cannot survive if subjected to book burning, thought control, condemnation without trial, proclamation of guilt by association—the very techniques of the Communists and Fascist regimes."[29] That news prompted the *Dallas Morning News* of January 28 to announce in the morning edition: "Museum Says Reds Can Stay." The inflammatory title was changed to "Museum Bans Politics Rule" for the city, or afternoon, edition. The identical articles stated the museum's policy not to withdraw any pictures from current or projected exhibitions.[30]

Members of the Council deplored the board's decision to exhibit art based on aesthetics and surmised that it would "permit the work of Red artists to be shown in the museum of our city."[31] They called a meeting on January 31, 1956. "The Reds are moving in upon us," warned Colonel Alvin Mansfield Owsley, former U.S. minister to Ireland and Denmark and a former commander of the American Legion. One hundred and fifty inflamed Council members cheered Owsley's words. Standing in front of American and Texas flags, he ended his speech triumphantly, "Let those who would plant a Red picture supplant it with the Red, White and Blue. White for purity, blue for fidelity as blue as our Texas Bluebonnets."[32]

Another speech by William Ware, also of the American Legion, charged that "the members of the board of trustees have been very cleverly maneuvered into the position of serving as a Communist Front for the protection of pro-Communist artists."[33] He also raised great concern among the group by saying that "our tax money is going into the pockets of artists devoted to the destruction of our way of life." By resolution, the Dallas County Patriotic Council appealed to the Park Board, which controlled the museum's budget, "to deny exhibition privileges of a public tax-maintained institution to persons with records of affiliation with subversive activities of Communist and Communist front organizations."[34]

It was generally agreed among members of the Council that censorship was a fair price to pay to save America from Communism. The tax issue became their banner. Handbills were circulated throughout Dallas and posted on the automobiles of museum visitors stating, "Your tax money is going through the Park Board to the museum for the aid, comfort, and prestige of your enemies. . . . Don't you think it's time to cut off Park Board funds from the Dallas Museum of Fine(?) Arts?"[35]

In a public statement, Gerald Mann defended the museum's policy and added, "The pictures you see at the Dallas Museum, whether in a traveling exhibit or purchased by the museum, do not cost the tax payers of Dallas a

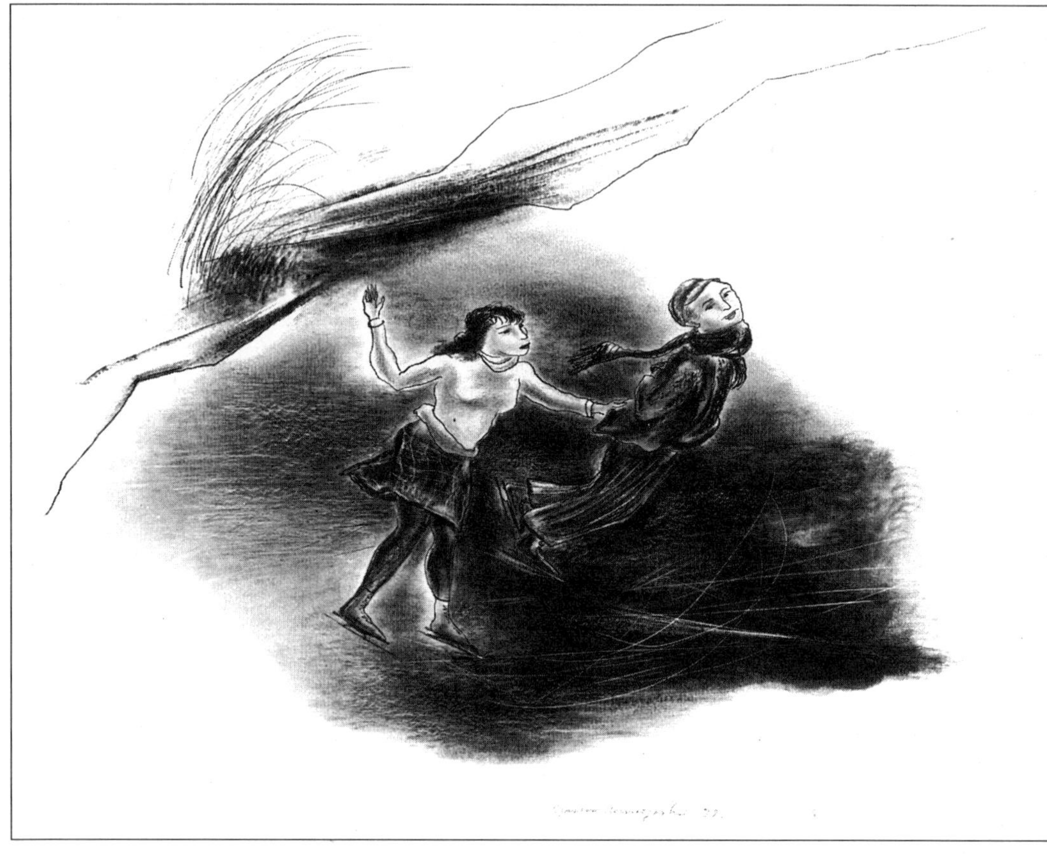

FIG. 4. Yasuo Kuniyoshi, *Skaters*, 1933.
Ink and charcoal on wove paper, 31.4×43.2 cm (12⅜×17 in.).
 Gift of Winslow Ames.

single cent."[36] The City of Dallas, through the Park Board, supplied the museum with an annual operating fund of $63,365 for the year 1955. The Council's appeal to the Park Board to cut off operating funds for the museum was a dangerous threat to the survival of the museum. They stated their argument succinctly, "Shall art by Reds be exhibited at taxpayers' expense in our museum?"[37] The issue remained the censoring of four works in the "Sport in Art" exhibition, and the Council promised to take its case to the Dallas City Council if the paintings were not censored from the exhibition. The Park

Board listened to the Council's complaints but upheld the museum's decision to exhibit the entire "Sport in Art" show.[38]

In an effort to stem the tide of negative criticism, John Rosenfield wrote a lengthy editorial in support of the museum which outlined the dangers of censorship as specifically applied to the Dallas controversy.[39] He quoted liberally from President Eisenhower's remarks on the occasion of the twenty-fifth anniversary of the Museum of Modern Art. Eisenhower made a clear statement in support of aesthetic freedom: "freedom of the arts is a basic freedom, one of the pillars of liberty in our land." Eisenhower stated not only that artists must have freedom of expression but also that "people must have unimpaired opportunity to see, to understand, and to profit from our artists' work." He called for "healthy controversy and progress in art" and reminded everyone "how different it is in tyranny. When artists are made the slaves and tools of the state; when artists become chief propagandists of a cause, progress is arrested and creation and genius are destroyed." The museum board reprinted the president's statement and circulated it. The statement substantiated their decisions and they felt that the words of the most revered Republican would carry a great deal of weight with their most ardent critics.

The week before the opening of the "Sport in Art" exhibition, the Council ran an elaborate advertisement in the *Dallas Times Herald* asking readers to clip a ballot and choose whether or not they wanted the art of "Communists or pro-Communists exhibited or honored in our Municipal Museum."[40] The paid editorial concluded, "The Dallas County Patriotic Council protests the use of public facilities for exhibiting or honoring Communists or pro-Communists. We urge you to express your opinion as a citizen of Dallas while there is still time!" Concurrently, *The Dan Smoot Report* recounted the entire Dallas controversy and stated emphatically: "The museum's exhibitions have become top-heavy with communist art—to the exclusion of works by American artists who are not communists."[41]

Reveau Bassett, the leader of the disgruntled artists and the most venomous in his attacks against the art museum, was a successful painter of landscapes and ducks whose work had appeared in many exhibitions at the museum. A Dondero disciple, Bassett peppered his public remarks with spicy language, and often said that the sight of a modern painting by a "Red" made him feel ill.[42] Using his own definition of art as beauty and sanity, Bassett pointed disparagingly to works by Expressionists, Cubists, and Futurists as examples of anti-beauty and anti-art. He repeatedly targeted the Dallas

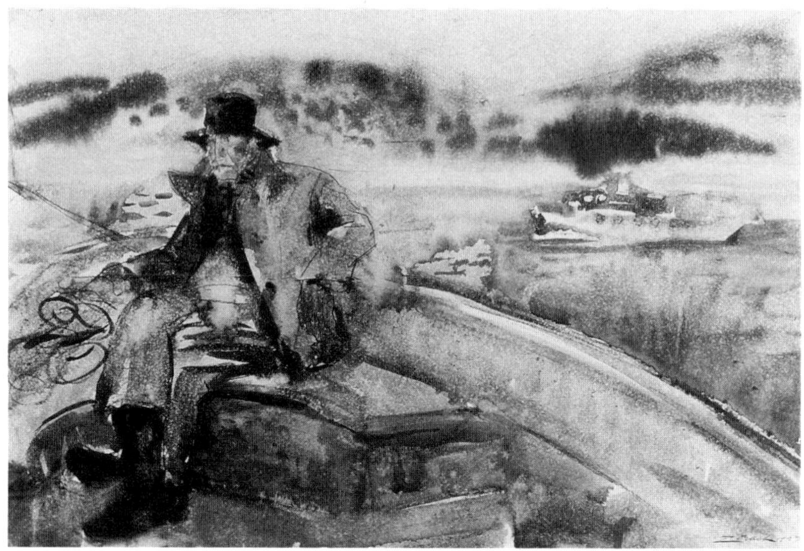

FIG. 5. William Zorach, *Fisherman*, 1927.
Watercolor and charcoal on paper, 38.5×56.2 cm (15⅛×22⅛ in.).
The Museum of Modern Art, New York. Given anonymously.
Photo: © 1997 The Museum of Modern Art, New York.

museum for supporting "commie artists" and he complained that "good American artists don't have a chance" because juries for competitive exhibitions were fixed.[43]

Other traditional artists in Dallas were also unhappy with the actions of the Dallas museum. "For years they have filled the Museum with modernistic paintings ignoring Dallas artists," complained the president of the Federation of Dallas Artists, who added that "exhibitions at the museum are closed affairs, the same people have won prizes for 15 years."[44] The Reaugh Club and the Klepper Club backed the charges, and a spokesman for the Aunspaugh Art Club made the argument clear: "We have not been given a room where we could exhibit our art. After all, we are taxpayers." This loose affiliation of artists joined the Dallas County Patriotic Council because they believed the museum had done some great injustice to them by not exhibiting their artwork.

The Dallas Women's Chamber of Commerce proposed a solution to the controversy between the avocational artists and the art museum by instructing the museum "to make a special gallery space available for local artists."[45] Such a plan was seen by the museum board as a viable means to win back the support of local art groups. However, the board's decision to offer a gallery to the local art groups placed Bywaters in an untenable position. In his tireless efforts to promote the art of the region, quality and professionalism were his main concerns. In February 1956, Gallery A of the museum was designated as the art clubs' turf; the clubs were in charge of assembling, jurying, and maintaining the standards of their shows. Bywaters did not have curatorial control of the work to be exhibited in Gallery A, but the museum staff was obliged to hang the art club exhibitions.

An exhibition of works by the members of the Aunspaugh Club inaugurated the shows. On that occasion the art critic of the *Dallas Times Herald* wrote, "These series of shows will give the public an idea of what the various art clubs around Dallas are up to currently. From a cursory examination we would say that they are mainly up to painting fruits and flowers."[46] When the Bassett Club opened its exhibition, *Dallas Morning News* art critic Rual Askew did not fail to point out the irony that Bassett, one of the museum's leading opponents, did not refuse to show his work in an institution that allegedly showed the work of Communist artists.[47] When the Federation of Dallas Artists opened its show, Askew assessed the work as "the noncommittal fare that is both the bane and life of avocational painting."[48] Another reviewer stated, "At the museum . . . the staff will change the signs in Gallery A, but the names, subject matter and quality will remain largely the same."[49] The Gallery A experiment proved to be a concession to local politics that seriously damaged the museum's credibility. The loss of curatorial control constituted a major defeat for Bywaters. Despite his efforts to maintain a high level of professionalism, amateur artists hung mediocre works on the walls of the Dallas Museum of Fine Arts.

After almost a year of controversy the events in Dallas were regionally and nationally debated. On March 12, 1956, *Time* magazine published an update on "the running battle between the Dallas Museum of Fine Arts and a band of vociferous Texas patriots."[50] The Sunday art page of the *New York Times* published an article supportive of the museum's position: "The courageous stand of the Dallas Art Association is of benefit not only to the Texas museum but also for every creative person in the land."[51]

On Sunday March 25, 1956, the "Sport in Art" exhibition opened at the Dallas Museum of Fine Arts. There was an unusually tense atmosphere that afternoon. The five museum galleries housing the show were packed. Members of the Patriotic Council mingled with the crowd and, according to newspaper reports, were outspoken in their disagreements with the show.[52]

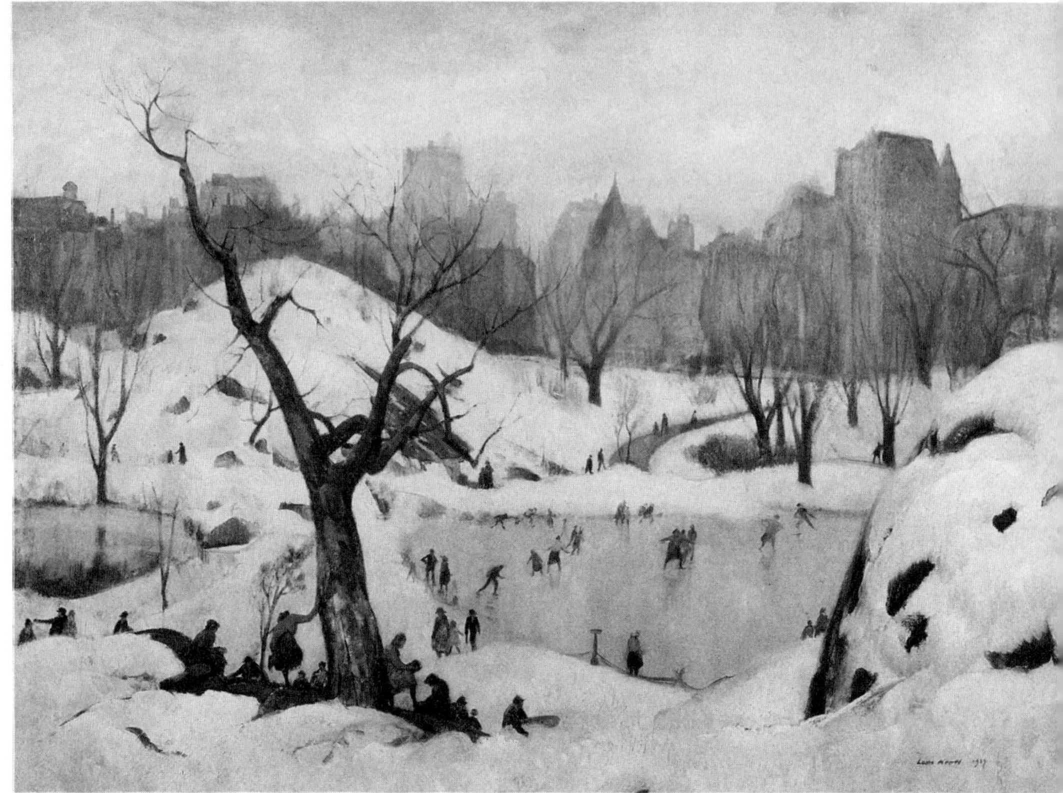

FIG. 6. Leon Kroll, *The Park, Winter*, 1923.
Oil on canvas, 91.5×122 cm (36×48 in.). © The Cleveland Museum of Art, Cleveland, 1997. Hinman B. Hurlbut Collection.

Extra armed guards were summoned for the occasion. An eight-page locally printed leaflet attacking the showing of four paintings by Shahn, Kuniyoshi, Kroll, and Zorach was found on the windshield of every car in the museum parking lot, but the infamous exhibition hung unmolested on the public walls of the Dallas museum. Also opening that day at the opposite end of the museum corridor in Gallery A was an exhibition of works by members of the Klepper Art Club, who served tea and tried to draw museum viewers into their show.

Attending the opening of the "Sport in Art" exhibition was journalist Charolette Devree, who was in Dallas specifically to write a story for *Art News* on the protracted controversy. In her article, published in September

1956, she tried to make sense of the events by listing key figures and presenting a chronology of events.[53]

There was more positive press. Finally, six months after the publication of Esther Pels's erroneous article, there was a rebuttal by a respected art journal. In an editorial, the editors of *Arts Magazine* discounted and disproved each of Pels's feeble arguments: "Miss Pels is really saying that anything imaginative, anything unfamiliar, or simply anything she does not like, is dangerous."[54] The most extensive and authoritative counter to the Pels article was written by René d'Harnoncourt, director of the Museum of Modern Art. He responded to the challenge of *Facts Forum* and countercharged: "To attack modern art, which is in itself a manifestation of individual freedom of expression, as part of the Communist conspiracy is to misunderstand the nature of the Communist conspiracy."[55]

By the end of the summer of 1956 the museum controversy occupied less space in the newspapers. The "Sport in Art" exhibition closed in Dallas and traveled on to open in Denver without incident. The Public Affairs Luncheon Club felt frustrated that their grievances were not heard in Dallas, so they took one final step to have the exhibition tour either censored or canceled. The women announced to the press that "the club appealed to the Un-American Activities Committee of the House, the International Security Committee of the Senate and the Department of State to take immediate action either to eliminate the works of Ben Shahn, Leon Kroll, Yasuo Kuniyoshi and Wiliam Zorach from the exhibit or refuse United States sponsorship of the exhibit."[56]

Sponsored by Time, Inc. and *Sports Illustrated* magazine in collaboration with the American Federation of Arts, from its inception "Sport in Art" was to travel to Australia during the 1956 Olympic Games. The United States Information Agency was the governmental agency responsible for touring the art exhibition. In May of that year the *New York Times* reported: "The United States Information Agency has canceled plans to send overseas a modern art exhibit that once incurred 'subversive' charges."[57] The article directly linked the controversy in Dallas to the U.S. government's decision to cancel the tour to Australia. The official reason was "due to over-all budgetary considerations." The USIA spokesman offered "No comment" when asked "whether the Dallas episode had played any part in the cancellation." Dondero was pleased with the cancellation of the show; his June 14, 1956, speech included a detailed rundown of the events in Dallas as he saw them.[58]

In an editorial entitled "Dondero, Dallas, and Defeatism," *Arts Magazine* also credited the Dallas controversy for the cancellation of the exhibition.[59]

An article by Ben Shahn in the *Atlantic Monthly*, entitled "Nonconformity," put the entire controversy in perspective. Shahn's essay was addressed to those who fear and misunderstand freedom of individualism and artistic expression. He referred to pressure groups for conformity in American art led by the fallacious assertions of Congressman Dondero. "The most recent of the civic crusades," Shahn pointed out, "was directed against a very large exhibition of sports themes." Referring to the Dallas controversy, he asserted, "so great was the Texas commotion . . . that the exhibition was not sent on to Australia."[60]

The cancellation of the "Sports in Art" exhibition marked a defeat for the Dallas Museum of Fine Arts. Throughout the controversy the museum could note with pride that the sponsorship of the exhibition by the United States Information Agency was proof that the artworks were not controversial. Also challenged was Bywaters's belief that a good work of art should be exhibited regardless of the artist's politics. And there was a larger defeat in the acquiescence to pressure groups. As the smoke of battle cleared, however, the museum emerged as a champion of artistic freedom. Bywaters's actions were commended by resolution at the 38th Annual Meeting of the American Association of Art Museum Directors, thus signifying the respect of the art world. *Life* included Bywaters in a feature article on museum directors, and *American Artist* congratulated him as "a progressive director who has worked hard at building a first-rate institution."[61]

The United States Information Agency's cancellation of the tour of "Sport in Art" was not the only instance of scandal involving art exhibitions. The government's policy of cultural exchange during the Cold War was initiated as a means to advertise the benefits of the "free world." The program of touring exhibitions was intended to demonstrate that the United States was as successful in culture as in war, and as rich in art as in business. The government, however, retreated from this program as an increasing number of complainants charged that modern art was motivated, either directly or remotely, by the Soviets. Before the Dallas controversy, the 1946 "Advancing American Art" exhibition, which was organized by the State Department to promote not only contemporary American art but also a positive American image, met a firestorm of criticism that stopped its international tour. In 1956 the USIA asked the American Federation of Arts to plan an exhibition of one hundred works by contemporary American artists to tour Europe. The exhibition "Twentieth Century American Painters" was canceled at the last minute amid a storm of controversy. Due to Dondero's accusations, ten of the artists were considered "social hazards" and forty of the artists represented in the exhibition were believed to be affiliated with the Communist Party. Also in 1956 an exhibition sponsored by the College Art Association of works by major contemporary European artists was scheduled to tour internationally as part of America's cultural exchange program, but was canceled due to political scandal. All of these exhibitions were canceled as a discordant chorus of anti-Communist alarmists voiced concern that modern art contained disturbing evidence of Communist infiltration and aggression. When politicians could no longer be certain that the message of the cultural exchange program was pro-American, the program and the exhibitions of suspect artworks were canceled. The Cold War collision of aesthetics, politics, and economics is most evident in the heated public debate and cancellation of these exhibitions.

The story of the Dallas controversy surrounding the "Sport in Art" exhibition should be remembered within the larger context of the history of American art in the Cold War era. The issues involved are larger than the aesthetic concerns of realism versus abstraction, or public discourse about freedom of expression versus national security, or political debate focused on Americanism versus Communism; and they are more complex than the effects of Red Scare hysteria.

NOTES

1. "Resolution on the Promotion of the Work of Communist Artists," The Public Affairs Luncheon Club of Dallas, March 16, 1955. Unpublished material, Jerry Bywaters Research Collection, Southern Methodist University, Dallas, Texas. Press coverage of the resolution included: "Women's Group Protests Policy of Art Presentation at Museum," *Dallas Morning News*, March 15, 1955; "Dallas Museum Heads Deny 'Communistic' Art Displayed," *Dallas Times Herald*, March 15, 1955; "Museum to Study Charges," *Dallas Times Herald*, March 16, 1955.

2. *Dallas Morning News*, August 14, 1955.

3. Don Carleton, *Red Scare: Right Wing Hysteria, Fifties Fanaticism and Their Legacy in Texas* (Austin: Texas Monthly Press, 1985).

4. Statement by Jerry Bywaters in a 1985 interview with Gerald Saxon, Dallas Public Library, Dallas, Texas.

5. "The Public Affairs Luncheon Club of Dallas," 1954–55 Year Book, Bywaters Research Collection, Southern Methodist University.

6. Hon. George A. Dondero, "Communist Conspiracy in Art Threatens American Museums," *Congressional Record*, March 17, 1952.

7. Ibid.

8. Public Affairs Club, "Resolution."

9. "Is There a Communist Conspiracy in the World of Art?" The Public Affairs Luncheon Club of Dallas, Handbill, 1955, Bywaters Research Collection, Southern Methodist University.

10. Vertical File, Dallas Museum of Fine Arts, Bywaters Research Collection, Southern Methodist University.

11. Stanley Marcus, *Minding the Store: A Memoir* (Boston: Little, Brown, 1974), 155–56.

12. Letter from Stanley Marcus to the author, July 8, 1991.

13. "Larger Sunday Crowd Visits Dallas Museum," *Dallas Morning News*, March 21, 1955.

14. Ibid.

15. "Debate Over Art Stirs Curiosity," *Dallas Times Herald*, March 20, 1955.

16. "Dallas Museum Is Criticized for 'Pink' Art," *Texas Observer*, March 21, 1955.

17. Col. John W. Mayo to the Dallas Art Association, March 21, 1955, Bywaters Research Collection, Southern Methodist University.

18. "Public Statement," Dallas Art Association for the Dallas Museum of Fine Arts, April 4, 1955, Bywaters Research Collection, Southern Methodist University.

19. *Dallas Times Herald*, April 11, 1955; *Dallas Morning News*, April 12, 1955.

20. *American National Research Record*, April 30, 1955.

21. Vertical Files, Bywaters Research Collection, Southern Methodist University.

22. *Dallas Times Herald*, April 5, 1955; *Dallas Morning News*, April 5, 1955.

23. Vertical Files, Bywaters Research Collection.

24. Esther Julia Pels, "Art for Whose Sake?" *American Legion Magazine*, October 1955.

25. *Facts Forum News*, February 1956. The magazine invited rebuttals to Pels's article.

26. Vertical File, Dallas Museum of Art, Bywaters Research Collection, Southern Methodist University.

27. Vertical Files, Bywaters Research Collection, Southern Methodist University. The museum's statement was derived from the "Statement of Artistic Freedom," American Federation of Arts, October 22, 1954, which included this statement: "artistic expression must be judged solely on its merits as a work of art and not by the political or social views of the artist. . . ."

28. Col. Mayo to Dallas Art Association, January 12, 1956, Bywaters Research Collection, Southern Methodist University.

29. Dallas Art Association to Col. Mayo, January 27, 1956, Bywaters Research Collection, Southern Methodist University.

30. "Museum Says Reds Can Stay," *Dallas Morning News*, January 28, 1956; "Museum Bans Politics Rule," *Dallas Morning News*, January 28, 1956.

31. "Dallas Art Museum Won't Ban Works on Political Basis," *Dallas Morning*

News, January 28, 1956; "City Will Be Asked to Ban Reds' Art," *Dallas Times Herald*, February 1, 1956; "More Action on Art Row Slated Here," *Dallas Morning News*, February 1, 1956.

32. *Dallas Morning News*, February 1, 1956.

33. Ibid.

34. "Resolution," Dallas County Patriotic Council, January 31, 1956, Bywaters Research Collection, Southern Methodist University.

35. Vertical Files, Bywaters Research Collection, Southern Methodist University.

36. Gerald B. Mann, "Essential Issue Is Our Freedom," *Dallas Morning News*, February 4, 1956.

37. "Patriot Group Gives Answer in Art Dispute," *Dallas Times Herald*, February 14, 1956.

38. "Second Round Set Wednesday in Art Dispute," *Dallas Times Herald*, February 22, 1956.

39. John Rosenfield, "Censorship in Art Might Be the Start," *Dallas Morning News*, February 22, 1956.

40. *Dallas Times Herald*, March 14, 1956.

41. "Art for Propaganda," *Dan Smoot Report*, March 16, 1956.

42. Charolette Devree, "The U.S. Government Vetoes Living Art," *Art News*, September 1956, p. 54.

43. Vertical Files, Bywaters Research Collection, Southern Methodist University.

44. Ibid.

45. "Women's Chamber Seeks to Resolve Art Controversy," *Dallas Times Herald*, May 22, 1955.

46. Eugene Lewis, "Museum Opens First of Art Club Shows," *Dallas Times Herald*, February 12, 1956.

47. Rual Askew, "Technical Assurance Dominates," *Dallas Morning News*, February 26, 1956.

48. Rual Askew, "One More Exhibit by Clubs," *Dallas Morning News*, March 11, 1956. Also see, Rual Askew, "Art and Artists: Points of View Clearly Drawn," *Dallas Morning News*, March 35, 1956.

49. *Dallas Times Herald*, February 12, 1956.

50. "Dallas Armistice," *Time*, March 12, 1956.

51. Aline B. Saarinen, "Art Storm Breaks on Dallas," *New York Times*, February 12, 1956.

52. Alice Murphy, "Art Show Viewed Despite Opposition," *Dallas Times Herald*, March 26, 1956.

53. Devree, *Art news*, September 1956.

54. "Spectrum: An Answer to Miss Pels," *Arts Magazine*, March 1956.

55. René D'Harnoncourt, "Modern Art and Freedom," *Facts Forum*, June 1956.

56. Ruby Clayton McKee, "Public Affairs Luncheon Club Backs Interposition Proposals," *Dallas Morning News*, February 28, 1956.

57. Anthony Lewis, "U.S. Bars Art Tour After 'Red' Charge," *New York Times*, May 26, 1956.

58. Dondero, "UNESCO—Communism and Modern Art," *Congressional Record* July 20, 1956.

59. "Dondero, Dallas, and Defeatism," *Arts Magazine*, July 1956.

60. Ben Shahn, "Nonconformity," *Atlantic Monthly*, September 1957.

61. Jacob Getlar Smith, "Deep Is the Art of Texas," *American Artist*, September 1956.

Censorship and Controversy in the Career of Edward Kienholz

GERALD SILK

EDWARD KIENHOLZ, A MAJOR AMERICAN environmental assemblage artist, had an uncanny ability for embroiling his art in controversy. While turmoil swirled around him throughout his career, the uproar was especially pronounced from the early 1960s to the mid-1970s, when he produced his most pointedly political and social pieces.[1] Because this was a period when society was undergoing radical upheaval, Kienholz's politically committed art should not seem surprising. Ironically at this time, the major visual artists of the alleged avant-garde were generally interpreted as emphasizing formal innovation and eschewing political involvement in their art.[2]

Kienholz was among a small cadre of contemporary artists who refocused attention on the political components of vanguardism. Using one possible strategy of the avant-garde, shock, he selected intentionally nettlesome subjects and presented them in unusual, if not bizarre, ways; his tactics seemed guaranteed to touch raw nerves of the public sensibility. In work he described as "social protest" propelled by the "pressures of today,"[3] Kienholz acutely and acerbically addressed such issues as the Vietnam War, the sexual revolution, the generation gap, American middle-class values, civil rights, abortion, birth control, obscenity and the arts, rape, capital punishment, and society's neglect, mistreatment, or brutalization of the mentally impaired and the elderly. (The continued relevance of these topics today is a testimony to his perspicacity.) His visual presentation of these subjects—environmental tableaux that conflate the vernacular and quotidian with the strange and nightmarish—operates much like a good horror movie, in which terror derives its power by lurking within the deceptively familiar.

Kienholz, who died in 1994, made a fair share of what I like to call "uneasy

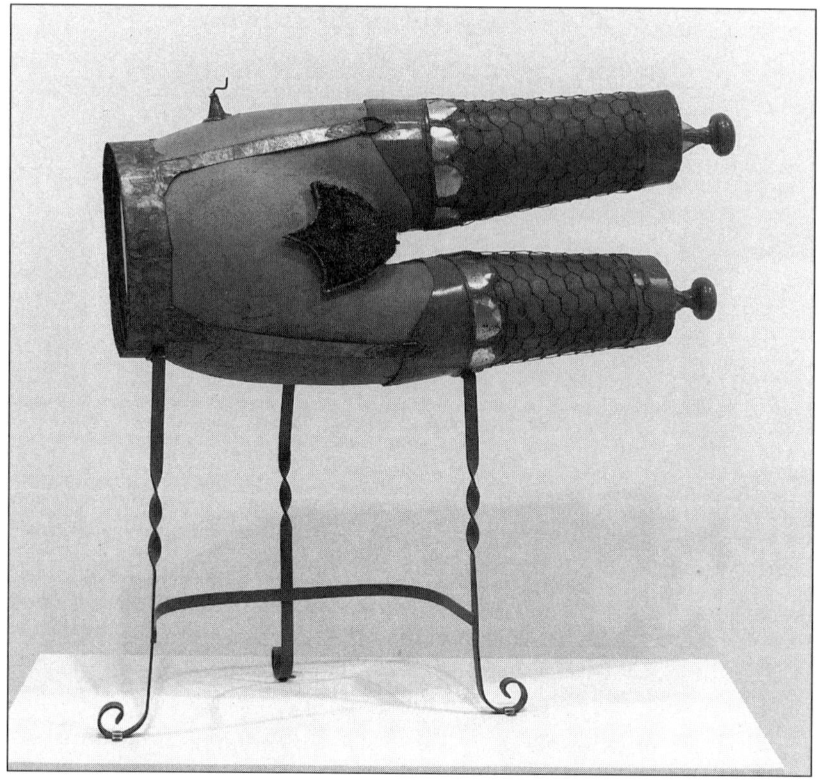

FIG. 1. Edward Kienholz, *Bunny, Bunny, You're So Funny*, 1962.
Mixed media, 82.6×84×32 cm (32½×33$\frac{1}{16}$×12⅝ in.). Williams College Museum of Art, Williamstown, Massachusetts. Gift of Susan W. and Stephen D. Paine (Class of 1954), 85.44.

pieces," or works of art so upsetting that they become the target of attempted censorship, by either modifying or removing pieces from display or literally changing or destroying work.[4] This essay will examine Kienholz's career within the context of several controversies that occurred between 1963 and 1974. Assaults on his art run the gamut of censorship: the outright suppression in 1963 of his assemblage *Bunny, Bunny, You're So Funny* (1962) (fig. 1); the threat in 1966 that a display of his would be banned, and ultimately two pieces were altered, *Back Seat Dodge '38* (fig. 2) of 1964 and *Roxys* (fig. 3) of 1961–62; and the forcible removal of his *Still Live* of 1974 (fig. 4) from exhibition. (The gamut is not quite complete, since the artist was never arrested or imprisoned because of his art.)[5]

The various justifications used by those who tried to censor Kienholz's

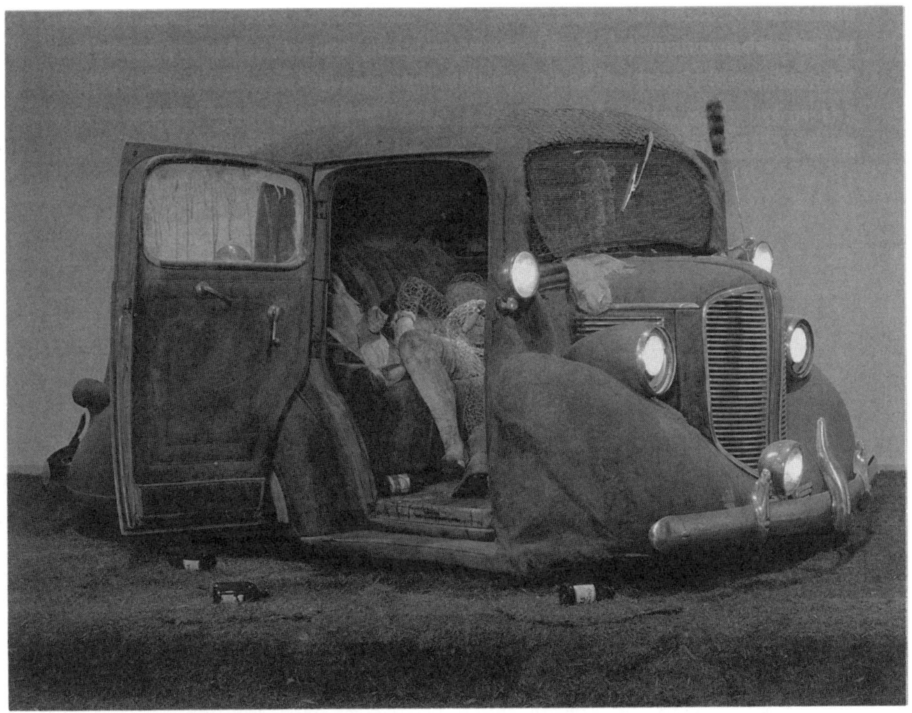

FIG. 2. Edward Kienholz, *Back Seat Dodge '38*, 1964.
Mixed materials tableau, 167.6×609.6×365.8 cm (66×240×144 in.).
Los Angeles County Museum of Art, Los Angeles,
purchased with funds provided by the Art Museum Council.
Courtesy of Nancy Reddin Kienholz.

works appear narrow, but the particulars of each brouhaha reveal more complex issues at stake. The objections concerning *Bunny, Bunny, You're So Funny*, *Back Seat Dodge '38* and *Roxys* arose because the pieces were deemed pornographic, obscene, or immoral. As any chronicle of censorship of the visual arts will show, issues of morality, along with those of politics (and of course morality and politics are intertwined), are often the ostensible reasons behind censorship. Since much of the art Kienholz made during this period could have been attacked on political and moral grounds, it is worth considering why these particular pieces were singled out.

It might be argued that these works were offensive morally or subversive politically. Certainly, a piece like *Back Seat Dodge '38* falls into these categories, even though its power derives from addressing a wide range of key so-

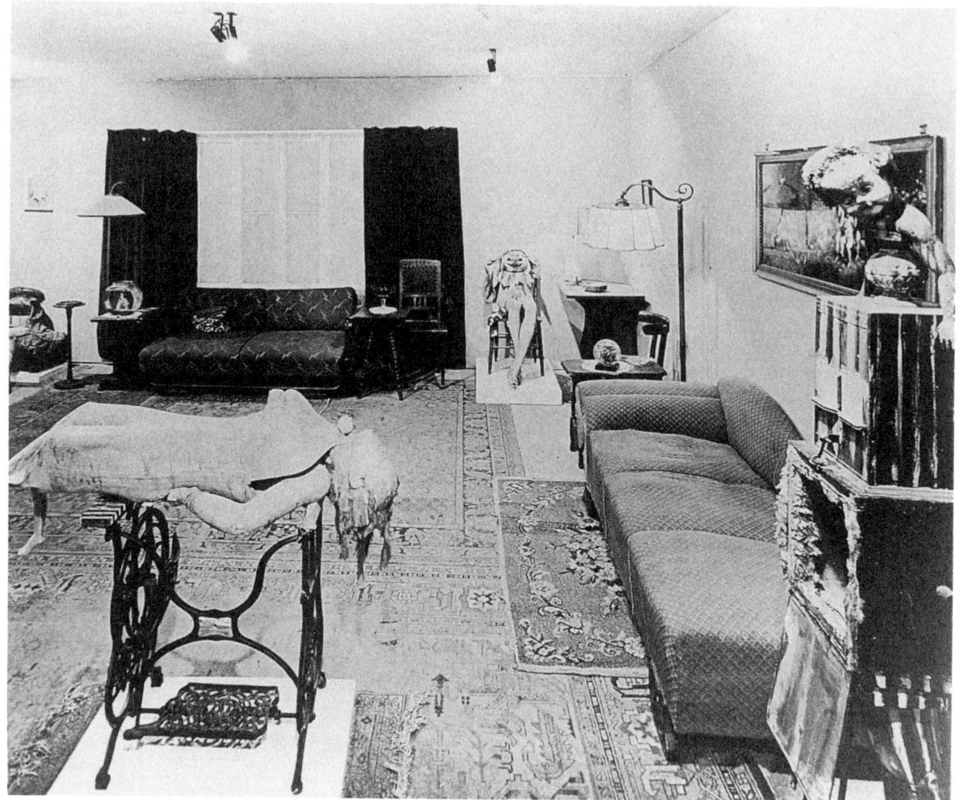

FIG. 3. Edward Kienholz, *Roxys*, 1961–62.
Mixed materials environment. Collection of Reinhard Onnasch, Berlin.

cial issues so sharply. More importantly, the work was also a victim of circumstances. The attack on *Back Seat Dodge '38* came at the time it did for a host of reasons, including a contemporaneous debate in the U.S. Supreme Court on the definition of obscenity; a history of bad blood between the board of trustees and staff of the Los Angeles County Museum, where Kienholz's work was on exhibit; and the political aspirations of members of the Los Angeles County board of supervisors, who controlled the purse strings of the museum. This case demonstrates that censorship does not issue exclusively from objective criteria (which are extremely hard to establish in any event), but is inspired and shaped by factors extraneous to the attempt to apply such standards to specific works of art.

The *Back Seat Dodge '38* controversy, like nearly all cases of censorship for

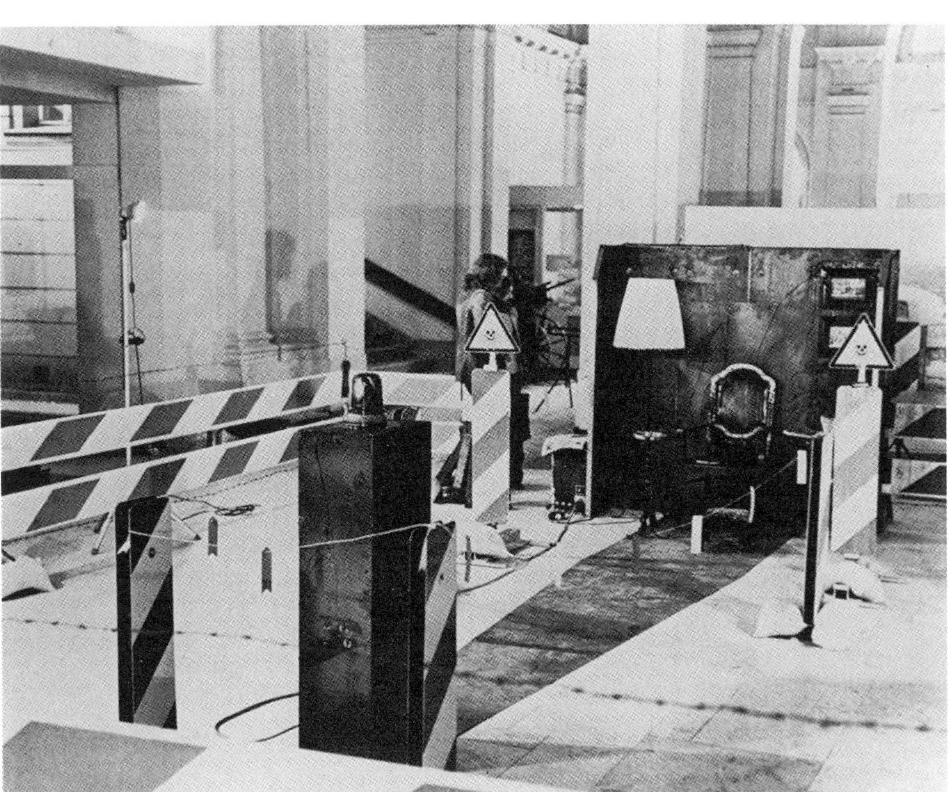

FIG. 4. Edward and Nancy Reddin Kienholz, *Still Live*, 1974.
Mixed materials environment. Collection of Nancy Reddin Kienholz.

moral reasons, is also about the fundamentally condescending and arrogant attempt to force one's morality on others. Contention arises for several reasons: lack of unanimity (again, no objective criteria) as to what is moral and what is not; objection to the imposition of a specific morality on others; and belief in the freedom of expression. Halting the display of Kienholz's *Still Live*, however, was a decision that possibly had far wider support than usual, since the piece was potentially a lethal threat to its audience. Such a work, in which a viewer could actually get shot, truly tests the outer limits of freedom of expression. Those who would protect such license, no matter how emotionally, psychologically, politically, or morally menacing a work might be, would perhaps draw the line at the boundary of physical harm. Of course, measuring the threat of nonphysical categories such as politics or morality is difficult and imprecise. Assessing the palpable damage of a bullet to the body is far easier.

Even before Kienholz and his art prompted a spate of major controversies in the early 1960s, he had achieved a certain notoriety. He made a splash in the art world in Los Angeles as a gallery owner and director, when in 1956 he opened the alternative space called the Now Gallery. "Now" folded, and in 1957 he started the Ferus Gallery with Walter Hopps, whom he later made the subject of a 1960 cutout sculpture, *Walter Hopps Hopps Hopps* (fig. 5). Attuned to art's ability to shock, Kienholz depicts the art historian, dealer, curator, and later museum director Hopps as a street hustler trading in questionable pictures. To the potential viewer/buyer, Hopps flashes from inside his jacket several images of abstract expressionist paintings, including one from Willem De Kooning's famous and controversial "Women" series. Kienholz both pays homage to abstract expressionism, especially its renegade status, and transforms critically "hot" works of art into illicitly and, in the case of De Kooning, sexually "hot" merchandise.

Kienholz's activities as gallery impresario were instrumental in the development of the Los Angeles art scene in the late 1950s. Even in this role, he courted trouble. After the opening of a Wallace Berman show at Ferus in 1957, the Hollywood Vice Squad arrived to investigate a complaint about "lewd, lascivious, and pornographic" art. The police viewed the show, removed a harmless piece (not even by Berman), and arrested the artist. Much to everyone's surprise and dismay, Berman was convicted and fined $150.[6]

Kienholz had been producing art since the early 1950s. One of the reasons he opened gallery spaces was because he was having little luck showing his own work. From the beginning, his oeuvre had the mark of something unusual. His earliest pieces, such as *Triptych* of 1956, consisted of broadly brushed, muddily colored canvases to which were attached scraps of plywood. His inclusion of detritus, linking the work to a tradition of collage and assemblage, and his application of paint with a broom—what he called "anti-gestures"—intentionally adulterate the sacred associations of the freely brushed abstraction that had been established in abstract expressionist art.

Kienholz dove directly into the topical in 1957 with another painted relief called *George Warshington in Drag* (fig. 6). The title, inscribed into the piece by a sharp object dragged through thick layers of paint, provides a series of puns. Like Marcel Duchamp transsexualizing the Mona Lisa by adding a mustache, Kienholz "transvestizes" the "father" of our country, noted for his wigged coiffure, by adding breasts and a vagina. The fact that he became the

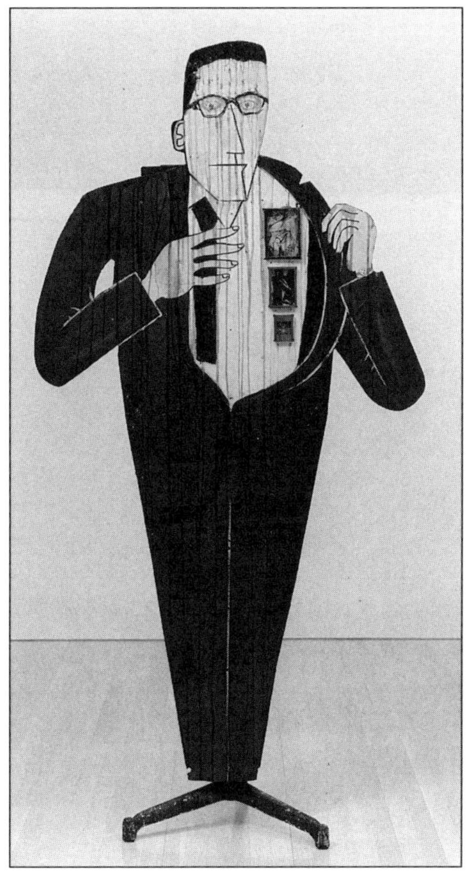

FIG. 5. Edward Kienholz,
Walter Hopps Hopps Hopps, 1959.
Mixed media construction,
221×106.7×53.3 cm (87×42×21 in.).
Collection Lannan Foundation, Los Angeles.

nation's patriarch because of his military prowess is indicated through the intercalated "r" in Washington. Father becomes mother, in part because Kienholz believed that a tough general had to be a real "mother." The artist was also thinking about then President Dwight D. Eisenhower, who, like Washington, became the country's leader through his success as a military general, and who, Kienholz felt, began to act and look much like an old woman.[7]

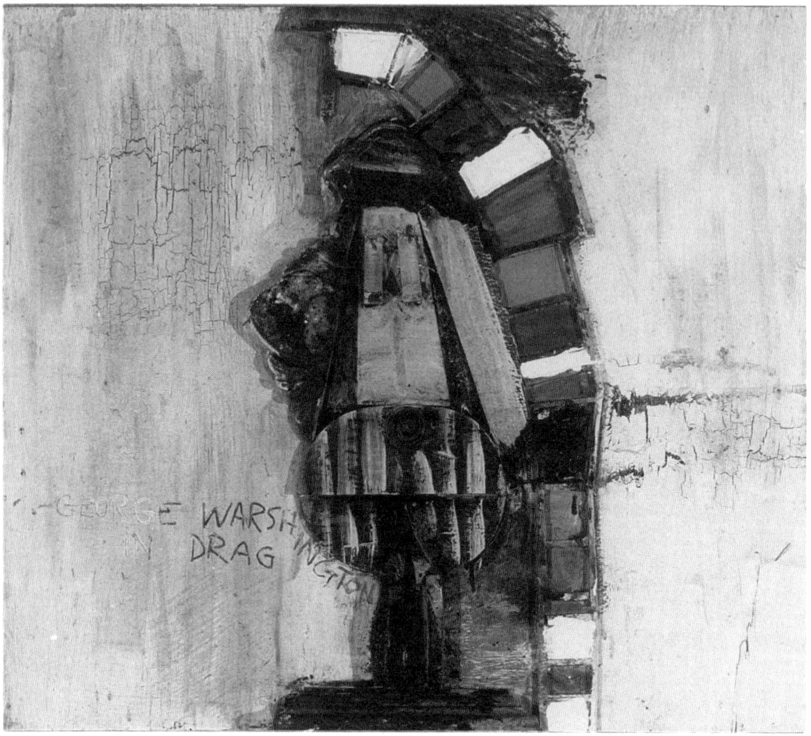

FIG. 6. Edward Kienholz, *George Warshington in Drag*, 1957.
Wall relief: paint and cut wood mounted on plywood, 82.6×91.4 cm (32½×36 in.).
Private collection, courtesy of The Menil Collection, Houston.

Kienholz addressed the issue of American military might (a subject he treated often), and perhaps that of a national or military machismo compensating for questionable masculinity. With San Francisco beatniks as friends, Kienholz also opened up the subject of homosexuality (obviously still sensitive today, and much in discussion in the 1940s and 1950s in the American art community). This was a time when, on the one hand, certain American artists and poets (many from the beat generation) declared or disguised their gay identities: poet Allen Ginsberg was a major declarer, and the artists Jasper Johns and Robert Rauschenberg were perhaps subtle declarers, but ultimately disguisers. On the other hand, artists such as the abstract expressionists Jackson Pollock, De Kooning, Franz Kline, and David Smith may have been trying, consciously or otherwise, to make the practice of art tougher and more macho, to counter the peculiarly American notion of art as an activity unfit for real men. The workings of the art world is another common Kienholz subject, and there may be a reference here to Larry Rivers's 1953 resurrection of Washington in his ironic updating of Emanuel Leutze's nineteenth-century war-horse, *Washington Crossing the Delaware.* Rivers later addressed the militarism-homosexuality nexus in *The Greatest Homosexual* (1964), based on the portrait of the French leader by Jacques-Louis David.

During a period when great emphasis was placed on the formal components of art, Kienholz defied that consensus, as he did the larger one associating art with beauty. He admits that he "conscientiously worked to make [these pieces] as ugly as possible." He also used chemically incompatible paints just to see what might happen, as well as to challenge the sacrosanct nature of art and to place in doubt the physical permanence of the work.[8] Testing aesthetic limits, preventing works from getting too pretty, maintaining the integrity of the raw junk, and exploring art's impermanence preoccupied Kienholz throughout his career, and these attributes contributed to the fundamental abrasiveness of much of his art.

In the late fifties and early sixties, Kienholz continued to do socially intense pieces, referring to race relations in both *The Little Eagle Rock Incident* of 1958 and *It Takes Two to Integrate, Cha Cha Cha* of 1961; the Russian launching of Sputnik in *The God Tracking Station no. 1* of 1958; rape and capital punishment, pointing to the Sacco-Vanzetti case (earlier approached in art by Ben Shahn), the Caryl Chessman trial, and perhaps the Rosenbergs' execution, in his 1960 box in the form of a Boy Scout knapsack, *The Psycho-Vendetta Case*; and selective amnesia toward Nazi atrocities in the 1961 *History as a Planter* (fig. 7), replete with a wandering Jew plant and Jew's harp and oven, all converted into a grisly domestic arrangement.[9] Again, these subjects—race relations, capital punishment, the killing of the Rosenbergs, the rewriting of Nazi history—remain controversial today.

Kienholz's involvement with topical subject matter in the late 1950s signals the beginning of a new era of explicitly social commitment in the arts. Growing up in the 1930s, Kienholz cut his social teeth in an atmosphere in which art and radical politics were closely linked. Yet the radicalism of the thirties was replaced in the 1940s and 1950s, in the midst of McCarthyism and the wake of the Rosenberg trial, by an art of detachment from and even atonement for such activism. As Morris Dickstein argued in his trenchant book, *Gates of Eden: American Culture in the Sixties*: "What was buried with the Rosenbergs . . . was two decades of American Marxism."[10]

But the death of American Marxism was not instantaneous. Many events

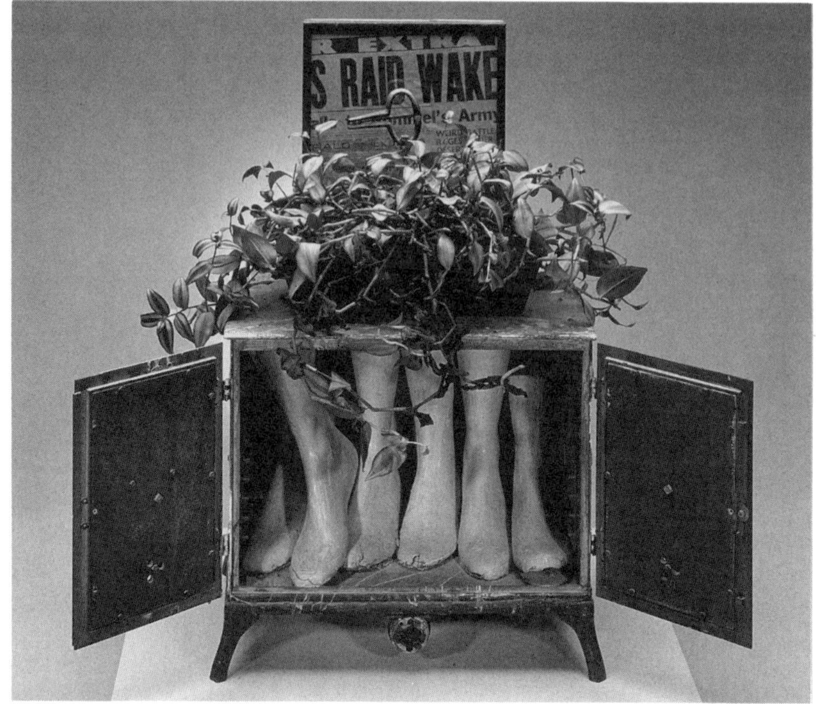

FIG. 7. Edward Kienholz, *History as a Planter*, 1961.
Mixed material assemblage, 83.8×47.3×31.4 cm (33×18$\frac{5}{8}$×12$\frac{3}{8}$ in.). Los Angeles County Museum of Art, Los Angeles, anonymous gift through the Contemporary Art Council. Courtesy of Nancy Reddin Kienholz.

contributed to its demise, including the growing awareness of Stalin's brutal totalitarianism, the Nazi-Soviet pact, the Russian invasion of Finland, the formation of the Popular Front, and the Cold War. And there was a shift in tone in the writings of major art philosophers, theorists, and critics, such as Leon Trotsky, the exiled Russian revolutionary, André Breton, a founder of the surrealist movement, and Meyer Schapiro, Clement Greenberg, and Harold Rosenberg, local champions of the avant-garde—all of whom paved the way philosophically for an art that no longer needed to be a mouthpiece or, as they seemed to put it, a patsy for specific social and political ideologies.[11] Consider how the explicitly political nature of the art of the thirties, such as that of Ben Shahn and the Soyers, was replaced by the morally austere and largely apolitical and unideological art of the abstract expressionists. Kienholz was part of a new generation of artists, writers, and theorists who reacted in various ways against the silence of the fifties. His resurrection of politically and socially sensitive topics, and his particular way of treating them—not in the social realist manner of the thirties, but in a savage, grisly, and outrageous fashion that owes much to surrealism—parallel a resurgence in literature in the 1960s that addressed prickly social themes in a bizarre and grotesque manner and took cues from surrealism.

Kienholz's pieces physically grew at this stage of his career. With *John Doe* (fig. 8) of 1959 and *Jane Doe* of 1960, he began a fruitful series of tableaux that most often suggest human presence through manikin or doll figures; are free-standing and occupy significant zones of space; mix the humorous with the grim; and continue involvement with topical subject matter, as much broadly social as specifically political.

John and Jane, portrayed as typical middle-class American citizens, are bizarre blends of the prim and proper with the grotesque and even violent. Kienholz seems to represent them as unquestioning recruits in, though perhaps bloody victims of, the great but barren American Dream. John, being part baby stroller, is pushed into that dream down an unswerving path. Jane is the appropriate wifely companion. Composed partly of a night stand, she has no movement. She stagnates on her anorexically skinny legs at John's side, attempting to remain proper while torn between conventional morality and a revulsion for her empty existence.

Although this kind of satire of American middle-class life may seem a cliché today, we must place "John" and "Jane" in their proper cultural context. Begun in 1959, they operate as a commentary on the values of a decade that poet Robert Lowell called the "tranquillized" fifties.[12] Lowell was not alone in his assessment of this eerily repressed and complacent time. Sociologist Paul Goodman, in his 1960 book *Growing Up Absurd*, cultural historian Irving Howe, in his essay "This Age of Conformity," and Norman Mailer, in his 1957 essay "The White Negro: Superficial Reflections on the Hipster," offered related analyses; for instance, Mailer compared America's focus on totalitarianism abroad with "the slow death by conformity" at home "with every creative and rebellious instinct stifled."[13] While a certain stridency accompanies these literary onslaughts against conventionality and disgust for the hypocrisy of American middle-class life (Mailer's being the most savage), Kienholz's unique approach arises from a distinctively West Coast milieu dovetailing from a late 1950s beat sensibility into a 1960s counterculture and eventual political activism.[14]

John Doe and *Jane Doe* function individually as traditional, free-standing,

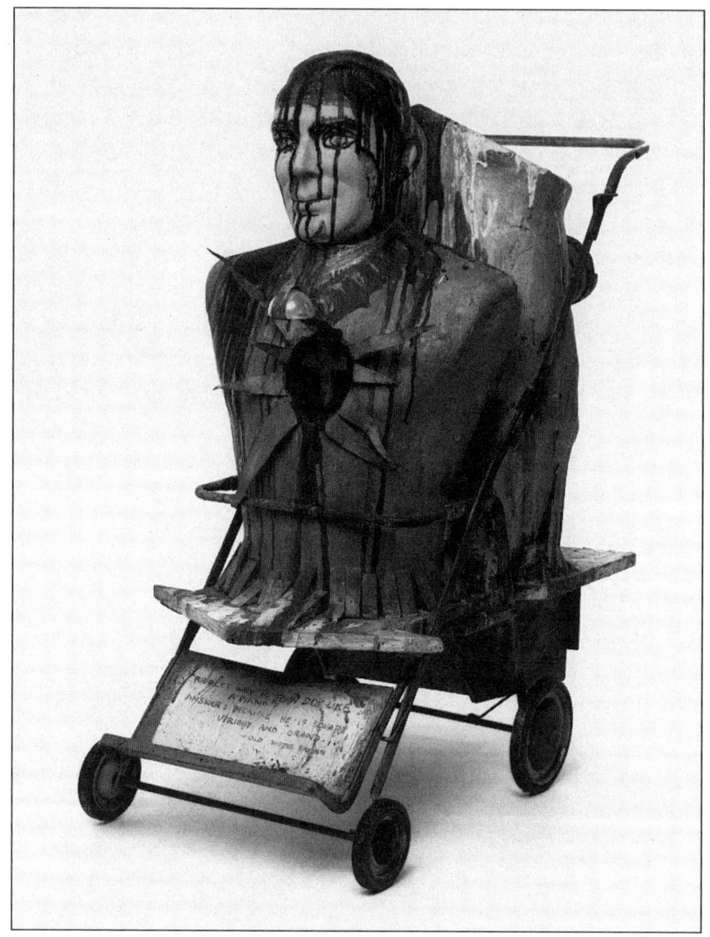

FIG. 8. Edward Kienholz, *John Doe*, 1959.
Free-standing, mixed materials assemblage, 100.3×48.3×79.4 cm (39½×19×31¼ in.).
The Menil Collection, Houston.

or—better yet—free-wheeling sculpture; together, they approach the concept of environmental art (in 1961 they were joined, as if in an actual birth, by *Boy, Son of John Doe*). Environmental art is a natural progression of collage developing into assemblage and construction art. Generally consisting of a variety of sculptural units that work together, environments may occupy substantial portions of a display space where the viewer is allowed to enter and become a participant. Such works may have great impact and immediacy; satisfy certain spatial, temporal, and conceptual ambitions; and create confusion between the boundaries of a work of art and the everyday world. Environments are undoubtedly theatrical, without the temporal and logistical constraints of a linearly unfolding performance. (In this context, it is tempting to think of Kienholz's politically charged art in connection with the contemporary emergence of guerrilla theater.) Many of the artists who produced assemblages and environments in the late 1950s—George Segal, Claes Oldenburg, and Red Grooms, to mention a few—also were involved in happenings, an ephemeral artform that mixes theater and art; at times, relocates art from the gallery to the streets; allows randomness and chance to enter a piece; can involve the audience; fuzzes art-life distinctions; attacks the permanence of art, making it less of a purchasable, possessible, and exchangeable commodity; and has sources in the sometimes political art performances of the Futurists, Dadaists, and Surrealists.

While the Doe family approaches the concept of an environment, Kienholz's first bona fide environment was *Roxys* (fig. 3), done in 1961. Where the "Does" might be grouped together in a gallery space, *Roxys* is intended to occupy an entire room to the exclusion of any other objects. Interestingly, *Roxys* evolved. Kienholz made several of the figures first as independent sculptural entities, such as *Fifi, A Lost Angel*; the accumulation of this batch of related characters seemed to cry out for a more specific home other than a neutral space. Thus Kienholz concocted the idea of a total environment, and since the characters were based on prostitutes from a Las Vegas brothel, the solution was to approximate a room in the brothel itself.

The approach to this piece is common to many of Kienholz's tableaux, and includes the use of altered manikins, the melding in his figures of the grotesque and the poignant, and an obsessiveness with details to produce situational and temporal specificity. Situationally, the seedy, patterned furniture, walls, and rugs, and the assignment of suggestive names to the girls (even the closed drawers of the furniture contain, among other things, sad letters written by them), all evoke pathetic and artificial attempts to achieve sensuality. Temporally, the calendar, magazines, style of clothing, jukebox, and exhortatory Douglas MacArthur photograph date the work to 1943.

Yet Kienholz was not interested in producing a piece of nostalgia. Allegedly "the world's oldest profession" and a subject that recurs throughout the history of art, prostitution can never be frozen in time. Kienholz also ensured that the work has an immediacy and contemporaneity by permitting the viewer to wander into this world. For its opening night at the Ferus Gallery in 1962 he insisted that all who came wear formal attire and be on their best behavior, in respect for the depicted prostitutes. Kienholz, the didactic moralist and exposer of hypocrisies, again operates as a quintessential 1960s commentator, suggesting that since, at one time or another, most people's integrity gets compromised, the viewer should not approach the theme of this tableau with condescension. Also, by issuing instructions to the spectator, he converts observing the work into an experience akin to theater, and thus to happenings. Increasingly, Kienholz demanded more of the viewer's attention and participation.

Roxys, when first shown in 1962, raised eyebrows. Four years later, when displayed as part of a major Kienholz retrospective at the Los Angeles County Museum of Art, it was at the center of a storm of controversy. But prior to the 1966 LACMA conflict, Kienholz's art was censored by San Fernando Valley State College. In 1963, his assemblage *Bunny, Bunny, You're So Funny* (1962) (fig. 1) was felt to be too disturbing for inclusion in a group show. It consists of a waist-to-knees fragment of a female manikin to which is attached steel-wool pubes and chicken-wire mesh stockings, mounted horizontally on a spindly wrought-iron base. Inside the body hangs a plastic baby doll that spins when the crank jutting from the upper thigh is turned. Despite majority support from the art faculty, a university official banned *Bunny, Bunny* from display. In response, the other artists removed their works from the gallery, and the university hastily assembled a replacement exhibition.[15]

The San Fernando fracas, however, was tame compared with the tempest Kienholz's 1966 LACMA exhibition provoked. While Kienholz's disquieting art might have spawned a dispute on its own, this, the museum's first retrospective of a West Coast artist at its newly built space, came at a stressful time for the institution. In November 1965, the board of directors of LACMA dismissed Dr. Richard F. Brown, the museum's director, even though such a move was illegal, and Brown had actually resigned from the post several weeks earlier.[16] His departure was the culmination of a bitter battle with the board, beginning when Brown felt that it had pushed through a design for the new museum that was more an overblown monument than a space hospitable to the exhibition of art and sensitive to the needs of the community. Continued meddling by the board in the daily affairs of the museum exacerbated already strained relations. The result was the attempt to fire Brown, amid accusations of administrative ineptitude, charges that most in the art community regarded as trumped up.[17] In response, a Save the Museum committee was formed to decry "trustee interference in museum policy."[18] Brown then accepted a job as director of the Kimbell Art Foundation in Fort

Worth, which was also engaged in new museum construction. The result—Louis Kahn's Kimbell Art Museum, generally regarded as one of the most sensitive and elegant in the world—served, in part, to vindicate Brown.

Ill feelings were rekindled early in March 1966 when Chief Curator James Elliot announced his resignation from LACMA in order to accept the position of director of the Wadsworth Atheneum in Hartford, Connecticut. Elliot fired a parting shot, remarking that he had been "deeply disturbed" by the events surrounding Brown's resignation, accusing the trustees of "inaccurate statements . . . to justify their position."[19] As the opening of the Kienholz exhibition approached on March 30, the eyes of the art community were trained on the museum. Considering Kienholz's notoriety, many anticipated further trouble. They were not to be disappointed.

Forty-seven works were scheduled for display in this midcareer retrospective organized by LACMA curator Maurice Tuchman. There was much in the exhibition to offend, as Kienholz, functioning as moralist and social critic, addressed sensitive issues, some of which have already been mentioned: homosexuality and militarism in *George Warshington in Drag* (fig. 6); civil rights and racism in *The Little Eagle Rock Incident* (1958) and *It Takes Two to Integrate, Cha Cha Cha* (1961); American concerns about Russian scientific superiority after the launching of Sputnik in *The God Tracking Station no. 1* (1959); American middle-class values in *John Doe* and *Jane Doe* (dated in the catalogue 1959); art, obscenity, and scandal in *Walter Hopps Hopps Hopps* (1960) (fig. 5); sexual and capital violence in *The Psycho-Vendetta Case* (1960); and efforts to redefine the holocaust in *History as a Planter* (1961) (fig. 7). Other issues he confronted included: U.S. humiliation at a recent international summit in *The U.S. Duck or Home from the Summit* (1960); religion in *The Nativity* (1961); birth-giving (probably out of wedlock) in *The Birthday* (1964); abortion in *The Illegal Operation* (1962) (fig. 9); sexual rituals and relations in *While Visions of Sugar Plums Danced in Their Heads* (1964); aging in *The Wait* (1964–65); and the impact of modern media and technology, such as the computer and television, in several pieces.[20] Two works provoked special antagonism: the aforementioned *Roxys*, dealing with prostitution, and *Back Seat Dodge '38* (fig. 2), a sardonic environment of lovemaking in an actual 1938 Dodge truncated to its hindquarters.

The chronology of events surrounding the furor over the Kienholz retrospective is not totally clear, and newspaper accounts and other documents offer conflicting evidence. Apparently at a luncheon on March 15, Warren Dorn, a member of the Los Angeles County board of supervisors, expressed concern over the upcoming Kienholz show to Edward W. Carter, president of

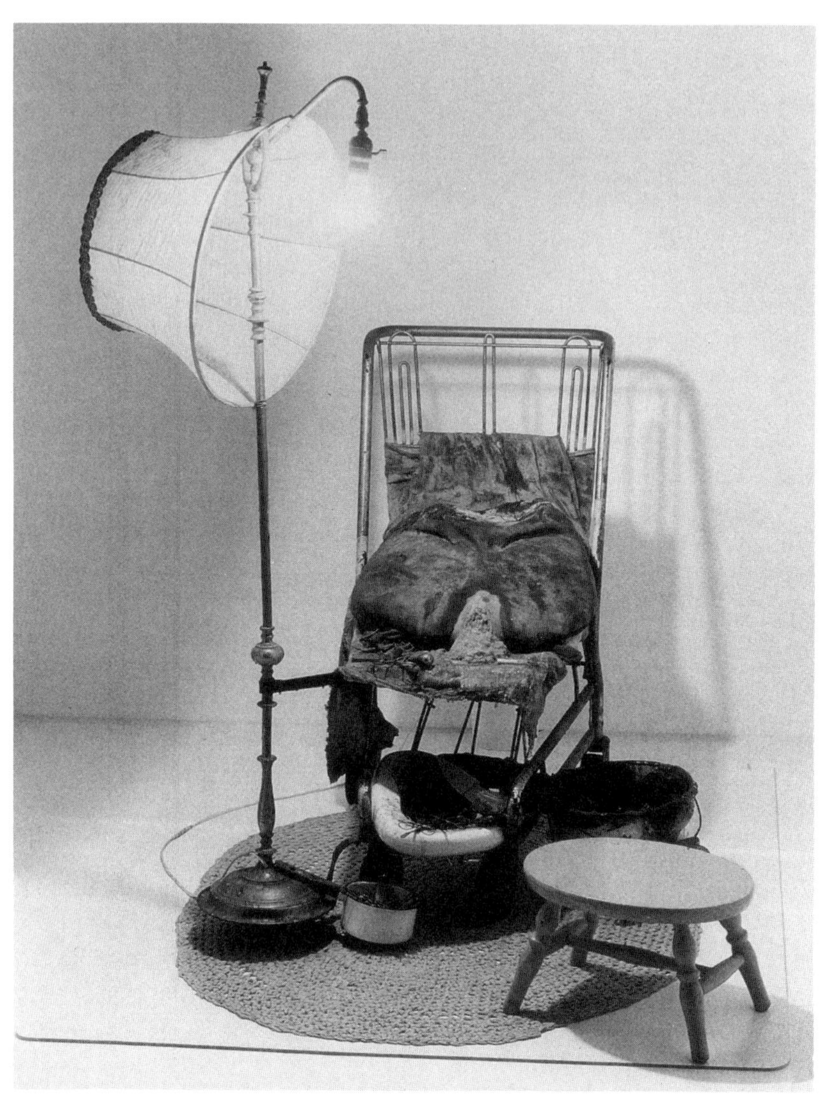

FIG. 9. Edward Kienholz, *The Illegal Operation*, 1962.
Mixed materials environment, 149.9×121.9×137.2 cm (59×48×54 in.).
Betty and Monte Factor Family Collection, Santa Monica, California.
Courtesy of Nancy Reddin Kienholz.

the board of trustees of the Los Angeles County Museum. Later that day, Dorn visited the exhibition, accompanied by a second supervisor, Kenneth Hahn. Afterward, Dorn said the show left him "sick and saddened,"[21] and on March 17, he penned a letter to Carter singling out two pieces as objectionable: *Back Seat Dodge '38* and *Roxys*. "I am most vehemently opposed to having this kind of expression shown by a public institution to the public at large," he wrote. "Certain of the objects or creations are most revolting, and I feel, pornographic in nature. In particular, I found the scene in the automobile and the House of Prostitution repugnant . . . and not art in any sense."[22]

Although there is a report that the two supervisors held a press conference following this viewing, there is no press mention of these events until March 24, casting some doubt on precisely when they first saw the show. One newspaper article suggests the visit took place on March 22,[23] with the letter coming two days after that, even though it bears the date March 17. What is clear is that on March 22, eight days before the official opening, the board of supervisors met. Based on the opinion of Dorn and Hahn, the only two members of the five-person board to view the exhibition at this point, the supervisors unanimously condemned the two objectionable works in the show and demanded that they be removed from display.

On either March 22 or 23, the museum board unanimously announced its support for the retrospective, calling it "an honest statement by a serious artist."[24] Although attributable in some accounts to a press conference following the initial Dorn-Hahn visit to the show, first reports of Dorn's catchy, amusing, and inadvertently revealing response to the show—"My wife knows art. I know pornography"—date it to March 23.[25] The same day, Dorn announced his entry into the Republican primary for governor of California (the primary and governorship were ultimately won by the already declared candidate Ronald Reagan).[26] Dorn then pledged to cancel speaking engagements connected to his candidacy in order to focus on the Kienholz affair, leading fellow supervisor Ernest E. Debs to brand the uproar "Dorn's baby."[27] Hahn considered, though never entered, the Republican race for lieutenant governor.

Charges and countercharges flew. On March 23, Hahn deemed the inclusion in *Roxys* of a portrait of General Douglas MacArthur "degrading."[28] After a second viewing on March 24, Dorn judged as "unpatriotic" the MacArthur allusion and an Army Eisenhower jacket pinned with a good conduct medal, and labeled one of the figures representing a prostitute in *Roxys* "obscene."[29] Some suggested that the exhibition, under way at the time Richard Brown departed as director, was part of a plot of "recrimination," that was "not only in bad taste but inconsistent with the [county] board['s] . . . efforts to halt the moral decline of the community."[30] The county board of supervisors also accused the museum board of trustees of not opposing the show for fear of aggravating an already tense relationship between the museum board and staff. The trustees's abdication of responsibility thus required that the supervisors step in as moral arbiters.[31]

Despite threats by Hahn on March 23 to strip top museum officials of their supplemental salaries, LACMA's board, previously the villain in the eyes of the art community and frequent antagonist to the museum's professional staff, acted in concert with the staff and refused to withdraw the works.[32] The museum then issued testimonials of leading art experts regarding the validity and importance of Kienholz's art.[33] Attempting to circumvent the museum, a third supervisor, Frank G. Bonelli, threatened to withhold over one million dollars in county funding unless the show was "cleaned up."[34] The county counsel ruled that this would violate the contract between the county board and the museum.

At a seven-hour closed door meeting held one day before the exhibition was to open, a compromise was reached involving the modification of the two most thorny pieces, and the board of supervisors voted four to one to permit the show to go on. *Five Dollar Billie*, one of the prostitute figures from *Roxys*, was placed on a larger plinth, making its ostensibly offensive elements less easy to see. The door to the back seat of the Dodge containing the copulating couple was to be open only during four daily museum tours, and the entire exhibition was to be closed to those under the age of eighteen (unless accompanied by parent or teacher).[35]

The exhibition opened as scheduled on March 30. The dispute had so piqued public interest that attendance broke museum records, turning what should have been an important midcareer retrospective into a titillating blockbuster.[36] Controversy continued to flare as the Los Angeles city council entered the fray, proposing a resolution that resulted in a split vote to commend the board of supervisors for their intervention in the Kienholz matter. At the same moment, the supervisors, in an effort to ease strained relations with the museum's trustees, whom they essentially had accused of cowardice, gave a vote of confidence to the museum board.[37]

On April 4, Dorn, unsatisfied with the alteration to *Five Dollar Billie* because two curse words on the sculpture were still visible, warned that someone might be arrested, despite the assertion by the deputy counsel of Los Angeles that neither Kienholz nor the museum was in violation of the law.[38] Dorn next attacked Kienholz's *The Nativity*, claiming it was sacrilegious to display it during the upcoming Easter Week. By this time, Dorn had become as much a spectacle as the show itself, and some of his previous supporters grew tired of a moral indignation that began to appear too much like the grandstanding of a candidate running for office. "You have milked this thing dry. Now let's drop it," admonished Supervisor Debs. Hahn, among the most outspoken critics of Kienholz on the county board, also seemed to relent: "What we should have done is just to give this whole thing the silent treatment."[39]

Eventually the furor subsided somewhat. But for several weeks, the *Los Angeles Times* ran daily articles on the exhibition turmoil. Throughout the affair, the *Times* expressed its opposition to censoring the show. After the first day of the exhibition, the paper published a story with the vindicating headline: "No Giggles in the Gallery: Public Sees Art Exhibition; Consensus: Not Pornographic." The article paid particular attention to the door of *Back Seat Dodge '38*, reporting that it was first opened "at 11:15 A.M. at the request of a . . . 25 [year-old] . . . art history graduate student who is writing a thesis on Kienholz" and that it "was opened 32 times during the day, enabling about 85% of the 1500 visitors to view the scene inside."[40] (Kienholz himself thought of the door as the psychological fulcrum of the piece. Because he so identified with and personalized his characters—assigning actual names, Mildred and Harold, to the lovers—he understood the opening of the door as a profound invasion of their privacy. He lamented: "I really felt almost like crying because Harold and Mildred became real in the process of making them—real enough that I felt like I betrayed them by making them subject to the will of anybody that wanted to take the handle and open the door.")[41] Although some spectators expressed shock at what they saw, museum officials reported that several of the complaints were raised by ill-informed attendees who mistook the museum's collection of seventeenth- and eighteenth-century paintings containing nudity for Kienholz's art.[42]

In addition to the articles in the *Los Angeles Times*, coverage was widespread, including pieces in most major newspapers and *Time* magazine. Kienholz became a local talk-show celebrity, his work the subject of newspaper editorials, letters to the editor, political cartoons (figs. 10–12), and even a topic of local sermons. After the board of supervisors arranged a special tour for some Los Angeles clergymen prior to the show's official opening, a Baptist minister called the exhibition "filthy, blasphemous, and offensive," and a female All-Saints reverend countered that "the exhibition has a much more important message than all the sermons that will be preached during Holy Week."[43] In defense of his work, Kienholz, at the inception of the affair, re-

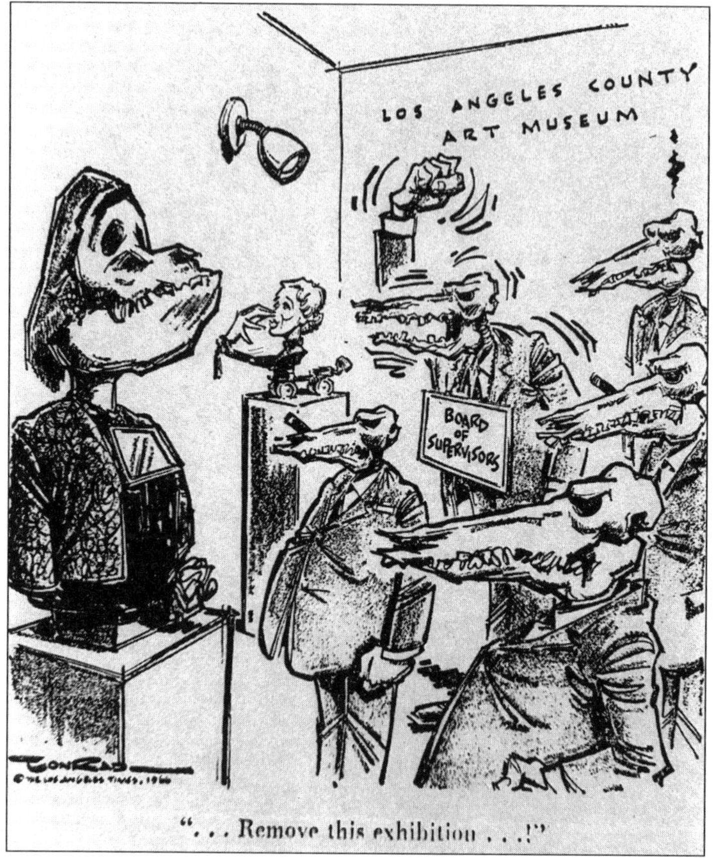

FIG. 10. Paul Conrad, "... Remove this exhibition ...!"
Political cartoon, *Los Angeles Times*, March 24, 1966. Copyright 1966.
Los Angeles Times Syndicate. Reprinted by permission.

marked that his work was "designed to show life stripped of its sham and hypocrisy."[44] In the press coverage that followed, this phrase became the "sound bite" most often used to describe the artist's characterization of his work.

Despite all the claims and posturings, what made the exhibition in general and works such as *Back Seat Dodge '38* and *Roxys* so problematic? It is certainly understandable why allusions to prostitution and sexual intercourse might have raised hackles, but the complex nature of the scandal made it clear that other issues were at stake. These include contemporaneous U.S.

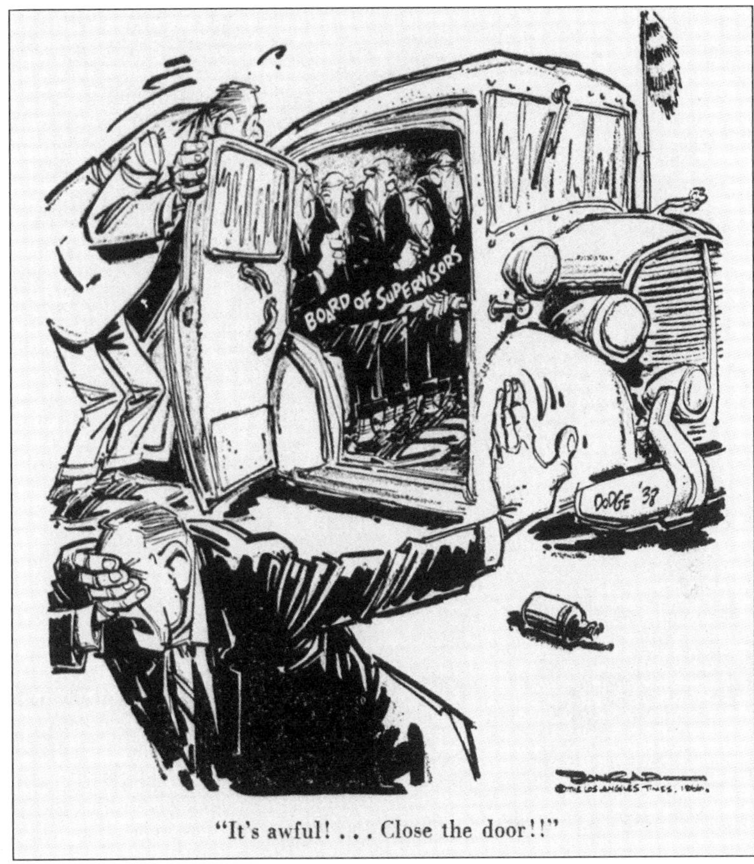

"It's awful! . . . Close the door!!"

FIG. 11. Paul Conrad, "It's awful! . . . Close the door!!" Political cartoon, *Los Angeles Times*, March 30, 1966. Copyright 1966. Los Angeles Times Syndicate. Reprinted by permission.

Supreme Court debates and rulings on the nettling definition of obscenity, and shifting sexual mores and political values in the turbulent 1960s, characterized and exacerbated, in part, by what became known as the generation gap.

Around the time of the Kienholz conflict, the Supreme Court was reviewing several obscenity cases (the debates received wide press coverage), including production, publicity, and sale of some Ralph Ginzburg publications, among them *Eros* magazine. After conducting hearings in December 1965, the Court made its ruling on Ginzburg on March 21, 1966, nine days be-

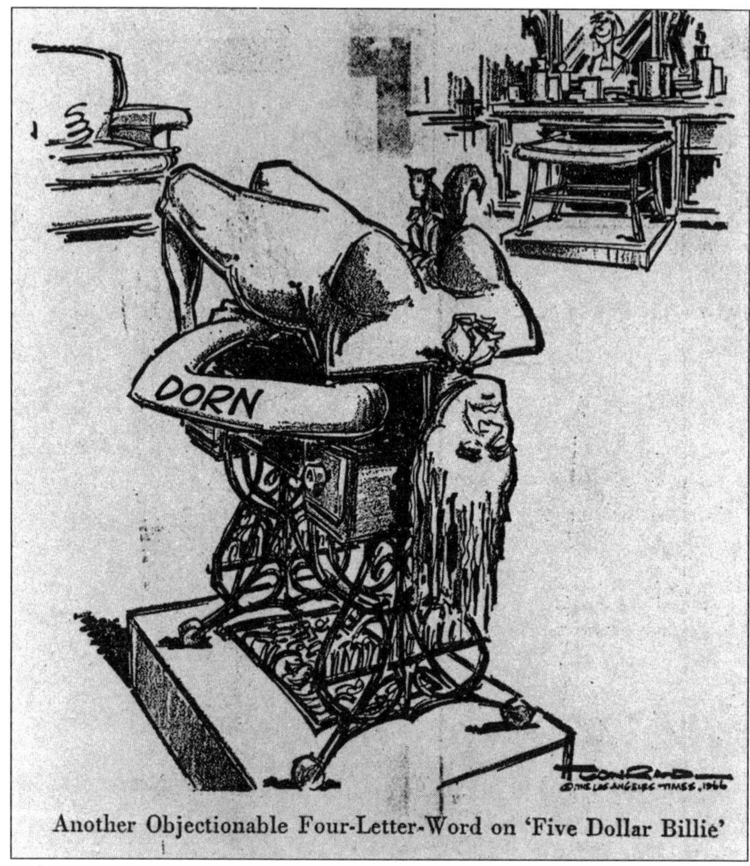

Another Objectionable Four-Letter-Word on 'Five Dollar Billie'

FIG. 12. Paul Conrad, "Another Objectionable Four-Letter Word on 'Five Dollar Billie.'" Political cartoon, *Los Angeles Times*, April 6, 1966. Copyright 1966. Los Angeles Times Syndicate. Reprinted by permission.

fore the Kienholz opening and one day before the Los Angeles county board labeled the show "pornographic." In a five to four ruling, the Court rejected Ginzburg's appeal of a lower court conviction for peddling pornography and its consequent $28,000 fine and five-year jail sentence (*Ginzburg v. United States*, 383 U.S. 463). In his dissenting opinion, Supreme Court Justice Potter Stewart elaborated on his well-known 1964 "I know it when I see it" definition of obscenity (*Jacobellis v. Ohio*, 378 U.S. 184), a phrase from which Dorn obviously took his "My wife knows art. I know pornography" cue.

As is often the case in obscenity charges, the leaders of such supposedly moral crusades are frequently running for office or up for reelection.[45] Dorn and Hahn, trying to position themselves as protectors of morality in prospective bids for governor and lieutenant governor of the state, instigated and capitalized on the Kienholz controversy, gaining much free publicity in the bargain. (In accusing "Five Dollar Billy" of being obscene, Dorn refers specifically to current Supreme Court rulings.)[46] Intriguingly, in the Ginzburg case, several experts testified to the effect that Ginzburg's publication was not pornography but art, similar to the defense of Kienholz's work by art professionals. Fearing increasing threats to freedom of expression, a group of well-known and respected intellectuals took out a full-page advertisement in the *New York Times* on April 3, 1966, defending First Amendment rights; among the signers was the noted art historian H. W. Janson.

A more detailed analysis of *Back Seat Dodge '38* should help to explain why the "generation gap" was central to the polemic. The piece consists of a shortened 1938 Dodge covered with electric blue flocking, with the bottom half of its rear (and only) wheels lopped off, all connected to casters resting on a bright green carpet of artificial grass, ringed by smaller patches of the grass serving as ersatz coasters for strewn bottles of Olympia beer. With the front seat excised, the automobile becomes a "bedroom-on-wheels," recalling John Steinbeck's often-quoted remark in *Cannery Row*: "Most of the babies of the period were conceived in Model T Fords and not a few were born in them."[47] The sexually engaged figures—a beer-drenched, chicken-wire male and a plaster female—fuse into a single faceless, conjugal head that contains a photograph of a salacious scene, suggesting the fantasy-reality interface of sexual activity, a kind of "eroticartesian" mind-body split.[48]

Voyeuristic in nature, the *Dodge* stirred up trouble because the artist, by lining the interior windows of the car with mirrors, short-circuits the pleasures of voyeurism, thus confronting the spectator with his own viewing of the work. *Back Seat Dodge '38*, temporally located by a variety of details in the mid-forties and exhibited in Los Angeles in the mid-sixties, exposes the true morals (or immorals) of an older generation who was currently criticizing the new morality (especially the sexual mores) of the sixties generation. (Intriguingly, a hypothetical child conceived in the *Dodge* would have been in his or her mid-twenties when the work was completed.) Kienholz cleverly intertwined the past and present by having the car's radio in operation at all times, thus perpetually keeping the work up to date. He further emphasized the universality of the image in the car's rear license plate that reads "C692 Everywhere U.S.A.," a detail seldom seen because *Back Seat Dodge '38* is often placed in the corner of a gallery, as if tucked away on a private lover's lane. In the *Dodge*, the middle-aged protectors of the public morality are "caught with their pants down," so to speak, and this exposure is made even more damning because they are revealed in perhaps the most favorite trysting spot of their youth—the car. The subject of *Back Seat Dodge '38* is based in part on Kienholz's memories of his own adolescent sexual experiences. His individual understanding of the car's role in rites of passage in American society thus maximizes the more collective impact of the piece. (*Roxys* works similarly: the sensitive subject issues from personal experience but has universal resonance. It is an environment that the spectator enters, is provided with a voyeuristic view of prostitutes on display, and is converted into a part of the piece that others see; and in its temporal location in 1943, it documents the morality of an earlier generation.)

That those who claimed to find these works scandalous and immoral in fact identified with the vexatious elements in the show appears to have been confirmed by recordings Kienholz surreptitiously made at the exhibition. Moral indignation functioned as a smokescreen for seeing one's own "reflection" in the pieces, as Kienholz's report of the supervisors' bugged conversation reveals:

> ... they'd say things like "Gee, Kenny [Hahn, a supervisor] look at this. I haven't been in a place like this in twenty years. Look at that over there." It was like old home week. They're in there, just having a ball. And the next thing you hear them come out of *Roxy's* and they're saying, "Why it's a moral outrage. Can you imagine women and children seeing that, I can't believe it."[49]

Again, the Ginzburg *Eros* decision comes to mind, for Ginzburg insisted that the Supreme Court ruling was much the reflection of a generation gap: "If the average age of the justices had been twenty-five years younger," Ginzburg stated, "it would have swung one or two votes and that's all we needed. I believe the decision is Old Guard America talking, not the Young America of today—they don't regard sex as dirty."[50]

The generation gap problem in the Ginzburg and Kienholz cases points up an issue common to much censorship. Censorship is often a means by which those in power try to maintain that power, suppressing any forms of expression that are fundamental threats to the status quo. One manifestation of censorship as an instrument of power is fear of the "other," since recognition of the "other" acknowledges the possibility of difference within society, a potential prod to change.[51] (As well, fear of difference in others is often a disguise for fear of the existence of such difference in ourselves, precisely the case in the *Back Seat Dodge* scandal.) Anxiety about what art might express is an admission of art's potency. Better to be feared, and on occasion, even deterred and quashed, than ignored. As the Peruvian writer and politician Mario Vargas Llosa put it: "If you are killed because you are a writer, that's the maximum expression of respect, you know."[52]

One of the compromises reached between the artist, museum, and board of supervisors, to place age restrictions on the viewing of the "objectionable" works, is another leitmotif in the history of censorship. The idea that art (or other questionable material) is appropriate for some, but not others, may go back at least as far as Aristotle, who in *Politics* argued that rulers should not allow children to hear or use "improper language," "should also banish pictures or speeches from the stage which are indecent," and should protect them from any "image or picture representing unseemly actions," because of "the evil influences of such representations."[53] The Los Angeles County Museum was hardly pioneering in its regulations; in the early eighteenth century, institutions such as the Pennsylvania Academy of Art established special "ladies days," when nude statuary was draped.

Censorship is commonly class, gender, or age determined. It is understandable why restrictions might apply to minors (and even this may be arguable), but placing others in that category implies that they are like children, and need to be protected from material that might offend, harm, or inflame them. The most egregious example of this reasoning is the famous 1868 "Hicklin rule," named after Benjamin Hicklin, Recorder of London and principal in the obscenity case *Regina v. Hicklin* (the "Regina" being Queen Victoria). Lord Chief Justice Sir Alexander Cockburn ruled in the appeal that the "test of obscenity" is "whether the tendency of the matter charged as obscenity is to deprave and corrupt those whose minds are open to such immoral influences and into whose hands a publication of this sort may fall."[54] The idea that susceptibility to social and moral corruption may be dependent on class, gender, education, age, or other social distinction or characteristic implies distrust and condescension toward those whom the censors are allegedly trying to protect, and can reveal the extraordinary, often paternalistic arrogance of censorship.

Although the artist claimed he did not appreciate all the difficulty the exhibition caused, and felt as a result people might come to see his work for the wrong reasons, he nonetheless believed that captivation is a prerequisite for communication, and the media circus surrounding this show can certainly be regarded as one form of captivation. The publicity provided a major boost to his reputation, and placed his art at the forefront of two major developments in the sixties: the efflorescence of assemblage and environments; and the production of inflammatory works during an age of heightened social and political awareness.

As to the first development, Kienholz was sometimes lumped together with artists such as Robert Rauschenberg, George Segal, and John Chamberlain. But a comparison between their work and that of Kienholz and other West Coast assemblagists, such as Wallace Berman, Bruce Conner, and George Herms, reveals the distinctions between East and West Coast activities. There is a repellent, belligerent, often grisly appearance and a more critical political tone to the West Coast work, far less tame than the aesthetically self-conscious art of Rauschenberg or Segal.[55] Kienholz perhaps made this difference explicit in a 1960 punning homage, an assemblage titled *Odious to Rauschenberg*. Although its intended delivery to Rauschenberg as an anonymous gift at a birthday celebration never occurred, the piece has a diathermic machine hidden within it, which would have seriously interfered with television reception in the area and would probably have brought the local authorities to Rauschenberg's place to investigate and possibly arrest the artist. As Robert L. Pincus points out, this work of art truly interacted with life, thus functioning as a wry commentary on Rauschenberg's famous statement of trying to work between the gap of art and life.[56]

A few reasons can be offered as to why West Coast art was more extreme: the potent doses of fantasy from Hollywood and Disneyland; the virulence of West Coast beat culture; California as the most conspicuous home of consumer culture; and the influence of glittery and often strange Mexican and Indian artifacts. Perhaps distance from New York encouraged the production of less safe art. And the smaller numbers of major public art collections may have made the weight of art historical tradition less onerous, thus prodding experimentation.

As to the political dimensions of Kienholz's work, a careful examination of the political nature of 1960s art still needs to be done. The age was one of social activism, but as mentioned, the visual (and performing) arts were frequently thought of as tranquil islands in a stormy sea. In "One Culture and the New Sensibility," the concluding essay of her important collection *Against Interpretation and Other Essays* of 1966, Susan Sontag noted the shift in importance of various arts at this time that reflects their involvement in social commentary. Literature, because of "its heavy burden of 'content,' both reportage and moral judgment," became subordinate. "But the model arts of our time," she wrote, "are actually those with much less content, and a much cooler mode of moral judgment—like music, films, dance, architecture, painting, sculpture."[57] A thorough investigation of the issue might prove otherwise; still, the role that modern art played in sixties activism, with notable exceptions, such as James Rosenquist's *F-111* (1965) and Claes Oldenburg's *Lipstick Ascending on Caterpillar Tractor* (1969), remains unclear. In this regard, Kienholz's art appears closer in sensibility to the "Howling" of Allen Ginsberg or the scatological and sardonic humor of Lenny Bruce or Mort Sahl than to that of many contemporary visual artists.[58]

Kienholz's preachy, nearly narrative style also brings him close to literature, with its heavy burden of content, as Sontag characterized it. Kienholz, however, charges this moral content with a surrealistic visionary strangeness. In this context, he becomes the visual equivalent to black humor writers emerging in the sixties, such as Kurt Vonnegut, Thomas Pynchon, Norman Mailer, and Philip Roth, whose work Dickstein sees as a reaction against the cautious realism and psychological inwardness dominating literature since World War II. He argued: "All black humor involves the unseemly, the forbidden, the exotic and the bizarre . . . always affronting taboos, giving offense, recalling people to their physical functions and gut reactions." He talks of its "absurdity and incongruity, its mixture of farce, violence, and hysteria," characterized by "its wild adventurousness of imagery," tellingly labeling it "the birth of a new surrealism."[59]

After the 1966 brouhaha, Kienholz continued to produce work destined to antagonize, including two explicitly antiwar tableaux, *The Eleventh Hour Final* and *The Portable War Memorial* (fig. 13), a piece that the artist said "has to do with the stupidity of war."[60] Both were done in 1968 and coincided with the increasingly outspoken protests against the Vietnam War, especially after word emerged about the Tet offensive, and after the United States became dramatically polarized because of the assassinations of Martin Luther King and Robert Kennedy and the riots outside the Democratic National Convention. Also, *Roxys* (fig. 3) figured in a further controversy when it was on display in 1968 at "Documenta IV," a major international art show held periodically in Kassel, Germany. As student protests spread in reaction to some of the events just described, art was sometimes perceived as a superfluous, bourgeois luxury and a capitalist phenomenon worthy of attack. Consequently, German students occupied "Documenta," and because *Roxys* is a habitable environment offering certain comfortable amenities, it became a hangout for some of the protestors.[61]

These are the last of Kienholz's major tableaux from the 1960s. He contin-

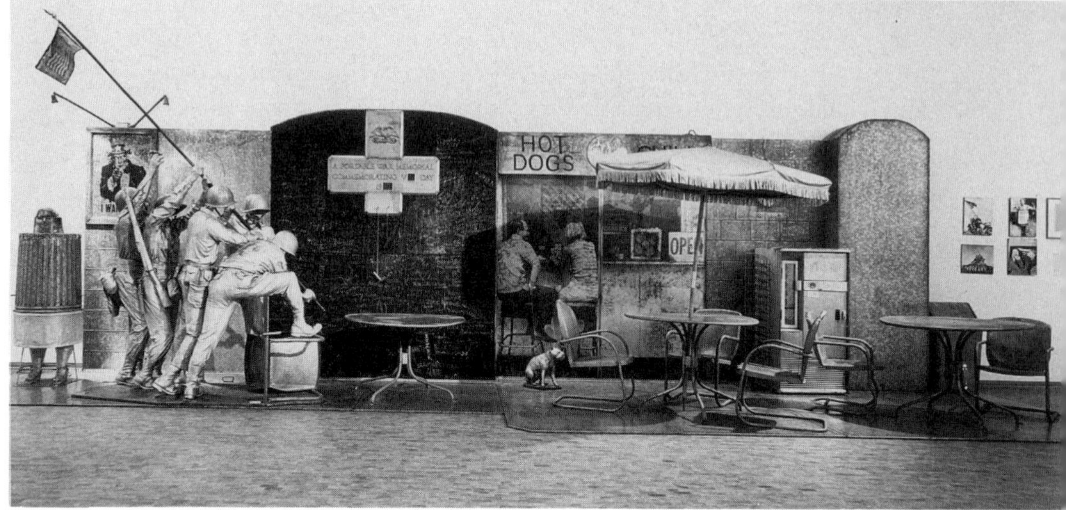

FIG. 13. Edward Kienholz, *The Portable War Memorial*, 1968.
Mixed materials tableau, 289.6×975.4×243.8 cm (114×384×96 in.). Collection of Museum Ludwig, Museen der Stadt, Cologne. Photo: Rheinisches Bildarchiv, Cologne.

ued to produce socially relevant work, but as the times became less responsive to such issues, when, ironically, more artists embraced politically biting art, Kienholz responded with several of his most extreme tableaux.

One of these is *Five Car Stud* (fig. 14), a parking-lot sized environment, consisting of four automobiles, a pickup truck, and nine figures. It was designed specifically for exhibition in a tent at "Documenta V" in Kassel in 1972. The title puns on a gambler's card game and refers to the number of vehicles in the piece and to one of its issues: masculinity. Like *Back Seat Dodge '38*, it combines cars and sex, but adds a potent dose of violence. The presumed narrative involves a nighttime attack by white males on a black man, who is on a date with a white woman. Four cars, headlights on, encircle and theatrically spotlight the brutal scene. Fitted with grotesque and bizarre Halloween masks, four of the white males pinion and castrate the black male, while a fifth holds his leg with a rope. A leering, shotgun toting white male stands guard at the pickup, where a white female, closed-eyed and vomiting, slumps in the passenger seat. A young boy (the son of one of the terrorizers?) looks on in fear (and fascination?) from inside a car. (Is he learning to abhor or embrace such violence?) The black male is made up of a double-faced cast—one expresses calm, the other torment—and an automobile oil-pan

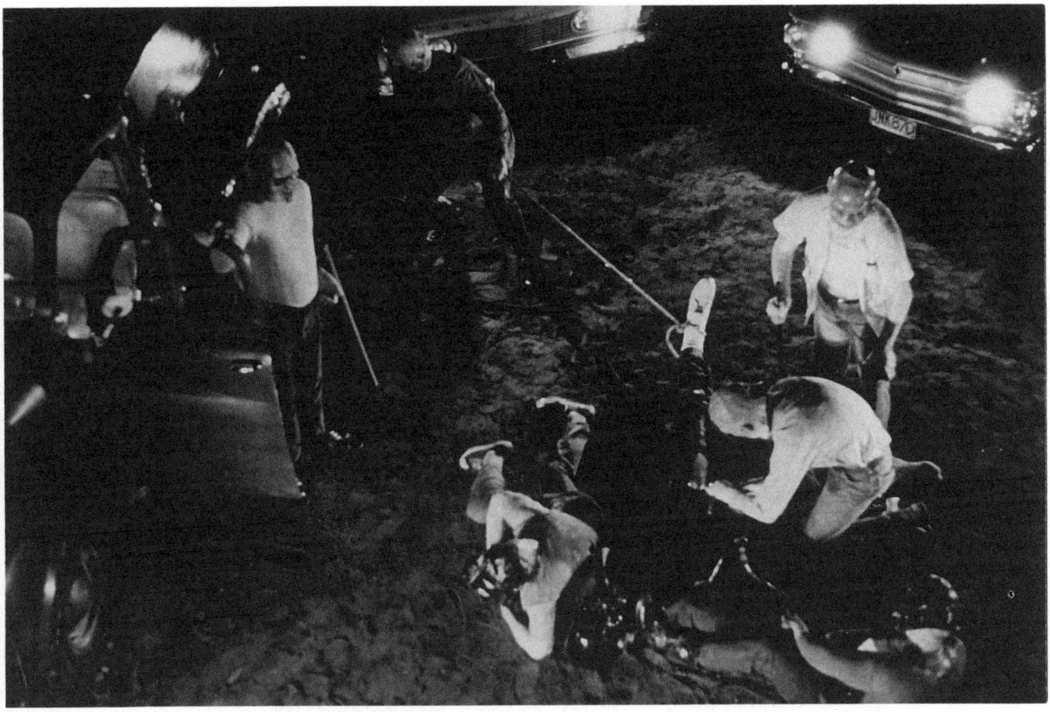

FIG. 14. Edward Kienholz, *Five Car Stud* (detail), 1969–72.
Mixed materials tableau. Kawamura Memorial Museum of Art, Sakura, Japan.

torso, filled with black liquid in which floats plastic letters that spell out in fractured form: "NIG-GER."

Kienholz said the tableau symbolizes "the social castration . . . of the black,"[62] and though not based on an actual event, the piece encapsulates centuries of brutal racism, sparks visions of lynchings and race riots (also the subject of works by white artists Andy Warhol and Duane Hanson), and foreshadows the Rodney King beating videotape and the inflammatory power of the "N" word in the O.J. Simpson trial. This life-sized environment produces a visceral immediacy meant to engage and ultimately implicate the assumed white viewer in the emasculation of African American culture, an idea reinforced by the license plates that ironically spell out "State of Brotherhood."

In a work related to *Five Car Stud*, titled *Sawdy* and also done in 1972, Kienholz points the accusing finger of racism directly at the viewer. This is a fifty-edition work: each piece is comprised of a Datsun pickup truck door that has a mirrored glass window, which when rolled down, reveals a second pane of glass bearing an image of *Five Car Stud*. Because the viewer first sees his own image reflected in the mirror, and then, after cranking it down, sees the *Five Car Stud* drama, he mentally imprints, locates, and implicates himself into the scenario. It is as if he has become an observer in one of the surrounding/strangleholding vehicles or a participant in the castration itself.

Even more threatening is Kienholz's *Still Live* (1974, fig. 4), one of the most outlandishly extreme works in the history of art.[63] The piece is attributable to him and his wife Nancy Reddin Kienholz, who was assigned co-authorship of all work done after 1972. *Still Live* is an environment which invites spectators, after they have signed a legal release, to sit in an old-fashioned armchair (surrounded by other deceptively domestic furnishings, including some still-life paintings) at which is pointed a rifle barrel encased in a black box triggered to detonate at a random moment within the next hundred years. The exact time is unknown to all. (The Kienholzes imposed a further restriction to the signing of a release: only those over eighteen would be allowed to participate, ironically recalling the age limit LACMA placed on the viewing of his contentious 1966 retrospective.) Although the odds of being shot were infinitesimally small, complaints were lodged two days after the September 27 installation at Berlin's art school, the Hochschule für bildende Künste, as part of the "Aktionen der Avantgarde" for the 1974 Berlin Festival. On October 3, German police confiscated the piece as a violation of an obscure firearms law. Legal battles ensued, the German district attorney arguing that Kienholz might be charged with attempted homicide, while his lawyers countered that the signed release absolved him of such a crime.

The incident took an international turn when the police insisted on opening the box, which the artist feared would effectively destroy the work, and the U.S. ambassador intervened, stating that American authorities should handle the situation. After much wrangling, a compromise was negotiated in March 1975, and *Still Live* was returned intact to the Kienholzes in exchange for its removal from German soil. Most likely the selection of Germany as the site of this installation further inflamed the situation; the country's past and its then divided present must have heightened sensitivity toward the issues of death, violence, and censorship.

Punning on the term "still life"—the French version *nature morte* literally translates as "dead nature"—the Keinholzes created in *Still Live* a modern-day *vanitas* image (the German authorities nicknamed it the "death-machine" and others described it as "death-art"). The artists add a new dimension to the more conventional modernist debate of "art versus life" (already skewered in *Odious to Rauschenberg*) with a riveting confrontation of "death versus life."[64] With frightening directness, the piece treats the life-death issues common to Kienholz's tableaux—war and violence in *George Warshington in Drag* (fig. 6), *The Eleventh Hour Final*, and *The Portable War Memorial* (fig. 13); birth, death, and approaching death in *The Illegal Operation* (fig. 9) and *The Wait*; and capital punishment in the *Psycho-Vendetta Case*. They also address the dilemma of the avant-garde artist. No matter how hard the artist tries to create work that is shocking and unacceptable, contemporary capitalist culture eventually, and often blithely, accepts and thus co-opts even the most outlandish piece. Kienholz tries but one more time, producing a work that, either in itself is desperate, or parodies the desperate dance and ultimate embrace continually performed by the antagonistic avant-garde artist and accepting public. At the same time, the artist insisted: "My purpose is not death. Quite the contrary, I would hope that this work may be able to invoke new and positive responses to the wonders of life."[65]

As outrageous as this piece may be, it has a modernist pedigree and contemporary parallels. Building actual violence into works of art was not unique to Kienholz. For the most part, however, such violence operated on the level of rhetoric or fantasy. As rhetoric, the nineteenth-century Russian anarchist Mikhail Bakunin's cry "destruction is creation" is developed in aesthetic theory in futurist Filippo Tommaso Marinetti's exhortation from the early teens that "Art can only be violence, cruelty, and injustice," and surrealist André Breton's insistence in the twenties that "The simplest surrealist act consists of dashing down into the street, pistol in hand, pulling the trigger and blindly and as fast as you can firing into the crowd." Examples range from fantasy, in several of Oldenburg's proposed monuments that could be injurious to passers-by, to reality in some happenings of the 1960s. With spontaneity and sometimes destructiveness programmed into them, happenings could erupt into genuine violence, including ones staged by Oldenburg, Wolf Vostell, Jean Tinguely, and Nam June Paik, to mention a few.

It seems no accident that the Kienholzes' incorporation of extreme violence into their art came at a time when the subject was being explored viscerally and empirically by contemporaneous body and performance artists, such as Vito Acconci and especially Chris Burden. Both made the testing of their own physical limits a key element of the work, offering sardonic variations on the modernist insistence that the artist must take risks and the popular mythology of artist as martyr. This type of work might also be understood as reflections of an increasingly violent culture and as allegedly heroic proclamations of control in an environment in which man appears to be losing control over even what is physically and psychologically harmful to him. (Censorship itself threatens an individual's sense of personal control.) In other words, if harm is going to come to me, artist and citizen, at least allow me to decide by whose hand and by what means.

Furthermore, such acts enact a basic mythology of art production, originating perhaps with Michelangelo, revered especially in romanticism, and played out with a vengeance in abstract expressionism: the artist is a tortured soul who must suffer for his calling. Kienholz extends that suffering for one's art to the viewer. Throughout his career, Kienholz sought to involve the spectator with disarming, often menacing directness; in *Still Live*, he satisfies this desire terroristically. As he put it: "I have long been interested in making an environment that could be dangerous to the viewer."[66] In so doing, the work became a test of censorship itself; it apparently crossed the line beyond which one could defend it against suppression when physical risk outweighed freedom of expression.

One might imagine that the extremism of *Still Live* could signal the end of an era for this artist, whose work was so often strongly based on biting social commentary and disturbing imagery and seemed to invite tangles with interdiction. The artist himself admitted in 1982 that the "adrenaline-producing . . . hard-cutting anger" that fueled his tough and dark early work "is now gone."[67] Also, times had changed, and as artists, in far greater numbers and in varying degrees of vitriol, began to incorporate social, political, and cultural themes into their work, Kienholz was no longer a rare renegade.

This is not to say that Kienholz (who died in 1994), and his wife and collaborator, Nancy Reddin Kienholz, avoided making controversial art after *Still Live*. Wittily, acutely, even savagely, the Kienholzes continued to address sensitive themes such as Nazism, militarism, religion, child abuse, racism, sexism, loneliness, dispossession, and prostitution. They even went after the Supreme Court, the ultimate arbiter of censorship issues, in *Caddy Court* of 1987 (fig. 15). It consists of a split and stretched 1978 white Cadillac housing a 1966 Dodge Van, which may refer to the 1966 LACMA censorship scandal involving *Back Seat Dodge '38*. When the van's doors are closed, the facade of the Supreme Court building is seen; when open, shelves of law books appear, along with a black curtain, which, when pushed aside, reveals the black-

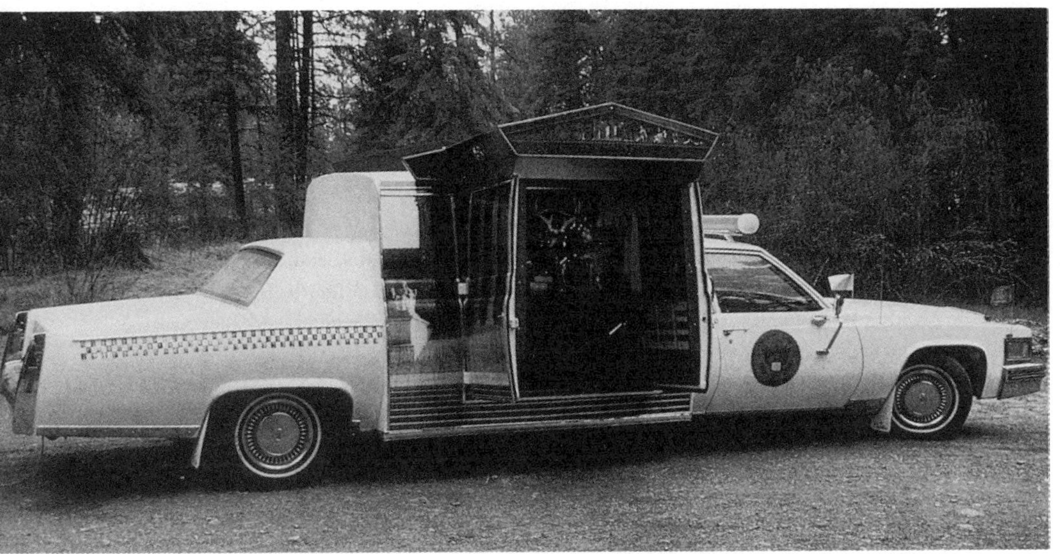

FIG. 15. Edward and Nancy Reddin Kienholz, *The Caddy Court*, 1986–87.
Mobile tableau, 213.4×702.3×254 cm (84×276½×100 in.).
Collection of Nancy Reddin Kienholz.

robed nine justices, fitted with grotesque animal heads, some teeth-baring, others skeletal. As a potentially mobile piece harking back to traveling circuit courts, *Caddy Court* signals how out of touch this predominantly white, male, Christian institution is.[68]

The issues surrounding the efforts to censor Edward Kienholz's art hold true today. With the exception of *Still Live*, the one instance in which something resembling objective standards might be applied for quashing a piece, the censoring of his work seems like "politics as usual." Assaults on art by politicians adopting self-righteously moral and patriotic stances, often designed to deflect the public from more substantive issues, are so common today as to appear hackneyed. From Jesse Helms to Pat Buchanan, from the cutting of funds for the National Endowment for the Arts to "oaths" that artists must sign to receive support, from "family values" to the questioning of one's patriotism, censorship can often appear to be little more than a publicity-grabbing tool of politics. These threats to freedom of expression are precisely the kinds of "sham and hypocrisy" that Kienholz, in his art, tried to strip away.

NOTES

This essay is based on my article "Ed Kienholz's *Back Seat Dodge '38*," published in *Arts Magazine* 52 (January 1978): 112–18. Some of the ideas were elaborated in a lecture at Middlebury College in 1986, "Controversy in the Career of Ed Kienholz." Although new literature on Kienholz has appeared since I wrote that article, my interpretation of his art remains fundamentally unchanged. I want to thank Janelle Wise and Jennifer Kahane for their help in the preparation of the current version. Maurice Tuchman kindly provided answers to queries I had about the artist. I am also indebted to the late Edward Kienholz and to Nancy Reddin Kienholz, with whom I spent a pleasant and provocative weekend in Hope, Idaho, before writing the 1978 article, and Walter Hopps who over the years has shared with me his insights and inside information on Kienholz. Nancy Kienholz and Alberta Mayo provided further help in the gathering of material for this essay.

1. All the works done by Edward Kienholz before 1972 are attributable to him. In 1981 he retroactively reassigned all his post-1972 works as a joint effort with his wife, Nancy Reddin Kienholz. From 1979 until his death in 1994, all the work has been cosigned.

2. The major developments in the visual arts of the 1960s are conventionally thought of as devoid of potent political content. Surely some of the important movements of that decade such as minimal art and color field painting seem politically bland or uninvolved. But I have always felt that certain developments, such as pop, op, happenings, and certain artists, such as Kienholz, Claes Oldenburg, Leon Golub, and Peter Saul, offered reasonably strong—if not explicitly political and social—commentary.

3. Quoted in Arthur Secunda, "Interview with John Bernhardt, Charles Frazier, Edward Kienholz," *Artforum*, November 1962, 31–32.

4. See Gerald Silk, guest ed., *Art Journal* ("Uneasy Pieces: Controversial Works in the History of Art: 1830–1950), 51 (Spring 1992): passim.

5. In the *Art Journal* "Uneasy Pieces" issue, there are examples of arrests and imprisonments for producing problematic art (see Elizabeth C. Childs, "Big Trouble: Daumier, *Gargantua*, and the Censorship of Political caricature," 26–37) and instances of giving up one's life to protect art under siege (see Danuta Batorska, "The Political Censorship of Jan Matejko," 57–63).

6. Betty Turnbull, *The Last Time I Saw Ferus*, exh. cat. (Newport Harbor, Calif.: Newport Harbor Art Museum, 1976), n.p.

7. Credit goes to Walter Hopps for this information.

8. *Kienholz*, exh. cat. (Helsinki: Galerie Christel, 1974), 6. See also Barbara Catoir, "Interview mit Edward Kienholz," *Kunstwerk*, March 1973, 49.

9. Julius and Ethel Rosenberg were Americans executed in 1953 by the U.S. government for alleged Soviet espionage, despite much doubt about their guilt and many

cries for clemency. The climate of the cold war and anti-Semitism were considered critical factors in their conviction and execution. Caryl Chessman was executed by the State of California after conviction on the charge of child molestation. His case became the centerpiece of a debate on capital punishment.

10. Morris Dickstein, *Gates of Eden: American Culture in the Sixties* (New York: Basic Books, 1977), 45. In addition to my own experiences growing up in the 1960s, Dickstein's book has been extremely useful as a guide to the pulse of that decade.

11. For a discussion of some of these ideas, see Francis Frascina, ed., *Pollock and After: The Critical Debate* (New York: Harper and Row, 1985).

12. Dickstein, *Gates of Eden*, 11.

13. Paul Goodman, *Growing Up Absurd* (New York: Random House, 1960). Cited ibid., 12. Norman Mailer, "The White Negro: Superficial Reflections on the Hipster," *Dissent*, Summer 1957, 277.

14. Several writers have suggested that the most compelling parallels to Kienholz's scathing social and political commentaries come from outside the visual arts. William Seitz made such connections in his ground-breaking exhibition, *The Art of Assemblage*, exh. cat. (New York: Museum of Modern Art, 1961). A selected and abbreviated cataloguing of discussions of Kienholz's extramural affinities include: references to comedian Lenny Bruce, beat poet Allen Ginsberg, and Walt Whitman in Philip Leider, "Art: Kienholz," *Frontier*, November 1964, 25; to playwrights Eugene O'Neill and Jean Genet and beat author Jack Kerouac in Frederick S. Wight and Henry T. Hopkins, "Two Views of Edward Kienholz," *Art in America* 53 (October–November 1965): 70–73; and to horror films in Max Kozloff, "Art," *The Nation*, January 1, 1968, 29–30. Robert L. Pincus, in his *On a Scale that Competes with the World: The Art of Edward and Nancy Reddin Kienholz* (Berkeley: University of California Press, 1990), explores literary and poetic connections to Kienholz's work in detail. In addition to some of the aforementioned writers, such as Ginsberg, he discusses Kienholz's kinship of sensibility with authors William Burroughs and Norman Mailer. Not surprisingly, the work of several of these writers and performers, including Bruce, Ginsberg, Sahl, Burroughs, and Genet, was subject to censorship.

15. For a discussion of this controversy, see Gerald Nordland, "The Suppression of Art," *Artforum*, November 1963, 25–26. See also Nordland, " 'Bunny, Bunny'—Not So Funny," *Frontier*, May 1963, 19–21.

16. "Los Angeles Art Museum Head Quits after Denouncing Trustees," *New York Times*, November 8, 1965, 42. For a discussion of the Kienholz controversy in the context of political dissent in California, see Richard Cándida Smith, *Utopia and Dissent: Art, Poetry, and Politics in California* (Berkeley: University of California Press, 1995), especially pp. 318–29.

17. Philip Leider, editor of the then West Coast based magazine *Artforum*, defended Brown in its December 1965 editorial, which was reprinted in *Art Journal*, one of the two major publications of the College Art Association, the professional organi-

zation of artists and art historians. It reads, in part: "it [should] be clear from the outset that Dr. Brown's resignation came about as a result not of his shortcomings, whatever they may have been, but out of his virtues; that a resignation was forced from Richard Brown not because of his inability but because of his singular refusal to permit . . . trustees . . . to 'establish . . . [their] taste as the official record.'" Quoted in *Art Journal*, Winter 1965–66, 192–94.

18. Peter Bart, "Museum on Coast Faces Big Protest," *New York Times*, November 13, 1965, 27.

19. Bart, "Curator of Los Angeles Museum in Aftermath of Dispute," *New York Times*, March 4, 1966, 30.

20. One of the works dealing with television was *The Big Eye* (*Homage to H.S.*) (1961), prompted by a negative review from the *Los Angeles Times* art critic, Henry Seldis. Atop a television set is a copy of Seldis's criticism; on the tube itself is a screenplay written in rhyming poetic meter about the art world. It includes characters such as "Ed Kienbusch, a carpenter person," referring to Kienholz and perhaps to the American landscape painter William Kienbusch; "Millard Threesheets, an art bore #2," referring to the conservative artist Millard Sheets and perhaps to the slang expression for drunkenness, "three sheets to the wind"; and "Henry J. Smellish, a witty art critic person," referring to Seldis. The piece had a certain prescience. Sheets was later at the center of the 1965 LACMA building controversy, since one of the most influential members on the board of trustees wanted him as the architect for the building. Seldis's continued diatribes against Kienholz probably helped fuel the sense of anxiety regarding the 1966 retrospective. In the script, Kienbusch, wondering why Smellish dislikes the artist's work, makes inquiries such as ". . . does my art offend you? . . . The things disgust you? . . . the colour's foul? . . . The shape's obscene?" Quoted in Maurice Tuchman, *Edward Kienholz*, exh. cat. (Los Angeles: Los Angeles County Museum, 1966), 47. See also, *Roxys and Other Works (aus der Sammlung Reinhard Onnasch)*, exh. cat. (Bremen: Gesellschaft für Aktuelle Kunst, 1982), n.p. Interestingly, Seldis's comments on the 1966 retrospective were mixed, calling *The Big Eye* itself a "childish, thin-skinned tantrum," saying that Kienholz's oeuvre "lack[ed] esthetic worth." Nonetheless, he admitted that some works expressed a "genuine and convincing fury against inhuman hypocrisies of American society," and were "often astonishingly imaginative and . . . craftily inventive." His concluding remark that "Kienholz's message . . . is certainly not beautiful but it deserves to be heard," implies that Seldis opposed censoring the exhibition. Henry J. Seldis, "Kienholz Art: Anything Goes," *Los Angeles Times*, March 27, 1966, 1, 16.

21. Harry Trimborn, "Background of Art Exhibit Controversy Told by Dorn," *Los Angeles Times*, March 25, 1966 I-24.

22. Letter from Warren M. Dorn to Edward W. Carter, in the Kienholz Scrapbooks. Also, "Museum Unit View in Art Feud Expected," *Los Angeles Times*, March 28, 1966, dates the letter to March 17.

23. Trimborn, "Background," I-24.

24. Harry Trimborn, "Kienholz Exhibit Will Be Shown Intact at the Museum," *Los Angeles Times*, March 29, 1966, 26, gives the March 22 date. Peter Bart, "Tableaus Revive Museum's Woes," *New York Times*, March 24, 1966, 47, offers a March 23 date.

25. Bart, "Tableaus Revive," 47.

26. "Seventh Aspirant Enters California Race," *New York Times*, March 24, 1966, 23.

27. Harry Trimborn, "Hahn Will Try to Block Extra Pay for Art Museum Officials," *Los Angeles Times*, March 24, 1966, 34.

28. Ibid.

29. Trimborn, "Background," I-24.

30. Philip Leider, "Los Angeles and the Kienholz Affair," *New York Times*, April 3, 1966, 23.

31. Trimborn, "Background," I-3, 24.

32. Trimborn, "Hahn Will Try," 1, 3, 34.

33. Peter Bart, "Los Angeles Museum Defies Censorship by County Board," *New York Times*, March 25, 1966, 36.

34. Harry Trimborn, "Museum Threatened with Loss of Funds," *Los Angeles Times*, March 26, 1966, 2. Also, Trimborn, "Kienholz Exhibit Will Be Shown," 26.

35. Trimborn, "Kienholz Exhibit Will Be Shown," 1, 26.

36. Associated Press, "Crowds Wild at L.A. Show," *San Francisco Chronicle*, March 31, 1966, 43.

37. Harry Trimborn, "Art Show to Open with Heavy Guard," *Los Angeles Times*, March 30, 1966, 3, 31.

38. Harry Trimborn, "Dorn Warns of Arrest over Art Works' 4-Letter Words," *Los Angeles Times*, April 5, 1966, 3, 18. Also, Associated Press, "'Two Little Words' that Shake L.A.," *San Francisco Chronicle*, April 5, 1966, 6. The words are "fuck" and "shit" presented in a thinly disguised manner as lovers' initials carved into a rock or tree.

S.H.
+
I.T.

appears in this configuration; F.U.C.K., periods fading with each successive letter, is inscribed into an arrow-pierced heart. I want to thank Judy Hecker of the Whitney Museum for her help with this information.

39. "Latest Word on Wild L.A. Art Show," *San Francisco Chronicle*, April 6, 1966, 2. Also, Harry Trimborn, "Debs Claims Dorn 'Milks' Art Dispute," *Los Angeles Times*, April 6, 1966, 3.

40. Harry Trimborn, "No Giggles in the Gallery: Public Sees Art Exhibition; Consensus: Not Pornographic," *Los Angeles Times*, March 31, 1966, 35.

41. Lawrence Weschler, ed., *Edward Kienholz* (Los Angeles: University of California, Los Angeles Oral History Program, 1977), 257–58; quoted in Pincus, *On a Scale*, 43.

42. Trimborn, "No Giggles in the Gallery," 3, 35.

43. Trimborn, "Museum Threatened," 2.

44. Trimborn, "Hahn Will Try," 34.

45. In an article on obscenity and the law, highlighting the Ginzburg case, *Newsweek* wrote: "In an election year government lawyers expect a heavy new wave of prosecutions as this governor or that DA seizes on smut-hunting as a sure-fire issue." "Obscenity Test—A Legal Poster," *Newsweek*, April 4, 1966, 21.

46. Trimborn, "Dorn Warns of Arrest," 3, 18. In the *Los Angeles Times*, the articles on the Kienholz affair and on Supreme Court obscenity deliberations sometimes appear in the same issue and on the same page, even abutting one another.

47. John Steinbeck, *Cannery Row*, 2d ed. (New York: Viking Press, 1963), 60, first published in 1945.

48. *Back Seat Dodge '38* may look back to Salvador Dalí's *Rainy Taxi*, shown in 1938 (same year as the vintage of Kienholz's Dodge) at the International Surrealist Exhibition in Paris. Dalí's assemblage consists of an abandoned cab, adorned with all manner of vegetation and rigged to unleash downpours on its two manikined occupants, one a shark-headed chauffeur, the other a blond female passenger ensconced on a bed of lettuce and crawling with live Burgundy snails. At this same exhibition was the famous *Rue Surrealiste* made up of a row of altered manikins done by several different surrealist artists. For a discussion of the significance of this exhibition for environmental artists of the 1960s and how it might have been known, see Sarah Ann Clark-Langager, "Sculptural Tableaux of the Sixties: Edward Kienholz, Claes Oldenburg, and George Segal," Ph.D. dissertation (New York and Ann Arbor: City College of New York and University Microfilms, 1988), 61–84.

49. Weschler, ed., *Edward Kienholz*, 387–88; quoted in Pincus, *On a Scale*, 33.

50. *Newsweek*, 19.

51. David Leavitt argued this point in his essay "Fears that Haunt a Scrubbed America" (*New York Times*, August 19, 1990, C1 and C27), noting, for example, how often work by or about homosexuality is singled out for excoriation. A *New York Times* editorial over six decades earlier, entitled "The Censorship Mania," offered a related analysis of the rise in censorious legislation in New York State, pointing to the Anglo-Saxon "overwhelming desire to make everybody else exactly like yourself" (*New York Times*, January 28, 1927, 16). Justice William Brennan similarly described "an acute ethnocentric myopia that enables the Court to approve . . . censorship" (*Hazelwood School District v. Kuhlmeier*, 1988); quoted in Barbara Hoffman, "Editor's Statement: A Tribute to Justice Brennan," *Art Journal* ("Censorship I") 50 (Fall 1991): 8. Also, the "other" often refers to foreigners and thus the close link between obscenity laws and customs and importation regulations.

52. Mario Vargas Llosa. Quoted in Joseph Kosuth, "A Play: News from Kafka and a Quote," *Art Journal* 51 (Spring 1992): 10. See also notes 4 and 5.

53. Benjamin Jowett, trans., "Politica," in W. D. Ross, ed., *The Works of Aristotle* (Oxford: Clarendon Press, 1966), volume X, book VII: 1336.

54. See "R vs. Hicklin" (1968) LR QB 360 at 371; quoted in P. R. MacMillan, *Censorship and Public Morality* (Aldershot, England: Gower Publishing, 1983), 5–8.

55. This is not to say that the work of Rauschenberg or Segal is devoid of topicality. Rauschenberg's *Dante's Inferno* series and many works by Segal address contemporary political and social issues critically. On several occasions Segal's art has provoked major controversy and been censored. A discussion of social critiques in the work of Segal, as well as in that of Kienholz and Claes Oldenburg, can be found in Clark-Langager, "Sculptural Tableaux of the Sixties," esp. 374–414.

56. Pincus, *On a Scale*, 39.

57. Susan Sontag, "One Culture and the New Sensibility," in *Against Interpretation and Other Essays* (New York: Farrar, Straus and Giroux, 1966), 298–99.

58. For bibliographic sources on the connections between Kienholz and those outside the visual arts, see note 14. Kienholz's awareness of and possible affinity with Sahl are revealed in his 1960 assemblage entitled *The Mort Soul Searcher.*

59. Dickstein, *Gates of Eden*, 100, 126, 16.

60. Quoted in Douglas Davis, "Art: Horror Show," *Time*, August 7, 1971, 65.

61. Jürgen Hart in *Edward and Nancy Kienholz: 1980's*, exh. cat. (Düsseldorf: Städtische Kunsthalle Düsseldorf, 1989).

62. Weschler, *Edward Kienholz*, 490; quoted in Pincus, *On a Scale*, 82. As seen in *The Little Eagle Rock Incident* (1958) and in *It Takes Two to Integrate, Cha Cha Cha* (1961), Kienholz showed a strong interest in race relations. In the Ginzburg *Eros* case, one of the images singled out as obscene was a relatively tame and artfully composed series of nude photographs of a black man and a white woman. It has been suggested that the interracial sex implied in the photos was the real problem, since far more explicitly pornographic material than that published in *Eros* was available. Ginzburg may have also run into trouble because he marketed *Eros* as art, not pornography, and law enforcement officials were most likely disturbed because the magazine was not intended to be limited to X-rated stores but for wide and open distribution. This points up a paradox regarding art and pornography. On the one hand, problematic material, such as sexually provocative imagery, if presented as art implies that it possesses a value beyond prurience and might not be regarded as pornographic. That is, something that might be interpreted as obscene in a conventional context might not be judged as such in an "art" context. On the other hand, sexually provocative material is often tolerated precisely because it admits to being pornographic, which tends to circumscribe its distribution and audience. If it professes to be art, it may have a wider and different audience and may be held to higher standards of beauty, edification, or improvement; thus its provocation or explicitness becomes more of a menace.

63. The best source of information on *Still Live* is *Edward Kienholz: Still Live, Aktionen der Avantgarde, Projekt für ADA2*, exh. cat. (Berlin: Neuer Berliner Kunstverein, 1975). It includes Kienholz's statement about the work and reprints an important newspaper account, Roland Wiegenstein's "How the Allies Kept a 'Death-Machine' Alive," *Frankfurter Rundschau*, March 7, 1975, 56. A further excellent accounting of the events can be found in Nancy Reddin Kienholz's "Chronology" in *Kienholz, a*

Retrospective: Edward and Nancy Reddin Kienholz, exh. cat. (New York: Whitney Museum of American Art, 1996), 257–59.

64. The "art world" is a leitmotif that runs throughout Kienholz's work. In addition to a work such as *Walter Hopps Hopps Hopps*, Kienholz satirized art criticism in his scatological *The Critic* (1961), and "art collecting [as] a glorified autograph hobby" (his words, quoted in Grace Glueck, "Peepshows and Put-Ons," *New York Times*, April 6, 1969), in a series of watercolors sold for the amount painted on them. His most famous lampoon is *The Art Show*, conceived first as a concept tableau in 1963, that was brought to one stage of completion in 1977 when it was given a trial run at the Galerie Folker Skulima in Berlin and then installed at the Pompidou Center in Paris.

65. Quoted in *Edward Kienholz: Still Live*, 3.

66. Ibid.

67. Pincus, *On a Scale*, 12.

68. See Rosetta Brooks's entry in *Kienholz, a Retrospective* (p. 210), for a good analysis of this piece.

Art Censorship in Socialist China: A Do-It-Yourself System

JEROME SILBERGELD

IMPERIAL CHINESE GOVERNMENTS, despite a long history of censoring literature, seem never to have engaged significantly in censoring visual arts. The painted image was rarely considered equal to the written word, and it never seemed enough of a threat to quite merit censorship. There were, to be sure, isolated incidents of painters getting into trouble for works made at the royal court, but even these often seem to have been cases where particular works provided rivals with a pretext for carrying out personal vendettas rather than being the initial cause.[1] Politics might get an artist in trouble, but art alone rarely seemed to do so. None of those artists known to have painted anti-government subject matter, as in the early years of Mongol and Manchu rule, seem to have gotten into any trouble for doing so.[2]

It could be argued that the imperial court in its role as dominant patron of the arts and molder of the nation's aesthetics represented a form of economic censorship. But that misconstrues the true nature of censorship. Powerful patrons, in their selection process, certainly helped shape public taste, and artists often conformed to that taste in response, but that is not the same thing as imposing involuntary constraints. If a Chinese painter found the constraints at court distasteful, he was always free to leave, to parlay his reputation there into financial success elsewhere.[3]

The earliest major examples of government repression in the visual arts did not occur until modern times, beginning with warlord Sun Quanfang's attempt in 1926 to thwart the introduction of Western-style nude models and expanding into Chiang Kaishek's brutal suppression of socialist printmakers in the 1930s.[4] But such violence was crude and sporadic compared to the subtle and pervasive system of censorship devised by Chinese Communists. The

Communist system of censorship bears little relationship to the popular image of hard-fisted bureaucrats who know only politics and little of art, and who are readily identifiable by artists as outsiders and enemy intruders. In fact, art censorship as the suppression of completed works of art scarcely exists in socialist China. Rather, the entire system is conceived of as benign and couched in terms of education, helping artists to understand what is expected of them so they might avoid anything that could cause trouble. The goal is to create compliance and thereby to avoid forcible intervention.

In historical times, while most Chinese were denied anything much more than the smallest measure of individuality in their lives, Confucianism rationalized in theory and helped bring about in fact a considerably higher degree of individuality in the lives of the scholar class. "Neo-Confucian" philosophy, which arose in the ninth century, helped to trigger an aesthetic reorientation of Chinese painting from the eleventh century on that was profoundly individualistic, not simply in terms of subject matter and style but in painting practices and viewing habits as well.[5] Maoist aesthetic theory was based on a redefinition of that view, transforming art from a largely esoteric medium into a tool for mass reeducation. Mao Zedong paid special attention to identifying the proper audience: limited in the literati tradition to the artists' fellow intellectuals, the audience for art was now redefined as the masses. Above all, Mao left no doubt about the subservience of art to politics: "Revolutionary literature and art are part of the whole revolutionary cause, they are cogs and wheels in it."[6] Hungarian dissident poet Miklós Haraszti has described the mechanistic reduction of artistic independence with an irony that leaves no doubt of its utility to the one-party state: "But there is, in fact, only one taboo: the recognition of a *variety* of realities is forbidden, including any separate reality of one's own. . . . You do not need much theoretical training to realize that there can be no 'real' reality where there are many realities."[7] After 1949, the individuality and relativism of traditional painting stood in fundamental contradiction to this new order, a minor threat to the centralization of authority ("democratic centralism"). It managed to survive the massive political attacks leveled against it in the 1950s, 1960s, and 1970s only because it was the prime representative, after all, of cultural nationalism.

Socialists (and Western iconoclasts) say that in modern capitalist societies the value of art lies in its impracticality and inherent uselessness, in its surplus or luxury value. But in Mao's realm, its value derived from revolutionary necessity. From this necessity came a heightened esteem and concern for artists—esteem for those who could hew to the specifications prescribed for all art work, and a wary concern for all. A combination of mechanisms has been used to maximize artistic compliance with these specifications.

Between 1949 and the mid-1980s, all art sales were centralized under the control of the Bureau of Cultural Relics, an agent of the State Council. This bureau intentionally limited most sales to antiquities, destroying thereby the market for contemporary art, so that artists were "free" to work in the service of politics rather than "bound" by the pursuit of profit. Liberated from dependence on private patrons, artists became creatures of China's state-run institutions, teaching academically and in cultural halls, and painting as propaganda artists for China's thousands of industrial production units.[8]

Access to the higher echelons of the art world has typically been influenced by artists associations. These associations are, in effect, a network of art workers' unions, membership in which is all but necessary for those who aspire to show their works in public exhibitions, to participate in collective artistic activity, or to teach others. China's artists associations are theoretically "mass organizations," generated by the artists themselves, but in reality they are organized from the top down, under the supervision of Communist Party propaganda departments at the national, provincial, and local levels.[9] Acceptance into an artists association requires careful scrutiny not only of one's work but of political attitudes and lifestyle. Academic units, on the other hand, are organized by the Ministry of Culture, that is, by the government rather than the Party. Here, the Party intrudes laterally, both by requiring artists association membership as a condition of appointment and through the appointment to each unit of a Party secretary, or commissar, who sees that the Party's cultural directives are carried out. Artists association and art academy membership both come with continuing infusions of indoctrination in the latest changes in Party line, along with regular criticism and self-criticism sessions.

Through these mechanisms, immediate control over artistic production is delivered into the hands of the artists themselves. While basic policy comes from the Party, the artists collectively are their own policemen. The implementation of Party directives is theirs to carry out, transforming artists into agents of the state, collaborators in a union of do-it-yourself censors. In his dark-humored book *The Velvet Prison: Artists Under State Socialism*, Haraszti described the Eastern European socialist system in terms applicable to China:

> Socialism, contrary to all appearances, does not suppress artists' Nietzschean desires but satisfies them. . . .
>
> Today every artist is a minor politician of culture. . . . In our eyes the state represents not a monolithic body of rules but rather a live network of lobbies. We play with it, we know how to use it, and we have allies and enemies at the controls. Today "censorship" works through this calculating and accommodating spirit rather than through any sense of defenselessness. . . .
>
> The state need not enforce obedience when everyone has learned to police himself. . . .[10]

The central, and seemingly most ironic feature of this system is the phenomenon of regulatory agencies serving at the same time as both chief patron and as censor of the arts, functions normally thought of (in America at least) as diametrically opposed.[11] At the unit level, members play an active role in carrying out the careful screening and selection of new members and of helping to apply to the arts those views which are promulgated from above. In each unit, works are subjected to mandatory critical reviews by all members. Above each unit lies layer upon layer of other bureaucratic units which also carry out constant reviews of the art and artists. Each work of art accepted by the unit or approved by some higher unit for a broader public function (exhibition, publication, or study) is in some regards a group work—art by committee.

What the socialist aesthetic failed to proscribe by theory has often been suppressed in practice. Perhaps the strongest disincentive in practice to the development and expression of individual personality has been the simple lack of theoretical consistency—the constant change of the Party's ideological "lines," the endless alternate "tightening" and "loosening" the degree of political control. This inconsistency alone has caused most artists not to venture forth stylistically, never knowing whether today's acceptable art might become a basis for tomorrow's recriminations. Entrance into a government-established artists association is extremely competitive; but once achieved, the artist's tenure there is relatively secure. Tenure is threatened only by doing something out of the ordinary, something that will attract criticism, something individualistic; otherwise, one is threatened only by the sheer irrationality of external events.

A typical career pattern has been for an artist to venture forth just enough to establish a reputation and secure official patronage, but then to take no additional artistic risks, turn no artistic corners, go no farther for fear of going too far. At some later point, it is common to try to secure a lasting reputa-

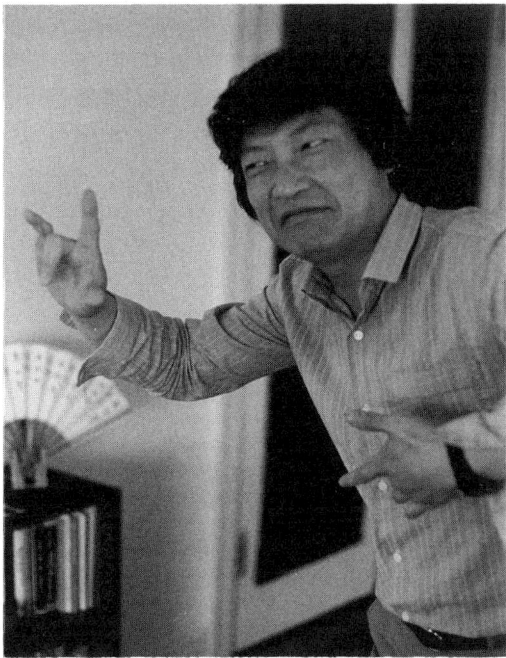

FIG. 1. Photograph of Li Huasheng pantomiming Sichuan-style opera.

tion by popularizing one's art—often by "sweetening" one's style in a way which is cloying to the educated taste. Artists who risk the security of their established reputation, who turn new corners in pursuit of some more progressive artistic accomplishment, who resist the sweetness of popular taste for the rugged self-expression or subtle understatement once found in traditional Chinese painting, or those who dare to explore a variety of media are rarely found in China today. In China, things are quite as Haraszti described sardonically in his comments on Communist Hungary:

> Artists are educated to be unable to create anything unpublishable. . . .
>
> Open resistance to the state is seen as professional cowardice. . . .
>
> Where the state is charitable, artists will try hard not to give offense. Generosity from on high will be matched by docility from below. . . .
>
> The figure of the independent artist is now to be found only in the waxworks museum, alongside that of the organized worker. Independent art is impossible because there is no independent audience. . . .

> The choice available to me is not between honest and lying art, not even between good and bad art, but between art and non-art. . . .
>
> If the expression of my artistic consciousness is made public, this will have happened only because I have employed a coauthor: the state. My audience knows that I am a permitted author with a permitted message.[12]

The Chinese network of censorship and the precise means by which it works can be well understood only in the context of individual application. Yet access to the documentation on socialist China's artistic regulation had been as tightly restricted as Chinese art itself. The detailed study of an individual painter's life became possible only during one brief period, in the late 1980s. And only an artist successful enough to penetrate the system yet nonconformist enough to violate the unspoken taboo against revealing its working details could provide a realistic depiction of the arts-management process. One such artist is the Sichuan painter Li Huasheng (b. 1944) (fig. 1). Through his career and that of his teacher, the late Chen Zizhuang (1913–76) (fig. 2), whose artistic careers stretch across the entire period of socialism in China, it is possible to observe in detail the administrative machinations of Maoist cultural politics in their native province of Sichuan and to chart the liberal transformation under Deng Xiaoping, since 1979, a process in which these two artists played a leading role. Both painters are traditional-style landscapists, more likely to be thought of as "reactionary" than as avant-garde radicals. But until the mid-1980s, theirs was the major threat to the Communist Party's official aesthetic socialist realism and revolutionary romanticism. With the liberal reforms of the 1980s, Chen Zizhuang emerged—posthumously—from three decades of official ostracism to become the figurehead of Sichuan's movement toward artistic moderation, while Li Huasheng rose almost overnight out of artistic obscurity to become the movement's foremost younger standard-bearer.

Chen Zizhuang would be an interesting character historically even if he had not so belatedly become a cultural symbol. He was born in 1913 in Sichuan. His father was a peasant, a painter, and a member of one of Sichuan's countless "secret societies"—in other words, a gangster and extortionist. Chen Zizhuang began his artistic career as a poor farm boy painting with mud when he could not afford pigments, but he still followed his father's ways. He became the head of a secret society and made his reputation as a martial arts expert by accidentally killing a leading opponent in public competition. This won him a job as chief bodyguard to Sichuan's warlord governor, Wang Zanxu, whom he also served as artistic consultant. When Chiang

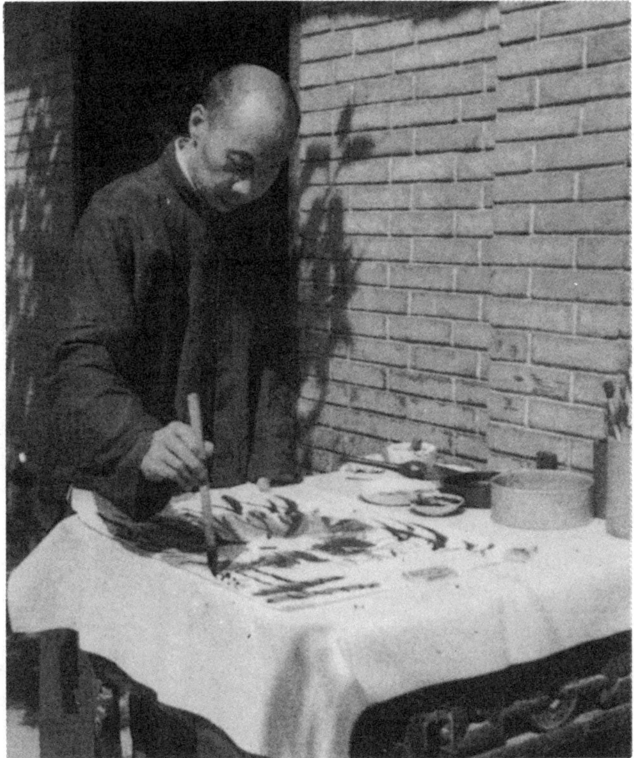

FIG. 2. Photograph of Chen Zizhuang at his small painting table. (After Wang Zhihai, *Shihu hua ji*, frontispiece.)

Kaishek fled the mainland in 1949, he flew to Taiwan from Chengdu, entrusting the final details of surrender to this governor; and reportedly it was Chen himself who delivered the Nationalists' surrender to the Communist troops. Needless to say, all this did not leave Chen much hope for a successful artistic career. The fact that he was an unsparing, sharp-tongued critic who alienated many of his fellow artists did not further his cause, and for decades after the Communist Revolution he maintained a fierce rivalry with the ideologically hard-line chief of Sichuan's artists association, Li Shaoyan.[13] Chen was forever barred by fellow artists from association membership and academic appointment. He was instead shepherded into an organization of which little is known in the West, the Hall of Culture and History (Wenshiguan), designed to assimilate the old literati—the deposed cultural elite, the "evil landlords" of Marxist rhetoric—into post-Revolutionary China and there to regulate their lives, to isolate them from the mainstream of Chinese society, and to maintain them in quiet submission to the new order. The Wenshiguan was a major element in the new government's seizing control of Chinese arts and culture.

Maintenance of the old literati, rather than crudely exterminating them, was part of the mission of socialist China's United Front, which publicly displayed the generosity of the state toward its vanquished foes while securing the appearance of a broad front of participation in China's socialist rebuilding. Membership in the Wenshiguan required acquiescence in ideological reeducation. On the other hand, it also permitted members to indulge in their old-fashioned activities of painting, calligraphy, music, and writing. Much of the writing was not spontaneous but was directed toward their production of historical memoirs. Thus the old gentry voluntarily disclosed the details of their political lives and provided basic data for the compilation of an official socialist history of the Nationalist period. Since most former enemies of the state were publicly branded and rejected by the mass of society, they were scarcely employable and membership in the Wenshiguan was actively sought after as a means of survival. Acceptance into the organization demanded their meeting particular standards and sometimes even required appropriate personal connections.[14] In 1955, at the age of forty-three, Chen Zizhuang was admitted into the Wenshiguan in Chengdu with the help of his powerful connections; as its youngest member, he was referred to as the Wenshiguan's "Young Pioneer."

The Wenshiguan provided a salary, cultural services, and an accepting community, along with the weekly study of Communist literature. For its deprived artists, it provided a room with painting tables and painting materials, and each year it purchased a large quantity of *xuan* painting-paper for their use (China's best, from Xuancheng in Anhui province). At the same time, it provided an opportunity to paint in the old-fashioned, no longer acceptable manner; yet most of these paintings would be buried away and only rarely, at best, be viewed by the public at large.[15] It was at an exhibition under Wenshiguan auspices, in 1962, that Li Huasheng first became aware of Chen's art.[16]

During the decade-long upheaval of the Cultural Revolution (1966–76), Maoist forces attempted to purge the Party and society of all remaining "feudalistic" vestiges, and anything "old" was forcibly rejected. The maintenance of the Wenshiguan withered, and its members suffered increasing hardship. Chen's home was broken into twice by Red Guards and ransacked during the early period of the Cultural Revolution, and his small but excellent collection of the painter's "four treasures" (antique paper, brushes, ink-sticks, and inkstones), which by then had lost all commercial value, was destroyed. Chen Zizhuang became so poor that he rarely attended the Wenshiguan, needing instead to stay home painting cheap fans and little bamboo hanging scrolls for a dollar each in order to support his family. In 1976, Chen died in extreme poverty and near-total isolation, one of many such victims in the arts. His painting table, the largest he could afford (fig. 2), was too small to permit the painting of anything much larger than an album leaf, typically a mere ten inches tall. The censorship of Chen's art in his lifetime achieved the desired results. His paintings, frequently modeled after individualistic masters of the "feudalistic" era like the seventeenth-century Bada Shanren, were permitted only because they never circulated publicly and because Chen himself was regarded as a "dead tiger," bad but no longer a threat to the socialist regime.

What were these paintings like, which the government preferred the general public not to see? As simple a painting as Chen's bamboo (fig. 3) might have seemed innocuous a few decades earlier, yet by 1963 it could only have been seen as a statement of political resistance to the imposition of a new culture based on peasant and working-class values. In traditional China, there was no subject with which aristocratic painters and writers were more directly identified than bamboo. They often, simply, referred to it as "this gentleman." Its flexible strength, its evergreen foliage, its hollow core and jointed segments, all represented in symbolic ways the scholarly virtues of China's social and political elite—China's scholars, poets, and painters. In painting bamboo, they subtly expressed themselves, vented their passing moods, and revealed their basic personalities, all for the benefit of a circumscribed audience of their peers. Once such traditional-style paintings had been branded as feudalistic, after 1949, then choosing to be a traditional painter was to risk being labeled a reactionary individualist.

Chen's paintings, however, were not fully typical even of the older values in art. Traditional Chinese bamboo paintings had been things of grace and elegance, symbolizing the literary elegance of the old scholar elite. But rather than displaying literary elegance and scholarly composure, or even the occasional hint of loneliness, Chen's bamboo reveals struggle, anger, and force. Shorn of its potential beauty, the bamboo stalk is squat and bent, its leaves seem to bristle with anger, reflecting Chen's degraded personal status and social alienation. Since the scholars' painting of bamboo came laden with well-established expectations, Chen could hardly have painted so homely a plant without anticipating the perceptions it would engender.

Only rarely did Chen paint anything overtly dissident in theme. Occa-

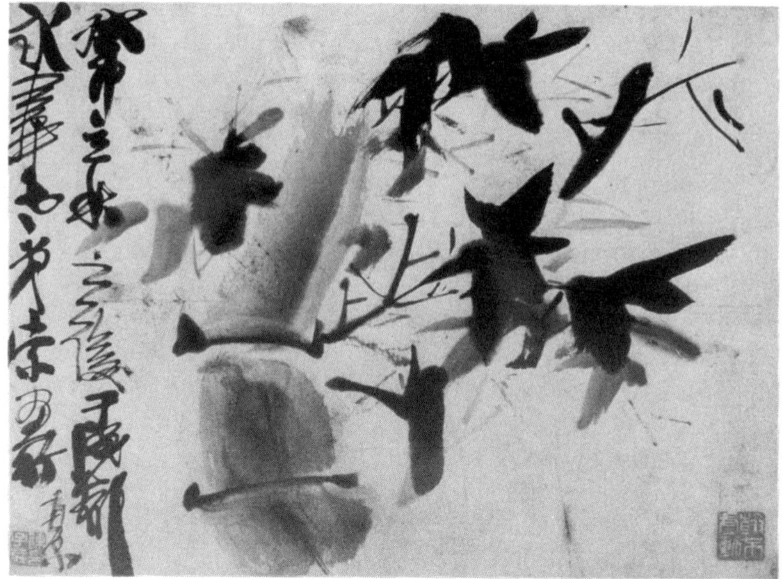

FIG. 3. Chen Zizhuang, *Bamboo*, 1963.
Ink and color on paper.
Collection of Li Huasheng, Chengdu.

sionally during the Cultural Revolution, he expressed his anti-government feelings by depicting Zhong Kui, the eighth-century spirit who helped chase devils from the royal palace (in other words, swept the political "bogeys" out of government), a risky topic that his ailing wife urged him not paint. On the other hand, many of Chen Zizhuang's delicately colored paintings—like a mountain hut from the mid-1960s (fig. 4) or his *Two Boats* (fig. 5)—are so pure and simple, so primitive and childlike, that they defy the miserable social circumstances under which they were produced. Such works created an alternate reality, a longed-for escape into rustic simplicity, something attainable in mind and in art, if not in the real world. From where did the calm simplicity of these paintings come, from what inner reserve of serenity? It can only be answered that such serenity is a mark of individuality, a statement of resistance, a refusal to be part of a society that demanded of its citizens participation in a collective orgy of political passion and class struggle. Chen Zizhuang once told a fellow artist, "The true painter must have the ability to rule the country, to kill the people and burn their houses." What he meant by this seemingly tasteless statement was simply this: to be a good art-

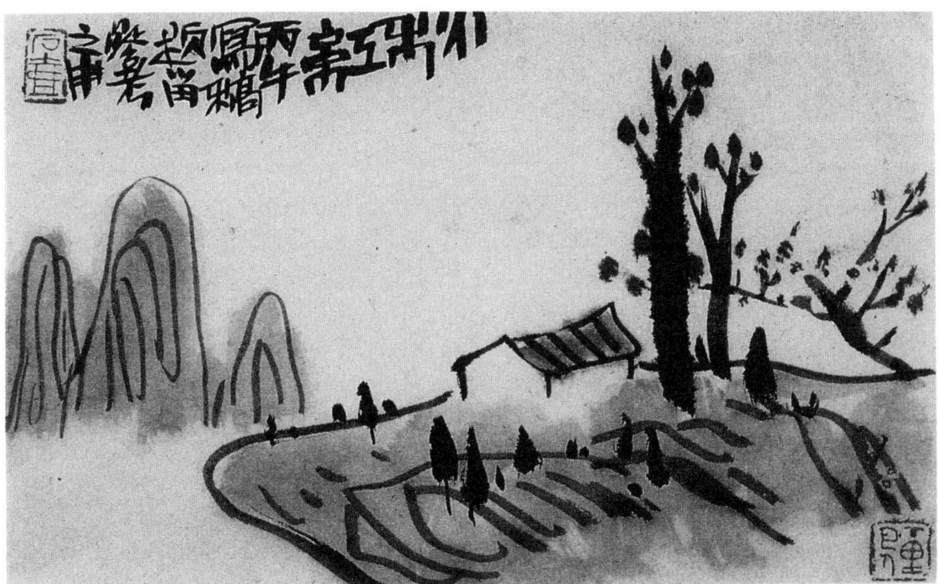

FIG. 4. Chen Zizhuang, *Autumn Red*, 1966.
Ink and color on paper. Unknown collection, China.
(After Wang Zhihai, *Shihu hua ji*, plate 35.)

ist in such times, one had to be steeled against all external pressures, to be a nonconformist totally at odds with society.

In March 1988, twelve years after his squalid death at the very end of the Cultural Revolution, in a China vastly changed by the leadership of Deng Xiaoping, an exhibition of Chen's work was held at the Chinese National Art Gallery in Beijing, the first posthumous solo exhibition ever held there. More than ten thousand visitors a day attended (setting a record at that time), not so much to see his artistry as to demonstrate political sympathy for this victim of cultural repression. Today, most of Sichuan's leading traditional painters have suddenly proclaimed themselves followers of Chen Zizhuang.

Chen Zizhuang's longtime follower, Li Huasheng (fig. 1), was born in February 1944, the son of a Yangzi River sailor. He began to paint at the age of five, in the final year of the Revolution. He received no formal training in the arts, only a technical training in the shipping school run by his father's company, for whom he later became a propaganda artist. From childhood on, Li Hua-

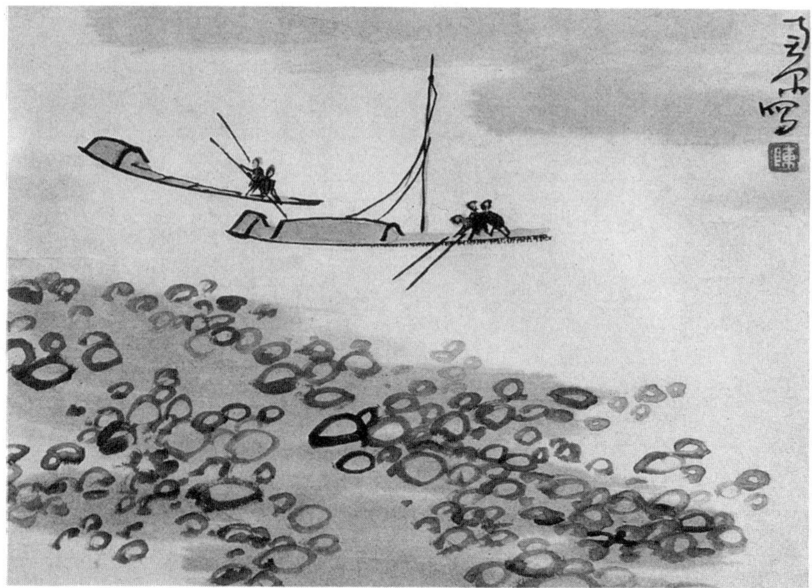

FIG. 5. Chen Zizhuang, *Two Boats*, undated.
Ink and color on paper. Unknown collection, China.
(After Zhang Zhengheng, *Chen Zizhuang hua ji*, p. 32.)

sheng was a rebellious personality whose first love was not art but theater; only his parents' refusal to let him sink so "low" led him into the study of painting as a substitute for a career in theater. (He has nevertheless publicly performed Chinese opera, and his third marriage was to a traditional Chinese opera performer and instructor.) By the time he was four or five, Li had organized the neighborhood children into a theatrical troupe, designed their stage, and painted their props and masks. By the age of fifteen, his paintings of theatrical personalities were exhibited in the halls of Chongqing's main theater. In a society that suppresses flamboyance and stresses conformity, the theater sanctions the expression of strong personality. Yet in daily life, one can get away with theatrical airs only by having the talent to back it up. Li is a strong personality who has always sought center stage. He has also carried his personal flamboyance into his art and artistic life; many of his landscape compositions, he claims, are transformed from stage actors in full costume, and his career has been laced with high drama.

Li's strong artistic impulses got him into serious political trouble three times, twice even before the advent of the Cultural Revolution. His first encounter with cultural repression came in 1963, when a group of young dissident intellectuals he joined for the sake of listening to Beethoven's music was broken up by police for indulging in a "capitalist life style." Li got off with merely being labeled a "problem individual," but others ultimately paid the price of labor camp imprisonment, in part because of a misunderstanding by the police. At the time of the arrest, the name of Beethoven (Bei Duofan) was mistaken for that of the nineteenth-century Hungarian poet Sándor Petöfi (Pei Duofei). Throughout the Marxist sphere after the Hungarian uprising of 1956, Petöfi had come to symbolize the counterrevolutionary spirit of the intellectual class. Li was fortunate that no attention was paid directly to his art, which at that time featured realistic oil paintings like one depicting Chongqing's waterfront looking as shabby as it really was, rather than the way the socialist realists wanted things to look (fig. 6). Works like this, done "on the dark side" in Maoist terminology, marked Li as a rebel and were never meant to be seen by others.

Li's second encounter with public censorship came in March 1966, during an intensification of the Socialist Education movement that ushered in the Cultural Revolution. At the time, everyone was obliged to engage in public debate and everybody's views were scrutinized for ideological flaws. Li was severely criticized for a traditional-style painting he had done on a dormitory wall, in which he had depicted a pair of rocks and a few bamboo plants. He was accused of representing weapons—sharpened spears and stones—which, it was claimed, he meant to be hurled against the Communist Party. There was also a landscape painting of campus scenery that he had done on paper, around which (for lack of affordable framing materials) he had painted a frame with brush and black ink; for that, he was accused of confining his socialist school in a "black, capitalist prison." The charges against Li may have been thin, to say the least, as charges at the time usually were. But as a political target, Li was well chosen. He was hardly a model of socialist enthusiasm, and he had scarcely any record of positive political behavior with which to defend himself. After being convinced it was better to confess his "crimes" than resist, he was labeled a "contradiction among the people" (ideologially criminal but correctable, and far better than being pronounced an "enemy of the people"). He was sentenced to reform at hard labor. Ironically, the initial upheaval of the Cultural Revolution, which threw nearly everything in China into reverse gear, led to his early release.

Despite his nonconformity, during the Cultural Revolution Li also produced many conformist works, socialist realist art like the jointly painted *Mao Zedong Inspects the Rivers of Sichuan* (fig. 7,) which appeared on the

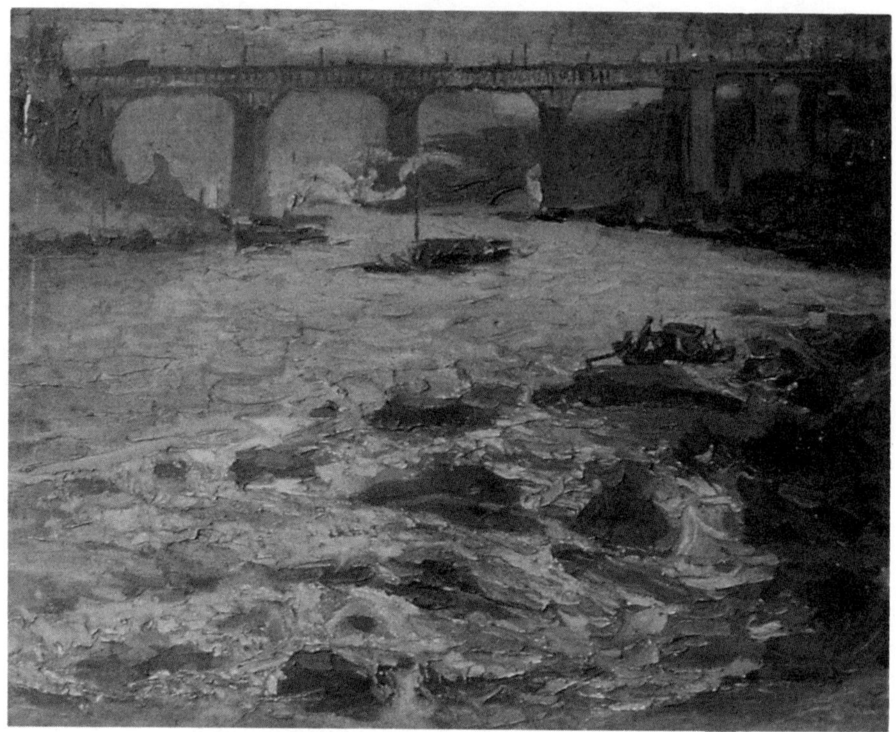

FIG. 6. Li Huasheng,
The Jialing River at Chongqing, ca. 1965.
Oil on canvas. Collection of the artist.

cover of *Sichuan Pictorial* in 1973), propaganda cartoons, sculpture, and prints. The model for one of his prints was Li's young first wife in their first year of marriage, and the resulting, somewhat romanticized work was criticized by his superiors—peasants, workers, and soldiers should be more robust, they told him. Subsequently, he conformed to this criticism in a sculptural rendition of the same figure. Some of this kind of work was forced on him violently in the late 1960s, literally, a "Do it, or we'll break your hands" threat by hard-line Red Guard factions, which led to an endless round of Mao Zedong portraits done to canonical standards; some of this work was expected of him professionally, later on, after he found employment as a propaganda artist for the Yangzi River Shipping Administration; and some of it he did of his own initiative toward the end of that era, once he realized the compromises needed to get ahead in the Sichuan art world.

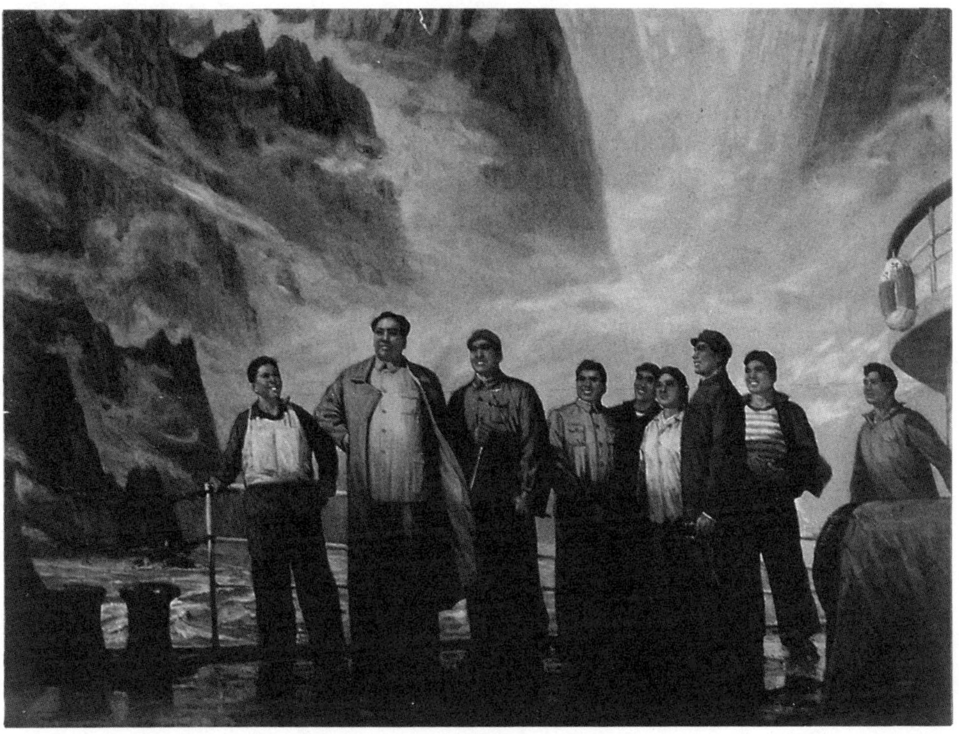

FIG. 7. Li Huasheng, Wu Youchang, and Lei Zuhua,
Mao Zedong Inspects the Rivers of Sichuan, 1972.
Oil on canvas. (After *Sichuan huabao*, January 1973, front cover.)

But Li also studied the nonconformist art of Chen Zizhuang, whom he met with the aid of the labor camp connection between a fellow member in the Beethoven fan club and an interned artist-friend of Chen's, a fallen leader of the Provincial Academy of Fine Arts. Li dared to befriend Chen when Chen and his art were politically least acceptable. Like Chen himself, he imbued his work with forbidden lessons learned from the great individualists of China's past, artists like Bada Shanren, Daoji, and Hongren. For the first six years of the Cultural Revolution, when the mere possession of traditional paintings, or even reproductions, could get one mercilessly beaten or sent off to a reform-through-labor camp, Li Huasheng spent every night locked secretly in a small room by friends, where he copied individualist artists of the seventeenth century from an old Japanese publication, *Shina nanga taisei*. Then for eleven more years, in new quarters provided after his marriage, Li worked at mastering the secrets of China's much-abused artistic tradition, often with his wife and child sleeping on half of his painting table while he worked on the other, with rats scurrying around the rafters overhead knocking dust onto his painting paper, and with a leaking roof and walls that brought an intrusion of poisonous insects and snakes and regularly forced them to abandon the building in the midst of heavy night rains. In one series of paintings, Li Huasheng gave both visual life and a thematic twist to Li Shangyin's famous ninth-century poem, *Night Rain in the Sichuan Mountains*, which he chose as a means to respond to the squalor of his life and to the hardships still being endured by so many millions of Chinese, some three decades after socialism had come on the scene with its promise of a brighter future (fig. 8). In these paintings, Li does not take to the stage or to combat but rather to flight from the system, proclaiming a desire to escape to the mountains, to live with the peasants, closer to nature and unpolluted by the grime and politics of urban life.

Another painting depicts the fabled scenery of Anhui's Yellow Mountains (*Mount Huang*, fig. 9). The poem overhead—this time his own—focuses on a narrow path, scarcely visible, that cuts a swath up the mountainside, and compares the tourists who enjoy such scenic paths with those peasant laborers whose blood and sweat produced them. It reads, in part:

Layers of trees: green, dark; mountain path: white.
Draped in clouds, dappled by fog, a dancing dragon-serpent.
Splitting the sky, these gathered stones, hewn by compass and square,
This carved cliff of inlaid steps, of carefully measured lines.
One thousand, ten thousand blows of hammer and chisel—so difficult each step;
One thousand steps, ten thousand steps, climbing toward Heaven's gate.
Tourists sit around, suffering from food too rich;
In the workers' mouths, just dry biscuit crumbs,
Their calloused hands painfully drawing water from the mountain stream,
Their dark sleeves sweat-drenched, by their own salt whitened. . . .

The real target here was not local tourists but the corruption of China's supposedly egalitarian system, seen by Li in 1980 as divided into rich Communist cadres and oppressed working people just as far apart as rich and poor had been in feudal times. This painting was in Li's first major exhibition, in Nanjing; but before the exhibition (extended, due to its initial success) traveled to the Chinese National Gallery in Beijing, he was obliged to pull it from the show and substitute a politically sanitized work. Li never knew: perhaps this was mandated not by some trouble-making antagonist but by a sympathetic bureaucrat, seeking to spare him more serious trouble in Beijing, China's trouble capital.

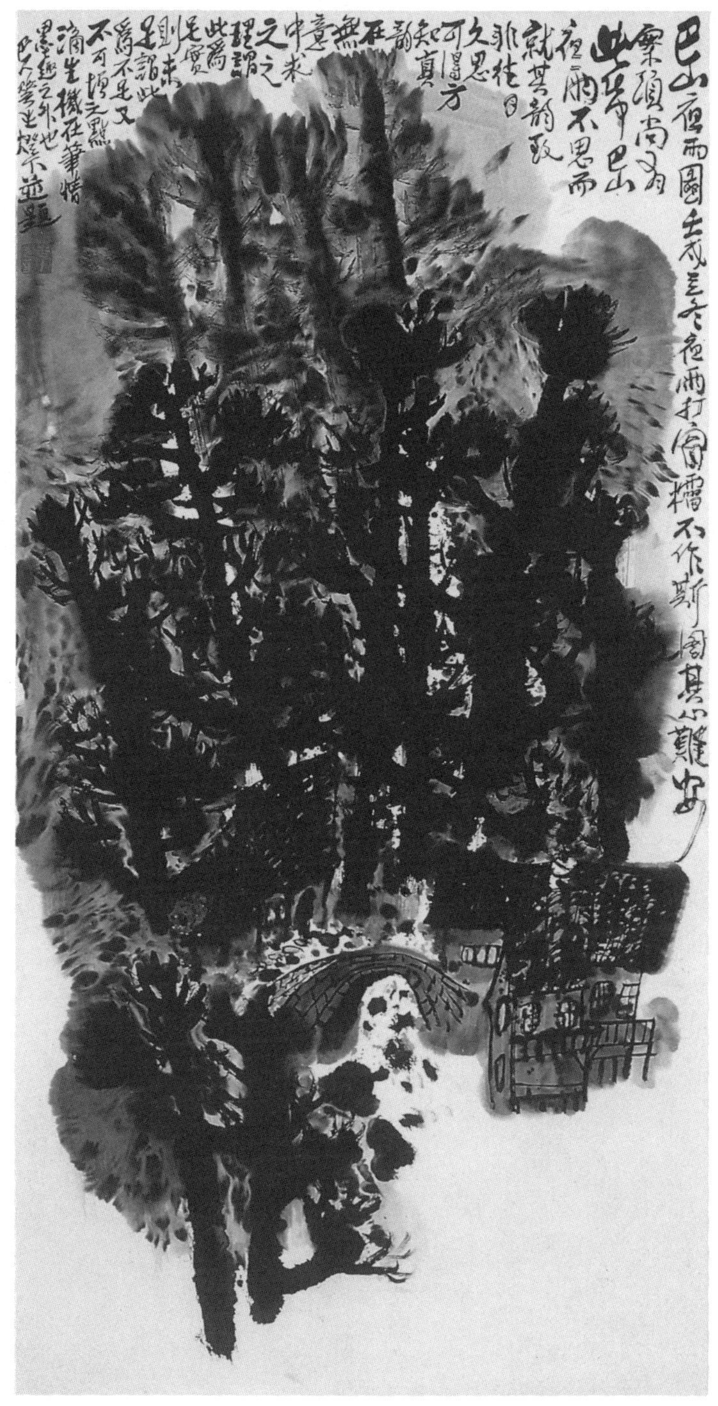

FIG. 8. Li Huasheng, *Night Rain in the Sichuan Mountains*, early winter 1982. Ink and color on paper, 99.7×67.3 cm (39¼×26½ in.). Private collection, United States.

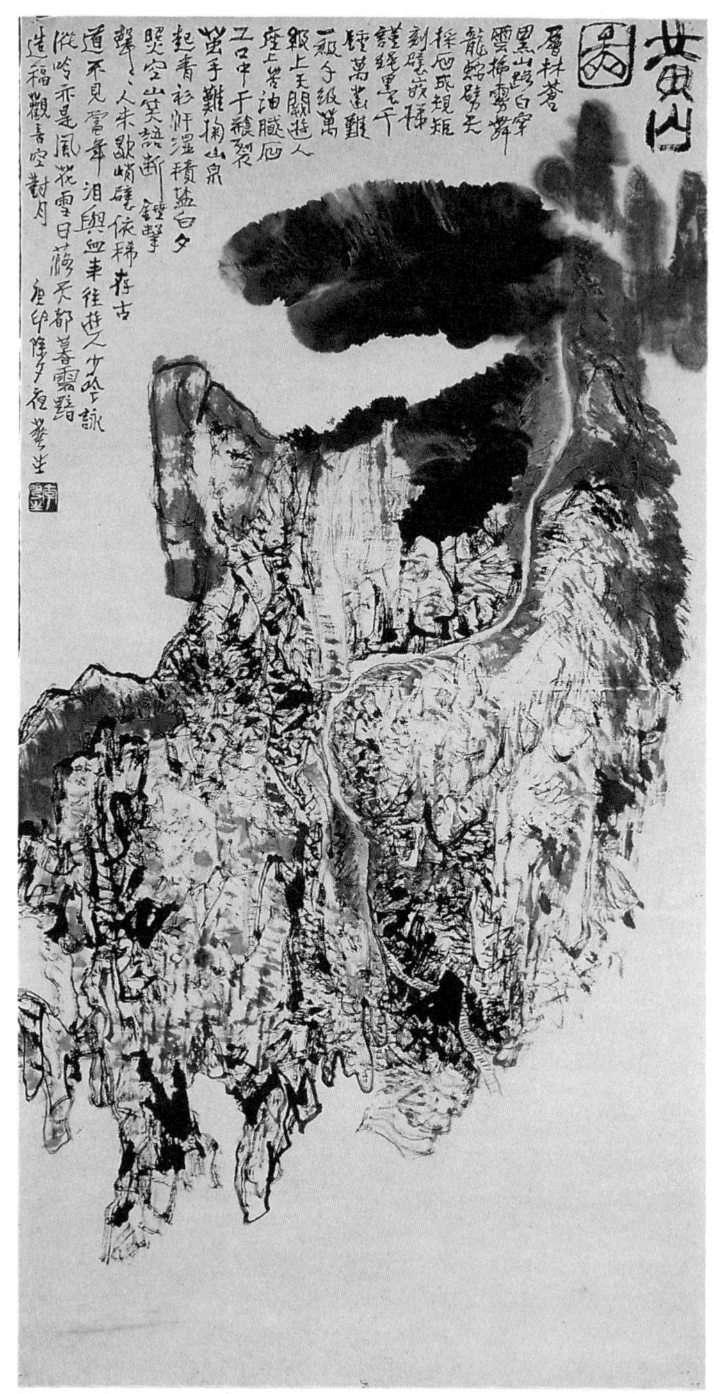

FIG. 9. Li Huasheng, *Mount Huang*, December 31, 1980.
Ink and color on paper, 139.4×66.7 cm (54⅞×26¼ in.). Private collection, United States.

On other occasions, Li or his friends knew enough to steer clear of such problems. For example, in 1979 he made a series of highly abstract works using thick ink mixed with glue and smeared on cardboard, which he called "picture-prints." It is easy enough to read these as landscapes, but in China in 1979 they could only be read as abstractions, as art for art's sake, solipsism, and nothing the masses could understand—thus, culturally intolerable. In his first emergence from obscurity, invited in that year to participate in a Chinese Painting Creativity Group in Beijing, Li carried these "picture-prints" with him. But in the end, he didn't dare show them to anyone. At about the same time, he made a painting of a pine tree, a common enough theme but displayed so close up that one could see only the bark of the tree. For Li, the aged skin represented the tree as a whole, which had stood through the years in silent witness to the political suffering of the Chinese people. But even his closest friends thought the work dangerously "formalistic," again meaning "art for art's sake," and they persuaded him to add a series of branches and needles. Once he had done this, Li felt the painting was spoiled, and he destroyed it.

Many of Li's critics were too obtuse to recognize such references, and indeed his work is usually less explicit. The majority of his paintings (like fig. 10) are simple evocations of Sichuan's timeless landscape, unchanged by the politics of socialism; but these works are still subject, thereby, to criticism as counterrevolutionary. In 1984, claims were made against Li that the houses in his paintings leaned this way and that rather than standing upright, like good socialist houses in a good, upright society. We may laugh, but Li's critics were actually right. Good Communists *don't* paint this way. Li didn't intend anything specific by this. But it was easy enough to see that he had a bad attitude.

In rapidly changing times, throughout the 1980s, China was uncertain about what was bad and what was good. In 1980, on Deng Xiaoping's first return to his native province after his rise to power, he approved a nonteaching art academy for Sichuan's finest, most innovative younger artists, designed to offset the hard-line Maoist arts administrators still in power there. Li Huasheng, just three weeks after his initiation into the artists association, was one who proposed the creation of this academy to Deng (fig. 11). Then, in 1982, in response to Deng's call for modernization, the chairman of the local artists association, Niu Wen, promoted Li Huasheng—thirty-eight years old, with no formal education in the arts—to the position of vice-chairman of the Chongqing association, propelling him ahead of all of Chongqing's other artists, many of them three to four decades his senior. This was unprec-

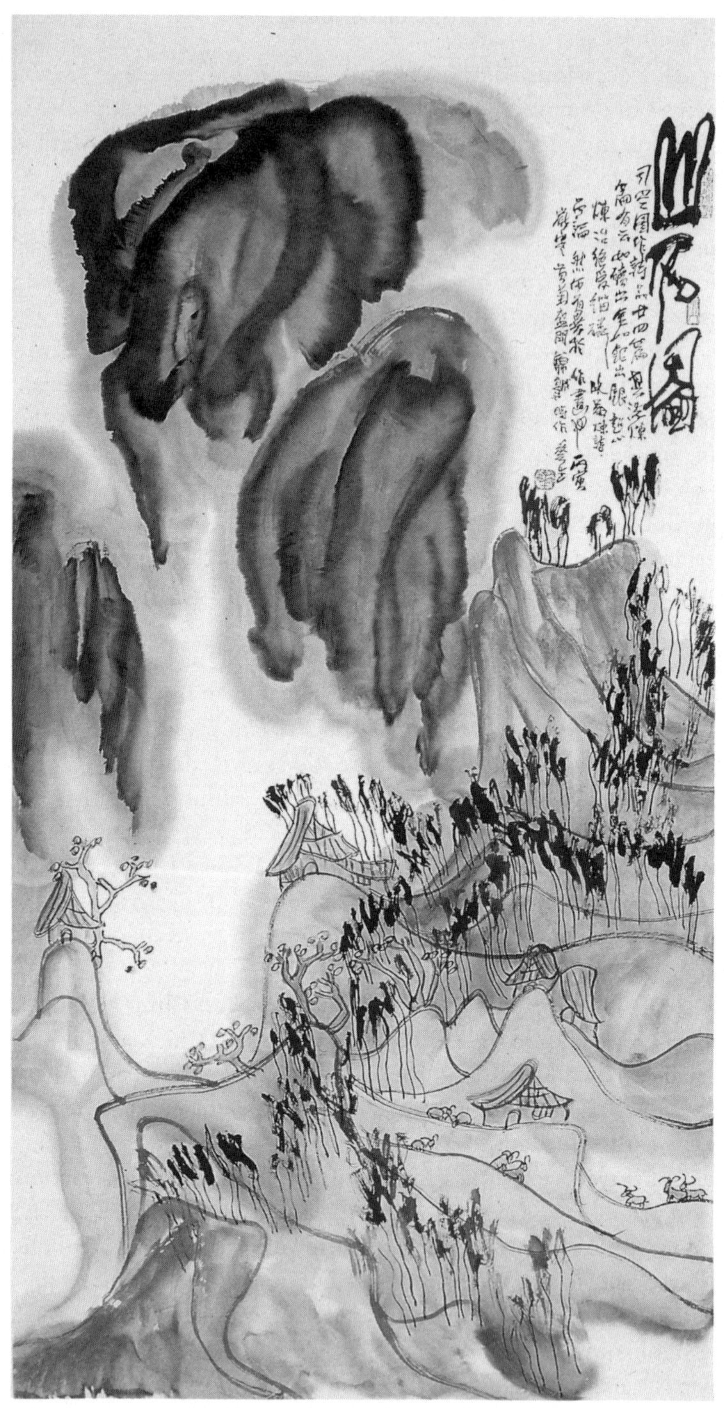

FIG. 10. Li Huasheng, *Mountain Dwelling*, winter 1986.
Ink and color on paper, 138.7×69.2 cm ($54\frac{5}{8}\times27\frac{1}{4}$ in.). Private collection, United States.

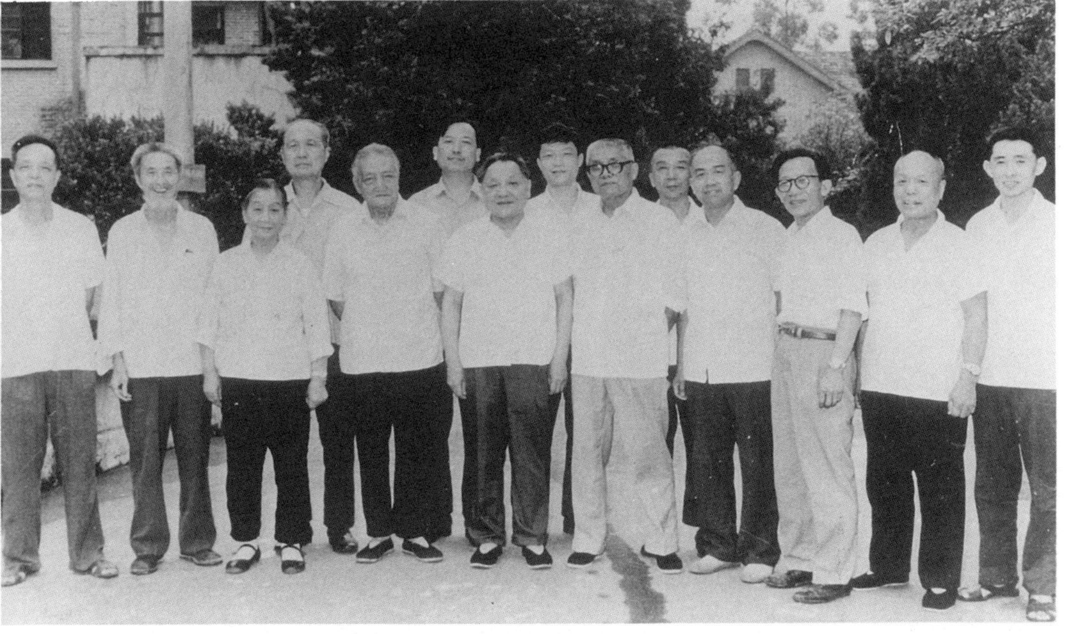

FIG. 11. Vice-premier Deng Xiaoping (seventh figure from left), Li Huasheng (eighth from left), and members of the Academic Research Group at the Golden Ox Hotel, Chengdu, July 1980.

edented. In the next year, working within the system rather than against it, LiHuasheng attempted to rejuvenate traditional painting by transferring support from the older, more conservative artists to the younger generation.

But given the inconstancy of Deng Xiaoping's policies, the outcome of this experiment was perhaps inevitable. By the end of Li's first year in office, in 1983, the Campaign Against Spiritual Pollution was launched in China, and the older artists—socialist realists and retrograde traditionalists alike—mounted a joint counteroffensive that charged him with propagating antisocialist art ("leaning houses" and so forth, although they failed to understand the more substantial dissidence of paintings like *Mount Huang*, fig. 9) and with other forms of counterrevolutionary behavior. They took advantage of an illicit love affair Li was engaged in to fabricate multiple charges of seduction and rape, capital offenses in China. Li was paraded before the local and national media as an example of bourgeois corruption in the arts. He was driven from office and soon fled Chongqing for his personal safety, to the hills west of Chengdu. By the time Sichuan's prestigious new art academy finally opened in 1984—the Sichuan Academy of Poetry, Calligraphy, and Painting,[17] in Chengdu—with Deng Xiaoping's calligraphy displayed on the outer gates, Li was in political disgrace and barred from membership. But ever flamboyant and bold, Li seized the occasion of the painting academy's opening exhibition to launch a solo exhibition of his own, an unprecedented individual exhibitor challenging an all-star show put on by the arts establishment.

Li's exhibition was held in Chengdu's vaunted Du Fu Thatched Hall, whose gallery was managed by a friend. Li's sales set a gallery record, and he was obliged to close the exhibition early for lack of remaining paintings to show. Among the works exhibited were scenes of the region Li had fled to several months earlier to avoid arrest, as well as a number of landcapes with the traditional theme of a rustic hermitage providing solace from politics. In these works, he joined spirits with the peasants, he fished with the fishermen. Though more escapist than Maoist (and therefore "solipsistic," "bourgeois"), Li's works nonetheless won great success in the mid-1980s, and with this success Li showed himself to be an individual force not easily dismissed. Even as reversal followed reversal in China's public policy throughout the 1980s, Li ably finessed the system, and with the aid of powerful political patrons, he finally joined the painting academy in 1985 and eventually, in 1989, became its first-ranked member.

His own artistic skill and personal flamboyance were not sufficient, of themselves, to ensure Li's survival and his successful return to artistic prominence. In this contentious and highly personalized environment, nothing could have been accomplished without adequate patronage. The art world of Li Huasheng has been one of uncertainty and massive contradictions, with great changes taking place since 1979. In the 1980s, as in pre-Revolutionary times, paintings and artistic fellowship were once again commonly exchanged for a variety of goods and services that money could not buy, ranging from extra coal for the kitchen stove to political protection. By the mid-1980s, a commercial market for contemporary painting was permitted to develop and a variety of new mechanisms for sales and exhibition were created, primarily directed toward foreign investors with the intent of building capital reserves.[18]

The introduction of market economics established a historical watershed and loosened the monopolistic grip of state control. Moreover, foreign patrons (especially Japanese and American) have brought not only money and prestige but also outside scrutiny, which given the government's new-found sensitivity to international opinion can be most valuable to artists threatened by internal sanctions. When Li Huasheng was in trouble in 1984, Japanese patrons bought up his works at the Du Fu Thatched Hall in record time, and the fact that two of his paintings were then touring to enthusiastic reviews in America's first major exhibition of traditional Chinese painting since 1949 (fig. 12) must have helped his defenders enormously.[19] Painters like Li have also reestablished traditional patronage bases in China's Buddhist and Daoist temples, those ancient centers of artistic interchange which have often shared a bond with artists of suffering under the socialist regime. Over the years, Li has been friendly with and patronized by the abbot of the famed Shangqing Daoist Temple on Mount Qingcheng near Chengdu, Fu Zhitian, vice-president of the Chinese Daoist association. While in hiding from Chongqing authorities in 1984, Li spent much of his time at Mount Qingcheng.

An artist needs promotion, but the more important he becomes, the greater his need for protection in a hostile environment where there is never enough protection to ensure anyone's political well-being. In this realm of institutionalized confrontation, with its absence of institutionalized protection, personal jealousy (which the Chinese call "red-eye disease") is rife. "Jealousy and blame," says Li, "are a disease that infects China. In China, if you criticize someone or say he could do better, he will store it away in his mind until he gets his revenge." Like the isolated boat in one of his paintings of Sichuan's Yangzi River gorges (fig. 13), the individualist Li Huasheng has had to steer a rugged course and weather many a storm. Ironically, since Mao Zedong's demise, the rulers of Marxist China have found that just as in ancient times, the aura of political legitimacy requires the trappings of high culture. Cadres throughout the country have gone scurrying to cultivate artistic relations with China's traditional painters, offering in return both positive support and protection from less sympathetic cadres.

The man most responsible for saving Li's career in 1984, and perhaps his life, is Ai Weiren, then the deputy political commissar for the 13th Army and later vice-commissar for Party affairs in Sichuan, Yunnan, Guizhou, and Tibet. With the arts administration taking its cues from politicians, a few appropriate words by such a man can outweigh the accumulated force of many jealous artistic rivals. At the height of Li's troubles, Ai merely told the head of the Chongqing Party's Propaganda Department, "Although you have said there are problems with Li Huasheng's painting, I cannot see where there is any problem," and the struggle against Li had to be wound down. More recently, asked why he appreciates a "rebellious" artist like Li Huasheng, Ai asserted that "actually, there is no contradiction between Li and myself, be-

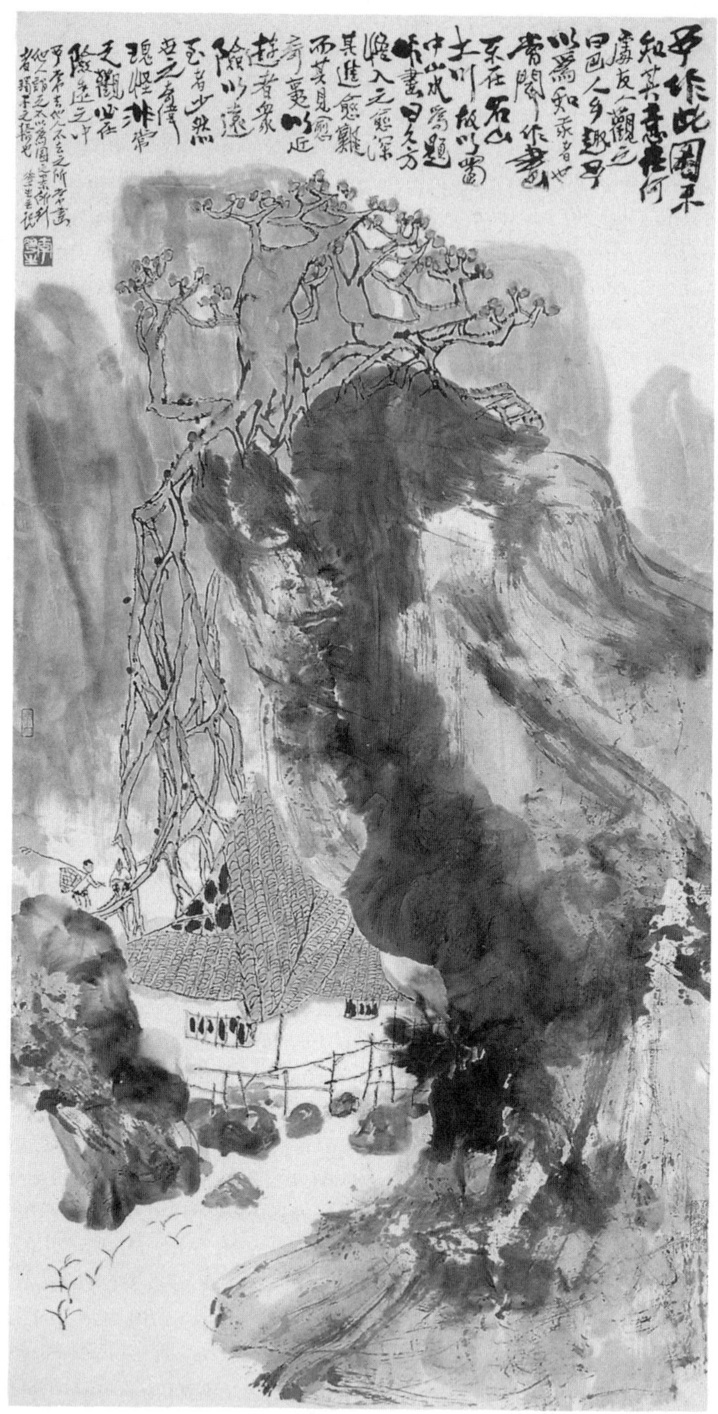

FIG. 12. Li Huasheng, *Rustic Scene*, summer 1982.
Ink and color on paper, 136×68 cm (53½×26¾ in.). Private collection, United States.

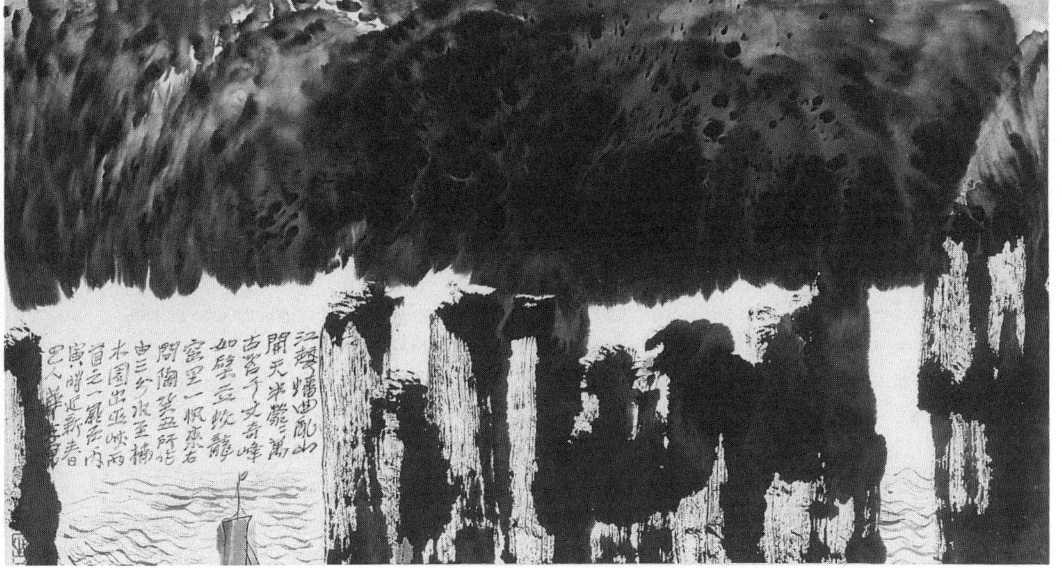

FIG. 13. Li Huasheng, *Traveling Through the Gorges*, late winter, 1986. Ink on paper, 54.3×98.7 cm (21⅓×38⅞ in.). Private collection, United States.

cause in military strategy you must be able to come up very quickly with new creative solutions. As Li is so good at doing this in art, I can learn from him."

Since the late 1970s, the reemergence of traditional modes of patronage, like the survival of traditional painting itself, has made evident the failure of Marxist policies to eradicate many of the patterns deeply etched in Chinese social history. Deng Xiaoping's new economics has allowed artists to sell their works commercially, generating a contemporary art market for the first time in half a century. A revival of traditional sources of private patronage combined with the development of new foreign markets to dilute, perhaps predictably, the dominant role of Party-engineered artists associations and state-managed art academies as exclusive sponsors of the arts; and this in turn has significantly eroded the censorial powers of Party and state.

By the mid-1980s, traditional Chinese painting—that persistent and unresolved contradiction to Maoist aesthetics—had clearly survived three decades of periodic attempts to eradicate it. As rapidly changing economic and social policy unleashed new artistic forces, among the factors helping finally to ensure traditional Chinese painting's survival was, ironically, the passing of dynamic oppositional leadership to newly emergent painting movements and to more progressive media. A realistic strain of art critical of both socialist "realism" and the excesses of the Cultural Revolution began to appear as early as 1977 and developed throughout the next several years. Oil painting was the favored medium of these artists, whose work paralleled and drew inspiration from a phenomenon in literature known as "Scar Literature." Still more iconoclastic, avant-garde painting, in league with installation and performance arts, began to emerge as a major force in the arts in the mid-to-late 1980s, experimenting with abstraction, mixed media, artistic nudity, and virtually all the latest "isms" of Western art.

Several of these elements first surfaced in 1979. The government was reluctant to tolerate this art but naive, perhaps, about the ease with which it could be suppressed: in 1980, Minister of Culture Jiang Feng briefly provided a niche in Beijing's National Gallery for an avant-garde group of artists called "The Stars," and he proclaimed to those who questioned this, "When these people realise that the mass of the people don't understand their work, they will learn, and change their ways."[20] But, to the contrary, by the mid-1980s, avant-garde styles began to emerge directly from several of the leading fine arts academies (public institutions, all), and from there China's diffusely scattered experimental artists linked forces nationally in what came to be known as the " '85 Movement." At first optimistic about the ability of culture to liberalize society, avant-garde enthusiasm soon began to decline as a result of China's gradual political retrenchment in the later 1980s. And in February 1989, this heretical movement finally overreached the government's own vaguely defined limits with the ill-fated "China/Avant-garde" exhibition at the National Gallery.[21] The Ministry of Culture intervened not once but twice to close down the "China/Avant-garde" exhibition, a visible sign (in retrospect) of the government's increasing readiness to react to unwanted cultural change.

Just a few months later, after the startling suppression of massive student demonstrations in Beijing, Chengdu, Xi'an, and elsewhere throughout the country, the ministry tightened its control over all public exhibitions, while the Bureau of Publications discontinued dozens of cultural journals. The censorship was demanded centrally but still mostly administered in the usual, decentralized fashion. Simultaneously, artists were called back to ideological study and self-criticism sessions in order to reengage the structures of self-censorship at all levels. China's self-censoring structures remained intact; but reportedly, compliance was at an all-time low, administrators and artists mostly going through the motions and more ready than in past times to reveal their hesitation.

The passage of time, up to the present day, has shown the Party and state increasingly hard-pressed to elicit support for their cultural mandates from China's do-it-yourself censors. A typical result has been that nonconformist works which could not even have been exhibited institutionally before the late 1980s are now able to win awards in national juried exhibitions. And while avant-garde ("New Wave") artists are still often denied the opportunity for major public exhibition, for them to succeed they no longer need to work in the official system at all, now that the government has permitted a popular market for their art. Many of these artists regularly exhibit their work at large gatherings in artists' apartments and studios, and the most successful of these export their work to waiting collectors in Hong Kong, Taiwan, Australia, Japan, Western Europe, and the United States. Being "banned" at home just drives up prices. Foreign customers now vastly outstrip the domestic market and provide safe passage abroad for works still taboo for domestic purchase in China. Expressions of subjectivity and ambiguity, irony and what has been called "rogue cynicism" now reign, mirroring a society once energized by Maoist certitudes but now shorn of common purpose (fig. 14).[22]

Looming even larger than the studio arts as a concern of central authorities by the mid-1980s was the film industry, awash in a liberalizing tide that flowed alike from senior directors working in older styles[23] and from the Beijing Film Academy's newly graduated class of 1982, the so-called Fifth Generation of art-filmmakers. Much of what Fifth Generation filmmakers like Chen Kaige, Zhang Yimou, Huang Jianxin, Tian Zhuangzhuang and Hu Mei brought to the cinema by the mid-1980s had already appeared in literature and painting of the previous few years, arts which replaced socialist "realism" by something profoundly real and engaged viewers in social criticism, satire, ambiguity, and subjective interpretation. But films like *Yellow Earth* (Chen Kaige and Zhang Yimou, 1984), *Black Canon Incident* (Huang Jianxin, 1985), *Horse Thief* (Tian Zhuangzhuang, 1985), *Girl from Hunan* (Xie Fei and Ulan, 1985), *Army Nurse* (Hu Mei and Li Xiaoqun, 1985), and *Sacrificed Youth* (Zhang Nuanxin, 1985) did this so well that their works produced a cultural shock. The audience for these films was relatively small, but that doesn't measure their impact among the intellectuals. And in 1988, Zhang Yimou's sexually rebellious *Red Sorghum* topped the national popularity chart (fig. 15).

Because of its huge viewing audience, its considerable expense, and its limited and controllable output, the state has always managed and controlled the Chinese film industry more closely than other cultural media.

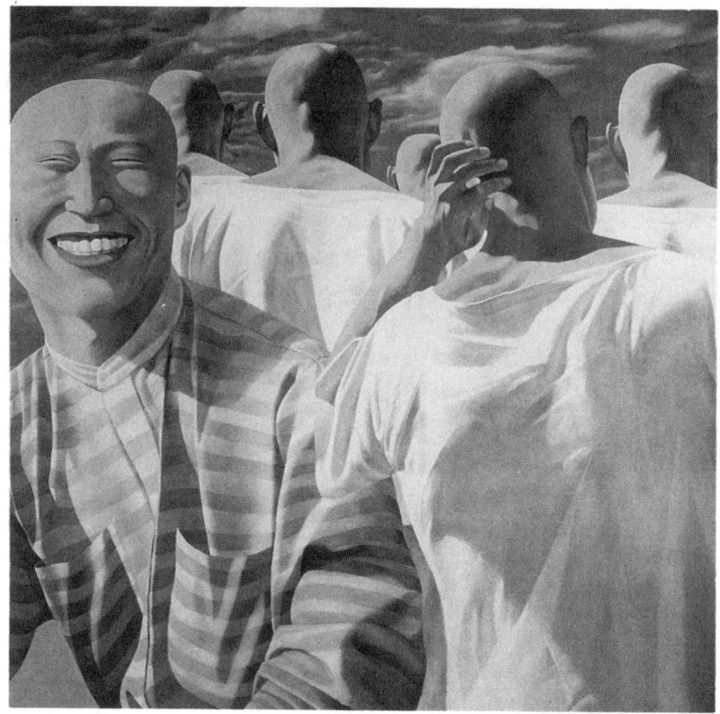

FIG. 14. Fang Lijun, *Group Two No. 3*, 1992.
Oil on canvas, 200×200 cm (78¾×78¾ in.). Private collection.
(After Haus der Kulturen der Welt, Berlin,
China Avant-garde: Counter-Currents in Art and Culture, p. 115.)

But as in all cultural media, change in the film industry flowed inexorably from Deng Xiaoping's economic reforms despite all efforts to control and limit cultural liberalization. After Mao's death, according to Paul Clark,

> What changed least was the formal structure of censorship and control, despite a lot of talk about the desirability of improvement: the film industry remained a centralized structure under Party control exercised through the Ministry of Culture at the top, local cultural offices in Shanghai, Changchun and elsewhere, down to studio-level Party committees. The attitudes, however, of those in control of this structure seemed different by the 1980s.[24]

That is to say, while the structures themselves changed little, the nature of these structures allowed for enormous changes in implementation. Increas-

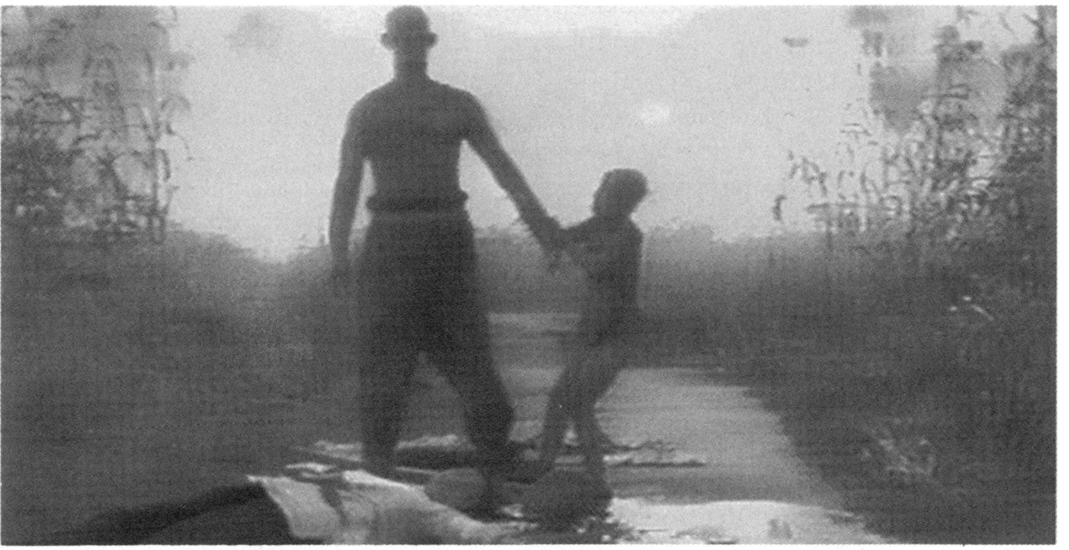

FIG. 15. *Red Sorghum*, Xi'an Film Studio, 1988, directed by Zhang Yimou, with Jiang Wen and Gong Li.

ingly, some Chinese films are internationally financed and produced so they can be shown in China as "imports." Even so, after 1989, Zhang Yimou has had four films banned from internal distribution (two were later released); Chen Kaige has had four films banned. The latest series of films banned, six in April–May 1996, offended primarily not through politics but through their treatment of sexual activity and drug addiction.[25]

So the government remains engaged in trying to set limits, while elements within the film industry remain engaged in trying to push these limits back, occasionally overstepping the government's willingness to engage in give and take. Usually, though not always, some accommodation is worked out through "voluntary" cuts made by the filmmakers, allowing for eventual public release of their work. On balance, censorship has effectively blunted the impact of art films on the Chinese audience and shifted the market for these films overseas.

With dramatic trends like these to set a pace in the 1980s and 1990s, traditional-style painting no longer seemed to the central authorities like the same old enemy it used to be. Once imagined as the fearsome agent of counterrevolution, traditional painting began instead to seem like a rather moderate and safe alternative to greater challenges emerging in the arts. In the 1980s, domestic enmity was no longer sought among the remnants of China's semifeudal past but instead within the corruption of Westernized culture, oozing through China's defensive walls—the spiritually polluted by-product of government-sponsored modernization. Hard-line Communist ideologues, once the loud trumpets of change in China, found themselves transformed into cultural conservatives trying to stem the tide of foreign values by appealing patriotically to traditional cultural identities. To them, traditional Chinese painting now seemed better to be wooed than scorned.

If the Chinese artists associations and art academies are increasingly obliged to compete with an independent art market for artists' support and affiliation, China's do-it-yourself system of censorship may eventually be done for. Before the early 1980s, there were only government-run, institutional channels to disseminate artistic work, but once a commercial market was called into being, everything was bound to change. Formerly all spokesmen for the government and as rigorously screened for thought as for talent, artists could now become entrepreneurs, self-employed, with no one to scrutinize their politics or social background. In 1993, one of many such artists leaving the old battleground behind, Li Huasheng resigned from the Sichuan Painting Academy he had fought so hard to enter and took to the open market.

Today, the Chinese government seems to be exploring a policy unthinkable to centuries of Confucianists and Maoists alike: unhooking culture from political ideology. Deng Xiaoping has already done this for economics, so that China remains politically Maoist but has economically embraced the policies of Milton Friedman. If cultural liberation gradually follows in the wake of economic liberalization, this would confine the Party's interest to policing the public order and perpetuating its own political survival. It would reduce the artists' former life-and-death struggle to mere artistic bickering, like that which prevails throughout the Western world. It would leave artists free to do and say most anything, as long as they keep it nonpolitical—a stunning contradiction of Mao's absolute emphasis on class-based politics as the superstructure of all cultural behavior. One can imagine a peculiarly un-Marxian resolution of contradictions here: not a Hegelian conquest but a pragmatic accommodation, with the people freed by the Party to get rich and enjoy a blossoming of cultural diversity, and the Party assured of a mandate to uphold public "safety" and the integrity of China's extensive borders. Even such an unorthodox compact as this might require new forms of censorship, but nothing so insinuating and pervasive as the do-it-yourself system of previous decades.

NOTES

This article is an outgrowth of my book *Contradictions: Artistic Life, the Socialist State, and the Chinese Painter Li Huasheng* (Seattle: University of Washington Press, 1993), produced with Gong Jisui. When research was begun in 1987, China had become the most liberal of Communist nations; by the time of its completion, China stood almost alone as a major Communist nation, its apparatus for artistic control challenged and no longer all-powerful but nonetheless intact and still formidable. For a parallel study which focuses on the major institutions, artists, and movements of the Maoist era, see Julia F. Andrews, *Painters and Politics in the People's Republic of China, 1949–1979* (Berkeley: University of California Press, 1994).

1. For example, the early Ming artist Dai Jin was denounced by artistic rivals at court for works purported to insult the emperor; see James Cahill, *Parting at the Shore: Chinese Painting of the Early and Middle Ming Dynasty, 1368–1580* (New York: Weatherhill, 1978), 45–47.

2. Politics spelled trouble for an entire generation of early Ming artists from Suzhou, including Wang Meng, Zhao Yuan, Xu Ben, Chen Ruyan, Zhang Yu, Zhou Wei, and Sheng Zhu. Though innocent in their art, they fell victim to imperial jealousy based on interregional rivalries. See James Cahill, *Hills Beyond a River: Chinese Painting of the Yüan Dynasty, 1279–1368* (New York: Weatherhill, 1968), 128–31; and Harrie Vanderstappen, "Painters at the Early Ming Court (1368–1435) and the Problem of a Ming Academy," *Monumenta Serica* 15 (1956): 283–302. On the other hand, the painting and poetry of Yuan artists like Zheng Sixiao, and early Qing artists like Bada Shanren and Gong Xian, reveal political dissent of the sort that failed to arouse the court's interest. Such artists typically chose to communicate personal grievances in a recondite fashion to a limited audience of intimate acquaintances, representing dissent rather than sedition. See Frederick Mote, "Confucian Eremitism in the Yüan Period," in Arthur Wright, ed., *The Confucian Persuasion* (Stanford: Stanford University Press, 1960), 209–12, 232–36; Jerome Silbergeld, "Kung Hsien's Self-Portrait in Willows, with Notes on the Willow in Chinese Painting and Literature," *Artibus Asiae* 42 (1980): 5–38; and Wang Fangyu and Richard Barnhart, *Master of the Lotus Garden: The Life and Art of Bada Shanren (1626–1705)* (New Haven: Yale University Press, 1990).

3. As Tai Chin seems to have done, at least for a while. A rare example to the contrary was the early-to-mid-eighth-century figure painter, Wu Daozi, whom the Xuanzong emperor liked so well that by decree he refused Wu permission to paint for anyone else.

4. Mayching Kao, "China's Response to the West in Art: 1898–1937," Ph.D. dissertation, Stanford University, 1972, 111; Shirley Sun, "Lu Hsün and the Chinese Woodcut Movement: 1929–1936," Ph.D. dissertation, Stanford University, 1974, 88 ff.

5. From among the numerous studies of later Chinese painting theory and style, see Max Loehr, "The Question of Individualism in Chinese Art," *Journal of the History of Ideas* 22 (1961): 147–58; James Cahill, "Confucian Elements in the Theory of Painting," in Arthur Wright, ed., *The Confucian Persuasion* (Stanford: Stanford University Press, 1969), 115–40; Susan Bush, *The Chinese Literati on Painting: Su Shih (1037–1101) to Tung Ch'i-ch'ang (1555–1636)* (Cambridge: Harvard University Press, 1971); James Cahill, "Style as Idea in Ming-Ch'ing Painting," in Maurice Meisner and Rhoads Murphy, eds., *The Mozartian Historian: Essays on the Works of Joseph R. Levenson* (Berkeley: University of California Press, 1978), 137–56.

6. Mao Zedong, from his canonical "Talks at the Yan'an Conference on Literature and Art," in *Selected Readings from the Works of Mao Tsetung* (Beijing: Foreign Languages Press, 1971), 271–72, borrowing the phrase "cogs and wheels" from Lenin's-famous 1905 article, "Party Organization and Literature," which became the cornerstone of Soviet aesthetic theory.

7. Miklós Haraszti, *The Velvet Prison: Artists Under State Socialism* (New York: New Republic/Basic Books, 1987), 121.

8. Until the early mid-1980s, aside from the salary provided by one's assigned work unit, the only additional compensation artists could realize came from the occasional publication of their work. Since that time, artists have become able to retain up to 50 percent of the sale price of their work.

9. The national-level Chinese Artists Association is supervised from above by the Chinese Federation of Literary and Art Circles (for short, Cultural Federation), in which the association of visual artists is paralleled by other associations which originally included writers, dramatists, musicians, and dancers. More recently, the array of associations under the umbrella federation has been expanded to embrace such areas as calligraphy, film, photography, television, folk artists, ballad singers, and acrobatics, while the Chinese Writers Association became so large that it has been delegated independent status, parallel to that of the Cultural Federation itself. The Cultural Federation, in turn, is controlled by the Communist Party's Propaganda Department (a unit of the party's Central Committee, as distinguished from a state agency). At the provincial level, the Cultural Federation operates primarily "horizontally" rather than "vertically," which is to say it takes political guidance from the provincial party Propaganda Department rather than from the national Cultural Federation. In the early Cultural Revolution period, before the functional demise of the Cultural Federation (and with it, all the artists associations) and again after its rehabilitation and reorganization in 1977, this control was facilitated by placing Propaganda Department personnel in the association bureaucracy. Before the Cultural Revolution (1966–76), the Ministry of Culture was also assured of a significant administrative voice in the associations through similar placement of its officials; but in

the reorganization of the late 1970s, the level of Ministry of Culture representation was reduced, purportedly to reduce bureaucratic interference in the work of artists and other cultural workers.

The organization of these cultural associations was derived from the Soviet literary model; for an overview, see John and Carol Garrard, *Inside the Soviet Writers' Union* (New York: Free Press, 1990), especially pages 8–9 for the matter of structural voluntarism.

10. Haraszti *Velvet Prison*, 26, 78–79, 96–97.

11. In America, with no history of state censorship, supportive patronage and censorial prohibition have largely been discrete, seemingly antithetical functions. In Europe, however, the role in art of church and state (including church-bound and modern-totalitarian states alike) has merged and blurred the functions of patronage and censorship.

12. Haraszti, *Velvet Prison*, 133, 137, 79, 19, 72, 119.

13. Li Shaoyan (b. 1918), with a background in journal-based propaganda illustration, typified the leadership of the new artists associations. He was a prominent woodblock print specialist who promoted that medium over all others, and particularly over traditional painting with its "feudalistic" associations. Woodblock illustration, in addition to being a Chinese invention (of the eighth century, in behalf of Buddhist propagation), was an inexpensive mass medium. In the 1930s and 1940s, it was the socialists' medium of choice, drawing heavily on European socialist models. Traditional painters like Li Huasheng have long derided Li Shaoyan's artists association as operating more like a "woodblock print association." Li Huasheng claims that "generally speaking, the policy for the Sichuan Artists Association was that painting and art should be tools of class struggle. They predetermined the subject matter and assigned the duty of creating this to the artists. Any works counter to this policy were criticized by Li Shaoyan." But Li Shaoyan's efforts met with great success, and he helped make Sichuan the foremost center for woodblock illustration in socialist China.

14. Initially, applicants were reviewed and accepted if they measured up to standards for literary background and sufficient age. In the 1960s, an additional criterion was added: poverty. The plan to establish these Wenshiguan had been decided upon by Mao Zedong and Zhou Enlai even before the Communist Revolution, in accordance with the Party principle of "honoring age and respecting literature." The first hall was established in Beijing in 1952, followed by others (including those in Sichuan) in the same year; all provinces were represented in the system by 1953. Eventually, all major cities in the country were provided with a unit. In Sichuan, the provincial unit was located in Chengdu, and Chongqing was provided a municipal unit. It was administered by the Political Consultative Conference and funded by the Ministry of Culture.

15. Today, throughout much of China, the Wenshiguan units possess an unassayed treasure of contemporary art of which Western and Japanese art historians still re-

main virtually unaware. The Chengdu branch has between 700 and 800 works, approximately half of them paintings and half calligraphy.

16. In 1962, more than a decade after the Revolution, Chen was given his first chance for public display in a five-artist exhibition organized by the Wenshiguan at the Sichuan Provincial Museum in Chengdu and afterward sent on to Chongqing. Partly commercial in intent, it enabled Chen to sell quite a few paintings.

17. Called the Sichuan Painting Academy for short.

18. In the 1980s, the Bureau of Cultural Relics (formerly under the State Council) became a unit of the Ministry of Culture and with its antique stores (*Wenwu Shangdian*, the best known of which is Beijing's Rongbaozhai) set out in full pursuit of the profits of art. Since the contemporary Chinese painting market has become a burgeoning enterprise, a wide variety of agencies, including artists associations, as well as individual artists, have been freed to compete with the Bureau in this pursuit.

19. See Lucy Lim, James Cahill, and Michael Sullivan, *Contemporary Chinese Painting: An Exhibition from the People's Republic of China* (San Francisco: Chinese Culture Foundation of San Francisco, 1983). Organizer Lucy Lim wrote of Li as "perhaps the most original and interesting painter on the contemporary Chinese art scene" (17), and one of Li's landscapes was used on invitations to the exhibition opening in San Francisco. The exhibition subsequently toured Birmingham, Ithaca, Denver, Indianapolis, Kansas City, and Minneapolis.

20. Quoted by Michael Sullivan in *The Stars: Ten Years* (Hong Kong: Hanart 2 Gallery, 1989), 6. Sullivan goes on to say, "He sincerely believed that the exhibition would defeat itself [but in] the two weeks that it ran, it attracted nearly two hundred thousand visitors."

21. For recent reviews of these movements, see Chiang Tsong-zung et al., *China's New Art, Post 1989, with a Retrospective, 1979–1989* (Hong Kong and Seattle: Hanart T Z Gallery and University of Washington Press, 1993); Haus der Kulturen der Welt (Berlin), *China Avant-garde: Counter-Currents in Art and Culture* (New York: Oxford University Press, 1993). See also Richard Strassberg, ed., *"I Don't Want to Play Cards with Cézanne" and Other Works: Selections from the Chinese "New Wave" and "Avant-garde" Art of the Eighties* (Pasadena: Pacific Asia Museum, 1991).

22. See the international exhibition catalogue cited in note 21, above.

23. Especially Xie Jin, China's most popular director of the 1980s, who turned the officially sanctioned melodramatic style of film against the Party itself in powerful films like *Legend of Tianyun Mountain* (1980) and *Hibiscus Town* (1986).

24. Paul Clark, "Two Hundred Flowers on China's Screens," in Chris Berry, ed., *Perspectives on Chinese Cinema*, 2d ed. (London: British Film Institute, 1991), 57. The Film Bureau, housed under the Ministry of Culture since 1949, became part of a new Ministry of Radio, Film, and Television in 1986.

25. Most notable among these was Chen Kaige's *Feng yue* (*Temptress Moon*), which offended on all counts, with an opium-smoking heroine, a gigolo scam artist for a hero, and insinuated allusions to contemporary politicians.

David Wojnarowicz: A Portrait of the Artist as X-Ray Technician

PETER F. SPOONER

To make the private into something public is an action that has terrific repercussions in the pre-invented world. Each public disclosure of a private reality becomes something of a magnet that can attract others with a similar frame of reference; thus each public disclosure of a fragment of private reality serves as a dismantling tool against the illusion of the ONE TRIBE NATION; it lifts the curtains for a brief peek and reveals the possible existence of literally millions of tribes; the term GENERAL PUBLIC disintegrates. If GENERAL PUBLIC disintegrates, what happens next is the possibility of an X-RAY OF CIVILIZATION, an examination of its foundations.

THE PASSAGE QUOTED ABOVE, by multimedia artist David Wojnarowicz (fig. 1), is one of many statements he made about the importance of art as an expression of "tribal" difference, and about the way in which it can and should serve diverse groups of people as a tool of inquiry.[1] Another statement, written in 1965 by Senator Claiborne Pell, Democrat from Rhode Island, as part of a report accompanying a bill to establish a National Foundation on the Arts and Humanities, embodies a similar awareness of art as a means of exploring the mutable facades and structures of American life:

> It is the intent of the committee that in the administration of this act there be given the fullest attention to freedom of artistic and humanistic expression. One of the artist's and the humanist's great values to society is the mirror of self-examination which they raise so that society can become aware of its shortcomings as well as its strengths. Moreover, modes of expression are not static but are constantly evolving. . . . Therefore, the committee affirms that the intent of this act should be the encouragement of free inquiry and expression.[2]

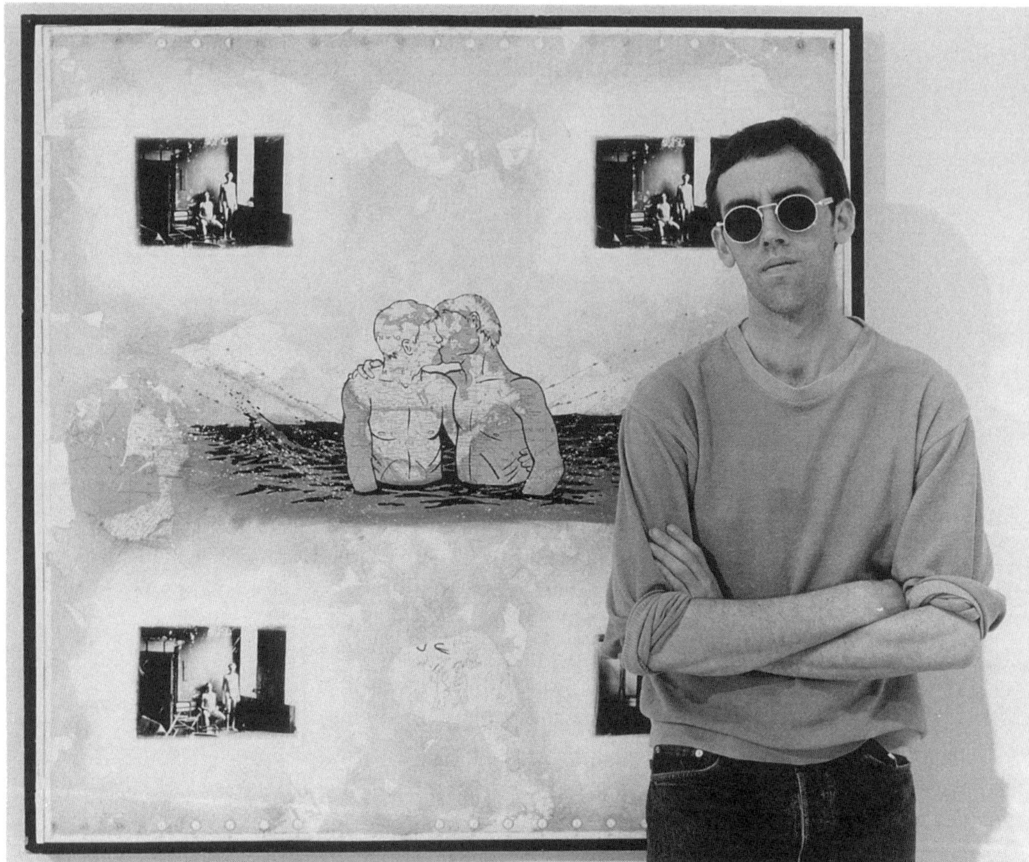

FIG. 1. David Wojnarowicz, *Fuck You Faggot Fucker*, 1984.
Acrylic and collage on masonite, 122×122 cm (48×48 in.). Private collection. Courtesy of the Estate of David Wojnarowicz and P.P.O.W., New York. Photo: Anna Maria Watkin.

Both statements offer visions of art as a tool for the unfettered exploration of a constantly changing world. Both celebrate art as a means of inclusion in society and as a challenge to totalitarian thinking. Both presume that an important function of art is to explore and present ideas that might at any time challenge the status quo. Given the events of recent years, however, we now see a great disparity between goals of certain contemporary artists, as characterized by Wojnarowicz's frank challenges, and the hopeful, though vague idealism of the American government thirty years ago as characterized by Pell's report.

Taking stock of what Wojnarowicz did as an artist, we will see that he most often made his work into a "mirror of self-examination," and practiced the "free inquiry and expression" of his life and unique experiences in America. An extremely versatile artist, Wojnarowicz employed painting, sculpture, photography, film, writing, music, and performance to illuminate his observations.[3] Like Wojnarowicz himself, the art is alternately angry and tender, filled with both poetry and rage. Perhaps more than any other artist in the past decade, he has generated an enormous, real, and ongoing discourse about our fears, pleasures, and actions. His work lends an affirming voice to many who live on the margins of society, and it strikes a deep chord of fear in many who claim to live at society's "moral center." Wojnarowicz's one resounding message was that positive change could be effected through a responsive, poetic examination of the diverse substructures—sociosexual, biological, spiritual, political, economic—underlying life in America. If art were medicine and society a free clinic, he would be the head of radiology. Stated in terms of the current battle for First Amendment rights, X-ray vision is his form of eternal vigilance.

In ten brief years,[4] Wojnarowicz accomplished exactly what Pell claimed would make artists of "great value" to society, yet he was denounced by conservatives because of the content of his work. More to the point, it was because Wojnarowicz was openly gay, had AIDS, and used his work to discuss issues of homophobia, discrimination against people living with AIDS, and other forms of social injustice, that he was caught in the middle of an ongoing battle between the conservative Right and the "cultural elite." Because they can easily appeal to moderates and conservatives alike by suggesting that "hard-earned tax dollars" are being channeled through the National Endowment for the Arts (NEA) to fund "pornographic" and "blasphemous" art, the Right has made a concentrated effort of attacking government funded artists, publications, and institutions. In 1990, Dana Rohrabacher, a Republican congressman from California, characterized the exhibition "David Wojnarowicz: Tongues of Flame,"[5] as "an orgy of degenerate depravity," describing his art as "sickeningly violent, sexually explicit, homoerotic, antireligious and nihilistic."[6]

The possibility of controversy over the content of works funded with taxpayer monies was foreseen and debated before the NEA and NEH ever received their first appropriations in 1965. The sponsors of the National Foundation on the Arts and Humanities Act (H.R. 9460, S.1483) had the foresight to include in the proposed legislation the following language: "In the administration of this act no department, agency, officer or employee of the United

States shall exercise any direction, supervision or control over the policy determination, personnel, or curriculum, or the administration or operation of any school, or other non-Federal agency, institution, organization, or association."[7] Six months before approving passage of a bill establishing the NEA and NEH, President Lyndon Johnson made it clear that noninterference in the support of the nation's artists was crucial:

> We fully recognize that no government can call artistic excellence into existence. It must flow from the quality of the society and the good fortune of the Nation. Nor should any government seek to restrict the freedom of the artist to pursue his calling in his own way. Freedom is an essential condition for the artist, and in proportion as freedom is diminished so is the prospect of artistic achievement.[8]

Some early opponents to government support for the arts cited the possible result of censorship and the encouragement of artistic mediocrity as leading causes for their disapproval. Arguing against H.R. 9460, Congressman William S. Broomfield (Republican from Michigan) said: "We are being urged to back a bill which will set up an official art czar similar to the cultural czar in the Soviet Union. . . . we can be sure that if this bill is passed, the day will not be far off before we demand political allegiance of those who receive Federal gifts, that we see the controversial ignored and the mediocre praised."[9] Conversely, Congressman Peter H. B. Frelinghuysen (Republican from New Jersey) felt that the Federal National Arts Council (an NEA forerunner) should be instituted precisely because "one of the areas of inquiry of such a council . . . would well be to look into the nature of programs which we subsidize and . . . if they are inappropriate, we would not do it. So there would be less chance of getting our taxpayers' money misused if we had a directly focused attack."[10] Without stretching the imagination, this "directly focused attack" can be equated with attempts to add content-restrictive language to appropriations bills for the NEA, like those recently proposed by Senator Jesse Helms (Republican from North Carolina).[11]

Flare-ups in the art censorship debate have been largely the result of a clash between artists who choose to address certain "taboo" themes and an increasingly powerful and vocal element of social, political, and religious conservatism. The power of fundamentalist groups like Reverend Donald Wildmon's American Family Association (AFA)[12] is amplified through greater access to the media and politial influence, which are in turn fueled by massive fundraising campaigns (some used "immoral art" like Wojnarowicz's as a rallying point) and by a much larger atmosphere of conservatism that accompanied twelve years of the Reagan and Bush presidencies. Hans Haacke, an artist whose works are often highly critical of corporate and governmental policies, and whose own exhibitions have been canceled because of the topics he addresses, said of the Helms amendment:

> A law stipulating that taxpayer's money must not be spent on artworks and institutional programs deemed offensive by certain politicians amounts to a hijacking of my taxes for the purpose of imposing their sectarian precepts on the entire country. It is just this danger, the infringement of free expression and the establishment of a state religion, that the First Amendment was meant to ward against. Instead, we now have government agencies that make compliance with an unconstitutional law a new criterion for receiving grants that we have financed through our tax payments.[13]

During his short and brilliant lifetime, Wojnarowicz was never the direct recipient of a government grant. He did, however, receive indirect support for his work from the government through institutions that were able to exhibit his visual art, publish his writings, and host his performances with the assitance of partial funding from the NEA, and from state art councils that routinely receive NEA funding. Born in Redbank, New Jersey, on September 14, 1954, Wojnarowicz died of AIDS related illnesses in New York City on July 22, 1992. His father was a sailor, who on his infrequent stays with the family was often drunk, abusive, and violent. His parents divorced when he was two, and Wojnarowicz and his siblings ended up in an equally abusive foster care situation. Soon remarried, the elder Wojnarowicz kidnapped his children a year later, and the abuse escalated to the point that he would shoot guns off in the house, often pointing them at the heads of his children. When David was nine his father sent them to New York City to live with their mother, who was supportive but extremely poor and on welfare. The survivor of a childhood of abuse and neglect, Wojnarowicz learned early to rely on his imagination for comfort and escape. By age eleven, Wojnarowicz was spending most of his time on the street, occasionally selling himself to men in Times Square for money, but still in school. In 1968 he was accepted at the High School of Music and Art, where he had his first experience with "official" censorship. At that time the subculture of the streets, where Wojnarowicz found a degree of acceptance and freedom, included violent demonstrations against the Vietnam War. Most of his work at Music and Art, he wrote, "consisted of 3-D street constructions filled with long hair radicals shooting policemen from windows and rooftops and hurling bombs and molotov cocktails. The cops were farm pigs in n.y.c. uniforms. When the principal made his rounds, the art teachers would dump all my work behind the radiators or toss them in the trash."[14]

By 1970, Wojnarowicz had dropped out of school and was living on the street full time, supporting himself by turning tricks and stealing food and clothes. During this period he narrowly escaped being murdered twice, and nearly starved to death. Through a halfway house for potential jail risks, he was able to find janitorial jobs and begin the slow process of coming off the street. For several years he had been taking photographs, making drawings, and keeping written journals of his life on the street. It was also during this time that he began living openly as a homosexual. According to his self-authored "Biographical Dateline," in 1972 he "lived openly as a queer and realized how healthy and calm I felt as a result. Realized that my queerness was a wedge that was slowly separating myself from a sick society." At this point, art became a means of emotional and psychic, if not material survival for Wojnarowicz, as he slowly began to trust making images and objects as a means of documenting his own history on his own terms: "Worked on a series of drawings that revealed everything people are pressured not to reveal. Shifted my ideas of what making things could be. Started developing ideas of making and preserving an authentic version of history in the form of images/writings/objects that would contest state-supported forms of 'history.' Didn't really believe that it would survive time."[15] He traveled to Central America, France, and all over the United States, recording his experiences in writing and photographs, later translating many of them into paintings and performances.

Previous to his entry into the "official" art world of gallery shows, museums, and collectors, Wojnarowicz stenciled images such as a burning house, a menacing dog, and a falling man on abandoned cars and buildings, garbage cans, and advertising posters. He also worked in the crumbling shipping warehouses along the Hudson River, documenting the activities of the sexual underground. Wojnarowicz's first widespread recognition in the art world came as part of the East Village art scene during the early 1980s, where he participated in the "Lower Manhattan Drawing Show" at the Mudd Club, the "Erotic Show" at Club 57, and solo exhibitions at Milliken Gallery, Hal Bromm Gallery, and Civilian Warfare, and later at P.P.O.W., all in New York City. From the start Wojnarowicz's works relied heavily on collage, through which he demonstrated his attraction to the groundless, stream-of-consciousness, and revelatory properties of surrealism (fig. 2). "The interplay of symbols established by the collage technique allows for a multiplicity of meanings," writes Andrew Norris. "Rather than reducing the meaning of

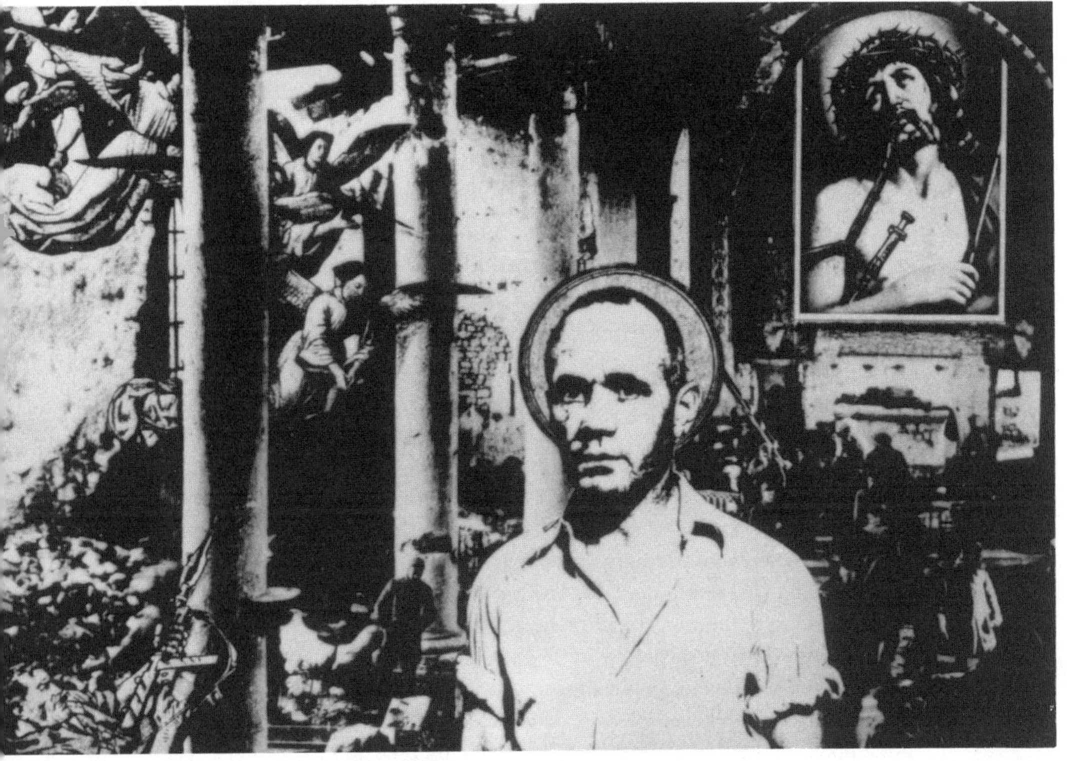

FIG. 2. David Wojnarowicz, *Untitled (Genet)*, 1979.
Xerox collage, 22×28 cm (8½×11 in.). Estate of the artist. Courtesy of the Estate of David Wojnarowicz and P.P.O.W., New York. Photo: Michael Sarver.

human experience to a set of 'central ideas,' Wojnarowicz's work sets in motion an endless expansion of concepts, each adding new insight into the main themes."[16] Collage techniques also allowed him to rearrange images and texts at will, to cut through, as he termed it, a "pre-invented world," and recreate it to reflect his own life experiences, including his homosexuality and experiences of repression from childhood and adolescence. The more he painted, photographed, wrote, and spoke, the more adept he became at delivering real-world issues with a poetic voice. The main strength of his work, and hence its threat to the Right's cultural hegemony, is concisely summarized by critic David Deitcher:

> There are languages of analysis and emotion that we tend, in this culture, to regard as mutually exclusive. But Wojnarowicz's texts are neither the reasoned

language of political discourse nor, strictly speaking, the stuff of fiction. Here, within the space of individual works of art, an emotional language manages to explicate a social condition, rather than leading, as it so often does in art, to vagueness and mythification.[17]

Eventually, Wojnarowicz's art allowed him to transcend the culture of repression in which he had lived for the first half of his life. Like so many individuals who are not members of the dominant (i.e., white, male, heterosexual, Christian, middle or upper-middle class) culture, Wojnarowicz rarely saw his own experience, or read or heard his own voice, reflected in popular culture *or* in high art. He witnessed censorship as a broad-based and far-reaching condition inherent in mainstream society, and not only as an isolated incident that resulted in squabbles over government arts funding. Writing from a feminist perspective, Carol Jacobsen notes:

> There is a gaping discrepancy between the way censorship has been defined and discussed and the way it has actually functioned through customs, practices and rules throughout its long history in Western culture. Despite the rampant and ongoing censorship of *artists themselves* . . . public discourse has limited the definition to the suppression, removal, or alteration of artists' work or the conditions of their display *after the fact*—when those works have already been accepted or installed for public exposition. This focus on overt . . . acts is actually a conservative brand of censorship based on the ideological assumption that public expression is a "natural" entitlement of the dominant . . . perspective. Its double standard serves to resuscitate a dying patriarchy while conveniently ignoring the most pervasive and obliterating uses to which censorship has been put.[18]

Censorship proves to be a slippery concept, in part because it can be applied to a wide variety of practices, but also because its definition seems to rely so much on official actions, particularly actions taken by established agencies. In other words, "we know it when we see it," or we know it when it is practiced "by certain officials or institutions." A narrowly focused definition might require censorship to be an *action* sanctioned by an institution (i.e., church, school, government) that knowingly keeps a product from being created, expressed, or consumed by an individual or a group of people. But attitudes precede actions. A broader definition might look behind censorial actions to include conditions and attitudes that make it difficult or impossible for people to express themselves or to gain exposure to the expressions of others. Among these conditions are the absence of minority art, literature, and recorded history from educational and cultural institutions, lack of access to high-level jobs or political office, the atmosphere of repression that results from constant worry about meeting basic (food, clothing, shelter) needs, "hate crimes" directed against members of particular races or lifestyles, the lack of representation for certain minorities and lifestyles in advertising and popular media, self-censorship based on fear of losing income or opportunity, or the use of any form of government to promote or give preference to the interests and expressions of any one group over those of another. Stepping even further back, we see that these conditions result from attitudes like racism, sexism, homophobia, greed, xenophobia, and that they are bred as easily in the private sphere as in the public. In effect, these covert forms of censorship restrict speech and access to speech as much as do the overt actions of banning books or removing artworks from exhibitions. An *atmosphere* of repression is a more insidious form of censorship within a society because it is invisible *as* censorship until it is born out in some covert action. "What they want to shut down," said Wojnarowicz of such cultural censors, "are tiny pieces of information that aren't played on television, that aren't played in the newspapers. . . . it's a smokescreen issue for them—their fear that art might be subsidized by a few public pennies. It's not that. It's the information that art contains that's most frightening for them. You control culture, you control dissemination of information, you control any of these aspects and essentially you control people."[19]

Until relatively recently, which is to say until controversies over the work of Andres Serrano, Robert Mapplethorpe,[20] and Wojnarowicz brought the arts funding debate into the national spotlight, censorship has been defined rather narrowly. As befits the sense of inclusiveness Wojnarowicz sought for his art, the question of what constitutes censorship and how it has or has not been practiced against the artist should be addressed broadly. It is far more enlightening to look at a broad range of conditions and attitudes that equal the deleterious effects of censorship on artistic freedom than it is to adhere only to a "dictionary definition."[21] Overt attempts to censor Wojnarowicz based on the content of his work have been tied directly to debates over the appropriateness of government funding of artwork which is critical of, or offensive to, some individuals. These instances adhere more to what might be described as "official" censorship, insofar as they ask a governmental agency to restrict speech. Wojnarowicz first became a target of anti-NEA sentiment in November 1989. Then, newly appointed NEA Chairman John Frohnmayer made a decision to withdraw a $10,000 grant from Artists Space (New York City) for "Witnesses: Against Our Vanishing," an exhibition curated by Nan Goldin that presented responses to the AIDS pandemic by twenty-three artists. A participant in the exhibition, Wojnarowicz was also asked to contribute an essay to the show's catalogue, which he titled "Postcards from America: X-Rays from Hell." Frohnmayer's decision to rescind the grant was based on the observation that its "artistic focus had eroded" and it had become "too political."[22]

Under enormous pressure from the arts community, Frohnmayer restored funding to the exhibition, but only on condition that it not be used for the catalogue, in which Wojnarowicz's essay openly criticized the repressive AIDS policies of Helms, John Cardinal O'Connor (Archdiocese, New York City), and William Dannemeyer, Republican congressman from California. As critic Elizabeth Hess wrote, "Wojnarowicz makes the same connections in his catalogue essay—between the disease, money, sex, the church and members of Congress—that he has all along in his artwork. But texts are difficult to read on a wall. Laid out on a page, Wojnarowicz's words became more dangerous."[23] Frohnmayer's decision to pull funding from the catalogue drew, at least temporarily, a line between what was and what was not appropriate for NEA funding; it was going too far, he implied, when an artist started naming the names of political and religious leaders. As writer Joyce Hanson has commented: "Wojnarowicz laid himself bare in his writing. He spoke not only of his rage, sadness and fears, but also attacked the lawmakers and clergymen whom he blamed for promoting instead of preventing the spread of AIDS. . . . Later in the essay—where Frohnmayer feared trouble for the endowment—Wojnarowicz named names."[24] It is likely, though impossible to prove, that "Witnesses: Against Our Vanishing" was initially seen as worthy of NEA funding because it was interpreted as a project that would express mourning, and not as a collection of visual and literary forms that challenged repressive AIDS policies and called for change and action. As Wojnarowicz said in reference to the exhibition, "Artists are supposed to mourn, but they're not allowed to protest."[25]

"Postcards from America: X-Rays from Hell" was reprinted along with five other prose works by the artist in the catalogue for "David Wojnarowicz: Tongues of Flame" at University Galleries of Illinois State University. The exhibition, catalogue, and related programming at University Galleries received a $15,000 NEA "Special Exhibitions" award, which was approved in the same cycle of grants that included the grant to Artists Space for "Witnesses: Against Our Vanishing." The publication of this particular work by Wojnarowicz in the University Galleries catalogue posed the question: How was it possible that the exact same piece of work could be denied NEA funding in one circumstance but approved for the same level of funding in another, nearly identical circumstance? One obvious answer is that in restoring the Artists Space grant Frohnmayer had won back some much-needed approval from arts supporters. To then turn around and challenge the University Galleries grant (even though University Galleries used NEA funds to publish the same essay that Artists Space could print only with a disclaimer clearly separating it from that exhibition's NEA funds) would be political suicide, inviting the full wrath of artists and arts supporters nationwide. According to Congressman Pat Williams (Democrat from Montana), chairman of the House subcommittee responsible for the NEA's reauthorization, Frohnmayer was responsible for a "bruising of freedom of artistic expression" by threatening to not fund "anything which is seen as affecting political discourse. If the cancellation [of the Artists Space grant] was because the work is political discourse then he [Frohnmayer] made a terrible decision. If it was because the nature of the work had changed from the time of the grant approval, then there is doubt as to his political judgment. Either way he has made a mistake."[26]

From Wojnarowicz's point of view, the Artists Space incident implicated not only the NEA and Frohnmayer, but also Artists Space (and its then director Susan Wyatt) for their acceptance of the funds on the condition that his essay be declared separate from the rest of the show. Wojnarowicz never hesitated to point out that the ultraconservative Right is not the only censor around and that, in general, art museums have never fully embraced art by gays, lesbians, minorities, and women, or art that is overtly political, sexual, or otherwise controversial in nature:

> The actions by Helms and [Alphonse] D'Amato [R-NY] only follow standards that have been formed and implemented by the "arts community" itself. . . . museums in New York, not to mention major museums around the country, are just as guilty of this kind of selective cultural support and denial. It is a standard practice to make invisible any kind of sexual imaging other than straight white male erotic fantasies—sex in america long ago slid into a small set of generic symbols. . . . So people have found it necessary to define their sexuality in images, in photographs and drawings and movies in order to not disappear. . . . Jesse Helms is, at the very least, making his attacks on freedom public; the collectors and museums responsible for censorship do theirs at elegant private parties or from the confines of their self-created closets.[27]

Writing in *The Nation*, Paul Mattick confirms Wojnarowicz's accusations:

> For art institutions . . . the struggle over the NEA provides a comfortable spot to take a stand. One museum curator remarked to me how handily protesting the

> threat of NEA censorship obviated paying attention to the everyday censorship that goes on in the bulwarks of culture. Every choice of an exhibition . . . implies a decision not to show or play something else. Such choices are powerfully subject to forces emanating from donors and potential donors, corporate sponsors and the tastes of the sought-after audience.[28]

Covert acts of censorship from within the art world itself, like the subtle forms of censorship that result from the culture of repression, are not always easy to see, and thus are more difficult to fight.

In their attempts to convince constituents and colleagues of the offensive and blasphemous nature of some contemporary art, a strategy commonly used by the Right is the selective editing of carefully chosen images. On March 28, 1990, the AFA placed a full-page anti-NEA advertisement in *USA Today.* Captioned "Is this how you want your tax dollars spent?" the advertisement called for an end to "support [for] pornographic, anti-Christian 'works of art.'" The advertisement described fourteen instances where NEA funds had allegedly been misused, including grants for exhibitions by Serrano, Mapplethorpe, and Wojnarowicz, along with a list of 252 members of Congress who had voted in favor of a motion by Ralph Regula which effectively struck down the Helms amendment. The only image in the advertisement was a portion (the upper right corner, approximately one-eighth of the total image) of Wojnarowicz's *Untitled (Genet)* (fig. 2). The same detail was used by Dana Rohrabacher in his "Dear Colleagues" letter of February 20, 1990, and by the weekly publication *Human Events* on February 24, 1990. Both the AFA advertisement and the *Human Events* issue used the image to raise funds for their respective organizations, since both included subscription or donor information along with the cropped Wojnarowicz artwork.[29] Beyond blinding people to Wojnarowicz's actual (and essentially positive) artistic intentions, groups like the AFA distribute mailers adorned with carefully selected examples of "offensive" or "blasphemous" artworks as fund-raising tools. In doing so they seem to suggest that if you send them a donation, "immoral" artists like Wojnarowicz will be put out of business, members of Congress who voted to reauthorize the NEA will be voted out of office, and "correct moral values" will prevail.

The next overt act of censorship against Wojnarowicz took place in April 1990, when the Reverend Donald Wildmon (executive director of the AFA) distributed an anti-NEA brochure that featured fourteen details of works by Wojnarowicz that had been reproduced in the University Galleries catalogue.[30] For example, the AFA reproduced a detail taken from the upper left corner of *Sex Series (Bridge)* (fig. 3). Entitled "Your Tax Dollars Helped Pay

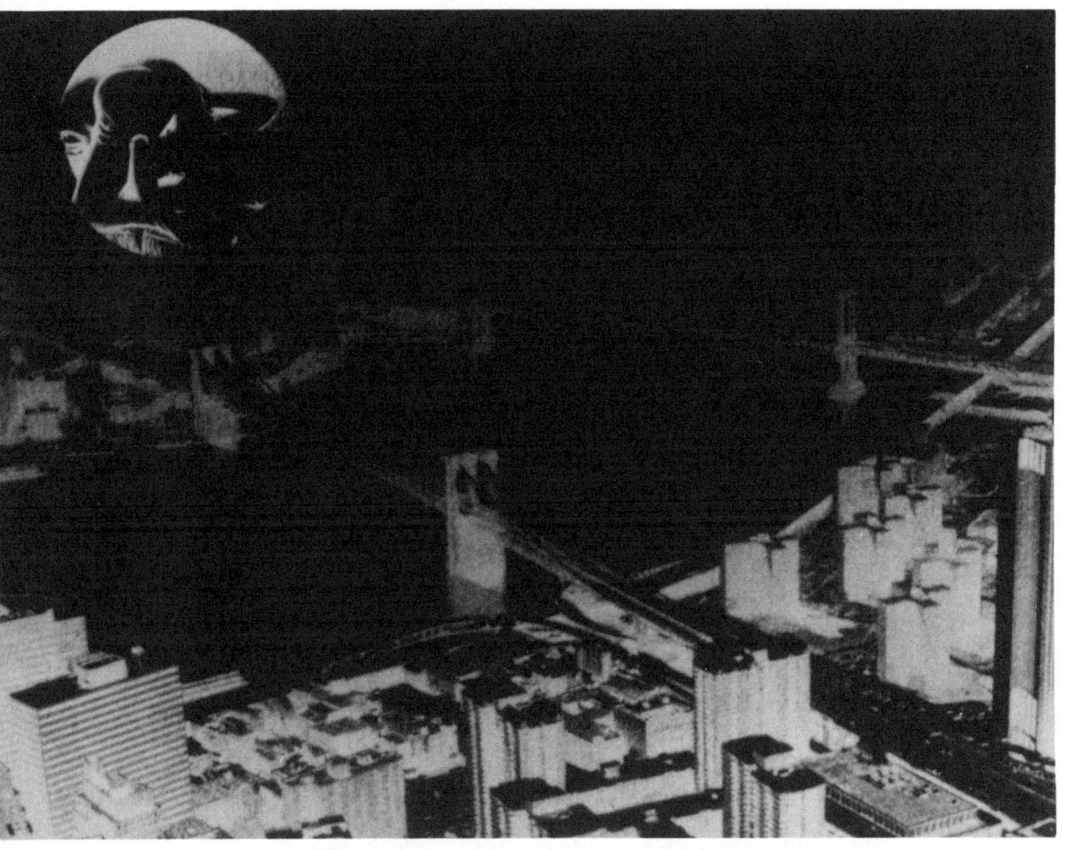

FIG. 3. David Wojnarowicz, *Sex Series (for Marion Schemama). Bridge*, 1988. Black and white photograph, 46×56 cm (18×22 in.). Private collection. Courtesy of the Estate of David Wojnarowicz and P.P.O.W., New York. Photo: Anna Maria Watkin.

for These 'Works of Art,'" the brochure was distributed to 523 members of Congress, 3,230 Christian church leaders, 947 Christian radio and TV stations, and 1,578 newspapers. Mailed in envelopes labeled "Caution: Contains Extremely Offensive Material" (presumably at nonprofit, bulk rates, since the AFA is tax exempt), the brochure failed to mention that the images reproduced were small parts of much larger works. This selective editing compromised a clear understanding of Wojnarowicz's works, rendering them indistinguishable from pornography. Elizabeth Hess reported: "'It's not my work,' said Wojnarowicz when he first saw the mailing. Indeed it's not. All the credit for this masterpiece goes to Wildmon, who has succeeded in making the artist look like a mediocre 'pornographer.' The mailing gives the distinct impression that these pictures are reproductions of *whole* objects from a consistent body of work, which couldn't be further from the truth."[31] As Carole Vance suggests: "In moral campaigns, fundamentalists select a negative symbol which is highly arousing to their own constituency and which is difficult or problematic for their opponents to defend. The symbol, often taken literally, out of context and always denying the possibility of irony or multiple interpretations, is waved like a red flag before their constituents."[32]

Wojnarowicz sued Wildmon and the AFA for copyright infringement, defamation of character, and breach of the Lanham Act and the New York Artists Authorship Rights Act, asking for a total of five million dollars in damages. On May 26, 1990, Judge William Connor of the U.S. District Court in Manhattan granted a preliminary injunction against further publication of the brochure, arguing that it "'could be construed by reasonable persons as misrepresenting the work of the artist, with likely damage to the artist's reputation and to the value of his works,' a violation of Wojnarowicz's rights under the New York Artists Authorship Rights Act."[33] The final ruling on August 8, 1990, held that "(1) the artist was entitled to an injunction under the New York Authorship Rights Act; (2) the pamphlet was not employed in the 'advertising or promotion' of goods or services within the meaning of the Lanham Act; and (3) the copying fell within the definition of fair use of copyrighted material. [T]he Authorship Rights Act specifically provides for a right of 'disattribution,' and the Court believes it just to require the defendants to distribute a corrective communication to all those to whom they sent the original pamphlet. . . . So far as the record shows, not one gallery or museum currently scheduled to exhibit plaintiff's work has cancelled; nor has one planned sale been cancelled. . . . Accordingly, the Court hereby awards plaintiff nominal damages in the amount of $1.00."[34]

That Judge Connor ruled in favor of Wojnarowicz on only one out of four complaints meant that the action against the AFA amounted to little more than a proverbial slap on the wrist. The trial itself was beneficial, however, because it was the first time since recent controversies over the NEA began that an artist fought a censor in court. The trial sent a clear message that such a gross misrepresentation of an artist's work could be declared illegal in some cases. As ordered by the court, the AFA produced and distributed a correction which said in part: "This correction is to advise you that the images were not reproductions of complete works of Mr. Wojnarowicz. They were fragments or parts of larger artworks and do not constitute the entire work from which they were reproduced."[35] It is ironic that the extreme degree of Wildmon's cropping of Wojnarowicz's original images may be just what saved him from being ruled against under the fair use provision. An important factor in deciding fair use cases has been the "amount and substantiality of the portion used in relation to the copyrighted work as a whole." The fair use provision states: "Generally speaking, the greater the amount copied, the less the likelihood that it constitutes fair use."[36]

Despite the 1990 court decision barring the AFA from distribution of its Wojnarowicz brochure, the same brochure was included in a package of information sent in response to a February 1991 request from a Chicago area resident. In a meeting between Wildmon, Judge Connor, and Wojnarowicz's lawyers, it was discovered that, indeed, two copies of the brochure had been sent out, but Judge Connor concluded that "the mailings were mistakes from which no malevolence could be presumed."[37] He then orderd Wildmon to send Wojnarowicz a letter of apology, but denied a motion to hold him in civil contempt.

Mailings of the type engineered by Wildmon and Rohrabacher are designed to create a kind of mass hysteria among recipients, and these did no less. Within days of both the Rohrabacher and Wildmon mailings, University Galleries (and its parent institution, Illinois State University) received a series of letters and phone calls from around the country, complaining about the exhibition. Not surprisingly, the images mentioned by letter writers and callers were the same ones used by Wildmon, and none of the complainants had seen the exhibition or even the entire catalogue from which the AFA had constructed its "calculated to offend" brochure. It is extremely important to point out that from among the more than six thousand viewers who saw the works in their entirety in the context of the University Galleries exhibition, with access to guided tours, a performance by Wojnarowicz (and his presence in the community for three weeks), panel discussions, videos, wall labels, brochures, and the exhibition catalogue, less than ten individuals registered any official form of complaint. I had the opportunity to speak with many persons who called to voice displeasure about the exhibition but who found that as they gained more information about the artist (and thus a broader understanding about the content and context of his work) they became less and less outraged. Some conversations ended with callers apologizing for their limited views of the artist and the exhibition. Misrepresenting an artist's work by showing only a small portion of it—without clearly labeling it as such—has the negative effect of destroying the work's intended meaning. For audiences unused to looking at art in the form of reproduction in books and magazines, the use of details, if not clearly identified as such, often gives the impression that what they are looking at is the entire artwork. The recycling of preproduced imagery (otherwise known as recontextualization, deconstruction, or appropriation) is a strategy practiced by many artists, including Wojnarowicz. But in their attempts to recontextualize Wojnarowicz's work as "pornography," Wildmon and Rohrabacher erroneously claimed that it was still Wojnarowicz's work, which it was not. Even though Wildmon sent out a correction stating that his previous mailing contained reproductions of details, and not complete works, by Wojnarowicz, the damage had been done.

Some of Wojnarowicz's images and writings directly address the many guises of censorship itself and the ways in which such actions result from ignorance, fear, xenophobia, cultural insularity, and greed. In a 1990 performance, Wojnarowicz suggested that certain preconceived notions of his homosexuality produced in the audience a social myopia that prevented his intended message from being received: "As time goes on I have come to believe that all things are not what they appear to be if you judge them only by their silence, or by their invisibility. . . . I wonder in my coming out here to talk, whether my being a queer who asserts his sexual identity publicly in any way causes some of you to see the word 'QUEER' somehow written across my forehead in capital letters, and whether or not that revelation prevents you from hearing anything else I say."[38] A complex blend of painted imagery, photographs, and preprinted materials, Wojnarowicz's collages are densely layered, with many diverse and at times disjunctive images. Viewers who cannot get past the fact that certain works contain vignettes of sexual activity, alongside less taboo images, are preventing themselves from "hearing anything else the artist has to say."

Understanding Wojnarowicz's art is never a matter of simply reading its form. Constructed of myriad poetic associations, his art tends to give rise in the viewer to more such associations. It is a poetry that works exponentially, by producing even more poetry in the beholder. Similarly, his writing is alternately heady, trailing off into memories and the reveries of dreams, and then editorially direct, jerking the reader back to bitter fact. There is a raw and intuitive emotionalism about his work that overanalysis only numbs, and yet underreading or misreading Wojnarowicz's work, as Helms and Wildmon have discovered, can lead to the impression that it is "about" its own sexual explicitness, that it merely intends to shock or offend, or that its only purpose is to "be controversial." Works like the *Sex Series (for Marion Schemama)* (figs. 3, 4) do *use* pornographic images, but that does not make them pornography, since their intended context is one of emotional and in-

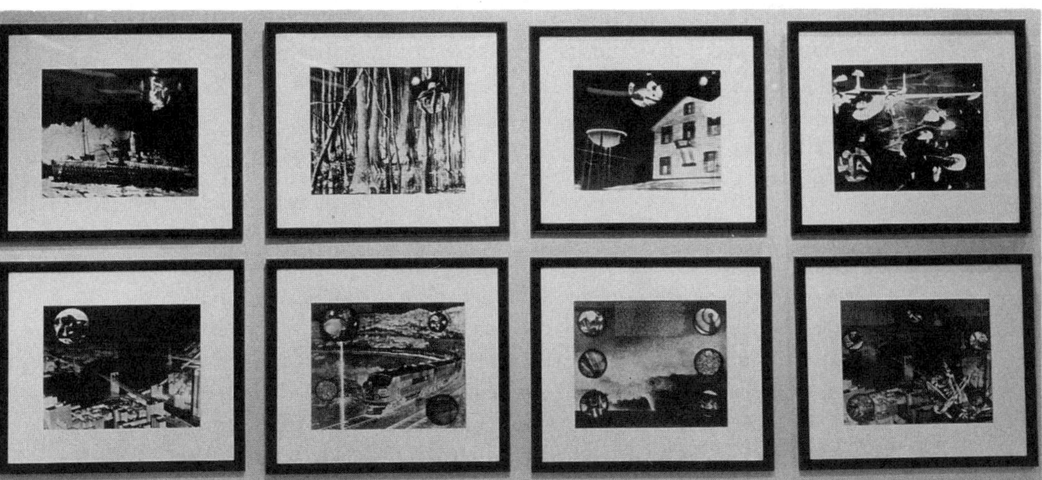

FIG. 4. David Wojnarowicz, *Sex Series (for Marion Schemama)*, 1988.
Eight black and white photographs, 46×56 cm (18×22 in.). Private collection. Courtesy of the Estate of David Wojnarowicz and P.P.O.W., New York. Photo: Anna Maria Watkin.

tellectual, not primarily sexual, stimulation. If he had intended any of his works to be pornographic, one would have to conclude that Wojnarowicz was a terribly inept pornographer, since the addition of so much nonsexually explicit material confuses, instead of excites, prurient interests. Lucy Lippard has written that as a homosexual, and particularly as a gay man with AIDS, "Wojnarowicz's refusal to deny his own sexuality and his insistence on publicly representing it is a potent form of resistance to the 'preinvented world.' [He says:] 'When I concentrate on issues of sexuality in my work . . . a lot of people say that's better left to the bedroom. I say bullshit, because I'm completely surrounded by one form of sexuality; it's represented in every ad—whether it's cigarettes or beer or whatever, there's always one prescribed sexuality that makes me feel invisible.'"[39] In discussing recent instances of censorship it is impossible to ignore society's deeply ingrained fear of the body, and the long-standing habit of repressing things sexual. The usual frames of reference for explicit sexual images are shrouded in taboo: in pornography, in art that is safely historicized, or in concurrent feelings of attraction/repulsion toward the other-cultural, which includes the other-culture of homosexuality. The task of seeing beyond the taboo surrounding artistic representations of homosexuality is difficult for many people, in light of years of cultural conditioning that homosexuality is "abnormal." The difficulty of breaking such conditioning is compounded by laws in some states that contend that homosexual acts are not only immoral but also illegal. Writing in *The Nation*, Gara Lamarche and William Rubenstein observed:

> Society's oppression of homosexuals is based on censorship—of speech as much, if not more than, conduct. Society rarely polices homosexual conduct directly, although the Supreme Court gave it the green light to do so in *Bowers v. Hardwick*, upholding Georgia's sodomy law. Instead, society polices the *expression* of sexual identity, turning "coming out" into a political declaration. As more lesbians and gay men make this declaration, society fights back by muzzling expression—increasingly, with violence. . . . speech by and about gay themes is inordinately censored because it is situated at the confluence of a number of other repressive forces within our society: the muting of discourse about sexuality of any kind; the cold rejection of "difference," whether based on race, gender, ethnicity, disability, sexual orientation or any other factor; and the packaging of sexual orientation as an issue of "morality."[40]

In the same way that heterosexuality is pervasive in advertising, in fine and popular art, and in language, Wojnarowicz used his art as a means of representing his own experience of sexuality. Despite what Helms or Wildmon would have us believe (and despite the artist's avowed intention of countering societal repression of other-sexuality) Wojnarowicz's oeuvre generally contains less direct reference to things sexual than does an equal measure of the average television program or popular magazine. This is in no way an apology for his forays into the representation of sexuality or an attempt to minimize their importance in his work. It is simply a way of stating that, mature and comfortable with his own preferences, Wojnarowicz depicts sex as a natural *part* of human experience. It is this directness and honesty, when viewed against the opaque backdrop of sexual repression, that might make his work appear to be "obsessed" with sex.

The photographs of the *Sex Series* contain small circular insets with scenes of homosexual and heterosexual lovemaking, images of technology, military action, money, and blood cells. These are situated within larger images of travel, nature, and domesticity, the whole of which Wojnarowicz printed in photographic negative. The insets are comments on surveillance, and on the secrecy imposed on those who act "differently," and on scientific scrutiny, as in the search for a genetic "cause" for sexual otherness. They also present "close-ups" of activities that go on within the larger landscapes that Wojnarowicz depicts, but that are usually hidden from view. Their representation in negative enforces the idea that what they depict is an alternative reality, no

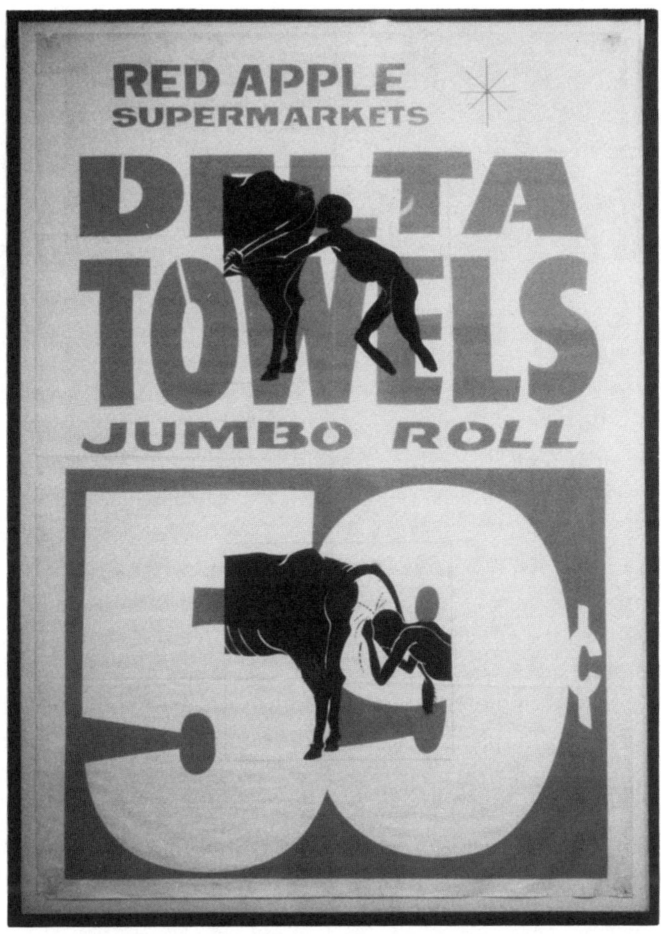

FIG. 5. David Wojnarowicz, *Delta Towels*, 1983.
Spray paint on poster, 76×51 cm (30×20 in.). Estate of the artist.
Courtesy of the Estate of David Wojnarowicz and P.P.O.W., New York.

less real and always possible behind the "positive" reality we are generally encouraged to see.

Delta Towels (fig. 5) is a wry comment on the blindness of first world sensibilities to the practices of third and fourth world cultures. Over an advertising poster for paper towels, Wojnarowicz stenciled an image, which he claimed to have seen in *National Geographic*, of an African youth practicing a cleansing ritual well known and effective for his (if not our) tribe. Among

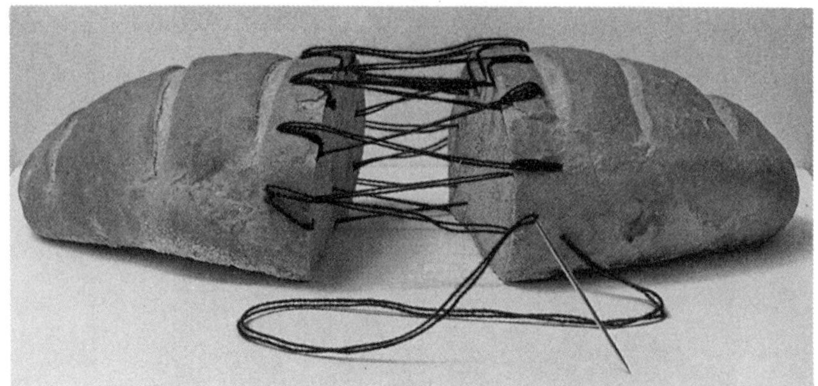

FIG. 6. David Wojnarowicz, *Bread Sculpture*, 1988–89.
Bread, string, needle, 8×33×15 cm (3×13×6 in.). Estate of the artist. Courtesy of the Estate of David Wojnarowicz and P.P.O.W., New York. Photo: Michael Sarver.

some desert peoples, cow urine is used to rid the head of lice, and in order to get the animal to urinate "on demand," air is blown into the animal's anus. In *Delta Towels* the artist confronts us with our feelings of discomfort and disgust at such a practice, which puts the individual in closer contact with nature than most of us would care to get. In our society, being clean means keeping a barrier (the paper towel) between ourselves and nature. The meaning of *Delta Towels* hinges on understanding that our feelings of comfort or disgust are conditioned by our knowledge, or lack thereof, of the beliefs and practices of different cultures. If we are open-minded and willing to learn about those who are different from ourselves, fear of the unfamiliar dissipates, understanding grows, and acts of repression or censorship are unnecessary.

Offering visions of the power structures embodied in history, science, politics, the media, organized religion, and capitalist economics, Wojnarowicz asks us to examine these forces and the control they exert on our perceptions and in our day-to-day lives. *Bread Sculpture* (fig. 6) produces a masterfully witty equation between poverty and voice. Joining an image of silencing (having one's lips sewn shut) with a symbol of basic sustenance, this deceptively simple work speaks to the difficulty of gaining political, social, and economic clout when all one's energies are directed toward maintaining basic needs (i.e., getting enough "bread" to survive). *Globe of the U.S.* is one of many works by Wojnarowicz using maps as a symbol of boundaries that are psychological, economic, and ideological, rather than simply geological, in

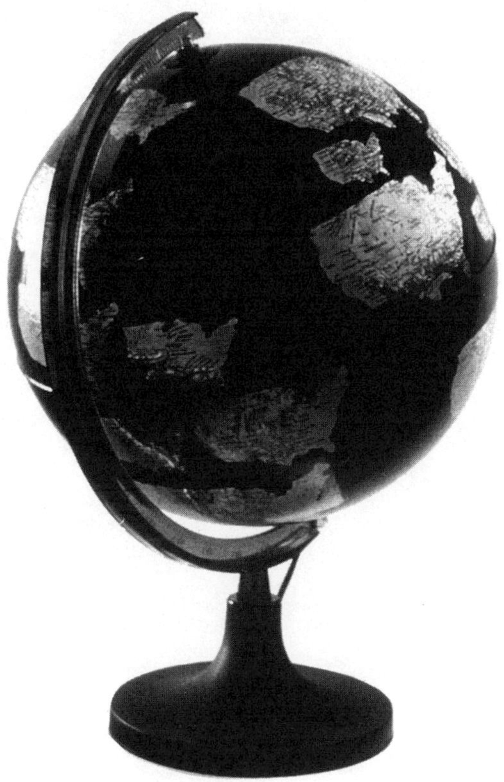

FIG. 7. David Wojnarowicz, *Globe of the U.S.*, 1990.
Collage on globe with working lamp, 41 cm high × 30 cm diameter
(16 in. high × 12 in. diameter). Estate of the artist.
Courtesy of the Estate of David Wojnarowicz
and P.P.O.W., New York. Photo: Michael Sarver.

nature (figs. 7, 8). Scattering maps of the United States all over a globe, he creates a powerful reminder of "one tribe" thinking and of the colonialistic urge to repress and conquer whatever is foreign and different. This work speaks to the homogenization of world cultures by a single (Western/capitalist/Christian) ideology. It proposes a social, political, and economic geography that overrides the literal geographical and cultural boundaries we were taught as children. The transgression of boundaries was both a matter of psychological and imaginative space, and an issue of practical, real-life concern for Wojnarowicz:

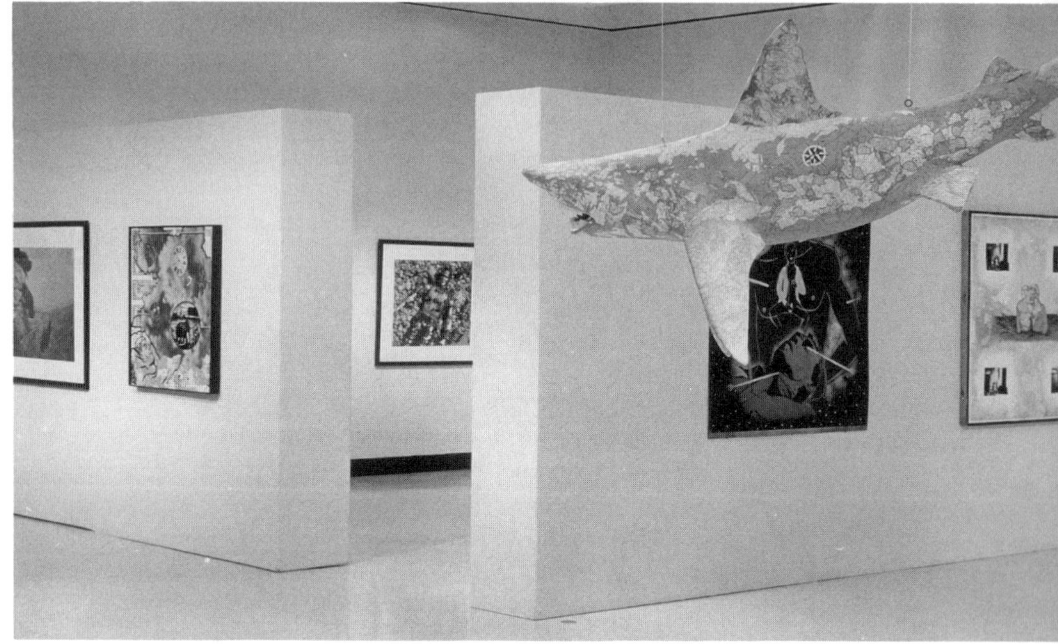

FIG. 8. Installation view, "David Wojnarowicz: Tongues of Flame," University Galleries, Illinois State University, Normal, January 23–March 4, 1990. Foreground: *Untitled (Shark)*, 1984.
Acrylic and collage on fiberglass, 130×56×66 cm (51×22×26 in.). Private collection. Courtesy of the Estate of David Wojnarowicz and P.P.O.W., New York. Photo: Anna Maria Watkin.

I'll use pre-printed material in order to illustrate something of the structure behind those . . . materials. . . . the concept of the map is contingent on people accepting that this is what landmasses look like from some point in outer space. Most people will never have that experience of being in outer space and yet they accept as a given that this is what the world looks like, they don't stop to think that the borders are really psychic things rather than actual physical things. . . . You can think of the map as a metaphor for government—that this is what the world looks like, this is who you are, this is your job, this is how things have to run, etc. . . . You question structures and you're suddenly in a minority and there's nothing as frightening as finding yourself a minority in a hostile environment. By ripping the map into pieces suddenly I've erased all these borders and I've completely joined opposing governments. It's a metaphor for a sense of groundlessness and anarchy.[41]

Untitled (Genet) (fig. 2) is the artist's homage to the French novelist and playwright Jean Genet, with whom he shared a common identity as a homosexual, and as an artist who lived on the fringes of "normal" society. Wojnarowicz saw Genet's *Un chant d'amour* in 1974, and the play's impact on him was such that it "confirmed that one could transcend society's hatred of diversity and loathing of homosexuals." In the same year he "read burroughs and others and realized clearly what american society had been suppressing beneath its skin—realized that had I seen some of these people or their work as a teenager I would have been more easily able to get off the streets without the national guilt on my shoulders."[42] In the small Xerox collage of appropriated imagery, the haloed figure of Genet is shown in the foreground, while behind him is the cavernous interior of what looks like a bombed-out church. Fluttering in the upper left are winged angels, and below a comic-book warrior aims a flaming machine gun toward the ceiling. In an altarlike alcove over Genet's right shoulder hangs a framed image of Christ wearing a crown of thorns, a syringe in his forearm and a rubber tube wrapped around his bicep, pulled tight by his teeth. This detail of *Untitled (Genet)* was seen by millions of people, since it was distributed by the AFA (in their newspaper advertisement and fundraising brochure), Dana Rohrabacher, and in the weekly publication *Human Events*. Rohrabacher's written interpretation of the image said that it was "a depiction of Jesus Christ shooting heroin." The AFA's cropped version of the work was captioned "Jesus depicted as a drug addict," and elsewhere in their anti-NEA advertisement it was described as "a photo of Christ in the process of injecting drugs into his arm using a needle and a syringe." Wojnarowicz's detractors automatically labeled the image as "anti-Christian" and "blasphemous." A bit of unbiased thought could just as easily have led to the conclusion that, projected into the twentieth century (Genet was born in 1909), Christ, in taking on the sufferings of mankind, would be confronted with drug (and other) addictions. The Christ image is a small element in the whole scene, a minor metaphor in a work that is really about Wojnarowicz's identification with Genet and the playwright's search for meaning in a life of contradiction and adversity. Since the work's main figure—Genet—was never correctly identified by them (even though his name is in the title), it is obvious that Rohrabacher and Wildmon made no attempt to understand and convey Wojnarowicz's intended meaning. Or perhaps they did understand it, and the full meaning of the work didn't suit their purpose, which was to suggest to constituents and supporters that *Untitled (Genet)* was a direct attack on Christianity. Informed of the figure's correct identity when he mistook it for a self-portrait of Wojnarowicz, Rohrabacher said that his opinion was not altered, because what was important was the initial reaction of a viewer: "You see Jesus Christ shooting heroin and a self-portrait of the artist with a halo. . . . That itself suggests that it shouldn't be getting government funds to have that kind of an attack on Christianity."[43]

An area of great importance, and one that has received surprisingly little discussion, is the relationship between literacy (particularly, visual literacy) and the need to censor images. Use of the term visual literacy here extends beyond the academic practice of decoding the formal elements of art and principles of design, referring more broadly to the ability to extrapolate (and in turn, communicate) a wide range of metaphors and statements from the images, symbols, *and* formal devices of art, and to interpret them in ways that relate to the life of the individual and of the society about which they comment. Wojnarowicz aspired to and often attained the admittedly idealistic goal of offering us an ever larger and sharper "mirror of society" through his art. At the same time an increasingly conservative, vocal, and politically influential segment of society either lacks, or wants to squelch, the broader view of cultural literacy required to understand and accept his poetic criticism and analysis. It can be assumed either that conservative leaders like Helms, Wildmon, and Rohrabacher know that they are stripping the poetry from Wojnarowicz's work by erasing its context or that they suffer from extreme ignorance and are incapable of understanding the artist's use of metaphor and symbol. It would be easy to explain and dismiss such actions as ignorance, but it is more likely true, as Carol Jacobsen says, that the religious Right and ultraconservatives "are not demonstrating visual illiteracy when they look at a flag and name it 'freedom,' or an image of sexual pleasure or desire for anyone other than straight-arrow white males and name it 'porn,' or a fetus and name it 'murder.' Their strategy is a calculated offensive meant to buttress the masculinist power structure—and not coincidentally to help get their candidates reelected."[44]

It no doubt helps the conservative cause when its leaders take what they see and hear in contemporary art and music very literally, and then promote such limited readings among their constituents. In this way the poetry, metaphor, and constructive social comment of artists like Wojnarowicz can be completely lost on hundreds of thousands of people. In their misinterpretations of Wojnarowicz's art, Helms, Rohrabacher, and Wildmon have expressed outrage at its "nihilistic," "degenerate," "anti-Christian," and "morally offensive" character. They sense, and rightly so, that the intent of Wojnarowicz's work is not to shock, but to empower—to give speech to previously dispossessed members of society and to decentralize the moral voice of church and state. As always, the most effective way to keep ideas away from people is not just to burn their books, but to convince them that they should not learn how to read in the first place.

Speaking to the issue of cultural politics just prior to the 1992 presidential election, David Ross, director of New York's Whitney Museum of American Art, said:

> . . . the greatest crisis we face as a country is a lack of educational opportunities sufficient to produce not merely productive citizens but *functionally enlightened* populations. Nearly all the subsidiary problems we face today, from homelessness to addiction to the monstrous forms of intolerance and divisiveness that we associate with reactionary forms of religious and ethnic bigotry, result directly from our comprehensive national crisis in education. . . . The questions that need to be addressed first are: In whose interest is this ongoing educational crisis maintained? And, what can we as individuals do about it?[45]

Since the advent of nonnarrative, modernist abstraction, the public, educated or not, has expressed suspicion and doubt about the meanings and intentions of "high" art in general. As Francine Carraro and Christoph Zuschlag have pointed out in their respective examinations (in this book) of modern art in the McCarthy era and "degenerate" art in Hitler's Germany, these suspicions spring from fear of what might be hidden in a work of art. Calculated promotions of the "evil" nature of artworks have convinced masses of people to distrust artists in the past, and no doubt continue to do so today.

These attitudes are to be expected in a society whose leaders place little emphasis on cultural education and who attempt to limit access to the diverse ideas that have always been expressed by artists. The antidote to censorship is discussion, not only about political or art issues, but about education that promotes visual and cultural literacy. To even begin looking at the problem, however, it is obvious that the smoke screen of censorship based on moral grounds must be cleared from the scene. When subjected only to literal or formal readings, art simply is not art. Or to put it differently, the real art of an artist's work depends upon the possibility of interpretation; where interpretation is limited, whether by ignorance, repression, or overt acts of censorship, so is art. Selective editing and unrepresentative selection severely limit or prevent interpretation of an artist's work, and thus are insidious forms of censorship. Many passive forms of censorship do exist and are reinforced from within educational institutions. In the public schools, there is an unwritten but self-enforced taboo against presenting and discussing nudity, sexuality, and controversial social or political content in art. Generally, university art education departments are among the most conservative in terms of the range of artworks and real-world issues they encourage future teachers to deal with. The whole history and the contemporary function of visual art would seem to be of paramount interest to them, but on the whole, programs in art education offer little instruction in integrating historical *or* contemporary art issues with effective classroom teaching strategies.[46] Often due to funding constraints, but just as often guided by the misconception that the arts are frivolous and thus expendable, elementary and secondary schools continue to place arts education at the bottom of a long list of priorities.

Another barrier to a more widespread understanding of contemporary art lies in the art marketplace itself, where public education about artistic meaning is a moot point as long as the work is moving, and "diversity" is often just another trend to be co-opted for economic gain. With their sound-bite mentality, popular print and electronic media only add to the possibility of censorship by picking up on and amplifying a sensationalized spectacle of obscenity. Although many fine analyses of the situation have appeared in specialized journals and on PBS (a company whose government funding Senator Helms has recently argued against), the mainstream media has more often than not discussed only those images and issues brought to their attention by the offended, keeping many readers and viewers ignorant about the underlying causes and implications of censorship in contemporary society. The works of artists like Wojnarowicz, Mapplethorpe, and Serrano have too often been examined in the popular press in relation to their opposition to "standards of decency," or in relation to the issue of government arts funding, and not in terms of the lives of the artists themselves, or the broad poetic analysis they offer. Similarly, the congressional debates about NEA reauthorization and appropriations have generally focused on the rhetoric of the controversy itself or on the NEA's track record, with little or no time spent exploring the intentions of the artists. To suggest that politicians, conservative or otherwise, are not art scholars and thus have no business discussing the meanings of artworks is to maintain the same separation that has long existed between artists and society at large. If art is to be debated in the American political arena (as it has been since 1988), the language of art needs to be more clearly recognized and understood by our elected officials. Turning either the interpretation or the defense of contemporary art over to "experts" or "specialists" reinforces Edward Said's declaration: "The particular mission of the humanities is, in the aggregate, to represent *noninterference* in the affairs of the everyday world. . . . Instead of noninterference and specialization, there must be *interference*, a crossing of borders and obstacles, a determined attempt to generalize exactly at those points where generalizations seem impossible to make."[47] In that sense, we have much to learn from Wojnarowicz, and by extension (if we can briefly forgive the results of their censorial actions) from Helms and Wildmon. It is precisely because they "interfered" in each other's specialized fields that the socially enforced boundaries separating art and religion, anarchy and morality, and homosexuality and Christianity were shown to be more permeable than we thought.

Perhaps the most important thing that can be said about controversies surrounding the work of Wojnarowicz and other artists against whom censorship has recently been practiced is that, for most people, the "controversy" subsides in direct proportion to the amount of information they have about these artists and their work. More (and less-restricted) speech about these challenging images clearly defuses controversy and fear of the "other." But as any cultural worker will confirm, the present atmosphere of censorship and self-censorship makes it more difficult than usual to convey to audiences accurate information about potentially controversial artworks.

Wojnarowicz put forth a great challenge, difficult, but as he demonstrated, certainly not impossible: Do we maintain our own repressive silences or do we begin to communicate openly and honestly about what we know our world to be? Do we continue to fear those different from ourselves, or do we cross predetermined boundaries and begin to accept diversity? The artist's own words offer us a succinct and poetic analysis of the conditions of, and perhaps the antidote to, censorship in our time:

> I found giant bird nests I could only assume were made by eagles, or maybe that was only a matter of perspective, given that I was once small in size, and when you're small in size things look monumental, and as you grow older things look less monumental, and things looking less monumental doesn't always have to do with vision, it can be affected by thought processes, and analysis. As I grow older my father looks less monumental both because he's dead . . and because I can see and understand a little better his humanity, and his demons. And he looks less monumental because I speak of him, and I bring the fear-charged

memories of him outside my head. Sound is so interesting this way. Words are so interesting this way. Words can strip the power from a memory or an event—words can cut the ropes of an experience. . . . Describing the once indescribable can dismantle the power of taboo. To speak about the once unspeakable can make the invisible familiar, if repeated often enough in clear and loud tones.[48]

NOTES

When an earlier version of this paper was presented at the College Art Association annual conference in 1991, I was assistant director/curator at University Galleries of Illinois State University, where Barry Blinderman had organized "David Wojnarowicz: Tongues of Flame." I would like to thank David Wojnarowicz, Barry Blinderman, and Elizabeth Childs for their help in refining the ideas presented here. This essay is dedicated to the memory of David Wojnarowicz.

1. David Wojnarowicz, "Postcards from America: X-Rays from Hell," *Witnesses: Against Our Vanishing*, exh. cat. (New York: Artists Space, 1989), 10–11. The phrases "pre-invented world" and "one tribe nation" occur throughout the artist's writing, as he constantly pointed out the confining parameters of life as he witnessed it.

2. Senate Report 300, submitted by Senator Claiborne Pell, Committee on Labor and Human Resources, to accompany S.1483, 1965. The NEA and NEH were established with the National Foundation on the Arts and Humanities Act of 1965 (Public Law 89-209). The report continues: "The committee wishes to make clear that conformity for its own sake is not to be encouraged, and that no undue preference should be given to any particular style or school of thought or expression."

3. Wojnarowicz was a prolific writer. His books include: *Sounds in the Distance* (London: Aloes Books, 1982), foreword by William S. Burroughs; *In the Shadow of Forward Motion* (New York: PPOW Gallery, 1982), introduction by Felix Guattari; "Postcards from America: X-Rays from Hell," in *Witnesses: Against Our Vanishing*, exh. cat. (New York: Artists Space, 1989); *David Wojnarowicz: Tongues of Flame*, exh. cat. with six essays by Wojnarowicz (Normal: University Galleries of Illinois State University, 1990); *Close to the Knives: A Memoir of Disintegration* (New York: Random House/Vintage Books, 1991); *Memories That Smell Like Gasoline* (San Francisco: Artspace Books, 1992).

4. Wojnarowicz died of AIDS-related illnesses on July 22, 1992. For background information, see David Wojnarowicz, "Biographical Dateline," and the chapters "Exhibitions" and "Bibliography," in *David Wojnarowicz: Tongues of Flame*, 113–25. See also C. Carr, "Portrait of the Artist in the Age of AIDS," *Village Voice*, February 13, 1990, 31–36.

5. The exhibition "David Wojnarowicz: Tongues of Flame" was organized by Barry Blinderman at University Galleries of Illinois State University, Normal. The exhibi-

tion and a 128-page catalogue were produced with the assistance of funding from the Paul Anderson Foundation and the National Endowment for the Arts. The exhibition was shown at the following places and times: University Galleries, Illinois State University, January 23–March 4, 1990; Santa Monica Museum of Art, July 27–September 5, 1990; Exit Art, New York, November 17, 1990–January 5, 1991; Temple and Tyler Galleries, Temple University, Philadelphia, February 1–March 2, 1991.

6. Dana Rohrabacher from material he distributed to members of Congress, February 20, 1990. Printed on Rohrabacher's congressional stationery and entitled "The National Endowment for the Arts is at it Again! Again!" the sheet was in the form of a letter to colleagues. Rohrabacher called it "our NEA decency quiz." It contained four brief, noninterpretative statements (for example, "A depiction of Jesus Christ shooting heroin," and "Explicit photographs of homosexual, anal sodomy") about selected portions of works by Wojnarowicz, and included a partial image of Wojnarowicz's *Untitled (Genet)*, 1979.

7. "Establishment of a National Foundation on the Arts and Humanities," *Congressional Record–Senate*, sec. 4(c), March 10, 1965, 4596.

8. Lyndon B. Johnson, "Statement on the Proposed National Foundation on the Arts and Humanities, March 10, 1965," *Public Papers of the Presidents of the United States* (Washington, D.C.: U.S. Government Printing Office, 1966), 273.

9. Representative Broomfield, *Congressional Record–House*, September 15, 1965, 23942.

10. Representative Frelinghuysen, *Congressional Record–House*, August 20, 1964, 20650.

11. A 1989 amendment to the Appropriations Bill for the Department of the Interior and Related Agencies, written by Helms and passed by the Senate as H.R. 2788 on July 26, 1989, proposed: "None of the funds authorized to be appropriated pursuant to this Act may be used to promote, disseminate, or produce—1) obscene or indecent materials, including but not limited to depictions of sadomasochism, homoeroticism, the exploitation of children, or individuals engaged in sex acts; or 2) material which denigrates the objects or beliefs of the adherents of a particular religion or nonreligion; or 3) material which denigrates, debases, or reviles a person, group, or class of citizens on the basis of race, creed, sex, handicap, age, or national origin." After much debate, a compromise amendment (no. 143) was passed by both the House and Senate in October 1989: "None of the funds authorized to be appropriated for the National Endowment for the Arts or the National Endowment for the Humanities may be used to promote, disseminate, or produce materials which in the judgment of the National Endowment for the Arts or the National Endowment for the Humanities may be considered obscene, including but not limited to depictions of sadomasochism, homoeroticism, the sexual exploitation of children, or individuals engaged in sex acts and which, taken as a whole, do not have serious literary, artistic, political or scientific value." On September 19, 1991, the Senate passed an amendment authored by Senator Helms which would prohibit the NEA from using funds "to pro-

mote, disseminate or produce materials that depict or describe, in a patently offensive way, sexual or excretory activities or organs." The restrictive language was struck down in the House on October 24 and in the Senate on October 31, 1991. For more information on Helms's 1991 proposed amendment see Philip Davis, "Appropriations," *Congressional Quarterly Weekly Report*, September 14, 21, October 12, 19, 26, and November 2, 1991.

12. See Bruce Selcraig, "Reverend Wildmon's War on the Arts," *New York Times Magazine*, September 2, 1990, 22–25, 43, 52–53. The AFA is a conservative "watchdog" group based in Tupelo, Mississippi.

13. Hans Haacke, "In the Vice," *Art Journal*, Fall 1991, 53.

14. Wojnarowicz, "Biographical Dateline," *David Wojnarowicz: Tongues of Flame*, 117.

15. Ibid.

16. Andrew Norris, "Fire and Pain," *Nassau Weekly*, February 7, 1991.

17. David Deitcher, "Ideas and Emotions," *Artforum*, May 1989, 125.

18. Carol Jacobsen, "Redefining Censorship: A Feminist View," *Art Journal*, Winter 1991, 42.

19. Wojnarowicz, in Stephen Salisbury, "A Brush with Outrage," *Philadelphia Inquirer*, July 17, 1990, 4E.

20. See William Honan, "Andres Serrano: Contradictions in Life and Work," *New York Times*, August 16, 1989, 22. See also Judith Tannenbaum, "Robert Mapplethorpe: The Philadelphia Story," *Art Journal*, Winter 1990, 71–76. The work of Andres Serrano was brought to the attention of Helms when it was included in the "Awards in the Visual Arts" exhibition series at the Southeastern Center for Contemporary Art, Winston-Salem, North Carolina, which had received partial funding from the NEA. "Robert Mapplethorpe: The Perfect Moment" was organized in 1988 by the Institute of Contemporary Art at the University of Pennsylvania, Philadelphia, with partial funding from the NEA. For a more detailed analysis, see the essay by Steven Dubin in this volume. See also Elizabeth Hess, "Mapplethorpe Goes to Washington," *Village Voice*, August 8, 1989, 27–30.

21. According to *Webster's New World Dictionary*, a censor is "an official with the power to examine publications, movies, television programs, etc. and to remove or prohibit anything considered obscene, libelous, politically objectionable, etc." Any definition of censorship is fraught with questions open to a variety of interpretations: Who is to be the "official"? What is the means of "examination"? How are "obscene," "libelous," or "politically objectionable" defined? Who decides what meets these criteria?

22. Joyce Hanson, "The Rage of David Wojnarowicz," *New City (Chicago)*, February 1, 1990, 7.

23. Elizabeth Hess, "It *Is* Political: Jesse Helms' Nightmare," *Village Voice*, November 28, 1989, 117. See also Elizabeth Hess, "Frohnmayer's Normal Waterloo?" *Village Voice*, December 12, 1989, 69.

24. Hanson, "The Rage of David Wojnarowicz," 7.

25. Hess, "It *Is* Political: Jesse Helms' Nightmare," 117.

26. Nichols Fox, "An Orderly Demise?" *New Art Examiner*, January 1992, 21. On February 21, 1992, Frohnmayer was forced to resign his post as NEA chairman, directly following (then presidential nomination challenger) Patrick Buchanan's TV ad criticizing President Bush for supporting the NEA. This ad cited NEA funding of filmmaker Marlon Riggs's *Tongues Untied*, which portrayed the experiences of black gay men. Bush replaced Frohnmayer with Dr. Anne-Imelda Radice, who in her first month as NEA chair vetoed two grants that had passed both the peer review panel and the National Council. She also demanded that a project that had received funding the previous year remove any notice of NEA support from its press and documentary materials. For more information on these events, see "Newsbriefs," *New Art Examiner*, April, June 1992; Bill Lichtenstein, "The Secret Battle for the NEA," *Village Voice*, March 10, 1992, 35–37; "Front Page," *Art in America*, July 1992, 27–28; and Mark Alice Durant, "Art and Politics I," *Art in America*, July 1992, 31–35.

27. David Wojnarowicz, "Postcards from America: X-Rays from Hell," *Witnesses: Against Our Vanishing*, 10.

28. Paul Mattick, "Arts and the State," *The Nation*, October 1, 1990, 356.

29. "New subscribers can receive *Human Events* weekly for $30 per year—$10 off the normal subscription rate. Write: Human Events, 422 First St., S.E., Washington, D.C. 20003. And indicate that you are a member of the American Family Association." *Human Events*, February 24, 1990. With the heading "How You Can Stay Informed," an order form for the AFA Journal and a solicitation for donations was printed at the lower right of the AFA's full-page anti-NEA advertisement in *USA Today*, March 28, 1990. An identical advertisement appeared in the *Washington Times* on February 13, 1990.

30. Brochure showing fourteen partial images selected and cropped from seven works by Wojnarowicz: *Untitled (Genet)*, 1979; *Bad Moon Rising*, 1989; *Sex Series (for Marion Schemama)*, 1988; *Delta Towels*, 1983; *Water*, 1987; *Rimbaud Masturbating* (from the *Rimbaud* series), 1978–79; and one video still from *ITSOFOMO Grid*, a thirty-image document of a Wojnarowicz performance at The Kitchen, New York City, 1989.

31. Elizabeth Hess, "Wojnarowicz to Sue Reverend Wildmon: Artist Doesn't Turn Other Cheek," *Village Voice*, May 22, 1990.

32. Carole S. Vance, "The War on Culture," *Art in America*, September 1989, 41.

33. Paula Span, "Judge Blocks Anti-NEA Pamphlet," *Washington Post*, June 26, 1990, D1, D4.

34. "David Wojnarowicz v. American Family Association and Donald E. Wildmon," *West's Federal Supplement, v. 745* (St. Paul: West Publishing Co., 1991), 130–49.

35. Unpublished letter from Rev. Donald E. Wildmon on AFA stationery. With the word "Correction" at top, the letter reads,

"On April 12, 1990, we mailed you a pamphlet entitled 'Your Tax Dollars Helped

Pay For These Works Of Art.' It included fourteen images and stated that 'The photographs appearing on this sheet were part of the David Wojnarowicz Tongues of Flame exhibit catalogue.'

This correction is to advise you that the images were not reproductions of complete works of Mr. Wojnarowicz. They were fragments or parts of larger artworks and do not constitute the entire work from which they were reproduced. This correction has been sent to you pursuant to the New York Artists Authorship Rights Act by order of a United States District Court."

36. "David Wojnarowicz v. American Family Association and Donald E. Wildmon," *West's Federal Supplement, v. 745*, 143.

37. Robert Atkins, "Scene & Heard," *Village Voice*, November 12, 1991, 105. I became aware of the continued distribution of the AFA's brochure when an Illinois State University professor informed me that a former student had received materials about Wojnarowicz from the AFA. Upon receiving copies of these materials (from the former student), I discovered that the brochure received was identical to the one the AFA had been ordered to cease distributing, and contacted Jonathan Olsoff, a lawyer who had worked on Wojnarowicz's case. According to Olsoff, in a meeting between himself, co-counsel Kathryn Barrett, Wildmon, and Judge Connor, Wildmon admitted that the copies most recently distributed were being kept for the AFA's archives, and were mistakenly sent out with requests for other material.

38. From a performance by Wojnarowicz on January 23, 1990, at University Galleries of Illinois State University, Normal. Later revised by the artist, this narrative appears in "Do Not Doubt the Dangerousness of the 12-Inch Politician," in his *Close to the Knives: A Memoir of Disintegration*.

39. Lucy Lippard, "Out of the Safety Zone," *Art in America*, December 1990, 136.

40. Gara Lamarche and William Rubenstein, "The Love That Dare Not Speak," *The Nation*, November 5, 1990, 524.

41. Wojnarowicz, in Barry Blinderman, "The Compression of Time: An Interview with David Wojnarowicz," *David Wojnarowicz: Tongues of Flame*, 61.

42. Wojnarowicz, "Biographical Dateline," *David Wojnarowicz: Tongues of Flame*, 117.

43. Allan Parachini, "Edited Photos Fueling NEA Confrontation," *Los Angeles Times*, April 25, 1990, F1, F6.

44. Jacobsen, "Redefining Censorship: A Feminist View," *Art Journal*, 42.

45. David Ross, in "Art and Politics: A Pre-Election Symposium," *Art in America*, October 1992, 42.

46. There are, of course, some more and less progressive programs. These statements are, perhaps, extreme generalizations, but they are based on my experiences as an undergraduate student in an art education program and as a graduate student in a studio program, both in public liberal arts institutions. At either institution I do not recall being presented with artworks identified as being made by a homosexual or

lesbian artist, or ever discussing strategies for presenting politically or sexually charged images to students I was being prepared to teach.

47. Edward Said, "Opponents, Audiences, Constituencies, and Community," *Critical Inquiry*, September 1982, 22, 24.

48. From a performance by Wojnarowicz on January 23, 1990, at University Galleries, Illinois State University. Later revised by the artist, this narrative appears in "Do Not Doubt the Dangerousness of the 12-Inch Politician," in Wojnarowicz, *Close to the Knives: A Memoir of Disintegration*, 150.

The Trials of Robert Mapplethorpe

STEVEN C. DUBIN

ONCE ARTISTS FINISH THEIR WORK, it is largely out of their control. To put it another way, artworks are *never* completed—they are continually reinterpreted and reevaluated by successive publics. Acceptance and rejection alternate in cycles, so that artists' intentions are only one factor contributing to the reception of anything they produce. Viewers project their anxieties and concerns onto a work of art much like subjects taking the Rorschach test see different things in the inkblots. In so doing, the audience reveals a great deal about the social contours of the times.

Critic Arthur C. Danto was shortsighted when he made the following remark after encountering a Robert Mapplethorpe self-portrait showing the photographer with a bullwhip inserted into his anus: "*It would be known in advance* that such an image would challenge, assault, provoke, dismay—with the hope that in some way consciousness would be transformed."[1] He failed to recognize that the same image might amuse or excite viewers—or confirm already established attitudes. And who can foretell what the reaction of future audiences will be: boredom, aversion, curiosity, repugnance? Danto may have recorded his own reaction accurately, but his response hardly exhausts the possibilities.

Robert Mapplethorpe's life was once summed up as "the middle of a contradiction—part altar boy and part leather bar."[2] At the early stages of his career he turned his creative eye to the fast-lane gay society of the 1970s and early 1980s, in which he was himself an active participant. Mapplethorpe captured a sense of post-Stonewall exuberance that pushed sexual frontiers—before the onset of the AIDS crisis. In the 1990s his images have become elegies to a lost world.

After his first gallery show in 1976, Mapplethorpe quickly became known for his work in three classic genres: male and female nudes, still lifes, and celebrity portraits. There is a cool, detached formality to Mapplethorpe's images, even when the subject matter is emotionally loaded. Much of his work is sexually charged, and a sense of fragile beauty, the inevitability of mortality, and even innocence runs through various photographs. He both anthropomorphized flowers into figures brimming with erotic power and objectified his human models. The title of his disputed exhibition "The Perfect Moment" reflects this attempt to capture the apex of beauty before decay commences.

Several "generations" of critics arose in response to Mapplethorpe's work. One of the most consistent points of dissension was that his work was overaestheticized. According to Mapplethorpe, "I don't think there's that much difference between a photograph of a fist up someone's ass and a photograph of carnations in a bowl."[3] But to many eyes this became boring and tedious, an approach that was all surface and no substance. In Donald Kuspit's estimation, there was "a hot emotional point to the cool visual tale Mapplethorpe tells,"[4] but one that largely was glossed over, sometimes in elaborate custom-designed frames incorporating mirrors and expensive fabrics. Some lamented the lack of moral evaluation in this body of work, comparing its "rhetoric of artifice" to fascist aesthetics.[5] Yet even his detractors conceded that Mapplethorpe was a serious artist, and his work became ordinary and acceptable as it became more well known within the art world: "Elegance spoils it as pornography," one critic remarked, "and avidity wrecks it as fashion."[6]

Mapplethorpe was also cited for the possible racist implications of his image making. One reviewer indicted him for removing his black models to a hermetic environment, thus cloaking the troubled history of race relations in the United States. But another felt that by placing black men on pedestals and highlighting the sensualness of their skin, Mapplethorpe subverted the racial hierarchy.[7]

"Thomas and Dovanna" (1987) embodies the prototypical white racist nightmare: a naked, muscular black man dances with a white woman clothed in a white gown, dipping her as she follows his lead. But was the photographer demolishing or confirming the cliché here? "Man in Polyester Suit" (1980) was routinely reproached for underscoring racial stereotypes of black men as hypersexed. The photograph shows a black man in a three-piece suit, the image cropped at about midchest and above the knee. In startling contrast is his imposing penis, heavily dangling from his unzipped pants. One possible reaction picks up the inherent humor and absurdity of the situation: it could be confronting racist assumptions by exposing them in a comical way. But according to another reading, this is a racist image itself.

The multivalence of Mapplethorpe's creations spawned dilemmas for some members of the gay community, particularly gays who are African American. What should they do if they found explicit sexuality (especially sadomasochism) offensive or the racial associations unsettling? If gays broke ranks and publicly criticized the photographs, their confreres could judge them to be an insidious third column, betraying the cause and playing into the hands of anti-gay foes. Nonetheless, some gays *were* troubled by these images.

For example, Essex Hemphill, a black gay man, argued that Mapplethorpe exploited and objectified black men by focusing on body parts, a practice reminiscent of assessing the work potential of slaves: "This blindness allows white males to pursue their sexual fantasies about black males without ever actually entering a ghetto, a jail, or a black man's shoes, or a black man's bad day to see if he feels like stripping down for aesthetic and/or erotic reasons."[8]

Such appraisals from people generally identifying themselves as political progressives were somewhat unusual in the initial stages of the Mapplethorpe controversy. But dissenting opinions increased over time, the fissures *within* certain embattled groups becoming as manifest as the gaps between them and their confirmed adversaries.

Kobena Mercer, another black, gay critic, continues to revise his own judgment of this work, declaring that "[Mapplethorpe's] images can elicit a homophobic reading as easily as a homoerotic one, can confirm a racist reading as much as produce an antiracist one."[9] His stance underscores the fact that there is not a monolithic black or gay view, but black and gay communi*ties* endorsing opinions of every political stripe.

Critics who are not gay have also registered their disapproval. The sexual orientation of a critic is relevant only if it appears to jaundice one's opinion. Danto cites, for example, "the perfect male nude, viewed from the rear—from its vulnerable side. . . ."[10] What an odd comment given the vulnerability of the naked male both fore and aft, except when considered in the context of the fear of sexual violation through penetration, a fear evidently heightened for this reviewer when he wrote about the depiction of homosexual desire.

In July 1989, in a home decorated with religious and nature scenes, Senator Jesse Helms, Republican from North Carolina, showed his wife Dorothy a catalogue of "The Perfect Moment." She quickly put it down and cried out in dismay, "Lord have mercy, Jesse, I'm not believing this." What upset the domestic tranquility of the Helms household that day was the challenge inherent within Mapplethorpe's photographs to at least two important social hierarchies, sexual and racial. Helms directed particular outrage against images that broached both interracial and homoerotic themes: "There's a big difference between 'The Merchant of Venice' and a photograph of two males of different races [in an erotic pose] on a marble table top," he argued.[11]

A debate was enjoined by a new generation of cultural critics. Richard Grenier, writing in the *Washington Times*, rekindled biblical fury by labeling Mapplethorpe "the great catamite." In the same publication antipornography crusader Judith Reisman equated Mapplethorpe's image "Honey" with child abuse (also known as "Rosie," a young girl between three and four years of age ingenuously lifts her dress, thereby exposing her genitals), and accused Mapplethorpe of "photographically lynching" the man in the polyester suit.[12] But it was Patrick Buchanan who launched the most sustained attack in print through a series of venomous newspaper columns.

Buchanan detected a struggle for the soul of America in the battle over the arts. On one side was a small band of arts and gay rights radicals, out of touch with most of society, and suffering from "an infantile disorder."[13] They promoted filth and degradation in the guise of mediocre art, and a lifestyle that was suicidal (Mapplethorpe's death from AIDS). In Buchanan's view the goal of this new Kulturkampf was to overturn tradition and create a pagan society.[14] On the other side were the stalwart defenders of the good, the true, and the traditional, such as himself.

Some established art critics sounded a similar alarm in reviewing "The Perfect Moment." Hilton Kramer had characterized a "tamer" retrospective at the Whitney in 1988 as "this bizarre exhibition."[15] Adopting the role of guardian of aesthetic standards and of the public's morals, he now decried what he saw as Mapplethorpe's attempt to "force" the public to accept "loathsome" sexual values by publicly exhibiting images "designed to aggrandize and abet erotic rituals involving coercion, degradation, bloodshed and the infliction of pain."[16] In making such judgments from an elevated position, Kramer inevitably short-circuits the public's opportunity to draw independent, informed conclusions.

Kramer most frequently referred to pictures from the *X*, *Y*, and *Z* portfolios. The *Y* portfolio contained flower photos, moderating the *X* portfolio that chronicled sadomasochistic homosexual behavior, and the *Z* portfolio that featured the sexuality of black men. But in Connecticut at the Hartford

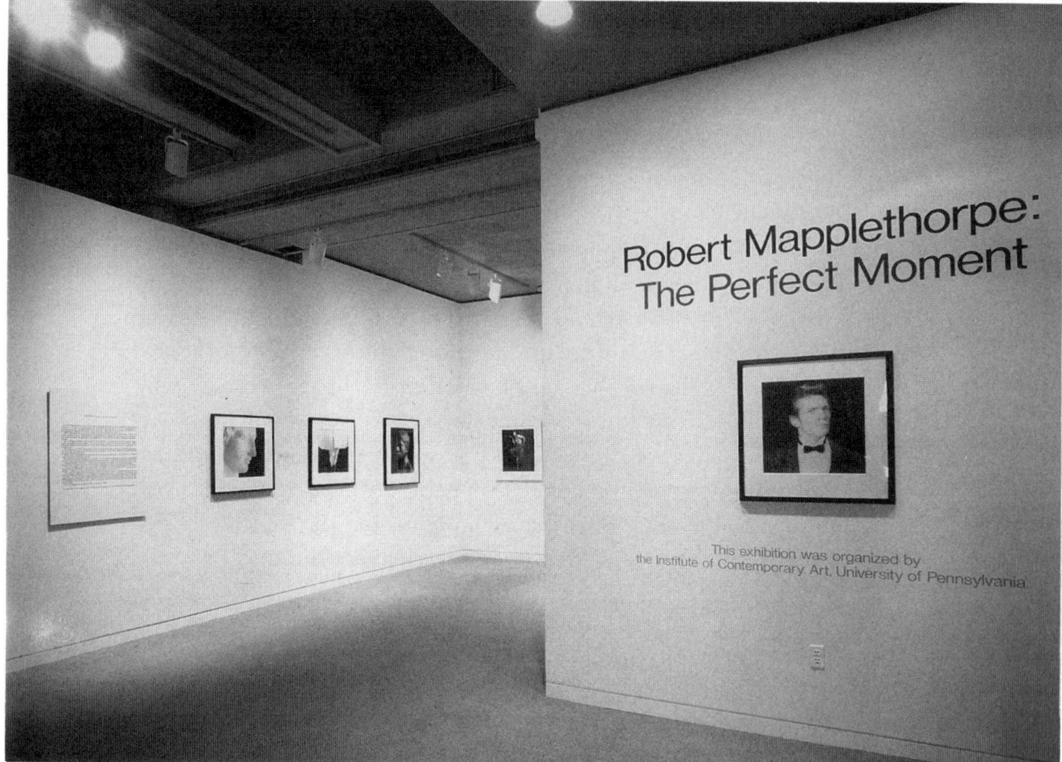

FIG. 1. Installation photograph of Robert Mapplethorpe, "The Perfect Moment," 1989.
Courtesy of Wadsworth Atheneum, Hartford, Connecticut.

Atheneum, for example, viewing these images was strictly a matter of choice. A separate admisson was charged at the museum's entrance, and the exhibit was shown in a series of upstairs galleries (fig. 1). There was no chance of accidentally stumbling into it, nor glimpsing any part of it in passing.

"The Perfect Moment" was scheduled for a tour of seven cities: Philadelphia, Chicago, Washington, D.C., Hartford, Berkeley, Cincinnati, and Boston. In Philadelphia and Chicago the show went largely unremarked, beyond generally amiable reviews. The next stop was Washington, D.C, and from there on the exhibit took on a controversial aura.

The range of reactions it evoked—from nonchalance to outrage to veneration—demonstrates that art and artists judged to be outlaws at one time and place can flourish elsewhere. To claim that Mapplethorpe's photographs were inherently scandalous misses an important point: for controversy to be activated, something must be added from the *outside*. This was more likely to occur once the photographs were subject to evaluation by people who were relatively unfamiliar with the contemporary art world, or by those who were automatically repelled by topics like homosexuality. Such opinions were the leavening which caused the conflict to rise.

The Corcoran Gallery of Art is the U.S. capital's oldest art museum, located just blocks from the White House. Engraved over an entrance is the motto "Dedicated to Art." It wasn't difficult to appreciate the irony of that epigram during the summer of 1989 when the museum canceled the Mapplethorpe exhibit at the eleventh hour.

On June 12, 1989, Director Christina Orr-Cahill announced that the heated political climate in Washington made it unwise for the Corcoran to host the Mapplethorpe retrospective. Vocal members of Congress were still steaming over government support of Andres Serrano's photograph "Piss Christ" with funds from the National Endowment for the Arts (NEA), and the Dread Scott affair a few months earlier (a student at the School of the Art Institute of Chicago had placed a U.S. flag on the floor as part of an installation piece) was fueling an explosion of official flag-waving that continued for the remainder of the summer.

Congressman Dick Armey, Republican from Texas, had collected one hundred signatures on a letter calling for a review of NEA procedures, and copies of "The Perfect Moment" catalogue were allegedly circulating in Congress. Orr-Cahill felt that the appearance of such controversial images in close proximity to Capitol Hill could jeopardize the NEA's future. The Corcoran was also vulnerable because it had no endowment of its own and depends on a federal program for a significant infusion of money.

Orr-Cahill defended her actions by saying, "I don't think there was censorship at all. The [show's catalogue] is out, the exhibit has been seen elsewhere and will be seen elsewhere. I think censorship would have been editing the show."[17] But many people took her to be naive at best, villainous at worst. Rather than squelching controversy, the Corcoran's director fanned the flames even higher.

The reaction of the artistic community was swift and creative. Three days after the cancellation was announced, up to one hundred protestors marched at the Corcoran in a demonstration coordinated by the D.C. Gay and Lesbian Activist Alliance, the National Gay and Lesbian Task Force, and Oppression Under Target (OUT).[18] On June 30, about one thousand demon-

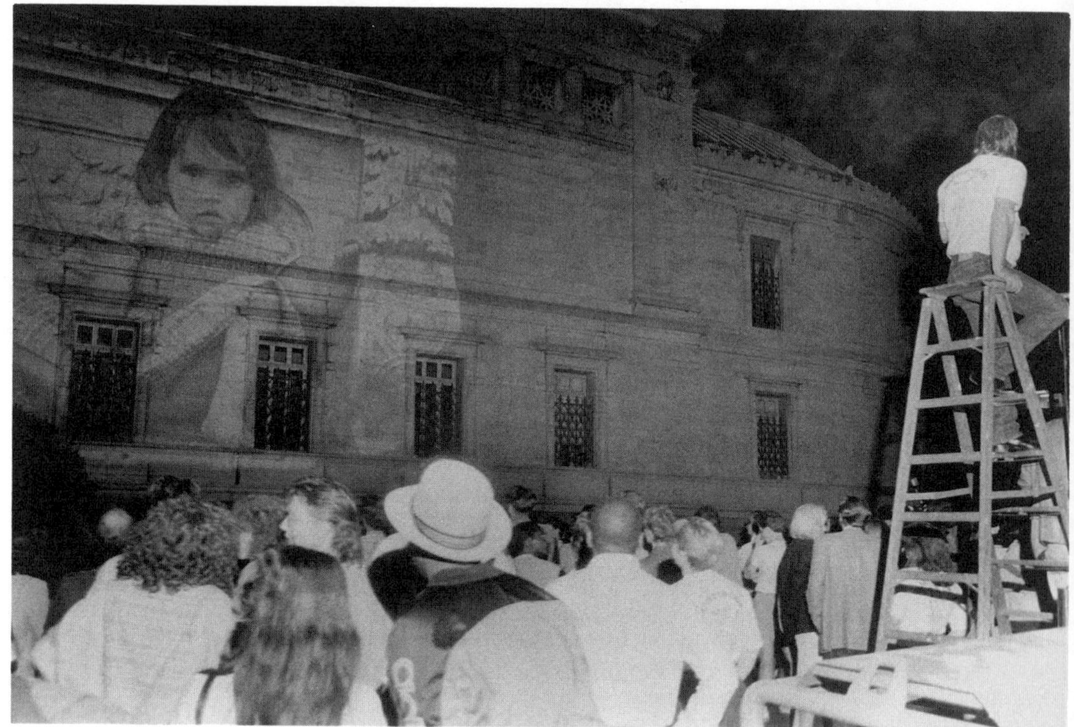

FIG. 2. Jim Marks, photograph of demonstration outside Corcoran Gallery of Art with projection of Robert Mapplethorpe's "Honey" [1976], June 30, 1989. Used by permission of Jim Marks.

strators witnessed an unconventional extension of the museum's walls when slides of Mapplethorpe's work were projected onto the Corcoran's facade (fig. 2).

Artists scheduled to exhibit at the Corcoran boycotted it, once they felt it had earned a reputation as an unpredictable and unreliable venue. Meanwhile, another institution—the small, artist-run Washington Project for the Arts (WPA)—stepped in as the new sponsor of the exhibit in the District of Columbia. A familiar pattern was established: publicity boosted attendance to nearly forty times normal.[19]

There was a conspicuous reluctance to rally around Mapplethorpe's sadomasochistic imagery at this time; it was simply too difficult for many people to come to terms with, especially on short notice. A series of similar incidents occurred before a public dialogue on antihomosexual bias began, either within the arts community or among the public at large.

Jesse Helms led the charge against art for five months in the summer and fall of 1989. His canny tactics kept his opponents dodging punches from several directions. He excelled at turning out memorable quotes: "If someone wants to write ugly nasty things on the men's room wall," he declared in a disparaging tone, "the taxpayers do not provide the crayons."[20]

Helms launched a three-pronged assault. His initial maneuver was a "sneak attack," bringing a measure attached to an appropriations bill to a voice vote when only a handful of senators were present. Known as the Helms amendment, it barred the use of federal funds to "promote, disseminate, or produce obscene or indecent materials, including but not limited to depictions of sadomasochism, homoeroticism, the exploitation of children, or individuals engaged in sexual acts; or material which denigrates the objects or beliefs of the adherents of a particular religion or nonreligion." It also cut $45,000 from the NEA's appropriation (an amount equal to the support for Seranno and the Mapplethorpe exhibit),[21] and proposed a five-year ban on the supporting institutions, the Southeastern Center for Contemporary Art (SECCA) and the Institute of Contemporary Art (ICA).

Helms deployed another strategem when a Senate and House Conference Committee was assembled to work out a compromise. He sent committee members a packet of Mapplethorpe photos: the children "Honey" and "Jesse McBride," as well as the man in the polyester suit and a picture of a penis perched upon a pedestal. On his scale of offensiveness, Helms rated these a "five" out of a possible ten.[22] But after the committee appeared to be leaning toward softening the bill, Helms requested that all the pages and the women ("ladies") leave the chamber so that he might show his colleagues the pictures. He hoped once again that a firsthand confrontation with the evidence would secure his victory. He was also vigilant to protect the sensibilities of those whom he believed might not be sufficiently robust, due to their age or gender, to tolerate such a visual assault.

Senator Helms's final tactic was to threaten to bring matters to a voice vote "so that whoever votes against it [the anti-obscenity clause] would be on record as favoring taxpayer funding for pornography."[23] Helms steered the debate in such a way that pornography—pro or con—was the main issue.

Helms's gambit had a mixed outcome: the conference committee eliminated the proposed five-year ban on SECCA and ICA, although it required the NEA to notify Congress before awarding any future grants to either institution.[24] It also prohibited federal funding of art that could be considered obscene, in accord with the 1973 Supreme Court decision *Miller v. California*. This was a relaxation from the original Helms proposal. *Miller* prescribes that three distinct tests must be met before the designation of obscenity applies; the vague notions of "indecency" and "denigration" were dropped from the bill.

Nevertheless, the arts community was not off the hook with this measure, the first content-specific restriction placed on the NEA. It was not completely clear who would apply the *Miller* test or where, even though under its principles the notion of "obscene art" is virtually an oxymoron. But the answers to these questions would soon be forthcoming.[25]

When "The Perfect Moment" moved from Washington to Hartford, and then to Berkeley, it enjoyed a momentary respite from notoriety. The large crowds continued and the peacefulness of the sojourn was maintained. It was a welcome lull: the reception in Cincinnati was to be vastly different.

Cincinnati was the major cultural center west of New York in the nineteenth century, and its leaders were convinced it was destined to become even more important as the country expanded. They grossly miscalculated. Post–Civil War growth in cities such as Chicago, Cleveland, and St. Louis elbowed out this city on the Ohio River, consigning it to a diminished role on the national stage. The arts did flourish there, however, from painting to literature, music to pottery. Many cultural institutions were established with nineteenth-century enthusiasm and wealth, leaving the city with a substantial legacy.[26]

The Contemporary Art Center, the host site, occupies a unique niche in the ecology of arts organizations in Cincinnati. It is the parvenu among the stodgy, nineteenth-century dowagers. According to CAC's (former) chief curator Jack Sawyer, "As a contemporary art museum, our mission is to be an outsider. . . . We haven't really collected objects, so that baggage is not on us. . . . We're alway seeking out art which doesn't have a place in the culture."[27] Even its locale is distinctive: it is housed above a Walgreen's Drug Store in downtown Cincinnati, part of a mercantile arcade where restaurants and shops link old structures with more modern ones.

Cincinnati's city fathers have taken advantage of its geographic location to rid it of the commercial sex industry: there are no X-rated movie theaters, video outlets, or bookstores in the city. Pornographic material is available for sale only across the river in Kentucky. Newport, Kentucky ("Sin City") has been a center of vice serving a tri-state area for decades. This marks a civic compartmentalizing of desire unmatched in other U.S. cities.

In recent times, a production of *Equus* was reviewed by the Cincinnati police before it was allowed on stage in 1989 (nudity had become a cause for concern). Religious organizations effectively blocked *The Last Temptation of Christ* from being screened until fourteen months after its release,[28] and *Hair*, *Oh! Calcutta*, and the Playboy Channel have all run into opposition. Cincinnati is also the place where Larry Flynt was convicted on obscenity charges for his magazine *Hustler*. But, as Peter Lefcourt pointedly posed the question in his satirical novel *The Dreyfus Affair*, "How could you trust a city with no hookers or X-rated movie houses? What did people do with their baser instincts?"[29]

Cincinnati is a prime instance of the nexus of values and power. According to research conducted at the University of Cincinnati's Institute for Policy Research, this city falls "in the center" on important social and economic questions. In other words, for midsize cities it is no more liberal or conservative than others on issues such as pornography, censorship, or abortion.[30] But values are merely one part of the equation. What makes the decisive difference in Cincinnati are seasoned moral crusaders and key government officials who can mobilize opposition against anything that violates their sense of propriety (fig. 3).

Local businessman Charles Keating—later notorious for his involvement in the Lincoln Savings and Loan scandal in California—founded Citizens for Decency Through Law in 1956. Cincinnati is the headquarters of the National Coalition Against Pornography, as well as a morality organization that spearheaded the anti-Mapplethorpe campaign, the Citizens for Community Values (CCV). The CCV initiated its campaign against the Mapplethorpe exhibit before it arrived in Cincinnati with a mass mailing of photographs reminiscent of Helms's techniques.

The Contemporary Art Center was the target of threatening phone calls, as were board members. Shortly before the opening of the exhibit, the chairman of CAC's board resigned; the bank where he was a vice-president had received calls of protest as well.[31] According to a CCV spokesperson, "Cincinnati is the pinnacle. We enforce the law to the nth degree."[32]

The CAC was determined that the show go on. The gallery was careful to dissociate itself from the public funding debate that had swirled around Andres Serrano and had dominated the Corcoran brouhaha. The retrospective was sponsored in Cincinnati by a grant from a local business, and by increas-

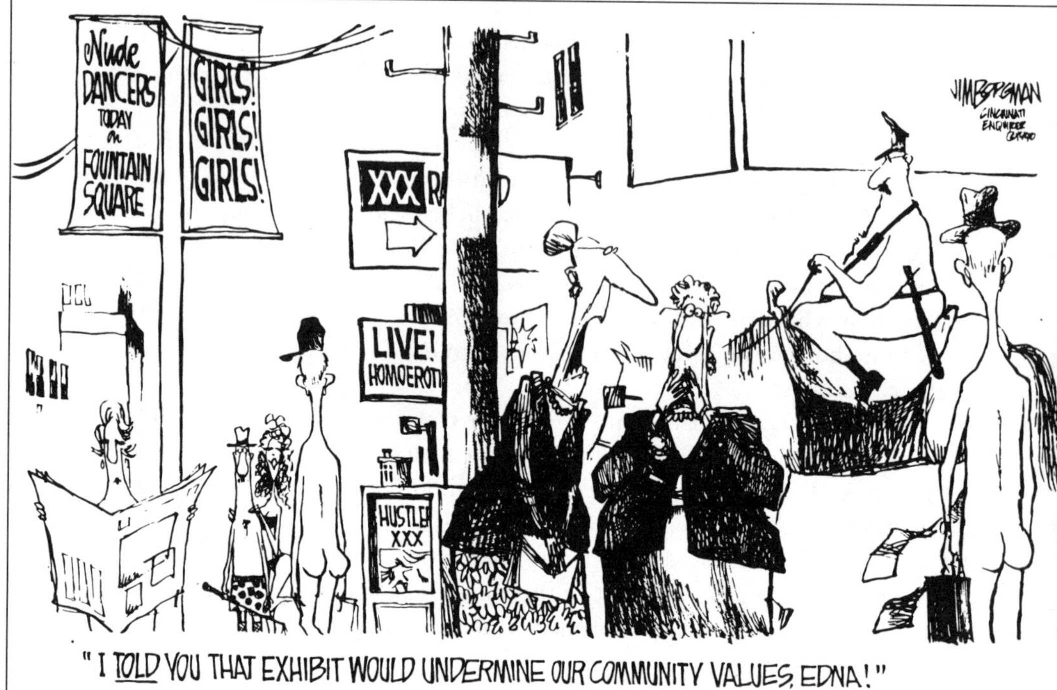

FIG. 3. Jim Borgman editorial cartoon, *The Cincinnati Enquirer*, April 8, 1990. Reprinted with special permission of King Features Syndicate.

ing the usual admission fee. The CAC also excluded itself from being a beneficiary of the Cincinnati Institute of Fine Arts, a local umbrella group that raises money to support a myriad of cultural endeavors. The CAC posted warning signs about the graphic nature of some of the photographs, and at this site no one under the age of eighteen was admitted to the exhibition.

The CAC attempted to clarify its legal situation before the exhibition opened by requesting that a jury examine the controversial images and determine whether they were obscene. A judge denied this request, forcing the CAC to proceed with the exhibit without knowing whether or not it could be held in violation of any criminal statutes. On the evening of April 6, thousands of people lined up for a members-only preview of the show. Their ranks were swelled by a flurry of new affiliates who suspected the exhbit might be shut down by a police raid once the public run commenced.

The mounting uncertainty over the exhibition's fate was terminated when a showdown occurred on the official opening day, April 7. Nine members of a Hamilton County, Ohio, grand jury were among the first visitors. After their viewing they decided that seven of the photographs were obscene, and charged the CAC and director Dennis Barrie with two misdemeanor counts each of pandering obscenity and illegal use of a child in nudity-related material.[33] Later that afternoon police, armed with a search warrant, cleared the gallery of visitors in order to videotape the exhibit.

This effort to collect evidence prompted an enraged crowd to shout "Gestapo go home" and "Sieg Heil." It was a highly emotional and hazardous situation, intensified because the enclosed arcade area was jammed with people, and the primary means of entry and egress from the gallery are two escalators connecting the first and second levels. In fact, over two thousand people filled the atrium and snaked in lines onto the sidewalks outside. Ex-curator Sawyer reports that the staff was stunned: "We really didn't believe it would come to police action. . . . I think if they had brought Dennis [Barrie] out in handcuffs there very well could have been a riot."

Several months of legal wrangling followed, during which the exhibit was allowed to remain open. When the case was eventually heard in September, the tour was completing its two-year journey, in Boston. Barrie was the first U.S. museum director indicted for obscenity in the course of doing his job. As he declaimed in the title of an op-ed piece, "Pandering? That's Nonsense . . . I'm a museum director."[34]

The results of a telephone poll of Hamilton County, Ohio, residents revealed that 63 percent of the respondents opposed the prosecution of the arts center.[35] And affirmative gestures were expressed by a number of national as well as local professional groups. But opponents were legion—and vocal—in Cincinnati. For example, a trio of doctors used their credentials to bulwark their claim that the disputed exhibit "forces upon us a bizarre, sexual vision" by presenting "degrading acts that diminish us all." And one of these physicians also asserted authoritatively on television that to people struggling with "addictions" to pornography, seeing the sadomasochistic or homoerotic images in an art museum could give them the green light to engage in similarly destructive behavior themselves.[36]

Appeals by the defense attorneys failed to derail the trial. Not even the argument that some of the contested photos appeared in books in the collection of the county public library was sufficient to cause the judge to dismiss the charges. In fact, decisions by the judge in the pretrial stage greatly distressed the defendants and their supporters. First, Judge F. David J. Albanese ruled that the jury could hear testimony about only the seven allegedly obscene images out of the 175 photographs in the retrospective. A key section of the Miller test states that to be judged obscene, "the work, *taken as a whole*, lacks serious literary, artistic, political, or scientific value."[37] The judge took this to mean each photograph as a whole, not the complete exhibition.

Second, Albanese denied a request for adjournment by ruling that the CAC was a gallery rather than a museum. Under Ohio law, museums are allowed to display obscene materials for educational and cultural purposes.[38] And finally, the judge refused to restrict the juror pool to the city of Cincinnati, which presumably would generate a more liberal panel. He instead ordered that it be drawn from Hamilton County as a whole.

Jury selection also troubled the defense. On the face of it, the jury pool did not offer people who appeared naturally inclined to endorse CAC's point of view. In the end, four men and four women were selected. Only one was a resident of the city, and one held a college degree. They were a predominantly working-class group, having little interest in or experience with art.[39]

The prosecution's case was rudimentary: they presented only three police officers, who confirmed that the photos were displayed at CAC. Their supposition was that the photos were prima facie evidence of guilt.[40] But the defense was intricate, backed by four days of expert testimony offered by male and female museum personnel chosen from around the country, representatives of CAC, and two local art critics. This group was assembled in anticipation of a much more formidable lineup of adversaries, so that this turned out to be a lopsided contest. The CAC had compiled a list of over fifty curators who were willing to talk about the merits of Mapplethorpe's work. CAC officials laid out the "intellectual geography" for the lawyers: the challenge was to display expert know-how without appearing effete or too well heeled.

Art professionals scrupulously presented a crash course in aesthetics and criticism to the relatively unsophisticated jurors. Defense witnesses were alchemists who recast images of extreme sexual acts into figure studies, and transformed the arc of the urine being directed into a man's mouth into a classical study of symmetry. This deflected attention away from the difficult subject matter of the photographs onto formalist considerations such as composition. In some instances these specialists also drew art historical analogies, such as likening the children's portraits to Renaissance putti. It was a well-conceived strategy, and extremely well executed.

The defense's case was also strengthened by affidavits of support signed by the parents of both of the children whose photos were in dispute. These were important because Ohio law prohibits "any material or performance that shows a minor who is not the person's child or ward in a state of nudity." Not only did the parents verify that the photos had been taken with their permission, but they were also dismayed that religious and political leaders were now presenting them as evidence of visual child abuse. They had never viewed them as anything but innocent and natural portrayals.[41] The little boy, Jesse McBride (age nineteen by the time of the trial), shared his parents' opinions, and contributed a unique display of support: he allowed himself to be rephotographed nude as an adult in the same pose, a portrait which was printed in New York City's *Village Voice*.[42]

But the defense did not go completely unchallenged. To rebut the testimony that championed the photographs as art, the prosecution called a single witness, Dr. Judith Reisman, whose credentials included writing songs for *Captain Kangaroo* and conducting research for the American Family Association (AFA). Reisman concentrated on the subject matter of the photos, not their formal qualities. She blasted the anonymity of the sex acts they portrayed, and dismissed the claims for them as art because they failed to express human emotion; for example, she noted that only one even showed a face. Her attack on the children's pictures was similarly disparaging; she assessed them as dangerous public displays that legitimated child abuse.[43]

The jury considered Reisman's criticisms to be opinion, not the statements of an expert. The "apple pie" approach of Barrie's attorney, H. Louis Sirkin, proved to be more persuasive. Sirkin compared the Miller standard to an apple pie. If a recipe called for three ingredients to make an apple pie, he argued, merely one or two of them would not be sufficient to yield the desired result. Mutatis mutandis, a ruling of obscenity could occur only if all three conditions of *Miller* were met. After only two and a half hours of deliberation, the jury acquitted Barrie and the CAC on all charges. Barrie had faced up to one year in jail and a fine of $2,000, and the CAC could have been fined $10,000.

The verdict was a surprise to many people, supporters and detractors of the Mapplethorpe exhibit alike (fig. 4). Some commentators touted this as a resounding victory for the American justice system and for freedom of artistic expression, in articles with titles such as "Grand Juries" and "Rank-and-File Rebuff to Censorship."[44] But beyond the gloating there was also a sense that a considerable degree of luck had been involved: the prosecution had essentially failed to assemble a plausible case.

It is disquieting to acknowledge that strong class elements were at work here, with elite intellectuals initiating their inexperienced fellows into the workings and understandings of the art world. In important respects the specialists finessed their way through without forthrightly addressing the explicit sexual content of a pivotal portion of Mapplethorpe's photos, which trouble viewers who are gay or straight, liberal or conservative, for a variety of reasons. They had not decisively won the cultural war.

Following the reception Cincinnati accorded the Mapplethorpe exhibit, there was every reason to believe that a similar challenge could be mounted in Boston. After all, its reputation as a bluenose burg was earned over decades of campaigning by vigilant anti-obscenity societies and by the activities of watchful public officials. But Mapplethorpe's supporters abandoned the defense and took an impressive proactive stance in Boston. They not only talked about freedom of expression. They asserted it.

Adversaries attempted to mobilize public sentiment against this show, without much success. A thirteen-member coalition of groups calling itself the First Amendment Common Sense Alliance was the primary opponent. But it was unable to convince Boston Mayor Raymond Flynn, the state attorney general, or a municipal magistrate to take action. The state house of representatives did pass some punitive legislation in a late-night session, only for it to be stalemated in the state senate.[45] And *The Pilot*, newspaper of the Catholic Archdiocese of Boston, ran an editorial, a commentary, and a full-page ad in protest, but the tabloid *Boston Herald* counseled "hands off."[46]

While the opposition was spotty and largely ineffective, supporters were shrewd. The strongest evidence of this was a number of "solidarity shows" installed at other Boston sites. The Museum of Fine Arts presented "Figuring the Body," an exhibit on the human form; Harvard's Fogg Museum displayed another selection of Mapplethorpe's work; and the Photographic Resource Center assembled "The Emperor's New Clothes: Censorship, Sexuality and the Body Politic," drawing on images from fashion, art, and pornography. Arts institutions had not joined in common cause like this in any other city, nor had the arts community gained the upper hand or controlled the terms of the debate so convincingly anywhere else.

The local public television affiliate WGBH upped the ante even further. In answer to many conservative critics who sneeringly noted that the photos generally had not been printed in newspapers or shown on TV because of their highly charged nature, WGBH broadcast them on the *10 O'Clock News* the evening before the exhibit opened to the public. The broadcast addressed but did not lay this issue to rest: Reverend Donald Wildmon of the AFA and at least two other individuals complained to the Federal Communications Commission. Wildmon sent a tape of the program to the FCC and claimed that it contained material that was indecent and obscene. The FCC rejected

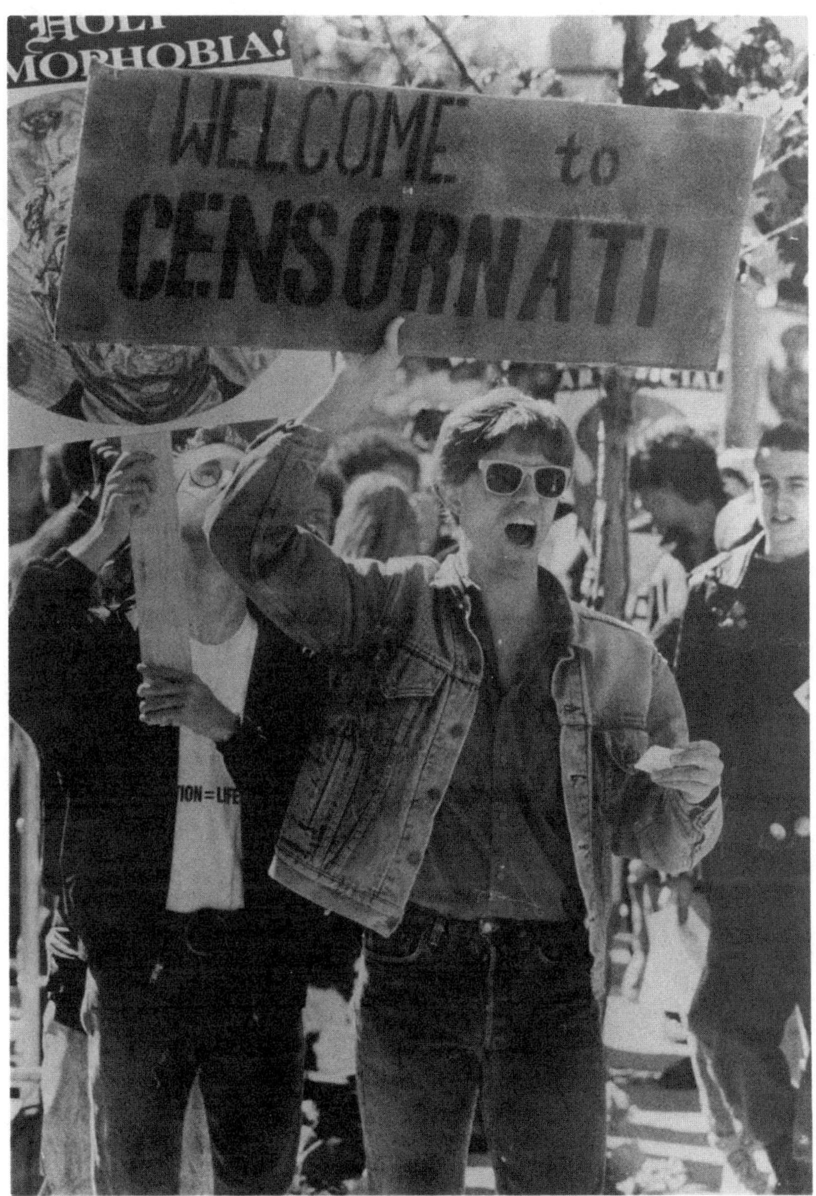

FIG. 4. Jim Callaway, photograph of pro-Mapplethorpe/anti-censorship rally in Cincinnati, Ohio, September 24, 1990. Used by permission of *The Cincinnati Enquirer*.

the indecency complaint on jurisdictional grounds (the broadcast was after 10 P.M.), and felt the obscenity charge was "unsustainable."[47]

A crowd of about 250 people demonstrated in support of the exhibit on its opening day, easily overwhelming those who opposed it. This event occurred just two days after the formation of a Queer Nation chapter in Boston, a branch of the militant direct action group that had been formed in New York City earlier in the summer.[48] The coalescence was fortuitous: Queer Nation had its first local opportunity to demonstrate against homophobia.

It was a fitting end to a tumultuous circuit through the country, and marked some distinctive changes in the gay community and in the public mood. The Mapplethorpe affair also confirmed two typical features of art controversies: since opposition breeds enormous interest, "The Perfect Moment" consistently established new levels of attendance wherever it was shown; and since controversy also adds cachet to a work, its market value rises. Record auction prices followed in the exhibit's wake, a boon to the coffers of the Mapplethorpe estate. The estate's commitment to AIDS research and promoting photography has been unwittingly strengthened by the actions of those who most feverishly oppose Mapplethorpe and his work. In 1992 the Mapplethorpe Foundation contributed $5 million in cash and artworks to the Guggenheim Museum to establish a photography collection, and Mapplethorpe's name now graces its new gallery. These are ironic lessons dating back at least to the time of Nero, which Tacitus observed in his *History*.[49]

Whither Cincinnati and Mapplethorpe, after the verdict? The prosecution opened up a rift in Cincinnati's art community: most of the major arts institutions were not willing to openly support the CAC in its struggle and jeopardize their own situations. The CAC was left in relative isolation, targeted by the collusion of politicians and moral leaders, too controversial to attract many corporate sponsors, and separated from its fellow arts organizations by its advocacy of difficult work.[50] It is only gradually being accepted back into the fold.

The city has been split over other public issues, in its continuing quest to define its civic character. Ku Klux Klan members have rallied and erected crosses downtown in Fountain Square during the Christmas season for the past several years. They have been met with jeers, injunctions, and the toppling of their displays.

But whatever this may signal about public intolerance of bigotry, the electorate turned vindictive when it voted to overturn a gay rights amendment in November 1993,[51] and the police and the gay community eye one another with suspicion: in 1994, for example, vice squad officers charged three employees of a gay bookstore with pandering obscenity after undercover cops rented Pier Paolo Pasolini's *Salo: 120 Days of Sodom*.[52] Yet in one of those "stranger than fiction" developments, Cincinnati was ranked number one by the *Places Rated Almanac* in 1993, the arts factoring into a complex calculus of assessment. It remains a city of vast contradictions.

The anti-gay sentiment which surfaced over Robert Mapplethorpe still simmers in American culture, and bubbles up recurrently. The identities of characters may change in each episode, but their roles are scripted in much the same fashion. Opponents are entwined in what Michel Foucault pithily characterizes as "perpetual spirals of power and pleasure."[53] Players derive satisfaction from exercising authority as well as from evading it or tweaking its agents on the nose. Nonetheless, one fact remains central: some individuals pay dearly when who they are or what they do opposes the status quo.

This sort of struggle was apparent in the saga of the "NEA Four," a quartet of self-consciously defiant performance artists—Karen Finley, John Fleck, Tim Miller, and Holly Hughes, an ardent feminist, two gay men, and a lesbian, respectively—who were denied NEA grants by Chairman John Frohnmayer in 1990, overruling the recommendations of a peer review panel. The artists prevailed in a lawsuit in 1992, invalidating the use of a "decency standard" as a condition for accepting NEA support. In 1993 they successfully demonstrated that they were denied their subsidies on political and not artistic grounds. At that time the court ordered the NEA to reinstate the grants and awarded each of the aggrieved artists an additional $6,000 in damages.

But victories for protection of free expression are regularly counterbalanced by contrary events. County commissioners in Cobb County, Georgia (suburban Atlanta), passed a resolution in 1993 condemning homosexuality as incompatible with "family values." They also considered requiring county-funded arts projects to reflect "community, family-oriented standards," but then backed off, fearing legal complications when it came to actually interpreting and enforcing these notions. Officials instead nixed *all* local support to the arts, rather than run the risk of sanctioning so-called deviant values.[54]

And in 1994, gay, HIV-positive artist Ron Athey was demonized after $150 of NEA funds supported his performance at the Walker Art Center in Minneapolis. Athey staged a ritualized scarification wherein he pierced himself and another man (who was non-HIV-infected) with acupuncture needles and a

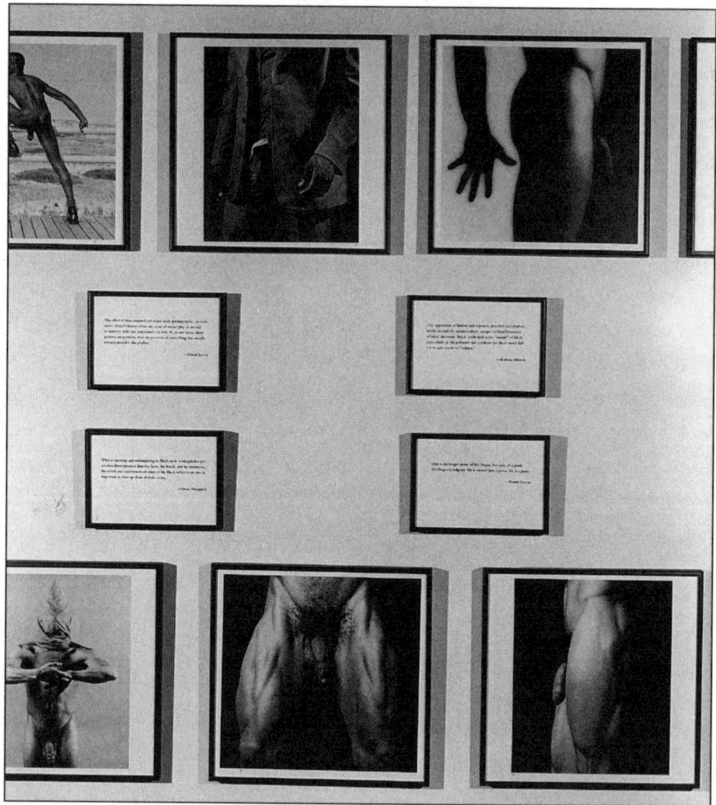

FIG. 5. Installation photograph (detail) of Glenn Ligon, "Notes on the Margin of the *Black Book*," 1993, at the Whitney Museum of American Art's 1993 Biennial Exhibition. Courtesy of Max Protetch Gallery; all Mapplethorpe works© The Estate of Robert Mapplethorpe, used by special permission, all rights reserved.

scalpel. Irate congressmen raised the specter of Athey endangering the health of observers after they heard that paper towels which blotted up the noninfected blood were suspended over the audience.

Never mind that the retellings exaggerated and distorted the situation; the audience was not, in fact, imperiled. Even so, some members of Congress used this opportunity to reduce the NEA's budget, and once again challenge the agency's right to make independent artistic judgments—or even to continue to exist. These sentiments snowballed into more drastic action after a

Republican-dominated Congress took office in 1995. It voted a draconian 40 percent budget cut for the NEA, and projected the agency's total demise by 1997, the lamentable cumulative effect of its critics' incessant pummelings over the preceding years.

One of the most exciting ramifications of the Mapplethorpe controversy is that the cycle of assessment and reassessment of the artist's work continues. Paul Rudnick's 1994 off-Broadway play *The Naked Truth* used a thinly disguised Mapplethorpe-like photographer to comically skewer high society pretensions, political ambitions, and many contemporary foibles.

In a much more serious vein, Glenn Ligon's contribution to the 1993 Whitney Biennial was "Notes on the Margin of the *Black Book*" (fig. 5):the artist arranged two rows of Mapplethorpe photographs along the walls. Sandwiched between them were two rows of framed quotations revealing every shade of opinion about this body of work. The viewer was nudged toward one political, aesthetic, or philosophical position and then another, with a dizzying multiplicity of voices.

No one has yet had the last word.

NOTES

1. Arthur C. Danto, *Encounters and Reflections: Art in the Historical Present* (New York: Farrar, Straus and Giroux, 1990), 21, emphasis added.

2. Dominick Dunne, "Robert Mapplethorpe's Proud Finale," *Vanity Fair*, February 1989, 132.

3. Quoted in Parker Hodges, "Robert Mapplethorpe, Photographer," *MANhattan Gaze*, December 10, 1979, 5. In an interview given ten years later, Mapplethorpe maintained the same position: "Whether it's a cock or a flower, I'm looking at it in the same way"; see the interview by Lawrence Chua, "Robert Mapplethorpe," *Flash Art*, January/February 1989, 103.

4. Donald Kuspit, "Robert Mapplethorpe: Aestheticizing the Perverse," *Artscribe International*, November/December 1988, 65.

5. Jorge Ribalta, "Decorative Heroism: The Death of Mapplethorpe," *Lapiz*, April 1989, 69.

6. Peter Schjeldahl, "The Mainstreaming of Mapplethorpe: Taste and Hunger," *7 Days*, August 10, 1988, 48.

7. Robert Rooney, "The Unambiguous Stare of Mapplethorpe's Lens," *Australian*, February 25, 1986, and Mark Schoofs, "Robert Mapplethorpe: Exquisite Subversions," *Windy City Times*, March 16, 1989, 28.

8. Ibid.

9. Kobena Mercer, "Looking for Trouble," in Henry Abelove, Michele Aina Barale, and David M. Halperin, eds., *The Lesbian and Gay Studies Reader* (New York: Routledge, 1993), 359.

10. Danto, *Encounters and Reflections*, 216.

11. Quoted in Maureen Dowd, "Unruffled Helms Basks in Eye of Arts Storm of His Own Making," *New York Times*, July 28, 1989, B6.

12. Richard Grenier, "A Burning Issue Lights Artistic Ire," *Washington Times*, June 28, 1989, F4, and Judith Reisman, "Promoting Child Abuse as Art," *Washington Times*, July 7, 1989, F1, 4.

13. Patrick J. Buchanan, "Why Subsidize Defamation?" *New York Post*, November 22, 1989, 31.

14. See Patrick J. Buchanan, "Jesse Helms' Valiant War Against Filth in the Arts," *New York Post*, August 2, 1989; "In the New *Kulturkampf*, the First Battles Are Being Fought," *Richmond* [Virginia] *Times-Dispatch*, June 19, 1989; and "Artists Seek to Create 'Pagan' Society," *Chicago Sun-Times*, March 23, 1990.

15. Hilton Kramer, "Mapplethorpe Show at the Whitney: A Big, Glossy, Offensive Exhibit," *New York Observer*, August 22, 1988, 12.

16. Hilton Kramer, "Is Art Above the Laws of Decency?" *New York Times*, July 2, 1989, H7.

17. Quoted in Elizabeth Kastor, "Corcoran Cancels Photo Exhibit," *Washington Post*, June 13, 1989, C1.

18. Elizabeth Kastor, "Gays, Artists to Protest at Corcoran," *Washington Post*, June 16, 1989, B1, 6, and Doug Hinckle, "Gay, Arts Communities Join Forces," *Washington Blade*, June 23, 1989, 4.

19. Todd Allan Yasui, "The Mapplethorpe Bonanza," *Washington Post*, August 21, 1989, B7.

20. Quoted in Dowd, "Unruffled Helms."

21. In the case of the Mapplethorpe retrospective, the NEA's $30,000 of support supplemented the $180,000 raised from private sources; see Glenn Collins, "On Helms and Grants with Poison Pills," *New York Times*, August 7, 1989, C11.

22. Kara Swisher, "Helms's 'Indecent' Sampler," *Washington Post*, August 8, 1989, B2.

23. Quoted in William H. Honan, "Compromise Is Proposed on Helms Amendment," *New York Times*, September 28, 1989, C14.

24. Punitive action was taken against ICA in the next grant-making cycle: two of three of their requests were approved by the peer panels, but overturned by NEA's National Council. According to council member Jacob Nuesner, awarding them at that time "would be tweaking the nose of Congress." See Kimberly Taylor, "NEA National Council Vetoes ICA Grants," *New Art Examiner*, Summer 1990, 11.

25. The NEA implemented the terms of the Helms amendment by requiring that artists sign a pledge affirming that they would not create obscene work. All recipients of NEA grants during the fiscal year ending October 1, 1990, were required to endorse

this anti-obscenity "loyalty oath" as a condition of receiving government support. It was struck down in a successful legal challenge by the Bella Lewitsky Dance Company and the Newport Harbor Art Museum, both based in California.

26. See Robert C. Vitz, *The Queen and the Arts: Cultural Life in Nineteenth-Century Cincinnati* (Kent, Ohio: Kent State University Press, 1989).

27. From an interview conducted August 26, 1991 (when Sawyer held the chief curator position). This and all subsequent unattributed quotes are from that interview.

28. Jim Knippenberg, "Have the Arts Gone Too Far? Or Are We More Conservative?" *Cincinnati Enquirer*, April 8, 1990, D5.

29. Peter Lefcourt, *The Dreyfus Affair* (New York: Random House, 1992), 254.

30. Knippenberg, "Have the Arts Gone Too Far?" D1.

31. See Steven Mannheimer, "Cincinnati Joins the Censorship Circus," *New Art Examiner*, June 1990, 33–35.

32. Isabel Wilkerson, "Trouble Right Here in Cincinnati: Furor Over Mapplethorpe Exhibit," *New York Times*, March 29, 1990, A21.

33. Jane Prendergast, "Grand Jury: Mapplethorpe Photos Obscene," *Cincinnati Enquirer*, April 8, 1990, A1.

34. *New York Times*, April 18, 1990, A25.

35. See CAA press release, April 9, 1990; Jane Prendergast, "CAC Gets National Support," *Cincinnati Enquirer*, April 14, 1990, A8; and Milo Geyelin, "Cincinnati Sends a Warning to Censors," *Wall Street Journal*, October 8, 1990, B1.

36. John W. Vester, William J. Gerhardt, and Mark Snyder, "Mapplethorpe in Cincinnati," *Cincinnati Enquirer*, March 24, 1990, 46, and Mark Snyder on *Nightline*, April 10, 1990.

37. *Three* conditions must be met to satisfy a *legal* definition of obscenity. First, "the average person, applying contemporary community standards, would find that the work, taken as a whole, appeals to the prurient interest [in sex]." Second, "the work depicts or describes, in a patently offensive way, sexual conduct specifically defined by the applicable state [or federal] law." *And* the third condition, as cited in the text, emphasis added. See *Final Report of the Attorney General's Commission on Pornography* (Nashville: Rutledge Hill Press, 1986), 17–18.

38. Owen Findsen, "Ruling that CAC Is Not a Museum Jolts Art World," *Cincinnati Enquirer*, June 21, 1990.

39. See two articles by Isabel Wilkerson: "Selection of Jury Begins in Ohio Obscenity Trial," *New York Times*, September 25, 1990, A16, and "Jury Selected in Ohio Obscenity Trial," *New York Times*, September 28, 1990, A10.

40. Jurors did not see the original photos, but "fuzzy copies." The homosexual pictures were larger than the originals, and the photos of the two children were smaller. See Jayne Merkel, "Art on Trial," *Art in America* 78 (December 1990): 46. Such "distortions" can be significant to how an image is received and evaluated.

41. Paula Span, "For His Friends, Portraits of Children's Beauty and Innocence," *Washington Post*, May 3, 1990, D1, 12.

42. See C. Carr, "Suffer the Children," *Village Voice*, June 5, 1990, 27.

43. See Eric Harrison, "Gallery Photos Compared to Child Porn," *Los Angeles Times*, October 5, 1990, A27, and Isabel Wilkerson, "Witness in Obscenity Trial Calls Explicit Photographs 'Destructive,'" *New York Times*, October 5, 1990, A20.

44. Anna Quindlen, *New York Times*, October 25, 1990, A27, and David Margolick, *New York Times*, October 6, 1990, 5.

45. See Patti Hartigan, "Mapplethorpe Show to Open Amid Controversy," *Boston Globe*, August 1, 1990, 1, 16; Peter Catalano, "Mapplethorpe Not Banned in Boston," *Los Angeles Times*, July 30, 1990, F1, 8; and "Mapplethorpe Complaints Denied," *Los Angeles Times*, September 6, 1990, F2. Hartigan reported that among the members of the coalition were representatives from Morality in Media, Citizens for Family First, and the Catholic League for Religious and Civil Rights.

46. Patti Hartigan, "The Pilot Joins Mapplethorpe Fray," *Boston Globe*, July 27, 1990, 29, 36, and Catalano, "Mapplethorpe Not Banned," F8.

47. Roy J. Stewart to Donald E. Wildmon, April 26, 1991; photocopy in author's personal archive.

48. See Desiree French and Vernon Silver, "Shouting Breaks the Calm at ICA," *Boston Globe*, August 2, 1990, and Kay Longcope, "Boston Gay Groups Vow New Militancy against Hate Crimes," *Boston Globe*, August 2, 1990, 25, 31.

49. See Sue Curry Jansen, *Censorship: The Knot That Binds Power and Knowledge* (New York: Oxford University Press, 1991), 41–42. Mapplethorpe's images *continue* to spark controversy worldwide: a Japanese businessman is pressing his government to return his copy of the catalogue from the 1988 Whitney retrospective, which was seized as obscene when it was brought into the country; and the Victoria and Albert Museum in London canceled an AIDS fundraiser that was slated to feature a slide show of Mapplethorpe's images, while Harrods stopped selling a book of the photos. In the first instance, the Japanese government wanted to prevent "causing offense," and in the second the museum and Harrods caved in to anticipated as well as actual customer complaints; see Kay Itoi, "Dirty Pictures?" *Art News*, February 1995, 52, and "Robert Mapplethorpe in Hot Water Again," *Twist Weekly* [Portland, Oregon], November 19, 1992, 7.

50. See, for example, Robin Cembalest, "After the Acquittal," *ARTnews*, February 1991, 31, and David Lyman, "Post-Mapplethorpe Blues in Cincinnati," *New Art Examiner*, January 1991, 56. But Sawyer reported that some conciliatory gestures were being made a year after the trial, including a degree of cooperation from the business community, which was making corporate-owned artwork available for loan to CAC shows.

51. Called Issue 3, the initiative blocked the government from prohibiting discrimination against gay men, lesbians, and bisexuals. It was similar to anti-gay initiatives on the ballot in Oregon and Colorado in November 1992. The Colorado bill passed, but was struck down by the Supreme Court as unconstitutional in May 1996. The Cincinnati bill was voided in August 1994 by a federal judge who determined the

measure was constitutionally vague and violated the First Amendment, but it was subsequently upheld by the U.S. Court of Appeals in May 1995. In the latest twist, the Supreme Court, after its decision in the Colorado case, ordered the Court of Appeals to reconsider its earlier decision in light of this new precedent.

52. "Vice Officers File Pandering Charge Against Gay Shop," *Stonewall News of NY*, July 18, 1994, 12.

53. Michel Foucault, *The History of Sexuality*, Vol. 1, *An Introduction* (New York: Vintage Books, 1980), 45.

54. Both Cobb County and Cincinnati have suffered economically for their repressive actions; proposed conventions have pulled out of both sites. The estimated loss in Cincinnati is $24 million since 1993, including the cancellation of meetings by the American Library Association and the American Historical Association, among others (*The Advocate*, December 12, 1995, 11). In addition, the Olympic torch bypassed Cobb County on its route to the 1996 Centennial Olympic Summer Games in Atlanta in July 1996, because of the anti-gay resolution there.

CONTRIBUTORS

CHRISTIANE ANDERSSON is Kress Professor of Art History at Bucknell University in Lewisburg, Pennsylvania. She has taught at Columbia University, the Johann Wolfgang Goethe University in Frankfurt, and the Williams College Graduate Program in Art History. She has written widely on the history of drawings and prints, including (with Charles Talbot) *From a Mighty Fortress: Prints, Drawings and Books in the Age of Luther* (Detroit Institute of Arts, 1983); *Dirnen, Krieger, Narren: Ausgewählte Zeichnungen von Urs Graf* (Gute Schrift Verlag, 1978); and "Polemical Prints in Reformation Nuremberg," in *New Perspectives on the Art of Reformation Nuremberg*, edited by Jeffrey C. Smith, 1985. Her current research focuses on the censorship of images in Reformation Germany.

BERNADINE BARNES is associate professor of art history at Wake Forest University. She received her Ph.D. at the University of Virginia in 1986. A specialist in Italian Renaissance art, she is particularly interested in the ways in which art reflects developments in social history. She has published several articles on Michelangelo's work, and is a contributor to *EVA/AVE: Images of Women in Renaissance and Baroque Prints* (National Gallery of Art, 1990). Her book, *Michelangelo's Last Judgment: The Renaissance Response*, was published by the University of California Press in 1997.

FRANCINE CARRARO is associate professor of art history at Southwest Texas State University, San Marcos, Texas. She received her Ph.D. from the University of Texas at Austin in 1989. A specialist in American art, she has focused on regional art and her essays have appeared in a variety of journals, including *American Craft* and *Southwestern Historical Quarterly.* She has served as curator and essayist for exhibitions at Laguna Gloria Art Museum, the Art Museum of Southeast Texas and Southwest Texas State University. She is the author of *Jerry Bywaters: A Life in Art* (University of Texas Press, 1994), and a contributor to *Prints and Printmakers of Texas* (Texas State Historical Association, 1997).

ELIZABETH C. CHILDS is assistant professor of art history at Washington University in St. Louis. She received her Ph.D. from Columbia University, where she wrote her dissertation on exoticism and international politics in the caricature of Honoré Daumier. She has edited *Honoré Daumier: A Thematic Guide to the Oeuvre* (Garland Press, 1989), and co-curated (with Kirsten Powell) the exhibition "Femmes d'Esprit: Women in Daumier's Caricature" (Middlebury College and the Neuberger Museum, Purchase College, 1990). She has published articles on exoticism in the work of various artists, including Daumier, Matisse, and Gauguin. During 1996–97, she had fellowships from the National Endowment for the Humanities and the National Gallery of Art to work on her book, *In Search of Paradise: Painting and Photography in Colonial Tahiti, 1880–1909.*

STEVEN C. DUBIN is associate professor of sociology at Purchase College, State University of New York, where he directs the Social Sciences and the Arts Program. He received his Ph.D. from the University of Chicago, and was a postdoctoral fellow at Yale University. He is the author of *Bureaucratizing the Muse: Public Funds and the Cultural Worker* (University of Chicago Press, 1987) and *Arresting Images: Impolitic Art and Uncivil Actions* (Routledge, 1992), which was cited by the *New York Times* as a Notable Book of 1992 and by the Gustavus Myers Center as an outstanding book on human rights. His articles and reviews have appeared in *Contemporary Sociology, American Journal of Sociology, Urban Life, Social Problems, Social Forces, Sociological Inquiry, Journal of Aesthetic Education, Journal of Arts Management and Law, New Art Examiner,* and *The Nation.*

JOHN HOUSE is professor of the history of art at the Courtauld Institute of Art, University of London. He was co-organiser of the "Post-Impressionism" exhibition at the Royal Academy of Arts, 1979–80, and of the "Renoir" exhibition, Hayward Gallery, London, and Museum of Fine Arts, Boston, 1985–86. He also was guest curator of "Impressions of France" at the Museum of Fine Arts, Boston, 1995–96. He is the author of *Monet: Nature into Art* (Yale University Press, 1986) and of many essays and articles on French nineteenth-century painting.

PAUL H.D. KAPLAN is associate professor of art history at Purchase College, State University of New York. He received his Ph.D. from Boston University in 1983; in 1993–94 he was an NEH Research Fellow. His two earlier essays on Veronese appeared in *Arte Veneta* and in the Acts of the 1988 symposium on that painter. He is also the author of *The Rise of the Black Magus in Western Art* (UMI Research Press, 1985) and of articles on Titian and Giorgione. He is presently completing a book entitled *The Storm of War: Martial and Erotic Themes in the Art of Giorgione.*

JEROME SILBERGELD is professor of art history at the University of Washington in Seattle, where he teaches Chinese art with particular interests in traditional and modern Chinese painting, architectural history, and Chinese cinema. He has published four books, including *Contradictions: Artistic Life, the Socialist State, and the Chinese Painter Li Hashing* (University of Washington Press), which was a *New York Times* Notable Book of 1993. He has published articles in numerous journals, including a state-of-the-field essay on Chinese painting studies in the West (*Journal of Asian Studies*, 1987) and a revised entry on the history of Chinese art for *The Encyclopedia Britannica* (1995). At the University of Washington, he has served as chair of Art History and as director of the School of Art.

GERALD SILK is associate professor of art history at Tyler School of Art, Temple University. He has written widely on modern and contemporary art, and his essays have appeared in a variety of publications, including the periodicals *Art Journal*, *Arts*, and *Art Criticism*, and the anthologies *World War II: A Fifty Year Perspective on 1939* (Siena College Research Institute Press, 1992), *art—public* (Acts of the International Association of Art Critics, 1992), *Twentieth Century Art Theory: Urbanism, Politics, and Mass Culture* (Prentice-Hall, 1990), *The Automobile and American Culture* (University of Michigan Press, 1983), and *The Great Drawings of All Time: The Twentieth Century* (Shorewood/Talisman, 1980). He is the author of *Automobile and Culture* (Abrams, 1984) and *Museums Discovered: The Wadsworth Atheneum* (Shorewood/Penshurt, 1982). He has been a curator and essayist for exhibitions at various museums, including the Museum of Contemporary Art, Los

Angeles; the Institute of Contemporary Art, Philadelphia; the National Air and Space Museum, Washington; the Portland Museum of Art, Portland, Maine; and the Hara Museum of Art, Tokyo.

PETER F. SPOONER is curator and registrar for the Tweed Museum of Art, University of Minnesota, Duluth, where he is currently curating an exhibition of the work of Rudy Autio. Formerly assistant director and curator for University Galleries, Illinois State University, he has written essays on the work of Alexis Rockman, Dennis Oppenheim, and David Moreno, as well as numerous essays for group exhibitions of contemporary art. He received a B.S. in art education from the University of Wisconsin-Stout, and M.S. and M.F.A. degrees in studio art from Illinois State University. He has taught art and art history in the public schools and at the college level, has worked as a museum educator, and has served as a selection panelist for the Minnesota State Arts Board and the Illinois Arts Council.

JANIS TOMLINSON's publications include *Goya: The Tapestry Cartoons and Early Career at the Court of Madrid* (Cambridge University Press, 1989), *Goya in the Twilight of Enlightenment* (Yale University Press, 1992), and *Francisco Goya and Lucientes* (Phaidon, 1994). On two occasions, she has won the Tufts Award for a distinguished publication on the arts of Iberia. She has taught at Columbia University and at Williams College and has received fellowships from the Comité Conjunto Hispano Norteamericano, the American Council of Learned Societies, the Woodrow Wilson Center, and the John Simon Guggenheim Foundation. Her current research involves national identity and the historiography of art in eighteenth- and nineteenth-century Europe.

CHRISTOPH ZUSCHLAG is assistant professor of art history at the University of Heidelberg/Germany. He was educated at the University of Vienna/Austria and at the University of Heidelberg/Germany, where he received his Ph.D. in 1991. He is author of "*Entartete Kunst*": *Ausstellungsstrategien im Nazi-Deutschland* (Wernersche Verlagsgesellschaft, 1995), and of several essays on art policy in the Third Reich. He contributed to the exhibition catalogue "*Degenerate Art*"—*The Fate of the Avant-Garde in Nazi Germany*, edited by Stephanie Barron (Los Angeles County Museum of Art and Abrams, 1991). He has also published on contemporary art.

INDEX

Boldface citations refer to pages with illustrations.